Ius Gentium: Comparative Perspectives on Law and Justice

Volume 70

More information about this series at http://www.springer.com/series/7888

Alan Uzelac · Cornelis Hendrik (Remco) van Rhee
Editors

Transformation of Civil Justice

Unity and Diversity

Springer

Editors
Alan Uzelac
Faculty of Law
University of Zagreb
Zagreb, Croatia

Cornelis Hendrik (Remco) van Rhee
Faculty of Law
Maastricht University
Maastricht, The Netherlands

ISSN 1534-6781 ISSN 2214-9902 (electronic)
Ius Gentium: Comparative Perspectives on Law and Justice
ISBN 978-3-030-07343-5 ISBN 978-3-319-97358-6 (eBook)
https://doi.org/10.1007/978-3-319-97358-6

This Springer imprint is published by the registered company Springer Nature Switzerland AG
The registered company address is: Gewerbestrasse 11, 6330 Cham, Switzerland

Preface

The civil justice systems of modern states are facing unprecedented challenges today, and they are—in most cases, unsuccessfully—struggling to find appropriate responses to them. At the same time, public confidence in the civil courts and their ability to protect and enforce civil rights and obligations is fading. The need to address this state of affairs through a broad international academic discussion is clear.

This book is the result of academic research on the transformations of contemporary civil justice systems. The contributions collected in this volume come from different regions of the globe, from (North and South) Europe to Africa and (North and South) America. They share, nonetheless, the same wish to explore whether the changes in the national justice systems appropriately address the needs of the present time. Both historical and contemporary contributions indicate that a profound change is now a *conditio sine qua non* for the survival of the civil courts as the principal protectors of the legal rights of those under the jurisdiction of modern nation states.

The core of this book is the research produced in the research project 6988 (TcJust-UD-IP-11-2013) that was funded by the Croatian Science Foundation (HRZZ). The international project team represented in this book by seven of its key researchers was reinforced by experienced, leading scholars of comparative civil procedure, but also by young and promising contributors interested in the topic. Most of them shared the experience of joint work and discussion at the postgraduate course and conference which took place at the Inter-University Centre Dubrovnik as part of the Public and Private Justice (PPJ) series. The editors would like to thank the Inter-University Centre, led by Secretary-General Ms. Nada Bruer, for their continuing kind assistance in providing an inspiring forum for high-quality, professional and academic debates.

The editors would also like to thank all of those who helped in the production and editing of the present volume. They are particularly grateful to Mr. Randolph W. Davidson (Pavia) for revising the contributions of the non-native English speakers. Valuable editing assistance was provided by Marko Bratković, who also contributed to this volume. Some pertinent language issues were resolved by the courtesy of John Sorabji (London).

Last but not least, we would like to express our gratitude to the Springer team, whose collaboration and understanding greatly helped us to bring this book project to a successful finish.

Zagreb, Croatia Alan Uzelac
Maastricht, The Netherlands Cornelis Hendrik (Remco) van Rhee
May 2018

Contents

Contributors

Sérgio Cruz Arenhart Faculty of Law, Federal University of Paraná, Curitiba, Brazil

Rashri Baboolal-Frank Faculty of Law, University of Pretoria, Hatfield, South Africa

Marko Bratković Faculty of Law, University of Zagreb, Zagreb, Croatia

Juraj Brozović Faculty of Law, University of Zagreb, Zagreb, Croatia

Fokke Fernhout Faculty of Law, Maastricht University, Maastricht, The Netherlands

Halvard Haukeland Fredriksen Faculty of Law, University of Bergen, Bergen, Norway

Aleš Galič Faculty of Law, University of Ljubljana, Ljubljana, Slovenia

Fernando Gascón Inchausti Complutense University of Madrid, Madrid, Spain

Erwin Giesen Faculty of Law, Maastricht University, Maastricht, The Netherlands

Henrik-Riko Held Faculty of Law, University of Zagreb, Zagreb, Croatia

Rob Jagtenberg Erasmus School of Law, Rotterdam, The Netherlands

Bartosz Karolczyk Faculty of Law, Kozminski University, Warsaw, Poland

Stephanie Law Max Planck Institute Luxembourg, Luxembourg, Luxembourg

Richard Marcus Hastings College of the Law, University of California, San Francisco, USA

Ivan Milotić Faculty of Law, University of Zagreb, Zagreb, Croatia

Annie de Roo Erasmus School of Law, Rotterdam, The Netherlands

Elisabetta Silvestri Department of Law, University of Pavia, Pavia, Italy

Jorg Sladič Faculty of Law, University of Maribor, Maribor, Slovenia

Magne Strandberg Faculty of Law, University of Bergen, Bergen, Norway

Alan Uzelac Faculty of Law, University of Zagreb, Zagreb, Croatia

Matthias Van Der Haegen Faculty of Law and Criminology, Ghent University, Ghent, Belgium

Cornelis Hendrik (Remco) van Rhee Faculty of Law, Maastricht University, Maastricht, The Netherlands

Oscar Vranken Faculty of Law, Maastricht University, Maastricht, The Netherlands

Matthias Weller Department of Law, University of Bonn, Bonn, Germany

Margaret Woo Northeastern University School of Law, Boston, USA

Part I
Introduction

The Metamorphoses of Civil Justice and Civil Procedure: The Challenges of New Paradigms—Unity and Diversity

Alan Uzelac and Cornelis Hendrik (Remco) van Rhee

In nova fert animus mutatas dicere formas corpora.
—Ovid, Metamorphoses

Abstract In 1975, Mauro Cappelletti predicted a profound transformation in the area of civil justice. In his view, the complexity of contemporary societies required new and enhanced methods of dispute resolution since the traditional means were increasingly insufficient to address societal (and even civilizational) challenges. It is questionable, however, whether this transformation has indeed occurred. In order to evaluate Cappelletti's prediction, the present contribution addresses a selection of changes in the area of civil justice that have occurred since Cappelletti's prediction and tries to identify the driving forces of change. Subsequently it identifies seven main transformation areas in civil procedure, evaluating both their present impact on civil justice and their possible future effects. The relevant areas are (1) Transformation by borrowing from national and transnational sources; (2) Transformation by technological modernization; (3) Transformation by the reorganization of courts and a redefinition of court functions; (4) Transformation by the establishment of a multi-dimensional procedure for civil cases; (5) Transformation by the pursuit of alternatives to litigation; (6) Transformation by the collectivization of decision-making processes; and (7) Transformation by 'dejudicialization' (privatization, outsourcing) of judicial tasks. The contribution serves as an introduction to the papers collected in the present volume, written by authors from a wide variety of jurisdictions in Europe and around the globe.

This contribution is the result of research supported by the Croatian Science Foundation (project no. 6988).

A. Uzelac (✉)
Faculty of Law, University of Zagreb, Zagreb, Croatia
e-mail: auzelac@pravo.hr

C. H. van Rhee
Faculty of Law, Maastricht University, Maastricht, The Netherlands
e-mail: remco.vanrhee@maastrichtuniversity.nl

A. Uzelac and C. H. van Rhee (eds.), *Transformation of Civil Justice*,
Ius Gentium: Comparative Perspectives on Law and Justice 70,
https://doi.org/10.1007/978-3-319-97358-6_1

1 Introduction

In 1975, Mauro Cappelletti, the father of comparative civil procedure, published a text on the metamorphoses of civil procedure. This text, devoted to the protection of group and collective interests, starts with a promising first section: *Une révolution en cours dans le droit judiciaire civil* (Cappelletti 1975, 571). The essence of Cappelletti's submission on a 'profound transformation' or a '*véritable révolution*' in the area of civil justice was the thesis that the complexity of contemporary societies requires new and enhanced methods of dispute resolution since the traditional means of individual redress are increasingly insufficient to address societal (and even civilizational) challenges.

Almost half a century later, Cappelletti's words still sound fresh—but only as a programmatic statement. As a description of the reality of national civil justice systems in Europe and the world, it can hardly be stated that they accurately depict the state of affairs in the first quarter of the 21st century. The main theme of Cappelletti's paper (and many of his other works), the establishment of adequate mechanisms of collective dispute resolution, is even today in an early stage. Doctrinal works produced on class actions, collective redress and the protection of group interests have rarely resulted in a broad and effective network of innovative judicial remedies. A revolution? A metamorphosis? Until well into the 21st century the new face of civil justice invoked by Cappelletti will be a wishful construct; new forms of judicial protection adjusted to process mass claims are—at least in Europe —not the reality but more like 'squeaking mice' (Harsági and Van Rhee 2014). The 'mighty cleavage' between private and public law (Merryman 1985, 91) is in most countries still present.

It should not, therefore, come as a surprise that, apart from a limited number of those interested in comparative law, scholars of civil procedure generally share the view that although civil justice does undergo changes, generally it does not radically alter its features—*plus ça change, plus c'est la même chose*. The inherited forms of civil justice, and the traditional doctrine of civil procedure, are taken for granted. Referring to the well-established human right to a fair trial for any dispute concerning civil rights and obligations, many think that the residual court monopoly on dispute resolution should not be put in jeopardy. Indeed, public criticism of civil justice is every now and then lively voiced, but is that not something that also shows the cyclic nature of history, as since Shakespeare's time there have been those who have complained about civil justice due to the 'law's delay' (Van Rhee 2004).

Current developments may, however, prove that Cappelletti's statements on the need for a profound transformation of civil justice are not inaccurate, only premature. There is no single factor which leads to this conclusion—it is rather a conjunction of several processes both outside and inside state judiciaries. An important process is the change in the social context and the methods of human interaction that is bringing Cappelletti's need for a 'profound transformation' to a whole new level.

Cappelletti most likely wrote his text with pen and paper—or maybe a typewriter. Back in 1975, personal computers were rare, and there were no mobile phones and no internet. Messages were sent by regular post office mail, as even the telefax did not acquire broad use until the 1980s and 1990s. With the fall of the Iron Curtain, economic globalization expanded, and integration processes, both in Europe and elsewhere, entered a new dimension despite all temporary difficulties. In the past 50 years, the world population has more than doubled. A 'profound transformation' can be noticed, but it is primarily a transformation of life outside national courtrooms. How much did this transformation affect civil justice, which in Cappelletti's time was already in need of a profound change?

One thing is certain: the present situation is more troublesome and uncertain than the picture painted by Cappelletti. The challenges have multiplied and intensified, and public dissatisfaction with the operation of contemporary judiciaries has accumulated. A *révolution véritable*, a rapid and adequate adjustment of civil justice systems to the requirements of the new social realities in most countries happened on a rather modest scale or did not happen at all. Where changes occurred, they often came with considerable delay, lagging far behind the overwhelming change in the social environment. It is well known that the national systems of civil procedure have a strong link to particular or even parochial characteristics specific to national legal systems and cultures (Deguchi and Storme 2008, 11) and consequently many reforms have been largely local and national in spite of economic and political integration processes.

The reactions of judicial systems to change are not only slow and indecisive, they are also going in rather different directions. For researchers of European procedural law, the current perception of European legal systems is one of 'unity and diversity' (Wijffels 2013, 14). In this introductory chapter, we will analyse the driving forces that motivate the transformation of civil justice systems. We will also try to synthesize several trends and reform processes in different jurisdictions, seeking to find some unity in the diversity of transformations. Additionally, we will show that the same unity and diversity is apparent in the contributions from different regions of the globe to the present volume.

2 The Driving Forces of Change in Contemporary Civil Justice Systems

The diversity of contemporary judicial systems is largely due to the nation state that promoted regulation, codification and an institutional framework exclusively linked to the sovereign power at the national level. The civil courts have for the longest period been immune to change, as they have their roots in the practices of local legal communities and largely deal with private interests which are not the first priority of national political elites [for a slightly different view, see Van Rhee (2012)]. However, with the European (and global) economic and political integration processes, the push towards harmonization and unification has become more pronounced. This started in specific areas of substantive law, but gradually also spilled over into procedural law, in the beginning limited to establishing mutual trust and cooperation among European judicial systems while preserving their specific features (Schwartze 2000; Gottwald and Klicka 2002). The basis for cooperation and mutual understanding in the field of civil procedure is, at least in continental Europe, also to be found in the common origins of the law of procedure in Romano-canonical models, which formed a 'procedural *ius commune*' for many European territories before the codification period (Van Rhee 2011; Petrak 2008).

The early projects aimed at harmonization ('approximation') of procedural laws in Europe date back to the 1980s and 1990s (Council of Europe 1984; Storme 1994), but the trend towards producing 'genuine' European instruments of procedure that not only deal with mutual recognition of judicial decisions but also create new unified European procedures in civil matters (payment orders, small claims) only started in the 2000s (Freudenthal 2010; Kramer 2010). Attempts to achieve harmonization even removing the borders between the common law-civil law divide also happened on a global scale, e.g. by way of defining common principles and rules of transnational civil procedure (Hazard et al. 2001; ALI/UNIDROIT 2006).

One of the driving forces of harmonization of civil procedure was the globalization of the economy and the move towards increasing economic and social welfare through international trade. In this context, a relatively high degree of harmonization was achieved in the area of international commercial arbitration through the work of UNCITRAL on model legislation and international rules, such as the UNCITRAL Model Law on International Commercial Arbitration and the UNCITRAL Conciliation Rules (Sanders 2004). Another trend that has received global attention is the use of alternative dispute resolution, which is a field where both the UN and the European Union undertook important activities that were intensified in the 2000s. In the EU, this development received particular attention after the enactment of the Directive on Mediation (AIA 2008), and in great part also due to the growing applicability of alternative dispute resolution in the context of consumer protection (Hodges et al. 2012).

There are several reasons for the approximation of laws and practices in the area of civil justice that are particularly important for Southern and Eastern Europe. One of the reasons relates to problems with respect to delay and inefficiency of judicial proceedings (Van Rhee 2004; Galič 2013). Others are connected with the common heritage of socialism (Uzelac 2010). Some, especially in the Mediterranean countries, are the result of a history of dysfunctional court practices (Uzelac 2008).

In Western Europe, the excessive costs of litigation are the common driving force behind a number of reforms that have become the focus of attention especially in the past decade (Hodges et al. 2010). In any case, since the beginning of the 21st century there has been a perception in many national civil justice systems of crisis accompanied by common attempts to introduce a new approach to civil procedure (Zuckerman 1999; Trocker et al. 2005). The establishment of a balanced system of legal aid and assistance in which access to justice is guaranteed also for the disadvantaged and legally illiterate members of the society is an issue in many jurisdictions, also in reform attempts in Southern and Eastern Europe (Uzelac and Preložnjak 2012).

Equally in the East and in the West, the sources of inspiration for legal reforms are often drawn from the activities of transnational bodies. Among others, a frame of reference was created by various documents of international organizations such as the UN and the Council of Europe. An even more precise and compelling source of motivation for reforms was the case law of transnational tribunals. For Europe, the major source is the case law of the European Court of Human Rights in Strasbourg, in particular concerning Article 6 of the European Convention on Human Rights (Van Dijk et al. 2018; Uzelac 2013). Successful or promising reform projects in other countries also play a major role: the global reputation of the reforms of the English Civil Procedure Rules by Lord Woolf is a good example (Andrews 2003; Van Rhee 2005; Gottwald 2010).

For some countries, a special source of reform involving harmonization was the EU accession process. The establishment of rules which make domestic legal systems of new Member States more compatible with the legal systems of existing EU Member States is not so problematic. The biggest stumbling block is the proper functioning of the justice system and ensuring effective and timely legal protection [for an example from Eastern Europe, see Uzelac et al. (2013), Uzelac (2009)].

3 The Forms of Transformation: Unity and Diversity in Seven Polycentric Steps

The metamorphoses discussed here are often not easy to spot and define. Why some forms change in a certain way depends on multiple factors. The judicial transformations, as described in the preceding paragraphs, also occur due to different factors and different local circumstances. Changes are sometimes subtle, sometimes abrupt, and very often interconnected. Still, it is possible to distinguish seven main transformation processes in civil procedure triggered by the contemporary challenges to the national justice systems. In the present introduction, these processes will be ordered based on their intensity and impact, from 'soft' and more conventional to more radical ones, including processes that may dramatically alter the very substance of our understanding of 'civil justice'. In real life, often these processes occur simultaneously and combined. Nevertheless, they can be distinguished and are characteristic of many legal justice systems irrespective of their geographic or cultural location. There is in our opinion no relation of hierarchy between the various forms or processes of transformation. The seven processes are truly polycentric, as the policies of judicial reform can involve one, several or all of them at the same time.

The seven transformation processes distinguished here are the following:

1. Transformation by borrowing from national and transnational sources;
2. Transformation by technological modernization;
3. Transformation by the reorganization of courts and a redefinition of court functions;
4. Transformation by the establishment of a multi-dimensional procedure for civil cases;
5. Transformation by the pursuit of alternatives to litigation;
6. Transformation by the collectivization of decision-making processes;
7. Transformation by 'dejudicialization' (privatization, outsourcing) of judicial tasks.

These processes of transformation of civil justice systems are visible in various contemporary legal systems, and their particular features largely depend on perceptions of the goals of civil justice (Uzelac 2014). However, these transformation processes are undeniably present, and concrete examples can be found in the contributions to this volume.

3.1 Borrowing from National and Transnational Sources: Change as a Legislative Mimicry and Transplantation of Concepts

The 'softest' and most conventional form of legal adaptation to new social circumstances is the borrowing of ideas from other legal systems. Comparative legal historians have argued that 'massive successful borrowing is common place in law' (Watson 2000; also see Watson 1974).

While the notion of legal transplants can be controversial, it is certainly widespread and originates in the past. It consists mainly of some form of emulation of legal rules or principles, either by copying or by rephrasing and adjustment. One may now ask whether there is anything decisively innovative in the legal transplants pertaining to the functioning of civil justice in the 21st century. The method is old, but a novel element is its universal application to national civil procedure and civil justice systems (court structures and the legal profession). Some forms of procedural transplants have indeed been undertaken in the past, with varying success, such as the introduction of the German model of civil litigation in Japan in 1890, or the literal translation of the Austrian ZPO in the Kingdom of Yugoslavia in 1929. But such all-encompassing transplants were more the exception than the rule. With the start of the 21st century, the procedural reforms based on transplants from other legal systems became mainstream, in particular where it concerns borrowing from transnational sources. In Europe, for example, the reconfirmed European Union competence in the field of civil procedure introduced by the Treaty of Amsterdam and expanded by the Treaty of Lisbon caused the Member States to regularly check their internal procedural design from the perspective of compatibility with EU law. Consequently, recent studies speak of a 'Europeanization' of civil procedure, announcing the introduction of common minimum standards (see Manko 2015; Tulibacka et al. 2016). The new case law of the European Court of Human Rights in the interpretation and application of the fair trial rights of Article 6 ECHR became indispensable in the reforms of civil procedure in a whole series of areas such as fairness, reasonable time, the means of recourse, effective remedies, the effective implementation of judgments and proportionality in the enforcement of civil judgments [*inter alia* see Van Dijk et al. (2018), Uzelac (2013, 2009)].

In a way, issues that used to be strictly national (for instance payment orders, or enforcement systems) are now increasingly 'trans-nationalized'. In economic and political integration such as in the European Union (where the notion of 'cross-border matters' became ubiquitous), the idea of mutual trust forces the legal reformers to resort to comparative law whenever a new reform of civil justice is planned.

Also, beyond membership in international organizations, procedural transplantation is becoming an indispensable technique. For example, the ambit of influence of EU law includes non-EU countries like Norway, among others, which follow the European *acquis* without wishing to become fully bound by EU membership (see *infra* the contribution of Fredriksen and Strandberg). In addition, the prospective members of closed clubs—such as the accession candidates to the EU—treat procedural models of the countries that have passed the test of compatibility in the accession process as best practices. The European Union as such may also have motives to regulate the judicial cooperation of its Members States with non-EU states (see the contribution of Weller to this volume).

Beyond transnational integration, the echo of successful reforms undertaken mainly for national reasons—like the Woolf reform in England and Wales—motivates national legislators, both in Europe (as in the Netherlands) and on the other side of the globe (as in Singapore, Hong Kong and China). There are mutual influences. Just as England may be a source of inspiration for Germany, the latter may be a source of inspiration for the former (cf. Gottwald 2010). The formation of bodies for the evaluation of the national justice systems such as the CEPEJ (European Commission for the Efficiency of Justice of the Council of Europe) motivates states to compare their laws and regulations with the laws and regulations of other states that are perceived to excel in efficiency and fairness. The easiest way to emulate (more) successful or efficient states are 'transplants' from foreign law even though these transplants sometimes 'go wild' (see the contribution of Galič to this volume), create 'legal irritants' (Teubner 1998) and generally raise further methodological issues (cf. Legrand 1997).

The principal agents of legislative borrowing that transform contemporary civil justice systems are currently official bodies involved in international processes. If scholars of civil procedure wish to retain their relevance, they need to study comparative law. While this is only partially true today, it is quite likely that the 'transplantational' nature of reforms in the national civil justice systems will transform not only civil justice, but also civil procedural scholarship, which will need to absorb comparative methodology, so far rarely employed in the study of civil procedure. Comparative law becomes the engine of change for civil procedure (Picker 2016). This trend is already noticeable in international projects for the creation of model rules for national civil justice systems. The ALI-UNIDROIT Transnational Principles are a genuine comparative product, which will be raised to the next level in the ongoing ELI-UNIDROIT project that aims to produce European Rules of Civil Procedure (Hazard et al. 2001; ALI/UNIDROIT 2006; Uzelac 2017, 3–4).

3.2 Technological Modernization: From 'Justice' to 'E-Justice'

The challenge of keeping pace with technological developments is also fundamentally transforming civil justice. The nature of this transformation should not be underestimated.

Technology today is not a tool which merely assists the administrators and judges to do whatever they have been doing in the past but a tool which assists them to do so with higher efficiency and lower costs. As described *supra,* technological changes in the past few decades have led to a true 'revolution'. The attempts of national reformers to maintain traditional procedural forms, employing new 'inventions' such as computers and video recording only superficially, have little prospect of success in the long run, as such forms of legal process are (or will soon be) perceived as hopelessly antiquated, in spite of the use of new 'gadgets'. Modern technology urges a fundamental transformation of justice systems, legal markets and the law itself (Susskind 2003).

At present, civil justice systems still struggle with the adoption of fundamental changes mandated by the developments of modern life, as is demonstrated by contemporary studies on electronic technology (see Kengyel and Nemessányi 2012). Even the very idea of a fully 'electronic', paperless procedure is still controversial, though the public at large has every right to expect completely digitized proceedings, i.e. proceedings that are conducted by electronic means in all important procedural steps—initiation of the proceedings, service of documents, evidence-taking, hearings and decisions.

Moreover, the establishment of 'e-justice' (a fashionable and frequently used notion in many states) should not create a justice system in which the 'electronic' element is an end in itself. Electronic litigation should not be just a functional equivalent of the older, paper-based procedure. It has the capacity to fundamentally change the procedure, just as paper-based litigation did not simply emulate but fundamentally transformed oral procedures in the past.

Electronic litigation, if properly employed, can revolutionize all dimensions of communication among the main actors in the lawsuit. The flow of information will not only be speedier, but also more complete and productive. Immediate communication is expedient, between the parties (or their representatives), between the parties and the court (including the court administration and other legal services and professions) and between different courts or their departments. Any decision made in a pending lawsuit can be announced and delivered instantly.

Such an immediate flow of communication is instrumental for the fulfilment of the goals of civil procedure. If all channels of communication are kept open, the various steps in the procedure can be openly discussed among all participants, and the ideal of an open justice system, in which the parties, their lawyers and the court collaborate in the execution of a common task—i.e. the conduct of a quick and inexpensive, but fair and accurate process—may be achieved. Electronic litigation is thus an optimal tool to neutralize the disadvantages of both adversarial and inquisitorial proceedings, contributing to a cooperative model that adjusts the procedure to its substance and optimizes the use of the necessary resources while reducing unnecessary litigation (Uzelac 2017; Van Rhee 2014).

Integral technological modernization as a form of thorough transformation of civil justice also has further positive features. It presupposes a system in which all necessary legal sources are freely accessible to and instantly searchable for the interested audience, from applicable laws and regulations to case law and commentaries. For the courts and lawyers it means that paper files are replaced by electronic files, transcripts by video recordings and public auctions in courts by digital bidding led by virtual auctioneers.

All of this has a number of side effects. The tremendous potential of new technologies does not only enable accelerated and cheaper proceedings, it also makes a number of conventional legal activities (and their agents) obsolete. Massive court archives, impressive court buildings and administrative staff (such as typists, drivers, administrators and bailiffs) may in the near future become unnecessary, replaced by only a handful of IT specialists. Moreover, the very essence of some legal professions that have built their portfolios on the classic written proceedings is put into jeopardy. For lawyers there is an urgent need to 'embrace new technologies and novel ways of sourcing legal work' in order to continue a prosperous, and avoid a disastrous, future (Susskind 2008, 269). Many aspects of the traditional operations of civil justice that are simple, routine and repetitive will be replaced by some form of automation. This, indeed, has the capacity to transform the profile of civil justice. In the future, civil justice will have to adopt a full spectrum of new technologies in order to become more flexible, more cost-efficient and leaner.

For many of the principal agents of the contemporary civil justice systems, who for ages have been pampered with high demand and high esteem for the services of their arcane profession—and abundant profits for low-tech legal work—this may not be good news. When paper-based industrial society changes into technology-based internet society (Susskind 2008), those professions which mainly survive on paper-based services—public notaries are a prominent example—may have tough times transforming, adapting, to new environments. However, adaptation is by no means impossible. From history we learn that the traditional understanding of notaries as agents who are exclusively linked to documents is factually incorrect, as is demonstrated in the historical contribution by Milotić to the present volume.

In any case, the fear of a transformation of the traditional legal professions is certainly among the reasons why the transformation by technological modernization happens in a slow, poorly designed and inefficient way in many civil justice systems. A second historical contribution to this volume provides an example of new procedures which were intentionally disregarded by legal elites in order to protect their imminent interests, thereby creating parallel and largely conflicting modes of procedure in which, at least for the time being, the old modes were prevalent (see the contribution of Held). But, just as in the past, in contemporary societies social pressure is mounting, in particular in countries which have a history of slow and inefficient courts and a low level of social trust in the traditional forms of justice. Thus, paradoxically, new technologies are being introduced faster in these civil justice systems which experience more dysfunctionalities than in countries where judicial institutions are more trusted and their users more satisfied (see the contribution of Karolczyk to this volume).

3.3 Reorganizing Justice: A Redefinition of Court Structures and Their Functions

The changes discussed above do not only affect the technological functioning of civil justice. As has been stated, the organizational components of civil justice are also affected. Starting with court structures, the introduction of new technologies, enhanced means of communication and travel and a change in the profile and number of cases are putting a redefinition of the role and function of courts on the agenda, as well as the overall composition of court structures. This trend has sometimes been referred to as 'developing a public administration perspective' on judicial systems (Fabri and Langbroek 2000).

There are at least three dimensions to this reorganization process. The first dimension is related to the size and number of court structures. In many countries, the structure of the court network dates back to the 18th and 19th centuries. In the light of new realities (such as better roads, faster trains, airplanes and instant communication), it is legitimate to ask whether there is a need for a court in every community, and whether, in general, the structure of the court network is adequate for meeting the current justice demands.

The second dimension concerns specialization. While the transformation of court procedures often rationalizes the influx of cases, it should be noted that in the future the remaining court cases are likely to be more complex. One may ask whether this should lead to the creation of new, specialized courts, or to some other forms of specialization, depending on many factors. As several examples show (see the contribution of Baboolal-Frank to this volume) the process of modernization of court structures may result in a move in the opposite direction, i.e. to the creation of a unified court system away from the decentralized and compartmentalized structures as they exist today in many jurisdictions. Such an amalgamated court system may bring advantages in terms of consistency, effectiveness and standardization of court functions while preserving specialist skills and knowledge.

The third dimension is a conceptual one and deals with rethinking the role and function of particular courts, especially those at the apex of the court pyramid. The new approach to justice systems as a public service offered to its users under favourable terms and for an affordable price motivates a reassessment of the role of the courts in the judicial hierarchy. Can a system of state courts afford multiple assessments of the same issue at three or more levels of adjudication? Should supreme courts be used for a private function, in order to correct errors in the factual and legal determination in a wide range of cases? The reforms of the supreme courts both in the East and in the West demonstrate a trend which focuses the role of these courts on specific, system-oriented issues. While this trend is not without difficulties, it is not likely that it will be stopped. As demonstrated by various contributions to this volume (see Bratković and Van Der Haegen), the past experience of slow procedures, backlogs and the poor quality of supreme adjudication transforms the very essence of the models upon which supreme courts are founded, shifting their attention from the mass processing of individual cases to a narrower range of systemically important issues, resulting in well-reasoned decisions of fundamental importance for the rule of law.

3.4 Multi-dimensional Procedures: From Speed and Costs to Proportionality, Access to Justice and Case Management

Technological modernization and court reorganization based on best international practices logically leads to another fundamental procedural transformation: the reshaping of the approach to cases processed by the civil justice system. The keywords of many reforms in different parts of the world since the beginning of the 21st century are *proportionality, access to justice* and *case management.* All of these notions are connected in the new, multi-dimensional perspective on the goals of civil justice.

While the conventional doctrine of civil procedure almost exclusively focused on substantive justice (i.e. on the accuracy of the decision-making process, the fairness of the judicial processes and the consistency of judicial decisions), the approach to reforms in the past two decades has raised to the same level of importance the element of appropriate time (i.e. the speed of decision-making), affordable costs (i.e. the reduction of unnecessary expenses) and the effectiveness of the enforcement of civil and commercial judgments (the timely and complete implementation of judicial decisions). There is a desire to distribute the means which are at the disposal of the national justice systems proportionally, based on the importance and social value of the matters at stake. This is not an entirely new approach; its most authoritative and prominent example is Lord Woolf's 'new theory of justice' in England and Wales (Sorabji 2014, 161–199).

Part of the proportionate allocation of resources related to the enhancement of access to justice for the ultimate court users is the establishment of a system in which the users will have a real and practical possibility to use the system in a way that is appropriate to protecting their rights. In the context of austerity policies and social priorities, the establishment of a legal aid system which does not merely provide an attractive normative framework, but which is functional in practice can be a significant challenge (as is demonstrated in the contribution of Brozović to this volume).

Another way to promote access to justice is the creation of special proceedings which can provide quick and affordable relief to a large circle of court users. Among these special proceedings are summary proceedings for the certification of uncontested debts such as payment orders, and special proceedings for the protection of consumers. As explained in the contribution of Stephanie Law to this volume, one way to reduce costs and provide access to justice is to provide the courts with more extensive *ex officio* powers to establish the facts relevant for the protection of consumers. Indeed, for managerial judges with broad powers it is essential to maintain impartiality. In this volume, a team led by Professor Fernhout developed a method of assessing the predicted effectiveness of measures for safeguarding such impartiality.

3.5 In Pursuit of the Best Alternatives: Consensual Dispute Resolution and ADR

A transformation of the approach to the goals of civil justice leads also to a different attitude towards conventional civil litigation. Contentious civil litigation once upon a time viewed as the pinnacle of the legal process—as a constitutionally guaranteed default method of legal protection with which each dispute starts and ends—is progressively regarded (at least by some scholars) as a costly and lengthy method of dispute resolution which should be avoided wherever possible. If law is regarded as a service industry and civil justice as another public service offered to the society, then litigation should be used only where ultimately necessary.

If civil litigation is the ultimate remedy (*ultimum remedium*), what then is the first and preferable remedy? As there is no need for state intervention where private persons can resolve their problems autonomously and consensually, the first preference of contemporary civil justice is a negotiated solution, reached either as a result of direct contact between the disputants or with the assistance of a third, neutral party in some form of alternative dispute resolution (ADR).

As argued by Professor Marcus in his contribution to this volume, the ADR movement in the USA was a 'reaction to costly and lengthy proceedings the United

States was coping with'. From the USA, this movement was exported to other countries and has become one of the most common trends in practically all civil justice systems worldwide. Invariably, national jurisdictions are today promoting ADR, as exemplified by the contribution on Spain (see Gascón Inchausti), sometimes adopting rather innovative methods for special cases, such as family group conferences (described by de Roo and Jagtenberg in this volume).

Admittedly, the results of the ADR movement are ambiguous. Only a handful of jurisdictions have opted for mandatory ADR on a large scale, and this is controversial (Lupoi 2014). The announced transformation has so far happened mainly at a normative and doctrinal level, but the real effects on the reduction of contentious cases and the expenses of dispute resolution are so far rather limited (De Palo et al. 2014). Two contributions to this volume criticize the ADR movement from the perspective of the public goals of civil justice (see Marcus and Woo). Nevertheless, it is certain that the ADR movement continues to contribute to the transformation of civil justice, at least where it concerns a change in the culture of litigation and the psychology of the litigants (and their lawyers).

3.6 Collectivizing Decision-Making: Group Actions

A global trend, optimistically asserted by Mauro Cappelletti in his 1975 text, concerns the promotion of collective dispute resolution. Cappelletti's optimism may have been based on the fact that in the United States class actions had been gaining momentum since the second half of the 1960s. US class actions have a global reputation and present one of the major hallmarks of the American civil justice system which is still broadly used in spite of recent developments aimed at constraining some of its excesses (on 'patent trolls' see Marcus in this volume). Driven by private interest, US class actions generally manage to be decent instruments by which private law serves the enforcement of public interests. One of the remarkable examples of the positive use of class actions—the bright side of class actions—is presented in this volume in the contribution on human rights class actions (see Silvestri).

Outside the United States, collective redress in Brazil has developed into an important and widely used instrument. In Brazil, however, public bodies like the Public Prosecutor's Office play a key role in collective redress. The *actio popularis* based on Roman antecedents is still a common practice in this country. Even more popular is the Brazilian-style class action (*ação civil pública*), in conjunction with some other techniques, such as 'public civil inquests'. These secure a large volume of Brazilian mass litigation (see Cruz Arenhart in this volume).

In the rest of the world, the (re)discovery of collective litigation is a by-product of the transformative movements of the 2000s. Like the ADR movement in the past, the 'collectivization' movement in civil justice is more likely to be present in speeches, programmatic documents and academic writings than in everyday reality. There are, however, no signs that promoting collective actions and other forms of collective decision-making will fade away. In the contemporary world of massification and automatization, it is somewhat logical to look for a functional equivalent of mass industrial processing in a document-based industrial society, although the mass processing of legal problems in a technology-based internet society can also be achieved by other means. A number of countries have enacted laws on collective redress. The Slovenian example shows that such legislation has a very high chance of being perceived as a legal irritant, due to unprepared transitional judiciaries (see Sladič in this volume).

In a limited number of areas such as consumer or financial services cases collective redress is gaining ground. A combination that has proved to operate well in the Netherlands is that of collective redress and ADR. Under Dutch law, some cases of mass damages may be decided by collective settlements concluded under court supervision. The experience with these settlements under the WCAM (Act on Collective Settlement of Mass Damage) are analysed by de Roo and Jagtenberg in the present volume.

3.7 Outsourcing, Privatization and Other Forms of Dejudicialization

A final trend of transformation is 'dejudicialization'. The notion of 'dejudicialization' is understood in this volume as encompassing all forms of a transfer of tasks from courts and judges to other, non-judicial persons and services.

In the words of Margaret Woo, the trigger for 'dejudicialization' is 'a renewed call for minimizing costs and maximizing efficiency' (*infra*). The starting point is the insufficiencies of modern judiciaries, primarily ineffectiveness due to an overburdening of the court system with non-essential tasks. Another reason for dejudicialization are the costs of the performance of judicial tasks, which can be considered excessive compared to the costs of some other, non-judicial arrangements. Dejudicialization is comparable to (and partly inspired by) the business strategy of outsourcing, by which companies subcontract their own internal activities to other, different companies.

In a broader sense, 'dejudicialization' can be either internal or external. Internal dejudicialization means the transfer of particular tasks from judges to other court staff or services. For instance, some time-consuming parts of the judicial process, like arranging the service of documents or the drafting of decisions, can be allocated to the court administration or to judicial assistants (for examples, see the contribution of Gascón Inchausti to this volume). Similarly, simple and routine judicial cases can be 'outsourced' to court clerks or land registrars. Such internal 'outsourcing' does not change the jurisdiction of the court, although it influences the internal competences and the internal division of labour within the court system. In a way, the promotion of (court-annexed) ADR as a replacement for civil litigation can be viewed as a form of internal outsourcing, as court cases are steered away from the judicial decision-making process (adjudication) to an extra-judicial dispute settlement process (mediation), usually—but not always—conducted by professionals who are not judges.

A more radical form of dejudicialization is the transfer of tasks of the state courts to the private professions or private companies. As noted in one of the contributions to this volume (see Marcus), the ADR movement in the USA was a form of 'outsourcing' the tasks of the public courts to the private sphere. In areas that are by their very nature private, like family relations, dealing with relevant issues is more appropriately done by private means. In this sense, mediation was found to be most successful in the domain of family law according to studies by the European Commission (de Roo and Jagtenberg in this volume).

A whole range of non-contentious cases can easily be 'dejudicialized', as legislators generally have a certain latitude in distributing these cases to various bodies or branches of state power. These cases are also the easiest to privatize. Recent experiences with non-contested divorce and separation proceedings in France and Spain show a trend of transferring such cases from courts to notaries (on Spain, see Gascón Inchausti in this volume).

Dejudicialization is not only a blessing for overburdened judicial systems—it is also an important warning for them. A transformation of civil justice systems which transfers many of their functions to the private sphere can be a signal that these systems are incapable of adapting to new circumstances. And, as an apocryphal statement attributed to Darwin tells us, 'It is not the strongest of the species that survives, nor the most intelligent, but the one most responsive to change.' In a similar sense, if the justice systems do not adequately respond to the requirements and expectations of the new age, their transformation may well mean their gradual fading away. Such a prophecy might seem to be too radical, as billions of euros and dollars are still being invested in civil justice systems, but the dominance of 'public court-based dispute resolution' is undeniably shrinking. As noted by Gascón Inchausti in this volume for Spain, civil justice systems are able to resolve average civil and commercial disputes reasonably well, but obviously this begs the question as to the 'less than average' cases.

If 'average' means cases that are average in size and complexity, the remaining cases are either complex or high-value cases important for the national economies, or small and routine cases which may be legally less interesting, but due to the high volume of these cases still economically important. As regards both categories, the public courts are rapidly losing ground, as is demonstrated in several contributions to this volume. In high-value/low-volume cases, this is noticeable in the trends of introducing mandatory pre-action procedures, the growth of international commercial arbitration and the recent controversies about investor-state dispute resolution. In low-value/high-volume cases, the courts and judges are being bypassed through the introduction of (automated and digitized) payment order schemes, the mandatory mediation of disputes and various private options for the collection of small and uncontested claims.

Should one be worried, or should one welcome the trends of the shrinking dominance of public courts in dispute resolution worldwide? On the one hand, modernization has always changed our lives, whether we like it or not. If other means of social regulation are better and more efficient than public courts, one should not feel too much sorrow when some matters are taken away from conventional civil dispute resolution. Many matters, in particular those related to the processing of non-contentious cases, were only by chance, i.e. through accidents of history, entrusted to courts. There are no good reasons for them to remain in court if other agents—or sophisticated machines—can decide them in a better and cheaper manner.

On the other hand, the extension of private and non-court mechanisms and the diminishing role of the state courts cause certain risks in contentious cases. While ADR may promote access to justice, it can also jeopardize access. In this context, Professor Marcus discusses in his contribution to this volume the risks of mandatory ADR, and the even greater risks of mandatory private arbitration. In the USA, where the privatization of justice has progressed further than elsewhere, consumers are bound by clauses that force them to waive their right to public litigation, and to arbitrate before consumer courts described as 'kangaroo courts'.

Consequently, one should be wary of the risks that accompany the erosion of access to public courts, and preserve and foster mechanisms that secure the equal protection of rights, especially between litigants of unequal power, wealth and experience. When dispute resolution schemes do not protect the rights of the weaker party in civil cases, these schemes cannot be a good replacement for a public and fair trial before an independent and impartial court of law. And, where civil justice cannot be qualified as 'civil' and does not provide justice, legal development is frustrated and at some point court users may resort to self-help.

4 Concluding Remarks

As has been demonstrated in this introduction, the global and European civil justice landscapes show considerable unity but also extreme diversity. It is obvious that the present changes in society and technology may have profound effects regarding the way disputes are resolved either in court (public justice) or out of court (private justice). In order to be able to compete with out-of-court solutions, the civil justice systems provided by the state courts are in need of reform. So far changes have not materialized on an all-compassing scale. Where changes have occurred it seems that the various implications of societal and technological developments have not been fully thought through (for example the implications of the availability of new technology). It is the conviction of the authors of the present introduction that the state courts serve important goals, not the least of which is in the area of the development and interpretation of the law. However, this goal will come under threat if the state court systems prove to be unable to meet the challenges posed by changes in society and technology. Private justice will fill the gap and obviously private justice will not be able to realize the public goals which state courts may serve. The future will show whether the necessary balance between public and private justice can be found, giving rise to a civil justice system where both the private interests of the litigants and the public interests of society will be served in an optimal manner, in part by way of out-of-court solutions, and in part by way of the state judiciary.

References

AIA (2008) Association for international arbitration (ed). In: The new EU directive on mediation. Maklu, Antwerpen-Apeldoorn

ALI/UNIDROIT (2006) Principles of transnational civil procedure. Cambridge UP, Cambridge

Andrews N (2003) English civil procedure: fundamentals of the new civil justice system. Oxford UP, Oxford, New York

Cappelletti M (1975) La protection d'intérêts collectifs et de groupe dans le procès civil (Métamorphoses de la procédure civile). Revue internationale de droit comparé 27(3):571–597

Council of Europe (1984) Principles of civil procedure. Recommendation No. R(84), 5, Council of Europe, Strasbourg

Deguchi M, Storme M (2008) The reception and transmission of civil procedural law in the global society. Maklu, Antwerpen-Apeldoorn

De Palo G, et al (2014) 'Rebooting' the mediation directive: assessing the limited impact of its implementation and proposing measures to increase the number of mediations in the EU. European Parliament Studies, Brussels – PE 493.042

Fabri M, Langbroek PM (2000) The challenge of change for European judicial systems: developing a public administration perspective. IOS Press, Amsterdam, Washington, Tokyo, Brussels

Freudenthal M (2010) Attitudes of EU MS towards the harmonisation of civil procedure. In: Van Rhee CH, Uzelac A (eds) Enforcement and enforceability. Intersentia, Antwerp, Oxford, Portland

Galič A (2013) Ograničenje mogućnosti iznošenja novota i cilj građanskoga parničnog postupka. In: Uzelac et al (eds) Djelotvorna pravna zaštita u pravičnom postupku. Izazovi pravosudnih transformacija na jugu Europe. Liber amicorum Mihajlo Dika. Pravni fakultet Sveučilišta u Zagrebu, Zagreb, pp 95–116

Gottwald P (2010) Litigation in England and Germany. Gieseking, Bielefeld

Gottwald P, Klicka T (2002) Procedural law on the threshold of a new millenium. CLC, Wien

Harsági V, Van Rhee CH (2014) Multi-party redress mechanisms in Europe: squeaking mice. Intersentia, Cambridge, Antwerp, Portland

Hazard GC Jr, Taruffo M, Sturner R et al (2001) Introduction to the principles and rules of transnational civil procedure. NY Univ J Int Law Politics 33:769–782

Hodges C, Vogenauer S, Tulibacka M (2010) The costs and funding of civil litigation. Hart, Oxford and Portland

Hodges C, Benöhr I, Creutzfeldt-Banda N (2012) Consumer ADR in Europe. Civil Justice Systems. CH Beck, Hart, Nomos

Kengyel M, Nemessányi Z (2012) Electronic technology and civil procedure. Springer, New York and London

Kramer XE (2010) Enhancing enforcement in the EU. The European order for payment procedure and its implementation in the member states. In: Van Rhee CH, Uzelac A (eds). Enforcement and Enforceability. Intersentia, Antwerp

Legrand P (1997) The impossibility of 'legal transplants'. Maastricht J European Comp Law 4 (2):111–124

Lupoi MA (2014) Facing the crisis: new Italian provisions to keep disputes out of the courtroom (or take them out of it). ZZPInt 19:95–108

Manko R (2015) Europeanisation of civil procedure. Towards common minimum standards? EPRS, European Parliament, June 2015, PE 559.499
Merryman JH (1985) The civil law tradition: an introduction to the legal systems of Western Europe and Latin America. Stanford University Press, Stanford
Petrak M (2008) The procedural Ius commune as a source of contemporary law: a croatian example in a European context. In: Van Rhee CH, Uzelac A (eds) Civil justice between efficiency and quality: from Ius commune to the CEPEJ. Intersentia, Antwerp, Oxford, Portland
Picker C (2016) Comparative law as an engine of change for civil procedure. In: Picker C, Seidman G (eds) The dynamism of civil procedure—global trends and developments. Springer, Cham
Sanders P (2004) The work of UNCITRAL on arbitration and conciliation. Kluwer, The Hague
Schwartze A (2000) Enforcement of private law: the missing link in the process of European harmonisation. European Rev Private Law 8(1):135–146
Sorabji J (2014) English civil justice after the Woolf and Jackson reforms. Cambridge UP, Cambridge
Storme M (1994) Rapprochement du droit judiciaire de l'Union europeenne/Approximation of judiciary law in the European Union. Nijhoff, Dordrecht-Boston
Susskind R (2003) Transforming the law: essays on technology, justice and the legal marketplace. Oxford UP, Oxford
Susskind R (2008) The end of lawyers? Rethinking the nature of legal service. Oxford UP, Oxford, New York
Teubner G (1998) Legal irritants: good faith in British law or how unifying law ends up in new divergences. The Modern Law Rev 61(1):11–32
Trocker N, Varano V, De Luca A (2005) The reforms of civil procedure in comparative perspective. Giappichelli, Torino
Tulibacka M, Sanz M, Blomeyer R (2016) Common minimum standards of civil procedure. European added value assessment annex I. EPRS, European Parliament, June 2016, PE 581.385
Uzelac A (2008) Reforming mediterranean civil procedure. In: Van Rhee CH, Uzelac A (eds) Civil justice between efficiency and quality. From Ius commune to the CEPEJ. Intersentia, Antwerp, Oxford, Portland, pp 71–99
Uzelac A (2009) In the quest for the Holy Grail of effectiveness. In: Council of Europe, The right to trial within a reasonable time and short-term reform of the European Court of Human Rights, Ljubljana
Uzelac A (2010) Survival of the third legal tradition? Supreme Court Law Review, 49 S.C.L.R. (2d):377–396
Uzelac A (2013) The European court of human rights. In: Wijffels AA, Van Rhee CH (eds) European Supreme Courts. A Portrait through History. Third Millenium Publishing, London, pp 274–284
Uzelac A (2014) Goals of civil justice and civil procedure in the contemporary world. In: Uzelac A (ed) Goals of civil justice and civil procedure in contemporary judicial systems. Springer, Cham, Heidelberg, New York, London, pp 3–31
Uzelac A (2017) Towards European civil procedure: rethinking procedural obligations. Hungarian J Legal Stud 58(1):3–18
Uzelac A, Preložnjak B (2012) The development of legal aid systems in the Western Balkans. A study of controversial reforms in Croatia and Serbia. Kritisk Iuss. Utgitt av Rettspolitisk Forening (Liber amicorum—Jon T. Johnsen) 38(3–4):261–287
Uzelac A, Garašić J, Maganić A (2013) Djelotvorna pravna zaštita u pravičnom postupku. Liber amicorum Mihajlo Dika. Narodne novine, Zagreb
Van Dijk P, Van Hoof F, Van Rijn A et al (2018) Theory and practice of the European convention on human rights. Intersentia, Antwerpen
Van Rhee CH (2004) The law's delay. Essays on undue delay in civil litigation. Intersentia, Antwerpen, Groningen

Van Rhee CH (2005) European traditions in civil procedure. Intersentia, Antwerpen, Oxford
Van Rhee CH (2011) Towards a procedural Ius commune? Russian Yearb Civ Proc Arbitr 7 (8):201–217
Van Rhee CH (2012) Harmonisation of civil procedure: an historical and comparative perspective. In: Van Rhee CH, Kramer XE (eds) Civil litigation in a globalising world. T.M.C. Asser Press, Springer, The Hague, pp 39–63
Van Rhee CH (2014) Obligations of the parties and their lawyers in civil litigation. In: Adolphsen et al (eds) Festschrift für Peter Gottwald zum 70. Geburtstag. Beck, München
Watson A (1974) Legal transplants. An approach to comparative law. University of Georgia, Athens
Watson A (2000) Legal transplants and European private law. Electron J Comp Law 4/4
Wijffels AA (2013) European legal history and the diversity of supreme judicatures. In: Wijffels AA, Van Rhee CH (eds) European supreme courts. 3rd Millenium Publishing, London, pp 14–37
Zuckerman AAS (1999) Civil justice in crisis. Oxford UP, Oxford

Alan Uzelac Professor of Law at the University of Zagreb, Croatia, where he teaches Civil Procedure and Comparative Civil Procedure, Organization of the Judiciary and Alternative Dispute Resolution. Founding Member of the European Commission for the Efficiency of Justice (CEPEJ) in Strasbourg. Delegate in the UNCITRAL Working Group on Arbitration and Conciliation. Co-director of the Public and Private Justice seminar at the Inter-University Centre, Dubrovnik, Croatia. Director of the research project Transformation of Civil Justice Under the Influence of Global and Regional Integration Processes.

Cornelis Hendrik (Remco) van Rhee Chair of European Legal History and Comparative Civil Procedure, Maastricht University, the Netherlands. Director of the research programme Foundations and Principles of Civil Procedure in Europe of the Ius Commune Research School. Co-director of the Public and Private Justice seminar at the Inter-University Centre, Dubrovnik, Croatia.

Part II
Impact of Regional and Global Developments: Cooperation, Borrowing, Transplants

Enforcement by Means of Periodic Penalties (Astreinte) in Slovenia: A Transplant Gone Wild

Aleš Galič

Abstract Already in 1978, undoubtedly as an implant from French law, the concept of *astreinte* was introduced as a means of indirect coercion to enforce judgments in the (then) Yugoslav legal order. In the Yugoslav era, however, the instrument of *astreinte* was never widely used in practice and it was mostly overlooked in legal writing as well. After the independence of Slovenia and in the era of socio-political, legal and economic transition, the situation changed. Creditors increasingly started to use the instrument of *astreinte*, and only then did it become apparent that its regulation did not contain sufficient guarantees against abuse. Rarely has any other concept of Slovenian private law sparked as many controversies in legal doctrine as the concept of *astreinte*. Nevertheless, in recent years the regulation of *astreinte* has to a certain degree developed through case law. Some of the disputed issues have been settled and certain necessary safeguards established.

1 Introduction

1.1 A General Outline of the Enforcement of Civil Judgments in Slovenia

In Slovenia, the procedure concerning the enforcement of civil judgments is divided into two steps. A creditor who is in possession of a valid *titre executoire*[1] must first

This contribution is the result of research supported by the Croatian Science Foundation (project no. 6988).

[1]In Slovenian law, only a final court judgment (*res iudicata*) is enforceable; there is no provisional enforceability of first instance judgments pending appeal. Other important types of *titre executoire* are settlements in court, enforceable notarial records, and arbitral awards; Article 17 EJPMA.

A. Galič (✉)
Faculty of Law, University of Ljubljana, Ljubljana, Slovenia
e-mail: ales.galic@pf.uni-lj.si

A. Uzelac and C. H. van Rhee (eds.), *Transformation of Civil Justice*,
Ius Gentium: Comparative Perspectives on Law and Justice 70,
https://doi.org/10.1007/978-3-319-97358-6_2

apply for a court order authorising the enforcement (a motion for enforcement; Article 40 of the Enforcement of Judgments and Protective Measures Act—hereinafter: EJPMA[2]). The "enforcement court" (the court vested with jurisdiction for enforcement proceedings) shall issue a warrant of execution (*sklep o izvršbi*) by which it verifies the title and orders enforcement measures (Article 44 EJPMA). The warrant of execution empowers the creditor to proceed with physical measures of enforcement—with the methods of enforcement and to the extent authorised in the warrant of execution. Thus, the warrant of execution not only confirms the enforceability of the judgment in general, but also defines the methods to be applied and to the extent to which the enforcement is authorised in the particular case.[3] With regard to the system whereby the creditor always needs to obtain an authorisation from the court, the Slovenian law on the enforcement of judgments in civil matters is (just like Slovenian civil procedural law in general) still similar to the Austrian law. After the warrant of execution has been rendered, the enforcement proceedings in the narrower sense may either remain in the domain of the court or be conducted by a private bailiff. The court undertakes enforcement measures in certain types of enforcement (e.g. garnishment of wages, enforcement against real estate, and enforcement of certain non-monetary claims such as prohibitory injunction judgments). The most important field where the responsibility for physical actions for enforcement is allotted to bailiffs as private enforcement agents is enforcement against movable property (attachment and sale by auction). Furthermore, bailiffs also carry out the enforcement of certain non-monetary claims such as the eviction of tenants who do not or no longer have a legal right of occupation.

1.2 The Imposition of Fines as the Primary Method of Enforcement of Certain Types of Permanent Injunctions

A pecuniary fine as a method of enforcement of a civil judgment may be threatened and ultimately imposed as a means of persuading the judgment debtor to fulfil his or her obligation. Where a judgment results in an individual being made subject to either a mandatory injunction (Article 226 EJPMA) or a prohibitory injunction (Article 227(1) EJPMA), enforcement may be effected through the imposition of a fine. Furthermore, fines can be imposed as a primary method of enforcement of

[2]*Zakon o izvršbi in zavarovanju*, consolidated text, Official Gazette, No. 3/2007.

[3]The warrant of execution should be distinguished from the so-called enforcement clause (*izvršilna klavzula*); the latter is obtained from the (clerk of the) court that rendered the judgment and is a matter of purely formal examination; it only confirms that the judgment is final and that the time limit for voluntary fulfilment has elapsed, but it does not refer to the authorisation of particular enforcement measures (Article 42 EJPMA). The enforcement clause therefore does not substitute for a warrant of execution.

judgments concerning the custody right of access to a child (Article 238d and 238f EJPMA[4]) as well as a labour court judgment ordering an employer to reinstate a worker in the workplace (Article 232 EJPMA). Thus, the system of fines as a method of enforcement only applies to such injunctions, the fulfilment of which ultimately depends on the willing cooperation of the judgment debtor. The fines are paid to the benefit of the state treasury.

In cases of judgments for specific performance where such cooperation of the debtor is not necessary for effective enforcement, other methods of enforcement are applied. The eviction of a tenant is achieved through direct enforcement by a bailiff (Article 221 EJPMA). If the creditor is entitled to the delivery of a specific asset, the bailiff shall seize the asset and hand it over to the creditor (Article 214 EJPMA). If the objects to be handed over cannot be found, the court shall, upon a motion of the judgment creditor, order the judgment debtor to repay their value (Article 215). If the asset is not individually determined, the court shall authorise the creditor to purchase such an asset at the expense of the debtor (Article 216 EJPMA). A similar rule applies for the enforcement of an obligation to carry out an act that can be performed equally well by other persons and not solely by the judgment debtor. The creditor may, upon the court's authorisation, have the work performed by a third party at the judgment debtor's expense (Article 225 EJPMA).

1.3 The Introduction of Astreinte as an "Implant" from the French Legal System

The described system of fines as a method of enforcing certain judgments entailing an injunction has a long tradition in Slovenia. It has basically been in force without interruption since the time when Slovenia was still a part of Austria (until 1918) and then in Yugoslavia (between 1918 and 1991). However, in 1978 an important reform of civil law took place in (the then) Yugoslavia. The concept of *astreinte* was introduced as an additional means of indirect enforcement of judgments in civil matters. This reform did not abolish the aforementioned system of fines; it just gave creditors another option to pursue the fulfilment of non-monetary claims affirmed by final court judgments. The (then) novelty of *astreinte* was introduced by the new Contracts and Torts Act[5] (whereby the Enforcement of Judgments Act was amended at the same time by the inclusion of a provision with a procedural character[6]). Undoubtedly, the introduction of *astreinte* into the (then) Yugoslav legal system was influenced by French law (Kresteš 2008, 1028). Also, the first

[4]The direct physical measure of handing over a child with the assistance of a bailiff can be applied as a subsidiary method of enforcement.

[5]*Zakon o obligacijskih razmerjih* (Official Gazette of the SFRY, No. 29/78).

[6]*Zakon o izvršilnem postopku* (Official Gazette of the SFRY, No. 20/78).

commentators on the newly introduced concept strongly relied on French doctrine (Cigoj 1984, 1010).

Today, the main provision concerning *astreinte* (in the Slovene language, *sodni penal*; literally translated: a "court penalty") is contained in Article 269(1) of the Slovenian Code of Obligations (formerly Article 294 of the Yugoslav Contracts and Torts Act). Pursuant to this provision, if the debtor fails to perform on time any non-pecuniary obligation as determined by a final judgment, the court may, upon a motion of the creditor, require the debtor to pay the creditor a specific sum of money for each day of delay or for any other unit of time. When imposing *astreinte*, the court sets an extended time limit for the voluntary fulfilment of the obligation. The amount of *astreinte* is determined and enforced without prejudice to any liability for harm caused by the party who fails to comply with the obligation imposed by the judgment. Although regulated by the law of obligations, and although *astreinte* is not in itself a method of execution, the rules concerning it clearly have the purpose of effecting enforcement. According to Article 269 of the Code of Obligations, *astreinte* is a means of exerting pressure in order to break the debtor's resistance to fulfilling the judgment. It is thus an indirect method of coercion.

The most significant difference between fines and *astreinte* is that the former are payable to the benefit of the state treasury. In contrast, the latter sum is paid in full to the party (the judgment creditor) who obtained an order for its payment.

Where applicable, the judgment creditor may freely choose between two tracks. He or she may either initiate an ordinary execution procedure (whereby indirect enforcement through fines shall be implemented in the case of mandatory or prohibitory injunctions) or request the imposition (and ultimately the enforcement) of *astreinte*. Nevertheless, once a motion for an ordinary execution procedure is filed, the creditor is no longer entitled to request *astreinte*.[7] If the creditor has first requested the imposition of *astreinte*, he or she may still subsequently avail him- or herself of an ordinary execution procedure. However, once a motion for the ordinary execution procedure is filed, the order for the payment of *astreinte* has no further effect.

The wording of Article 269(1) of the Obligations Code might suggest that the court exercises discretion as to deciding whether to impose *astreinte* or not, as it states that the court "*may*" impose *astreinte*. However, the position in the legal doctrine and case law has always been that the court is obliged to impose *astreinte* if the conditions determined by law are met and the creditor files an appropriate motion (Juhart et al. 1995, 221).

[7]Even if the creditor withdraws the request for execution, he or she is no longer entitled to claim *astreinte*. Conclusion of the General Session of the Supreme Court of Slovenia of 18 June 1986, Poročilo VSS 1/86.

2 The Mixed Elements of *Astreinte* and Its Legislative Goal

Whereas the concept of fines payable to the state treasury is exclusively a matter of the enforcement of judgments, the legal nature and purpose of *astreinte* is mixed (Cigoj 1981, 497; Berden 2004, 15). *Astreinte* is a private penalty that should grant the creditor a sort of satisfaction for the frustration caused by the failure of the debtor to perform the obligation imposed by a final court judgment. *Astreinte* is, as alluded to above, determined irrespective of any loss incurred by the creditor. Thus, the creditor may request both *astreinte* as well as the recovery of damages for the harm caused by the non-performance of the obligation. However, it needs to be stressed that under Slovenian law in such a case the creditor may only request the recovery of pecuniary loss. Concerning moral (non-pecuniary) damage, a *numerus clausus* applies in Slovenian law (Strohsack 1990, 225) and thus only legally recognised moral (non-pecuniary) damages can be compensated for. The harm in the form of the creditor's suffering, pain, and feeling of frustration or helplessness caused by the debtor's failure to comply with the judgment is not a harm for which damages are recoverable. In this sense, *astreinte* is a substitution for the creditor's moral damage caused by the debtor's non-compliance with the final judgment. Furthermore, the possibility of invoking *astreinte* also puts the creditor of a monetary claim and the creditor of a non-monetary claim on more equal footing. In the case of monetary judgments, default interest may be automatically claimed in the event of the debtor's default. In the case of non-monetary claims, *astreinte* plays a similar role (Wedam Lukić 1992, 110). However, *astreinte* also has another purpose—it is a means of enforcement of judgments.[8] In fact, this is the main purpose of *astreinte*, whereas the purpose of compensation for moral damage is only secondary. As the Constitutional Court has confirmed, *astreinte* is an important instrument for the enforcement of judgments.[9] An effective enforcement procedure is an inseparable element of the right of access to court, as guaranteed by Article 23 of the Slovenian Constitution and Article 6 of the European Convention on Human Rights. In addition, ensuring that the final decisions of courts are enforced and respected is also important for the implementation of the principle of a state governed by the rule of law, as determined by Article 2 of the Slovenian Constitution.[10] The Constitutional Court has drawn attention to the provision of Article 269(2) of the Code of Obligations, pursuant to which a debtor may subsequently request that a portion of the *astreinte* already paid be returned, but only after he or she has performed the obligation imposed by the judgment. This provision shows, as held by the Constitutional Court, that the main purpose of *astreinte* is the enforcement of

[8]Cf. Decision of the Ljubljana Court of Appeal, I Ip 4440/2014 of 4 December 2014.

[9]Decision of the Constitutional Court No. Up 181/99 of 18 December 2002.

[10]In general on this issue, see Decision of the Constitutional Court No. U-I-344/06 of 20 November 2008.

judgments, and not the recovery of damages.[11] From these important findings it follows, *inter alia*, that when determining the amount of *astreinte* (and when reducing such amount *ex post facto*) the court does not need to take into account the (non) existence or amount of actual loss suffered by the creditor (Dika 2003, 23).

The procedure for an *astreinte* order is a *sui generis* procedure with mixed elements: firstly, it establishes a civil claim (as the *astreinte* order forms a title for a new monetary claim) and, secondly, it is a means of enforcement of a non-monetary claim (Dika 2003, 23). Therefore, there are doubts as to whether it is appropriate that an *astreinte* order is rendered in the same kind of procedure as ordinary enforcement orders—a simplified written procedure, conducted *ex parte*, whereas the debtor may only subsequently oppose the order (Berden 2004, 20).

Concerning both fines[12] as well as *astreinte*,[13] the Constitutional Court rejects the viewpoint that they have a penal nature. It has confirmed that they are not aimed at punishment. It is consequently not necessary for the principles that apply in criminal procedure to apply also to these sanctions (for example: a strict requirement as to proportionality between the severity of the sanction and the nature of the wrongdoer's act). The Constitutional Court has affirmed that fines and *astreinte* are not imposed as measures of punishment, but pursue the aim of ensuring the execution of a judgment in cases in which imposing sanctions is a means intended to influence the willingness of the debtor to perform the obligation.[14] Thus, their purpose is to encourage compliance rather than to punish past non-compliance.

3 Scope of Application

It has already been mentioned that the system of fines as a method of enforcement only applies to such injunctions whose fulfilment ultimately depends on the willing cooperation of the judgment debtor. In contrast, the scope of the possible application of *astreinte* is considerably broader. *Astreinte* can be imposed in connection with *any non-monetary obligation* (specific performance), thus not only in cases of mandatory and prohibitory injunctions, but also for the delivery of goods, for the carrying out of an act that can be performed equally well by another person at the debtor's expense, and for the eviction of a tenant. This broad possibility of seeking *astreinte* is heavily criticised in Slovenian legal doctrine (see Sect. 8 below). It is conceded that *astreinte* is a useful means of coercion in cases where ultimately the active and willing participation of the debtor is necessary for adequate fulfilment of the judgment. On the other hand, there seems to be no such justification for

[11]Ibid.

[12]Decision of the Constitutional Court No. U-I-339/98 of 21 January 1999.

[13]Decision of the Constitutional Court No. Up 181/99 of 18 December 2002.

[14]See also Decision of the Constitutional Court No. U-I-344/06 of 20 November 2008.

astreinte in cases where enforcement could be achieved through methods of direct constraint (such as substitute performance or substitute purchase).

Concerning fines imposed as a means of enforcement both of mandatory injunctions and of prohibitory injunctions, as well as *astreinte*, there are no exceptions as to who may be subject thereto. The State may be subject to *astreinte* (payable to the creditor) and, in theory, also to fines payable to the state treasury. The latter is not necessarily without any practical effects, as the consequence is that the money is transferred to different beneficiaries within the state treasury. The concept of enforcement through fines payable to the state treasury applies also to the enforcement of prohibitory injunctions in certain other fields of law (competition and anti-trust[15] matters, administrative matters[16]), but the concept of *astreinte* is known solely in the field of private law.

4 Determination of the Amount of Fines and Astreinte

When filing a motion for an *astreinte* order the claimant must specify the amount sought. This is in line with the principle of party disposition, which is strictly applied in Slovenian civil procedure (for example, when filing a monetary claim the claimant must always specify the amount of money requested, and the court has no power to grant the claimant more or other than that requested—*ultra* or *extra petita*; Article 2 of the Civil Procedure Act—CPA). On the other hand, when initiating enforcement proceedings where fines are imposed, the creditor does not need to specify the amount of fine to be imposed. This is understandable, as these fines are paid to the State and not to the creditor.

When imposing a fine, the court immediately determines the specific amount. However, the fine is not immediately enforced, but first only threatened, if the debtor fails to perform the obligation within an additional period of time. If the debtor (still) fails to perform, the fine is enforced *ex officio* and another fine can be imposed. *Astreinte* may not be fixed as a simple lump sum but rather by reference to periods of time. A specific amount must be determined already in the *astreinte* order. It is then for the judgment creditor to decide when he or she will seek enforcement of the *astreinte* order.

Concerning fines, the amount should depend on the circumstances of the case, but the amount of a single fine may not exceed EUR10,000 for a physical person or EUR500,000 for a legal entity or a sole trader. If the debtor still fails to accomplish the required act, the fine is enforced *ex officio* and another fine can be imposed, until the whole amount of the imposed fines has reached a sum ten times the aforementioned amounts (EUR50,000 or EUR5 million; Article 226 EJPMA). Thus, the

[15]Article 31 of the Act on the Prevention of Restriction of Competition (Official Gazette No. 36/2008).

[16]Article 298 of the Administrative Procedure Act (Official Gazette Nos. 80/99, etc.).

fine is imposed per violation. If a prohibitory injunction is rendered against the debtor, the course of enforcement is practically the same as described in the preceding paragraph, except that there is no upper limit as to the level of the overall amount of the fines that may be imposed (Article 227(1) EJPMA). The same system applies with regard to the enforcement of judgments concerning labour law relations and judgments concerning custody and visitation rights over a child (Article 238c and Article 238 EJPMA).

The amount to be paid pursuant to an *astreinte* order is defined per day or per some other amount of time, but not per violation.[17] The law provides no explicit guidance concerning setting the amount of *astreinte*; however, doctrine and case law have developed certain criteria. The question whether the creditor has suffered any pecuniary loss due to the debtor's non-performance is not an important factor, as an *astreinte* order is issued without prejudice to any loss suffered (Cigoj 1984, 1015). On the other hand, it should be observed that, partially, *astreinte* also has the role of offering the creditor just satisfaction for the suffering sustained by the debtor's non-observance of the final judgment of a court of law. The debtor's financial condition is also a factor that the court should take into consideration. As the main purpose of *astreinte* is to apply pressure on the debtor in order to break resistance to the court order, the amount that would be sufficient to influence the debtor's will must be assessed.[18] This assessment, however, also depends on the overall financial condition of the debtor (Cigoj 1984, 1015; Keresteš 2008, 1028).

The law imposes no maximum amount, and for a long time the prevailing view rejected the possibility that the aforementioned limits concerning fines should *per analogiam* also apply with regard to *astreinte*. However, some cases, heavily criticised by legal scholars (Berden 2004, 15; Wedam Lukić 2000, 3),[19] as well as in the media, in which enormous debts were built up due to continuous non-performance, caused a shift in the case law. Now it is accepted that when imposing an *astreinte* order the court is authorised to establish an overall maximum amount that the defendant may become liable to pay—*per analogiam* with the aforementioned provisions of the EJMPA on the maximum amounts of fines.[20]

The court may not set any further conditions when imposing *astreinte* or fines. The only condition is that *astreinte* or fines may be enforced if the debtor fails to

[17] An important question for the legal practice was whether default interest can be claimed if the debtor fails to pay the amount of *astreinte* due. Certain parties advocated the viewpoint that the obligation to pay the amount imposed by an *astreinte* order is just like any other monetary claim, and, therefore, in the event of late performance the debtor should be liable to pay default interest on the due amount of *astreinte* as well. However, this view was rejected in the case law, as *astreinte* is, per se, a penalty for a default and therefore it cannot result in a double sanction (Decision of the Ljubljana Court of Appeals No. III Cp 480/99).

[18] Decision of the Ljubljana Court of Appeals, No. III Cp 157/2007 of 7 February 2007.

[19] See also the dissenting opinion of Judge Wedam Lukić to the Decision of the Constitutional Court No. Up-181/99 of 17 January 2000.

[20] See Decisions of the Ljubljana Court of Appeals III Cp 157/2007 of 7 February 2007 and III Cp 2178/2004 of 4 May 2005.

perform the obligation by an extended time limit specified by the court. It follows from the general rules on conditions for a *titre executoire* that *astreinte* cannot be ordered before the debtor has been served the judgment that the *astreinte* order relates to. The creditor may request an *astreinte* order only after the debtor is in default as to the fulfilment of the judgment (Article 269(1) Code of Obligations). However, such default cannot occur before the judgment has been duly served on the debtor. According to Article 19 of the EJPMA, the time limit by which the debtor should voluntarily fulfil the obligation determined in the judgment, before the creditor may initiate enforcement proceedings, starts to run on the day when the judgment is served on the debtor. It must be stressed that if the debtor files an appeal against an *astreinte* order, *astreinte* does not start to run until the court of appeals reaches a final decision. The extended time limit for voluntary performance starts to run only after the decision of the appellate court is served on the debtor. Until then, the effect of the *astreinte* order is suspended.[21] The other restriction is that the *astreinte* order ceases to apply once the creditor files a request for regular enforcement (Article 212(3) EJPMA).

5 Motion for the Partial Return of Paid *Astreinte* Following Fulfilment of the Obligation

The sanction of *astreinte*, once imposed, may not be lifted in response to a mere indication by the sanctioned party that it is willing to perform. However, the law also allows the debtor to request that the amount of *astreinte* be reduced after he or she has performed the obligation (Article 269(2) Code of Obligations). This rule is in line with the main purpose of *astreinte*, i.e. to coerce compliance, rather than to punish non-compliance. When deciding on a motion for an *ex post* reduction of *astreinte*, the court must take into account all the particulars of the case—the purpose of the measure, the reasons for the belated performance, the importance of the matter for the creditor, etc. (Cigoj 1984, 1015; Dika 2003, 29). The possibility of an *ex post* reduction in *astreinte* is or at least should be a guarantee that there will be no exorbitant disproportionality between the amount of *astreinte* due and the economic value of the dispute.[22] When deciding on a request for the reduction of *astreinte* the court should not take into account whether the claimant has suffered any pecuniary loss due to non-performance, as *astreinte* is determined without prejudice to any claims for the recovery of damages (Cigoj 1984, 1015).

---

[21] E.g. Decision of the Ljubljana Court of Appeals No. III Cp 1361/2000 of 26 October 2000.

[22] Decision of the Constitutional Court No. Up 181/99 of 17 January 2000. See also Decision of the Ljubljana Court of Appeals No. VSL sklep II Ip 2201/2015 of 15 July 2015.

6 Procedure

The local court (*okrajno sodišče*) is vested with jurisdiction for all matters of enforcement. Thus, it also has jurisdiction both for imposing fines in the course of enforcement as well as for imposing *astreinte*. In the case of enforcement through fines as a means of the enforcement of mandatory and prohibitory injunctions, territorial jurisdiction is vested with the court of the place where the obligation must be performed (Article 224 EJPMA). The law contains no provision as to territorial jurisdiction for issuing an *astreinte* order (Article 212). The prevailing view is that the jurisdiction is determined by the general rules of the Civil Procedure Act[23] (domicile of the defendant; Article 46 CPA). From an alternative viewpoint, the jurisdiction to issue an *astreinte* order should be vested with the court that would have the jurisdiction for the enforcement of the non-monetary judgment—thus the court where the obligation in question must be performed (Poznić 1987, 471). As an *astreinte* order is then enforced in separate proceedings, just like any other judgment concerning a monetary claim, the jurisdiction for the proceedings for the enforcement of *astreinte* depends on the method of enforcement.[24] The court that rendered the *astreinte* order also has jurisdiction for deciding on the debtor's request for the reduction of *astreinte* (after the debtor has performed his or her primary non-monetary obligation).[25] An appeal may be lodged with a court of appeals against an enforcement measure of the local court imposing *astreinte*.

The law is silent as to the issue of whether the court may impose an *astreinte* order in an *ex parte* procedure or in an adversarial procedure. As to the latter procedure, another issue arises with regard to the question of whether the court needs to hold an oral hearing or if it is sufficient to allow the parties to state their view in written pleadings. Until recently, the position in the case law was that an *astreinte* order may be rendered in an *ex parte* procedure, just like any other decision rendered pursuant to the EJPMA (Bizjak 2004, 15). In ordinary enforcement proceedings, the court may issue a warrant of execution *ex parte*. The debtor may then file an objection that is decided by the court of first instance (thus, the court that issued the warrant for execution), and if the objection is dismissed, the debtor can file an appeal with the court of appeals. However, it is questionable whether it is possible to apply this system *per analogiam* also in cases when the court decides on the creditor's request for an *astreinte* order. It should be taken into account that the debtor cannot file an objection against an *astreinte* order, but only an appeal with the court of appeals.[26] Hence, if we accept the viewpoint that an

---

[23]*Zakon o pravdnem postopku*, Official Gazette RS, Nos. 26/99, etc.

[24]E.g.: if an attachment and the sale of real estate is requested as a method of enforcing a monetary claim based on *astreinte*, jurisdiction shall be vested with the court of the place where the land is situated; Article 166 EJPMA.

[25]Conclusion of the meeting of the Yugoslav Federal Court from 10 June 1981, published in the Bulletin of the Serbian Supreme Court, 1982, Nos. 7–8, p. 14.

[26]See, e.g., Decision of the Koper Court of Appeals No. II Cp 9/2005 of 15 March 2005.

astreinte order may be issued in an *ex parte* procedure, then the debtor is bereft of the right to be heard in the first instance court. This, however, is not in line with the position of the Constitutional Court, which has conceded that in certain cases urgency or the need to achieve a surprise effect justifies a restriction of the right to be heard; such right is only guaranteed after the court order has been rendered and become effective.[27] However, the right to be heard should be recognised before the same court that issued the decision in question, in order to enable that court to review its decision in light of the new arguments of the opposing party. It is not sufficient if this party can only be heard in proceedings at the appellate court.[28] The same approach should apply with regard to *astreinte* orders: if the debtor has no right to request that the first instance court review an *astreinte* order issued in an *ex parte* procedure, then he or she should be given an opportunity to be heard before the *astreinte* order is rendered.

7 Enforcement of Fines and Astreinte Orders

Upon the motion of a claimant in whose favour a court has issued either a mandatory or a prohibitory injunction, the court shall issue a warrant of execution in which it determines an extended time limit for voluntary performance. At the same time, the court imposes a fine that shall be effective if the obligation remains unperformed. This, in fact, means that the fine is first imposed only conditionally—the debtor may prevent its execution if he or she performs the obligation by the extended time limit. If the debtor still fails to perform, Article 226(2) of the EJMPA provides for enforcement *ex officio*. However, in practice, an appropriate motion by the claimant is necessary, as it is otherwise impossible for the court to know whether the debtor failed to perform the obligation. Upon the claimant's motion, the court then enforces the fine (and imposes another fine if the obligation is still not performed by the new time limit). The debtor may then object to the enforcement of the fine and argue that the obligation in question was fulfilled (Article 55 EJPMA). In order to decide on such an objection, the court may fix a date for a hearing and take evidence. If the objection is dismissed, the debtor may file an action with a regular court for a declaration that the enforcement is inadmissible (Article 59 EJPMA). The filing of such an action does not, however, suspend the enforcement proceedings.

Whereas fines are imposed and ultimately enforced in the same enforcement proceedings, in the case of *astreinte*, two separate proceedings must be distinguished. In the first procedure, the claimant requests that the court issue an *astreinte* order due to the debtor's failure to comply with a non-monetary final judgment (Article 212 EJPMA). The amount that the creditor is entitled to due to the debtor's

---

[27]Decision of the Constitutional Court No. Up 10/99 of 25 May 1999.

[28]Ibid.

continuing non-performance is then enforced in regular enforcement proceedings, just like any other monetary claim.

When the extended time limit[29] for the performance of the obligation has lapsed, the creditor may request the enforcement of *astreinte*. It is enforced in the same manner as any other *titre executoire* concerning a monetary obligation. It is sufficient that the claimant assert that *astreinte* is due, which means that the debtor has neither paid *astreinte* nor performed the obligation ordered by the judgment to be performed. The burden is on the debtor to file an objection that the obligation to pay *astreinte* has ceased or that it never came into existence if he or she performed the obligation without default. The court where the enforcement proceedings are pending may take evidence concerning this objection (Article 55 EJPMA). If the objection is dismissed, the debtor may file an action with an ordinary civil court for a declaration that the enforcement proceedings are inadmissible due to the orderly performance of the obligation (Article 59 EJPMA). It is questionable whether the debtor may also argue that *astreinte* should not have been imposed at all as he or she had fulfilled the required obligation even before it was imposed. The case law is divided on this point, but the more plausible view is that such an objection should be filed in the proceedings in which *astreinte* was imposed and not in the proceedings in which it is enforced (Berden and Kleindienst 2005, 20).

The forfeited sum is collected in the same manner as in the case of any other enforcement of a monetary obligation (garnishment procedures, attachment and the sale of movable or immovable property, etc.). Enforcement is initiated upon the request of the creditor. In the case of fines, such are imposed upon the request of the claimant; however, the forfeited sum is then collected *ex officio* in the same manner as enforcement in matters of taxation. The difference between *astreinte* and fines with regard to the method of the collection of money is understandable, as in the case of *astreinte* the creditor is entitled to the collected sum, whereas in the case of fines, they are collected to the benefit of the state treasury. The payment (either voluntary or in the course of execution) of *astreinte* does not extinguish the debtor's original obligation to perform the non-monetary obligation.

There is no fixed period of time in which the creditor may request the enforcement of *astreinte* [except the general provision that an obligation for which a *titre executoire* already exists becomes statute-barred after ten years have elapsed (Article 356 Code of Obligations)]. With regard to certain specific types of claims, the law imposes a time limit by which the creditor may request enforcement (judgments concerning disturbance of possession: 30 days—Article 429 Civil Procedure Act; judgments rendered in labour disputes concerning the reinstatement of a worker: six months—Article 231 EJPMA). In such cases, a creditor who has not requested regular enforcement within the aforementioned time limits will also

[29]When determining the extended time limit by which a debtor may still perform the original obligation without *astreinte* starting to build up, the courts should take into account the nature of the obligation and the estimated time needed for the debtor's compliance with the original obligation, as well as the importance of the matter for the creditor. See, e.g., Decisions of the Ljubljana Court of Appeals No. II Cpg 281/97, II Cpg 86/2000, III Cp 480/96, and III Cp 369/97.

lose the right to file a motion for an *astreinte* order.[30] The general rule is that when there can be no enforcement, there can be no imposition of an *astreinte* order either (for example, in the event of objective inability to perform). In such cases, also an *astreinte* order ceases to apply after the primary non-monetary obligation is no longer enforceable or ceases to exist.[31]

8 Controversy Over the Concept of *Astreinte* in Slovenian Legal Doctrine

The system of fines, as the regular method of the enforcement of mandatory and prohibitory injunctions, is well accepted in doctrine and practice. As already mentioned, it has a long tradition, the regulation in the EJPMA is sufficiently detailed, and the case law sufficiently developed. The same conclusion, however, cannot be reached with regard to *astreinte*. Only rarely has any other concept of Slovenian private law sparked as many controversies in the legal doctrine as the concept of *astreinte*. The objections against *astreinte* in the legal doctrine are numerous. It is argued that the concept of *astreinte* is "alien" to the Slovenian system of enforcement (Berden 2004, 15). The concept of *astreinte* was, it is argued, transplanted from French law, but just, however, on a principled level, without all the necessary measures required for adequate implementation. There is only one article in the Code of Obligations and one article in the EJPMA regarding this matter, which are insufficient, and this drastically diminishes legal certainty and predictability in this field. Dilemmas arise, for example, as to whether an *astreinte* order may be issued in an *ex parte* procedure; what the grounds for appeal are; in which kind of procedure a reduction in *astreinte* can be sought; etc. (Keresteš 2008, 1033; Berden and Kleindienst 2005, 20). This situation is aggravated by the fact that *astreinte* has no tradition in Slovenia (the concept was only introduced in 1978) and there exist very few judicial decisions on this matter issued by the highest courts. Due to the insufficient case law and legislative regulation, there is a serious lack of safeguards concerning the principle of proportionality (enormous debts totally disproportionate to the value of the claim were built up in certain cases, as also reported in the media[32]) and the prevention of the abuse of this right by the creditor.[33] Furthermore, unlike fines, *astreinte* can be applied with regard to a final judgment for any non-pecuniary obligation—such as the delivery of goods or the

[30]On the other hand, if an *astreinte* order has been filed within the aforementioned time limit in a labour dispute and the dispute concerns the disturbance of possession, it does not lose effect when the time limit expires; Decision of the Constitutional Court No. Up 181/99 of 17 January 2000.

[31]Decision of the Ljubljana Court of Appeals No. III Cp 802/2003 of 7 January 2004.

[32]E.g. articles in "*Nedeljski dnevnik*", dated 2 (all of page 8), 8, 13 and 29 (page 11) February 2004.

[33]See the dissenting opinion of Judge Wedam Lukić to the Decision of the Constitutional Court No. 181/99 of 17 January 2000.

carrying out of an act whose performance is not exclusively dependent on one particular person (and which can therefore be adequately performed also by another person). Therefore, many advocate the possible introduction of the restriction that *astreinte* should *de lege ferenda* be possible only in the same cases as the imposition of fines in ordinary enforcement procedures (mandatory and prohibitory injunctions).[34] The legal nature of *astreinte* is rather unclear. Its main purpose is, as explained above, to offer the creditor an additional tool (besides regular enforcement through fines) for enforcement of (foremost) mandatory and prohibitory injunctions. Therefore, one would expect to find provisions on *astreinte* in the chapter of the EJPMA concerning the enforcement of such obligations. However, they are placed in the chapter of the EJPMA dealing with the enforcement of monetary claims because *astreinte*, once imposed, requires the debtor to pay a certain amount of money, and the creditor may directly move to enforce it just as with any other monetary claim (Keresteš 2008, 1029). Although the EJPMA contains provisions on *astreinte* in the chapter regulating the enforcement of monetary claims, legal scholars usually consider *astreinte* in the context of the enforcement of non-monetary claims, because *astreinte* was introduced as a penalty for the non-performance of such obligations (Rijavec 2003, 325; Wedam Lukić 1992, 110). The fact that the Constitutional Court had to decide whether the regulation of *astreinte* is in conformity with the Constitution is also a sign of the described controversy concerning *astreinte*. In the end, the Constitutional Court confirmed that the regulation of *astreinte* in EJPMA is not contrary to the Constitution, but it also needs to be noted that the decision was reached by a slight majority (5:4) and the matter was highly controversial within the Court itself as well.[35]

9 Conclusion

Although the instrument of *astreinte* remains one of the more hotly debated issues in the Slovenian law on the enforcement of civil judgments, it seems that in recent years there have been positive developments in the case law. Many of the disputed issues have been settled and clarified, and certain necessary safeguards established. Experience has proved that it was not necessary to amend the legislation in order to enable the courts to set limits concerning the maximum amounts and that the same result could be reached through more adequate case law. The courts can now determine limits with regard to the maximum amount or maximum duration of *astreinte* and they can also apply general principles regarding the prevention of the abuse of rights. Nevertheless, certain clarifications and improvements at the

[34]Ibid.

[35]Decision of the Constitutional Court No. Up 181/99 of 18 December 2002. See also the dissenting opinion of Judge Wedam Lukić regarding the aforementioned decision.

legislative level are still needed. On the other hand, the positive effects of *astreinte* as a mechanism of indirect compulsion should not be overlooked, especially in a country like Slovenia, where (from the viewpoint of an individual creditor) ordinary enforcement proceedings are often excessively time-consuming and where (from the viewpoint of the interests of the judicial system as a whole) there is still a great need to promote the legal interest that the final decisions of the judiciary should not remain disrespected and ignored.

References

Berden A (2004) Sodni penali [Court penalties]. Pravna praksa 11:15–18

Berden A, Kleindienst I (2005) Sodni penali—2 [Court penalties—2]. Pravna praksa 9:20–22

Bizjak A (2004) Sodni penali [Court penalties]. Pravna praksa 11:14–16

Cigoj S (1981) Sodni penali [Court penalties]. Združeno delo 3:496–502

Cigoj S (1984) Komentar obligacijskih razmerij [Commentary on legal relations out of obligations]. ČZ Uradni list, Ljubljana

Dika M (2003) Sudski penali [Court penalties]. In: Buljan V et al (eds) Ovrha i stečaj—aktualnosti zakonodavstva i sudske prakse. Inženjerski biro, Zagreb, pp 22–28

Juhart M, Grilc P, Ilešič M et al (1995) Zavarovanje in utrditev obveznosti [Securing and Consolidating Claims]. GV Založba, Ljubljana

Keresteš T (2008) Kazni in sodni penali v izvršilnem postopku [Fines and court penalties in enforcement proceedings]. Podjetje in delo 6–7:1027–1036

Poznić B (1987) Gradjansko procesno pravo [Civil procedure]. Savremena administracija, Beograd

Rijavec V (2003) Civilno izvršilno pravo [Law on the enforcement of judgments in civil matters]. GV Založba, Ljubljana

Strohsack B (1990) Odškodninsko pravo in druge neposlovne obveznosti [Law of torts and other non-contractual obligations]. ČZ Uradni list, Ljubljana

Wedam Lukić D (1992) Civilno izvršilno pravo [Law on the enforcement of judgments in civil matters]. ČZ Uradni list, Ljubljana

Aleš Galič Professor at the Faculty of Law, University of Ljubljana, Slovenia, where he is engaged in teaching and research in the areas of Civil Procedure, International Private Law, Arbitration and ADR.

Norwegian Civil Procedure Under the Influence of EU Law

Halvard Haukeland Fredriksen and Magne Strandberg

Abstract The influence of the European Union on the civil justice systems of European countries is remarkable, also on those of the non-EU Member States. One example is Norway, which has integrated EU rules on jurisdiction and the recognition and enforcement of judgments in civil and commercial matters, thereby recognizing the judgments of the Court of Justice of the EU as legal sources. However, there are also other indirect ways in which the EU manages to affect Norwegian law, since Norway is a part of the European economic area. This contribution addresses the indirect influence of the EU Charter of Fundamental Rights, the general principles of non-discrimination on grounds of nationality, and principles of equivalence and effectiveness, as well as EU secondary law on the Norwegian legal system.

1 Introduction

Although Norway is not a member of the European Union, EU law influences Norwegian civil procedural law in a number of ways. A clear example of this is the EU rules on jurisdiction and the recognition and enforcement of judgments in civil and commercial matters, which now apply to Norway by virtue of the 2007 Lugano Convention.[1] The Convention's object and purpose of extending the EU regime (now found in the recast Brussels I Regulation of 2012) to the participating

[1]Convention on jurisdiction and the recognition and enforcement of judgments in civil and commercial matters, 30 October 2007 (entry into force 1 January 2010). The 2007 Convention replaced the 1988 Lugano convention on jurisdiction and the recognition and enforcement of judgments in civil and commercial matters in order to reflect subsequent changes in EU law. Norway was also a contracting party to the 1988 convention.

H. H. Fredriksen · M. Strandberg (✉)
Faculty of Law, University of Bergen, Bergen, Norway
e-mail: magne.strandberg@uib.no

H. H. Fredriksen
e-mail: halvard.fredriksen@uib.no

A. Uzelac and C. H. van Rhee (eds.), *Transformation of Civil Justice*,
Ius Gentium: Comparative Perspectives on Law and Justice 70,
https://doi.org/10.1007/978-3-319-97358-6_3

European Free Trade Association (EFTA) States has caused the Norwegian Supreme Court to recognize that the Convention, as incorporated into Norwegian law, is to be interpreted and applied in line with the case law of the EU Court of Justice (ECJ), thus opening the way for the continued influence of ECJ rulings on this part of Norwegian civil procedural law.[2]

A more indirect example is the EU Charter of Fundamental Rights (EUCFR) and ECJ case law concerning the EU law principle of effective judicial protection as sources of inspiration for the European Court of Human Rights (ECtHR) when interpreting the European Convention on Human Rights (ECHR). Norway is a party to the ECHR, and the impact of Articles 6(1) and 13 of the Convention on Norwegian civil procedural law has long been recognized by Norwegian courts and by the Norwegian legislator alike. To the extent that developments in ECJ case law impact the ECtHR's interpretation of Articles 6(1) and/or 13 ECHR, the result will thus be the indirect and somewhat "hidden" influence of EU law on Norwegian civil procedural law.[3]

A third basis for the influence of EU law on Norwegian civil procedural law, and the main object of this contribution, is the 1992 Agreement on the European Economic Area (EEA). The object and purpose of the EEA Agreement is to provide for the fullest possible realisation of the free movement of goods, persons, services and capital within the whole European Economic Area, so that the internal market established within the European Union is extended to the participating EFTA States (Iceland, Liechtenstein and Norway, but not Switzerland).[4] As made clear already in the Preamble to the EEA Agreement, equal conditions for competition in a "dynamic and homogeneous European Economic Area" presupposes not only common rules, but also "adequate means of enforcement including at the judicial level".[5] Acknowledging this, the EFTA Court has repeatedly held that access to justice and effective judicial protection are essential elements in the EEA legal framework.[6] Furthermore, the objective of establishing a dynamic and homogeneous European Economic Area can only be achieved if EFTA and EU nationals and economic operators enjoy equal access to the courts in both the EU and EFTA pillars of the EEA to ensure their rights which they derive from the EEA Agreement.[7] Thus, as a starting point and main rule, the limitations on the so-called procedural autonomy of the EU Member States developed by the ECJ—the

[2]See further in Sect. 6 below.

[3]As is well known, the "judicial dialogue" between the ECtHR and the ECJ goes both ways, but for our present purposes the point is that Arts. 6 and 13(1) ECHR may serve as a vehicle for Norwegian reception of ECJ case law concerning the principle of effective judicial protection and the right to a fair trial.

[4]As explained by the ECJ in Case C-452/01, *Ospelt*, ECLI:EU:C:2003:493, para. 29. For a recent analysis of the Agreement's achievements and future challenges, see Fredriksen and Franklin (2015, 629–684).

[5]Fourth recital of the Preamble to the EEA Agreement.

[6]See, e.g., Case E-11/12 *Koch* [2013] EFTA Court Report 272, para. 117 and case law cited.

[7]Ibid.

well-known EU law principles of equivalence and effectiveness—apply also to the EFTA States that are parties to the EEA Agreement. In Case E-11/12 *Koch*, the EFTA Court referred to the ECJ's judgment in Case C-432/05 *Unibet* and put this as follows:

> In the absence of EEA rules in the field it is for the domestic legal system of each EEA State to designate the courts and tribunals having jurisdiction and to lay down the detailed procedural rules governing actions for safeguarding rights which EFTA and EU citizens and economic operators derive from EEA law … provided, first, that such rules are no less favourable than those governing similar domestic actions (principle of equivalence) and, second, that they do not render practically impossible or excessively difficult the exercise of rights conferred by EEA law (principle of effectiveness) (see, mutatis mutandis, *Unibet*, cited above, paragraph 43).[8]

In addition to the general limitations brought about by the principles of equivalence and effectiveness, the EEA Agreement includes several EU legal acts which contain procedural rules—recent examples include Directive 2013/11/EU on alternative dispute resolution for consumer disputes (the ADR Directive) and Regulation (EU) No. 524/2013 on online dispute resolution for consumer disputes (the ODR Regulation), both of which were incorporated into the EEA Agreement by the EEA Joint Committee in 2016.[9] EU legal acts with procedural rules are also to be found in the related Agreement between the EFTA States on the Establishment of a Surveillance Authority and a Court of Justice (the so-called Surveillance and Court Agreement—SCA),[10] in particular with reference to the enforcement within the EFTA pillar of the EEA Agreement's provision on competition law and state aid (for all the details, see Arnesen et al. 2018).

However, there are limits to the scope of the EEA Agreement which need to be taken into account when assessing the influence of EU law on Norwegian civil procedural law. As the EEA Agreement was negotiated in 1990–1991, the scope of the Agreement essentially reflects the scope of the EC Treaty as it stood prior to the Treaty of Maastricht.[11] Thus, the EEA Agreement knows of no parallel to Article 81 TFEU on judicial cooperation in civil matters. As a result, none of the EU legal acts based on Article 81 TFEU have been incorporated into the EEA Agreement. As far as the Brussel I Regulation on jurisdiction and the recognition and enforcement of judgments in civil and commercial matters is concerned, this is largely remedied

[8]Ibid., para. 121.

[9]EEA Joint Committee Decision No. 194/2016 of 23 September 2016 amending Annex XIX (Consumer protection) to the EEA Agreement.

[10]The EEA Agreement is characterized by its two-pillar structure: enforcement of EEA law within the EU was entrusted to the pre-existing EU institutions, whereas the fulfilment by the EFTA States of their obligations is overseen by the EFTA Surveillance Authority and the EFTA Court. For reasons of reciprocity, the EFTA Surveillance Authority and the EFTA Court were established through a separate agreement to which only the participating EFTA States are contracting parties (as the EFTA States are not contracting parties to the EU treaties establishing the EU institutions).

[11]In order to maintain a level playing field with equal conditions, the Annexes to the EEA Agreement are continuously updated with new EU legal acts of EEA relevance, but the scope of the Agreement has not been widened to include new fields of EU law.

by the above-mentioned Lugano Convention, but Norway's interest in similar agreements concerning certain other parts of the EU rules on judicial cooperation in civil matters has so far not been acted upon by the EU.[12]

Furthermore, and more problematic for the daily functioning of the EEA Agreement, the fact that the EU rules on judicial cooperation in civil matters fall outside the scope of the EEA Agreement appears to have caused Norwegian authorities to believe that the influence of EEA law on Norwegian civil procedural law in general is more limited than the influence of EU law on the national civil procedural law of EU Member States. Thus, also a number of EU legal acts based on the EU's competence to regulate the internal market (Article 114 TFEU) have been held by Norwegian authorities to fall outside the scope of the EEA Agreement, as they are considered to primarily deal with harmonization of national procedural law.[13] And even though the general limitations brought about by the EU law principles of equivalence and effectiveness were recognized by the Expert Committee that wrote the draft for what was to be the Act of 17 June 2005 No. 90 relating to mediation and procedure in civil disputes ("the Dispute Act"),[14] the committee (and later on in the process also the Ministry of Justice) clearly regarded the practical implications for Norwegian civil procedural law as very limited indeed.[15] However, during the last couple of decades, Norwegian scholars have slowly begun to challenge that view and acknowledge the potential influence of EEA law on Norwegian civil procedure (see e.g., Utgård 2005, 131–140; Fredriksen 2008, 289–359; Nylund 2011, 131–133; Nylund 2014, 31–51; Nylund 2016, 101–114).[16]

In this contribution, we will provide an overview of the influence of EU law on Norwegian civil procedure. The potential impact on Norwegian law of the EU Charter of Fundamental Rights will be addressed (Sect. 2), followed by a presentation of the procedural side to the general EU/EEA law prohibition of discrimination on grounds of nationality (Sect. 3) and then the general EU/EEA law principles of equivalence and effectiveness will be addressed (Sect. 4). Thereafter follows a presentation of Norway's position with regard to EU secondary law which

[12]See further in Sect. 5 below.

[13]See further in Sect. 5 below.

[14]In force since 2008. The Act is regularly referred to in English as "the Dispute Act" despite the fact that it is a full-blown Code of Civil Procedure in the Continental tradition. Somewhat reluctantly, we too will refer to it as the Dispute Act in this contribution. An English translation of the Act can be found by searching for "tvisteloven" at http://app.uio.no/ub/ujur/oversatte-lover/english.shtml. Accessed 7 June 2018. Note that the translation has not been updated, but so far the number of amendments is fairly limited. For an informative introduction in the English language, see Backer (2007) and several of the contributions in Fredriksen and Lipp (eds) (2011).

[15]NOU 2001: 32, *Rett på sak*, pp 154, 155, Ot.prp. No. 51, *Om lov om mekling og rettergang i sivile tvister (tvisteloven)*, (2004–2005) p 32.

[16]See also Viken (2012, 43–45) on EU law concerning evidential use of surveys in trademark and marketing practice litigation.

harmonizes national procedural law (Sect. 5), before the contribution is rounded off with some thoughts about the future influence of EU law on Norwegian civil procedure (Sect. 6).

2 The Potential Impact of the EU Charter of Fundamental Rights on Norwegian Civil Procedure

2.1 Article 47(1) EUCFR as an Expression of the Principle of Effective Judicial Protection

Article 47(1) EUCFR states that "everyone whose rights and freedoms guaranteed by the law of the Union are violated has the right to an effective remedy before a tribunal". The provision is inspired by Article 13 of the ECHR, but the protection offered is more extensive since it guarantees the right to an effective remedy before a court (not only before "a national authority").[17] Even more importantly, Article 47 (1) EUCFR extends the right to an effective remedy well beyond the rights and freedoms as set forth in the ECHR—it encompasses all rights and freedoms guaranteed by EU law.

The EU Charter has not been made part of the EEA Agreement or in any other way been formally recognized by Norway or any other of the participating EFTA States. This matters little, however, as far as the right to an effective remedy is concerned. As noted already in the introduction at the start of this contribution, the EFTA Court has repeatedly held that access to justice and effective judicial protection are essential elements in the EEA legal framework.[18] For more than 20 years now, the EFTA Court has demonstrated its willingness to do everything within its power to achieve and maintain homogeneity between EU and EEA law (Baudenbacher 2016, 179–194). It may thus be safely assumed that the EFTA Court will develop the EEA law principle of effective judicial protection in line with the ECJ's interpretation of Article 47(1) EUCFR.

In general, the right to an effective remedy expressed in Article 47(1) EUCFR is unlikely to add much to Norwegian procedural law. Since 2014, Article 95(1) of the Norwegian Constitution guarantees everyone the right "to have their case tried by an independent and impartial court within reasonable time".[19] The scope of this provision is neither limited to certain fundamental rights (such as Article 13 ECHR)

[17]See the Explanations relating to the Charter of Fundamental Rights, Official Journal of the European Union C 303/17; Explanation on Art. 47.

[18]See, e.g., Case E-11/12 *Koch* [2013] EFTA Court Report 272, para. 117 and case law cited.

[19]The full text of the provision is as follows: "Everyone has the right to have their case tried by an independent and impartial court within reasonable time. Legal proceedings shall be fair and public. The court may however conduct proceedings in camera if considerations of the privacy of the parties concerned or if weighty and significant public interests necessitate this".

nor limited to EEA law (such as the EEA law principle of effective judicial protection). Both ECtHR case law concerning Article 13 ECHR and, which is more important for our present purposes, ECJ case law concerning Article 47(1) EUCFR must be presumed to be relevant sources of inspiration for the Norwegian Supreme Court in the future development of the effective remedy clause of the Norwegian Constitution, but the Supreme Court has also made very clear that it is for the Supreme Court itself to decide on the interpretation of the Constitution.[20]

However, there is one "hot topic" of Norwegian constitutional/procedural law where Article 47(1) EUCFR may have practical consequences. In a couple of controversial decisions, the Supreme Court has held that the corresponding provision in Article 13 ECHR supports a right to a declaratory judgment from a Norwegian court that rights under the Convention have been violated. Initially, the right to a declaratory judgment was limited to situations where the victim had no other way to get the courts to assess the alleged violation of the ECHR, e.g., in the context of a claim for damages.[21] More recently, however, the Supreme Court has held that a declaratory judgment can be sought even if the alleged violation could have been brought before the courts by way of a claim for damages.[22] This is an understanding of the right to an effective remedy for violations of the ECHR which goes beyond the demands of the ECtHR (see Application No. 51374/16), and it has therefore been subject to criticism from academic quarters (Backer 2015, 213). It remains to be seen whether the Supreme Court will extend this approach also to the field of EEA law. The ECJ's judgment in Case C-432/05 *Unibet* makes quite clear that EU law (and, as a result of the homogeneity objective, EEA law) as such does not require a self-standing action to challenge the compatibility of a national provision with EU law provided that other effective legal remedies, which are no less favourable than those governing similar domestic actions, make it possible for such a question of compatibility to be determined as a preliminary issue.[23] However, this does not in any way hinder the Supreme Court from offering better judicial protection than required by EU/EEA law. Arguably, the principle of equivalence[24] demands that the Supreme Court either changes course on the question of declaratory judgments for violations of the ECHR or extends this remedy also to the field of EEA law.[25] When the majority of the Supreme Court held in 2012 that Norwegian law does not offer a self-standing action for alleged violations of the UN Convention on the rights of the Child, it did so with a reference to the fact that that

[20]E.g., Rt. 2015 p 93 *Maria,* para. 57. See further, in English, the speech by Supreme Court Justice A Bårdsen, "Interpreting the Norwegian Bill of Rights", Annual Seminar on Comparative Constitutionalism 21–22 November 2016, Faculty of Law, University of Oslo, available from the Supreme Court's homepage at http://www.hoyesterett.no. Accessed 7 June 2018.

[21]Rt. 1994 p 1244 *Kvinnefengsel*, Rt. 2003 p 301 and Rt. 2009s. 477 *Nordsjødykker*.

[22]Rt. 2015s. 93 *Maria* (Sec. 42), HR-2016-2178-U *Universitetssykehuset i Nord-Norge*.

[23]Case C-432/05 *Unibet*, ECLI:EU:C:2007:163.

[24]Further explained in Sect. 4 below.

[25]Cf. the reasoning of the ECJ in Case C-118/08 *Transportes Urbanos*, ECLI:EU:C:2010:39.

convention does not include a provision corresponding to Article 13 ECHR.[26] In light of Article 47(1) EUCHR and the EFTA Court's case law concerning an EEA law principle of effective judicial protection, this reasoning can hardly be extended to the EEA Agreement.

2.2 *Article 47(2) EUCFR as an Expression of the Right to a Fair Trial*

Article 47(2) EUCFR states that everyone is entitled to a fair and public hearing within a reasonable time by an independent and impartial tribunal previously established by law. As suggested by its wording, this provision is essentially taken from Article 6(1) ECHR. However, it may well, through the case law of the ECJ, develop in ways which do not fully concur with the interpretation of Article 6(1) ECHR favoured by the ECtHR.[27]

As noted above, the EU Charter has not been made part of the EEA Agreement or in any other way been formally recognized by Norway or any other of the participating EFTA States. Still, all of the EU and EFTA States parties to the EEA Agreement are also parties to the Convention and there is general agreement in the case law and literature that provisions of the EEA Agreement are to be interpreted and applied in a manner which is consistent with the contracting parties' obligations under the Convention (for a recent analysis, see Björgvinsson 2014, 263–280).

The EFTA Court has referred to Article 6 ECHR in several cases. In Case E-15/10 *Posten Norge (Norwegian Mail)*, a case about the public enforcement of competition law, the EFTA Court for the first time also included a reference to Article 47 EUCFR:

> The principle of effective judicial protection including the right to a fair trial, which is *inter alia* enshrined in Article 6 ECHR, is a general principle of EEA law. It may be noted that expression to the principle of effective judicial protection is now also given by Article 47 of the Charter of Fundamental Rights of the European Union (see on the latter point Case C-389/10 P *KME v Commission*, judgment of 8 December 2011, not yet reported, paragraph 119; and concerning the right of access to justice, Case E-2/02 *Bellona* [2003] EFTA Ct. Rep. 52, paragraph 36 and Case E-3/11 *Sigmarsson*, [2011] EFTA Ct. Rep. 430, paragraph 29).[28]

It is worth noting that the reference to Article 47 was couched in a way that plays down the potential "added value" of the Charter (Wahl 2014, 291), but also that the

---

[26]Rt. 2012 p 2039. Cf. Skoghøy (2017, 406), who argues that there is a requirement of an effective remedy in that Convention and therefore also a right to a declaratory judgment.

[27]The complex interaction and coexistence between the ECJ and the ECtHR falls outside the scope of this contribution. For present purposes, it suffices to note that there is no formal hierarchy between the two and that diverging interpretations of Art. 47 EUCFR and Arts. 6 and 13 ECHR cannot be excluded.

[28]Case E-15/10, *Posten Norge* [2012] EFTA Court Report 246, para. 86.

EFTA Court portrays both Article 6 ECHR and Article 47 EUCFR as mere expressions of a general principle already recognized by EEA law. By this, the EFTA Court may have laid the groundwork necessary to keep up with ECJ case law even beyond the scope of the Convention (Fredriksen and Franklin 2015, 646, 647).

To Norwegian civil procedure, the potential importance of Article 47(2) EUCFR in EEA-related matters further complicates a legal landscape where a number of abstract "over-arching" minimum criteria have been developed. In addition to Article 6(1) ECHR, a reform in 2014 added a new provision to the Norwegian Constitution which *inter alia* declares that "[l]egal proceedings shall be fair and public".[29] The provision was inspired by Article 6,[30] and the committee preparing the constitutional reform recommended that ECtHR case law should be "relevant" for its interpretation.[31] Acknowledging this, the Norwegian Supreme Court regards case law from the Strasbourg Court as not only relevant, but an important source for the interpretation of the new human rights provisions of the Norwegian Constitution.[32] However, as noted above, the Supreme Court has also made very clear that it is for the Supreme Court itself to decide on the interpretation of the Constitution.[33]

There is a chance, then, for future development of the "fair trial" standard in Article 95 of the Constitution which deviates from both the one advocated by the ECtHR under Article 6(1) ECHR and the one advocated by the ECJ under Article 47(2) EUCFR. It may be that the right to a fair trial has a somewhat different meaning when interpreted by the Strasbourg court in a geographically wide European context, by the ECJ within an integrationist and market-oriented EU law context, or by the Norwegian Supreme Court in a combined domestic and European context. Further complexity is brought about by the older Norwegian principle of "sound proceedings" which was developed by the Supreme Court and is now codified in Section 1-1(1) of the Dispute Act.[34] Whether this principle still has any practical importance after the 2014 constitutional amendments is a matter of discussion (cf. Skoghøy 2017, 540–545; Robberstad 2015, 27, 28), but it cannot be excluded that this "home-made" principle still has a role to play in addition to the constitutional and international standards.

---

[29]Art. 95(1) of the Norwegian Constitution. The full text of the provision is reproduced in n. 19 above.

[30]*Rapport til Stortingets presidentskap fra Menneskerettighetsutvalget om menneskerettigheter i Grunnloven,* Dokument 16 (2011–2012), pp 121–125.

[31]Ibid., p. 122. The committee did not comment on the potential impact of EU and EEA law in this regard.

[32]E.g., Rt. 2014 p 1292, para. 21.

[33]See Sect. 2.1 above (n. 20 and accompanying text).

[34]In the English translation, Sec. 1-1(1) of the Dispute Act makes clear that the purpose of the Act is to "provide a basis for hearing civil disputes in a fair, sound, swift, efficient and confidence inspiring manner through public proceedings before independent and impartial courts".

2.3 *Other Provisions of the EU Charter of Potential Relevance for Norwegian Procedural Law*

Although Article 47 is clearly the most significant provision of the EU Charter as seen from a civil procedure perspective, other articles may also be of importance.

Firstly, it is well known that also the presumption of innocence in Article 6(2) ECHR affects cases concerning administrative sanctions that are criminal charges under the Convention but not defined as such under national law. In such cases, the Norwegian Supreme Court has held that Article 6(2) requires a relatively high standard of evidence—at least a qualified preponderance of the evidence.[35] Article 48 EUCHR corresponds to Article 6(2) ECHR, but may perhaps prove to offer "added value" if the ECtHR's margin of appreciation-doctrine leaves the ECHR contracting parties with more discretion than the ECJ and the EFTA Court, with their focus on equal conditions for competition throughout the EU and the EEA, are prepared to offer to the EU/EEA Member States. The EEA-relevance of the presumption of innocence is clearly demonstrated by the fact that two of the cases where the Supreme Court discussed the matter were cases concerning the public enforcement of EEA competition rules.[36]

Secondly, the right to privacy in Article 7 EUCFR and the right to the protection of personal data in Article 8 EUCFR can be relevant for, *inter alia*, the interpretation and application of national rules concerning access to evidence. The corresponding provision in the ECHR—Article 8 ECHR—has been considered in this regard by the Norwegian Supreme Court[37] and has proven to be especially relevant when access to evidence is required in a pre-trial stage under the rules in Chapter 28 of the Dispute Act (Hjort 2016a, 224–231). It may well be questioned whether Articles 7 and 8 EUCFR offer any "added value" as compared to Article 8 ECHR, but the ECJ's judgments in a number of high-profile data protection cases in the last couple of years may suggest an answer in the affirmative.[38]

---

[35]See Rt. 2007 p 1217 *ulovlig fiske* (dissent 3-2), Rt. 2008 p 1409 *tilleggsskatt* (dissent 6-5), Rt. 2011 p 910 *Tine*, Rt. 2012 p 1556 *Gran & Ekran* (dissent 3-2). Note, however, that it is far from clear that the Strasbourg court in fact requires such a standard of evidence in these cases; see for instance the Swedish case *Lucky Dev v Sweden* (application 7356/10), para. 65–69, where a standard of evidence called "sannolikt" ("probable") did not constitute a violation of Art. 6(2). See also Strandberg (2017, 115–134).

[36]Rt. 2011 p 910 *Tine* and Rt. 2012 p 1556 *Gran & Ekran*.

[37]Rt. 2012 p 1819 para. 35, Rt. 2014 p 1084 para. 12, HR-2014-962-U. See also the ECtHR's judgment in *Bernhard Larsen Holding AS and others v Norway*, Application No. 24117/08.

[38]See Joined Cases C-293 and 594/12 *Digital Rights Ireland*, ECLI:EU:C:2014:238; Case C-131/12 *Google Spain*, ECLI:EU:C:2014:317; Case C-362/14 *Schrems*, ECLI:EU:C:2015:650; Joined Cases C-203 and 698/15 *Tele2 Sverige*, ECLI:EU:C:2016:970 and Opinion 1/15 *EU-Canada transfer of passenger name record data*, ECLI:EU:C:2017:592.

3 The Procedural Side to the General Prohibition of Discrimination on Grounds of Nationality

Article 4 of the EEA Agreement includes a general prohibition of discrimination on grounds of nationality, essentially mirroring what is now Article 18 TFEU. As is well known by EU lawyers, this prohibition also applies to civil procedural law, limiting the procedural autonomy that the EU Member States enjoy in the absence of EEA rules governing procedural matters.[39] The EFTA Court has also recognized this in Case E-5/10 *Kottke*:

> In the absence of EEA rules governing the matter, it is for the domestic legal system of each EEA State to lay down the detailed procedural rules governing actions for safeguarding rights which individuals derive from EEA law. Nevertheless, EEA law imposes certain limits on that competence (see, for comparison, *Data Delecta*, cited above, paragraph 12; Case C-323/95 *Hayes* [1997] ECR I-1711, paragraph 13, and Case C-122/96 *Saldanha and MTS* [1997] ECR I-5325, paragraph 19). In particular, legislative provisions on national procedure may not discriminate against persons to whom EEA law gives the right to equal treatment or restrict the fundamental freedoms guaranteed by EEA law (see, for comparison, Case C-186/87 *Cowan* [1989] ECR 195, paragraph 19).[40]

The *Kottke* case was about a Liechtenstein rule that requires plaintiffs residing in another EEA State to lodge security for legal costs. Unlike the other EFTA States parties to the EEA Agreement, Liechtenstein has not acceded to the Lugano Convention (neither the original one from 1988 nor the new one from 2007). This forced the EFTA Court to concede that a requirement to lodge security for legal costs in civil proceedings may be justified even though such a rule would, in the setting of EU law, be caught by the general prohibition of discrimination on grounds of nationality now found in Article 18 TFEU.[41] The EFTA Court tried to limit the consequences of this finding by stressing that such security could not be required in a manner disproportionately affecting the interests of a non-resident plaintiff in being able to commence legal proceedings.[42] The fact nevertheless remains that Liechtenstein's decision not to sign up to the Lugano Convention may serve to justify discrimination which cannot be justified in an EU law context.

Norwegian law now recognizes the impact of Article 4 EEA on rules concerning security for costs. Traditionally, Section 182 of the 1915 Norwegian Dispute Act made clear that any litigant not resident in Norway could be ordered to provide security for the other party's legal costs. After the entry into force of the EEA

[39]See, e.g., Case C-186/87 *Cowan* ECLI:EU:C:1989:47 and Case C-43/95 *Data Delecta*, ECLI:EU:C:1996:357.

[40]Case E-5/10, *Kottke* [2009–2010] EFTA Ct. Rep. 320, para. 27.

[41]The relevant difference in legal context is that within the EU, the Brussels I Regulation makes sure that a cost award can be enforced in the plaintiff's home state. As long as this is the case, the indirect discrimination entailed by national provisions requiring a plaintiff from another EEA State to provide security for costs cannot be justified.

[42]Para. 52.

Agreement in 1994, the compatibility of this provision with the EEA Agreement's general prohibition of discrimination on grounds of nationality was a matter of dispute between the EFTA Surveillance Authority and the Norwegian Ministry of Justice.[43] In the end, Norwegian authorities gave in and agreed to amend the Dispute Act so that security could no longer be required if the claim in dispute fell within the scope of the EEA Agreement.[44] Acknowledging this, the new Dispute Act of 2005 included the following provision on security for costs in its Section 20-11(1):

> The defendant may demand that a claimant who is not habitually resident in Norway shall provide security for his potential liability for costs in the current instance. Security cannot be required if it would violate an obligation in international law on equal treatment of parties resident abroad and parties resident in Norway, or if it would seem disproportionate in view of the nature of the case, the relationship between the parties and other circumstances.

The intention of the second sentence was to ensure that security of costs was not required if such an order would violate the EEA Agreement, but the wording was kept general and unspecified so that also other binding international agreements were included, for instance if Norway had entered a treaty with a particular state to which the party is a citizen.[45] Unfortunately, however, the ambiguous wording of Section 20-11(1) of the new Dispute Act resulted in a number of court decisions in which security for costs were imposed on claimants from other EEA States and where the compatibility of these orders with Article 4 EEA was questionable at best.[46] Thus, acting upon a complaint, the EFTA Surveillance Authority raised the matter with the Norwegian government and concluded that Section 20-11(1) in the new Dispute Act, or at least parts of the case law based on it, violated Article 4 of the EEA Agreement.[47]

---

[43]See, e.g., the EFTA Surveillance Authority's Letter of Formal Notice to Norway of 7 December 1999 (Doc No. 99-8844-D) as well as the Norwegian Ministry of Justice's presentation of the matter (in the Norwegian language) in Ot.prp. No. 63 (2000–2001).

[44]Act of 15 June 2001 No. 58, amending Sec. 182 of the 1915 Dispute Act.

[45]NOU 2001: 32, pp 937, 938.

[46]Mostly decisions from lower courts, but also one from the Supreme Court; see the order in Rt. 2008 p 1459, where an Icelandic company was required to provide security for costs when bringing a matter concerning a petition for seizure of a specific company's property, following the alleged failure of that company to attend to a pecuniary claim linked to the purchase of fishing equipment.

[47]See the EFTA Surveillance Authority's letter of 5 November 2014 (Doc No. 727963), Letter of formal notice of 24 June 2015 (Doc No. 749608) and Reasoned Opinion of 13 July 2016 (Doc No. 807176), all of which can be obtained from the Authority's Public document database at http://www.eftasurv.int/press–publications/public-documents/. Accessed 7 June 2018. In addition to the alleged breach of Art. 4 EEA, the EFTA Surveillance Authority opined that the provision could also, depending on the circumstances, entail an unjustifiable restriction under Art. 28 EEA on the free movement of workers, Art. 31 EEA on the freedom of establishment, Art. 36 EEA on the freedom to provide services and Art. 40 EEA on the free movement of capital.

The Norwegian Ministry of Justice replied that it was of the opinion that Section 20-11(1) of the Dispute Act was in line with Norway's obligations under the EEA Agreement, but that it nonetheless would amend the provision in order to clarify this. Two alternatives were proposed; Section 20-11(1) was either to be amended to the effect that a plaintiff could not be asked to provide security for legal costs if the subject under dispute fell within the scope of the EEA Agreement ("first alternative") or that plaintiffs resident within the European Economic Area should not be required to furnish security for costs of legal proceedings before Norwegian courts where no such requirement is imposed on plaintiffs residing in Norway ("second alternative").[48] The choice between these two alternatives caused a somewhat heated discussion between the Ministry and the EFTA Surveillance Authority. The Ministry of Justice argued that the first alternative would suffice to meet Norway's EEA law obligations, whereas the EFTA Surveillance Authority opined that such a rule would make it "at best" more cumbersome for a national of another EEA State to bring an action before the Norwegian courts.[49] According to the EFTA Surveillance Authority, it was "possible and/or likely" that the first alternative would result in security for costs being demanded much more frequently from EEA plaintiffs than from Norwegian nationals. In the Authority's opinion, EEA States could not subject non-citizens or non-residents to systematically different rules on security for costs. The Ministry of Justice disagreed, but still opted for the second alternative, as it became clear that most of the respondents in the consultative round preferred this for reasons of legal clarity and predictability.[50] Parliament agreed, so that Section 20-11(1) second sentence of the Dispute Act now reads:

> Security cannot be required if the claimant is resident in an EEA State, if it would violate an obligation in international law on equal treatment of parties resident abroad and parties resident in Norway, or if it would seem disproportionate in view of the nature of the case, the relationship between the parties and other circumstances.

Thus, as of 1 July 2017, security for costs cannot be required if the claimant is resident in an EEA State no matter whether the claim in dispute is within the scope of the EEA Agreement or not. If a claimant resident in an EEA State is party to a case that is not affected by substantial EEA law, for instance an inheritance case, the prohibition against a requirement for security still applies. Arguably, this is not an obligation under the EEA Agreement; it is a spillover effect of such an obligation.

---

[48]Letter to the EFTA Surveillance Authority of 4 December 2015 (Doc No. 784247).

[49]Letter to Norway of 2 February 2016 (Doc No. 789453).

[50]Prop. 42 L (2016–2017) *Endringer i tvisteloven (sikkerhet for sakskostnader)*, pp. 7, 8.

4 The EU/EEA Law Principles of Effectiveness and Equivalence

Further, both the Norwegian Supreme Court[51] and the EFTA Court[52] have held that the case law of the ECJ concerning the principles of effectiveness and equivalence applies *mutatis mutandis* in the EEA context. In its 2005 decision in *Allseas Marine Contractors*, the Supreme Court quoted with approval the following standard phrase from the ECJ's judgment in *Safalero*:

> As a preliminary point, it should be recalled that, in the absence of Community rules governing the matter, it is for the domestic legal system of each Member State to designate the courts and tribunals having jurisdiction and to lay down the detailed procedural rules governing actions for safeguarding rights which individuals derive directly from Community law, provided that such rules are not less favourable than those governing similar domestic actions (principle of equivalence) and that they do not render practically impossible or excessively difficult the exercise of rights conferred by Community law (principle of effectiveness).[53]

The applicability of the general requirements flowing from the ECJ's case law also in the EEA context implies that Norwegian judges will face similar procedural challenges as their colleagues from EU Member States. In cases concerning EEA rights, the principles of effectiveness and equivalence may come to influence any part of civil procedural law—everything from rules on standing and limitation periods to obligations of the courts to raise and consider points of European law of their own motion, evidentiary rules, costs, the right of foreign advocates to act as counsel in national courts, the conditions under which interim relief may be granted, the conditions under which leave to appeal to the higher courts may be granted and possibly even national rules on *res judicata* and reopening of decided cases, just as in the EU Member States.[54]

In Case E-11/12 *Koch*, the EFTA Court explained the principle of equivalence as follows, closely following ECJ case law:

> [...] the principle of equivalence requires that the national rule in question be applied without distinction, whether the infringement alleged is of EEA law or national law, where the purpose and cause of action are similar [...]
>
> In other words, the principle of equivalence extends the general principle of equality to the law of remedies. National procedural law must remain neutral in relation to the origin of the rights invoked, under the conditions set out below.

---

[51]Cf., e.g., Rt. 1996 p 282 *Wilhelmsen*, Rt. 2005 p 597 *Allseas Marine Contractors* and Rt. 2010 p 1500 *Elkem*.

[52]Case E-11/12 *Koch* [2013] EFTA Court Report 272, para. 117 and case law cited.

[53]Case C-13/01 *Safalero*, ECLI:EU:C:2003:447, para. 49, as quoted by the Norwegian Supreme Court in Rt. 2005 p 597 *Allseas Marine Contractors*, para. 39.

[54]For an overview from the perspective of Dutch law, see Krans (2015, 567–588).

> In order to establish whether the principle of equivalence has been complied with in the case in the main proceedings, it is for the national court, which alone has direct knowledge of the procedural rules governing actions in national civil law, to consider the purpose, cause of action and the essential characteristics of allegedly similar domestic actions [...]
>
> Moreover, every case in which the question arises as to whether a national provision is less favourable than those concerning similar domestic actions must be analysed by the national court by reference to the role of that provision in the procedure, its conduct and its special features, viewed as a whole, before the various national bodies [...].[55]

The Court then gave the following presentation of the principle of effectiveness, again closely following the ECJ's lead:

> [...] as regards application of the principle of effectiveness, every case in which the question arises as to whether a national procedural provision makes the application of EEA law impossible or excessively difficult must be analysed by reference to the role of that provision in the procedure, its conduct and its special features, viewed as a whole, before the various national bodies. For those purposes, account must be taken, where appropriate, of the basic principles of the domestic judicial system, such as protection of the rights of the defence, the principle of legal certainty and the proper conduct of procedure [...].[56]

So far, the practical application of the principle of effectiveness in Norwegian civil procedural law has been dominated by issues concerning access to court, at least if we concentrate on the decisions by the Supreme Court.

Already in 1996, the Supreme Court (Interlocutory Appeals Committee) held in the *Wilhelmsen* case that national rules on standing must not make it excessively difficult to challenge the compatibility of a national provision with EEA law.[57] The case concerned several merchants who had lost their municipal concessions to sell beer with more than 4.7% alcohol as a result of a legislative amendment in 1993 which reserved this right to a state-controlled monopoly. The merchants decided to bring an action directly against the State, but the Attorney General replied that they should have applied to the municipality for renewals of their concessions and then, when none were issued, sue the municipality. The claimants argued that such a course of action would have no purpose, as it was obvious that the municipality was not allowed to issue any new concessions. The Supreme Court acknowledged that the outcome of an application to the municipality was given, but still concluded that this was the right course of action, presumably in order to avoid a self-standing action to challenge the compatibility of a statutory provision with the EEA Agreement. The statement as to the importance of access to court was nevertheless important because it made clear that the municipality, if and when a case was brought against it, could not argue that the case should rather have been filed against the State.[58]

---

[55]Case E-11/12 *Koch* [2013] EFTA Court Report 272, para. 122–125 (references to ECJ case law omitted).

[56]Ibid., para. 132.

[57]Rt. 1996 p 282 on p 287.

[58]The merchants did bring an action against the municipality, but they lost on the merits after the Oslo City Court referred the matter to the EFTA Court, which held the monopoly to be lawful; see Case E-6/96 *Wilhelmsen* [1997] EFTA Court Report 53.

The above-mentioned decision in the 2005 *Allseas Marine Contractors* case also concerned legal standing. The case was brought by a group of employees who argued that the tax authorities' decision that their employer—a Swiss company engaged in subsea activities on the Norwegian continental shelf—had to pay social security contributions to Norway even though they neither had nor wanted membership in the Norwegian national insurance system, violated the right to free movement of workers as guaranteed by the EEA Agreement. The Supreme Court held that the employees clearly lacked standing under the Tax Payment Act, but proceeded to assess whether they had to be given legal standing due to the EEA law principle of effectiveness. However, the answer was in the negative, as the tax decision was imposed on the company only and had minor and indirect effects for the employees.[59]

In the *Elkem* case from 2010, the Supreme Court once again acknowledged the general requirements of effectiveness and equivalence.[60] The case concerned the lawfulness of a limitation period imposed by the Tax Payment Act. Citing ECJ case law, the Supreme Court held that a limitation period of six months was not a violation of the principle of effectiveness.[61]

Although not yet present in the jurisprudence of Norwegian courts, a debate on ECJ's case law concerning *ex officio* application of EU consumer law by national courts has emerged in the legal literature (Robberstad 2002, 195–223; Fredriksen 2008, 326–328; Giertsen 2014, 215, 216; Skoghøy 2017, 600–604; Nylund 2014, 107, 108; Eldjarn 2016, 237–243). As is well known to EU lawyers, the ECJ ruled in *Oceano Grupo Editorial* from 2000 that national courts must have the power to apply EU consumer protection law on their own motion[62] and later on made clear that domestic courts are obliged to make use of these powers.[63] Since the relevant parts of EU consumer protection law are part of the EEA Agreement, the EU law obligation on national courts to apply them *ex officio* must apply also to Norwegian courts. However, a transformation of these obligations into Norwegian civil procedural law is far from straightforward.

Although Norwegian judges, pursuant to the *iura novit curia* principle contained in Section 11-3 of the Dispute Act, are under an obligation to apply any relevant substantive or procedural law, difficulties arise when the ECJ requires national courts to apply EU consumer protection law even if this demands inclusion of other facts than those pleaded by the parties. One way for Norwegian judges to fulfil the ECJ's demands within the existing structure of Norwegian civil procedure is by regarding EEA-related consumer protection cases as cases where public policy limits the parties' rights of disposition in the legal action (Skoghøy 2017, 600–602).

---

[59]Rt. 2005 p 597, para. 42–46.

[60]Rt. 2010 p 1500, para. 65.

[61]Para. 66.

[62]C-240/98-C-244/98 *Oceano Grupo Editorial*.

[63]E.g., Case C-473/00 *Cofidis*, Case C-168/05 *Mostaza Claro*, Case C-243/08 *Pannon*, Case C-618/10 *Banco Español de Crédito* and Case C-497/13 *Froukje Faber*.

In such cases, a judge is not bound by the parties' dispositions on facts and evidence,[64] and is "under a duty to ensure that the presentation of evidence provides a sound factual basis for the ruling".[65] Regarding EU consumer protection law as a matter where the parties' rights of disposition in a legal action are limited by public policy consideration thus clearly fulfils the obligations of judge-activity advanced by the ECJ. One may argue, though, that such a move is an unnecessarily drastic limitation of the autonomy of consumers, especially because it will deprive the consumers of the possibility to settle the case. A less drastic alternative within the existing structure of Norwegian civil procedure is to regard EU/EEA consumer protection law as matters of which a Norwegian judge is under an obligation to provide active guidance to the weaker party. Inspired by German rules on *materielle Prozessleitung*,[66] Section 11-5 of the Dispute Act contains rules on judges' guidance to the parties on procedural and substantive matters.[67] However, the Norwegian rules, in contrast to the German rules (Braun 2014, 597, 598; Haas 2011, 99, 100–104), only provide judges with the competence to guide on substantive matters. A judge is under an obligation to provide such guidance only if extraordinary circumstances occur, for instance if especially important values are at stake for a party and he or she lacks the knowledge, skills or resources necessary to present his case (Schei et al. 2013, 416).[68] An obligation to provide guidance on matters of EU/EEA consumer protection law will obviously widen these obligations, and thereby represent a modification of Norwegian procedural law, but it is not a drastic change. Such a modification is preferable because active guidance will enlighten a consumer as to his or her rights, and at the same time respect the choices made by an enlightened or well-informed consumer.

Fulfilment of these *ex officio* obligations in Norwegian civil procedural law may also meet institutional challenges. The obligation of *ex officio* application of

[64]Sec. 11-4 of the Dispute Act.

[65]Sec. 21-3(2) first sentence of the Dispute Act.

[66]*Zivilprozessordnung* § 139.

[67]The provision reads as follows: (1) The court shall give the parties such guidance on procedural rules and routines and other formalities as is necessary to enable them to safeguard their interests in the case. The court shall seek to prevent errors and shall give such guidance as is necessary to enable errors to be rectified. Section 16-5 applies to the right to rectify errors. (2) The court shall, in accordance with subsections (3) to (7), give guidance that contributes to a correct ruling in the case based on the facts and the applicable rules. (3) The court shall endeavour to clarify disputed issues and ensure that the parties' prayers for relief and their positions regarding factual and legal issues are clarified. (4) The court may encourage a party to take a position on factual and legal issues that appear to be important to the case. (5) The court may encourage a party to offer evidence. (6) The court shall during the proceedings show particular consideration for the need for guidance of parties not represented by counsel. (7) The court shall provide its guidance in a manner that is not liable to impair confidence in its impartiality. The court shall not advise the parties on the position they should take on disputed issues in the case or on procedural steps they should take.

[68]NOU 2001: 32 p. 709.

consumer law obviously applies to national courts, but most of consumer protection in Norway is in practice taken care of by informal complaints boards.

5 Procedural Harmonization Through EU Secondary Law Within and Outside the Scope of the EEA Agreement—Consequences for Norway

As noted in the introduction, the national procedural laws of EU Member States are influenced not only by primary EU law (the treaties and general principles), but also by secondary law (directives and regulations in particular) which wholly or partially harmonize procedural matters. Examples include the EU legal acts on:

- Jurisdiction, applicable law, recognition and enforcement of decisions and cooperation in matters relating to maintenance obligations (Reg No. 4/2009)
- Alternative dispute resolution: mediation (Dir 2008/52/EC)
- Service of judicial and extrajudicial documents (Reg No. 1393/2007)
- European small claims procedure (Reg No. 861/2007)
- European order for payment procedure (Reg No. 1896/2006)
- European enforcement order for uncontested claims (Reg No. 805/2004)
- Jurisdiction, recognition and enforcement of judgments in matrimonial matters and matters of parental responsibility (Reg No. 2201/2003—Brussels II)
- Taking of evidence in civil and commercial matters (Reg No. 1206/2001)
- Insolvency proceedings (Reg No. 1346/2000)
- Common minimum rules relating to legal aid (Dir 2003/8/EC)
- Review procedures concerning the award of public contracts (Dir 2007/66/EC)
- Injunctions for the protection of consumers' interests (Dir 2009/22/EC)
- Alternative dispute resolution for consumer disputes (Dir 2013/11/EU)
- Online dispute resolution for consumer disputes (Reg No. 524/2013).

As has been mentioned already, many of these legal acts are based on Article 81 TFEU and are for that reason alone deemed by the EEA Joint Committee to fall outside the scope of the EEA Agreement. Given the fact that Article 81 TFEU refers to, *inter alia*, measures "necessary for the proper functioning of the internal market" (into which Norway is integrated through the EEA Agreement), this limitation on the scope of the EEA Agreement is not unproblematic.

As far as the Brussel I Regulation on jurisdiction and the recognition and enforcement of judgments in civil and commercial matters is concerned, this is largely remedied by the 2007 Lugano Convention. Still, unlike the EEA Agreement, the Lugano Convention is essentially static in nature—it has no simplified procedure that allows for updating of the Convention to keep up with changes in EU law. As a result, the changes to the EU rules introduced by the recast Brussels I Regulation of 2012 (Reg No. 1215/2012) are so far not reflected in the Lugano Convention, thus creating certain differences between the Lugano and the

Brussels Regimes. Apparently, the Lugano Convention's Standing Committee has not considered the divergences serious enough to justify a full revision of the Convention.

With a caveat for matters where there is no longer full parallelism between the Lugano and the Brussels Regimes, the Lugano Convention serves as an effective vehicle for the reception of ECJ case law into Norwegian law. Through Section 4-8 of the Dispute Act, the entire Lugano Convention, protocols and annexes included, has the status of a Norwegian statute. This includes Protocol 2 on the uniform interpretation of the Convention, whose Article 1 obliges national courts to pay "due account" to, *inter alia*, ECJ case law concerning the Brussels I Regulation.[69] Acknowledging this, the Norwegian Supreme Court regularly underlines that ECJ case law is a weighty source for Norwegian courts faced with interpreting the Lugano Convention.[70] In practice, the effect of ECJ case law concerning the EU rules on jurisdiction and the recognition and enforcement of judgments in civil and commercial matters is no different in Norway than in EU Member States.

As to the other EU legal acts based on Article 81 TFEU, Norway has shown an interest in at least some of them. There are ongoing negotiations between Norway, Denmark, Iceland and Switzerland and the EU concerning the Regulation on taking of evidence in civil and commercial matters (Reg No. 1206/2001). Norway is reportedly also interested in other agreements concerning, for example, service of judicial and extrajudicial documents (Reg No. 1393/2007), but the EU has so far not followed up on this.

As to EU legal acts based on EEA-relevant parts of the TFEU, notably the EU's competences to regulate the internal market (Article 114 TFEU), the picture is more nuanced. However, as noted in the introduction, the EFTA States in general and, reportedly, Norway in particular have been reluctant to accept novel legal acts which harmonize national civil procedural law. Directive 2004/48/EC on the enforcement of intellectual property rights is an (in)famous example. The European Commission marked the Directive as "Text with EEA relevance", and the substantive rules on intellectual property rights are clearly part of the EEA Agreement. Still, Norway refused to accept the EEA-relevance of the Directive due to its "procedural character":

> The Directive is not taken into the EEA Agreement, which means that Norway is not obliged to implement it. This is because the Directive contains a number of procedural rules. Such rules are outside the scope of the EEA Agreement.[71]

---

[69] In theory, this Protocol applies also to the ECJ and obliges it to pay due account to decisions from, *inter alia*, the Norwegian Supreme Court, but this is clearly not followed up by the ECJ in practice.

[70] See, e.g., HR-2017-1297-A *Bergen Bunkers*, para. 37 and case law cited. This is in line with the Supreme Court's approach to ECJ case law of relevance for the 1988 Lugano Convention; see Rt. 2004 p 981 *Agrimann Norge* (para. 22) and Rt. 2011 p 987 *Marin Alpin* (para. 35).

[71] Prop. 81 L (2012–2013) *Endringer i lovgivningen om industrielt rettsvern m.m. (styrking av håndhevingsreglene)* pp. 8, 9.

The EU apparently accepted Norway's stance on this; the EEA-relevance of the Directive appears not to have been raised as a matter of concern in the EEA Joint Committee.

A further example is Directive 2014/104/EU on actions for damages under national law for infringements of EU competition law. This Directive contains both substantive and procedural rules; the procedural rules are primarily several provisions on evidence. The Directive is marked as "Text with EEA relevance" by the EU. In its proposal for the Directive, the Commission explained this as follows:

> The proposed Directive contributes to the proper functioning of the internal market as it creates a more level playing field both for the undertakings that infringe the competition rules and for the victims of this illegal behaviour. Due to these objectives in the fields of competition and the internal market, which form part of the EEA legal rules, the proposal is relevant for the EEA.[72]

However, a comment from the Standing Committee of the EFTA States on the Commission's proposal for the Directive suggests that the EFTA States consider the Directive not to be EEA relevant:

> The EEA EFTA States do not want to prejudge the conclusion of whether the draft Directive is considered to be EEA relevant or not. A final position on the issue of EEA relevance can only be taken after the adoption of the Directive in its final wording. The EEA EFTA States would, however, strongly underline that provisions on civil procedure are, in general, not EEA relevant and fall outside the scope of the EEA Agreement.[73]

Given the fact that the harmonization of national procedural law foreseen by these directives is considered by the EU legislator to be necessary for the proper functioning of the internal market (Article 114 TFEU), this stance is, of course, not unproblematic.

Perhaps somewhat paradoxically, Norwegian authorities seem to have acknowledged this. Although Norway insisted that Dir 2004/48/EC fell outside the scope of the EEA Agreement, the relevant Norwegian statutes were subsequently amended in order to make sure that the enforcement of intellectual property rights in Norwegian law meets the requirements set by the Directive.[74] The "voluntary" implementation of the Directive included the introduction of a new Chapter 28A into the Civil Procedure Act on discovery in these cases, which essentially mirrors the right of information provided for in Article 8 of the Directive.[75] The Norwegian government explained this course of action as follows:

> The interests of Norwegian trade and industry still call for Norway as a part of the EEA market to have rules on enforcement of intellectual property rights that at least fulfil the

[72]COM/2013/0404 final.

[73]EEA EFTA Comment on the proposal for a directive of the European Parliament and of the Council on certain rules governing actions for damages under national law for infringements of the competition law provisions of the Member States and of the European Union, 13 November 2013.

[74]See Act of 31 May 2013 No. 25.

[75]The inclusion of a new chapter which only concerns one specific sort of cases in the Dispute Act has met criticism; see Hjort (2016b, 277–290).

> minimum requirements of the Directive. Substantive EU-rules on industrial property rights that do not concern enforcement are a part of the EEA Agreement. It is important that the law is at least as favourable to right holders in Norway as in the EU also when it comes to enforcement. This has been normative for the shaping of the suggestion in the proposition.[76]

Thus, the Ministry of Justice recognized the problems that arise when Norway is obliged to implement certain substantial EU rules but not the procedural rules constructed to effectuate those substantive rules. Leaving harmonization of national procedural law outside the scope of the EEA Agreement may put Norwegian contractors in a weaker legal position than their European competitors. The reason for developing the new Chapter 28A in the Dispute Act was to counterbalance these negative effects for Norwegian businesses. Still, such "voluntary" implementation has certain drawbacks, among them the fact that Norwegian courts cannot ask the EFTA Court to clarify the interpretation of EU rules that are not part of the EEA Agreement.[77] Perhaps somewhat paradoxically, this probably only increases the influence of ECJ case law, as Norwegian courts will have to look directly to the ECJ for guidance on the interpretation of the Directive.[78]

On this background, it is hardly surprising that Norwegian scepticism towards EU legal acts that harmonize national procedural law appears to have softened considerably in recent years. As to the above-mentioned Directive 2014/104/EU on actions for damages under national law for infringements of EU competition law, the Norwegian government now seems ready to accept its EEA-relevance if only the EU will let Norwegian competition authorities participate fully in the EU's European Competition Network and accept decentralized enforcement of the EEA competition rules also within the EU. The reason why the Directive still has not been incorporated into the EEA Agreement (as of August 2017) is that it remains uncertain whether the EU is prepared to accept full and symmetrical decentralized enforcement of EEA competition law throughout the EEA and full participation of the national competition authorities of the EFTA States (and the EFTA Surveillance Authority) in an "EEA-wide" European Competition Network (see further on this, Franklin et al. 2016, 665–691).

Furthermore, a number of EU legal acts that contain procedural rules which harmonize national procedural law have been incorporated into the Agreement in recent years, including Directive 2009/22/EC on injunctions for the protection of consumers' interests, Directive 2013/11/EU on alternative dispute resolution for consumer disputes and Regulation No. 524/2013 on online dispute resolution for consumer disputes.

---

[76]Prop. 81 L (2012–2013) p. 13 (our translation).

[77]The EFTA Court's jurisdiction under Art. 34 of the Surveillance and Court Agreement is limited to giving Advisory Opinions on the interpretation of the EEA Agreement.

[78]As the purpose of creating at least as effective rules as in the EU for the enforcement of intellectual property rights clearly suggests that ECJ case law is relevant for Norwegian courts when interpreting Chapter 28A in the Dispute Act.

Still, divergences between EU and EEA law remain when it comes to harmonization of national civil procedural law. A difficult and sensitive question in cases of such divergences is the extent to which they can be remedied by the general EU/EEA law principle of effectiveness. Certain provisions of a remedial or procedural character in EU secondary law do arguably "only" define and give concrete expression to the principle of effectiveness. Still, it is naturally a sensitive matter for any court—be it the EFTA Court or the Norwegian Supreme Court—to deduce obligations from the general principle of effectiveness which parallels obligations flowing from EU legal acts that have not been made part of the EEA Agreement (see further on this, Fredriksen 2016, 109).

6 Concluding Remarks

The understanding of the potential impact of EU law on Norwegian civil procedural law is gradually emerging in Norway. In many ways, the combined effect of the EEA Agreement and the Lugano Convention is that Norwegian judges find themselves in a situation very similar to that of their colleagues from EU Member States. Still, as explained above, there are limits to both the EEA Agreement and the Lugano Convention which complicate the matter. So far, this has not caused considerable problems for the functioning of either agreement, but future developments in EU law may of course alter this assessment. Depending on the development of EU law, amendments to both the EEA Agreement and the Lugano Convention may become necessary.

References

Arnesen F, Fredriksen HH, Graver HP et al (eds) (2018) Agreement on the European economic area: a commentary. CH Beck/Hart/Nomo, Baden-Baden/München/Oxford

Backer IL (2007) The Norwegian reform of civil procedure. Scand Stud Law 51:41–75

Backer IL (2015) Norsk sivilprosess. Universitetsforlaget, Oslo

Baudenbacher C (2016) The relationship between the EFTA court and the court of justice of the European union. In: Baudenbacher C (ed) The handbook of EEA law. Springer, Cham, pp 179–194

Björgvinsson DT (2014) Fundamental rights in EEA law. In: Court EFTA (ed) The EEA and the EFTA court: decentred integration. Hart Publishing, Oxford/Portland, pp 263–280

Braun J (2014) Lehrbuch des Zivilprozeßrechts. Mohr Siebeck, Tübingen

Eldjarn E (2016) Materiell prosessledelse. Cappelen Damm akademisk, Oslo

Franklin CNK, Fredriksen HH, Halvorsen Barlund IM (2016) National report on private enforcement of European competition law in Norway. Private enforcement and collective redress in European competition law (2015 FIDE Congress). Wolters Kluwer, Budapest, pp 665–691

Fredriksen HH (2008) Tvisteloven og EØS-avtalen. Tidsskrift for Rettsvitenskap 121(3):289–359

Fredriksen HH (2016) EEA main agreement and secondary EU law incorporated into the annexes and protocols. In: Baudenbacher C (ed) The handbook of EEA law. Springer, Cham, pp 95–110

Fredriksen HH, Franklin CNK (2015) Of pragmatism and principles: the EEA agreement 20 years on. Common Market Law Rev 52(3):629–684

Fredriksen HH, Lipp V (eds) (2011) Reforms of civil procedure in Germany and Norway. Mohr Siebeck, Tübingen

Giertsen J (2014) Avtaler, 3rd edn. Universitetsforlaget, Bergen

Haas U (2011) The relationship between the judge and the parties under German law. In: Fredriksen HH, Lipp V (eds) Reforms of civil procedure in Germany and Norway. Mohr Siebeck, Tübingen, pp 87–123

Hjort MA (2016a) Tilgang til bevis i sivile saker. Universitetsforlaget, Oslo, Særlig om digitale bevis

Hjort MA (2016b) Gjennomføring av internasjonale forpliktelser i sivilprosessen. Om lovgivningsteknikk og påvirkningstendenser i Norge, Sverige og Danmark. In: Bugge HC, Indreberg H, Syse A et al (eds) Lov, liv og lære. Festskrift til Inge Lorange Backer 70 år. Universitetsforlaget, Oslo, pp 277–290

Krans B (2015) EU law and national civil procedure law: an invisible pillar. European Rev Private Law 23(4):567–588

Nylund A (2011) Europeanization of Norwegian civil procedure. In: Fredriksen HH, Lipp V (eds) Reforms of civil procedure in Germany and Norway. Mohr Siebeck, Tübingen, pp 125–134

Nylund A (2014) European integration and Nordic civil procedure. In: Nylund A, Ervo L (eds) The future of civil litigation: access to courts and court-annexed mediation in the Nordic countries. Springer, London, pp 31–51

Nylund A (2016) Norway: an insider outside—or an outsider inside—European civil justice. In: Nylund A, Krans B (eds) The European union and national civil procedure. Intersentia, Cambridge, pp 101–114

Robberstad A (2002) Norske dommeres plikt til å veilede om EØS-retten. Lov og Rett 41(4): 195–223

Robberstad A (2015) Sivilprosess, 3rd edn. Fagbokforlaget, Bergen

Schei T, Nordén DB, Bårdsen A et al (2013) Tvisteloven: Kommentarutgave, 2nd edn. Universitetsforlaget, Oslo

Skoghøy JEA (2017) Tvisteløsning, 3rd edn. Universitetsforlaget, Oslo

Strandberg M (2017) The presumption of innocence in civil cases. In: Uzelac A, Van Rhee CH (eds) Revisiting procedural human rights. Intersenita, Cambridge, pp 115–134

Utgård KA (2005) Procedural aspects of homogeneity: international coordination and harmonisation in the area of civil procedure. In: Baudenbacher C, Tresselt P, Örlygsson T (eds) The Efta court—ten years on. Hart Publishing, Oxford/Portland, pp 131–140

Viken M (2012) Markedsundersøkelser som bevis i varemerke- og markedsføringsrett. Gyldendal Akademisk, Oslo

Wahl N (2014) Uncharted waters: reflections on the legal significance of the charter under EEA law and judicial cross-fertilisation in the field of fundamental rights. In: Court EFTA (ed) The EEA and the EFTA court—decentred integration. Hart Publishing, Oxford/Portland, pp 281–298

Halvard Haukeland Fredriksen Professor of European Law and Civil Procedure at the University of Bergen, Norway. Dr. iur from the University of Göttingen, Germany. Ph.D. from the University of Bergen, Norway. Co-chair of the Research Group on Civil Procedure at the Faculty of Law in Bergen.

Magne Strandberg Professor of Law at the University of Bergen, Faculty of Law, Norway, where he teaches Procedure Law. Co-chair of the Research Group on Civil Procedure.

Judicial Cooperation of the EU in Civil Matters in Its Relations with Non-EU States—A Blind Spot?

Matthias Weller

Abstract Mutual trust is the bedrock of the EU's internal policy regarding judicial cooperation. When it comes to cooperation with third States, however, there seems to be a blind spot. Indeed, despite the increasing importance of foreign trade, most—if not all—FTAs concluded by the EU remain silent on judicial cooperation. Such a result is unfortunate, since the combination of trade agreements and judicial cooperation measures would certainly foster foreign trade. Therefore, this contribution discusses possible options, including grounds of competency of the EU, that could improve the current situation.

1 Introduction

"Mutual trust" is one of the most prominent claims of the EU to justify the Member States' obligations under EU secondary law for judicial cooperation within the Area of Freedom, Security and Justice (Weller 2017/2, 1–21; 2015, 65–102). Technically, mutual trust is implemented through far-reaching mechanisms for recognition of public acts of other Member States such as foreign judgments, administrative acts, etc. The EU legislator is convinced that judicial cooperation in civil matters or, in more general and less EU-specific terminology, private international law (Van Calster 2016; Weller 2016, para. 1)[1] is an integral part of a functioning internal market.[2]

---

[1]See also Institut de Droit International (Session de Genève 1874) Resolution "Utilité d'un accord commun des règles uniformes de droit international privé". http://www.idi-iil.org/app/uploads/2017/06/1874_gen_01_fr.pdf. Accessed 7 June 2018.

[2]See e.g. Recital 3 of Regulation (EU) No. 1215/2012 of the European Parliament and of the Council of 12 December 2012 on jurisdiction and the recognition and enforcement of judgments in civil and commercial matters (recast), OJ L 351, pp. 1–32.

M. Weller (✉)
Department of Law, University of Bonn, Bonn, Germany
e-mail: weller@jura.uni-bonn.de

A. Uzelac and C. H. van Rhee (eds.), *Transformation of Civil Justice*,
Ius Gentium: Comparative Perspectives on Law and Justice 70,
https://doi.org/10.1007/978-3-319-97358-6_4

However, when it comes to judicial cooperation of the EU with third states, in particular within its foreign trade relations, there seems to be a blind spot: no coherent strategy, no theories about suitable tools and mechanisms, and no awareness. I submit that this is a deficiency in the EU's foreign trade policy and that this should be changed.

2 Relevance of Foreign Trade for the EU: Some Facts and Figures

On the basis of the most recent data published in March 2017, Eurostat explains that:

> The EU-28, China and the United States have been the three largest global players for international trade since 2004 when China passed Japan. In 2015, the total level of trade in goods (exports and imports) recorded for the EU-28, China and the United States was almost identical, peaking at EUR 3 633 billion in the United States, which was EUR 61 billion higher than for China and EUR 115 billion above the level recorded for the EU-28 (note the latter does not include intra-EU trade); Japan had the fourth highest level of trade in goods, at EUR 1 127 billion.[3]

And:

> Looking at the flows of exports and imports, the EU-28 had the second largest share of global exports and imports of goods in 2015: the EU-28's exports of goods were equivalent to 15.5% of the world total, and in 2014 were surpassed for the first time since the EU was founded by those of China (16.1% in 2014, rising to 17.8% in 2015), but still ahead of the United States (13.4%); the United States had a larger share of world imports (17.4%) than either the EU-28 (14.5%) or China (12.7%).[4]

Most importantly for the purposes of this text:

> EU-28 international trade in goods with the rest of the world (the sum of extra-EU exports and imports) was valued at EUR 3 453 billion in 2016.[5]

On the basis of these facts and figures, it cannot be a surprise that "[t]he EU is the biggest trading partner for 59 countries as compared to 36 for China and 24 for

---

[3]http://ec.europa.eu/eurostat/statistics-explained/index.php/International_trade_in_goods. Accessed 7 June 2018.

[4]Ibid.

[5]Even larger is the volume of Intra-EU trade, see Eurostat, n. 4: "Trade in goods between EU Member States (intra-EU trade) was valued—in terms of dispatches—at EUR 3110 billion in 2016. This was 78% higher than the level recorded for exports leaving the EU-28 to non-member countries of EUR 1745 billion (extra-EU trade)." Taking intra-EU exports and imports together, these trade flows almost double the size of extra-EU trade.

the US. European external trade in goods and services accounts for 35% of EU GDP […]. Trade has never been more important for the EU economy."[6]

And each single transaction that contributes to this large volume of foreign trade takes place within the applicable framework of private international law—a fact that does not seem to be perceived as strongly as the relevance of foreign trade as such.

3 The EU's Future Plans to Intensify Foreign Trade

In the European Commission, the Directorate General for Trade ("DG Trade") "is in charge of developing and implementing the common trade policy of the European Union in accordance with the objectives set out in Article 207 of the Treaty on the Functioning of the EU (TFEU)".[7] And DG Trade explains that "[t]he EU's trade policy is an integral part of its wider 2020 strategy to boost employment and create a more modern, viable and sustainable economy. A vibrant domestic economy requires the Union to be increasingly competitive abroad."[8] Therefore, "[t]rade will be an even more important source of growth in the future. Approximately 90% of global economic growth in the next 10–15 years is expected to be generated outside Europe. Economic recovery will need to be consolidated through stronger links with the new centres of global growth."

To put it differently, economic integration with third states and non-EU trade blocks is considered to be essential for the future welfare of the EU, its Member States and all of its citizens. Against this background, it cannot be a surprise that intensifying and extending trade relations with non-EU states is one of the top priorities of the current Commission.[9] And indeed, the numbers of trade agreements of the EU[10] and ongoing negotiations[11] are vast and cover almost the whole world ("extended regionalism"[12])—despite setbacks and delays that occur from time to time.

In addition, in the EU's perspective, trade is no longer just about trade, as the College of Commissioners explained in its Communication on Trade and Investment Policy Strategy "Trade for All—Towards a More Responsible Trade

[6]DG Trade (2016) Strategic Plan 2016–2020. http://trade.ec.europa.eu/doclib/docs/2016/august/tradoc_154919.pdf and https://ec.europa.eu/info/sites/info/files/strategic-plan-2016-2020-dg-estat_march2016_en.pdf, p. 6. Accessed 7 June 2018.

[7]Ibid., p. 4.

[8]Ibid., p. 6.

[9]Ibid.

[10]http://ec.europa.eu/trade/policy/countries-and-regions/agreements. Accessed 7 June 2018.

[11]European Commission (2017) Overview of FTA and Other Trade Negotiations. http://trade.ec.europa.eu/doclib/docs/2006/december/tradoc_118238.pdf. Accessed 7 June 2018.

[12]European Commission (2016) The European Union Trade Policy 2016. http://trade.ec.europa.eu/doclib/docs/2011/august/tradoc_148181.pdf, p. 22. Accessed 7 June 2018.

and Investment Policy" of 14 October 2015.[13] Rather, trade is more and more understood as a vehicle to promote the values of the EU such as human rights, social welfare, sustainable development and inclusion, etc.[14] Free Trade Agreements (FTAs) more and more include supplemental areas of "cooperation". This is not an entirely new development. For example, the EU-Mexico FTA 2000[15] already contained several provisions on cooperation.[16] Further, the EU-Vietnam FTA Text 2016[17] provides for a Chap. 16 on "cooperation and capacity building". Article 1 of this Chapter reads:

1. The Parties affirm the importance of co-operation and capacity building in contributing to the efficient implementation of this Agreement, which will support the continued expansion of trade and investment activities between Viet Nam and the EU and create new opportunities for trade and investment.
2. The Parties commit to deepen co-operation activities in areas of mutual interest, taking into consideration the different levels of development between the EU and Viet Nam.

Article 2(2) specifies:

> To achieve the objectives referred to in Article 1, the Parties attach particular importance to cooperating in the following areas: (a) Regional cooperation and integration; (b) Trade facilitation; (c) Trade policy and regulations; (d) Trade-related aspects of agriculture, fishery and forestry; (e) Sustainable development, notably in its environmental and labour dimensions; (f) Small and medium-sized enterprises; (g) Other areas identified under specific chapters of the present Agreement; (h) Other areas of mutual interest related to the present Agreement.

Article 3 of Chap. 16, for example, specifically provides for cooperation on animal welfare.

---

[13]European Commission (2015) Trade for All. Towards a More Responsible Trade and Investment Policy. http://trade.ec.europa.eu/doclib/docs/2015/october/tradoc_153846.pdf, p. 22, sub 4.2.: "A trade agenda to promote sustainable development, human rights and good governance". Accessed 7 June 2018.

[14]To conceive (somewhat idealistically) of trade as a vehicle for deeper values than just economic benefits has roots in, inter alia, e.g. the conceptual thinking of the time of the Enlightenment, see Kant (1795/96), in translation (provided by the author of this text): "It is the spirit of trade that cannot go together with war, and sooner or later this spirit will cast its spell on each and every people.".

[15]Currently under renegotiation. http://ec.europa.eu/trade/policy/countries-and-regions/countries/mexico. Accessed 7 June 2018.

[16]See e.g. Article 20: Cooperation in relation to matters of the information society; Article 21: Cooperation in agriculture and the rural sector; Article 22: Cooperation on mining; Article 23: Cooperation on energy; Article 24: Cooperation on transport; Article 25: Cooperation on tourism.

[17]The text was finalized in 2016, but is currently undergoing legal review. http://ec.europa.eu/trade/policy/countries-and-regions/countries/vietnam. Accessed 7 June 2018.

4 Judicial Cooperation: An (Almost) Blind Spot

Nothing against animal welfare—an important ethical need. But compared to this (and other) rather specific topics of cooperation, it appears to me all the more striking that the EU-Vietnam FTA remains entirely silent on judicial cooperation. And this is symptomatic. There is no FTA to my knowledge that addresses this issue expressly—although under the TFEU judicial cooperation is a central and highly dynamic policy considered to have a serious impact on internal integration. Judicial cooperation is simply out of sight for DG Trade. Perhaps the most telling proof of this blindness is that the "College of Commission" that DG Trade assembled around its work includes nearly anybody one could think of, but not DG Justice.[18]

Likewise, many international organizations are shown in the chart on the "operating context" of DG Trade, but none of those organizations that deal with "judicial cooperation" appear, in particular not the Hague Conference on Private International Law. This separation results in a complete detachment of trade negotiations from the accession of trade partners to the Hague Conventions on judicial cooperation in civil matters. For example, whereas Mexico, an old trade partner of the EU, is a Contracting Party to the 1965 Hague Convention on the Service of Process, the 1970 Hague Convention on the Taking of Evidence, and the 2005 Hague Convention on Choice of Court Agreements, the prospective trade partner Singapore is only a Party to the 1970 and 2005 Conventions,[19] and another prospective trade partner, Vietnam, does not participate in any of these conventions. Obviously, there is no strategy and not even concern by DG Trade in this respect.

However, there should be such strategy and such concern. The European Council, in its 2005 Hague Programme, stated at the very end, after outlining its strategy on establishing the "area of freedom, security and justice, responding to a central concern of the peoples of the States brought together in the Union"[20]:

> External Relations: The European Council considers the development of a coherent external dimension of the Union policy of freedom, security and justice as a growing priority. In addition to the aspects already addressed in the previous chapters, the European Council calls on the Commission and the Secretary-General / High Representative to present, by the end of 2005, a strategy covering all external aspects of the Union policy on freedom, security and justice, based on the measures developed in this programme to the Council. The strategy should reflect the Union's special relations with third countries, groups of countries and regions, and focus on the specific needs for JHA cooperation with them. All powers available to the Union, including external relations, should be used in an integrated

[18]See European Commission (2015) n. 14 at p. 4.

[19]The consequence is that if, for example, a German claimant wants to serve process against a Singaporean Party, this will have to be done under the Convention between His Majesty and the President of the German Reich regarding Legal Proceedings in Civil and Commercial Matters of London, March 28, 1928.

[20]European Council (3 March 2005) Hague Programme: Strengthening Freedom, Security and Justice in the European Union, OJ C 53, pp. 1–14.

> and consistent way to establish the area of freedom, security and justice. The following guidelines (established at the European Council meeting in Feira in 2000) should be taken into account: the existence of internal policies as the major parameter justifying external action; need for value added in relation to projects carried out by the Member States; contribution to the general political objectives of the foreign policies of the Union; possibility of achieving the goals during a period of reasonable time; the possibility of long-term action.[21]

Shortly afterwards, the Council, in a note of 11 April 2006 from the Presidency to Coreper/Council on "Aspects of judicial cooperation in civil matters in the framework of the Strategy for the External Dimension of JHA: Global Freedom, Security and Justice",[22] identified as "method of work"[23]:

> To the greatest extent possible, cooperation in the field of judicial cooperation in civil matters with third countries should follow the general framework for the relations between the EU and a particular third country. Account should be taken of the existing level of cooperation, of the legal framework and of reciprocal interest in deepening cooperation in the field of judicial cooperation in civil matters.

And "it should also be noted that depending on the status of the country with respect to the European Union (e.g. a possible candidate country or close economic ties), the objectives and the level of detail of such cooperation vary significantly".[24]

Close economic ties—this sounds to me as though FTA partners of the EU would be clearly covered. However, the Council does not address this question more expressly. As "means of cooperation", the Council lists[25] "international negotiations at multilateral level" or "in the form of bilateral agreements" (to which FTAs with a single third state evidently belong). And:

> In particular, the work undertaken within the Hague Conference on Private International Law has provided for useful exchanges with third countries. With more than 60 member countries representing all continents and different legal traditions, the Hague Conference on Private International Law is an international organization reinforcing legal certainty and security on a global scale in the area of judicial cooperation in civil matters. In addition, similar approach should be taken as regards other forums such as the Council of Europe, UNIDROIT, UNCITRAL and others.[26]

However, "[i]n certain fields and with respect to some partners, it may be useful to proceed by way of concluding bilateral agreements between the EU and a respective third country in the field of judicial cooperation in civil matters. This method offers more flexibility and enables tailor-made solutions …".[27]

---

[21]Ibid., p. 14, sub 4.

[22]European Council (11 April 2006) Council Doc. 8140/06, http://register.consilium.europa.eu/doc/srv?l=EN&f=ST%208140%202006%20INIT. Accessed 7 June 2018.

[23]Ibid., p. 3, sub II.2.a., para. 8.

[24]Ibid., para. 9.

[25]Ibid., para. 13 et seq.

[26]Ibid., para. 16 and 17.

[27]Ibid., para. 18 and 19.

"Target countries" are (of course) primarily acceding and candidate countries as well as Lugano States and European Neighbourhood Policy countries, but also the USA, Canada and Russia,[28] and, most telling in this context, "other countries … with close commercial ties",[29] i.e., one is tempted to add, FTA partners. "As a first priority, cooperation should focus on the possibility of those countries acceding to certain key instruments of the Hague Conference on Private International Law."[30]

To summarize the Council's view: economic integration should go hand in hand with judicial integration, both internally and externally. However, nothing of this view has become reality in the EU's external relations so far.

5 Measures

What are the possible measures to take?

5.1 No Measures at All—Commercial Arbitration Takes Care of Everything

First of all, one might think that commercial arbitration fills the gap sufficiently. Indeed, Mexico, Vietnam and Singapore and, given the number of 157 Contracting States worldwide, presumably all other FTA partners of the EU are Parties to the 1958 UNCITRAL Convention on the Recognition and Enforcement of Foreign Arbitral Awards ("New York Convention").[31] It is certainly fair to say that a large number of commercial disputes that arise from and within foreign trade relations of the EU with third states will be taken care of within the elaborated structures of international commercial arbitration.

Yet, consent-based commercial arbitration has its limits when it comes to tort cases and multiparty arbitration (Menon 2015, 219–245). In addition, there is much debate as to the validity and scope of arbitration agreements. And it would be somewhat surprising if externally judicial cooperation could be fully substituted by arbitration when at the same time there is such a strong EU policy internally to intensify judicial cooperation. Then again, other regional integration communities have not (yet?) developed (such an intense) judicial cooperation,

[28]Ibid., para. 29.

[29]Ibid., para. 31.

[30]Ibid., para. 32.

[31]http://www.uncitral.org/uncitral/en/uncitral_texts/arbitration/NYConvention_status.html. Accessed 7 June 2018.

e.g. MERCOSUR[32] or ASEAN and in particular its newly established ASEAN Economic Union (Weller 2017/1, 789 et seq.), but this seems to be due to a lack of mutual trust amongst the participating states rather than to an assumed irrelevance of judicial cooperation beyond arbitration. The crucial question therefore is: What tools can be offered for trust management within relations of trading, but otherwise quite disintegrated states?

5.2 *Inserting a Chapter on Judicial Cooperation in All FTAs*

First of all, all future FTAs should include a chapter on judicial cooperation or integration as a natural supplement to the overall objective of the FTA, which is intensifying economic integration, thereby increasing the number of transactions and thus the number of disputes.

5.2.1 Along the Lines of Article 220 EEC

A politically rather subtle and careful first step could be inserting a provision along the lines of Article 220 EEC (Article 293 EC).[33] This provision was the starting point of intense judicial cooperation in civil matters within the EU. Along the lines of this provision, a respective provision in an FTA would read: "The [FTA] Parties shall, so far as is necessary, enter into negotiations with each other with a view to securing for the benefit of their nationals the simplification of formalities governing the reciprocal recognition and enforcement of judgments of courts."

Of course, this is no more than a kind reminder for the State Parties to become active within their full sovereignty on a purely intergovernmental level. Naturally, this reminder turned out to be effective for the then EEC only, because there was a Community institution like the European Commission that immediately pushed things forward, and even then it took until 1968 to bring about the Convention on jurisdiction and the enforcement of judgments in civil and commercial matters

---

[32]MERCOSUR can be characterized by its piecemeal legislation on judicial cooperation. In particular, the following instruments have been adopted: the Las Leñas Protocol on judicial cooperation, the Buenos Aires Protocol on international jurisdiction in contractual matters, the Protocol on precautionary measures, the International Commercial Arbitration Agreement, and the Agreement on legal assistance, all available at http://www.sice.oas.org/Mercosur/instmt_e.asp. Accessed 7 June 2018. The most comprehensive instrument, the Las Leñas Protocol, deals with judicial cooperation and assistance in civil, commercial, labour and administrative matters. The Protocol adopted a system of cooperation based on letters rogatory, which evidently does not reflect a high level of mutual trust between the states of MERCOSUR. For a deeper analysis on judicial cooperation in MERCOSUR, see Arroyo (2010); Tiburcio (2010); Weller (2017/1, 785 et seq.).

[33]This provision has no equivalent in the TFEU because its mission was entirely accomplished once the competency of Article 81 TFEU was established.

("Brussels Convention"[34]). And had there not been a(nother) deplorable phase of cross-border terrorism during the 1970s, there might not have been enough political impetus to overcome classic sovereignty concerns in judicial cooperation in criminal matters. And had there not been these initiatives in criminal law, there might not have been consecutive political initiatives for cooperation and integration in civil law. However, against this specific background of cross-border terrorism and organized crime, the European Council of Brussels of 5 and 6 December 1977 could draw the conclusion:[35] "Judicial cooperation: The European Council noted with interest a communication from the President of the French Republic on development of judicial co-operation between the Member States. It requested that active consideration be given to the proposals made in this respect."

The then French President Valéry Giscard d'Estaing had proposed to establish, as a necessary supplement to the internal market, "un espace judiciaire unique":[36]

> Je propose que nous franchissions un nouveau pas dans l'organisation de l'Union de l'Europe. Les pays membres de la Communauté sont engagés dans un processus qui doit les conduire à l'union, c'est-à-dire à la création d'un espace organisé. Les Traités de Paris et Rome ont jeté les bases d'un espace économique, le Marché commun, et aussi celui d'un espace commercial. … La construction de l'Europe devrait s'enrichir d'un nouveau concept, celui de l'espace judiciaire. … Je suggère donc que, par l'adoption d'une convention d'extradition automatique assortie des garanties appropriées pour les cas de crimes particulièrement graves, quels qu'en soient les mobiles, les Neuf mettent en place le premier élément d'un espace judiciaire unique.

Even then it took another two decades to arrive at a (limited) community competency for judicial cooperation introduced by the Treaty of Amsterdam in 1998.[37] Only afterwards, the concept of mutual trust could unfold to today's dynamics (Weller 2017/2, 1, 6 et seq.). Part of the initial impetus was the 2005 Hague Programme as well as the positions taken by the Council on judicial cooperation with third states, both explored and cited above. Thus, even though Article 220 EEC might have been a successful and, for the purposes and structures of the EU, politically clever kick-off for judicial cooperation within the European Union, it took half a century to bring about substantial proceeds. Therefore, the question must be whether there are better options that would bring about quicker progress.

---

[34]https://curia.europa.eu/common/recdoc/convention/en/c-textes/brux-idx.htm. Accessed 7 June 2018.

[35]European Council (5–6 December 1977) Conclusions of the Presidency. http://www.consilium.europa.eu/media/20779/bruxelles_december_1977__eng_.pdf, sub VIII (at the very end). Accessed 7 June 2018.

[36]Proposition de Valéry Giscard d'Estaing sur la mise en place d'un espace judiciaire européen (5 December 1977). http://www.cvce.eu/obj/proposition_de_valery_giscard_d_estaing_sur_la_mise_en_place_d_un_espace_judiciaire_europeen_bruxelles_5_decembre_1977-fr-c7f7171f-f73a-4ab4-829e-faa221acaeca.html. Accessed 7 June 2018. On details of the history see Menuet (2006, 21 et seq.).

[37]See Arts. 61 lit.c, 65 EC.

5.2.2 Declaration of Intention for Accession to the Core Hague Instruments on Judicial Cooperation

Alternatively, the proposed Chapter on judicial cooperation in a standard FTA of the EU with third states could provide for a declaration of intent by the Parties to accede to the core Hague instruments on judicial cooperation. This option would be nothing else than implementing the European Council's proposal discussed above. And indeed, this seems to be one of the most recent approaches taken by the EU, at least in respect of neighbouring countries. In the Association Agreements with Georgia[38] and Moldova,[39] both as of 1 July 2016, Article 21 (Georgia) and Article 20 (Moldova) provide: "Legal cooperation: 1. The Parties agree to develop judicial cooperation in civil and commercial matters as regards the negotiation, ratification and implementation of multilateral conventions on civil judicial cooperation and, in particular, the conventions of the Hague Conference on Private International Law in the field of international legal cooperation and litigation as well as the protection of children." Article 24 of the Association Agreement of 29 May 2014 with the Ukraine[40] reads slightly differently:

> Legal cooperation: 1. The Parties agree to further develop judicial cooperation in civil and criminal matters, making full use of the relevant international and bilateral instruments and based on the principles of legal certainty and the right to a fair trial. 2. The Parties agree to facilitate further EU-Ukraine judicial cooperation in civil matters on the basis of the applicable multilateral legal instruments, especially the Conventions of the Hague Conference on Private International Law in the field of international Legal Cooperation and Litigation as well as the Protection of Children.

So far, however, no steps towards a deeper judicial integration under these provisions have become apparent. But still, these provisions could serve as a model for future FTAs with other than neighbouring countries. On the other hand, acceding the Hague instruments might result in judicial cooperation with many more states than perhaps wanted, because the Hague instruments are of course open for accession to all states, and in regard to some trade partners, the EU might wish to install tailor-made bilateral solutions, as was considered by the European Council

[38] Association agreement between the European Union and the European Atomic Energy Community and their Member States, of the one part, and Georgia, of the other part (30 August 2014), OJ L 261/4, pp. 4–743.

[39] Association agreement between the European Union and the European Atomic Energy Community and their Member States, of the one part, and the Republic of Moldova, of the other part (30 August 2014), OJ L 260/4, pp. 4–738.

[40] Association agreement between the European Union and its Member States, of the one part, and Ukraine, of the other part (29 May 2014), OJ L 161/3, pp. 3–2137.

in its Communication explored above.[41] Thus, the next question must be whether such tailor-made solutions would be available in principle and, if so, how they could look.

5.2.3 Tailor-Made Bilateral Solutions in FTAs

So far there seems to be no example for a tailor-made instrument or chapter on judicial cooperation in an existing FTA text.

EU Competency

Before reflecting on how such instruments could look, it is necessary to verify that the EU has the competency to regulate judicial cooperation within an FTA.

Article 81 TFEU

Article 81(1) TFEU provides that "[t]he Union shall develop judicial cooperation in civil matters having cross-border implications based on the principle of mutual recognition of judgments and of decisions in extrajudicial cases"—wording that does not expressly restrict itself to intra-EU instruments. Further, according to sentence 2, "[s]uch cooperation may include the adoption of measures for the approximation of the laws and regulations of the Member States", including, one is tempted to add, measures for the approximation of the laws and regulations of the Member States in relation to extra-EU trade partners.

However, as is generally known, paragraph 2 of Article 81 TFEU allows only "measures … aimed at ensuring: (a) the mutual recognition and enforcement *between* Member States of judgments and of decisions in extrajudicial cases".[42] And even though the following aims listed in paragraph 2 again do not limit themselves expressly to measures "between Member States", it would be systematically unconvincing to argue that in respect of these latter measures instruments in relation to extra-EU states would be covered whereas such instruments would be excluded by *litera* a for the most important area of judicial cooperation. Thus, instruments on judicial cooperation with extra-EU states cannot be directly based on Article 81 TFEU.

And indeed, in its Lugano Opinion,[43] the European Court of Justice (ECJ) noted that, "[t]he Council, supported in this respect by all the Member States which submitted observations to the Court and by the Parliament and the Commission, points out that the subject-matter of the agreement envisaged falls within the scope

[41] European Council (11 April 2006), n. 23, p. 5 para. 19.

[42] Emphasis added by this author.

[43] ECJ, Opinion 1/03 of 7 February 2006—Lugano Convention. http://eur-lex.europa.eu/LexUriServ/LexUriServ.do?uri=CELEX:62003CV0001:EN:HTML. Accessed 7 June 2018.

of Article 61(c) EC and Article 67 ECJ. That legal basis does not expressly give the Community external competence",[44] even though the wording of Article 65(a) lemma 3 EC did not expressly limit itself to intra-EU measures.[45] Yet, as is again generally known, the ECJ inferred an implicit exclusive competency for the EU to conclude the Lugano Convention based on the ERTA doctrine.[46] Under the TFEU, this doctrine has been laid down in Article 216(1) TFEU,[47] combined with Article 3 (2) TFEU.[48] The doctrine's application in the area of judicial cooperation requires that the envisaged international agreement must affect the uniform and consistent application of the EU's rules, for example on jurisdiction and recognition and enforcement of judgments, as laid down by the Brussels I and Brussels Ibis Regulations and the proper functioning of the system established by those rules.[49]

Obviously, these requirements are likewise fulfilled by tailor-made instruments on jurisdiction and recognition and enforcement included in FTAs of the EU with non-EU trade partners. This is less obvious for the EU's common rules on the

---

[44]Ibid., para. 34.

[45]Article 65(a) lemma 3 EC: "Measures in the field of judicial cooperation in civil matters having cross-border implications, to be taken in accordance with Article 67 and insofar as necessary for the proper functioning of the internal market, shall include: the recognition and enforcement of decisions in civil and commercial cases, including decisions in extrajudicial cases."

[46]Ibid., para. 114: "The competence of the Community to conclude international agreements may arise not only from an express conferment by the Treaty but may equally flow implicitly from other provisions of the Treaty and from measures adopted, within the framework of those provisions, by the Community institutions (see ERTA, paragraph 16). The Court has also held that whenever Community law created for those institutions powers within its internal system for the purpose of attaining a specific objective, the Community had authority to undertake international commitments necessary for the attainment of that objective even in the absence of an express provision to that effect (Opinion 1/76, paragraph 3, and Opinion 2/91, paragraph 7)." And further in para. 116: "In paragraph 17 of the ERTA judgment, the Court established the principle that, where common rules have been adopted, the Member States no longer have the right, acting individually or even collectively, to undertake obligations with non-member countries which affect those rules. In such a case, the Community also has exclusive competence to conclude international agreements."

[47]Article 216(1) TFEU: "The Union may conclude an agreement with one or more third countries or international organisations where the Treaties so provide or *where the conclusion of an agreement is necessary in order to achieve, within the framework of the Union's policies, one of the objectives referred to in the Treaties*, or is provided for in a legally binding Union act *or is likely to affect common rules or alter their scope*" (emphasis added by this author).

[48]Article 3(2) TFEU: "The Union shall also have exclusive competence for the conclusion of an international agreement when its conclusion is provided for in a legislative act of the Union or is necessary to enable the Union to exercise its internal competence, or *in so far as its conclusion may affect common rules or alter their scope*" (emphasis added by this author).

[49]ECJ, n. 46, para. 172 et seq.: para. 172 f.: "The new Lugano Convention would affect the uniform and consistent application of the Community rules as regards both the jurisdiction of courts and the recognition and enforcement of judgments and the proper functioning of the unified system established by those rules. It follows … that the Community has exclusive competence to conclude the new Lugano Convention."

service of process[50] and the taking of evidence.[51] Yet, it is common ground (now[52]) that the EU has been empowered to accede to the Hague Conference as such[53] and that it thereby is empowered to either accede itself to Hague instruments on judicial cooperation[54] or to authorize Member States to do so, including e.g. the Hague Convention on the Service of Process.[55]

Thus, there cannot be any doubt anymore that measures of the EU on judicial cooperation with extra-EU trade partners are covered by Article 81 TFEU. However, since Ireland and the UK[56] as well as Denmark[57] do not or not unconditionally participate in measures based on this ground of competency, there might be an even better and more comprehensive ground of competency for measures on judicial cooperation of the EU with non-EU trade partners, namely the expressly exclusive competency of the EU for the common commercial policy, including the conclusion of international agreements, vis-à-vis third states under Articles 207, 216, 3(1) TFEU. The key question of course here is whether judicial cooperation with foreign extra-EU trade partners can be considered an element of the "common commercial policy" in the sense of Article 207 TFEU.

Article 207 TFEU—Common Commercial Policy

According to this provision, the EU's common commercial policy

> shall be based on uniform principles, particularly with regard to changes in tariff rates, the conclusion of tariff and trade agreements relating to trade in goods and services, and the commercial aspects of intellectual property, foreign direct investment, the achievement of uniformity in measures of liberalisation, export policy and measures to protect trade such as those to be taken in the event of dumping or subsidies. The common commercial policy shall be conducted in the context of the principles and objectives of the Union's external action.

---

[50]Regulation (EC) No. 1393/2007 of the European Parliament and of the Council of 13 November 2007 on the service in the Member States of judicial and extrajudicial documents in civil or commercial matters (service of documents), and repealing Council Regulation (EC) No. 1348/2000, OJ L 324, pp. 79–120.

[51]Council Regulation (EC) No. 1206/2001 of 28 May 2001 on cooperation between the courts of the Member States in the taking of evidence in civil or commercial matters, OJ L 174, pp. 1–24.

[52]On the controversy over this issue see e.g. Schulze (2007), 942 et seq.

[53]Council Decision 2006/719/EC of 5 October 2006 on the accession of the Community to the Hague Conference on Private International Law, OJ L 297/1, pp. 1–14.

[54]Council Decision 2014/887/EU of 4 December 2014 on the approval, on behalf of the European Union, of the Hague Convention of 30 June 2005 on Choice of Court Agreements, OJ L 353, pp. 5–8.

[55]Council Decision 2016/414/EU of 10 March 2016 authorising Austria to sign and ratify, and Malta to accede to, the Hague Service Convention 1965, OJ L 75, pp. 1, 2.

[56]Protocol 21 to the Lisbon Treaty.

[57]Protocol 22 to the Lisbon Treaty.

Obviously, there is no direct reference to judicial cooperation, nor is there a tradition of understanding open terms such as "trade agreements" or "measures to protect trade" as extending to judicial cooperation with the respective trade partner. On the contrary, it seems that this interpretation has never been put forward so far (Geiger 2015; Cottier and Trinberg 2015). Yet, according to Article 207 Sentence 2, the common commercial policy is to be conducted in the context of the principles and objectives of the Union's external action. Article 205 TFEU sets out in this respect: "The Union's action on the international scene, pursuant to this part, shall be guided by the principles of, pursue the objectives and be conducted in accordance with the general provisions laid down in Chap. 1 of Title V of the Treaty of the European Union." And Article 21 TEU provides:

(1) The Union's action on the international scene shall be guided by the principles which have inspired its own creation, development and enlargement, and which it seeks to advance in the wider world: democracy, the rule of law, the universality and indivisibility of human rights and fundamental freedoms, respect for human dignity, the principles of equality and solidarity, and respect for the principles of the United Nations Charter and international law.

These principles are certainly too abstract and general to cover the rather specific topic of judicial cooperation. However, Article 21(2) TEU, in *litera* h, provides for the following: "The Union shall define and pursue common policies and actions, and shall work for a high degree of cooperation in all fields of international relations, in order to promote an international system based on stronger multilateral cooperation and good global governance."

A high degree of cooperation in all fields of international relations, in order to promote an international system based on stronger multilateral cooperation—this wording sounds quite attuned to judicial cooperation, and given that a good governance of judicial cooperation in a trade relation with extra-EU trade partners obviously supports the overall objective of this relation, which is increasing cross-border trade amongst the trade partners, it appears to me to be a small step to conclude that judicial cooperation must be an integral part of the EU's common commercial policy vis-à-vis third states.

However, in its recent opinion on the EU-Singapore FTA,[58] the ECJ held that:[59]

> A regime [like the regime for investor-state dispute settlement envisaged in Chapter 9 B of the EU-Singapore FTA], which removes disputes from the jurisdiction of the courts of the Member States, cannot be of a purely ancillary nature … and cannot, therefore, be established without the Member States' consent. It follows that approval of Section B of

[58]ECJ, Opinion 2/15 of 16 May 2017.

[59]Ibid., para. 292.

> Chapter 9 of the envisaged agreement falls not within the exclusive competence of the European Union, but within a competence shared between the European Union and the Member States.[60]

Since measures on judicial cooperation for disputes between commercial parties from the Contracting States equally remove disputes from the jurisdiction of the courts of the Member States, i.e. those in which the defendant is not domiciled in a Member State, it looks at the moment as if the European Court of Justice would likewise reject an exclusive competence for commercial dispute resolution within FTAs.

One might still argue that commercial disputes are so much an integral part of an increase of commercial activity within an FTA that dispute resolution on this level is of a "purely ancillary nature" or "accessory"[61] as opposed to investor-state dispute resolution—at least *de lege ferenda.*

Which Tailor-Made Bilateral Measures?

The last question to pose is, which measures could be recommended? As opposed to intra-EU relations, extra-EU relations will often occur with states whose understanding and/or practice of the rule of law and administration of justice differs, sometimes fundamentally, from EU standards and expectations. At the same time, these differences are not to be taken as obstacles to intensify trade. Rather, and as has been explained above, trade is to bring about not only economic benefits but also changes in values and standards, including legal standards. Yet, EU enterprises, in particular those of a small and medium size (SMEs), must be protected adequately from the very beginning of a trade relation and must have access to effective justice. Thus, a tailor-made trust management for judicial cooperation is necessary. In general, mutual trust will have to be reduced, if not entirely excluded, compared to the level appropriate amongst EU Member States.

For example, one could think of a protective design of jurisdiction to the effect that the EU party will more often than otherwise be able to sue at home. One could think of concretizing the general public policy exception against recognition and enforcement of judgments from the foreign state and reinforce this exception by rules of evidence for cases of violation of the rule of law in the foreign proceeding which make it easier to establish such violation. One might further want to think of increasing the threshold for recognizing pending proceedings in the foreign forum in order to allow more easily proceedings at home. However, all of these measures

---

[60]Compare GA Eleanor Sharpston, Opinion 2/15 of 21 December 2016, para. 525: "Where the European Union has competence as regards the substantive provisions of an international agreement, it also enjoys competence as regards the dispute settlement mechanisms which aim to ensure that those provisions are effectively enforced. Such mechanisms merely help to achieve the primary objectives of the agreement and are thus accessory to the (substantive) rules to which they relate."

[61]Ibid.

are of a unilateralist and even hostile nature in that they expressly presume that the foreign state's administration of justice is considered deficient, which negates the principal claim of equality of each of the state trade partners. This is certainly not the atmosphere in which trade negotiations will prosper. Therefore, a more cooperative approach is necessary, for example institutionalized court-to-court cooperation or even common commercial state courts.

One further option could be "default arbitration" (Cuniberti 2017). A model for installing such a dispute resolution mechanism specifically within FTAs, or by a self-standing "Bilateral Arbitration Treaty" (BAT) or even multilateral agreements, designed along the lines of bilateral investment treaties (BITs), was submitted by Gary Born (Born 2013, 138).[62] Politically, it might not be the optimal time to submit proposals for expanding the concept and the structures of bilateral investment treaties. However, this should not stop academic analysis from checking out the benefits, but also the limits, of such proposals. According to Born, a (self-standing or FTA-integrated) BAT would provide, in essence, for cross-border commercial disputes within the respective trade relation that, by virtue of the treaty, arbitration takes place unless the commercial parties have agreed or agree otherwise or settle their dispute amicably within a certain period of time after notice about the dispute was received by the other party. Of course, such a structure raises a number of questions, including the following.[63]

Firstly, some proponents, including Born, argue that even though there is no actual consent in default arbitration, a form of constructive consent or an extensive interpretation of an international commercial contract without an express arbitration clause suffices on the grounds that arbitration would evidently have been the choice of the parties (or at least reasonable business parties) had they considered the issue. However, this would at least seriously stretch the limits of traditional notions of consent.

Secondly, a default or "opt-out" arbitration structure needs to provide for default rules on the composition of the tribunal and on the selection of the applicable procedure. Technically, these issues are easy to resolve. Born, for example, suggests as default setting the UNCITRAL Arbitration Rules and appointment authority of the Secretary General of the Permanent Court of Arbitration (PCA), and then leaves it to the respective tribunal to determine the seat.

Thirdly, the award resulting from arbitration under a BAT or BAT-like chapter of an FTA would not qualify as an award in the sense of the New York Convention, because the New York Convention considers decisions of tribunals to be "awards" in the sense of the Convention only if derived from consent-based proceedings, and "constructive" consent does not suffice (Wolff 2012, para. 57). Therefore, Born's model BAT contains a provision that mirrors the New York Convention and provides for recognition and enforcement along the same lines. But obviously, the

[62]See also Born's and Butler's draft Model BAT. https://www.victoria.ac.nz/law/about/staff/petra-butler/Draft-Model-BAT.pdf. Accessed 7 June 2018.

[63]For an in-depth analysis (with a very liberal approach) see Cuniberti (2017).

provisions of the BAT or FTA only bind the Contracting State Parties. Third states and their courts are not bound. This is certainly a severe drawback even though all Contracting States to the New York Convention are free to go beyond the Convention in recognizing and enforcing foreign awards[64] (but again would probably not consider the decision from BAT proceedings as an arbitral award).

Despite these (and other) issues, a treaty-based dispute resolution mechanism providing for neutral judges and state-of-the-art procedures might be a solution for judicial cooperation of the EU with—territorially and legally—remote extra-EU trade partners.

6 Conclusions

Trust management for judicial cooperation is crucial for each and every regional economic integration community, both for an internal common market and in its external trade relations. Whereas the EU has pushed mutual trust to the maximum internally, there is a strange lacuna in this respect externally, even though it is a declared policy objective of the EU to expand and intensify trade with extra-EU states. Yet, in (virtually) no free trade agreement of the EU with extra-EU states is there a chapter on judicial cooperation as part of the FTA, not even a single provision. At the same time, "add-on" topics to trade are increasingly dealt with in FTAs. No strategy outside the respective FTAs becomes apparent, such as e.g. concluding FTAs only on condition that the prospective trade partner will accede to the most important Hague instruments on judicial cooperation. The reason cannot be a lack of competency. There is Article 81 TFEU. Additionally, Article 207 TFEU should, at least *de lege ferenda*, be recognized as an even stronger exclusive competency for regulating judicial cooperation within trade relations. Options for specific trust management in trade relations with territorially and legally "remote" states are on the table. To come back to the initial thesis: The EU's judicial cooperation and common commercial policy must be connected.[65] Private international law must no longer be a blind spot in building trade relations.

References

Arroyo DPF (2010) Main characteristics of the new private international law of the Argentinian Republic. RabelsZ 80:130–150

---

[64]See Article VII (1) New York Convention.

[65]See Forster EM, Howards End, 1910: "Only connect the prose and the passion, and both will be exalted, and human love will be seen at its height. Live in fragments no longer. Only connect, and the beast and the monk, robbed of the isolation that is life to either, will die", if it is appropriate to cite an English novelist in the sober context of judicial cooperation.

Born GB (2013) BIT's, BAT's and Buts. Rev Bras de Arbitragem 10:138–144
Cottier T, Trinberg L (2015) Art. 207. In: Von der Groeben H, Schwarze J, Hatje A (eds) Europäisches Unionsrecht, 7th edn. Nomos, Baden-Baden
Cuniberti G (2017) Rethinking international commercial arbitration—Towards default arbitration. Edward Elgar, Cheltenham/Northampton
Geiger R (2015) Art. 207. In: Geiger R, Khan DE, Kotzur M (eds) European Union treaties. CH Beck, Munich
Kant I (1795/96) Zum Ewigen Frieden (Towards Eternal Peace)
Menon S (2015) Transnational protection of private rights. Asian J Int'l Law 5:219–245
Menuet L (2006) Le discours sur l'espace judiciaire européen: analyse du discours et sémantique argumentative. Dissertation, Université de Nantes. https://halshs.archives-ouvertes.fr/tel-00133442/document. Accessed 7 June 2018
Schulze A (2007) The accession of the European Community to the Hague Conference on private international law. Int'l Comp Law Q 56:939–949
Tiburcio C (2010) Cooperation in civil judicial matters. In: Franca Filhio MT et al (eds) The law of MERCOSUR (Chapter 11). Hart Publishing
Van Calster G (2016) European private international law, 2nd edn. Oxford/Portland, Oregon
Weller M (2015) Mutual trust: in search of the future of private international law. J Private Int'l Law 1:65–102
Weller M (ed) (2016) Europäisches Kollisionsrecht. Allgemeine Lehren. Baden-Baden, Teil A
Weller M (2017/2) Mutual trust within the judicial cooperation in civil matters: a normative cornerstone—a factual chimera—a constitutional challenge. Ned Int Privaatrecht 35(1):1–21
Wolff R (2012) Article II. In: Wolff R (ed) New York convention on the recognition and enforcement of foreign arbitral awards—commentary. CH Beck, Munich

Matthias Weller Alfried Krupp von Bohlen und Halbach Professor for Civil Law, Art and Cultural Property Law at the University of Bonn, Germany. Director of the Institute for German and International Civil Procedure and Dispute Resolution. Member of the International Association of Procedural Law, the German Association of Professors for Civil Procedure, the German Scientific Association for International Civil Procedure and the German Institution for Arbitration.

Civil Litigation in Tribunals in South Africa: Creating a Unified Tribunal System

Rashri Baboolal-Frank

Abstract The global establishment of tribunals has a deep history extending over a period in excess of 2000 years. South African tribunals proclaim more than 500 years of existence. It is essential to demonstrate the beginnings of tribunals in order to grasp the context within which tribunals operate. Furthermore, the historical context elucidates the establishment and development of changes tribunals have experienced and which have resulted in their transformation up to the present day. The tribunals forming the basis of this study were established in South Africa during the twentieth century and the opening years of the twenty-first century. Currently, in the South African context, it is submitted that the separate operation of tribunals disconnects each one from the others and is therefore counter-productive in that each tribunal creates a duplication of the system, as opposed to a single system with a unified pool of resources that ensures standardisation of functions. An amalgamated tribunal system under a unified tribunal system is proposed as more suitable for users and one which encourages consistency, which in turn eradicates any faults in the system that hamper its smooth operation. A unified tribunal system fosters the development of skills, efficiency and effectiveness through one mode of operation whilst the rationalisation of tribunal rules cultivates a harmonised tribunal system. The tribunals illustrated in this study are administrative, for they exercise public power, and are a tier of the executive, providing the realisation of policy and legislation through their decisions. As a result, the civil litigation of a unified tribunal system enhances access to justice and administrative justice.

R. Baboolal-Frank (✉)
Faculty of Law, University of Pretoria, Hatfield, South Africa
e-mail: rashri.baboolal@up.ac.za

A. Uzelac and C. H. van Rhee (eds.), *Transformation of Civil Justice*,
Ius Gentium: Comparative Perspectives on Law and Justice 70,
https://doi.org/10.1007/978-3-319-97358-6_5

1 General Overview

This study consists of two focal points: to address the historical journey of tribunals from a global perspective; and within a South African context, to briefly highlight aspects of five tribunals to illustrate the development of, and to argue the role of, a unified tribunal system in transforming access to justice in civil litigation.

The five tribunals forming the basis of this study were chosen due to, among other reasons, the similarity of their structure, rules of procedure and the manner in which they operate. It is evident that each tribunal has its own set of rules that are a duplication of those of the others. All the tribunals in this study utilise the High Court rules in instances where the prescribed rules of the tribunal do not make provision for certain operational aspects. To address this unnecessary duplication it is proposed to have a unified set of rules that provides comprehensively for the daily operation of the tribunals through rationalisation of all the current rules. The purpose of this research is to reveal the strengths and expose the shortcomings of the tribunals with the aim of proposing a unified and harmonised tribunal system that will operate more effectively and efficiently, and of illustrating that the tribunal system is transformative for civil litigation.

2 Introduction

Viewed from a global, universal perspective tribunals possess a profound history of over 2000 years[1] (Austin and Vidal-Naquet 1977, 297). Seen within the context of South Africa tribunals portray a story that is more than 500 years old.[2] In light of these facts, it is apparent that a study of the beginnings of tribunals enables an understanding of the context within which tribunals operate. Furthermore, the historical context of tribunals elucidates their evolution and continuous changes, which resulted in their transformation to the present-day tribunals of this study. In order to have a comprehensive understanding of their origin, establishment, development and relevance in current South African society, this study proposes to analyse five particular tribunals: the Rental Housing Tribunal,[3] the Companies Tribunal,[4] the Competition Tribunal,[5] the National Consumer Tribunal[6] and the Water Tribunal.[7] All were established in South Africa during the twentieth century

[1]Reference is made to the Koresos tribunal and, in the second instance, the Athenian tribunals, where matters were heard in a speedier manner around the period of 402 BC.

[2]Tribunals can be traced as far back as the time of the indigenous tribes of Africa.

[3]Established in terms of the Rental Housing Act 50 of 1999.

[4]Established in terms of the Companies Act 71 of 2008.

[5]Established in terms of the Competition Act 89 of 1998.

[6]Established in terms of the National Credit Act 34 of 2005.

[7]Established in terms of the National Water Act 36 of 1998.

and the opening years of the twenty-first century, and were selected for this study based on their similarity, nature of their mode of operation and are duly representative of the tribunals across the country. These five tribunals will be analysed in terms of the system of operation of tribunals[8] with the view to enhancing efficiency for the development and creation of a unified tribunal system in South Africa.

From a historical perspective, tribunals were created to hear disputes in a forum other than a court of law, in an informal, cheap, efficient and expeditious manner. It is argued that,

> [T]he image of tribunals seems to have gone through several evolutionary changes, from enemies of the rule of law, to useful but rather marginal entities, floating around in a no man's land somewhere between the judicial and the administrative systems, towards becoming fully-fledged, professionally accredited bodies set in the mainstream of a modernised and better integrated system of administrative justice. (Drewry 2009, 47)

This study argues a similar pattern of evolutionary changes within a South African context and attempts to draw a distinction between the implications of administrative justice and access to justice. The characteristics and purpose of tribunals are interlinked in order to enhance access to justice. However, it is important to mention that tribunals and courts are inherently different. It is therefore crucial to understand some of these distinctions. Characteristically, tribunals reflect in their membership the respective specific areas of expertise, whilst courts have a generalist expertise (Hoexter 2006, 52). In the same vein, tribunals in South Africa are inquisitorial, whereas courts are adversarial. Another distinctive difference between the two is that tribunals utilise application proceedings for hearings, whereas courts provide the option to the parties to elect either action or application proceedings depending on the nature of the dispute (Hoexter 2006, 52, 53). It is important to bear in mind these differences because in terms of procedure tribunals operate in an almost cloned procedure to that of the courts and confusion may otherwise arise, as both are seemingly indistinct in this aspect (with the exception that tribunals attempt a more relaxed approach than the formal approach of the courts).[9] Still, the application of the tribunal rules is still perceived as more flexible vis-à-vis the traditional inflexible court rules.

Moreover, this study argues that alternative dispute resolution (ADR) is an important trend for the resolution of disputes. Alternative dispute resolution is a mechanism that has been utilised by indigenous tribunals and tribes of Africa in the early resolution of disputes (Aiyedun and Ordor 2016, 163, 164). Currently, the Rental Housing Tribunal, the Water Tribunal and the Companies Tribunal employ ADR techniques. However, it is not a uniform mechanism across all of the tribunals

---

[8]This reference to tribunals is to all five South African tribunals in this study.

[9]*BMW South Africa (Pty) Ltd v NCC & JSN Motors (Pty) Ltd* NCT/2679/2011/101(1)(P); NCT/2807/2011/101(1)(P); NCT/2806/2011/101(1)(P). The National Consumer Tribunal applied the High Court rules in the consideration for an application of joinder. *Willem HW Makkink v Accordian Investments (Pty) Ltd NCT/8473/2013/75(1)(b)* in this matter, though the tribunal employed a flexible approach, the requirements of default judgment were not satisfied as condonation was not requested and proper service was not undertaken.

of this study. This study proposes uniform mechanisms through an amalgamated tribunal system aimed at enhancing access to justice. There are a range of benefits and advantages in the adoption of ADR techniques as an early resolution tactic, which results in the saving of, among other things, costs and time. This study elucidates these ADR advantages for their adoption in a unified tribunal system, whose net effect intensifies administrative justice.

With reference to the term 'access to justice', the word 'access' denotes means, opportunity, even the right, to approach, use, or benefit from, something, whereas the concept of 'justice' has a more complex history of deconstruction. It has been argued that, '[J]ustice is a central moral standard against which social conduct, practices, and institutions are evaluated, and this is as it should be' (Cohen 1986, 4). And it is evident, as remarked by Cappelletti and Garth (1977–1978, 183), that, '[T] he concept of access to justice has been undergoing an important transformation, corresponding to a comparable change in civil procedural scholarship and teaching.' Access to justice has been considered a natural right that was confined to the rigid structure of procedure as a formal right, with an absence of its impact and challenges (Cappelletti and Garth 1977–1978, 181, 182). Prior to the French Revolution in 1789, access to justice was considered within an individualistic silo, indifferent to the lack of accessibility in terms of costs and resources of the working class. The advent of the French Constitution of 1946 and the growth of the working class contributed to the change of the face of access to justice to one of being all-inclusive and classified as a basic human right of everyone. This transformation has been encapsulated as three waves in a worldwide movement to overcome the well-known barriers to access to justice (Cappelletti and Garth 1977–1978, 183–195). The first wave began in the period 1965 to the 1970s, and relates to the enhancement of legal aid in an attempt to overcome the barriers. There was a general improvement in legal aid in that it was state-funded instead of legal services being offered pro bono and stringent requirements applied in order to qualify for legal aid (Cappelletti and Garth 1977–1978, 197–199). This wave addressed the barrier regarding costs for litigants who were not receiving adequate representation. In the 1970s, the second wave was the representation of diffuse interests, which was also known as a revolution in civil procedure. The second wave made provision for class actions of public-interest law, which previously had no place in traditional civil procedure. This transition is remarked upon by Cappelletti and Garth (1977–1978, 209) as follows:

> The traditional conception of civil procedure left no room for the private, non-governmental protection of diffuse interests. Litigation was seen as merely a two-party affair, aimed at settling a controversy between the parties about their own individual rights. Rights tending to belong to a group, to the public or to a segment of the public did not fit well into that scheme. The laws of standing, the rules of procedure, and the roles of the judges were simply not designed to facilitate private enforcement of the rights of diffuse interests.

Hence, collective social interests were now provided for in terms of civil litigation and procedure.

The improvement of legal aid and protection of class action litigation led to the third wave of a new approach to access to justice (Cappelletti and Garth 1977–1978, 222). The third wave incorporated both of the preceding waves, which created the dimension of a refurbishing of the old lens through which access to justice was viewed. The consequence was the redesign of the rules of procedure and ensuring the balance of powers between litigants to reform the legal system. This third wave of the mid-1970s created an expansive aspect of reform in terms of procedure and structure, incorporating dispute resolution mechanisms together with radical innovative ideas, for the continuous process of reforming civil procedure (Cappelletti and Garth 1977–1978, 222–225). Cappelletti and Garth (1977–1978, 225) summarise this wave succinctly:

> This approach, in short, is not afraid of comprehensive, radical innovations, which go much beyond the sphere of legal representation. Further, this approach recognizes the need to relate and adapt the civil process to the type of dispute.

Some of the innovative techniques proposed were the forming of tribunals to address disputes and conflicts so as to reduce the workload of the courts. Another recommendation was to simplify the law for the users, so as to enhance access to justice in tribunals, courts and ADR mechanisms (Cappelletti and Garth 1977–1978, 286, 287). Cappelletti and Garth highlight the need for the establishment and development of tribunals. The creation of a landlord-tenant tribunal might ease the burden on the regular courts and, if designed to obviate the need for lawyers, it might reduce the need for legal services (Cappelletti and Garth 1977–1978, 227).

From the 1980s onwards the law, procedures and the abovementioned techniques were in a constant state of flux, as human justice is ever changing and adapting to the different needs and circumstances of individuals and communities.[10] References to the landlord-tenant tribunals are styled differently in different jurisdictions. In the 1990s the third wave reached the shores of South Africa, where the landlord-tenant tribunal became known as the Rental Housing Tribunal (Cappelletti and Garth 1977–1978, 260–265). Another tribunal was established for consumers facing financial hardship, namely the consumer tribunal for debt collection and restructuring (Cappelletti and Garth 1977–1978, 260–265). In South Africa, this

[10]Cappelletti (1985–1986) explained: 'What "human justice" can do is solve, or attempt to solve, concrete problems of individual and societal life: to enact and enforce norms, to create institutions, to design processes, all with that one goal in mind-to solve actual problems. But human problems continuously change, and so do norms, processes, and institutions. Human justice is changing justice whether or not there is, at a final point, an all-encompassing permanence, an Absolute which gives pause, and meaning, and light to all this moving and striving and passing which is human life.'

tribunal is known as the National Consumer Tribunal.[11] The development of tribunals in South Africa continued in that period and in the years that soon followed with the formation of the other three tribunals of this study.[12]

The historical milieu is significant, as it traces the beginnings of tribunals through their establishment and development to the present day. The origin is important because it creates the framework for the use of tribunals from their inception at a time when law first played a role in governing the ancient civilisation of Greece. The word 'tribunal' is a Western term, as its origins are found in the Roman and Greek civilisations[13] (Austin and Vidal-Naquet 1977, 297). In an African context, 'tribunal' was not coined in indigenous systems, which instead relied on a practice known as *makgotla* (meeting) (Choudree 1999, 20–22), which fostered the principles of *Ubuntu*. *Ubuntu* encourages the nurturing of community development seen as the development of the unit or tribe through the recognition of an ethical standard of common humaneness (Velthuizen 2012, 78, 79). The practice of *Ubuntu* espouses ADR mechanisms in terms of mediation of disputes (Aiyedun and Ordor 2016, 163, 164). It is apparent that 'the heart of African adjudication lies in the notion of reconciliation or restoration of harmony' (Allott 1968, 145). Although the term 'tribunal' is not used in the oral tradition of indigenous African communities, it is evident that there were indeed structures akin to tribunals in the resolution of disputes.

3 The Rental Housing Tribunal

3.1 Overview of the Rental Housing Tribunal

The Rental Housing Tribunal was established in order to ensure the balance and protection of rights between landlords and tenants.[14] The aim of discussing the Rental Housing Tribunal is to illustrate its mode of operation, rules of procedure and the cases it hears. All these aspects culminate to elucidate its strengths and shortcomings. A harmonised tribunal system aims to address the shortfalls of the current tribunal and, inadvertently, enhances access to justice by creating an amalgamated tribunal system.

---

[11]Established in terms of the National Credit Act 34 of 2005.

[12]Water Tribunal established in terms of the National Water Act 36 of 1998. Competition Tribunal established in terms of the Competition Act 89 of 1998. Companies Tribunal established in terms of the Companies Act 71 of 2008.

[13]See also Carnwath et al. (2008).

[14]Rental Housing Act 50 of 1999, Preamble.

3.2 *The Historical Significance of the Rental Housing Tribunal*

The Organisation of Civic Rights (OCR) has a long history of lobbying for the rights of tenants. The OCR aims to protect tenants from illegal lock-outs, disconnection of water and electricity, high rents, refusal of landlords to refund deposits held in trust and their not attending to repairs and necessary maintenance. In 1994, the year of democracy in South Africa, an ideal platform was created for OCR to consult with the national government and Minister of Housing to introduce new laws to protect both tenants and landlords, thereby ensuring that both parties understand their rights and obligations. A new task team was formed to meet with the Minister of Housing to deliberate upon the new laws (Mohamed 2010, 1). The deliberations culminated in legislation in August 2000, when the government introduced the new law of the Rental Housing Act 50 of 1999 across all provinces, and which included all the proposals made by the OCR (Mohamed 2010, 2). The Preamble to the Act made provision for the establishment of the Rental Housing Tribunal that would in turn be the custodian responsible for ensuring the balance of rights between landlords and tenants.

3.3 *Deconstructing the Rental Housing Tribunal*

The Rental Housing Tribunal is a tribunal of first instance. The Magistrates' Court may refer matters to be heard before the tribunal.[15] The tribunal's enforcement mechanisms fall within the jurisdiction of the Magistrates' Court. The tribunal thus does not have its own enforcement mechanisms. No decisions may be appealed, although they may be referred for review to the High Court. However, if there are grounds to appeal the review decision of the High Court to the Supreme Court of Appeal, then this is an appeal option. Usually the matter is finalised before the High Court. The Rental Housing Tribunal is unlike the other tribunals referred to in this study, because they are three-tiered. This means the first tier is a commission, the second tier of second instance is a tribunal and the third tier is an appeal/review mechanism to a specialised court or High Court. The Rental Housing Tribunal is two-tiered: the tribunal acts as the forum of first instance; at the second tier is the High Court, which is the forum of review and second instance, for there are no appeal mechanisms or remedies. The Rental Housing Tribunal does not have the jurisdiction to hear evictions; this matter is heard only by the Magistrates' Court and the High Court, which is a shortcoming. Another shortcoming of the tribunal is that there is a public perception that the tribunal tends to favour the tenant and not give an equal hearing to the landlord (Ardé 2017). A further shortcoming of the

[15]Sec. 13 (11) of the Rental Housing Act 50 of 1999.

tribunal is that there are no enforcement mechanisms nor appeal procedures. Moreover, the tribunal is an administrative body and subject to the Promotion of Administrative Justice Act, meaning that the tribunal is expected to be transparent and its failure to publish its decisions goes against the ethos of transparency for the public. Individuals must lodge the relevant applications for access to information to request previous decisions, which results in an expensive and lengthy process. The only judicial review mechanism is to the High Court. In addition, the Rental Housing Tribunal rules are for the most part a duplication of what is set down in the Rental Housing Act. This is something which is unnecessary, as the aim of the rules is to regulate the procedure, which then serves as little use to the users. Despite these shortcomings, there is a demand for the tribunal since it frequently handles matters that require resolution more robustly than what the ordinary court system can provide. A harmonised tribunal system will address these shortcomings by ensuring a tiered system that allows for enforcement mechanisms, appeal and review mechanisms, publication of decisions in a single database and an amalgamated set of rules that also allows for the hearing of eviction orders, which are sought simultaneously.

4 The Companies Tribunal

4.1 Overview of the Companies Tribunal

The Companies Tribunal was established by the Companies Act 71 of 2008. With the advent of the Act, the King III Report was propelled into addressing the new Act and ensuring that there was guidance regarding the amendments before the Act was promulgated in 2011.[16] The King III Report addressed the aspect of alternative dispute resolution as a technique utilised to resolve disputes at an early stage and through mediation and arbitration, thereby ensuring that matters are resolved expeditiously. The Companies Tribunal ensures that it addresses constitutional rights in upholding company law and regulation with relation to transparency, dignity, equality, privacy, administrative justice and accountability.[17] The aim of

[16]King III Report on Corporate Governance in South Africa, Introduction and Background, September 2009.

[17]Companies Tribunal Annual Report 2012/13 at 4. The rights in the Constitution which are applicable: Sec. 9, equality clause, '[T]hrough remaining accessible to diverse groupings of consumers and business, the Tribunal plays its role in ensuring that parties have the right to equal protection and benefit of the law'; also Sec. 10, in relation to human dignity, '[T]hrough the adjudication process, the Tribunal ensures that prohibited conduct, as well as the relevant action thereto, does not impair human dignity'; and Sec. 14, right to privacy, '[W]hile adhering to its founding legislation, and as part of the adjudicative role, the Tribunal ensures that the privacy of persons is protected'; Sec. 33, just administrative action, '[T]he Tribunal ensures it hears both sides to a dispute and that it issues reasons for its decisions.'

analysing the Companies Tribunal is to expose the shortcomings of the tribunal, and to propose the harmonised tribunal system for resolving the shortcomings.

4.2 The Historical Significance of the Companies Tribunal

The outdated Companies Act 61 of 1973 did not cater for the ever-changing current trends of corporate developments such as advancements in information technology and the evolving concept of alternative dispute resolution in the resolution and negotiation of corporate and commercial transactions. As such, the repeal and replacement of the Act was a necessary stride in terms of the promulgation of the Companies Act 71 of 2008 which was promulgated in 2011. Following the adoption of the new Companies Act, the King III Report addressed the new provisions of the Act and in turn ensured corporate governance across South Africa. The King III Report made provision for ADR mechanisms, as it recognised that statistics revealed that most matters are more quickly resolved through such mechanisms in an expeditious, efficient and effective manner.[18] The Companies Tribunal was a forum established by the new Act to ensure that matters are resolved robustly using ADR as a mechanism tool.

4.3 Deconstructing the Companies Tribunal

The Companies Tribunal is part of a three-tiered system. The first tier is the Companies Intellectual Property Commission and Takeover Regulation Panel. The second tier is the Companies Tribunal. Sometimes the Panel and the Commission refer matters to the Companies Tribunal, and a number of these matters are heard at first instance. The third tier is the High Court as the forum of review or appeal; or as the forum in which to make the decision of the tribunal an order of the court. The rules of the tribunal are comprehensive in making provision for its daily operations; the rules are influenced and based on the High Court rules. However, the influence of the High Court rules causes the Companies Tribunal to be formal, and as a result it loses its informality in relation to making the proceedings as expeditious and informal as possible. The tribunal attempts to cure this shortcoming through its authority to formulate its own procedures depending on the circumstances of the case; nonetheless the rigidity of the rules confines the tribunal to certain parameters and procedures. Another shortcoming is that the tribunal lacks enforcement

[18]King III Report, Chapter 8.8 at '39. Alternative dispute resolution (ADR) has been a most effective and efficient methodology to address the costly and time consuming features associated with more formal litigation. Statistics related to success range from a low of 50%, for those situations in which the courts have handed down a case for ADR, to an average of 85–90% where both parties are willing participants.'

mechanisms, and it is dependent on the High Court through application proceedings to make its decision an order of the court. It is the same procedure as that followed in making an arbitral award an order of the court. This is a drawback in that once a decision is received from the Companies Tribunal, and if there is non-compliance by one party pertaining to the decision, then the only remedy available is to approach the High Court to compel the other party to adhere to the decision. This is done by applying to have the decision made an order of the court. A unified tribunal system will address these drawbacks, because the tribunal system will have enforcement mechanisms, meaning that no party has to approach the court to make the decision enforceable and executable. The unified tribunal system will ensure uniform rules that allow for both matters to be resolved expeditiously and informally. A strength of the Companies Tribunal is that ADR mechanisms are utilised, which means that ADR mechanisms can be enhanced through a single system, with a unified pool of resources, in cases where ADR is encouraged as an early form of resolution.

5 The Competition Tribunal

5.1 *Overview of the Competition Tribunal*

The Competition Tribunal was established by the Competition Act 89 of 1998. The Preamble to the Act aims at redressing the inequalities caused by the apartheid regime in relation to unfair competition practices. As a consequence of apartheid, ownership was concentrated in the hands of a small number of people, and there were inadequate restraints on anti-competitive trade practices which would allow all South Africans to freely participate in the economy.[19] The Preamble encourages equality amongst all workers, consumers and owners in a competitive, economically balanced environment. The Competition Tribunal was established to adjudicate on competition disputes that arise in addressing the creation of the balance between all parties in competitive activities in relation to the diversification of the economy. The Competition Tribunal is a tribunal of second instance, in that the Competition Commission is the forum of first instance and the Competition Appeal Court is the forum of third instance, namely the specialised court that hears the appeal and review applications. The Competition Tribunal's strengths and shortcomings will be discussed to elucidate on the motivation for a unified tribunal system in order to address the shortcomings as exposed in this discussion.

[19] Competition Act 89 of 1998, Preamble.

5.2 *The Historical Significance of the Competition Tribunal*

The common law of South Africa did not address rules that could efficiently dispose of anti-competitive practices. There was also no legislation that dealt with the promotion of competition. This stimulated a debate over the need for legislation to address these gaps and lack of legislative guidance. The Minister of Economic Affairs directed that the Board of Trade and Industry investigate anti-competitive practices such as monopolisation of the market. The Board released the report on its findings in 1951.[20] Among other actions, the report recommended new legislation regulating and solely dedicated to competition law. Finally in 1956 the legislature obliged and the Regulation of Monopolistic Conditions 24 of 1955 was promulgated; it was the first of its kind regulating competition law in South Africa. This legislation had several shortcomings that needed to be addressed, such as enforcement. In 1975, the President of South Africa appointed a Commission to investigate competition policy. The findings of this Commission culminated with the Report of the Commission of Inquiry into the Regulation of Monopolistic Conditions Act (also known as the Mouton Commission Report), which was published in 1978. The Commission proposed new legislation, namely the Maintenance and Promotion of Competition Act 1979, which was promulgated in 1980. The Act was amended in 1985 and 1990. There were suggestions of a merger tribunal and a specialised court. The year 1992 sparked the advent of great political transformation, because at that time South Africa was on the brink of a democratic government. In 1994, radical change was proposed by the African National Congress (ANC) political party in the form of the Reconstruction and Development Programme. There was a macroeconomic policy for Growth, Employment and Redistribution in relation to competition law. The Department of Trade and Industry published their guidelines in relation to the reform of competition law in order to cure the injustices of the past. The Competition Bill was introduced in 1998 and eventually the Competition Act was promulgated, which allowed for the creation of the Competition Commission, the Competition Tribunal as the adjudicative body and the specialised court of the Competition Appeal Court (Sutherland and Kemp 2017, 3.2).

5.3 *Deconstructing the Competition Tribunal*

The Competition Tribunal has a difficult issue with enforcement, in that the tribunal cannot enforce its decisions and enforcement lies with the High Court. The enforcement of the decisions is not only confined to those of the tribunal but also to those of the Competition Commission and the Competition Appeal Court. All the decisions of the Commission, the Tribunal and the Appeal Court are considered to

[20]See also Board of Trade and Industry Report 327 of 1951.

be orders of the High Court, and for enforcement purposes they must be brought on application proceedings for the decision to be made an order of the court. This inevitably delays proceedings from reaching finality expeditiously because the application must be issued, served, filed and set down for hearing. This indicates that the Competition Tribunal's decisions have no strength, if its decisions cannot be enforced by the tribunal itself and are reliant on the High Court. This therefore contributes to the heavy caseload already on the court's rolls, creating an additional burden on the court system for a matter that could have been dealt with by the body hearing the matter with similar powers. The recommendation of the unified tribunal system will assist in addressing this shortcoming, as the power of enforcement will lie within the confines of the tribunal system and not with the courts. The Competition Appeal Court decisions carry the same status as High Court orders and not the same status as the decisions of the Supreme Court of Appeal. This means that judicial review and appeal of its decisions remain with the two courts, i.e. the Supreme Court of Appeal and the Constitutional Court, before finalisation, should there be grounds for appeal or should a constitutional issue arise. This is another drawback of the Competition Tribunal and its hierarchical tiers, because it is acknowledged that judicial review is not a problem and is a necessary measure to allow for access to the courts. Since the Competition Appeal Tribunal is a specialised court that functions as a court of appeal and review, it begs the question whether the process regarding finalisation should not end there. If the tribunal already performs the function of review and appeal and is equivalent in status to the High Court, then surely the specialised court should be the equivalent to the Supreme Court of Appeal to ensure that the process ends with the specialised court. Once again, this is a shortcoming and defeats the role of the specialised court, as enforcement and execution thereof lie with the High Court to address. The unified tribunal system will address these shortcomings by ensuring that the recognised status of any appeal or review mechanism other than the tribunal lies with the Supreme Court of Appeal. This process will unfold, because the unified tribunal system consists of hierarchical tiers with the same status as the Supreme Court of Appeal to eradicate the duplication of hearing the same matter on the same platform.

6 The National Consumer Tribunal

6.1 Overview of the National Consumer Tribunal

The National Credit Act and the Consumer Protection Act were promulgated to protect consumers, creditors, debtors and all parties concerned regarding credit agreements and consumer-related matters. South African consumers and debtors were previously heavily indebted and abused by exorbitant interest rate charges that saw consumers financially crippled. The legislation aimed at protecting and preventing the past abuses from occurring again, at ensuring that debtors were financially knowledgeable, and at creating onerous laws upon the creditors regarding lending and borrowing so as to avoid reckless lending from credit providers. The National Credit Regulator played the role of consumer watchdog to prevent consumer and credit abuse. The National Consumer Tribunal ensured that there was compliance with the abovementioned Acts and that there were consequences in terms of the Act when parties failed to comply with its provisions.

6.2 *The Historical Significance of the National Consumer Tribunal*

The Hire Purchase Act 36 of 1942 provided for the Hire-Purchase agreement which was promulgated in 1942 to uphold the rights of hire purchasers. A drawback of this Act was that it only provided protection for a small number of transactions. New areas arose that evaded the Act, which made it necessary for new legislation to address these shortcomings, and consequently the Credit Agreements Act 75 of 1980 was promulgated and the Hire Purchase Act was repealed. The Usury Act 37 of 1926 influenced the subsequent Usury Act 73 of 1968, and together these Acts regulated the credit industry for many years (Otto and Otto 2015, 3). However, as time passed it was decided to regulate the industry with one piece of legislation alone, which led to the adoption of the National Credit Act 34 of 2005. The genesis of the Consumer Protection Act 68 of 2008 was the Draft Green Paper, published by the Minister of Trade and Industry, which laid the foundation for the formation of the Consumer Protection Act (Eiselen 2014, 18–20).

6.3 *Deconstructing the National Consumer Tribunal*

The National Consumer Tribunal is a tribunal which, according to legislation, is supposed to be inquisitorial, informal and expeditious in the resolution of disputes. Despite this, the rules of the tribunal allow for the proceedings and formalities to be conducted in a formal manner. The tribunal meets its objective in that disputes are indeed resolved in a robust manner. The National Consumer Tribunal, Commission and Regulator decisions are all given the same status as High Court orders. However, the tribunal cannot provide for the enforcement of its decisions. As a result, once again the applicant needs to appear before the High Court for the decision to be made an order of the court. Hence, this means that the decisions of the tribunal have the same status in name alone, because application proceedings still need to be launched, with the net effect being that the decisions lose their strength and cannot be considered in these circumstances equal to a High Court order in action or in practice. A unified tribunal system addresses these shortcomings in that it provides for informal and simplified rules and, furthermore, provides for the tribunal system to possess the power of enforcement mechanisms.

7 The Water Tribunal

7.1 Overview of the Water Tribunal

The Water Tribunal was established in 1998. It aimed at ensuring the promotion of water usage, licence and catchment rights. The decisions of the Water Tribunal possess the same status as the Magistrates' Court. The tribunal's decisions are taken on appeal to the High Court. As with all tribunals, the Water Tribunal is not immune from having shortcomings. For example, due to the lack of experience and knowledge by the previous chairperson of the tribunal, as revealed by an appeal judgment from the Water Tribunal, administrative issues were created when the chairperson resigned and the minister delayed in appointing a replacement, which resulted in the tribunal not operating due to the Executive's failure to act.

This analysis of the Water Tribunal describes the procedure, mode of operation, functions and shortcomings which will be addressed through the establishment of a unified tribunal system.

7.2 The Historical Significance of the Water Tribunal

The period of the formation of the Water Tribunal (established in 1998) was significant because it began just four years after democracy was achieved in the nation. It is a tribunal that was created to address the obstacles faced during apartheid in protecting water as a resource for all of the people in terms of permits for irrigation farming and commercial use. Water is regarded as a sacred resource that all South Africans must have access to use and enjoy without prejudice of any kind. The Water Tribunal aims at regulating the use, enjoyment and access to water for commercial purposes. It is important that the government recognise that water belongs to the nation and is for the benefit of all its inhabitants.

7.3 Deconstructing the Water Tribunal

The Water Tribunal operates in an informal manner. It hears a limited number of cases annually, which illustrates that the tribunal is not in demand, nor is it a frequent choice for litigants. For a certain period of time the Water Tribunal was not in operation because (as already mentioned) there was a delay in appointing the necessary staff—that is to say, the chairperson, deputy chairperson and tribunal members—to facilitate the hearing of matters. Subsequently, in 2015 the requisite staff were appointed, and the tribunal is now in normal operation, once again holding hearings on relevant matters (Couzens et al. 2017, 19, 20). The decisions of the tribunal are equivalent to the decisions of the Magistrates' Court. The tribunal does not possess enforcement mechanisms and relies on the High Court to ensure the enforcement of decisions through application proceedings in order to make its decisions an order of the court. A unified tribunal system will ensure that the staff are appointed in a timely manner so that the tribunal system is always in operation and that the decisions of the tribunal are enforced without reliance on the High Court.

8 Concluding Remarks

The tribunals forming the basis of this study are not without their flaws. The common trend, with the exception of the caseload of the National Consumer Tribunal, is that the tribunals possess an insignificant caseload. This means that the tribunals are not being utilised enough by litigants to disputes. More matters heard before tribunals will ensure that caseload traffic is steered away from the courts. In this way, courts will be afforded an opportunity to reduce their backlog and hear more matters (themselves) each year. Enforcement mechanisms are again a common shortcoming of all the tribunals of this study, in that once the tribunal makes a decision, that decision must appear before the court on application proceedings to ensure the court makes the decision an order of the court, so as to ensure its enforcement. A unified tribunal system ensures the internal mechanism of enforcement so that a party does not have to go to court to enforce the decision should the other party not perform. Alternative dispute resolution is not utilised to its full potential within the tribunals of this study, and a unified tribunal system will incorporate ADR as an option for early resolution for every dispute.

This research aimed at illustrating the shortcomings of the South African tribunals under study and the manner in which they can be addressed through a unified tribunal system. The creation of tribunals, their development, the current tribunals and the proposed unified tribunal system reflect the story of the transformation of the tribunals towards their improvement and enhancement.

References

Aiyedun A, Ordor A (2016) Integrating the traditional with the contemporary in dispute resolution in African law. Democracy Develop 20:154–173

Allott AN (1968) African law. In: Derrett JDM (ed) An introduction to legal systems. Praeger, New York, pp 131–145

Ardé A (2017) Free tribunal protects tenants and landlords. https://www.businesslive.co.za/bt/business-and-economy/2017-07-01-free-tribunal-protects-tenants-and-landlords/. BusinessLive, 2 July 2017. Accessed 7 June 2018
Austin MM, Vidal-Naquet P (1977) The Greek cities and economic problems. California Univ Press, California
Cappelletti M (1985–1986) Repudiating montesquieu? The expansion and legitimacy of constitutional justice. Catholic Univ Law Rev 35(1):1
Cappelletti M, Garth B (1977–1978) Access to justice: the newest wave in the worldwide movement to make rights effective. Buffalo Law Rev 22:181–292
Carnwath LJ, Chitra M, Downes G et al (2008) An overview of the tribunal scenes in Australia, Canada, New Zealand and the United Kingdom. In: Creyke R (ed) Tribunals in the common law world. The Federation Press
Choudree R (1999) Traditions of conflict resolution in South Africa. ACCORD 9–28
Cohen RL (1986) Introduction. In: Cohen RL (ed) Justice. Plenum Press, New York and London
Couzens E, Maduramuthu D, Bellengere A (2017) Water security and judicial and administrative confusion in South Africa: the trustees of the time being of the Lucas Scheepers Trust, IT 633/96 v MEC for the department of water affairs, Gauteng 2015 ZAGPPHC 211 (17 April 2015) PER 20 (1):1–26. http://www.scielo.org.za/scielo.php?script=sci_arttext&pid=S1727-37812017000100010. Accessed 7 June 2018
Drewry G (2009) The judicialisation of 'Administrative' tribunals in the UK: From Hewart to Leggatt. Transylvanian Rev of Adm Sci 28(1):45–64
Eiselen N (2014) Commentary on the consumer protection act. Juta, South Africa
Hoexter C (2006) Administrative law in South Africa. Juta, Cape Town
Mohamed SI (2010) Tenant and landlord in South Africa, 2nd edn. Organisation of Civic Rights, Durban
Otto JM, Otto RL (2015) The national credit act explained. LexisNexis, South Africa
Sutherland P, Kemp K (2017) Competition law of South Africa. LexisNexis, South Africa
Velthuizen A (2012) Applying endogenous knowledge in the African context. Africa Insight 42 (1):73–86

Rashri Baboolal-Frank Lecturer in the Department of Procedural Law. Lectures in Civil Procedure, Alternative Dispute Resolution and Legal Practice, and for the LLM Civil Litigation Programme. Certified arbitrator and mediator for the Arbitration Foundation of Southern Africa. Advocate of the High Court of South Africa having previously practised as an attorney in the lower and higher courts. Currently finalising her doctoral studies at the University of Pretoria, South Africa.

Part III
Unity and Diversity: Civil Justice Between Modernization and Dejudicialization

Informatization of the Civil Justice System in Poland: An Overview of Recent Changes

Bartosz Karolczyk

Abstract In this contribution the author presents recent changes in the administration of justice in Poland, in particular civil litigation, involving the use of information technology (IT) systems. The introduction and expansion of such systems seems only natural, if not belated, in societies which have already embraced this phenomenon in other areas of life. While a sociologist or psychologist could argue over how this adversely affects humans or human interactions, the benefits of instant access to online or digital sources are there for everyone to see and experience. In the area of law some developments, such as the digitalization of public registers or access to judicial decisions, are clearly beneficial. Others, in particular in the area of civil litigation, are more complex or problematic due to, arguably, the very nature of procedural principles, most of which originated in the 19th century, in the times of quill pens and paper. Still, while the process surely brings its own challenges, they should not be a reason to stop, or should they be? As will be seen from the discussion below, investments in IT require prudent decision-making since what is useful (and costly) today may be obsolete tomorrow. Much attention should be paid while making such decisions because ultimately IT systems can hardly be perceived as a remedy to ever-present delays in the administration of justice.

1 Introduction

Recently, Polish legislation relating to the informatization of the civil justice system, and in particular civil procedure, has expanded in an unprecedented manner.

In this paper, I will outline two key areas: where Poland is with such legislation and to what extent the said system and the manner in which civil cases are processed have been digitalized.

B. Karolczyk (✉)
Faculty of Law, Kozminski University, Warsaw, Poland
e-mail: bkarolczyk@kozminski.edu.pl

A. Uzelac and C. H. van Rhee (eds.), *Transformation of Civil Justice*, Ius Gentium: Comparative Perspectives on Law and Justice 70, https://doi.org/10.1007/978-3-319-97358-6_6

Clearly, informatization—understood here as the provision of services or functions, including the processing of information, through information technology (IT) systems—can be beneficial. Primarily, it can significantly reduce the costs which a particular human activity, in this case the administration of justice, generates. For example, ten years ago commercial transactions involving a company and real estate would require a visit to two different courts, often located in different places. One would be to the Central Information of the National Court's Register to obtain a copy of a document confirming a variety of important information about the company. The other would be to the Mortgage Court to obtain a copy of the land and mortgage register for a particular plot of land. These two visits would also involve the payment of a fee for each document, to be made at a cashier's desk, and, naturally, standing in lines (time).

Since January 2012 the National Court's Register has been undergoing digitalization. It cost PLN1,499,930 (approx. EUR349,634) to build and implement this database (2012–2015). The cost of maintenance up to 2015 amounted to almost PLN2,000,000 (approx. EUR470,000).[1]

The register can be accessed from any computer connected to the Internet. A search engine is provided. PDF documents can be obtained free of charge. Generally, these documents have the same "legal power" as printed documents physically obtained from the Central Information of the National Court's Register.

Moreover, all proceedings relating to the establishment of business organizations disclosed in the National Court's Register can take place electronically.[2]

The land and mortgage register has undergone a similar change. It cost PLN3,862,146 (approx. EUR900,233) to build and implement this database (2010–2015). The annual contractual maintenance cost is PLN1,044,400 (approx. EUR480,000).[3]

The mortgage register can also be accessed from any computer connected to the Internet. The user must know the number of the plot in the register.[4] The user can then review the register and obtain a copy in a PDF format for free. A printout of the document is legally sufficient to execute a real estate transaction before a notary public.

[1]Data provided by the Ministry of Justice at the request of the author. On file with the author.

[2]Since 1 April 2016 these proceedings can be initiated electronically provided that the user has set up a free trusted profile within the e-administration program called Electronic Platform of Public Administration Services. See http://epuap.gov.pl/wps/portal for details. According to the information on the website, the Electronic Platform of Public Administration Services (ePUAP) is a coherent and systematic action program developed to allow public institutions to make their electronic services available to the public. The website enables defining citizen and businesses service processes, creates channels of access to different systems of public administration and extends the package of public services provided electronically. See generally the Act on Informatization of Entities Providing Public Services dated 17 February 2005.

[3]Data provided by the Ministry of Justice at the request of the author. On file with the author.

[4]There is also a "qualified user" who can search the database using names of individuals or entities.

Moreover, since July 2017 some qualified users (e.g. notaries or bailiffs) must file motions with the mortgage court electronically.

I will not hesitate to call this a digital revolution. It is an ongoing process. Some parts of it, such as the ones described above, are a success story, while others, such as the 2001 Act on the electronic signature (now repealed and replaced), simply failed to succeed despite initially being advertised as revolutionary. Some (discussed below) exist merely as a normative framework and have not yet been implemented as an actual IT infrastructure.

Is this revolution also taking place in the area of the courts and civil procedure? Importantly, is the provision of court services or functions to the members of society through IT systems even possible, as such?

The answer seems pretty obvious. In certain areas the judicial process is already digitalized. On a very basic level, one is more likely to obtain credible information faster by going online than by calling the court. On a systemic level, an electronic order for payment procedure is used to process approximately 3 million claims annually. Soon, litigants in Poland will be able to submit pleadings electronically in all cases. Service of process will be effected in this manner as well (more on this below).

These questions are perhaps too big for this short paper to fully explore. Still, there are certainly areas which, if subject to digitalization/informatization, would allow both the users and the state to save their limited resources. After all, litigation is basically the processing and storing of information.[5] However, intuitively one can certainly argue that the court system is a far more complex creature than simple data banks (which company or mortgage registers are).

Indeed, the system is a two-way street. There are end users (the litigants) and there are the courts, a conglomerate of various functions and people including clerks, assistants and judges. Thus, when discussing informatization one must be equally interested in facilitating the work of the courts and judges, and not only in the convenience of the users, so they too may directly benefit from informatization.

In any case, the benefits are there for everyone to see, and so are the challenges, the least of which are intellectual. Digitalization of the justice system naturally exposes the state and the society to cyber attacks, black-outs and, arguably, pushes the boundaries of actually understanding the system by the average person farther away due to dominant IT aspects.

The structure of this short paper is as follows.

First, inquiry into the simpler issue is warranted—the data banks.

Litigation generates at least two types of data banks. One, the judgments along with written reasoning (explanation).[6] Two, detailed information collected or generated in each individual case. I shall examine these two data banks below.

---

[5]Cf. Flaga-Gieruszyńska et al. (2016, at 2).

[6]The court writes the reasoning after it has delivered the judgment, provided a proper motion has been filed by a party. In practice, this is done by litigants and their attorneys as a matter of course. Cf. Uzelac (2011). It may be argued that this will change (at least with regard to certain cases), given the changes introduced in 2014. Specifically, if the hearings have been recorded (cf. main

Second, I will look at how the Polish legislator tries to digitalize judicial proceedings in civil cases.

2 Data Banks Related to Courts and Civil Litigation

2.1 Free and Public Electronic Access (E-Access) to Judgments

Free and public e-access to court decisions[7] resolving a dispute on the merits is essential to the existence and development of modern civic society. Court decisions represent law in action. These documents reflect how law is understood and applied by judges. As such, they are studied and analyzed, albeit for different purposes, by both academics and practitioners. Simply put, in theory they should provide guidelines and allow everyone to assess legal risks involved in a particular transaction, thus minimizing potential costs.

For many years after 1989 access to court decisions was limited to commercial and expensive databases. Generally, this changed in 2001 due to the Act on Access to Public Information. According to Article 4 § 1 of the Act, public authorities are under the duty to disclose public information. The term "public authorities" includes the judiciary as the third branch of the government. Further, according to Article 6 § 1 point 4, public information which is subject to disclosure includes court decisions (since they are considered official documents that are produced by public authorities in the process of discharging their duties).

Then, in early 2005 the Act on Informatization of Entities Providing Public Services was passed. Generally speaking, this law provided the comprehensive groundwork for the creation of e-government, including public data banks (registers) and IT systems for disclosure of public information.

As a result, the Portal for the Decisions of Common Courts (the "Portal") was created. Interestingly, strictly speaking there is no dedicated statutory basis for the existence of these portals. Each is set up pursuant to an internal order issued by the President of the Court of Appeals.[8]

---

text below), the court may provide reasoning orally after the delivery of the judgment. In such a case, if a motion for written reasoning is filed, the court will provide the moving party with a transcript of the oral reasoning. Arguably, this is a way to significantly reduce the workload generated by the requirement to write reasons for the decision, which, by the way, is a major chunk of what Polish judges actually do. In the bill amending the Code of Civil Procedure and other Acts dated 27 November 2017, there are further changes to this area of procedure.

[7]By court decisions I mean judgments by common courts (in Poland, courts of first instance and courts of appeals), which conclude the proceedings at a given instance, as well as by the Supreme Court.

[8]There are 11 Courts of Appeals in Poland.

The Portal is a database of court decisions (along with written reasoning) given by Polish common courts.[9] It can be accessed from any computer connected to the Web, does not require a user to set up a profile and is free of charge.

The Portal has a rather extensive, yet user-friendly search engine. Among other options, the user can search the database by reference to location, a division of a particular court, the law on which the judgment is based or the name of the judge. The result is displayed in HMTL format or can be easily exported into a PDF file.[10]

As of 18 August 2016, the Portal contained 168,299 court decisions.

As of 10 December 2017, the Portal contained 237,826 court decisions. In this respect it has eliminated the hegemony of commercial databases, thus becoming—as I would imagine—a mandatory working tool of every litigation lawyer in Poland.

The infrastructure of the Portal serves as the foundation for other search engines that enhance the Portal's utility, in particular analysis.[11]

Finally, the webpage of the Supreme Court[12] serves as a place of publication for many of its decisions. Nonetheless, some argue that—to the detriment of the civic society—the process of selecting cases for publication is not transparent. In addition, the Supreme Court has contractual relations with commercial publishers[13] that thus receive content which is generally not released into the public domain.[14]

2.2 *E-Access to Individual Cases*

Although somewhat limited, e-access to the file of individual cases is available to the litigants (and their attorneys) through Information Portals. There are 11 such portals, each linked to a territorial jurisdiction of the 11 Courts of Appeals.

The portals were built and implemented between 2013 and 2015, which cost PLN1,467,431 (approx. EUR342,058). Maintenance costs for 2014–2015 were PLN611,348 (approx. EUR142,505).[15]

The use of portals is free, but requires users to set up a profile. This is done by providing detailed, personal information, including an email address, which is very important because all notifications are sent by email. Once the online application

---

[9]Some decisions are generally excluded, e.g. divorce cases and those concerning sexual crimes. The list is set down in each internal order that serves as a normative foundation for any given portal.

[10]Published materials do not contain any personal information.

[11]System for the Analysis of Judicial Decisions at https://www.saos.org.pl/. Accessed 7 June 2018.

[12]http://www.sn.pl/en/SitePages/Main.aspx. Accessed 7 June 2018.

[13]There was a four-year-long litigation regarding disclosure of such contracts. The Supreme Court has been vehement in its refusal to disclose such contracts (pursuant to the Act on Access to Public Information).

[14]It can, of course, still be obtained on a motion pursuant to the Act on Access to Public Information.

[15]Data provided by the Ministry of Justice at the request of the author. On file with the author.

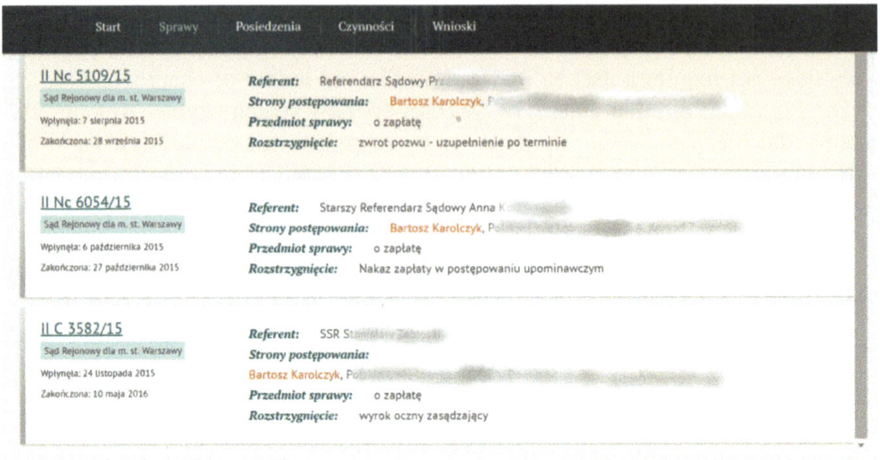

Fig. 1 "Cases" interface (reproduced from https://portal.waw.sa.gov.pl/)

has been filed (online), a person then needs to visit a court in order to have his or her personal information verified by a clerk. The profile then becomes active and can be automatically copied from one portal to another.

Access to specific cases requires a motion, in which the applicant identifies the court, the division, case number, year and capacity in which he or she acts in the case. The motion is filed through the portal (online). If the motion is approved, the applicant is granted access to that particular case.

The "Cases" interface is depicted in Fig. 1.

The cases to which I have access (and act as an attorney for one of the parties) are listed. Basic information is organized and provided: the case number, the court, the judge or (as in the first two cases listed, magistrate judge), the initiation date, the parties, the type of claim and the status (closed/ongoing). The name of the party I represent (here: myself) is displayed in orange color.

Clicking on a link to a particular case—like in Fig. 2—provides the user with further details, including addresses and hearing dates (both past and future).

At the very bottom of this tab, the user can write down his or her own comments.

Clicking on the second tab (Actions, marked by a star) reveals actions taken both by the litigants and the court. So, as mentioned, because I will receive email notification about each action in a given case, I will usually know my opponent has filed a document before I get it by post. Also, I will usually know what kind of action the court took and when it took the action.

However, the portal does not contain digitalized copies of pleadings or motions filed by the litigants. Still, in the third tab (Documents) I will have access to all documents (in DOC or PDF format) the court has produced, e.g. an order setting a deadline for my next submission. Thus, again, I will usually know about this before I get a copy of the order by post. Moreover, I will also know about orders directed

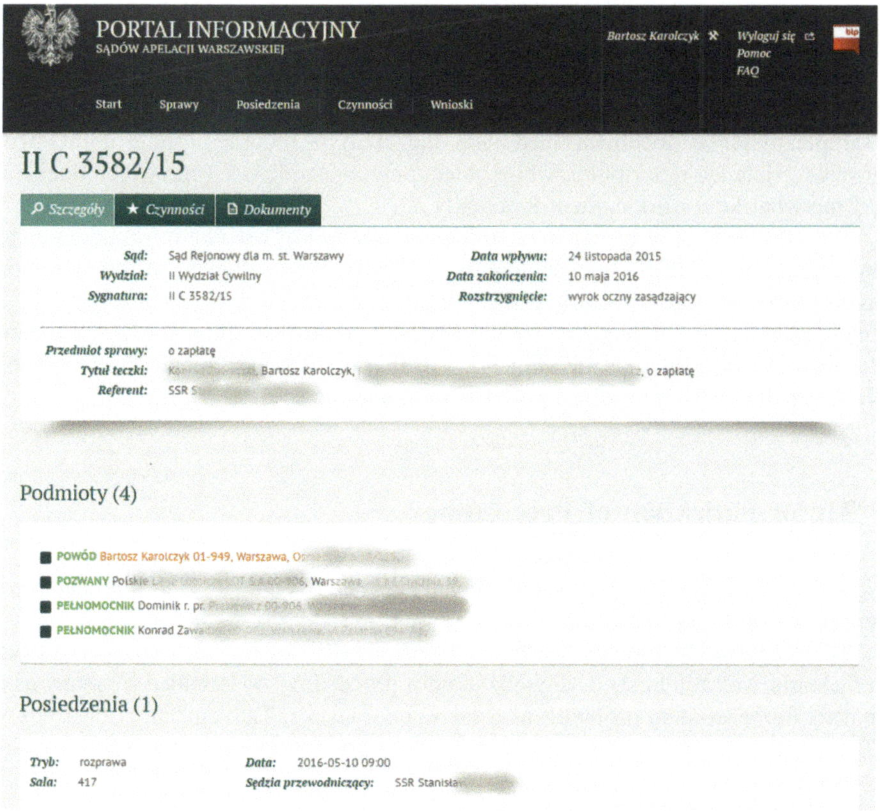

Fig. 2 "Cases" interface—further details (reproduced from https://portal.waw.sa.gov.pl/)

to my opponents, which I do not receive, as well as which witness has been summoned to the next hearing.

The final, fourth tab (E-transcript) contains downloadable audio files, if the hearings have been recorded (please note that Fig. 2 does not contain such a tab, which means recording is not available).

To summarize, this is a very, very useful tool, one that I use on a daily basis in my legal practice. As brilliant as it is, there are some minor problems.

One, similarly to the Portal for the Decisions of Common Courts, there is no dedicated statutory basis for the existence of these portals. Each exists and operates pursuant to an order by the president of any given common court.[16]

---

[16]The authority for such an order is found in Article 22 of the Act on the Organization of Common Courts of 2001 in connection with § 106 sec 1 of the Regulation of the Minister of Justice of 2015—Rules pertaining to the operation of common courts. This provision stipulates that the president of the court may decide to provide the litigants and their attorneys with information about the case, as well as copies of transcripts, judicial decisions and parties' submissions through a dedicated IT

Since there is no uniform regulation, the contents of each tab differ from one portal to another. For example, in one the summons sent to witnesses will be uploaded, while in another they will not (which will warrant a telephone call to the court, which in turn might yield that information, but not necessarily so). Another example: when a document filed with the court is recorded, some courts will provide a detailed description, while others only a generic one (one which does not tell me what kind of document it actually is).

Two, the level of diligence in or simply the practice of keeping information up to date differs dramatically between courts.[17] Clearly, the usefulness of the system is significantly reduced or outright eliminated if information is not disclosed in a timely manner. As pointed out by the Ministry of Justice, the use of Information Portals saves litigants time and money, as well as eases the workload of secretariats. However, this is only true if a portal is duly kept up-to-date.[18]

3 Informatization of Proceedings

Now that I have briefly discussed data banks related to courts and civil procedure, I will move on to digitalization of proceedings.

That process has already started. For reasons that, in my view, have not been sufficiently well established, digitalization of proceedings is heralded by many as a remedy to the existing problems of delay in civil justice. The legislator consistently

system. This is now being changed. The bill amending the Code of Civil Procedure and other Acts dated 27 November 2017 provides such a basis by amending the Law on the organization of common courts of 27 July 2001. Pursuant to a proposed provision (Article 175 h) the Minister of Justice will be formally in charge of the Portal. Still, the Minister will be able to delegate this task to a court. Moreover, the normative content regarding the public (open) character of proceedings was changed in September 2016. Specifically, Article 9 of the Polish Code of Civil Procedure now expressly states that minutes of hearings, pleadings as well as audio/video recordings can be provided to the parties through a dedicated IT system.

[17]According to the information I have received from the Ministry of Justice, disclosure of information is within the authority of each particular division. So, apparently there is no central hub for any given court to perform the task. Instead, every division takes care of its own business, so to speak. Perhaps a bit surprisingly, the dividing line does not run between congested urban courts—courts in a more remote location, with a (presumably) lighter workload. There are some remote courts that are exceptionally diligent in keeping their portals updated (i.e. if a hearing was held at 9:00 a.m., the transcript will be uploaded to the portal at 2:00 p.m. on the same day), while others apparently ignore it almost completely. Courts of Appeals are notorious for not disclosing information in a timely fashion.

[18]Fortunately, an online system for notification of errors or delays exists and works rather well. Problems are usually resolved within 48 h.

states that digitalization reduces costs, increases efficiency and expands access to the courts.[19] At the same time, discussion about potential practical risks is basically nonexistent.

The items below are presented in chronological order.

3.1 Recording of Hearings (E-Protocol/E-Transcript)

The first form of digitalization of proceedings[20] was the gradual (2011–2015) introduction of a countrywide system allowing for audio/video recording of court hearings.[21] This became known as e-transcript. The project covered proceedings in both civil and criminal cases.

The cost of the project—PLN191,017,736 (approx. EUR44,526,278).[22] Eighty-five per cent of that amount was provided by the European Union.

One may wonder, Why this? Presumably, the reason was the way in which the proceedings were recorded (in the traditional meaning). Generally, at a hearing, sitting next to the judge(s) was a clerk, who typed the transcript under the guidance of the presiding judge. As a matter of course, the presiding judge would dictate words to the clerk, and simultaneously look at his or her own, separate computer screen, to make sure the clerk transcribed the words accurately. Since there was no culture of proper questioning, during witness testimony the judge would paraphrase or rephrase what the witness said, so that the clerk could type more efficiently. As one can imagine, it took forever, and had other detrimental effects, the least of which was dividing the judge's attention. It was a significant delaying factor.

So, now, the vast majority of courtrooms in Poland allow for audio recording. My understanding is that one of the goals was to get rid of the paraphrasing/rephrasing, which would in turn significantly reduce the time required to collect testimony. Accordingly, pursuant to Article 157 § 1 of the Polish Code of Civil Procedure (CCP), the minutes of a public hearing are produced in a form of audio/video recording as well as in writing, under the guidance of the presiding judge. If the hearing is recorded, the part of the written minutes devoted to evidence should be limited to "a summary of results of evidence taking".

---

[19]See e.g. written opinion to the bill amending the Civil Code, the Code of Civil Procedure and other Acts dated 10 July 2015, at 1. On file with the author. Sections of that bill, which eventually became law, are discussed below.

[20]Technically speaking, the first form of digitalization was the introduction of computers. This, however, is now ancient history.

[21]Some courts of first instance (district courts, Polish *sądy rejonowe*) were left out. In total, the system was implemented in 2267 courtrooms. Data provided by the Ministry of Justice at the request of the author. On file with the author. See also Gołaczyński (2016).

[22]Data provided by the Ministry of Justice at the request of the author. On file with the author.

The practice?

Some judges have embraced the system—they got rid of paraphrasing/ rephrasing entirely and do not even care about "a summary". There is simply no content in the written minutes.[23] Others still diligently paraphrase every statement, effectively negating the entire purpose of spending almost 45 million euros.

It is worth noting that the audio recording system comes with very useful software which allows the recorder to mark a specific time in the recording with written information in the left margin of the screen. For example, at 6:00 p.m. witness A started testifying, at 6:28:43 p.m. witness B, etc. Unfortunately, in practice hardly anyone bothers. As a result, one may end up with a 4–5-h recording and no written material.

If you were not at the hearing, this may present somewhat of a challenge, especially if you are an appellate judge. Imagine having no written, official record of witness testimony. Instead you have 12 h of recordings.

Of course, under the CCP a judge may order the preparation of a transcript, if such is necessary to decide the case. This is often done if the testimony is long and no summary minutes have been made during the hearing. Apart from the money and time needed, however, transcripts are done automatically. Therefore, without human verification, they are often useless.

Logically then, in a response to a legal question by the Circuit Court in Warsaw, the Supreme Court recently held that: (1) the transcript of a recording is not an official document (in contrast to "classic" written minutes, which is an official document, and thus benefits from certain evidentiary privileges[24]); (2) if an audio recording does not allow the listener to understand its contents, that part of the proceedings, if decisive, needs to be repeated, i.e. the court must take evidence again.[25]

It is safe to say that nowadays everyone has an audio recording device on them at all times.[26] The Polish legislator took notice. Starting in September 2016, the court allows a party to record the hearing on its own device, unless this would adversely affect the proceedings[27] (and it is hard to imagine it somehow would). The bill amending the Code of Civil Procedure and other Acts dated 27 November 2017 takes this idea even further. All that will be required from the participant who wishes to record the hearing on his or her own device is to give notice to the

[23]Some judges will simply make their own (private), handwritten notes during the hearing.

[24]See Sect. 3.3 below.

[25]Supreme Court resolution dated 23 March 2016, III CZP 102/15. Available online at http://www.sn.pl/sites/orzecznictwo/Orzeczenia3/III%20CZP%20102-15.pdf. Accessed 7 June 2018.

[26]For a discussion about how this affects the law of evidence, see Karolczyk (2013).

[27]See CCP Article 162^1.

court.[28] The authors of the bill correctly point out, that: (1) recording of hearings only pursuant to the court's permission is contrary to the modern understanding and realities of the administration of justice; (2) the enforcement of the court's decision in this respect is in fact impossible due to advancements in technology, and the rule is therefore as harmful as it is impractical; and (3) generally, there is no reason to limit a party's private record to handwritten notes.[29] Thus, the court can only object if the hearing is to be held behind closed doors or if it would adversely affect the proceedings (and it is hard to imagine it somehow would).

One my wonder whether spending almost 45 million euros on this system was a good idea in the first place.

It is tempting to respond in the negative. After the fact it is easy to question the apparent lack of imagination that resulted in the introduction of a system which currently can be seen as superfluous due to the proliferation of smart phones. This story arguably illustrates the challenges that come with rapidly changing technology. It should also serve as a warning against the implementation of solutions which may quickly become outdated or the benefits of which, in the long run, do not seem to justify the expense.

On the other hand, the introduction of e-protocols has far-reaching consequences in terms of transparency, accessibility, legal culture and efficiency.[30] In a society suffering from post-transformational lack of institutional trust, the recording of proceedings probably has a positive psychological effect on the litigants. The reasoning is that any injustice that may occur will be there for everyone to see or hear, and therefore it is less likely to occur. Thus, recording enhances institutional trust in the area of civil justice.[31]

In addition, it is a commonly held belief among practicing attorneys that the recording of hearings has significantly improved the way in which both the court and the litigants behave, in particular towards each other, simply because that behavior is verbatim preserved for future reference. While that positive effect may diminish in the future as the digital society is continually pushing the boundaries of what is acceptable behavior, what matters is that it took place.

Finally, if the e-protocol is properly used, it allows the judge to be fully focused on the testimony, which will be performed without interruptions. Thus, efficiency of the hearing is improved—the collection of evidence is better and faster (Flaga-Gieruszyńska et al. 2016, 74, 75).

[28]See Article 1 point 2 of the bill amending the Code of Civil Procedure and other Acts dated 27 November 2017 (proposed CCP Article 9 § 1).

[29]See written opinion to the bill amending the Code of Civil Procedure and other Acts dated 27 November 2017, at 125. On file with the author.

[30]Similarly Flaga-Gieruszyńska et al. (2016, at 73–77).

[31]This was one of the goals indicated by the Ministry of Justice in its strategy regarding the introduction of e-protocol. See Flaga-Gieruszyńska et al. (2016, at 74).

3.2 Electronic Order for Payment Procedure (EPU)

The first procedure to be fully digitalized was the order for payment procedure (EPU).[32]

In 2010, a dedicated court for handling exclusively EPU was established in the City of Lublin (e-court). E-court is accessed via https://www.e-sad.gov.pl/default.aspx. It has subject matter and territorial jurisdiction irrespective of the amount in dispute (max. PLN100,000,000). The use of EPU requires a verified account, which can be set up at the website of the court.

As everywhere, the benefits of EUP are simplification of procedure, significant reduction of costs[33] and time necessary to obtain an order, provided the case is simple and does not, basically, require a hearing to collect evidence. The submission of a statement of claim is streamlined through the use of mandatory electronic/editable online forms. Evidence should be indicated in the statement of claim, but does not need to be attached.

Communication between the claimant and the court is exclusively electronic, whereas it takes the traditional form with the defendant, unless the defendant chooses the former.

While EPU's reception has overall been positive, it was initially viewed with caution as something of an experiment, and concerns were expressed about equality of arms, automation of adjudication and users' security (safety) [Flaga-Gieruszyńska et al. (2016, at 4, 109–118)]. Since in practice EPU is mostly utilized (and sometimes abused) by securitization funds active in the consumer debt-collection market,[34] some of these concerns indeed have merit. On the other hand, it has been argued that orders for payment are now being issued too cautiously, which undermines the entire purpose of EPU. Rather than hinder EPU, safety nets should be moved to the enforcement stage.[35] In any case, some of the solutions tested in EPU have proved successful enough to warrant their transfer to general proceedings [Golaszynski and Szostek (2016, at X)].

---

[32]See CCP Arts. 505^{28}–505^{37}.

[33]The court fee is 1.25% of the amount in dispute in comparison to 5% in regular court proceedings.

[34]In fact, but for EPU these businesses would find it more difficult to achieve economies of scale. Given the volume at which they operate and the fact that most business processes are automated, each digital advancement in the area of civil procedure is likely directly beneficial to such market actors.

[35]See Flaga-Gieruszyńska et al. (2016), 115.

3.3 *Expansion of Sources of Evidence*

Major amendments to the CCP were introduced in September 2016. Some of them were related to the legal definition of "document", introduced to the Polish Civil Code at the same time, but equally important was the creation of a normative framework for further digitalization of procedure.[36]

Until 8 September 2016 there was no legal definition of a document in Polish law (only in legal doctrine and case law). From a procedural standpoint, a document required a signature and authentication. As a result, a paper copy was not considered a document, and neither was a digital one (scan, PDF or a file). In addition, irrespective of the theory of open sources of evidence, which was almost uniformly disregarded in practice, and due to lack of provisions that would expressly allow the courts to treat such materials as evidence, the use of digital documents was problematic for the court and risky for the litigant. Moreover, this made courts look inadequately equipped to handle cases in the 21st century, in which paper is not the dominant medium to preserve information any more.

Under the modified Article 77^1 of the Polish Civil Code, a document is a data carrier (source, medium) which allows for the examination of the data. The focus is now on the content rather than on the form, which is an almost philosophical shift in perspective. Still, content needs to be accessible, and therefore the carrier is the second element constituting a document. For example, in the case of digital documents, a file is the carrier of content. Importantly, legislative materials expressly state that a signature does not constitute an essential element of a document.[37]

Procedurally, documents have been divided into two categories, i.e. one in which the content is expressed in an alphabet and language (textual or written document), and one in which it is expressed in other ways.[38]

The first category of documents will continue to benefit from certain evidentiary presumptions that are given to private[39] and official[40] documents.

---

[36]See e.g. Gołaczyński (2016), 1022.

[37]See written opinion to the bill amending the Civil Code, the Code of Civil Procedure and other Acts dated 10 July 2015, at 3.

[38]See written opinion to the bill amending the Civil Code, the Code of Civil Procedure and other Acts dated 10 July 2015, at 7. On file with the author. Other categories can be established, especially regarding the form, i.e. written (classic form) and electronic (digital).

[39]CCP Article 245. [Private documents] A private written or electronic document is a proof that its signatory has made a statement contained in such document.

[40]CCP Article 244 [Official documents]

§ 1. Official documents drawn up in the form prescribed by relevant public authorities and other state authorities constitute proof of the facts officially stated therein.

§ 2. The provisions of § 1 apply *mutatis mutandis* to official documents issued by authorities other than those provided for in § 1 within the scope of public administration tasks delegated to them by the law.

However, according to CCP Article 243[1] these and other special provisions pertaining to documents[41] apply to documents containing text which allows for identification of the issuer. So, while the presumption given to a private document is hardly a game-changer in real litigation, this is a limitation that needs to be kept in mind. In particular, the issuer of a written document still needs to be shown, albeit apparently a signature is not the only way in which this can be done.

The second category, broadly referred to as other documents (e.g. drawings, photos, designs, plans, all manner of recordings), is principally governed by CCP Article 308. Thus, the court shall take evidence in the form of such document, in particular containing an image or sound, by adequately applying the provisions on inspection and written documents.

3.4 E-Court

As mentioned, in September 2016 the Polish legislator took another big step towards the creation of a comprehensive legal environment which allows for digitalized processing of all civil cases.

Until these changes took effect, digitalized submissions were legally possible only in EPU, the mortgage register, the entrepreneurs' register and registered pledge proceedings.[42]

First, the normative content regarding the public (open) character of proceedings has changed. Specifically, CCP Article 9 now expressly states that minutes of hearings, pleadings as well as audio/video recordings can be provided to the parties through a dedicated IT system, i.e. electronically.[43] This assumes, that—at some point in time—the entire case file will be available in digital form and will be treated as equal to printed documents.

Second, in every case pleadings or motions can be submitted to the court electronically (e-submission). If this manner of submission is optional, the user needs to choose it in the system. In principle, the user can also switch back to the traditional, paper method.

---

[41]For example, the CCP provides restrictions with regard to the use of testimony to prove a fact against or beyond the contents of a document. Also, it introduces certain burden-shifting rules if authenticity is challenged.

[42]See Kościółek (2017), 3.

[43]The legislator is deliberate in the use of the term "through the IT system" and specifically distinguishes this method from "electronic". Thus, the term "electronically" is not a legal term and is used here generally, for the sake of simplicity.

Submission takes place upon uploading the document to the system. A qualified electronic signature[44] or an ePUAP profile[45] is required. If the user chooses this method, or if digitalized submissions are mandatory, then a traditional, written submission will be ineffective. The system will give the user notice of this rule. In addition, the court will give notice to the litigant that his or her submission is ineffective due to non-compliance with the required method of submission.

If a submission cannot be effected due to a failure of the system, this will be a cause for reinstatement of the deadline.

Still, even if the user chooses digital submission, submission of evidence in paper form will still be possible.

Thus, one party can go digital, while the other may go paper. This may cause some practical difficulties for the courts. In the long run, however, I imagine this to be a transitory problem.

In the light of the above the question has been posed as to how to ensure that courts will not be turned into printing offices. Arguably, the question is based on the false premise that a printed document is needed. Given the entire legal framework, however, this premise is not correct. It seems, therefore, that the question is—legally—not relevant. It may have some practical relevance, though, since lawyers are creatures of habit and many simply prefer or even enjoy working with paper.

The system is to be implemented until the end of 2019. According to estimates of the Ministry of Justice from 2015, it will cost approximately 19,000,000 (EUR5,000,000) to set up and PLN800,000 (EUR200,000) to maintain annually.

Third, similarly, service of process can also be effected electronically.[46] Traditional (postal) service of process is considered by some as one of the most dysfunctional (ineffective, inefficient) elements of the Polish justice system [Flaga-Gieruszyńska et al. (2016, at 5)].

Until these changes took effect, e-service was legally possible only in EPU, in labor and social security cases, and simplified, registration and EPU proceedings.[47]

In 2015, the Ministry of Justice estimated that traditional postal service of process just between trial courts and attorneys had an annual cost of approximately PLN122,000,000 (EUR30,500,000).[48] On top of that, attorneys alone paid over

[44]See Regulation (EU) No. 910/2014 of The European Parliament and of the Council of 23 July 2014 on electronic identification and trust services for electronic transactions in the internal market and repealing Directive 1999/93/EC. This Act has been partially implemented in Poland. On 5 September 2016 the Polish Parliament passed the Act on Trust Services and Electronic Identification.

[45]See n. 2 above.

[46]See generally CCP Article 131^1 § 1.

[47]See Kościółek (2017, 5).

[48]See written opinion to the bill amending the Civil Code, the Code of Civil Procedure and other Acts dated 10 July 2015, at 54. On file with the author.

PLN51,000,000 (EUR12,750,000) annually for this service. Additionally, the reduction in the courts' operating costs that would be generated by electronic confirmation of receipt was estimated at almost PLN14,000,000 (EUR3,500,000) annually starting from 2016. Assuming the accuracy of these (most recently available) estimates, the amounts are significant, and a result of electronic service of process will be the freeing of funds which can then be allocated elsewhere. Transactional costs will thus be reduced. From this perspective, e-service of process is clearly a beneficial solution.

At the same time, Poczta Polska [Polish Post] S. A., which holds a monopoly over postal services in the justice system,[49] is likely to be adversely affected, financially, once the system becomes operational.

If a party chooses the digital form, service of process will also be digital, unless a party chooses otherwise. If, however, e-submission is mandatory, e-service will also be mandatory, with no opt-out available.

Strictly speaking, service is effected by uploading a document to the system so that the user can learn its content.[50] Yet, practically speaking, service will take place upon logging in, irrespective of whether the user has actually learned the contents of the uploaded document. Thus, service can take place anywhere, anytime. The system will ask for or automatically provide the user with a confirmation of receipt,[51] which will serve as proof of service.[52] If the user does not confirm (or does not log into the system), the service is deemed effective upon the lapse of 14 days following the uploading of the document.[53]

The system is to be implemented until the end of 2020. According to estimates of the Ministry of Justice from 2015, the total cost of set-up and maintenance between 2012 and 2020 will be approximately PLN8,000,000 (EUR2,000,000).

In November 2017, some expectations regarding the establishment of a system for e-service found confirmation in another round of proposed amendments to the

[49]The battle over Poczta Polska S. A.'s monopoly in the justice system warrants a separate paper. Suffice it to say that there are Supreme Court rulings according to which in order to submit a motion or a pleading on time, it must be dispatched at Poczta Polska, even though the courts (at the time) could use a different postal operator to effect service of process. See e.g. the Supreme Court's ruling dated 14 July 2015, II UZ 10/15. Interestingly, the Supreme Administrative Court, during the same period, ruled the opposite for judicial administrative proceedings, saying that it was the only constitutionally sound result. See e.g. Supreme Administrative Court's ruling 22 April 2015, I OZ 343/15. Finally, on 19 July 2017 the Polish Supreme Court (III UZP 3/17) asked the Court of Justice of the European Union to resolve this strictly procedural matter, linking it to the interpretation of provisions of Directive 97/67/EC of the European Parliament and of the Council of 15 December 1997 on common rules for the development of the internal market of Community postal services and the improvement of the quality of service.

[50]See § 3 of the Minister of Justice Regulation on procedure and manner of electronic service of process dated 20 October 2015 (Dz.U. z 2015 r. poz. 1776).

[51]For details see § 4 of the Minister of Justice Regulation on procedure and manner of electronic service of process dated 20 October 2015 (Dz.U. z 2015 r. poz. 1776).

[52]See CCP Article 142 § 1.

[53]This is the rule in the EPU procedure described above.

law. Specifically, it was proposed that Information Portals (see Sect. 2.2) serve this purpose. According to the new CCP Article 131^2 § 1, learning the contents of a file uploaded to the Information Portal shall be deemed service of such document to the user. The details are to be provided by the Minister of Justice in the form of a regulation.

At first sight, it is clear that if the bill of 27 November 2017 amending the Code of Civil Procedure and other Acts becomes law, there will be two sets of rules for two different IT systems. One, a rather abstract system that perhaps will be created one day, and in which service takes place upon logging in, and a second system, based on the infrastructure of Information Portals described above, in which service takes place upon learning the contents of an uploaded file. This is clearly a confusing state of affairs, one that will hopefully be ironed out before the bill becomes law.

For a long time now, the CCP has allowed for a direct exchange of most pleadings between attorneys of record. The assumption here is correct: since attorneys represent a licensed profession of public trust, there is no need for a middleman. Since September 2016 attorneys do not need to present to the court proof of dispatch to the opponent, a simple statement to this effect in the document submitted to the court is sufficient.[54]

Following this pragmatic approach, the bill introduces yet another, simplified manner of service between attorneys.[55] Namely, attorneys will be allowed to serve upon each other exclusively in electronic form provided that they make a joint statement to this effect and provide the court with contact details for such service, in particular an email address or fax number. The said statement cannot be revoked and will be ineffective if made conditionally or with an expiration date. If deemed justified, the court may disallow this manner of service.

Fourth, it is now legally possible to hold hearings with the use of equipment that makes it possible to hold such hearings at a distance (telephone-conference, video-conference). Of course, the practical possibility depends exclusively on the availability of properly equipped rooms.

Fifth, electronic judgment. If the process has been initiated through the IT system, then the judgment can be given in an electronic form (and signed with a certified e-signature).[56] Pursuant to Article 53a of the Act on the Organization of Common Courts, a document obtained from the IT system and utilized in judicial proceedings has value equal to a document issued by a court, provided it has features that allow for its verification in the system.[57]

---

[54]See CCP Article 132 § 1.

[55]See proposed Article 132 § 1^3.

[56]See CCP Article 324 § 4.

[57]The details are set down in the Minister of Justice Regulation regarding the manner and features allowing for verification of the existence and contents of a document in the IT system utilized in judicial proceedings dated 7 September 2016 (Dz.U. z 2016 r. poz. 1422).

4 Random, Automated Allocation of Cases[58]

On 16 October 2017 the Ministry of Justice presented a new, operational IT system that randomly allocates cases to judges called System for Random Allocation of Cases (SLPS). Since then the system has been tested in selected courts in Poland. Starting from 1 January 2018 the system will be implemented in all 374 courts around the country. Before discussing a number of the features of the system, it is worth shedding some light on how the allocation of cases worked in the past and currently.

Generally, what was practiced was called a numerical system.

Pursuant to the Act on the Organization of Common Courts of 2001, in its original wording, rules pertaining to the allocation of cases should be set forth by the chief judge of the court of appeals, or chief judge of the district court. According to some, there was no uniformity between the courts in this respect. In particular, often it was the chief judge's decision to leave the allocation of cases within the authority of the president of a division, which, arguably, was contrary to what the law said. It should be noted, for the record, that the president of a division is appointed by the chief judge.

Hence, the key figure in this system was often the president, who kept an alphabetical list of judges, to whom cases were allocated chronologically (as they were filed with the court). However, the president could set this system aside if a case was connected to another case already being handled by a particular judge or if it was necessary to allocate workload evenly among judges.

In practice, cases regarding a particular subject matter were often given to a specific judge who had acquired a reputation as a specialist in such matters.

Therefore, lawyers with extensive practice before a specific court in specific matters could with relative probability of success bet on who would get the case. Combining this with a review of that judge's prior decisions, if publicly available (through the Portal, see above), it was possible to obtain a rough understanding of how the case might be adjudicated.

Minister of Justice Regulation of 2007—Rules pertaining to the operation of common courts[59] contained the normative basis of the said system. However, a subsequent Regulation of 2015, in its original wording, introduced the president's full freedom and authority in allocating cases. This was changed in December 2015, barely six months after the new regulation entered into force, when the 2007 system was re-introduced.

---

[58]This section is based on information available at: https://www.ms.gov.pl/pl/informacje/news,9881,losowy-przydzial-spraw-sedziom-gwarancja.html; http://www.rp.pl/Sady-i-prokuratura/310289966-Klamstwa-na-temat-losowego-przydzialu-spraw-sedziom.html; http://www.rp.pl/Sady-i-prokuratura/310119985-Losowanie-spraw-bedzie-w-ministerstwie.html; http://www.rp.pl/Sedzi owie-i-sady/312119900-Sa-problemy-z-losowaniem-skladow-trzyosobowych.html. Accessed 7 June 2018.

[59]Issued based on statutory delegation contained in the Act on the Organization of Common Courts of 2001.

It does not take much imagination to understand this system's potential for imperfect results.

Only in July 2017 was the Act on the Organization of Common Courts of 2001 changed to expressly provide that the allocation of cases shall be random, equal and done on a chronological basis.

SLPS covers the entire country. It is based on three key principles, which are (numerical) equality, randomness and chronological attribution. It works as follows. Each day all new cases are entered into SLPS. After the close of business hours for the courts, SLPS then "approaches" each division and randomly allocates all the new cases entered on that day to judges. SLPS will also factor absences (e.g. holidays, sick leave), additional functions performed by a judge (president, chief judge, etc.) as well as specializations, i.e. a judge handling divorce cases will not get a case regarding unfair competition. Family matters are excluded from SLPS. The system does not cover the Supreme Court.

On the next day, SLPS will notify each court about the outcome of the draw. The report is later printed and inserted into the case file.

According to the Ministry of Justice, any and all activity by or within SLPS is monitored and recorded, allowing for review, should it be needed.

References

Flaga-Gieruszyńska K, Gołaczyński J, Szostek D (eds) (2016) Informatyzacja postępowania cywilnego. Teoria i praktyka, CH Beck, Warszawa

Gołaczyński J (2016) Elektronizacja postępowania cywilnego—nowelizacja KPC i KC wchodząca w życie 8.9.2016, Monitor Prawniczy 19:1024

Gołaszyński J, Szostek D (eds) (2016) Informatyzacja postępowania cywilnego. CH Beck, Warszawa

Karolczyk B (2013) Admissibility of "illegal evidence" in civil procedure: a comparative look through Polish and American lenses. ZZPInt 18:189–221

Kościółek A (2017) Elektroniczne czynności procesowe w świetle nowelizacji z 10.7.2015, PME 1:3

Uzelac A (2011) The need to provide reasons in court judgments: some developments in East and West. In: Gudowski J, Weitz K (eds) Aurea praxis, aurea theoria. Księga Pamiatkowa ku czci Profesora Tadeusza Erecinskiego, LexisNexis, Waszawa, pp 1547–1566

Bartosz Karolczyk Senior Attorney in the law firm of Domański Zakrzewski Palinka sp.k., Warsaw, Poland, with practice focused on civil commercial litigation and arbitration. Senior Lecturer in Civil Procedure at the Faculty of Law, Koźmiński University, Warsaw.

Between Reform and Dejudicialization: Current Trends in Spanish Civil Litigation

Fernando Gascón Inchausti

Abstract Over the last 20 years the Spanish civil justice system has been very significantly transformed. The starting point was the new Code of Civil Procedure (2000), the main goal of which was to improve the quality of first instance proceedings and to secure greater efficiency in enforcement. From then, the whole Spanish dispute resolution system has been changed through further reforms. The role of the judge in the civil lawsuit has been partially modified and there has been strong reliance on the positive trend towards promoting mediation and other forms of ADR.

1 Introduction

Spanish civil procedure has experienced one of the biggest reforms thus far of the 21st century and one of the most far-reaching. Prior to the reforms there was a long thread of continuity running through Spain's civil procedural code. The *Ley de Enjuiciamiento Civil*, which was replaced by the reforms, had been in place since it was formally enacted in 1881. It was, however, almost a copy of its immediate predecessor, the first real code of civil procedure in Spain's legal history, which was enacted in 1855. It, and therefore the 1881 Code, could however be seen in terms of their structure as a direct inheritance, and evolution, from the Roman-canonic *solemnis ordo judiciorum*.[1] This was an inheritance that was broadly speaking untouched by influence from the French *Code de procédure civile*; the only

This paper is one of the results of a research Project funded by the Spanish Ministry for Economy and Competitiveness (DER2015-64756-P).

[1]See Fairén Guillén (1953), Montero Aroca (1982) and Montero Aroca (1996), 189–275.

F. Gascón Inchausti (✉)
Complutense University of Madrid, Madrid, Spain
e-mail: fgascon@der.ucm.es

A. Uzelac and C. H. van Rhee (eds.), *Transformation of Civil Justice*,
Ius Gentium: Comparative Perspectives on Law and Justice 70,
https://doi.org/10.1007/978-3-319-97358-6_7

institution whose French origin can be ascertained is the appeal for cassation, but even there significant differences are present (De Benito Llopis-Llombart 2017a).

The system did not experience significant changes during most of the 20th century. The Civil War (1936–1939) and the subsequent Franco authoritarian regime left no real room for change (Cachón Cadenas 2012). Consequently, Spain ended the 20th century with a procedural system which was entirely unsuitable as a means to provide a modern and efficient dispute resolution: it was primarily a written procedure, with a minimal role for the judge; it was too lengthy; and, it produced unsatisfactory outcomes (the main complaint lawyers made at the time was that judges were simply unable to "understand the dispute").

The 1978 Constitution and, from 1981, the Constitutional Court started to change this picture. Article 24 of the Spanish Constitution establishes the right of access to justice and to an efficient judicial remedy, as well as to a fair procedure. Additionally, the Constitutional Court is competent to hear challenges to judicial decisions for the infringement of fundamental rights (in a similar way to the German *Verfassungsbeschwerde*). The most frequently alleged infringements concern Article 24 of the Constitution. This means that the Constitutional Court was often given the opportunity to scrutinize how the civil justice system operated. As a result, it started to identify shortcomings in terms of procedural safeguards. During the 1980s and early 1990s the Constitutional Court's case law showed how inefficient the civil justice system, including the procedural code, was: while it was not unconstitutional, it did not facilitate the achievement of speedy and efficient resolution of disputes (Borrajo Iniesta et al. 1995). For instance, the Court reacted against undue formalism in the interpretation of the prerequisites to the right of action; it required higher standards as regards the reasons provided in judicial decisions, as a safeguard against arbitrariness; the right to enforcement was given constitutional significance; the legislature was urged to provide litigants with a well-functioning system of provisional relief in order to ensure the effectiveness of civil proceedings.

Further to these developments, some reforms were made in 1984 and 1992.[2] These were aimed at simplifying proceedings and reducing their duration; both were unsuccessful in practice (de la Oliva Santos and Fernández 1995). The opinion eventually prevailed that the problems associated with the system's operation were not just ones relating to financial and human resources. It was finally understood that the Code itself had to undergo radical reform in order to render it functional and efficient (Díez-Picazo Giménez 1999). In 1996, the work to prepare a new code of civil procedure started. It concluded with the new Code's official publication in

[2]*Ley 34/1984, de 6 de agosto, de reforma urgente de la Ley de Enjuiciamiento Civil*: the extent of the reform was wide: suppression of mandatory conciliation; introduction of a new preliminary hearing; reform of the appeal for cassation. This reform, however, was enacted before a relevant reform of the judiciary was put into place in 1985. The 1992 reform was put into effect by *Ley 10/ 1992, de 30 de abril, de Medidas Urgentes de Reforma Procesal*, mainly affecting the appeal for cassation and enforcement proceedings.

January 2000 (*Ley 1/2000, de 7 de enero, de Enjuiciamiento Civil*, hereinafter LEC) and its entry into force a year later, in January 2001.[3]

2 The Main Features of the New Code and the New Procedure

2.1 Scope

The new Code does not include arbitration, mediation or conciliation. These are regulated in separate Acts.[4] This would be meaningless in itself, but it can also be taken as hinting at a cultural state of mind: there is no "holistic" perception of dispute resolution mechanisms, at least from the lawmaker's point of view. Insolvency proceedings are also addressed in a different Act.[5]

2.2 Influences

If one addresses the structure of proceedings, there is a clear German-Austrian influence, which is due to the academic prevalence of German authors and of "Germanized" Italian authors on Spanish scholarship. This influence started in the 1920s and kept growing. Of course, this is mixed with a strong tribute to the national legal tradition, which is more visible when analysing the roles of the judges and the parties, as well as the position of the legal profession (no bailiffs or *huissiers*, for instance, but rather *procuradores*). It also has, however, important repercussions on the proceedings, such as the role of preclusion, the inception of appeals as *revisio prioris instantiae* rather than as *novum iudicium*. In any event, the search for efficiency, and not "loyalty to the legal family" or to "tradition", has been a relevant factor in respect of reform; some comparatist "cherry-picking", therefore, can also be traced: the order for payment procedure, for instance, belongs to the Romanistic tradition as it has a documentary basis while the French *référé*

---

[3]See, among many other handbooks: de la Oliva Santos et al. (2017); de la Oliva Santos et al. (2016); Ortells Ramos (2017); Armenta Deu (2017); and Nieva Fenoll (2016). Statistical data in this paper have been retrieved from an official publication of the Spanish General Council of the Judiciary (Consejo General del Poder Judicial) appearing yearly, titled La Justicia Dato a Dato—The Spanish Judiciary in figures, published both in Spanish and in English. See http://www.poderjudicial.es/cgpj/es/Temas/Estadistica-Judicial/Estudios-e-Informes/Justicia-Dato-a-Dato/. Accessed 7 June 2018. I have used the data that appear in the 2016 report.

[4]See *Ley 60/2003, de 23 de diciembre, de Arbitraje*, for arbitration; *Ley 5/2012, de 6 de julio, de mediación en asuntos civiles y mercantiles*, for mediation; and *Ley 15/2015, de 2 de julio, de la Jurisdicción Voluntaria* (Arts. 139–148), for conciliation.

[5]See *Ley 22/2003, de 9 de julio, Concursal.*

proceedings, although initially proposed in earlier drafts, were rejected and a strict vision of the instrumentality of provisional and protective measures still prevails.

2.3 Overriding Principles

The new Code, as enacted in 2000, follows some general overriding principles, which need to be taken account of if it is to be understood properly.[6]

A lawyers' procedure Spanish procedure is, in general terms, a procedure meant to be used and driven by lawyers, not by laypeople. Legal representation is mandatory if the value of a claim exceeds €2000.[7] In practice, however, it is common to have lawyers in cases where the amount at stake is lower. Historical tradition and the high number of lawyers could be an explanation for this.

The number of practising lawyers in 2016 was 152,373, for a population of around 46 million; this means more than 300 lawyers for every 100,000 persons, whereas there are only 12.2 judges per 100,000 inhabitants,[8] and 26.8 lawyers per judge (The Spanish Judiciary in figures 2016, 12, 22).

In fact, in Spain litigants are required to act under the assistance of two different legal professionals (Arts. 23 and 31 LEC): a lawyer (*abogado*), who will sign the pleadings and is responsible for legal assistance in a broad sense; and a *procurador*, a specific representative for court proceedings,[9] who presents the written pleadings of the parties and receives any judicial notifications addressed to them. This is a feature of systems based on the Romano-canonical procedure, and it fulfils a role that in most modern jurisdictions is performed by lawyers; in practice, the generalization of electronic communications is putting into question the survival of *procuradores*, whose fees are starting to be perceived more and more as unjustified.

The number of *procuradores* in 2016 was 10,347 (The Spanish Judiciary in figures 2016, 22).

The Spanish way of understanding the principle of party disposition and judicial impartiality Spanish civil procedure places great weight and importance on the principles of party disposition and party autonomy (Article 216 LEC). They are understood in a very strict and rigid way, sometimes hard to explain to a foreign observer. This rigidity is especially visible regarding two issues.

(a) On the one hand, a claimant bears the burden of identifying not only the factual, but also the legal grounds sustaining the claim; as a consequence, the court is not allowed to change nor to amend them (Article 218.1 II LEC, Section VI of the preamble). The *iura novit curia* principle, hence, has a narrow scope of

[6]See de la Oliva Santos (2000); de la Oliva Santos (2012) and Montero Aroca (2001).

[7]Article 31 LEC.

[8]There were 5692 judges in Spain in 2016 (The Spanish Judiciary in figures 2016, 11).

[9]The document "The Spanish Judiciary in figures" uses the term "solicitor" in its English version to refer to *procuradores*, although there are relevant differences between both legal professionals.

application: the court may consider legal provisions different from those put forward by the claimant, but the legal grounds (i.e. the legal perspective) cannot be altered.[10] Consequently a claim founded on contract could not be granted by the court on the basis of tort. The real extent of this provision is still controversial, as there is, on occasion, a very fine line between different possible legal grounds (e.g. *culpa in eligendo* v. *culpa in vigilando* when attributing responsibility arising from the conduct of a third party or an employee). The same burden applies to the defendant's defences. Except where a contract is void or there is a nullity, legal grounds cannot be taken account of *ex officio* by the court if they have not been properly alleged by the defendant.

(b) On the other hand, when it comes to evidence, it is the exclusive prerogative of the parties to produce evidence and to propose the taking of evidence (Article 282 LEC). The court can by no means order, on its own motion, the taking of evidence, and this includes expert reports, or requiring the presentation of a specific document, except in proceedings that are not governed by the principle of party disposition e.g., some family law cases. The only active role the court can play at this point is to suggest to the parties the possible additional evidence to be produced (Article 429 LEC), although it remains for the parties to accept it. This "suggestion" occurs only infrequently.

It could be said that such a limitation on the evidentiary powers of the court, as well as to the possibility to change the legal grounds of a case, could entail unfair consequences. According to traditional Spanish legal thinking, however, the answer is different: the parties are expected to act under the guidance of a qualified lawyer, whose duty is to provide the correct legal ground or to submit, in the alternative, different possible legal grounds to the court, and the same applies to evidence. If the court could change the legal grounds of a claim on its own motion, or if it could order the taking of evidence on its own motion, it would be perceived as doing the lawyer's work. Worse than that it could be perceived to be correcting the lawyer's poor quality work. Under Spanish legal thinking, this would infringe the principle of judicial impartiality and fair proceedings.

Preclusion and procedural rigidity A strong role for preclusion is also one of the defining features of Spanish civil procedure. Again this leads to a very rigid procedural development.[11] The new Code establishes a fixed track for each kind of procedure, as well as the timing and the deadlines for each of the parts or elements of every procedure: the space left for real case management is therefore very small. The Code contains detailed provisions concerning the way in which the case management process can develop. Parties are not allowed to agree any amendment or variation of the case management process which would deviate from what is legally established, e.g., expanding the deadline for the defendant to submit the written answer to the claim, or establishing that the court will determine liability

[10]On this issue, see de la Oliva Santos (2005); Tapia Fernández (2000) and Ormazábal Sánchez (2007).

[11]See Vallines García (2004).

before it then may go to determine the claim's quantum. The approach is anything but flexible. Judicial thinking and judicial training help maintain this *status quo*. Judges are not expected to be creative, and many lawyers are also used to this way of proceeding. There is, therefore, no real challenge to this practice. Problems, however, may arise in cross-border litigation, as foreign actors might not expect this rigidity.

Great weight is also given to preclusion. A heavy burden is placed on parties to include all possible contentions of fact and of law in their initial written pleadings; any contention which would have been possible at that time will no longer be permitted at any subsequent stage of the proceedings, including the appeal phase) (Article 400 LEC). In the later stages of proceedings, only new or newly discovered facts, as well as new or newly discovered evidence, can be successfully introduced (Article 286 LEC). The purpose of this rigid preclusion is to prevent the parties from keeping contentions out of the proceedings and to force them to present their position in a clear and extensive manner. This is intended to facilitate an early disposition of the dispute, as each party will know at an early stage all the "weapons" in the hands of the opponent. It is also seen as a means to reinforce the relevance of first instance proceedings: contentions and arguments cannot be reserved for the superior court.

2.4 Main Innovations and the Structure of Contentious Civil Proceedings

The main purpose of the reform of Spanish civil procedure in 2000 was to reinforce the quality and relevance of first instance proceedings.

Under the previous regulation, contentious civil proceedings were in practice completely written and there was no real need for the judge to be present, or to make a real follow-up of the case until it was "mature" for decision; oral meetings were in practice replaced by written submissions; questioning parties and witnesses was done before judicial officers, on the basis of previously written questionnaires (allegedly approved by a judge); judicial deadlines were systematically not respected, not least the deadline to give judgment. As a result, judgments were always belated and their quality was perceived as poor, due to the reduced contact of the court with the subject matter of the case. This also explained the high rates of default proceedings, taking into account that default did not lead to an automatic upholding of the claim.

The new Code of Civil Procedure has tried to arrange the course of the proceedings, as well as the duties of the parties and judges, in order to put the first instance judge in the best possible position to render the best possible decision in the dispute at hand. The strict preclusive rule is kept, since it is helpful to achieve the goal of having all factual and legal elements of the dispute presented before the court of first instance. And the new structure of first instance proceedings also aims at involving the judge from the beginning with the development of the procedure; the judge is now somehow "forced" to have direct contact with the contentions of the parties and, in a very significant way, with all sorts of evidence.

One of the basic tools, given the starting point, was the introduction of a significant dose of orality into the course of the proceedings, with its associate principles of concentration and immediacy: the German model was followed to place the judge at the centre of the procedure, although, maybe paradoxically, with reduced case management powers.

The structure of contentious proceedings in the first instance is rather simple, if one analyses the main elements of ordinary proceedings.

To commence proceedings, the claimant will file a statement of claim with the competent court (Article 399 LEC). The statement of claim will have to be submitted in writing and, as mentioned, all relevant facts and legal grounds must be included (Article 400 LEC); otherwise they will be considered precluded and the claimant will not be able to introduce a new (parallel or successive) claim founded on facts and/or legal grounds that he/she could have included in the first claim.

Together with the statement of claim the claimant must produce all relevant documents (in a broad sense) for evidentiary purposes: documents, files, electronically stored information and written reports prepared by experts appointed by the claimant (Article 265 LEC).

The court will decide on the admissibility of the statement of claim (Articles 403 and 404 LEC). Inadmissibility can only be founded on procedural grounds, not on grounds linked to the merits of the case.

If the statement of claim is admissible, the court will immediately order that notice be served on the defendant, accompanied by a hard copy of the claim and of the documents produced with it. The defendant is granted a deadline of 20 working days to present a written response, accompanied by all relevant documents, electronically stored information and reports drafted by party-appointed experts (the party can also announce that they will produce them as soon as they are received, in the event the party shows reasonable grounds for not having been able to do so within the deadline of 20 days). The 20-day deadline is fixed: no additional time will be granted. Given the case, within ten working days after service, and prior to submitting the answer to the claim, the defendant can submit a special written motion to challenge the jurisdiction of the court (*declinatoria*) with suspensive effect on the main proceedings (Articles 63 to 65 LEC).

The next step will be a preliminary hearing (*audiencia previa al juicio*), to take place 20 days after receipt of the answer to the claim (Article 414 LEC), serving different purposes: to try to conciliate the parties; to decide on procedural defences (except those concerning jurisdiction); final definition of the scope of proceedings; proposal of evidence and judicial decision on admission of evidence. It is a very relevant element of the proceedings, and a very active involvement and management from the judge is expected.

Finally, a main hearing (*juicio*) will ordinarily be held a month after the closing of the preliminary hearing, where evidence will be elicited and the parties will submit final arguments in the case. The main hearing has to be concentrated, following the idea of the German *Hauptverhandlung*. In exceptional cases, evidence that could not be elicited during the main hearing will be taken separately.

The judgment will follow, within a deadline of 20 days.

If the value of the case does not exceed €6000 or the case relates to some specific matters (Article 250 LEC), the procedural track is simplified (*juicio verbal*): the deadline to present the written answer to the claim is reduced to ten days and no preliminary hearing will take place, so that most of the procedural activity will be concentrated in a single hearing, encompassing decisions on procedural issues, parties' proposals, admissibility and the taking of evidence.

In general terms, the structure of Spanish contentious civil proceedings consists of a combination of written and oral elements. Pleadings will always have to be presented in writing. From that point on, the procedure becomes oral and concentrated in order to ensure immediacy and direct contact of the judge with the evidence. Aware of past abuses, the legislator has introduced some measures to ensure that oral activity will not be replaced by written submissions.

In the first place, as a procedural safeguard the principle of immediacy is given significant weight. It is compulsory for a judge to be present at the hearing and only the judge who attended the hearing will be entitled to give judgment. Additionally, the Code specifies in a very clear manner the set of activities where the judge needs to be present: examination of parties, witnesses and experts; inspection of premises, objects or persons; and the exhibition of audio, video or data recordings. Any infringement of the rules on immediacy will lead to the nullity—totally or partially—of the proceedings (Article 137 LEC). If a judge has to be replaced during the proceedings, the possibility arises that a hearing will have to be repeated.

The rules on concentration also serve the purpose of preserving immediacy. Hearings have to take place on a single or consecutive days. Interruptions, for different reasons, are possible, of course. However, if the suspension of the hearing lasts longer than 20 days, it may have to be repeated from the beginning, in order to prevent the risk of evidence taken after resuming the proceedings from gaining more weight than evidence taken previously (Article 193 LEC).

Furthermore, there is an additional element, apparently more "innocent", which has, in practice, turned out to be a key element in the reform's success: the means to document and to leave a record of the hearings. Traditionally, the court clerk would draft the minutes of the hearing, which in practice were not always sufficiently accurate or detailed. The new Code now requires all hearings to be video-recorded (Articles 147 and 187 LEC); written minutes have indeed been suppressed and a written transcription of the recordings is also prohibited now (Article 230.3 of the Ley Orgánica del Poder Judicial, Act on the Judiciary). Although these last requirements might be arguable, video-recording has produced many beneficial results:

(i) Lawyers better prepare their presentations, and judges are also expected to have prepared the hearing properly. This is especially true of preliminary hearings.

(ii) Orality is real. Oral pleadings cannot be replaced with written submissions, as was unfortunately the rule for the rare hearings established under the older regulation.

(iii) Evidence other than documents and expert reports has been reinforced: examination of parties and factual witnesses is now normal and judges have got accustomed to seriously taking it into account; the oral explanation of expert reports has also become common practice, allowing these reports to be evaluated more effectively. When necessary, judges (re)view the recording in their offices when drafting the judgment, in order to better evaluate the evidence.

(iv) Control over the evaluation of evidence at the appeal stage is more feasible, although this is subject to obvious limitations e.g., watching a video-recording is not the same as having been present during the hearing.

(v) The principle of public proceedings has also been improved and reinforced: a judge is now not only facing lawyers, parties and the public during the hearing, but also any other competent authority entitled to view the recording in the future e.g., an appellate court or disciplinary board.

The new structure of the proceedings which imposes an immediate link between the judge and the facts and evidence of the case allows the Code to presume that the first instance decision is correct. The legislator shows such a level of trust in this conclusion that it has established the direct provisional enforceability of all judgments, without the need to present any sort of security. If requested by the winning party, the court will order enforcement even if an appeal has been or can still be lodged. The court cannot require security from the claimant, who is therefore free to decide whether or not to wait for the judgment to be final (Article 526 LEC).

The strict respect given to the rules on orality, ensured by the requirements mentioned, and the "faith" put by the lawmaker in the first instance lie in the clear improvement of the Spanish civil justice system after the reform, in terms of time and quality. The length of proceedings has clearly decreased, at least according to the statistics; and the number of first instance decisions against which an appeal is lodged is also more than acceptable.

As to the length of first instance proceedings, the average in 2016 varied, as shown in Table 1: 6.1 months in first instance courts, 4.6 months in family courts, and 7.3 months in first instance and enquiry courts (mixed jurisdictions for civil matters and the direction of the preliminary phase of criminal proceedings).[12]

As to the perceived quality of first instance judgments, as shown in Table 2, in 2016 only 13.3% of first instance judgments were appealed. The courts of appeal confirmed 67.5% of the decisions; 14.2% were totally revoked and 17.8% were partially revoked.

[12]The data for commercial courts seem alarming: 44.8 months. However, they relate only to insolvency proceedings, which overburdened those courts during the "heavy" years of economic downturn.

Table 1 Civil courts—average length in months of proceedings per year 2012–2016 (The Spanish Judiciary in figures 2016, 94)

Civil courts	2016	2015	2014	2013	2012
First instance courts	6.1	5.6	6.2	7.1	7.2
Family courts	4.6	4.7	4.5	4.7	4.6
First instance and enquiry courts	7.3	7.0	7.6	8.8	9.2
Commercial courts	44.8	41.6	40.0	38.1	34.8
Provincial courts	6.7	6.1	6.5	7.0	6.3
H.C.J.—civil and criminal chamber	4.6	4.6	4.7	4.7	5.8
High court—1st chamber	14.9	5.4	13.3	11.7	11.1

Table 2 Civil courts—appeals submitted and returned in 2016 (The Spanish Judiciary in figures 2016, 89)

Civil courts	Appeals submitted higher court/judgments (%)	Upheld (%)	Appeals returned in the year		
			Reversed fully (%)	Revoked partially (%)	Remitted (%)
First instance courts and first instance enquiry courts	13.3	67.5	14.2	17.8	0.5
Commercial courts	13.6	59.8	18.5	20.2	1.6
Provincial courts	7.2	82.7	12.7	4.2	0.5

Apart from the rationalization of civil proceedings, the other main innovation in this field was the introduction of the order for payment procedure (*proceso monitorio*), which was unknown previously. The percentage of civil cases where the defendant did not take part in the proceedings was unsustainable (38.6% according to the statistics published in 1997).[13] Such system-inefficiency and the fact that default did not lead to the automatic success of the claimant explains why so many defendants did not even make the effort to react. The possibility of introducing default judgments according to the German or French model was dismissed due to reasons of legal culture. The alternative solution was the order for payment procedure, which, once introduced very quickly, absorbed almost half of civil litigation. Again, taking account of legal culture, the Italian document-based approach was taken as the model. Some technicalities and, more specifically, the consequences of the European Court of Justice (ECJ) judgment in the *Banco Español de*

[13] In the so-called *Libro Blanco de la Justicia*, approved by the Spanish General Council of the Judiciary, p 67.

Crédito case[14] have, however, had a negative impact on this procedure, and it is now regarded with a certain degree of mistrust.

In 2016, there were 1,868,228 new cases before the Spanish civil courts; 537,054 of them were order for payment procedures (around 35% of the whole number) (The Spanish Judiciary in figures 2016, 38, 65).

In addition to this, the new Code provided a systematic set of rules concerning provisional and protective measures, with common provisions on the prerequisites and the procedure to grant them (Article 721 ff. LEC). The type and number of possible measures is flexible (*numerus apertus*), although a range of typical measures which are considered suitable and effective for certain kinds of claims is specified. There are, however, two main differences—perhaps shortcomings—with other neighbouring legal systems on this point.

(i) As regards content: as a rule, provisional payments are not permitted (i.e. there were no pecuniary *Leistungsverfügung*, *kort geding* or *référé-provision* under Spanish procedural law).
(ii) As regards instrumentality: the problem here is, once again, a lack of flexibility concerning the relationship between the provisional measure and the proceeding on the merits, since it is mandatory for the applicant to file a claim on the merits if the measures were granted *ante demandam* (Article 730.2 LEC). A more flexible approach e.g., the German or Italian way, could have been more useful, especially in the case of provisional injunctions.

Of course, the system is far from being perfect, especially when it comes to putting it into practice with those human and financial resources that are available. From the point of view of legal design, it could be said that the Spanish civil justice system is quite fit for "middle-class" litigation: average civil and commercial disputes can be resolved reasonably well, and at reasonable cost, with more than acceptable "value for money"; it is a "highway" rather than a "motorway" or "freeway". One of its main features, the rigidity or the lack of flexibility, causes no real difficulties in average cases, always bearing in mind that such an approach belongs to the Spanish procedural legal culture. This rigidity may, however turn out to be more problematic for complex litigation and, within it, for cross-border cases and for collective redress.

2.5 Main Innovations and Structure of Enforcement Proceedings

The other pillar of the reconstruction of Spanish civil justice in 2000 is the aim of improving the efficacy of enforcement proceedings. This was one of the areas in which litigants showed a high rate of dissatisfaction. In everyday life, indeed, there

[14]Judgment of 14 June 2012, C-618/10, *Banco Español de Crédito*, ECLI:EU:C:2012:349.

is a traditional curse, which is very hard to translate into English, wishing someone to win a lawsuit (*pleitos tengas y los ganes*)[15]: the frustration that will appear when trying to enforce the judgment will overcome the feeling of victory i.e., you will be left with the feeling of having obtained a pyrrhic victory.

In 2016, 523,978 new enforcement proceedings were commenced, 678,754 were terminated with 1,987,702 remaining unresolved at the end of the year (The Spanish Judiciary in figures 2016, 38).

In 2000, the legislator introduced some reforms in order to improve the effectiveness of enforcement proceedings. One of the main fields addressed was the location of the debtor's assets, with stronger duties being placed on debtors and third parties to co-operate with each other (Arts. 589 to 591 LEC). Over the past few years information and communication technologies (ICT) have also been introduced, so that court officers, from their computers, are able to have immediate access to information coming from banks, social security and, of course, tax authorities. Additional improvements were also made to the development of enforcement proceedings, suppressing unnecessary formalism in the process of seizing and selling assets; with additional improvements to this aspect of procedure also coming from greater use of ICT. Since 2015 it is been compulsory for all judicial auctions to take place online, using a specific official platform, with a system similar to the one first initiated by eBay[16]: the aim here is to secure as much publicity as possible, in order to obtain the highest possible number of offers. A flexible regulation for the enforcement of non-pecuniary claims was also introduced, which was missing in the old code of civil procedure.

The measures taken in this field are limited by strong judicial participation in enforcement proceedings, which is established at a constitutional level. It is mainly the court's task to enforce judgments; *huissiers de justice* or bailiffs do not exist as such, although some hints of privatization are beginning to appear. On the one hand, the Code permits seized assets to be sold by private entities, if the court so orders upon application by the parties (Article 641 LEC): this could be suitable for the sale of valuable immovable property or works of art, but it is not as frequently used in practice as could be expected. On the other hand, there is a trend to transform the Spanish *procuradores* into something similar to the French *huissiers de justice*, although the difficulties in implementing this should not be underestimated (*procuradores* are not public authorities, but private legal professionals).

The constraints arising from the presence of the judge and the court clerk as the central actors in the enforcement process sometimes undermine the efficacy of the enforcement process, particularly from the creditor's point of view, but they are also to be seen as procedural safeguards benefitting the judgment debtor. Paradoxically, the European Court of Justice's case law has recently criticized the

[15]According to the *Instituto Cervantes*, an English translation could be: "Let's hope you have lawsuits, and that you win them" (https://cvc.cervantes.es/lengua/refranero/Ficha.aspx?Par=59297&Lng=0). Accessed 7 June 2018.

[16]The following link will lead to that platform: https://subastas.boe.es/. Accessed 7 June 2018.

protection granted to the debtor in the context of enforcement proceedings, when they are consumers and the enforceable title is a notarial deed or a mortgage. The ECJ judgment in the *Aziz* case, and many others,[17] has put pressure on the Spanish legislator, requiring amendments to be made to the structure of enforcement proceedings in order to enable *ex officio* and *ex parte* control of possible unfair contractual terms.[18]

3 What Has Come Afterwards?

One could expect that such a major reform, as the one experienced in 2000, would be followed by a period of relative tranquillity, which would allow the new system to get progressively adopted and assumed by all legal operators. The transition was both short and successful, probably for one reason: in the years prior to the new Code entering into force the public budget still allowed for the appointment of new and additional judges, so there were many first instance judges—the main addressees of the reform—who were relatively young, unaccustomed to the previous ways of administering civil justice, and were very enthusiastic about the new system. Lawyers offered more resistance during the Code's drafting process, but had no other option than to adapt. Extensive training was offered and provided to judges and lawyers during the *vacatio legis* period, which lasted one year.

The expected tranquillity did not last long, if it ever really arrived: the civil justice system still experiences transformations, which are occurring quite quickly, and it is still not certain whether the reform is moving in a clear and positive direction. This has caused scholars, lawyers and judges to forget that the system is still new; they deal with it as though it has already grown old.

[17]The leading case law can be found in the Judgment of 14 March 2013, C-415/11, *Aziz* (ECLI:EU:C:2013:164), followed by the Order of 14 November 2011, C-537/12, *Banco Popular Español* (ECLI:EU:C:2013:759); and in the Judgment of 17 July 2014, C-169/14, *Sánchez Morcillo and Abril García* (ECLI:EU:C:2014:2099), followed by the Order of 16 July 2015, C-539/14, *Sánchez Morcillo and Abril García* (ECLI:EU:C:2015:508).

[18]This adaptation to the ECJ case law was not performed at one time, but through four different acts amending the Code: (i) *Ley 1/2013, de 14 de mayo, de medidas para reforzar la protección a los deudores hipotecarios, reestructuración de deuda y alquiler social* (just two months after the ECJ *Aziz* Judgment); (ii) *Ley 8/2013, de 26 de junio, de rehabilitación, regeneración y renovación urbanas*; (iii) *Real Decreto-ley 11/2014, de 5 de septiembre, de medidas urgentes en materia concursal* (once again, two months after the ECJ *Sánchez Morcillo* Judgment, followed by *Ley 9/2015, de 25 de mayo, de medidas urgentes en materia concursal*; (iv) and *Ley 42/2015, de 5 de octubre, de reforma de la Ley 1/2000, de 7 de enero, de Enjuiciamiento Civil* (as a belated answer to the ECJ *Banco Español de Crédito* Judgment).

3.1 Context

The most recent transformations that are now affecting the evolution of civil justice can only be understood if they are properly put into context. This context is defined by, at least, four relevant elements.

3.1.1 Economic Downturn

As from 2008, and more acutely from 2011, the Spanish economy suffered one of the most severe downturns in recent history. Many financial entities needed to be rescued due to the negative impact of the "housing bubble burst"; public revenues fell sharply and deep budget cuts had to be adopted. In short, less money for (public) justice.

3.1.2 Case Overload

Budget cuts reduced the capability of the system to continue to process cases at the same pace as before. The fact is, however, that over the last few years there has been a huge overload of civil cases due to the economic crisis. On the one hand, many private households could not repay their debts, and creditors—mostly banks—lodged enforcement claims that, in many cases, ended up with the bank acquiring the ownership of the house as nobody would buy it: instead of getting cash, the banks found themselves with a huge "stock of brick" while, at the same time, enforcement proceedings overburdened the court system. Additionally, mass-cases appeared, linked to the mis-selling of financial products: entrepreneurial law firms induced hundreds of thousands of consumers to litigate against the banks, on the basis of unfair contractual terms provisions, to recover the losses from ruinous investments, allegedly induced by aggressive and misleading bank activity. In short, extra work for the courts, with fewer resources, and with legal difficulties, to handle mass-cases.

The graph in Fig. 1 shows the evolution in the number of new cases lodged with Spanish civil courts during the last ten years and the impact of the economic situation.

More specifically, the information in Table 3 shows the impact of the downturn on the number of mortgage enforcement proceedings (much higher during the "hard" years and progressively diminishing as the situation evolved positively).

3.1.3 Staff Difficulties and Internal Organization of Courts

The traditional structure of Spanish civil courts included, besides the judge, a court clerk (*secretario judicial*) whose main function was "giving faith" to judicial

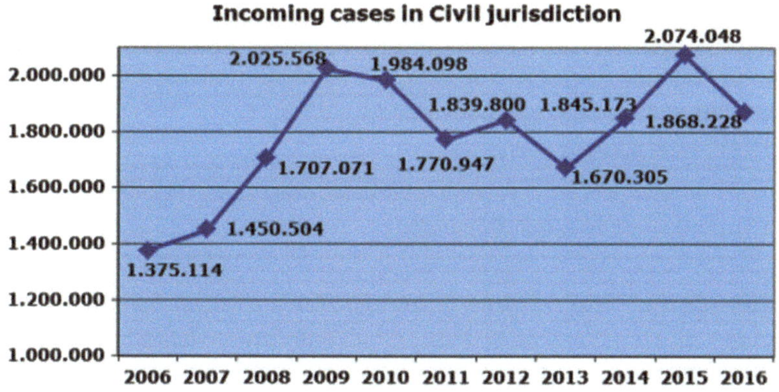

Fig. 1 Number of new cases in civil courts (The Spanish Judiciary in figures 2016, 48)

Table 3 Number of mortgage enforcement proceedings 2007–2016

2007	2008	2009	2010	2011	2012	2013	2014	2015	2016
25,943	58,686	93,319	93,636	77,854	91,622	82,688	80,785	68,165	48,410

These data have been retrieved from a different document, *Estadística sobre Ejecuciones Hipotecarias*, also available at the website of the General Council of the Judiciary: http://www.poderjudicial.es/cgpj/es/Temas/Estadistica-Judicial/Estadistica-por-temas/Datos-penales–civiles-y-laborales/Civil-y-laboral/Estadistica-sobre-Ejecuciones-Hipotecarias/. Accessed 7 June 2018

activity and, of course, helping the judge during the course of proceedings. Court clerks are law graduates who have passed a difficult state examination. They are perhaps overqualified and, perhaps for that reason, in practice judges entrusted them with some of their own tasks e.g., certain tasks relating to enforcement proceedings. The new Code of Civil Procedure, however, placed the judge at the centre of the procedure and also reduced the relevance of the "giving faith" task, due to the mandatory video-recording of hearings. What then should be the role of the court clerk? A feeling of collective frustration among court clerks led to a collective claim to be assigned additional functions, and, of course, remuneration (De Benito Llopis-Llombart 2017b).

3.1.4 European "Pressure" on the System

Several ECJ rulings have criticized Spanish civil procedure, mostly from the perspective of Council Directive 93/13 on unfair terms in consumer contracts.[19] They

[19]Apart from the decisions already mentioned in n. 18 above and 22 below, see also Judgment of 6 October 2009, C-40/08, *Asturcom Telecomunicaciones* (ECLI:EU:C:2009:615), on *ex officio* control of unfair contract terms during the enforcement of arbitral awards; Judgment of 3 October 2013, C-32/12, *Duarte Hueros* (ECLI:EU:C:2013:637); Judgment of 5 December 2013, C-413/12,

have done so as, apparently, Spanish procedural provisions do not leave sufficient room for the effective application of EU consumer protection legislation; the "neutral" and rather "passive" position of the judge, as well as the rules on preclusion, have therefore been questioned by the ECJ.

3.2 Consequences and Remedies

As can be imagined, too many obstacles exist for a peaceful transition to a more effective model. The responses to those stimuli have caused important malfunctions and shortcomings.

3.2.1 Court Clerks and the "*Dépeçage*" of the Procedure

Problems relating to court clerks have been resolved, at least in my opinion, in the worst possible manner. A very subtle distinction—a sophisticated one, in my view and in the view of many others[20]—was proposed, between "strict judicial" tasks and "mere procedural" decisions. The former remain the responsibility of judges e.g., resolving controversial issues during proceedings and, of course, giving judgment. The latter, however, can be handled by other qualified officers, that is, court clerks. A very significant reform in 2009[21] put this distinction into practice, opening the door to many difficulties that still hinder the structure of civil proceedings.

Asociación de Consumidores Independientes de Castilla y León (ECLI:EU:C:2013:800); Judgment of 21 January 2015, C-482/13, *Unicaja Banco* (ECLI:EU:C:2015:21); Order of 11 June 2015, C-602/13, *Banco Bilbao Vizcaya Argentaria* (ECLI:EU:C:2015:397); Judgment of 29 October 2015, C-8/14, *BBVA* (ECLI:EU:C:2015:731); Judgment of 18 February 2016, C-49/14, *Finanmadrid EFC* (ECLI:EU:C:2016:98); Order of 8 July 2015, C-90/14, *Banco Grupo Cajatres* (ECLI:EU:C:2015:465); Judgment of 14 April 2016, C-381/14, *Sales Sinués* (ECLI:EU:C:2016:252), addressing the relationship between collective and individual proceedings; Order of 21 June 2016, C-122/14, *Aktiv Kapital Portfolio* (ECLI:EU:C:2016:486); Judgment of 26 January 2017, C-421/14, *Banco Primus* (ECLI:EU:C:2017:60); Order of 26 October 2016, C-568/14, *Fernández Oliva* (ECLI:EU:C:2016:828), criticizing that provisional measures cannot be granted ex *officio* by civil courts in cases dealing with unfair contract terms; Order of 17 March 2016, C-613/15, *Ibercaja Banco* (ECLI:EU:C:2016:195). This large number of decisions shows how Spanish courts of instance had no confidence in the Spanish Supreme Court to provide a reasonable interpretation on EU consumer protective statutes, and instead submitted requests for preliminary rulings to the ECJ; the inherent criticism directed towards superior courts, however, is not always justified.

[20]See Banacloche Palao (2009); Blasco Soto (2010) and de Benito Llopis-Llombart (2017b).

[21]See *Ley 13/2009, de 3 de noviembre, de reforma de la legislación procesal para la implantación de la nueva Oficina judicial*, which amended all procedural codes (not only the civil procedural code).

(i) The tasks assigned to the court clerks have greatly exceeded the mere organization of proceedings: for instance, it is for them to declare whether statements of claim are admissible but not to rule that they are inadmissible; that can only be done by a judge; putting an end to the procedure if the case ceases to be contentious or if the claimant abandons the proceeding, provided there is no objection from the parties; setting aside a provisional measure if the claimant has not filed the claim within the established deadline and ordering them to reimburse the defendant for all losses and damages. Enforcement proceedings must be formally opened by the judge but, afterwards, the court clerk will be fully in charge, unless the debtor or a third party raises an objection. This means, in practice, that the clerk takes important material decisions such as, for instance, the distribution of what remains of the proceeds after an asset has been sold and the judgment creditor has been paid.

(ii) Judicial control over the clerk's decisions is not completely clear; some decisions, indeed, were intended to remain out of judicial control, but the Constitutional Court has already stated that such provisions are unconstitutional, although no legal amendment has been drawn up to correct the wording on this point.[22]

(iii) The fact that procedure is divided into two parts: in the 2000 procedural model the judge was meant to be at the centre of the procedure, as a means to ensure direct contact with the case from the very beginning. The new situation splits the procedure into two parts and the judge is excluded from the initial one: his first contact does not take place any longer at the phase of the initial admissibility check, but later on, at the preliminary hearing.

(iv) Last, but not least, the fact that court clerks are not independent: they have been organized following a hierarchical structure that ends up at the Ministry of Justice, which is authorized to address orders, instructions and protocols on the interpretation of procedural rules. This fact, indeed, has led the ECJ to rule that they cannot be considered "courts or tribunals" in the sense of Article 267 TFEU in order to submit requests for preliminary rulings.[23]

It is difficult to explain to a foreign observer how this parochialism and corporatism have hindered the functioning of the civil justice system, but it has happened and lawyers have the feeling they now have to deal with two different authorities which are not always well coordinated between them, so there is a feeling of more uncertainty than before. In addition, court clerks have not received the social consideration they expected and, more significantly, they have not received an increase in salary that they thought they deserved, so the underlying problem—an "identity" problem—remains unsolved: in 2015 they were given a new name, *Letrados de la Administración de Justicia*, much more grandiloquent, but nothing more than that.

---

[22]See Banacloche Palao (2016).

[23]Judgment of 16 February 2017, C-503/15, *Margarit Panicello* (ECLI:EU:C:2017:126).

3.2.2 Financial Issues and Case Overload: Dejudicialization

Financial issues and case overload difficulties have been tackled together, with solutions that present light and shadow. Two "mottos" or "slogans" have been disseminated by the government over the last few years:

First, "Spanish society has a culture that sticks too much to formalized litigation as the best way to solve disputes"; and this is a trend that should be corrected. There is a kernel of truth in this assertion; but it also shows the confidence of civil society in the court system, which is a basic foundation for the legitimacy of the system itself.

Secondly, "It is not possible to allocate more resources to the court system" (the official version) or "It is not worth allocating more resources to the court system, considered as old-fashioned and inefficient" (the unofficial version). These assertions may not be totally fair if we take account of the large amounts of money that are being invested in the implementation of e-Justice systems and in the digitalization of proceedings. But the fact is, e-Justice seems to attract the lion's share of expenditure, leaving human and other material resources quite disregarded. The official way of thinking, with its pros and cons, has entailed a number of actions, some of which belong to current trends in the European context.

Court Fees

A simple solution to the financial issue was, from 2012, the introduction of court fees as a means of securing additional resources.[24] The Act introducing them specified that these resources should, in turn, be dedicated to help sustain the national legal aid system and the implementation of e-Justice. This reform was very controversial: in 2015 fees were prohibited for natural persons, albeit they remained permissible for legal persons; while, in 2016 the Constitutional Court declared them partially unconstitutional.[25]

In 2014, before they were partially prohibited, €297 million in fee income was generated; in 2015, the year they were partially prohibited, this amount declined to €206 million; and in 2016, the first complete year when the partial prohibition was in force, income generation further declined to only €117 million (The Spanish Judiciary in figures 2016, 32).

[24]See *Ley 10/2012, de 20 de noviembre, por la que se regulan determinadas tasas en el ámbito de la Administración de Justicia y del Instituto Nacional de Toxicología y Ciencias Forenses*; the step was first taken by *Real Decreto-ley 1/2015, de 27 de febrero, de mecanismo de segunda oportunidad, reducción de carga financiera y otras medidas de orden social*, eventually enacted as *Ley 25/2015, de 28 de julio, de mecanismo de segunda oportunidad, reducción de la carga financiera y otras medidas de orden social.*

[25]Judgment of the Spanish Constitutional Court 140/2016 of 21 July 2016.

ADR

Another option, of course, has been the promotion of ADR mechanisms in order to reduce the court's caseload. The idea is positive in itself, but fostering arbitration and mediation has been presented as a pretext to justify lack of investment in the proper functioning of the court system. For instance, the ratio of judges to citizens in Spain remains very low: 12.2 judges per 100,000 inhabitants. The budget for the administration of justice in respect of GDP is also low: 0.33%. And so is the budget for the administration of justice per inhabitant: €78.90 (The Spanish Judiciary in figures 2016, 13, 29). Notwithstanding ADR's promotion it is important to note, however, that this trend has not been particularly successful in achieving its aims.

Arbitration, on the one hand, has only succeeded in its natural and predictable domain: high-value commercial cases. Consumer arbitration also has its scope of application, but it remains limited. The experience of arbitration in financial products cases has been disappointing, at least from the consumer's perspective: arbitral awards have been more favourable to financial litigants than to the consumer. Additionally, Spain exceeded by much the deadline to implement the 2013 Directive on Consumer ADR,[26] which demonstrates the weak commitment governmental authorities have to their own slogans.

Mediation, on the other hand, should have benefitted from the momentum associated with the implementation of the 2008 Directive. As happened in almost all EU Member States, the Directive's implementation was used to present mediation as the panacea for many civil and commercial disputes. Many legal provisions have been enacted or modified in order to make this possible: discontinuing civil proceedings to make mediation feasible; granting mediation agreements the value of enforceable titles; offering training to become mediators; and so on. More coercive measures, such as, for instance, mandatory mediation as endorsed by the ECJ in the *Alassini* and *Menini* cases,[27] have not been envisaged. The figures, nevertheless, continue to be disappointing. Mediation does not seem to be flourishing in Spanish soil.

Mediation has also started to play a role in the field of family law, where the number of cases redirected to court-annexed mediation has been rising[28]: 1642 cases in 2009; 2242 in 2010; 3206 in 2011; 3608 in 2012; 3736 in 2013; 5723 in 2014; 7485 in 2015; and 7336 in 2016. In the rest of civil matters, only 567 cases were redirected to court-annexed mediation in 2016.

---

[26]Through *Ley 7/2017, de 2 de noviembre, por la que se incorpora al ordenamiento jurídico español la Directiva 2013/11/UE, del Parlamento Europeo y del Consejo, de 21 de mayo de 2013, relativa a la resolución alternativa de litigios en materia de consumo*.

[27]See Judgment of 18 March 2010, C-317/08, *Alassini and Others* (ECLI:EU:C:2010:146) and Judgment of 14 June 2017, C-75/16, *Menini and Rampanelli* (ECLI:EU:C:2017:457).

[28]The information is also provided by the General Council of the Judiciary on its website http://www.poderjudicial.es/cgpj/es/Temas/Estadistica-Judicial/Estadistica-por-temas/Medios-alternativos-de-resolucion-de-conflictos/Mediacion-Intrajudicial/. Accessed 7 June 2018.

Dejudicialization of Some Proceedings

The workload of courts can also be reduced through the dejudicialization of proceedings where they can be carried out by other public bodies or officers. This trend can be seen in three main areas.

Non-contentious Proceedings

As an additional way to relieve pressure on the court system, the 2015 Act on Voluntary Jurisdiction has attempted to dejudicialize as many proceedings as possible, where there is no real dispute, where judicial involvement was simply justified on historical grounds, and where some "public authority" is necessary for certain acts to be legally acceptable, e.g. adoption, redefining the borders of a property or validating a handwritten testament, among many others. The 2015 Act provides that only those non-contentious proceedings most directly linked to the personal status of natural persons and to family law should still be handled by a judge. The rest, which constitute a very long list of matters, are assigned to court clerks, notaries or public officers in charge of the land registers or other public registers. The aim is very reasonable: to reduce the workload of the judiciary. But it must be noted that in practice such matters were not too burdensome[29]; additionally, in many cases the competence of court clerks, notaries and land registrars to deal with the matter is an alternative form of procedure that the applicant can elect to use, thus it can be expected that many cases remain inside the court system, although no longer in the hands of the judge, since they will be less expensive.

Divorce and Separation Proceedings

These proceedings were traditionally in the hands of judges and form part of the civil justice caseload. From 2015, when both spouses agree (i.e., there is no underlying dispute) and there are no minor children or persons with a reduced legal capacity dependent on their parents, such proceedings are either assigned to a court clerk or to a notary. The judge is, therefore, excluded. The task of both authorities is limited to ascertaining that the divorce agreement is not to the detriment of any of the spouses, or of any affected adult children. If that is the case, the court clerk or the notary will end the procedure and the parties will have to submit the application to a judge. The potential reach of this measure is still unclear, as official statistics do not distinguish cases that take into account the presence of minors or children who otherwise lack capacity.[30]

---

[29]In 2015, the number of new cases was 60,861 (The Spanish Judiciary in figures 2015, 62). The 2016 report shows a much higher number of new non-contentious proceedings: 116,944 (The Spanish Judiciary in figures 2016, 67). The report explains that as from 2016 the statistics include among the notion of non-contentious proceedings settlements before court clerks.

[30]In 2016, there were 71,101 new cases of undisputed divorce or separation, against 48,758 new contentious proceedings (The Spanish Judiciary in figures 2016, 66).

Order for Payment Procedure

In 2009, with the above-mentioned distribution of tasks between judges and court clerks, the order for payment procedure was put in the hands of the court clerks, except where the clerk considered that the document presented together with the application was not sufficient proof of the claim. In such circumstances the clerk could not refuse the application, but had to refer it to a judge, who should determine the matter (Article 815 LEC). In 2015, another step was taken: as an alternative to the court system, the creditor could also apply to a notary to issue an order for payment, with similar effects (Arts. 70 and 71 of the Notaries Act).[31] The application is equivalent in its scope to that of the judicial order for payment procedure: a claim for payment of a specific sum of money that has fallen due and that has some documentary support. There is, however, a very important limitation. This notarial procedure cannot be used to collect monetary claims where the debtor is a consumer and the creditor a business entity. Its process is similar to the judicial process: the notary will require the debtor to pay within a deadline of 20 working days, and three possibilities are open: payment; opposition, which is not formalistic and leads to the termination of proceedings; and default, in which case the notary will draft a document that is granted direct enforceability, in equivalent terms to those granted to a notarial deed.

The legislator has through introducing this process created an alternative "privatized" procedure. This process may be more expensive, although not necessarily so, as no lawyer is needed and no court fees should be paid by creditors who are legal persons; but it should be much faster and more efficient (the current case overload does not help in having a speedy processing of orders for payment). It will be the creditor's choice to opt for one or the other way.

Anything to Resolve Mass Litigation?

No procedural means have been taken to resolve mass litigation. It remains a minefield in Spanish civil litigation. The Spanish Code of Civil Procedure includes a system of collective redress based on the standing of consumer associations and other representative entities to file injunctions as well as compensatory claims to protect the rights and interests of consumers affected by a harmful event (Article 11 LEC). It is a form of mandatory collective action, where individuals are not provided with an express right to opt-out, although notice is required to file the claim and they are allowed to intervene in the proceedings to secure a better defence of their individual position (Article 15 LEC). According to Article 222 LEC, individuals will be bound by the *res judicata* effect of the judgment, even if they did not take part in the proceedings. This sort of collective redress is, however, not used very frequently in practice. This is so because consumer associations do not always commence proceedings due to funding issues. Additionally, many of the cases that

[31] *Ley del Notariado de 28 de mayo de 1862.*

have led to consumer mass litigation recently have not been considered appropriate for collective redress, as the assessment of the unfairness and voidness of a contractual term depends on the specific circumstances of each case and each claimant.

Two further measures have been considered to deal with mass litigation:

(i) Court Specialization. From 1 January 2017 in some judicial districts certain courts of first instance have been specialized to handle cases linked to consumer financial disputes and unfair contractual terms. It is important to note that those are not collective claims, but a multitude of single claims or claims involving joinder of actions.[32]

(ii) A sort of pre-action protocol has also been established in order to foster the settlement of cases involving the presence of unfair contractual terms in mortgage-backed loans, before they arrive at court (banks are forced to make some offers to their clients and a preliminary proceeding should also be available).[33] It is still too early to assess the impact of this measure, although the high rate of litigation in this field is not a good symptom.

3.2.3 European "Pressure" on Civil Procedure

As mentioned earlier, the case law of the ECJ has questioned the adequacy of some rules and principles of Spanish civil procedure in respect of EU law. There are several concerns, at least in my view, regarding the way the ECJ was informed of the way in which Spanish civil procedure actually operates before it took some of its decisions (this is, however, a topic for a different paper).[34]

The main focus of the reaction, however, has been concentrated on how to deal with enforcement and with specific proceedings concerning consumer protection that arise from Council Directive 93/13 on unfair terms in consumer contracts. And the visible results have been a number of relevant reforms to the Code of Civil Procedure.

On the one hand, debtors in enforcement proceedings concerning mortgage-backed loans or notarial deeds (i.e. non-judicial enforceable titles) will always be given the opportunity to challenge enforcement; the challenge being based on a claim that it arose from unfair contractual terms.[35] This was not possible

[32]In their first three months of functioning, these specialized courts have received more than 57,000 new claims, according to press releases issued by the General Council of the Judiciary.

[33]See *Real Decreto-ley 1/2017, de 20 de enero, de medidas urgentes de protección de consumidores en materia de cláusulas suelo*.

[34]The clearest example can be found in the Judgment of 3 October 2013, C-32/12, *Duarte Hueros* (ECLI:EU:C:2013:637), where criticisms to the rule on preclusion of Article 400 LEC were founded on a serious misrepresentation of its wording and meaning.

[35]Arts. 557.1.7 LEC and 695.1.4 LEC after the 2013 reform (put into effect by the *Ley 1/2013, de 14 de mayo, de medidas para reforzar la protección a los deudores hipotecarios, reestructuración de deuda y alquiler social*).

before the reform, where such a challenge could not be raised within the enforcement proceeding itself and had to be postponed to a parallel or subsequent declaratory proceedings. On the other hand, additional reforms have been introduced in order to put into place *ex officio* control over the existence of potential unfair contractual terms:

(i) in enforcement proceedings based on notarial deeds and in mortgage enforcement proceedings: before ordering the commencement of enforcement proceeding against a consumer, the judge has to ensure that no unfair contractual terms form the basis of the debt to be collected; if any doubt arises, a preliminary hearing will be arranged to determine this question (Article 552.1 LEC). This appears to result in a higher rate of opposition in such proceedings and a reduced effectiveness in terms of time;

(ii) a similar device has been introduced in the order for payment procedure: if the creditor is a business entity and the debtor a consumer, the court clerk must defer the decision whether to issue the application to a judge, who will in turn analyse whether there is any potential unfair contractual term adduced in the grounds of the claim. If there is, a hearing will be held (Article 815.4 LEC). In practice, the effectiveness of the procedure has again been reduced. Furthermore, this pre-emptive protection of consumer debtors explains the above-mentioned limitations on the notarial order for payment.

4 Balance

The purpose of this contribution was modest. It sought to familiarize the reader with the way in which Spanish civil procedure has evolved over the last 20 years. It has done so because this has been a period of significant transformation, both negative and positive, as can be seen from the two trends illustrated in the foregoing.

Initially, there was a very optimistic trend, aimed at reforming civil proceedings *stricto* sensu. This adhered to a very careful assessment of the situation, a clear definition of the aims, and a reasonable definition and legal enactment of the tools to achieve them. Of course, political issues were at stake and legal political decisions were taken, which can be considered as positive or negative, according to the personal position of the observer: a rigid procedure, carefully managed by the judge, based in turn on the activities of the parties' lawyers. But the reform that concluded with the enactment of the 2000 LEC was the result of a well-designed plan.

Subsequent events have led to a different trend: dejudicialization in a broad sense. This is a sensitive idea, at least in some fields and for some purposes. My feeling is that we are rushing in this direction in a more improvised manner, imposed by the force of circumstances. Reflection and public discussion of this policy—and of the consequences it might entail—are unfortunately missing. Civil justice and dispute resolution are too serious to be left to the pressures of externalities and to the need to give urgent solutions to minor problems, as has recently been the case.

References

Armenta Deu T (2017) Lecciones de Derecho Procesal Civil, 10th edn. Marcial Pons, Madrid-Barcelona
Banacloche Palao J (2009) El proyecto de nueva oficina judicial: ¿hacia un nuevo proceso administrativizado? Diario La Ley 7251
Banacloche Palao J (2016) Todas las resoluciones de los Letrados de la Administración de Justicia son revisables en todas las jurisdicciones. La inevitable extensión de la STC 58/2016, de 17 de marzo. Diario La Ley 8779
Blasco Soto MC (2010) La nueva estructura (o desestructura) del proceso: La admisión de la demanda en el proceso civil (Ley 13/2009 de 3 de noviembre). Diario La Ley 7325
Borrajo Iniesta I, Fernández Farreres G, Díez-Picazo Giménez I (1995) El derecho a la tutela judicial y el recurso de amparo: una reflexión sobre la jurisprudencia constitucional. Civitas, Madrid
Cachón Cadenas M (2012) Historias de procesalistas, universidades y una guerra civil (1900–1950). Universidad Carlos III de Madrid, Madrid
De Benito Llopis-Llombart M (2017a) Civil cassation in Spain: past, present, and future. In: van Rhee CH, Fu Y (eds) Supreme courts in transition in China and the West. Adjudication at the service of public goals, Springer, pp 97–130
De Benito Llopis-Llombart M (2017b) Justicia o burocracia. Civitas, Madrid
De la Oliva Santos A (2000) Sobre la Ley 1/2000, de 7 de enero, de Enjuiciamiento Civil: criterios inspiradores e innovaciones principals. Tribunales de Justicia 2:127–141
De la Oliva Santos A (2005) Objeto del proceso y cosa juzgada en el proceso civil. Civitas, Madrid
De la Oliva Santos A (2012) El papel del juez en el proceso civil. Civitas, Madrid
De la Oliva Santos A, Fernández MA (1995) Derecho Procesal Civil, II, 4th edn. Centro de Estudios Ramón Areces, Madrid
De la Oliva Santos A, Díez-Picazo Giménez I, Vegas Torres J (2016) Curso de Derecho Procesal Civil Civil II. Parte Especial, 3rd edn. Ed Univ Ramón Areces, Madrid
De la Oliva Santos A, Díez-Picazo Giménez I, Vegas Torres J (2017) Curso de Derecho Procesal Civil I. Parte General. 3rd edn. Ed Univ Ramón Areces, Madrid
Díez-Picazo Giménez I (1999) La reforma necesaria del proceso civil. Tribunales de Justicia 2:79–92
Fairén Guillén V (1953) El juicio ordinario y los plenarios rápidos. Bosch, Barcelona
Montero Aroca J (1982) Análisis crítico de la Ley de Enjuiciamiento Civil en su centenario. Civitas, Madrid
Montero Aroca J (1996) La Ley de Enjuiciamiento Civil española de 1855. La consolidación del proceso común. Ensayos de Derecho Procesal, Bosch, Barcelona
Montero Aroca J (2001) Los principios políticos de la nueva Ley de enjuiciamiento civil. Los poderes del juez y la oralidad, Tirant lo Blanch, Valencia
Nieva Fenoll J (2016) Derecho Procesal II. Proceso civil, Marcial Pons, Madrid-Barcelona
Ormazábal Sánchez G (2007) Iura novit curia. Marcial Pons, Madrid-Barcelona
Ortells Ramos M (2017) Derecho Procesal Civil, 16th edn. Aranzadi, Cizur Menor
Tapia Fernández I (2000) Objeto del proceso. Alegaciones. Sentencia. Cosa juzgada, La Ley, Madrid

The Spanish Judiciary in figures (2015). http://www.poderjudicial.es/cgpj/es/Temas/Estadistica-Judicial/Estudios-e-Informes/Justicia-Dato-a-Dato/. Accessed 7 June 2018
The Spanish Judiciary in figures (2016). http://www.poderjudicial.es/cgpj/es/Temas/Estadistica-Judicial/Estudios-e-Informes/Justicia-Dato-a-Dato/. Accessed 7 June 2018
Vallines García E (2004) La preclusión en el proceso civil. Civitas, Madrid

Fernando Gascón Inchausti Professor of Civil and Criminal Procedural Law at the Complutense University of Madrid, Spain. Director of the Research Group on Current Problems of Justice and Procedure and the research project The Harmonization of Civil Procedure in the European Union.

The Disappearing Trial: Retrenchment of Litigation in North America

Margaret Woo

Abstract Concerned with the rising rate of litigation and seemingly unchecked litigation abuse, countries, such as the U.S. and Canada, are making changes to their civil justice systems. It is a renewed call for minimizing costs and maximizing efficiency. Through legislative actions as well as judicial decisions both countries have moved towards greater encouragement of alternative dispute resolution and efforts to weigh the cost of the litigation against the value of the litigation, and, in some instances, they have heightened the barriers to the courts by restricting jurisdiction and raising pleading requirements. But has the protection of rights been subsumed by concerns over efficiency and cost containment? This contribution assesses these most recent limits in the United States and Canada—in personal jurisdiction, class actions, discovery, and the effects of upholding arbitration clauses that prohibit collective actions—and their likely effects on access to justice.

1 Introduction

Concerned with the rising rate of litigation and seemingly unchecked litigation abuse, countries, such as the U.S. and Canada, are making changes to their civil justice systems. It is a renewed call for minimizing costs and maximizing efficiency. Through legislative actions as well as judicial decisions both countries have moved towards even greater encouragement of alternative dispute resolution and efforts to weigh the cost of the litigation against the value of the litigation, and, in some instances, they have heightened barriers to the courts by restricting jurisdiction and raising pleading requirements.

But has the protection of rights been subsumed by concerns over efficiency and cost containment? Has the view that "expedience is at the service of accuracy" been replaced by the view that litigation is a *problem* to be managed and contained? Have some of these measures unduly moved the legal system's focus from ensuring

M. Woo (✉)
Northeastern University School of Law, Boston, USA
e-mail: m.woo@northeastern.edu

A. Uzelac and C. H. van Rhee (eds.), *Transformation of Civil Justice*,
Ius Gentium: Comparative Perspectives on Law and Justice 70,
https://doi.org/10.1007/978-3-319-97358-6_8

substantively correct outcomes to one that seeks to ensure each lawsuit does not utilize more than a proportionate share of the court's resources? Indeed, a "market" and economic view of litigation could inevitably reduce our vision of justice to one limited to individual rather than collective disputes, that litigation is more appropriate for seeking enforcement of private rather than public norms, and, finally, that the importance of the dispute is measured by the size of the financial costs involved rather than by the issues involved.

This contribution comes out of the author's report on recent developments in civil procedure in the U.S. and Canada presented at the International Association of Procedural Law 2018 meeting. Recent trends (from the mid 2010s onward) in the United States and to a lesser extent in Canada suggest that litigation in these countries is increasingly perceived as a problem and the messy process of litigation as unproductive. And so, efforts to contain the number of cases may have led to the result of eliminating litigation. Instead of a process in which efficiency and cost are at the service of accuracy and justice, we now have a process that favors simplicity over complexity, individual over collective actions, and settlement over adjudication. Trials in the U.S. federal courts have decreased to less than one per cent of cases, meaning that most cases do not reach the merits through a public trial. And as we attempt to process better the private function of litigation, we may in turn be compromising the public function served by the judge in adjudication. Rather than deciding right from wrong, judges are more burdened by processing cases and measured by their managerial skills. Civil litigation is reduced and returned to a more limited role as resolving private individual disputes rather than declaring public collective norms, and in some cases taken out of the judicial system completely.

I would like to believe that civil litigation is not simply a method of resolving disputes and maintaining peace between private individuals. It can have an important role in the public function of enforcing agreed upon legal and societal norms. In giving private citizens a voice in the application of legal norms in individual disputes, civil litigation can enforce public rights, forge community ownership of these norms, and instill greater public knowledge on policy issues. Most importantly, in treating litigants as equal citizens before the court, civil litigation can be a leveler and momentarily alter the configurations of authority between otherwise imbalanced parties, and alleviate inequality in society.

This was the view towards civil litigation in the United States that began with the civil rights movement in the 1960s and 70s. It was through private civil litigation that important social and civil legal rights were enforced. Yet much has changed in this view towards litigation, and in turn, in civil procedure. As the number of lawsuits increased and perceptions of litigation abuses spread, judicial reformers turned their attention to efficiency and case management. The latest set of civil procedural reforms is what my colleague Steve Subrin has called "a fourth era in civil procedure"—an era that seeks to manage litigation to the point where bringing suit is discouraged and going to trial is seen as a failure. It is also, I would argue, a period of retrenchment and containment of litigation to the point of derailing civil litigation and risking the erasure of substantive rights.

This trend of retrenchment and containment may also be found in Canada, albeit perhaps for slightly different reasons. A big issue currently in the Canadian system is the shortage of judges. As of 19 December 2016, there were 43 vacancies for judges in the superior courts of the provinces and territories even following the appointment of 39 superior court judges during 2016.[1] In addition to the shortage of judges, a lack of monetary resources has placed additional strains on the court system. The four different Federal Courts within Canada face inadequate funding which impacts their technological improvements, translation costs, and retention of files.[2] Given the critical scarcity of resources, Canada has also turned to efforts to decrease caseload and contain litigation.

Several areas in civil procedure from this past year are indicative of an inward turn towards containing litigation that has evolved with or, more specifically, under the guise of case management. These measures are in addition to the already controversial decisions, such as those in the U.S., to heighten the pleading standard, allowing judges greater ease to dismiss cases. Indeed, in two cases, the U.S. Supreme Court has already shifted from a prior "notice" standard to a "plausibility" standard for complaints.[3] While before, a complaint in the U.S. need only give notice to the other side of the nature of the dispute, today's complaint must first convince the court of its "plausibility." This "plausibility" standard has allowed U.S. courts to dispose of cases at the early stages of the complaint.

Since 2017, there are additional changes in civil procedure in the areas of restricting personal jurisdiction, raising the bar for class actions, weighing discovery, and upholding arbitration clauses that preclude court access for collective actions. In each of these areas, the United States and Canada have moved not only in the direction of increased case management, but also in the direction of retrenching civil litigation, curtailing collective action, and restricting the power of the courts.[4] Certainly, the importance of efficiency is undisputed. Justice delayed is justice denied. But has the call for efficiency led to a redefinition of the role of civil litigation and, in turn, the role of the courts themselves? What is the cost of judicial efficiency?

---

[1]In addition, some areas are finding a need to create more judicial positions, including Quebec, which introduced a bill to add two judicial positions to the Court of Appeal and five positions to their Superior Court. This information can be found at https://www.cba.org/CMSPages/GetFile.aspx?guid=0b6a021b-fe48-418f-9763-a1e2f1fc2ce2. Accessed 7 June 2018. Updated statistics as of August 1, 2017, show a shortage of 45 federally appointed judges out of the 1157 total number of judges that are appointed by the federal government. This information can be found at http://www.fja.gc.ca/appointments-nominations/judges-juges-eng.aspx. Accessed 7 June 2018.

[2]This information is found at https://www.cba.org/CMSPages/GetFile.aspx?guid=5daaa44d-c13f-4556-8d1e-84a1409465ce. Accessed 7 June 2018.

[3]See *Bell Atlantic v. Twombly*, 550 U.S. 544 (2007); *Igbal v. Ashcroft*, 556 U.S. 662 (2009).

[4]President Trump's quick appointment of Supreme Court Justice Gorsuch to replace conservative Justice Antonin Scalia left court-watchers speculating on the direction of the court. Justice Scalia had been a strong voice for corporate America, states' rights and limited judicial powers. It is widely believed that Justice Gorsuch will continue the pro-business tradition, but may be more unpredictable on civil and social rights issues.

2 Personal Jurisdiction

After more than two decades of silence on the subject, the U.S. Supreme Court heard a series of personal jurisdiction cases between 2011 and 2017, with *Bristol Myers Squibb Co. v. Superior Court* being the latest case decided. At a very general level, these decisions are part of a restrictive attitude towards the jurisdictional reach of the state courts and limit the ability of the plaintiff to bring litigation in a convenient forum. In combination, these decisions also have a particular impact against lawsuits formulated as collective actions.

In *Bristol Myers*, a joint litigation with several hundred in-state and out-of-state plaintiffs, the Supreme Court now requires *each* joined plaintiff to individually demonstrate that his claim *arose out* of the defendant's contacts with the forum state. This is required even if the defendant was already brought into the forum state on the same claim by in-state joined plaintiffs and has substantial other contacts with the forum state.[5] This ruling rejected the idea of pendent personal jurisdiction, at least for collective litigation in the state courts. In the past, pendent personal jurisdiction in collective actions might have been justified by the more flexible interpretation of "general jurisdiction." Under the prior "general jurisdiction" interpretation, pendent personal jurisdiction might be allowed over claims against the defendant that were not caused by its forum state contacts so long as the defendant had "substantial and continuous" other contacts with the forum state.

This general jurisdiction, however, was curtailed by the Supreme Court in 2011 with *Goodyear v. Brown*[6] and in 2014 with *Daimler AG v. Bauman*[7] to an "at home" test for corporations. The "at home" test in practice meant that general jurisdiction could only be asserted against the defendant corporation in its place of incorporation and principal place of business. *Goodyear* and *Daimler's* more limited definition of general jurisdiction, along with *Bristol Myers,* sounded the death knell for joint litigation by plaintiffs from different states. It is unclear whether *Bristol Myers* applies to class actions. However, as to other mass joinder cases, plaintiffs are now limited to filing in a defendant corporation's home state or must meet this relatedness test by showing that each joined plaintiff's claim "arose out" of the defendant's activities in that forum state.

The alternative, of course, would be for each plaintiff to file an individual action under case-specific jurisdiction in different states. However, case-specific jurisdiction has also been restricted under recent U.S. Supreme Court decisions. In the past,

[5]In *Bristol-Myers*, several hundred individuals from 33 states (along with 86 California residents) brought suit in California state court. Bristol-Myers did not develop or manufacture the drug in California and there was no reason to think that marketing, promotion, or distribution in California was involved in the injuries of the out-of-state plaintiffs. The only way in which the nonresidents' claims related to California was that the marketing and promotion of the pharmaceutical was conducted on a nationwide basis.

[6]*Goodyear v. Brown*, 131 S.Ct. 2846 (2011).

[7]*Daimler Ag v. Bauman*, 135 S.Ct. 746 (2014).

case-specific jurisdiction might be found in any forum state where the defendant had "minimum contacts"—defined simply as any state in which the defendant's products could "foreseeably" cause injury and lead the defendant to anticipate litigation. But in *McIntyre v. Nicastro*, the U.S. Supreme Court found no case-specific personal jurisdiction (no "minimum contacts") in the state where the defendant manufacturer's product caused injury simply because the offending product had entered the state through a retailer. It was the retailer, the Supreme Court reasoned, rather than the defendant manufacturer who had sufficient "minimum contacts" or the "foreseeability" with the forum state to be subject to case-specific jurisdiction. Under this rationale, then, global manufacturers can insulate themselves through their retailers even in forum states where their products ultimately cause injury. In sum, the *McIntyre* decision allows global manufacturers to evade a finding of such "in-state" contacts through the use of middlemen retailers and distributors even if they can "foresee" their products might and did cause injury in-state.

Indeed, previously, the U.S. personal jurisdiction standard was an outlier in the international context as most countries require something more than "minimum contacts" to render an out-of-state defendant susceptible to the forum state's authority. Today's decisions in *McIntyre* and *Bristol Myers*, *Goodyear* and *Daimler* may have tightened personal jurisdiction even beyond the requirements of other countries. In the U.S., plaintiffs from separate states must now split their cause of action unless each plaintiff can demonstrate in-state causation. This is required even if other in-state joint plaintiffs have already brought the defendant into the forum state. Secondly, big corporate defendants may not be susceptible to suit in a forum state even though the injury occurred in the forum state if in fact the product entered the forum state through a retailer middleman.[8]

In Canada, the Supreme Court of Canada, in the 2012 cases *Club Resorts Ltd. v. Van Breda* and *Club Resorts Ltd. v. Charron* ("*Van Breda*"),[9] updated and clarified the "real and substantial connection test" that Canadian courts must apply to

---

[8]The petitioner in *Bristol-Myers* seems to be advocating the cutting up of nationwide lawsuits into 50 separate suits and dispersing such cases to multiple states regardless of the convenience to the courts or any of the litigants, including the defendants themselves. See Brief of *Amici Curiae* Civil Procedure Professors in Support of Respondents.

[9]Both cases involved actions for personal injuries suffered by Canadian tourists at resorts in Cuba. The defendant Club Resorts is incorporated in the Cayman Islands and manages the hotels where the accidents occurred. In both cases, Club Resorts sought to dismiss or stay the proceedings, arguing that the Ontario courts lacked jurisdiction and, in the alternative, that a Cuban court would be a more appropriate forum. In both instances, the motion judges dismissed Club Resorts' motions, finding that Club Resorts had a sufficient connection to Ontario to permit the assumption of jurisdiction. These decisions were appealed to the Ontario Court of Appeal, which convened a special five-judge panel to reconsider the content of the real and substantial connection test. The Court of Appeal rearticulated the test in an attempt to increase the consistency and predictability of the jurisdictional determinations of Ontario courts. The Court of Appeal's decision was then appealed to the Supreme Court, which unanimously endorsed a new framework for the real and substantial connection test.

determine whether they have jurisdiction over foreign and out-of-province defendants. The *Van Breda* case set out a two-step analysis.

The first step is to determine whether any of four non-exhaustive and rebuttable presumptive connecting factors exists for personal jurisdiction: whether the defendant is domiciled or a resident in the province, the defendant carries on business in the province, the tort was committed in the province, or a contract connected with the dispute was made in the province. Similarly, as in the United States, an allegation that the plaintiff has suffered damages in the jurisdiction is insufficient. The second step would then be, if the plaintiff succeeds in establishing that a presumptive connecting factor exists, the defendant has the opportunity to rebut the presumption of jurisdiction by showing that, on the facts of the particular case, the connection is insufficient to establish a real and substantial connection. For example, where the presumptive connecting factor is a contract made within the jurisdiction, the presumption can be rebutted by showing that the contract does not relate to the subject matter of the litigation.

Though it is not clear whether *Van Breda v. Village Resorts Ltd.*, 2012 SCC 17, expanded or contracted personal jurisdiction, one article did specify that it seems to have brought Canadian personal jurisdiction more in line with the U.S. system. This is because the presumptive factors encapsulate both a defendant-centric and a subject matter approach, whereas the previous system had focused on the plaintiff.[10] Others have criticized the Court as moving too far in the direction of order, sacrificing fairness.[11]

3 Class Actions

In *Wal-Mart Stores Inc. v. Dukes*, the U.S. Supreme Court denied class certification for lack of "commonality" under Rule 23 of the Federal Rules of Civil Procedure in a class action suit for gender discrimination. In *Wal-Mart*, the more than one million female employees of Wal-Mart would have to demonstrate that they were all subject to the same discriminatory employment policy in the same manner before they could be found to satisfy the "commonality" requirement and be certified as a class. After *Wal-Mart*, the Supreme Court addressed class actions in three cases,[12] and in 2017 the Court decided in a unanimous decision that federal courts

[10]See http://elibrary.law.psu.edu/cgi/viewcontent.cgi?article=1123&context=jlia. Accessed 7 June 2018.

[11]See http://ir.lawnet.fordham.edu/cgi/viewcontent.cgi?article=2613&context=ilj. Accessed 7 June 2018.

[12]In *Spokeo v. Robins,* 136 S.Ct. 1540 (2016), the U.S. Supreme Court held that allegations of a "bare procedural violation divorced from any concrete harm" (that is, simply a technical violation of a federal statute) is insufficient to establish Article III standing, which requires that all matters in federal court be a "case or controversy." In *Campbell-Ewald Co. v. Gomez*, 136 S.Ct. 663 (2016), the Supreme Court concluded that an unaccepted Rule 68 offer made to the class representative for

of appeal lack jurisdiction to review a motion denying the certification of a class action after the named plaintiffs voluntarily dismiss their individual claims with prejudice.[13]

Justice Neil Gorsuch, the newest member of the U.S. Supreme Court, will likely maintain the Court's current pro-business approach to class action questions. The prediction is that the outcome of class actions will increasingly turn on whether membership in the class is ascertainable. A continuing circuit split in this area of the law has caused confusion and uncertainty, resulting in additional litigation to determine whether the class is ascertainable under the applicable law.[14]

Efforts to amend Rule 23 (the class action rule) continue to garner attention[15] with a 2016 proposal regarding electronic notice and stricter management of objections to class action settlements. But it is the persistent efforts to curtail class

---

full individual relief did not moot the named plaintiff's individual claim. One case in particular, *Tyson Foods, Inc. v. Bouaphakeo*, 136 S. Ct. 1036 (2016), presented the Court with an opportunity to revisit the pro-defendant assertions made by Justice Scalia in *Wal-Mart v. Dukes*, suggesting that the plaintiffs could not use representative proof to prove a defendant's liability (i.e., "trial by formula"). In *Tyson Foods*, the Court held that workers in a food processing facility could rely on representative sampling regarding hours worked "to fill an evidentiary gap" created by Tyson's failure to keep adequate records to establish class-wide liability for alleged violations of the Fair Labor Standards Act.

[13]The opinion emphasized that federal courts of appeals may review final judgments from district courts, but denial of class certification was not considered a final judgment. The Court spoke to the fear that allowing plaintiffs to create *pseudo*-interlocutory appeals would allow indiscriminate appellate review of interlocutory orders, outcomes that, as the Court explained, both the final judgment rule and Rule 23(f) were intended to prevent. In Justice Clarence Thomas' concurring opinion, he reasoned that federal courts of appeals lack jurisdiction to review an order denying class certification after the named plaintiffs had voluntarily dismissed their claims with prejudice because there was no longer a case or controversy as required by Article III. Chief Justice John G. Roberts, Jr. and Justice Samuel A. Alito, Jr. joined the opinion.

[14]For example, the Third and Eleventh Circuits have adopted a rigorous and strict inquiry into the existence of an ascertainable class, requiring a plaintiff to demonstrate by a preponderance of the evidence that (1) the class is "defined with reference to objective criteria" and (2) there is "a reliable and administratively feasible mechanism for determining whether putative class members fall within the class definition." *Carrera v. Bayer Corp.*, 727 F.3d 300 (3d Cir. 2013); see also *Karhu v. Vital Pharmaceuticals, Inc.*, 2015 U.S. App. Lexis 9576 (11th Cir. 2015). In contrast, the Seventh Circuit has adopted a more plaintiff-friendly approach pursuant to which proposed classes fail to satisfy the ascertainability requirement only if they are (1) vague and lack a "clear definition" (that is, one that "identif[ies] a particular group, harmed during a particular time frame, in a particular location, in a particular way"); (2) defined by subjective criteria; or (3) defined based on the merits of the claims (also known as a "fail-safe" class). See, e.g., *Mullins v. Direct Digital, LLC*, 795 F. 3d 654 (7th Cir. 2015). Thus, depending on the jurisdiction, the ascertainability requirement may preclude class certification or have no impact at all. We predict continued litigation and division among the circuits and lower courts regarding the ascertainability requirement unless and until the Supreme Court addresses the issue.

[15]The 2016 proposed amendments under consideration included electronic notice, as well as provisions to check frivolous objections and appeals in the class action settlement. These proposals would require objectors to state the grounds for objection with specificity and court approval for any payments to an objector or the objector's counsel for withdrawal of their objections or abandonment of appeals.

actions through legislation that are more troubling. Proposed legislation continues to surface, and if passed as introduced, would dramatically alter the class action landscape.[16] A recently proposed bill in the U.S. House of Representatives seeks to amend the procedures used in federal court class actions and multidistrict litigation proceedings arguably "to assure fairer, more efficient outcomes for claimants and defendants." The proposed bill's significant changes to current class action law include, but are not limited to: (1) prohibiting a federal court from granting class certification unless each class member suffered "the same type and scope of injury" based on "a rigorous analysis of the evidence presented;" (2) heightening the standard for certifying "issues" classes; (3) prohibiting class certification unless the class is defined by "reference to objective criteria," requiring class representatives to "affirmatively demonstrate that there is a reliable and administratively feasible mechanism" to identify class members and distribute monetary relief directly to a substantial majority of the class.[17] On 9 March 2017, the bill passed in the U.S. House of Representatives without any substantive amendments on a 220 to 201 vote; it was then sent on to the Senate for consideration. Needless to say, if the bill becomes law, it will be a game-changer and courts will grapple with its impact for many years to come.[18]

Class actions have also garnered attention in Canada. By early 2000, class action procedures had been implemented with comprehensive reforms by almost all of the provinces and territories, through legislation, and by the Federal Court of Canada, by amendment to its rules of practice (Bogart et al. 2007). In 2015, however, the Supreme Court of Canada considered for the first time the standard for granting a plaintiff leave to proceed with a statutory secondary-market securities class action. Previously, lower courts considering the issue arrived at inconsistent results, arming plaintiffs with precedents to support a very low threshold for leave. In *Theratechnologies Inc. v. 121851 Canada Inc.,* the Supreme Court held that the threshold for obtaining leave to proceed with such class actions should be more than a "speed bump" and that courts must undertake a reasoned consideration of the evidence to ensure the action has some merit. The Court noted that "[w]hat is required is sufficient evidence to persuade the court that there is a reasonable possibility that the action will be resolved in the claimant's favour."

---

[16]Representative Bob Goodlatte (R-VA) introduced H.R. 985, the Fairness in Class Action Litigation Act, on 9 February 2017. The Act, co-sponsored by Representatives Pete Sessions (R-TX) and Glenn Grothman (R-WI), would bring about dramatic and wide-ranging changes to the law governing class actions under Rule 23 of the Federal Rules of Civil Procedure.

[17]Additional proposed provisions include (4) automatically staying discovery during the pendency of motions to transfer, dismiss, and strike class allegations unless "the particularized discovery is necessary to preserve evidence or prevent undue prejudice;" (5) prohibiting class counsel from representing a client in more than one class action, among other "conflicts" prohibitions; (6) mandating the reporting of settlement data to the Federal Judicial Center; and (7) providing an automatic right to appeal an order certifying a class.

[18]The bill's ultimate fate continues to rest with the U.S. Senate, where the Senate Judiciary Committee has thus far taken no action on the bill, whose prospects for passage remain unclear at the time of this writing.

The parameters set by the Supreme Court were employed in a series of 2015 decisions and reinforced in the Court's decision in the limitation period trilogy of cases released in December 2015. Going forward, Canadian courts are expected to follow the Supreme Court's approach when considering whether to grant leave to proceed with statutory secondary-market securities class actions. This development has affected and is expected to continue to affect the quantity and quality of evidence adduced by both plaintiffs and defendants on leave motions.

4 Discovery

In the United States, an amendment to Rule 26 limited discovery to (1) "matter that is relevant to any party's *claim or defense*" (emphasis added) and (2) "proportional to the needs of the case." The change from discoverable matter "relating to the subject matter of the lawsuit" to "relating to a claim or defense" narrows the scope of discoverable materials. Additionally, while proportionality is not necessarily new to Rule 26, proportionality is now elevated and made explicit by the amendment. "Proportionality is an important principle to be applied to all of discovery," the Advisory Committee explained. Thus, the Committee justified that this change "neither places the burden of addressing all proportionality considerations on the party seeking discovery nor permits the opposing party to refuse discovery by making boilerplate objections based on proportionality." The Rule seeks a balance in discovery requests, i.e. that they are not unduly broad, and in discovery refusals, i.e. that they are not so automatic.

The proportionality requirement is further bolstered by adding to Rule 34(b)(2)(B), which requires that a response must plead "with specificity the grounds for objecting to the request," and the amendment to Rule 37(e) deals specifically with what a court may do if it determines that a party "lost" Electronically Stored Information with the "intent to deprive the other party."

Similar to what was already required in U.S. procedure, Canadian civil procedure added a requirement that parties agree to a discovery plan before they can obtain evidence by "discovery of documents, examination for discovery, inspection of property, medical examination or written questions" (Rule 29.1). Much as in the United States, discovery should embrace the proportionality principle. Parties should consider the nature of the litigation, the relevance of the electronic evidence, its importance to adjudication, and the cost and delay that may be imposed to deal with electronic documents.[19] For example, Quebec's New Code of Civil Procedure (NCCP) spells out the "guiding principles of procedure," which includes proportionality, whereby each party must ensure that each step in the proceedings (not only discovery) is proportionate, in terms of the cost and time involved, to the

[19]See further description of rule changes at https://www.attorneygeneral.jus.gov.on.ca/english/courts/civil/changes_to_rules_of_civil_procedure.php. Accessed 7 June 2018.

nature and complexity of the matter.[20] Most of the Superior Courts in Canada's other provinces have also added proportionality as one of the guiding principles of procedure.[21]

5 Arbitration

Finally, U.S. Supreme Court decisions have so far consistently upheld clauses that mandate individual arbitration and prohibit collective actions. In a series of decisions, including *AT&T Mobility LLC v. Concepcion* and *American Express Corp. v. Italian Colors Restaurant*, the Supreme Court rejected the "policing" of arbitration clauses to instead uphold these clauses regardless of their "unconscionability." The Court stated, "Courts must rigorously enforce arbitration agreements according to their terms, including terms that specify with whom the parties choose to arbitrate their disputes, and the rules under which that arbitration will be conducted."[22] Since then, arbitration clauses including class action waivers and other onerous provisions have become ubiquitous in employment and consumer contracts (Malin 2016).

This past fall, the U.S. Supreme Court heard *Epic Systems Corp. v. Lewis*, an employee class action suing for overtime wages denied in violation of the Fair Labor Standards Act of 1938. Epic moved to dismiss the complaint and cited the "waiver of class action" clause of its arbitration agreement. The question is whether the "waiver of class action" clause is unenforceable when it is in conflict with the right of employees to engage in "concerted activities" as provided by the National Labor Relations Act.[23] At issue then is whether these arbitration agreements

---

[20]Quebec's New Code of Civil Procedure, available at http://legisquebec.gouv.qc.ca/en/ShowDoc/cs/C-25.01. Accessed 7 June 2018.

[21]See, for example, Ontario's interpretation of ***General Principle*** 1.04 (1) "These rules shall be liberally construed to secure the just, most expeditious and least expensive determination of every civil proceeding on its merits." ***Proportionality*** (1.1) "In applying these rules, the court shall make orders and give directions that are proportionate to the importance and complexity of the issues, and to the amount involved, in the proceeding".

[22]The Court held that the Federal Arbitration Act preempted the California precedent that had previously held that, in certain circumstances, arbitration clauses in customer agreements were unenforceable. In *DirectTV, Inc.*, the Court took on the question of whether a reference to state law in an arbitration clause required the application of that state law despite its preemption by the Federal Arbitration Act. The Court held that requiring contract enforcement under California state law that the Supreme Court had held was invalid in *AT&T Mobility LLCConcepcion* would conflict with the Federal Arbitration Act. Also, there was no language in the contract referring to invalid state law. The Court also noted that there was no indication that a California court would apply state law that has been held to be invalid when it conflicts with federal law in any other context. See *AT&T Mobility LLC v. Concepcion.*

[23]The agency, the National Labor Relations Board (NLRB), had concluded that employer-mandated class action waivers violate section 8 of the NLRA by interfering with employees' rights under section 7 to engage in "concerted activity" for mutual aid and protection. In *D.R. Horton, Inc. v. NLRB*, a divided Court of Appeals for the Fifth Circuit reversed the

including a waiver against class actions should be upheld even when it is contrary to an underlying statutory policy favoring collective action, such as the National Labor Relations Act (NLRA).[24] Arguments were heard this fall, and in May, the Supreme Court issued the long expected opinion to rigorously uphold arbitration agreements. In upholding the arbitration clause against class actions, the Supreme Court narrowly construed the NLRA to say that, while the NLRA guarantees employees the right to bargain collectively and to engage in other concerted activities for the purpose of collective bargaining, 29 U.S.C. 157, the NLRA did not mention class or collective actions nor did it indicate a clear and manifest wish to displace the Federal.Arbitration Act, the Act which generally requires courts to enforce arbitration agreements as written.[25]

In sum, the Supreme Court has ruled that arbitration agreements can be used to bar access to the courts in collective actions. This has been done when individuals claim breaches of federal securities laws[26]; when employees allege age discrimination[27] and sex discrimination[28]; and in respect of consumer protection.[29] Scholars such as Judith Resnik are concerned with how the two practices—adjudication and arbitration—are coming to be styled as fungible options on a "dispute resolution" spectrum. Where courts used to be equated with public processes and arbitration with private consensual agreements, the mixing of the two undermines the political and moral legitimacy of the courts (Resnik 2015).

In Canada, the emphasis has long been in favor of individual arbitration and mediation. However, in the New Code of Civil Procedure which came into force in 2016, Quebec now requires parties to establish a mandatory case management

---

NLRB's holding that a class or collective action waiver imposed by an employer as a condition of employment violated section 8(a)(1) of the NLRA. The NLRB declared that the waiver interfered with, restrained, or coerced employees in the exercise of their right under section 7 of the NLRA to engage in "concerted activity" for mutual aid and protection. The Fifth Circuit majority recognized that the NLRB's holding that section 7 protected the employees' right to sue collectively to improve their working conditions was supported by NLRB and court authority. However, relying heavily on *Concepcion* and the Court's determination that the FAA favors enforcing arbitration agreements in accordance with their terms, the majority concluded that section 7 of the NLRA must yield to the conflicting policies of the FAA, the idea being that "concerted activity" does not clearly guarantee the right to class action, whereas the direction in the FAA clearly commands that arbitration agreements be enforced as written.

[24]"Epic Systems Corp. v. Lewis." *Oyez,* 7 Oct. 2017, www.oyez.org/cases/2017/16-285. Accessed 7 June 2018; consolidated with *Ernst & Young v. Morris* and *National Labor Relations Board v. Murphy Oil USA, Inc.*, both of which are cases that dealt with the relationship between the FAA and the NLRA.

[25]See Epic Systems v. Lewis, 584 U.S. (2018) at https://supreme.justia.com/cases/federal/us/584/16-285/? See https://www.nytimes.com/2017/10/02/us/politics/supreme-court-workplace-arbitration.html. Accessed 7 June 2018.

[26]*Rodriguez de Quijas v. Shearson/Am. Express, Inc.*, 490 U.S. 477 (1989), *Shearson/Am. Express Inc. v. McMahan*, 482 U.S. 220.

[27]*Gilmer v. Interstate/Johnson Lane Corp.*, 500 U.S. 20 (1991).

[28]Ada, s.532I/S/at 1-5/.

[29]*ATT & Concepcion*, 131 S.Ct. 1740.

regime before proceeding with the action including consideration of mediation.[30] As such, the NCCP places greater emphasis on private and alternate modes of dispute resolution, such as mediation, arbitration, and out-of-court settlement conferences. Parties will be obligated under the NCCP to consider private dispute prevention and resolution processes before going to court. Although mandatory mediation is not anticipated, the parties will have to inform the court whether such processes were considered. The consequences for failing to comply with this new obligation remain undefined. But the NCCP undeniably encourages more disputes to be resolved out of court, and interest in private mediations in the early stages of a dispute is also expected (Jolin 2016).

This shift carries with it many of the hopes that accompanied the original move in favor of arbitration in the United States, the idea being that arbitration can be more efficient and more accessible than litigation. Ideally, the (increased) use of alternative dispute resolution processes would prove to be a better forum for smaller claims brought by parties with minimal resources. Additionally, in combination with the emphasis on the "proportionality principle," litigants will also be asked to be more cost conscience and efficient and, thereby, alleviate some of the backlog in the Canadian courts. Time will tell whether this goal will be realized or if the Canadian system will develop arbitration and mediation issues similar to those of the United States. This will depend on, among other things, the frequency with which arbitration clauses are used in Canada, the language of those clauses, and the willingness of the courts to police and review such clauses.

6 Conclusion

Looking at case management as only having the aim of minimizing costs and maximizing efficiency is to miss the trend that has been underway in North America over the last 30 years. At least in the United States, the focus on cost and efficiency has resulted in the perception of lawsuits as problems. Rather than managing cases with an eye towards deciding the case on the merits, we are seeing a diversion of these cases. Indeed, the entire litigation system is under siege through what Judith Resnik (2015) has called "Dispute Diffusion," propelled by revised mandates to judges about how to handle cases by disfavoring collective actions, and by the U.S. Supreme Court's new approach to arbitration clauses.

Rather than diffusing disputes, we should remember the importance of courts and the public role of litigation. Government benefits from judges who gain their legitimacy and protect their independence through the discipline of making their procedures known and doing much of their work before the public. Filings are one measure of the judiciary's success, but so are correct adjudicated outcomes. Courts

[30]Quebec's New Code of Civil Procedure, available at http://legisquebec.gouv.qc.ca/en/ShowDoc/cs/C-25.01. Accessed 7 June 2018.

are seen as hospitable to a variety of claimants, proceeding under a system not of their users' design but fashioned by bodies of rule-makers committed to procedural neutrality and subject to public scrutiny. Courts are the rare venue aspiring to treat all comers equally and to level the playing field. They announce public norms and not simply settle private disputes. In the procedural rules, then, this will mean enabling rather than curbing collective actions, easing court access through jurisdiction, lowering pleading requirements, determining the amount of resources utilized by the importance of the issues, and policing arbitration agreements to ensure their conscionability.

References

Bogart WA, Kalajdzic J, Matthews I (2007) Class actions in Canada: a national procedure in a multi-jurisdictional society? A report prepared for The Globalization of Class Actions Conference, Oxford University. Available at http://globalclassactions.stanford.edu/sites/default/files/documents/Canada_National_Report.pdf. Accessed 7 June 2018

Jolin B (2016) Quebec's new code of civil procedure. The Canadian Lawyer, 29 Feb 2016. Available at http://www.canadianlawyermag.com/author/sandra-shutt/quebecs-new-code-of-civil-procedure-3193/. Accessed 7 June 2018

Malin M (2016) The three phases of the supreme court's arbitration jurisprudence: Empowering the already-empowered. Nevada Law J 17(23)

Resnik J (2015) Diffusing disputes: the public in the private of arbitration, the private in courts, and the erasure of rights. Yale Law J 124:2804–2939

Margaret Woo Professor of Law and Associate Dean of Research and Interdisciplinary Education at the Northeastern University School of Law, where she teaches Civil Procedure, Administrative Law and Comparative Law. Expert on the Anglo-American legal system and the Chinese socialist legal system. Former Fellow of the Bunting Institute (Radcliffe College). Associate of the East Asian Legal Studies Program at Harvard University.

Private Justice in the Domain of Family Law: The Place of Family Group Conferences Within the Range of ADR Methods

Annie de Roo and Rob Jagtenberg

Abstract In this contribution, the success of family mediation and collaborative practices across Europe will be briefly touched upon, but the focus will be on a less known method (or rather a decision-making model): 'family group conferences'. The concept of family group conferences originated in New Zealand in 1989; less than 15 years later the proliferation of the concept had led to the adoption of such conferences in over 30 countries worldwide. This contribution analyses how referrals to family group conferences have been organized and regulated in three of those jurisdictions, New Zealand, England and Wales and the Netherlands. Among the issues to be dealt with are: the problems that crop up in the (judicial) assessment of requests for referrals, the nature of 'a right to direct' one's own family affairs and the legal status of 'plans' concluded during a family group conference. The analysis ends with a preliminary assessment of the value added by this specific ADR variety, while further longitudinal, empirical research by the authors is in progress.

1 Mediation: The 2016 European Commission Report on Directive 2008/52/EC

Private justice—where parties directly involved in a conflict attempt to engineer a solution themselves—is often associated with ADR methods such as mediation. In the domain of family law, mediation is well established, but many more private justice varieties can be found there.

As mediation is likely the best known and most commonly used ADR method in the domain of family law, a few words need to be said first about the recently

A. de Roo · R. Jagtenberg (✉)
Erasmus School of Law, Rotterdam, The Netherlands
e-mail: jagtenberg@law.eur.nl

A. de Roo
e-mail: deroo@law.eur.nl

A. Uzelac and C. H. van Rhee (eds.), *Transformation of Civil Justice*,
Ius Gentium: Comparative Perspectives on Law and Justice 70,
https://doi.org/10.1007/978-3-319-97358-6_9

published *Report from the European Commission on the application of Directive 2008/52/EC on mediation in civil and commercial matters.*[1] This evaluation Report, published on 26 August 2016, integrates the outcomes of two earlier projects. First, a study titled 'The Mediation Directive', carried out in 2013–2014 by two consultancies, involving desktop research and small-scale consultations among stakeholders, particularly mediators (Milieu Ltd and Consulting 2014). Second, the Commission conducted a public online consultation in the fall of 2015, during which 562 responses were received, from the mediator community, but also from academics and public authorities.[2]

In its Report, the Commission concludes, among other findings, that across Europe mediation seems most successful in the domain of family law, this despite the difficulty in obtaining comprehensive statistical data on mediation.[3] Especially mentioned are divorce cases between spouses with children. According to the Commission, it is in the best interests of children that a constructive atmosphere is created to ensure fair access and maintenance arrangements, while minimizing (further) emotional trauma.

To give just one example: in the Netherlands today, approximately 20% of couples contemplating a divorce will jointly engage a single lawyer-mediator to help them make the necessary arrangements and prepare the documents that can be submitted together with the divorce petition, reducing the court's role to rubber-stamping the divorce, and everything even without the inconveniences of a hearing (Ter Voert and Klein Haarhuis 2015).[4]

The Report also summarizes a number of best practices. For instance, litigants 'should be required to state in their court applications whether mediation has been attempted'. Particularly in family law matters, '[L]itigants should be *obliged* to attend information sessions on mediation.'[5]

It is clear that the Commission thus seems to favour a cautious move into the direction of *mandatory referral* of litigants to mediation in family matters, arguably in the interest of children, although this is not specified in so many words.

One is reminded that in the 2013–2014 Study mentioned earlier data collection took place primarily among the community of private mediation providers. These respondents were overwhelmingly *in favour* of making court referrals to mediation mandatory. In the later *online consultation*, however, many government officials (including representatives from the judiciary) and academics responded, and they were largely *opposed* to making referrals mandatory.

[1]COM (2016) 542 final (Commission Report).

[2]The online consultation was open to the public from 18 September to 11 December 2015; parallel to this open consultation, national representatives within the EJN network were invited to give their views.

[3]Commission Report, p. 5: 'Family law appears to be the area where mediation is used to the greatest extent'.

[4]For completeness sake: 1 in 3 Dutch marriages ends in divorce; the single ground 'permanent disruption' is accepted without evidence.

[5]Commission Report, p. 12.

The best practices thus seem to embody a diplomatic compromise.

The Report does not specify the arguments on which the pro and con stances towards mandatory referral are based. As far as academics are concerned, one might expect this has to do with the current lack of conclusive evidence for the effectiveness of either voluntary or mandatory referral in generating friendly and enduring solutions.

This lack of evidence was also brought to the fore in a recent international study commissioned by the research unit of the Dutch Ministry of Justice (WODC) into the effectiveness of mandatory mediation in fiercely contested divorces, the so-called diWARce cases, or in Dutch *vechtscheidingen* (Geurts and Sportel 2015).

The effectiveness—with regard to the well-being of children particularly—can only be ascertained through sophisticated research designs, such as randomized, controlled trials (RCT), but such robust experimental studies are not available as yet. Empirical studies with less robust designs can provide indications at the most, but even then the emerging picture is still unclear. Hence, the researchers had to abstain from advising the Ministry to introduce mandatory mediation.

2 Collaborative Practice: An Increasingly Familiar Mediation Variety

Possibly due to the success of mediators 'taking over the business' of family lawyers, a practice has developed, first in the United States, for each of the spouses contemplating a divorce to engage their own lawyer, but under the proviso that litigation should be avoided (Tesler 2001). For such a collaborative approach, a so-called Participation Agreement is concluded at the outset, wherein it is stipulated that the parties will disclose all relevant information. Moreover, the Agreement provides that the parties will make good faith efforts to reach a mutually acceptable settlement and that the lawyers' roles will terminate in the event and as soon as negotiations fail and contested court proceedings are resorted to.

3 From State Abstention to State Intervention in Family Life

In view of the widespread use of mediation and similar collaborative practices in family disputes, the imposition of divorce arrangements by a court may be perceived as an intrusion into private family life, albeit an intrusion that logically follows the inability of parents to come to an agreement themselves.

A different situation arises where families with children are found to be in such deep trouble that the public authorities are authorized to step in. This is expressly so in cases of neglect or abuse, where a child may even be separated from his/her parent(s) in order to safeguard the child's well-being and security in the light of the parents' inability to raise their child in a safe and responsible manner. Child protection authorities and/or professional guardians are usually the designated agents that request the family courts to endorse such measures. Therefore, courts may issue 'supervision' or 'care and protection' or 'placement' orders, as they are most commonly referred to, although the exact name may differ as per jurisdiction. Such orders roughly extend to the (continued) appointment of a guardian to supervise the parents, to the removal of a child from its parents to a foster parent family, or even to a special-purpose facility run by psychologists and other professional social care workers. Parents will regard such court-endorsed measures as by far the most intrusive (and unwanted) interference with their family life. Most supervision or placement order cases therefore epitomize fierce disputes, this time between the parents and the public authority, such as the child protection authority that requested the court order. A typical characteristic of such disputes is, moreover, that the parents tend to lack the (mental) capacity or (socio-economic) means to such an extent that this makes them unfit to raise their child properly themselves.

It was for such situations that the concept of the 'family group conference' (FGC) was initially developed and introduced in New Zealand.

4 The FGC in New Zealand

The idea of the family group conference originated in New Zealand in response to an over-representation of Maori children in the state care system. The indigenous Maori pride themselves on their strong sense of community and close-knit social texture. They requested an opportunity to utilize the human resources in their own community—notably extended family networks—to care for children identified as suffering from neglect or abuse by their own parent(s), rather than having 'alien' state agencies take over.

The Maori request was honoured through adoption of the 1989 Children, Young Persons, and Their Families Act, which granted not only to the Maori but also to every family in New Zealand the right to a 'family group conference'. This right to a family group conference is essentially a decision-making process, where the child involved and the members of the wider family network come together to make a plan regarding the safety and welfare of the child. In this way, intervention by the State (*casu quo* the Department of Social Work) can be avoided.

A typical family group conference will unfold in four stages.

- Stage 1: a coordinator, who speaks the language of the family/community, and who is independent from the public authorities, will help the family prepare for the meeting, e.g. by locating more remote family members (or others in the community) who may assist in looking after the child.
- Stage 2: the conference itself gets started and professionals (social workers, guardians) may clarify their concerns about the upbringing of the child.

- Stage 3: the professionals leave and the family is left alone to discuss these concerns amongst themselves, and make a plan to address them. The plan may have to conform to bottom-line stipulations provided by the professionals.
- Stage 4: finally, the professionals are called in again and the plan is presented and (possibly after some refinements) approved.

These four stages are known as the preparatory, information-sharing, private family time and presentation stage, respectively.

Section 13 of the Children, Young Persons, and Their Families Act provides that every court and every social worker *must* be guided by the principle that children have to be protected from harm, as well as by the principle that the primary role in caring for and protecting a child lies with the child's (extended) family. The referral to a family group conference is mandatory for the Department of Social Work (DSW), as Section 18 of the Act provides that a family group conference must be convened if the DSW believes a child is in need of care. Section 34 of the Act further provides that a family plan as the outcome of a successful family group conference is basically binding, as DSW shall give effect to such plans, unless this would be unreasonable. It appears then that a clinical margin of appreciation is built into the system, both on the 'entry' (referral) side and on the 'exit' (plan) side.

A leading scholar in the field has observed that in the course of a decade the statutory right to a family group conference resulted in a 60% decline in court supervision orders (Doolan 2007).

From the perspective of the United Nations Human Rights Committee, a supervision or placement order does not constitute a violation of one's right to family life if the avenue of a family group conference has been offered.[6]

The family group conference has developed as a device to give 'voice' to the wider family (or community) and to mobilize support among its members to the benefit of the child.

Many commentators and scholars hailed the 1989 Act as an outstanding piece of 'responsive regulation', enabling 'problem solving' and 'therapeutic jurisprudence' (Levine 2000).

[6]View of the Human Rights Committee under the UN Covenant for Civil and Political Rights: Communication No. 858/1999 *Margaret Buckle v New Zealand.* The Committee found no violation of Arts. 17 and 23 of the Covenant, as an FGC had been convened. No cases have yet been published under the 1989 UN Convention on the Rights of the Child. Article 9 of the Convention provides that *all interested parties* shall be given an opportunity to participate in removal and placement proceedings.

5 Reception of the FGC in Europe—General Observations

In Europe, the concept of the family group conference as a fundamental right was well received in a number of countries, among them the UK and the Netherlands, the two countries to which we will confine ourselves here. Unlike in mediation, professionals in the field who were critical of the top-down, 'system-based' way of operating established private organizations such as the Family Rights Group in the UK and the *Eigen Kracht Centr*ale in the Netherlands. Their goal was to promote the FGC philosophy and to train independent coordinators in techniques to stimulate initiative and resourcefulness among family members, while at the same time respecting their autonomy.

The family group conference has strong potential to actively engage families that might otherwise remain 'passive consumers' of welfare. *It is the family* that decides how they are going to *take action*, to address the professional concerns, rather than being the *recipients* of imposed professional decision-making. This aspect in particular appeared to fit in well with the desire for more direct participation of citizens, the new buzzwords being 'empowerment', 'right to challenge' and 'the Big Society' (Taylor 2012). One is reminded of David Cameron's maxim: 'Society is not a spectator sport'. As observed in a comprehensive evaluation of the Big Society ideal, however, the idealistic motive of 'empowerment' went hand in hand with the somewhat more cynical motive of 'austerity' (Civil Exchange 2015). These same dual forces have also shaped the development of mediation.

In view of these strong parallels, the question presents itself whether the European agencies have laid down a similar regulatory framework for family group conferences as for mediation. The answer is no, although indirectly the steadily expanding case law of the European Court of Human Rights (ECtHR) on Article 8 of the European Convention on Human Rights (ECHR), bringing 'the mutual enjoyment by parent and child of each other's company' within the ambit of the right to family life, definitely provides support to the idea.[7]

6 Reception in the UK: The FGC as a Judicial Case Management Tool?

In the UK, Smith and Hennessey conducted an early family group conference experiment in Essex (Smith and Hennessey 1998). They found that family plans prevented 32% of children from entering local authority care and 47% of cases from proceeding to court. Cost savings were thus generated in respect of publicly funded care professionals as well as the publicly funded court system.

---

[7]ECtHR, 12 July 2001 *K and T v Finland,* held that Article 8 ECHR encompasses a positive duty to facilitate family reunification whenever a (justified) external placement order is renewed.

These outcomes were undoubtedly instrumental in the Ministry of Justice recommending the use of family group conferences to social workers and courts in its guidance that accompanied the introduction of the so-called Public Law Outline (PLO) in 2008 (Evans 2011).

The PLO is not a statute, but essentially a case management tool that specifies the steps to be taken by the local authorities whenever they intend to seek care and protection—and placement—orders from the family court. The aim is to ensure timely care proceedings (to be completed within 26 weeks), compelling the authorities to do their preparatory work well, demanding specified reports and care plans to be submitted during the 'pre-proceedings stage'.

During this stage, it is also peremptory that the professional social workers discuss their concerns with the family: the children and their immediate and wider family should be involved in addressing the concerns or in identifying alternative kinship care. The objective should be to keep the children with their (wider) families whenever possible in view of their safety and well-being.

Care proceedings were reformed following a 2011 review. Since then they provide an even stronger impetus to use the pre-proceedings process. However, there is a real danger that work during this stage becomes entirely focused on *preparing for court*, rather than *supporting families to avoid court*.

The main practical problem that has emerged is the very tight schedule within which a family group conference has to be organized: if a family plan is to be presented at the first court hearing, there is only a two-week window available as from the moment the 'letter before proceedings' (the document that starts the procedure) is issued.

This is a problem, because the preparatory work for a family group conference tends to be time-consuming. Family members not only have to be traced and child carers identified, but time is also needed for a face-to-face meeting of all the family members, and for all to get accustomed to the idea that they have to assume responsibility for making important decisions.

Several authors have wondered whether the very principles underlying FGCs are not compromised by this paramount need to avoid delays (Connolly and Masson 2014).

Meanwhile, the Court of Appeal of England and Wales in a 2013 landmark case laid down the principles to be observed by local authorities.[8] The court will expect the local authority to consider the pros and cons of all realistic options for the child in their care proposals, and explain why the preferred option is a proportionate intervention in the family life. It thus has become all the more important that all actions are reasoned and that options for alternative care in the family are fully explored.

Therefore, unlike in New Zealand, in the UK family group conferences have not become a statutory right, but are merely recommended in various guidance notes within the PLO. The courts have laid down specific standards by which they will

[8]Re B-S (Children) [2013] EWCA Civ 1146.

critically assess the reasons purported by the local authority to pass over the family network. Yet the time pressure, which was simultaneously introduced in the PLO, puts the very concept of the FGC in jeopardy.

7 Reception in the Netherlands: The FGC as Camouflage for Self-help Duties?

In the Netherlands, the concept of the FGC, heralding private family autonomy, has become even further squeezed between countervailing pressures. There, the Dutch provider Eigen Kracht Centrale (EKC), in a larger variety of areas than just child protection cases, has engineered the family group conference approach since 2000.

Early studies indicated that solutions thought out by families actively engaged were overall as viable as professional interventions, but came at a considerably lower cost (de Roo and Jagtenberg 2012).

In 2011, a Member of Parliament took up the concept when a new youth protection bill was discussed in the Dutch parliament. The MP, Mr. Voordewind, viewed a new statutory right to a family group conference essential in order to counterbalance the expanded powers that the bill granted to public authorities.[9] Therefore, in the Netherlands, as in New Zealand, the family group conference would constitute an emancipatory alternative to government intervention.

This bill was withdrawn, however, to make room for a more fundamental reconstruction of the entire care system. This included both youth protection (with public authorities in a supervisory role) as well as publicly funded support by professionals, which is often *hoped for* by families in need of professional support. Underlying this fundamental reconstruction was the consideration that the entire (youth) care system had become over-compartmentalized and supply-driven.

High profile care dramas, where, for example, twenty different care professionals had worked without any coordination on a single case, fuelled the idea that the care system should be anchored locally, in neighbourhoods, with *one generalist* as a designated contact person. This contact person was to decide about the care needed, but only after having inquired into the capacity of the family network to provide assistance in the first place. The expectation was, and remains, that this approach will generate cost savings as well.

To underscore the desired transformation of former passive ‘care consumers’ into ‘co-producers of care’, the new youth bill replaced the pre-existing statutory *right* to designated subsidized care that had accrued to parents and their children with a (allegedly non-enforceable) general *duty* of local authorities to help out. However, this duty was made *conditional* on families demonstrating their *inability* to help themselves.[10]

---

[9]Kamerstukken (Dutch parliamentary papers) II 2010/11, 32 015 nr. 23.

[10]Article 2.3 Jeugdwet 2015.

It is in this particular context that MP Voordewind, in 2013, again proposed to introduce a right to a family plan, this time in the comprehensive youth bill. At that time, the underlying idea seems to have been where a family is under an *obligation* to try to help itself, it should also have the *right* to help itself, as a corollary.[11]

MP Voordewinds's proposals were adopted. The new 2015 Youth Act, to be clear, covers *all* areas of youth care, which is the domain of youth protection including the array of interventions that may be imposed, such as supervision and placement orders, *and* the domain of publicly funded professional support applied for by families.

With regard to the *first* domain, the family group conference could be said to still function as an *emancipatory alternative* to authoritative intervention, but as for the *second* domain the family group conference serves as a *tool* to manage (i.e. to *reduce*) care *support applications*. One could argue that in the Netherlands as well as in the UK the idea underlying the FGC concept is compromised, but in different ways: in the UK due to the time pressure in pre-proceedings, in the Netherlands due to the considerably wider application of the family group conference well beyond the mere domain of youth protection.

8 The FGC and the Dutch Courts: Are Professionals Made the Gatekeepers for Family Autonomy?

It is fascinating to see how the Dutch courts have dealt with the right to a family group conference (or the duty to family self-help) in both domains, youth protection and hoped for professional care support. In the first domain, the family divisions within the regular courts have jurisdiction. In most of the published cases, the parents invoke the right to make a family plan in order to fend off requests for removal/placement orders. It is noteworthy that Dutch family courts (unlike UK family courts) have hardly formulated any specific guidelines. The pattern one can discern in the judgments on the merits is that the courts mostly rely on the professional's (guardian's) assessment, which a reliable family network that could offer alternative care is lacking.

Occasionally, courts use the argument that parents should have invoked their right the very first time that a supervision or placement order was sought.[12] If parents let one year pass by, they are denied a legal interest to vindicate this right. This finding infringes the case law of the ECtHR.

In the second domain, the *administrative courts* have jurisdiction, as publicly funded professional care support is now the responsibility of municipal governments (i.e. the mayor and his/her aldermen). In these courts, parents have precisely *sought* that professional support be provided by the local authorities. Here one

[11] Kamerstukken II 2012/2013, 33 684 nr. 57.

[12] ECLI:NL:RBNHO:2017:988.

comes across cases where municipalities use the duty to organize self-help first (or put differently, the duty to invoke one's right to a family group conference first) *against* citizens who have applied for support.

A recent landmark case by the Dutch Central Court of Appeals addressed the decision of a local authority *to discontinue* professional support to a daughter with mental retardation: in the opinion of the authority, *her mother* could take over.[13]

The Central Court of Appeals laid down a three-step model that is likely to *reverse* the roles of the family and the (publicly funded) expert professional.

According to the court, first, the request for care and support should be carefully analysed; second, a professional expert should specify the nature of the (mental) problems and indicate what exact care would be needed; third (*and only third*), the authority should ascertain whether the care needed (according to the expert) can indeed be provided by the family network itself.

The fascinating picture that emerges is that in both domains—that is, (1) the domain of child protection where family group conferences present an alternative to government intervention, and (2) the domain of hoped for professional support where family group conferences and family autonomy are used to curb the volume of applications for assistance—the Dutch courts thus far have strongly mitigated the envisaged role of family autonomy while giving the publicly funded care professional pride of place (again). The professional is thus bound to become the gatekeeper of family party autonomy.

9 FGCs and 'Regular' Modes of ADR: A Provisional Assessment

The problems and disputes for which family group conferences were designed are of a special nature: these are essentially disputes between a nuclear family (often a single parent trying to raise one or more children) on one side and an authority on the other. This authority can be a body of professional care workers (in the child protection domain) or it can be the municipal government (which is to decide about granting professional support that the family applied for). In both scenarios, there is apparently a serious problem with one of the parties in the dispute, i.e. the parent(s) who lack the capacity or means to perform their role as a parent properly. The idea underlying the original New Zealand FGC (where conferences are only used in the child protection domain to avert government intervention) was to replace the ill-performing parent(s) as a party with a caretaker, i.e. the wider family network. In this way, the greatly desired family (or rather, community) autonomy could (often) be preserved.

In *regular* ADR, such a 'subrogation' of one of the disputing parties is hardly conceivable, as it is exactly the disputants themselves who are expected to solve

[13] CRvB 1 May 2017 (*Steenwijkerland*) ECLI:NL:CRVB:2017:1477.

their problem. The option of 'extending' a party with problems might deserve further study though, particularly as the 'private life' notion in Article 8 ECHR has gradually been expanded in European case law.

At the same time, such an 'extension' or 'subrogation' of one of the parties in a dispute does raise a potential complication: a first prerequisite is that there *actually is* a (family) network trusted by the disputant (the parent); and a second prerequisite is that the network members themselves are *willing* to cooperate in providing a care solution vis-à-vis the child. Here, it does not take just two, but many more participants to tango.

This takes us to the other party in the dispute. In child protection cases, this is the party (child protection board, family guardian) with a statutory duty to protect the child from neglect and abuse. Always the interest of the child is (or should be) paramount. This means that if a family network is willing and able to conceive of a plan to take care of the child, the other party, the child or the protection agent must screen that plan. This is not different from regular ADR, with one exception: the screening is aimed at the interests of a third party, i.e. the child, and a risk assessment of what may happen if control over the further raising of the child is relinquished to the family. If things go wrong, could the child protection agent be held liable then, in view of his/her statutory duties?

Then again, can an unwilling adversary just preclude a family from exercising its right to a family group conference? The statutory rules in New Zealand and the Netherlands and the judicial criteria in the UK suggest the (wider) family is not to be lightly put aside, although some discretionary margin remains for the child protection authority.

The right to a family group conference could be regarded as a right not to be subjected to top-down professional interventions. However, there are other rights involved here: the neglected or abused child's right to adequate protection, and the statutory duty resting upon the child protection authority to provide this protection.

All the same, the right to a family group conference opens up the possibility for more reasoned decisions by the authority whether or not such protection could alternatively be afforded by the child's own family network. A form of 'collaborative governance' between professional and lay members of the family may be required here. Such a cooperative approach might even generate cost savings.

This cost aspect brings us finally to the standards for assessing the right to a family group conference, and indeed for assessing ADR/private justice generally. Two very different standards of evaluation that are familiar from the ADR debate were also encountered in the recent history of family group conferences:

(1) the potential to reduce costs (in this case not only in court administration, but even more so in state-funded youth care); and
(2) the potential to devise solutions oneself—the potential to empower people.

However, if there is the threat of child neglect or abuse, or a mental disorder complication that has also affected the child, is that a problem that *can* be solved by the extended family? How much can a layperson reasonably be expected to 'solve'?

What—in other words—is the therapeutic effectiveness of autonomous help or (alternatively) a professional intervention? Should that *also* be a standard for evaluation?

This creates a formidable obstacle by itself in making 'the right to direct one's own family' a reality. Owing to the judgment of the Central Court of Appeals of 1 May 2017 that we discussed earlier, the Dutch courts at any rate will seriously check how professionals think about the family's therapeutic potential.

There is in these cases a major power imbalance between the parties (professional authority versus lay family members) anyway, if only because families may not even be aware of the existence of this fairly novel right to make their own plan. Do professionals bring it to their attention? And to round off with a rhetorical question: following the Central Court of Appeals 2017 criteria, would a Dutch care professional, who is remunerated for his/her expertise, likely inform a court that the care problem at hand does not require his/her expertise as a care professional?

In the end, there will always be a host of diverging interests to reckon with. The main thing for researchers in this area is, in our view, not to overlook any of them. That, at least, is a lesson to remember from interest-based approaches in ADR such as mediation.

Acknowledgements This longitudinal, socio-legal empirical research project (2015–2019) is subsidized by the Netherlands Organization for Scientific Research NWO, together with the city of Rotterdam, under the aegis of the national *Smart Governance* programme.

References

Civil Exchange (2015) Whose society? The final big society audit. http://www.civilexchange.org.uk/whose-society-the-final-big-society-audit. Accessed 7 June 2018

Connolly M, Masson J (2014) Private and public voices: does family group conferencing privilege the voice of children and families in child welfare? J Soc Welf Fam Law 36(4):403–414

de Roo A, Jagtenberg R (2012) Socio-economic returns on FGC for Dutch multi-problem families. In: Clarijs R, Malmberg Th (eds) The quiet revolution. SWP Publishers, Amsterdam

Doolan M (2007) Duty calls: the response of law, policy and practice to participation rights in child welfare systems. Prot Child 22(1):10–18

European Commission (2016), Report on the Application of Directive 2008/52/EC on Mediation in Civil and Commercial Matters. Brussels: European Union, document COM 542 final

Evans C (2011) The public law outline and family group conferences. Child Care Pract 17(1):3–15

Geurts T, Sportel IDA (2015) Voorkomen van vechtscheidingen. Research Memorandum 2. Wetenschappelijk Onderzoeks - en Documentatie Centrum, The Hague

Levine J (2000) The family group conference in the New Zealand CYP&F Act of 1989: review and evaluation. Behav Sci Law 18:517–566

Milieu Ltd and ICF Consulting (2014) Study for an evaluation of the Mediation Directive. Brussels/London

Smith L, Hennessey J (1998) Making a difference: the Essex family group conference project. Essex Social Service publications, Chelmsford

Taylor M (2012) The big society and family group conferences: explanations and reflections. In: Clarijs R, Malmberg Th (eds) The quiet revolution. SWP Publishers, Amsterdam

Ter Voert MJ, Klein Haarhuis CM (2015) Geschilbeslechtingsdelta 2014. Wetenschappelijk Onderzoeks - en Documentatie Centrum, The Hague, 109
Tesler PH (2001) Collaborative law: achieving effective resolution in divorce without litigation. American Bar Association and Later Editions, Washington, D.C.

Annie de Roo Associate Professor of ADR and Comparative Law at Erasmus University Rotterdam, the Netherlands. Director of the Netherlands Organization for Scientific Research (N. W.O.) sponsored project on Hybrid Governance in the Social Domain. Vice-chair of the Exams Committee of the Mediators Federation of the Netherlands (MFN). Editor-in-Chief of *TMD*, the Dutch-Flemish Mediation & Conflict Management Quarterly.

Rob Jagtenberg Senior Research Fellow of Erasmus University Rotterdam, the Netherlands. Former member of the Supervisory Committee for the national Dutch project on court-connected mediation, and Principal Researcher in projects commissioned by the World Bank and The Council for the Judiciary, the Netherlands.

Reassessing the Essential Role of Public Courts: Learning from the American Experience

Richard Marcus

Abstract Over the years, the United States has introduced different alternative dispute resolution mechanisms, thus 'outsourcing' some of the court's tasks. The ADR movement was a reaction to costly and lengthy proceedings the United States was coping with. It is doubtful whether such 'outsourcing' indeed routinely saves time and money and contributes to the public goals of civil justice. This contribution describes the evolution of American civil procedure, thereby explaining the issues that the American civil justice system has faced over the years and mechanisms which have been identified and chosen to fight those challenges. This experience is a lesson to other countries trying to reach the same goals.

1 Introduction

This book addresses a key set of issues that have occupied proceduralists in many different systems—the centrality of relying on *public* courts to resolve disputes, and the centrality of public courts in resolving critical social issues. Of course, in all nations dispute resolution has existed outside the public courts, and often outside the public sphere. In the US, at least, courts have assumed a much greater importance than has reportedly been true in other societies. One manifestation of that centrality is the striking use of American courts to achieve social changes in the mid 20th century.

Somewhat in reaction to that 'judicial activism,' the US Supreme Court embarked more than a generation ago on a relatively broad embrace of alternatives to litigation, and hence to public court resolution, of many disputes. A good deal of the bloom has come off that rose. Nonetheless, the Supreme Court has adopted an increasingly aggressive attitude toward application of the 1925 federal arbitration law to compel private resolution of a large number of disputes, heightening the concern about pushing dispute resolution out of the public realm.

R. Marcus (✉)
Hastings College of the Law, University of California, San Francisco, USA
e-mail: marcusr@uchastings.edu

A. Uzelac and C. H. van Rhee (eds.), *Transformation of Civil Justice*,
Ius Gentium: Comparative Perspectives on Law and Justice 70,
https://doi.org/10.1007/978-3-319-97358-6_10

Meanwhile, in a number of respects, American public courts have been 'outsourcing' their tasks. To some extent, these developments can be linked to distinctive aspects of American procedure that prompt potential litigants to seek alternatives to the public courts. The alternative dispute resolution (ADR) movement that emerged in the 1980s was largely a product of disaffection from the rigors, cost, and duration of public civil litigation. Indeed, some in America have even sought to 'privatize' aspects of criminal justice; 'private' prisons have appeared in a number of places. In all likelihood, similar developments can be identified in other countries.

The issues raised by these developments are both basic and wide-ranging. This contribution cannot do more than introduce a few of them and report on some American developments that bear on those issues, in hopes that this American experience will prove informative for others who confront similar issues in their systems. At its most basic, one might say that the core question is whether some private disputes really ought not be in public courts. In 1979, Professor Fiss noted that 'some disputes may not threaten or otherwise implicate a public value. All the disputants may, for example, acknowledge the norms and confine their dispute to the interpretation of the words of the contract.' He added that '[s]uch disputes may wind their way into court, and judges may spend time on these purely private disputes [...]. That seems, however, an extravagant use of public resources, and thus it seems quite appropriate for those disputes to be handled not by courts, but by arbitrators' (1979, 30).

Also in 1979, then-Professor Posner noted that '[a]djudication is normally regarded as a government function and judges as public officials,' but added 'that the provision of judicial services precedes the formation of the state, that many formally public courts long had important characteristics of private institutions, and that even today much adjudication is private' (Landes and Posner 1979, 235). Indeed, Dean Carrington urged at the same time that '[t]he costs in time, treasure, and stress that are associated with public intervention into a dispute can be justified, and are justified, only by reference to public needs, interests, objectives, or "goods"' (1979, 304).

So these issues have been with us for some time, and they are unlikely to go away. Indeed, they form the heart of the contributions in this book. To introduce the American experience, I intend to focus on several themes: (1) The distinctive evolution of American procedure and the common law aspects that make 'public' adjudication arguably more important than in other systems; (2) The emergence in the mid 20th century of 'structural' constitutional litigation, private enforcement, and commercial litigation between businesses as recurrent themes built on American procedural arrangements; (3) The recoil from various aspects of that mid-century development and efforts to constrain some of the most aggressive features of American procedure; (4) The emergence of case management as a method of confining American procedure; (5) The relatively simultaneous growth of interest in expanding decision-making capacity by conferring decision-making authority on people who are not traditional 'judges;' (6) the flowering of ADR and seeming disappointment with arbitration as a method of resolving commercial disputes; and (7) the current controversy about enforcing consumer and other 'contracts' to arbitrate rather than use the public courts.

2 The 20th Century-Evolution of American Procedure

The public role of common law courts is, almost by definition, more significant than the role of civil law courts. At least from a distance, it seems that civil law courts are not authorized to 'make' law. That authority rests with the legislature. Even the decisions of civil law courts may not be regarded as 'precedent' that governs the resolution of later cases. Perhaps it was inevitable that the public role of American courts would be more prominent than in other systems; de Tocqueville observed in the early 19th century that Americans already tended to define or refine many issues that would be addressed in other ways in other nations into legal disputes suitable for resolution in court.[1]

That reality did not immediately cause American court systems to diverge from other common law systems, but the 'shared sovereignty' aspects of the American political union produced tensions about the role of courts in the 19th century. The key question was what the 'common law' was, and where it came from. In a civil law system, one suspects that this sort of question may not arise because the answer would be that the legislature would be the source of the law. But in the US, there was a complication—there were arguably *two* parallel common law court systems in operation throughout the country, one operated by the state in which the court sat, and the other by the federal government. When it created lower federal courts, Congress directed that they apply state 'law,'[2] but the Supreme Court ruled in 1842 that state court decisions did not constitute 'laws' that federal judges had to follow.[3] In significant ways, the 'law' announced by state courts diverged from the 'law' announced by federal courts until, in 1938, the Supreme Court reversed course and declared that federal courts did not have any general law-making power: '[T]he law to be applied in any case is the law of the state. And whether the law of the state shall be declared by its Legislature in a statute or by its highest court in a decision is not a matter of federal concern.'[4]

So long as the decisions of courts are, therefore, on equal footing with the decisions of legislatures, the public importance of those decisions is apparent. Besides recognizing this basic point, it is also important to appreciate two procedural features.

[1]See generally de Tocqueville (1835).

[2]28 U.S.C. § 1652 provides that 'the laws of the several states, except where the constitution, treaties, or statutes of the United States shall otherwise require or provide, shall be regarded as rules of decision in trials at common law in the courts of the United States.'

[3]Swift v. Tyson, 41 U.S. 1 (1842).

[4]Erie Railroad Co. v. Tompkins, 304 U.S. 64 (1938).

2.1 The Centrality of Trial in America's Public Procedure

There is a considerable temptation to lapse into what some have called 'litigation romanticism' (Menkel-Meadow 1995, 2669) when discussing American procedure. And there is considerable reason to view American procedure that way. Indeed, aspects of it have found their way into many Hollywood movies. The American jury trial is the stuff of legend, and also could be the stuff of direct democracy. American courts, in particular, would often announce legal rules that depend on the 'reasonable person' standard or some other multifactor test that would be applied by an American jury (operating under 'instructions' from an American judge). As recognized by Professors Burbank and Subrin in 2011, in an essay decrying the declining frequency of trials in American civil cases:

> [M]any legal norms need community input for the decisions applying them to be accepted by that community. Issues such a negligence, intentional discrimination, material breach of contract, and unfair competition are not facts capable of scientific demonstration. Nor are these issues pure questions of law. Rather, they are concepts mixing elements of fact and law that become legitimate behavioral norms when the citizenry at large, acting through jury representatives, decides what the community deems acceptable. (Burbank and Subrin 2011, 401, 402)

So one can say there is an inevitable 'public' aspect to the very application of many American legal rules.

A century ago, it seems that some American jury trials served not only that function, but also provided a broader public involvement in litigation. Consider the following description of trials handled early in his legal career by Robert Jackson, who later served on the US Supreme Court and also was a prosecutor at the Nuremburg trials of former Nazis:

> With the financial stakes typically tiny, the cases Jackson took early in his career were as much theater as they were law. The local community treated a day's worth of trials as entertainment. Court was not held before a judge, but in front of a justice of the peace who was not a lawyer. Trials took place not in a regular courtroom, but wherever there was space to gather; in a school, a church, or the dance hall of a Masonic Temple. (Feldman 2010, 45)

The innate 'publicness' of an American jury trial has much to commend it. Because the jury is drawn from the lay population and permitted only to consider the evidence presented in court, the presentation in court must be adequate to inform the jury, and hence also the attending public. Moving away from that model could weaken or undermine the public value of a trial.[5]

[5]See Marcus (1989, 778–782) (discussing what could be lost if the American system shifted to reliance on written materials submitted to the judge rather than relying on the in-court presentation of live witnesses before a jury).

2.2 *The Frustrations of 19th-Century US Procedure, and the Embrace of the 1938 Federal Rules*

Lest the description above invite 'litigation romanticism,' it is important to add that many found much to deplore in American 19th-century procedure. Dean Roscoe Pound famously denounced popular dissatisfaction with prevailing American procedure in a 1906 speech to the American Bar Association (1906). That speech, and other events, led to a 30-year reform effort that culminated in the adoption in 1938 of the Federal Rules of Civil Procedure, which came with their hallmarks—relaxed pleadings, broad discovery, and expansive remedies—that form the heart of contemporary American procedural exceptionalism, particularly when combined with the jury trial.

For some mid-century observers, the increased flexibility of American procedure seemed an inevitable process. Professor Millar, for example, posited that 'as procedure develops the advance is from rigidity to flexibility' (1952, 5). For some time, that seemed to be the way the wind was blowing. In the 1960s, for example, the federal discovery rules were relaxed further. And in 1966, the class-action rule was transformed in ways that proved over the following decades to make it a very formidable litigation instrument. Meanwhile, a majority of American states adopted procedure rules modeled on the federal rules, and even those states (like California) that did not do so relaxed their procedural rules so that they resembled the federal approach. But as explored below, counterpressures began to emerge in the 1970s, and they seemed to play a considerable role in the 'privatization' of some American litigation.

3 American Litigation in the 'Golden Age'

For those who indulge in nostalgia, there is usually a 'golden age' that some fear has been lost and seek to restore. Whether or not they were 'golden,' it seems that several developments followed the mid-century American relaxation of procedure and were fed by it. It seems also that they play a considerable role in the current debate about privatization of American litigation.

3.1 *'Public Law' Litigation*

When Professor Fiss suggested in 1979 that it would be wasteful for purely private disputes to occupy public courts (1979, 30), he was focused on what Professor Chayes had recently labeled 'public law litigation' (Chayes 1976). Chayes urged that America had, after World War II, produced 'a new model of civil litigation' in which 'the object of litigation is the vindication of constitutional or statutory policies' (1976, 1282, 1284). Fiss thus posited that the purpose of public courts is to give voice and effect to public values, and regarded using public courts for 'private' disputes as wasteful. The problem, then, is to determine when there is not a public interest in litigation. In all likelihood, Fiss would argue (1984) that there actually never is litigation in which the public has no interest, and for that reason by the mid 1980s he launched a scathing critique of the growing popularity of judicial settlement promotion.

The importance of public law litigation in the US cannot easily be overstated. In important ways, it replaced the legislature as the source of social and political progress for disadvantaged groups. Indeed, it was said that the US Supreme Court's desegregation rulings in part resulted from the failure of the other branches of government to address the need to renounce race-based and other discriminatory de jure and de facto practices.

To some extent, this form of litigation depended on mid-century procedural innovations. A key antidiscrimination case was the source of the Supreme Court's announcement in 1957 that 'notice pleading' should prevail under the Federal Rules.[6] Lower courts emphasized the need for broad discovery to obtain evidence of discriminatory practices or motives. Consider the following explanation of an appellate court for holding that the lower court in an age discrimination case had improperly refused to require the employer to disclose the name of every person over the age of 40 terminated during a six-year period: 'Because employers rarely leave a paper trail—or "smoking gun"—attesting to a discriminatory intent, disparate treatment plaintiffs often must build their cases from pieces of circumstantial evidence which cumulatively undercut the credibility of various explanations offered by the employer.'[7]

It need hardly be emphasized that having this sort of litigation decided in a public court is extremely important. Indeed, the very structure of a court system that authorizes all judges—not only a specialized Constitutional Court—to pass on the constitutionality of legislative and other governmental acts places court functions at the core of the public sphere. And some such cases continue to occupy the courts. A prominent recent example is litigation challenging conditions in the California prison system.[8] But as Judge Easterbrook said in 2008, the federal courts do not often entertain such cases now.[9]

---

[6]Conley v. Gibson, 355 U.S. 41 (1957). This case announced the 'slightest doubt' standard for dismissal on the pleadings that was 'retired' by the Supreme Court in its decision in Bell Atlantic Corp. v. Twombly, 550 U.S. 544 (2007). The case was about discrimination by a southern union against its African American members. For a discussion of the case, see Sherwin (2008).

[7]Hollander v. American Cyanamid Co., 895 F.2d 80, 84–85 (2d Cir. 1990).

[8]See Brown v. Plata, 131 S.Ct. 1910 (2011).

[9]Rahman v. Chertoff, 530 F.3d 622, 626 (7th Cir. 2008), criticizing the suit as 'a relic of a time when the federal judiciary thought that structural injunctions taking control of executive functions were sensible. That time is past.'

3.2 Private Enforcement by Private Attorneys General

Curiously, an important present feature of American public procedure is to facilitate the private enforcement of public norms.[10] For most modern industrial societies, the main (or only) enforcer of public norms is the state. From that perspective, it may seem odd that one would worry that the 'privatization' of judicial functions might undermine the enforcement of public norms, for public authorities surely could not be barred from the public courts.

Partly due to legislative successes in the effort to combat discrimination, private enforcement of public norms has achieved a central role that American procedure implements. The relatively relaxed pleading standards, along with broad willingness to permit amendment of pleadings, open the courthouse door to private lawyers who claim to serve the public good. The broad discovery American courts authorize enables private lawyers to use the subpoena to root out alleged wrongdoing. The jury trial enables lawyers to put their evidence before fellow citizens, who will sit in judgment. The absence of a 'loser pays' regime means that a litigation loss is much less costly.

A half-century ago, the American Congress elected to place primary responsibility to enforce anti-discrimination law under Title VII of the 1964 Civil Rights Act on private plaintiffs rather than an administrative agency.[11] Thereafter, it adopted the same format for a variety of other anti-discrimination statutes. It also used a similar approach to a variety of other statutes such as the Truth in Lending Act, authorizing those who contend that there has been a statutory violation to sue and recover their attorney fees if they win. These statutes often promise a minimum recovery (of $1000 or so) as an inducement to sue. As the Supreme Court put it in 1975, 'Congress has opted to rely heavily on private enforcement to implement public policy.'[12] Many states have followed the same pattern, authorizing victims of such things as 'junk' faxes, misleading product labels and the like to sue to enforce statutory requirements applicable to such activities. And such statutory regimes are often accompanied by one-way fee-shifting provisions—the successful plaintiff lawyer ends up being paid by the losing defendant, while a successful defendant cannot obtain reimbursement for its attorney fees. So the American bar has developed a considerable contingent of 'private attorney general' specialist lawyers.[13]

A somewhat similar enforcement-based argument has emerged in connection with modern American tort litigation. Unlike the statutory arrangements noted above, this litigation does not authorize recovery of attorney fees (although there are often contingency fee arrangements that can provide a handsome payday for the lawyer). But the prevailing orientation of American tort law to force providers of

[10]See generally Burbank et al. (2013).

[11]For an extensive review of this development, see Farhang (2010).

[12]Alyeska Pipeline Serv. Co. v. Wilderness Soc'y, 421 U.S. 240, 263 (1975).

[13]For discussion, see Rubenstein (2004).

goods and services to 'internalize' the costs resulting from their activities means that lawyers engaged in this activity have a plausible claim that they also serve the public interest by seeking private recoveries. Moreover, the possibility of a large recovery for 'pain and suffering,' and sometimes punitive damages as well, can mean that the incentives for potential defendants to avoid conduct that might expose them to liability are very large. And many in the defendant group claim that they attend closely to this risk, although they also deplore the expensive measures they have to take to stave off tort liability.

One can raise reasonable questions about whether such private, profit-oriented enforcement always serves public interests. The argument of potential defendants about tort liability is that the very large costs of litigation, along with the possibility (even remote) of a whopping verdict, actually deter them from producing products and services that are socially useful. And statutory claims can be used to achieve results that the legislators who enacted them never intended. For example, allegedly environmental suits are sometimes filed to stop public projects by people who have entirely different concerns but exploit the opportunity to prevent the project from going forward. To take a noteworthy example, the *San Francisco Chronicle* published an editorial attacking an anti-abortion group that sued to prevent the opening of a Planned Parenthood 'family planning' clinic in South San Francisco on the ground that the environmental impact report did not give enough emphasis on the disruption that would be likely due to 'reasonably probable First Amendment activity.' As the newspaper urged, 'the opponents of reproductive freedom are arguing that their own movement's protests would have a disruptive effect on downtown South San Francisco. … Meanwhile, Planned Parenthood is being forced to spend money on legal fees that could have gone into health care' (San Francisco Chronicle 2015). The point here is that a significant portion of the clout that those who bring such suits can wield is due to the distinctive features of American procedure. That clout is not always used in pursuit of what most would call the 'public interest,' much less to further the goals envisioned by those who authorized the private suits.

3.3 The Upsurge in Business Litigation

Until World War II, American business scorned litigation. It could not avoid being sued, but it could decline to initiate litigation. When he was US Secretary of Commerce, Herbert Hoover (later President) expressed this view very firmly: 'Next to war, commercial litigation is the largest item of preventable loss in civilization' (Institute of Law 1931, 1). As a consequence, until 1950 or so litigation departments of major law firms were poor stepchildren, there to do the bidding of the firms' business clients when they were dragged into court (Galanter and Palay 1991). In the 1950s and 1960s, this attitude gradually changed, and litigation departments in leading firms became profitable in their own right.

Two decades ago Dean Garth described the remarkable change in corporate attitudes toward litigation. By the 1980s, corporate clients began to shop for lawyers, producing competition among law firms to land corporate litigation business. Meanwhile: '[T]he business world's increased competitiveness made businesses eager to take advantage of whatever was available for economic warfare, including the law. … Business litigation increased, and there was competition within business litigation. The principal forms of innovation in litigation, it appears, were methods that escalated legal conflicts. Every aspect of lawsuits became contested' (Garth 1993, 942).

At that time, some attributed this development to the declining ability of lawyers to dissuade their clients from pursuing litigation, or at least to dissuade them from pursuing it in a scorched earth manner.[14] In the late 1990s, Dean Garth elaborated on the relationship between these developments and the escalating discovery problems reported in some cases:

> [L]awyers in the ordinary cases have learned how to manage time and expense. They have had to do so, since their clients will not pay for scorched earth tactics. On the other hand, the high-stakes, high-conflict cases involve clients who pay for the services of lawyers as warriors, and that is what they usually get. In terms of the legal services market and the civil discovery problem, it appears that clients seek the elite of the bar only when they believe that the nature of the problem and the stakes are sufficiently high to justify a major investment in legal services (or, in the contingent fee area, are sufficient for the lawyer to invest substantially in the case). It is likely that only a fraction of lawyers can claim the fees or attract the cases that justify (in terms of the stakes) investment in litigation as full-scale warfare. (Garth 1998, 605)

Ironically, these developments in business litigation came at the same time that businesses were decrying the high cost of litigation, and of discovery in particular. Thus, one could say that scorched earth commercial litigation was sometimes the cause of the very sorts of excessive litigation costs that businesses emphasized in their efforts to justify changes in the American procedural paradigm. We turn to those developments now.

4 The Reaction—Constraining American Procedure

In a real sense, the high water point for expansive American procedure was around 1970. The class-action rule had been reoriented in 1966, and in 1970 new and more expansive discovery rules come into effect. At around the same time, Congress and state legislatures were enacting a variety of new regulatory statutes that often

[14]See Gilson (1990, 899–903); Kronman (1993, 290) (lamenting the declining ability of lawyers to influence or guide their clients in making business decisions, as opposed to facilitating decisions the clients made without lawyer guidance).

included private rights to sue, and courts were sometimes finding 'implied' private rights of action even when the legislature did not expressly provide a private right to sue.

Whether or not a reaction was inevitable, it is clear that one happened. For more than 40 years, a recurrent theme has been that the procedural relaxation went too far, and that American businesses have been unduly hobbled by the litigation that results from this expansive procedure. Hence, various moves have occurred to constrain various aspects of American procedure. Initially, those focused principally on discovery,[15] but discovery has continued to have a central role in US litigation (Marcus 2014, 1707–1721). In 1995, Congress responded to protests about rampant securities litigation by adopting the Private Securities Litigation Reform Act,[16] which tightened pleading standards in securities fraud cases and also altered the handling of securities fraud class actions. In 2005, Congress adopted the Class Action Fairness Act,[17] which greatly expanded federal court jurisdiction to hear class actions based on state law claims, and also imposed some regulations on the settlement of class actions.

Attention to both discovery and class actions has continued; in 2006, discovery amendments to deal with production of electronically stored information went into effect, and another package of discovery amendments was approved by the Supreme Court in April 2015. Meanwhile, the federal rule-makers have again considered the possibility of amending the class-action rule, eventually leading to modest amendments that may go into effect in 2018 (Marcus 2015a, 2018).

Congress has also seen a number of bills introduced to change procedure outside the rulemaking process. One prominent example has been discussion of legislation to deal with the reported problem of 'patent trolls,' 'nonpracticing entities' that assert patent infringement claims in hopes of extracting lucrative licensing settlements. The White House issued a report in 2013 about this activity.[18] The reported objections echo the ones urged to justify broad changes in the handling of litigation —lax pleading standards, broad and costly discovery, and uncertainties of a jury trial. Proposed legislation[19] sought to solve the problems both by imposing more specific pleading requirements and by imposing a 'requester pays' regime for any discovery beyond somewhat limited 'core discovery.' It also directed the rule-makers to consider new rules to achieve those goals.

More recently, despite the decision of the federal rules-makers to adopt reforms of the class-action rule, Congress is considering a much more aggressive package of

[15]For a discussion of the changes between 1975 and 1995, see Marcus (1998).

[16]Private Securities Litigation Reform Act, Pub. L. 104–67, 109 Stat. 737, 1995.

[17]Class Action Fairness Act, Pub. L. 109-2, 119 Stat. 4–14, 2005.

[18]See Executive Office of the President (2013).

[19]See Innovation Act of 2015, H.R. 9, 114th Cong., 1st. Sess.

changes.[20] Should that legislation be adopted, it will likely cause significant changes to US class-action litigation.[21]

For the present, then, it is impossible to foresee exactly what further changes will emerge for American civil litigation. At least some observers urge rather radical changes in various aspects of American litigation. Ironically, given that the sources of many of those proposals are entities that generally do not favor a shift toward the governing principles of Western Europe, it does seem that the proposals themselves would bring American procedure much closer to the Western European model.[22] But the rule-makers have not lost faith with the basic mid-century commitment to broad access to court and significant discovery rights, and the rule changes that have occurred have basically adhered to the mid-century aspiration.

5 An Alternative Response—Case Management

Rather than cut back on discovery in a draconian manner, the rule-makers have instead urged (and sometimes tried to compel) judges to become more active in managing their cases, in hopes this individualized restraint will work better at constraining abusive behavior than some system-wide 'cures' or all-purpose objective definitions of 'abuse.' Beginning with the Woolf Reforms in the UK in the 1990s, the case management impulse spread beyond America's borders.

From one perspective, this response is a perfectly reasonable one to the alternative of unrestrained lawyer latitude.[23] But it has nevertheless provoked strong opposition on the ground that it compromises the commitment to public justice. A prominent example is Professor Resnik, who has campaigned since 1982 against managerial judging.[24] Professor Miller, a former Reporter for the federal rule-makers, has also inveighed against this evolution for more than a decade.[25]

The critics have a point, if the current reality is compared to the 'litigation romanticism' view that American trials are a critical feature of American democracy. Even within the common law tradition, as I observed in 1989, the emerging American method of deciding more cases using summary judgment and recognizing somewhat broader authority for judges to 'take the case from the jury' at trial

[20]See Fairness in Class Action Litigation Act of 2017, H.R. 985. The House of Representatives passed this bill in March 2017. It is uncertain whether the Senate will also pass it.

[21]For discussion of the legislation, see Marcus (2018).

[22]For discussion, see Marcus (2013).

[23]For an argument to this effect, see Marcus (2003).

[24]See, e.g., Resnik (1982).

[25]See Miller (2003).

resembles the practices of the English equity courts.[26] Rather than stressing live testimony in court, summary judgment relies on written alternatives, including deposition testimony and documents produced in discovery. Rather than affording the public access to a trial that serves as a quasi-theatrical event in which the litigants bring the controversy 'to life' for a jury (and also the observing public), managerial judging leading to summary judgment happens 'behind closed doors.' As Professor Resnik has objected, due to these changes 'the occasions for public observation and involvement in adjudication are diminishing' (2014, 18).

That is not the only way to view American procedural history, however. Recall that a century ago—when the 'democratic' features of civil litigation may have been at their height—Dean Pound denounced the reality of litigation as usually turning on procedural maneuvering and surprise. The Federal Rules were, in fact, designed to cure those problems. And it seems many believe that they did so by the middle of the century, when relaxed pleading and broad discovery minimized those problems.

But those distinctly American procedural features could also be used to wear down or overwhelm adversaries who have a just claim or defense but do not have sufficient treasure for the costly American litigation contest, or perhaps are not willing to spend that treasure to win in the unpredictable (as well as expensive) American system. One need not say that such experiences are universal, or even commonplace, to regard them as important. Thus, in the 1980s a prominent judicial supporter of active case management asserted that Professor Resnik 'wishes to preserve the *laissez faire* character of our adversarial system,' which the judge thought had 'run amok,' creating a serious risk of 'one party's collapse in the face of the other party's unsupervised dilatory tactics' (Peckham 1985, 265).

From the perspective of the rest of the world, where the 'single continuous trial' involving live testimony may be unknown, or a recent development, it may seem odd to regard the advent of judicial management of discovery and similar case development activities by the judge as a threat to the public nature of public justice. And it may also seem strange to regard this American development as a symptom of incipient 'privatizing' of civil justice. But that argument has stirred much controversy in the US. As noted below, that controversy exists in a system in which ready (in the Digital Age very ready) access not only to court decisions, but also to the materials on which they might be based, remains the norm, and unsupervised lawyer latitude to use subpoenas and party discovery to compel disclosure of material thought 'confidential' is also commonplace. For some, at least, the vision embraced by these voices decrying case management might be regarded as romanticism.

[26]See Marcus (1989).

6 The Independence of Ordinary Public Judges, and Expanding Judicial Capacity to Include Less Traditional 'Judges'

As all must by now be aware, governmental budgets around the world have been affected by austerity, which has an impact on procedure.[27] One way that governments might seek to save money is to delegate decision-making responsibilities to less expensive judicial adjuncts rather than to more expensive 'real' judges. Of course, that raises the question who is a 'real' judge. Although judicial independence is an international norm, what exactly that means is subject to debate. At one end of the spectrum might be Professor Redish, who has argued that the Due Process Clause of the American Constitution requires that judges have lifetime tenure and protection against diminution of salary.[28]

American judges who sit on what we call 'Article III courts'—US circuit court and district court judges—have constitutional guarantees of the protection Redish stressed. But it cannot be said that most 'public' judges in the US enjoy similar security. Certainly, few if any judges of state courts have similar protections. So from one perspective, one could say that almost all civil cases in the US are decided by judges who operate in a compromised condition. Even the federal courts have additional 'judges' who lack those protections, although they have considerable insulation against political pressures. Magistrate judges and bankruptcy court judges are appointed for a set term of eight years, and not guaranteed reappointment at the end of that period. And all federal judges are subject to statutory requirements that they remove themselves from cases in which they have a financial interest.[29] Finally, American federal judges are subject to judicial discipline for failure to satisfy their professional obligations.[30]

Beyond that augmentation of decision-making power, the US government has created a number of 'Article I courts,' which function like labor courts or other courts in other countries, housed in the administrative agency that is the source of their cases. On the one hand, these are surely 'public' employees engaged in 'public' business. But one may object that they are not 'public' enough. Professor Resnik has lamented the prominence of these judges in the US:

> In 2008, four times more judges (often called hearing officers or administrative judges) sat in federal agencies than in federal courts. These administrative judges rendered tens of thousands of decisions in disputes … Yet, unlike judges sitting in courts, administrative judges have less independence because Congress and the executive branch may seek to affect their decision-making. Further, and again unlike court-based judges, administrative judges work at sites that are often inaccessible to outsiders; hence the public can neither

[27]For a general discussion of these issues, see Marcus (2013b, 2015b).

[28]See Redish and Marshall (1984).

[29]See, e.g., 28 U.S.C. 455.

[30]See Marcus (1993) for discussion of judicial discipline.

provide a buffer against interference nor evaluate the processes and outcomes. (Resnik 2014, 17)

Experience with some categories of federal administrative judges has been disappointing. A prime example is provided by recent experience with immigration judges, whose decisions are reviewed by ordinary federal courts. The US courts of appeals routinely found that the adjudicative decisions of these officers are unsustainable.[31] But there is no general disdain for decisions of federal administrative agencies. Indeed, in 2015 the Supreme Court affirmed that decisions of administrative agencies are entitled to issue preclusive (*res judicata*) effect in court proceedings.[32]

Judges on US state courts do not have the job protections that federal judges enjoy. So though they are 'public,' they may be subject to pressures that could affect their decisions. In many places, judges are elected in ordinary elections, something that is evidently unique in the world (Pildes 2014, 810). Even where they are appointed, judges often must stand in 'retention' elections, and sometimes they may lose. A prominent example was in 1986 in California, when three of the seven justices of the state supreme court were removed from office by the electorate after a vigorous campaign attacking their alleged 'coddling' of criminals that was reportedly financed by businesses that disliked their decisions about such things as businesses' tort liability.[33] There have been other instances of judges who made unpopular decisions being removed from office due to aggressive campaigns against them, such as the superior court judge in Los Angeles who ordered school desegregation and was removed from office at the next election.[34]

This sort of influence over judges—particularly on state supreme courts—may increase in the wake of the US Supreme Court's ruling that corporations are 'persons' that have the constitutional right to make unlimited contributions to political campaigns. In 2009, the US Supreme Court ruled that a state supreme court justice who had received a huge political contribution from a company with a case pending before that court should have refused to participate in the decision of the

---

[31]See Musalo et al. (2011, 990, 991), reporting that as a result of 'streamlining' of administrative decisions 'federal court judges began to receive and directly review the decisions of the immigration judges' and 'began to express shock, dismay, and incredulity at both the quality of the legal decision-making, as well as the abusive and unprofessional behavior of the judges in the treatment of the applicants before them.'

[32]H & B Hardware v. Hargis Industries, 135 S.Ct. 1293, 1303 (2015): '[I]ssue preclusion is not limited to those situations in which the same issue is before two *courts*. [...] [B]ecause the principle of issue preclusion was so "well established" at common law, in those situations in which Congress has authorized agencies to resolve disputes, "courts may take it as given that Congress has legislated with the expectation that the principle of issue preclusion will apply except when a statutory purpose to the contrary is evident."'

[33]For an in-depth review of the campaign that removed three justices from the Supreme Court of California in 1986, see Grodin (1989).

[34]See Stolberg (1992), reporting that in 1970, then-Los Angeles Superior Court Judge Alfred Gitelson was defeated for election after 'a campaign that focused almost totally on his controversial order to desegregate the Los Angeles School System.'

donor's case.[35] Since then, there has been an upsurge in donations to judicial elections, seemingly from those who may hope to tilt those courts in a more 'conservative' direction. An article in the *New York Times* in March 2015, addressed this issue: 'Concerns Grow as Court Races Draw Big Cash.'[36] Although a recent decision by the US Supreme Court regarding limits on fund-raising activities by judges may slightly reduce this concern,[37] it reinforces the reality that judicial selection—and the evaluation of judicial performance—are distinctive in the US with regard to 'public' judges. It may seem that the public has a heightened role, but it surely does not ensure judicial independence.

What all of this means is that 'public' judges may fall short of the idealized role (some might say the 'romanticized' ideal) embraced by some. When one considers efforts to obtain decision-making assistance from those who are not 'public' judges, one must recognize that questions can be raised about those judges who are indisputably 'public.'

7 The Flowering and Partial Disappointment with ADR

By the 1970s, many in the US were disenchanted with the reality of American litigation and asking, 'Isn't there a better way?' The costs of at least some litigation had risen to a point that caused some to say court access was a myth for many. At least equally importantly, many resisted the supposed American penchant for adversary disputation and favored a more moderate attitude toward disputes. The American generation of the 1960s grew up with the slogan 'Make Love, Not War,' and something like that attitude could be translated into the litigation context.[38] At least in family law matters, it became a matter of law in some places. In California, for example, mediation was required by statute in all divorce cases when the couple had children.[39] This attitude could even rise to the level of religious doctrine; in 1986 the US Supreme Court dealt with a case involving a teacher in a Christian school who was fired for disregarding the 'biblical chain of command' by taking a complaint about working conditions to a public agency. According to the Court,

---

[35]Caperton v. A.T. Massey Coal Co, 556 U.S. 868 (2009), holding that under the 'extreme facts' of the case the US Constitution required that the state court justice be recused.

[36]Davey (2015); see also Smith (2015) (reporting that the challenger seeking a position on the Wisconsin Supreme Court in an election asserted that the incumbent justice was motivated by 'extreme liberal personal politics').

[37]See Williams-Yulee v. Florida Bar Ass'n, 135 S.Ct. 1656 (2015), upholding discipline imposed on a judge for personally soliciting campaign donations from lawyers who might appear in the judge's court.

[38]For an example, see Shaffer and Mcthenia (1985).

[39]See Cal. Civil Code 4607(a).

'the core of this doctrine … is that one Christian should not take another Christian into the courts of the State.'[40]

For a long time, American courts have favored settlements, and by the 1980s that enthusiasm prompted judges to become increasingly active in promoting settlement of cases before them. Almost by definition, settlements (except settlements in class actions, which require judicial approval) are private affairs. Professor Fiss found it necessary to argue against this attitude in his 1984 polemic *Against Settlement* (1984). But writing a decade later on *Settlements and the Erosion of the Public Realm*, Professor Luban asked, 'Can anybody realistically continue to be against settlements?' and answered that 'imaginary legal systems in which no cases settle, like those in which all cases settle, would be thoroughly undesirable' (1995, 2620). Not surprisingly, the Federal Rules have been amended to clarify and strengthen the judge's authority to promote settlements.[41] Congress adopted a statute to require US district courts to adopt some sort of ADR procedure to promote settlements.[42]

This enthusiasm for 'private' settlement of disputes may come at a public cost. But it is worth noting that there is something to be said for the widespread enthusiasm for this manner of disposing of cases. As Professor Cavanagh put it recently: 'The federal civil justice system is now at the crossroads. Many putative litigants have chosen to opt out of the courts in favor of some form of alternative dispute resolution, which they perceive as cheaper, faster, more private, and less risky than the court system' (2015, 633). It is worthwhile to catalog the potentially attractive features.

Reduced cost: Because cost plays such a prominent role in American litigation, the prospect that there are much cheaper ways of resolving disputes could be found to have great appeal. Litigation involves not only expensive lawyers, but much formalistic posturing that can obscure matters and make resolution more difficult. Cutting through all that might enable parties to save hugely on transaction costs, leaving more money for resolving the case on the merits. Indeed, this seemed for a long time such an attractive feature of ADR that people might treat it as dispositive in the contest between public and private adjudication.

Better results: A primary argument for ADR has long been that it produces better results. American courts have a limited set of remedies they can provide, and other solutions may better satisfy the litigants. For example, it may be that a plaintiff would very much value an apology from the defendant, but American courts do not have authority to order such things. A settlement, on the other hand, could so provide. Particularly in mediation, one goal is creativity in devising tailored, if unorthodox, solutions to disputes. As two proselytizers for ADR in the 1980s put it, 'participants in ADR are free to go beyond the legal definition of the scope of their

---

[40]Ohio Civil Rights Comm'n v. Dayton Christian Schools, 477 U.S. 619 (1986).

[41]See Fed. R. Civ. P. 16(b) (permitting the judge to require that parties attend pretrial conferences 'to consider possible settlement') and 16(c)(2)(I) (authorizing considering of 'settling the case and using special procedures to assist in resolving the dispute').

[42]See 28 U.S.C. § 651.

dispute. They can search for creative solutions to the problem that gave rise to the dispute, and those solutions may be far more novel than any remedy a court has the power to provide' (Lieberman and Henry 1986, 429).

Not only is there a much wider range of possible measures, an agreed resolution may actually be more effective than a litigated court judgment. Although many court judgments are enforceable and enforced, a significant number turn out to be 'paper decrees,' ineffective in changing real-life relationships. At least with mediation, it is said that things are different:

> The internal and interactional dynamics of consensual settlement processes combine to create pressures toward compliance that are largely lacking in adjudication. … Consent, unlike command, brings with it an assumption of responsibility for the settlement and its implementation. … [T]he personal and immediate commitments generated by consensual processes bind people more strongly to compliance than the relatively distant, impersonal obligations imposed by authorities. (McEwen and Maiman 1984, 44, 45)

Confidentiality: In the US, litigation is a very public activity. Only in rare circumstances is a plaintiff permitted to proceed anonymously.[43] Normally, however, plaintiffs must reveal their identities and—even though American pleading requirements are relatively lax—also provide significant detail about what they are complaining about. Sometimes courts will nevertheless permit anonymity, up to a point. Thus, in a case alleging that plaintiff was sexually abused as a child by a priest, the court directed that plaintiff would be allowed to proceed anonymously until trial.[44] On the other hand, an illegal immigrant suing to challenge the policies of colleges to exclude such persons was not permitted to keep secret her identity as an illegal immigrant.[45]

Confidentiality concerns go far beyond the pleadings, however, due to broad American discovery. Can the fruits of that discovery be kept confidential? Almost by definition, most of the material produced through discovery will be of little importance to resolving the lawsuit. And much of it may be regarded as very confidential. As a federal judge noted, 'Except for a few privileged matters, nothing is sacred in civil litigation.'[46] Accordingly, this judge ordered the Coca-Cola Company to turn over the top secret formula for Coca-Cola to the plaintiffs. Other judges frequently order disclosure of highly confidential matters like private diaries, confidential social media material, and the like. Until 2000, discovery materials in federal cases were routinely filed in court, and they may still be filed in many state courts. And court files are presumptively public. Given that even such sensitive materials as the formula for Coca-Cola could be caught up in the discovery net, and thereby become public, it is not surprising that some would prefer a nonpublic alternative process.

---

[43]See Rice (1996); Steinman (1985).

[44]Doe v. Archdiocese of Portland, 249 F.R.D. 358 (D. Ore. 2008).

[45]Doe v. Merten, 219 F.R.D. 387 (E.D. Va. 2004).

[46]Coca-Cola Bottling Co. v. Coca-Cola Co., 107 F.R.D. 288, 290 (D. Del. 1985).

Beyond that, some courts even seemed to invite the filing of lawsuits to reveal otherwise nonpublic information. Consider the following views of a federal appellate court in 1976: '[M]any important social issues become entangled to some degree in civil litigation. Indeed, certain civil suits may be instigated for the very purpose of gaining information for the public. [...] Civil litigation in general often exposes the need for governmental action or correction. Such revelations should not be kept from the public.'[47] This impulse has drawn support from those who seem to regard American discovery as an adjunct to America's Freedom of Information Act, although it has also drawn criticism.[48] It surely explains why the confidentiality of ADR could be a big plus factor.

Until recently, the presumptive publicness of court files, including discovery results included in those files, was not as significant as it has become in the Digital Age, because one who wanted to read the court files had to show up at the court clerk's office during regular business hours. That put practical limits on actual public access; only the persistent would really gain access. The whole idea of public access to court files may strike some as an invasion of privacy. In Germany, for example, court files are not open to the public.[49] In the US, the advent of online access to public records, including court records, has placed stress on this commitment to openness. When state courts in Ohio introduced online access, many rebelled: 'Divorce lawyers say clients are furious that neighbors are combing through the details of their cases (and are even brazen enough to discuss them with them). A teenager was confronted by his father about a speeding ticket. A man complained to [the court clerk's] office because his friends discovered his history of domestic violence' (Lee 2002, G1).

Given the wealth of detail in public court records, Congress directed that, although court records should be made accessible online, rules should be adopted to protect certain confidential information. The rule-makers, in turn, adopted a rule that precludes the filing of certain personal details, such as the entire Social Security number of a person, some financial account numbers, and the like.[50] But the basic point is that litigating in the public courts is likely to make public a great deal that would otherwise remain private. It is not surprising, therefore, that many may prefer private alternatives that do not carry the cost of public access. In California, for example, a significant number of divorcing couples use private judges to avoid the spotlight that would result from a public filing (O'Shea 2005).

---

[47]Chicago Council of Lawyers v. Bauer, 522 F.2d 242, 258 (7th Cir. 1976).

[48]For one criticism, see Marcus (1983).

[49]See Murray and Stürner (2004, 182): 'Case records in civil cases in Germany are not open to the public, either before or after judgment. The parties and their counsel are entitled to free access to the official records of their cases, but others may look at case records only with the consent of the parties involved or by order of the chief judge of the court upon a showing of some legitimate interest in so doing.' Contrast Japan: 'As a general matter, the court records of a case in Japan are public records just as the trial itself is a public event. Any person may seek to review the records of a case' (Goodman 2004, 341).

[50]See Fed. R. Civ. P. 5.2.

8 The Risks of Compelled ADR, Particularly Arbitration

As always, there are costs that come along with benefits, and some of them may threaten highly important matters.

Illusory cost savings: As noted above, cost savings (and prompt resolution) were among the prime motivators of ADR efforts. Those who signed up early—often businesses tired of the growing cost of litigating in the public courts—anticipated that they could short-circuit the wasteful aspects of public litigation. This hope was particularly pronounced in relation to arbitration, which allows final decisions by private decision makers, obviating any occasion for submitting one's fate to the costly public court system. As one lawyer wrote, in the 1990s 'arbitration was the proverbial fair-haired kid. It was touted as being cheaper, faster, and less confrontational than litigation' (Barkoff 2007).

At least for arbitration, anecdotal evidence suggests that the appeal of this alternative to litigation has declined. The *New York Law Journal* reported in 2007 that 'arbitration may be losing some of its luster. Some attorneys complain that its costs and complexity have been rising, while losing parties express dissatisfaction at the difficulty of appealing in court what they regard as unfair verdicts' (Bar 2007). A leading study of contracts by publicly held firms showed that only about 11% had arbitration clauses, prompting the authors to ask whether there had been a 'flight from arbitration' (Eisenberg and Miller 2007). But others writing in 2008 and focusing on franchising agreements found little evidence of a flight from arbitration comparing data over a ten-year period (Drahozal and Wittorck 2008).

Trying to unravel the data is beyond the scope of this paper, but it does not seem that businesses have universally found private arbitration to offer such a cost savings that they will abandon the public court system in droves.[51] In part, one suspects, that is because it turns out that they want many of the costly opportunities that the court system affords. Recall that a major feature of American litigation in the second half of the 20th century was the growth of litigation initiated by businesses.[52] Indeed, many of the examples of high discovery and other litigation costs in court cases seem to be in exactly those cases. Those high costs occur because the litigants take an uncompromising approach to litigation and can pay to fight every battle. So they probably do the same thing in arbitration. Moreover, if they fight their battles out in arbitration, they have to pay the arbitrators as well, a cost that can mount in complex cases. So it is not surprising that many major companies end up

[51]That is not to say that all businesses shy away from arbitration. For example, an article reported that many law firms prefer arbitration for legal malpractice claims. See Rogers (2015). But one lawyer interviewed for the article had a counter example that sounds as though it shows that arbitration can be just as costly as in-court litigation, if not costlier: 'She described an ongoing "runaway arbitration" in which the arbitrator has held 70 days of hearings over two years and has issued more than 500 "partial interim" orders. … "It's a nightmare."'

[52]See text accompanying ns. 28–32 above.

fighting their fights in public court. A prime example is the patent litigation between Apple Corporation and Samsung Corporation, which is being fought out in US District Court in San Jose, California.

Nullifying private enforcement: The previous section was about business v. business litigation, which seems not to have gone over to the arbitration side. Whether or not there is a 'flight from arbitration' in those situations, there clearly is not in many consumer settings. For a long time, the US Supreme Court (like many courts) refused to enforce agreements to accept a nonjudicial resolution of disputes; despite signing agreements to arbitrate, the parties could go to court if they wanted to. Indeed, the judicial hostility to enforcing arbitration clauses was so strong that in 1925 Congress passed the Federal Arbitration Act to require the courts to enforce such contracts.[53] Until the 1970s, however, the Supreme Court did not aggressively enforce the Act's provisions, but then it began to require that state courts enforce arbitration agreements. It has increasingly rejected arguments that agreements to arbitrate are unconscionable, even when state law has long so provided, ruling that those state laws have been preempted by the federal Act.

Many Americans are upset about the Supreme Court's pro-arbitration stance, emphasizing that in 1925 Congress was thinking about agreements between businesses when it authorized enforcing arbitration clauses. And as noted already, it seems that businesses have stopped flocking to arbitration (barely one in ten contracts involving publicly traded companies include arbitration clauses), if they ever did flock to arbitration.

There is really only one major 'growth' area in arbitration agreements—contracts between businesses and their employees and consumers. In a series of decisions, the Supreme Court has rejected arguments that state unconscionability doctrine can invalidate those provisions, and upheld the primacy of arbitration. One might regard this as uncontroversial, or even a boon for consumers. If arbitration is cheaper, simpler, and faster, that might mean that consumers who could not afford formal court procedures would be able to obtain nonjudicial relief. It may be that recent experience in the EU shows that this hope can be realized. Professor Hodges and his colleagues conclude in their recent book that in the EU '[o]ut-of-court redress mechanisms are increasingly recognized as an important element to strengthen access to justice' (2012, 23). So it does seem that this sort of alternative *can* work.

But there are considerable reasons for uneasiness about whether it *does* work for American consumers or employees bound by arbitration clauses. Certainly the popular press conveys the impression that it does not work. For example, in 2014 the *San Francisco Chronicle* ran a story entitled 'When Arbitration Causes Frustration,' about a car purchaser who claimed that the car she was sold as 'new' was in fact a used car. But she was bound by an arbitration clause, and she lost. In the consumer's view, the arbitration proceeding 'was like a kangaroo court. Arbitration is bought and paid for by the other side' (Said 2014). The story quoted a

[53]United States Arbitration Act, Pub. L. 68-401, 43 Stat. 883, codified at 9 U.S.C. §§ 1–10.

staffer from the California legislature as saying: 'These guys [arbitrators] are totally under the radar, working without any public oversight or regulations. […]. There are more rules about who can be a plumber or a massage therapist than an arbitrator or an arbitration company.'

It bears emphasis that newspaper reports are no substitute for the sort of scholarly analysis done by Professor Hodges and his colleagues. But it also bears emphasis that public perceptions matter, and sometimes they make a difference. Thus, when General Mills Company in 2014 purported to bind consumers by an arbitration clause, there was a huge public outcry. In what the *New York Times* called a 'stunning about face' and a 'stunning reversal for the company,' General Mills then abandoned the arbitration requirement (Strom 2014). At a minimum, it appears that mandatory arbitration has a very poor public image in the US. But at the same time, it is likely that few consumer complaints are of sufficient magnitude to support costly American litigation.

From an academic perspective, a greater concern in the US may be about the private enforcement feature of American civil litigation. This concern builds on the notion that arbitrators will bend their decisions to please their repeat customers—not the consumers or employees who initiate claims—and thus defeat or devalue the very rights that legislatures have sought to provide by permitting private suits. The heart of this concern is largely that agreements to arbitrate will preclude class-action litigation, which has been obstructed by recent Supreme Court decisions enforcing 'class action waivers' in arbitration agreements. This development presents a conundrum; although some consumer class actions seem to involve exploitive overkill by lawyers who use the costs and burdens of American litigation to capitalize on technical violations of rules (the sort of thing governmental regulators would likely overlook), there must be other instances in which class actions are essential to private enforcement.[54] In a 2013 decision, the Supreme Court rejected this concern in deciding whether to enforce a class action waiver in an arbitration agreement.[55] The level of worry has grown apace.

And there is reason to worry that ADR could more generally defeat or weaken adjudication where it is most needed. Judge Edwards addressed these concerns in 1986, after acknowledging that '[i]n strictly private disputes, ADR mechanisms such as arbitration are often superior to adjudication' (1986, 676). But '[i]nexpensive, expeditious, and informal adjudication is not always synonymous with fair and just adjudication,' for 'there are some disputes that cannot be resolved simply by mutual agreement and good faith. It is a fact of political life that many disputes reflect sharply contrasting views about fundamental public values that can never be eliminated by techniques that encourage disputants to "understand" each other. Indeed, many disputants understand each other all too well' (Edwards 1986, 678). Particularly with regard to the sorts of laws that legislatures enact to protect the

[54]For discussion of 'the private enforcement puzzle' in evaluating American class actions, see Marcus (2016).

[55]American Express Co. v. Italian Colors Restaurant, 133 S.Ct. 2304 (2013).

'little guy,' the risk created by relying on standardized arbitration agreements, and therefore private 'judges,' arouses particular concern. Recall that institutional litigation and antidiscrimination litigation have long been a distinctive feature of American litigation. For Americans, eroding access to public courts for such cases is problematical, but it must be recognized also that extraordinary involvement of judicially deputized assistants is often essential to public resolution of such cases.[56] So even when the litigation is 'public,' it often involves important participation by somewhat 'private' actors.

Inviting self-help: At some point, the unavailability of public courts may prompt people to engage in self-help. They may even seek assistance from alternative sources. For example, a *New York Times* story in 1992 reported that in Japan citizens resorted to help from yakuza gangsters because the public courts were not accessible:

> [T]he yakuza have been able to work their way into legitimate society by offering their services for resolving disputes where no other efficient means exists. While Americans enjoy access to the courts to resolve disputes, in Japan litigation is almost unheard of because it is so expensive, time-consuming (cases can take 10 years and more) and rarely produces results that challenge the status quo. Therefore to collect on an overdue loan, you can hire a member of a yakuza group to stand outside the home of the debtor and hurl obscenities and insults until the debtor caves. Disputed traffic accidents are handled at times by one party hiring a mobster to intimidate the other into agreeing to a resolution. (Sterngold 1992)

In the US, there are already many modes of self-help. Repossession is often done without governmental assistance. In many states, lenders can foreclose extrajudicially on homes when borrowers miss payments. And no doubt there are some parallels to the yakuza involving strong-arm tactics in this country. Determining when one is approaching a 'tipping point' where the risks of self-help become palpable is difficult. But there is a reason why people form governments, and a reason why governments create court systems. Should the court systems not respond, the people are likely to improvise.

Preventing or frustrating legal development: As noted above, in a common law system courts as well as legislatures 'make' law. As Professor Brunet argued: 'The output of conventional litigation should be viewed as a public good—society gains more from litigation than would be produced if litigation were left to the private market. … Litigation results in written opinions that apply necessarily vague positive law to concrete fact situations' (1987, 19, 20). As Professors Mnookin and Kornhauser recognized, settlements and other arrangements are devised 'in the shadow of the law,' (1979) and private resolution of disputes does not produce law that provides such a shadow.

---

[56]The whole issue of using special masters, Fed. R. Civ. P. 53, and other representatives of the court to achieve institutional reform is beyond the scope of this paper. Suffice it to say that such activity is itself 'private' in some senses, and that something like it could probably be constructed through private ADR.

Perhaps equally significantly, private dispute resolution may actually disdain the applicable legal rules. For example, divorce mediators in the US expressed antagonism toward the governing legal rules:

> Divorce mediation rejects the idea that legal rules should be used as weapons to improve one party's position at the expense of the other. Similarly, it rejects the idea that these legal rules and principles embody any necessary wisdom or logic. In fact, it views them as being arbitrary principles, having little to do with the realities of the couple's life and not superior to the judgments that the couple could make on their own. (Marlow 1985, 5)

Coupled with existing concerns about private enforcement of public norms, the possibility that private 'judges' would regard public norms as 'arbitrary' is unnerving. In all likelihood, divorce is a special case due to the singular importance (particularly if there are children involved) of the parties' ongoing relationship,[57] and a more general application of this skepticism toward legal rules is not at hand. But given that decisions by arbitrators, at least, are not subject to court review on the merits, the possibility must be kept in mind.

9 Conclusion: Whither (or Wither) the Courts?

The American courts never resolved most disputes, and they never will. Sensible people would not want them to; most disputes do not cry out for a 'legal' solution. But the whole fabric of any society ultimately depends in part on an effective, sensible, and fair way for government to resolve disputes. The American experience shows that trying to build the 'perfect' litigation machine may be a self-defeating effort. The unique features of American litigation that many American lawyers take as God-given tend to provoke horror in the rest of the world. They also have tended to fuel an effort in the US to find alternatives to litigation, including increasing reliance on judicial promotion of settlement and increasingly aggressive enforcement of agreements to submit disputes to private arbitration.

For the rest of the world, then, it may be that the first lesson provided by the American experience is: Be careful about adopting US litigation techniques. Unhappiness with the costs and other features typical of American litigation plays a major role in the American ADR movement. But at the same time, it must be recognized that when litigation addresses important issues, particularly issues involving a lot of money, disinterested action is rarer than self-interested action. Ultimately *somebody* has to decide who wins. Probably it is best that the person be

[57]On this score, consider the advent of 'collaborative divorce' efforts to persuade divorcing spouses to agree not to seek contested court hearings, disclose all relevant financial information, and generally refrain from acting in a manner detrimental to the future relationship of the parties. For a description, see Herman (2001).

a public official, and probably a judge is the best kind of public official to make such decisions. As we explore a variety of specific examples from a variety of countries, these basic issues can be kept in mind.

References

Bar B (2007) Some attorneys questioning advantages of arbitration. New York Law J, 17 May 2007
Barkoff R (2007) Is the bloom off the rose of alternative dispute resolution? Franchise Update, 4 Dec 2007. http://www.franchise-update.com/articles/335. Accessed 7 June 2018
Brunet E (1987) Questioning the quality of alternative dispute resolution. Tulane Law Rev 62:1–56
Burbank S, Subrin S (2011) Litigation and democracy: Reassessing a realistic prospect of trial. Harvard Civ Rights-Civ Liberties Law Rev 46:399–414
Burbank S, Farhang S, Kritzer H (2013) Private enforcement. Lewis & Clark Law Rev 17:637–722
Carrington P (1979) Adjudication as a private good: a comment. J Legal Stud 8:303–318
Cavanagh E (2015) Federal civil litigation at the crossroads: reshaping the role of the federal courts in twenty-first century dispute resolution. Oregon Law Rev 93:631–685
Chayes A (1976) The role of the judge in public law litigation. Harvard Law Rev 89:1281–1316
Davey M (2015) Concerns grow as court races draw big cash. New York Times, 28 March 2015
de Tocqueville A (1835) Democracy in America
Drahozal C, Wittorck Q (2008) Is there a flight from arbitration? Hofstra Law Rev 37:71–116
Edwards H (1986) Alternative dispute resolution: Panacea or Anathema? Harvard Law Rev 99:668–684
Eisenberg T, Miller G (2007) The flight from arbitration: an empirical study of ex ante arbitration clauses in the contracts of publicly held companies. DePaul Law Rev 56:335–374
Executive Office of the President (2013) Patent Assertion and U.S. Innovation, Washington, D.C
Farhang S (2010) The litigation state. Princeton University Press, Princeton and Oxford
Feldman N (2010) Scorpions: the battles and triumphs of FDR's great supreme court justices. Random House, New York
Fiss O (1979) Foreword: the forms of justice. Harvard Law Rev 93:1–58
Fiss O (1984) Against settlement. Yale Law J 93:1073–1092
Galanter M, Palay T (1991) Tournament of lawyers. University of Chicago Press, Chicago
Garth B (1993) From civil litigation to private justice: legal practice at war with the profession and its values. Brooklyn Law Rev 59:931–960
Garth B (1998) The worlds of civil discovery: from studies of cost and delay to the markets in legal services and legal reform. Boston Coll Law Rev 39:597–612
Gilson R (1990) The devolution of the legal profession: a demand side perspective. Maryland Law Rev 49:869–916
Goodman C (2004) Justice and civil procedure in Japan. Oceana Publications, Dobbs Ferry, New York
Grodin J (1989) In pursuit of justice: reflections of a state supreme court justice. University of California Press, Berkeley
Herman G (2001) Collaborative divorce: a short overview. Divorce Litigation 4:68–79
Hodges C, Benöhr I, Creutzfeldg-Banda N (2012) Consumer ADR in Europe. Hart Publishing, Oxford & Portland
Kronman A (1993) The lost lawyer. Harvard University Press, Cambridge
Landes WZ, Posner R (1979) Adjudication as a private good. J Legal Stud 8:235–284
Lee J (2002) Dirty laundry: online for all to see. New York Times, 5 Sept 2002

Lieberman J, Henry J (1986) Lessons from the alternative dispute movement. Univ Chicago Law Rev 53:424–439
Luban D (1995) Settlements and the erosion of the public realm. Georgetown Law J 83:2619–2651
Marcus R (1983) Myth and reality in protective order litigation. Cornell Law Rev 69:1–75
Marcus R (1989) Completing equity's conquest? Reflections on the future of trial under the federal rules of civil procedure. Univ Pittsburgh Law Rev 50:725–788
Marcus R (1993) Who should discipline federal judges, and how? Fed Rules Decis 149:375–434
Marcus R (1998) Discovery containment redux. Boston Coll Law Rev 39:747–784
Marcus R (2003) Reining in the American litigator: the new role of American judges. Hastings Int Comp Law J 27:3–30
Marcus R (2013a) Bomb throwing, democratic theory, and basic values—a new path to procedural harmonization. Northwest Univ Law Rev 107:475–510
Marcus R (2013b) Procedure in a time of austerity. Int J Procedural Law 3:133–158
Marcus R (2014) Looking backward to 1938. Univ Pennsylvania Law Rev 162:1691–1730
Marcus R (2015a) Once more into the breach? Further possible amendments to Rule 23. Judicature 99:57–66
Marcus R (2015b) A genuine civil justice crisis. XVth international association of procedural law world congress. Onikilevha, Istanbul, pp 27–54
Marcus R (2016) Bending in the breeze: American class actions in the 21st century. DePaul Law Rev 65:497–534
Marcus R (2018) Evolution v. Revolution in class action reform. North Carolina Law Rev (in press)
Marlow L (1985) The rule of law in divorce mediation. Mediation Q 9:5–13
McEwen C, Maiman R (1984) Mediation in small claims court: achieving compliance through consent. Law SocRev 18:11–50
Menkel-Meadow C (1995) Whose dispute is it anyway? A philosophical and democratic defense of settlement (in some cases). Georgetown Law J 83:2663–2696
Millar R (1952) Procedure in the trial court in historical perspective. Law Center of New York University, New York
Miller A (2003) The pretrial rush to judgment: are the 'litigation explosion,' 'liability crisis,' and efficiency clichés eroding our day in court and jury trial commitments? New York U Law Rev 78:982–1134
Mnookin R, Kornhauser L (1979) Bargaining in the shadow of the law: the case of divorce. Yale Law J 88:950–997
Murray P, Stürner R (2004) German civil justice. Carolina Academic Press, Durham
Musalo K, Moore J, Boswell R (2011) Refugee law and policy: a comparative and international approach. Carolina Academic Press, Durham
O'Shea J (2005) Private judges keep divorce quiet. San Francisco Recorder, 13 Jun 2005
Peckham R (1985) A judicial response to the cost of litigation: case management, two-stage discovery planning and alternative dispute resolution. Rutgers Law Rev 37:253–278
Pildes R (2014) Romanticizing democracy, political fragmentation, and the decline in American Government. Yale Law J 124:804–852
Pound R (1906) The causes of popular dissatisfaction with the administration of justice. Rep Am Bar Assoc 29:395–417
Redish M, Marshall L (1984) Adjudicatory independence and the values of procedural due process. Yale Law J 95:455–505
Resnik J (1982) Managerial judges. Harvard Law Rev 96:374–448
Resnik J (2014) Reinventing courts as democratic institutions. Daedalus 143(3):9–27
Rice C (1996) Meet John Doe: is it time for federal civil procedure to recognize John Doe parties? Univ Pittsburgh Law Rev 57:883–958
Rogers J (2015) Firms like arbitration for malpractice claims, but it's not without downsides, experts say. Bloomberg BNA Class Action Litigation Rep 16:292

Rubenstein W (2004) On what a 'private attorney general' is—and why it matters. Vanderbilt Law Rev 57:2129–2173
Said C (2014) When arbitration causes frustration. San Francisco Chronicle, 13 Jan 2014
San Francisco Chronicle (2015) Abuse of law. San Francisco Chronicle, 13 April 2015
Shaffer T, Mcthenia A (1985) For reconciliation. Yale Law J 94:1661–1705
Sherwin E (2008) Precedent by accident: the story of Conley. In: Clermont K (ed) Civil procedure stories, 2d edn. Thomson/Foundation Press, New York, pp 295–322
Smith M (2015) Partisanship a worry in Wisconsin supreme court election. New York Times, 6 April 2015
Steinman J (1985) Pseudonymous parties: when should litigants be permitted to keep their identifies confidential? Hastings Law J 37:1–90
Sterngold J (1992) Japan's rigged Casino. New York Times, 26 April 1992
Stolberg S (1992) Politics and the judiciary coexist, but often uneasily. Los Angeles Times, 21 Mar 1992
Strom S (2014) General Mills reverses itself on consumers' right to sue. New York Times, 20 April 2014
Survey of Civil Justice in New York (1931) Institute of law, Johns Hopkins University

Richard Marcus Horace O. Coil Chair in Litigation, UC Hastings College of Law, San Francisco. Co-author of leading American casebooks on complex litigation and civil procedure, and author of the discovery volumes of the leading US treatise on federal practice and procedure. Associate Reporter of the Advisory Committee on Civil Rules of the U.S. Judicial Conference. Principal author of rules for discovery and class actions adopted for U.S. federal courts since 1998.

Part IV
Global Trends: From Individual to Collective Justice

Human Rights Class Actions

Elisabetta Silvestri

Abstract One common imagining of class actions is associated with a few popular novels and films in which aggressive and unscrupulous lawyers sue giant corporations with a view to extorting financial settlements that will be highly profitable for the lawyers themselves but rarely for the members of the class action, the individual men and women who actually suffered injury. This is the dark side of class actions, one which is widely known by the public. But there is also a bright side, even though less glamorous and hardly appreciated, at least outside the United States: it is the experience of human rights class actions, namely the experience of class actions used as a form of civil redress available to the victims of mass violation of fundamental human rights. This contribution focuses on a number of particular aspects of human rights class actions, expounding on the controversial concept of universal civil jurisdiction.

1 Introduction

What do class actions have to do with human rights? Apparently, not much. In general, when we think about human rights and their infringement we do not think about civil remedies: certainly, damages paid to the victims of human rights violations seem to be poor compensation for injuries from which very often no recovery is possible. At the same time, when we consider class actions (and, in particular, U.S. class actions) we are met with two completely different images. On the one hand, we think of the positive aspects of class actions, personified by the champions of consumer rights (Ralph Nader and, more recently, Erin Brockovich, just to mention two of the most famous), who challenge in court giant corporations

This contribution is the result of research supported by the Croatian Science Foundation (project no. 6988).

E. Silvestri (✉)
Department of Law, University of Pavia, Pavia, Italy
e-mail: elisabetta.silvestri@unipv.it

A. Uzelac and C. H. van Rhee (eds.), *Transformation of Civil Justice*,
Ius Gentium: Comparative Perspectives on Law and Justice 70,
https://doi.org/10.1007/978-3-319-97358-6_11

and are able to force them to change their policies and behaviour for the benefit of the class members. On the other hand, we think of the dark side of class actions (a side well-illustrated by successful novels and movies), and what comes to mind is the image of aggressive and unscrupulous lawyers who are able to fabricate abusive class actions with the only aim of extorting lucrative settlements from the defendants: settlements that will greatly profit the lawyers themselves, and not so much, if at all, the class they represent.

In any event, it is hard to deny that, at first sight, the combination of human rights and class actions is not exactly a marriage made in heaven. In spite of that, the purpose of this essay is to show that even class actions can be put at the service of the enforcement of human rights: human rights class actions serve this very purpose, and this essay describes their development in the United States, their place of birth. This American experience is intriguing, since it is still quite unknown outside the United States, but also because of the uncertainties surrounding the possibility of conceiving class actions as procedural tools available under international law (Bassett 2011, 21–29).

Having said that the United States has served as the frontrunner for human rights class actions, one must yet acknowledge that in recent years this particular type of class actions has had its ups and downs. In spite of that, human rights class actions deserve to be studied carefully, since they can offer invaluable food for thought to those who believe that human rights violations cannot be cured only through criminal prosecution of the offenders.

2 Human Rights Class Actions: What They Are, How They Work

Human rights class actions are group actions that can be commenced before U.S. district courts (district courts being the courts of first instance in the U.S. federal judiciary) for the protection of the victims of human rights violations: they have a few particular features that make them a powerful procedural tool for the enforcement of human rights worldwide.

The remedy sought can be either an award of damages or an injunction preventing the repetition of the violation and—if possible—ordering measures for the elimination of the prejudicial effects of previous violations. As a matter of fact, when fundamental human rights have been infringed, both remedies appear inadequate: damages, in particular, almost seem an offensive tactic to silence the victims. Actually, though, the goal pursued by human rights class actions is to obtain neither damages nor injunctions against the defendant: both remedies have 'added value', but the main goal is to expose the wrongdoer to the judgment of public opinion (Stephens 2002, 13, 14).

It does not seem necessary to expand on the concept of class actions, since one may say that some basic ideas of this procedural device that makes it possible to aggregate in a single action the claims of an unidentified number of individuals all equally affected by the wrongful behaviour of a single defendant have become part of the conventional wisdom. By the same token, readers are likely to be familiar with the distinction between the so-called opt-in and opt-out models, the former preferred by European legal systems that require members of the class to join the action, and the latter typical of U.S. class actions, which have an inclusive nature, meaning that those who meet the parameters of the class are automatically included in the class itself unless they exclude themselves from the class.[1]

Against this background, the most interesting features of human rights class actions can be listed as follows: (1) the members of the class are not U.S. citizens; (2) the infringement of human rights did not take place in the territory of the United States, but in another country(ies); (3) the wrongdoer is in general an alien (i.e. not a U.S. citizen).

The legal bases for the development of human rights class actions are two U.S. federal statutes issued in very different times: the Alien Tort Claims Act of 1789 (also known as the Alien Tort Statute; hereinafter, ATCA) and the Torture Victim Protection Act of 1991 (hereinafter, TVPA).

The ATCA was adopted in the first session of the first U.S. Congress as part of the Judiciary Act that established the federal judiciary. The statute has been colourfully defined as a true 'legal Lohengrin', since apparently nobody knows how and why it ended up in the Judiciary Act.[2] According to the relevant provision of the ATCA, at present laid down by Paragraph 1350, Title 28 of the United States Code:

> The district courts shall have original jurisdiction of any civil action by an alien for a tort only, committed in violation of the law of nations or a treaty of the United States.

The TVPA grants subject matter jurisdiction to federal courts over torture committed by subjects under the authority of foreign governments (the so-called official torture, meaning torture committed by individuals acting in an official capacity, either real or apparent) in their own countries or elsewhere; the victims can be either citizens of the United States or aliens. With the adoption of the TVPA, the United States became the first country in the world to pass a statute affording the

---

[1]The literature on U.S. class actions is so vast that any attempt at sketching even a basic bibliography is bound to fail. In spite of that, it seems useful to mention that at present the judgments on the effectiveness of class actions and their future developments are mixed and debatable: for two radically different approaches, see, for instance, Marcus (2016) and Fitzpatrick (2015). In any event, nowadays as in the past the approach to class actions does not seem to contemplate half measures: either you love them or you hate them. As one author has written, the literature on class actions has always relied on competing, often 'romantic' narratives, so that 'the debate over class action litigation reform often is reduced to hyperbolic, rhetorical posturing': Mullenix (2014/2015, 447). As far as the European trends in the field of group actions are concerned, see the essays collected in Harsági and Van Rhee (eds) (2014).

[2]The definition is attributed to Judge Henry Friendly: Lewis Humphrey (1980/1981, 327–354).

victims of torture the right to sue their persecutors for civil damages (Schwartz 1994, 271–338; Drinan and Kuo 1993, 605–624). The TVPA reads:

SEC. 2 ESTABLISHMENT OF CIVIL ACTION

> (a) LIABILITY. – An individual who, under actual or apparent authority, or color of law, of any foreign nation –
> (1) subjects an individual to torture shall, in a civil action, be liable for damages to that individual; or
> (2) subjects an individual to extrajudicial killing shall, in a civil action, be liable for damages to the individual's legal representative, or to any person who may be a claimant in an action for wrongful death.

Often, these statutes are referred to jointly,[3] since they both provide for the jurisdiction of federal courts as regards civil actions brought against defendants who are deemed to be responsible for violations of the 'law of nations' (meaning the core principles of customary international law) or for acts of torture perpetrated against one or more individuals.[4]

U.S. district courts have jurisdiction no matter if the parties are aliens, the wrongful event took place outside the United States or the wrongdoer claims that he acted lawfully while exercising a power legally conferred on him. All that may sound strange to lawyers trained according to the tenets of the civil law tradition. It must be remembered, though, that the American concept of civil jurisdiction is quite different from the continental European concept. If, according to a U.S. federal statute, a certain civil action falls within the jurisdiction of a district court, that is it, and nothing else is necessary to start a proceeding. No other requirement is necessary: the plaintiff can be an alien and the event may have occurred on the other side of the world. What is imperative, though, is that the defendant is physically on

[3]According to scholarly opinions as well as courts, the two statutes are strictly connected—the TVPA being almost a sort of modern development of the ATCA—even though they provide for distinct and separate causes of actions: see extensively Apostolova (2010, 643–652).

[4]The TVPA adopts a very broad notion of 'torture'. The relevant rule provides as follows: 'Section 3. DEFINITIONS. (b) TORTURE—For the purposes of this Act—(1) the term "torture" means any act, directed against an individual in the offender's custody or physical control, by which severe pain or suffering (other than pain or suffering arising only from or inherent in, or incidental to, lawful sanctions), whether physical or mental, is intentionally inflicted on that individual for such purposes as obtaining from that individual or a third person information or a confession, punishing that individual for an act that individual or a third person has committed or is suspected of having committed, intimidating or coercing that individual or a third person, or for any reason based on discrimination of any kind; and—(2) mental pain or suffering refers to prolonged mental harm caused by or resulting from—(A) the intentional infliction or threatened infliction of severe physical pain or suffering;—(B) the administration or application, or threatened administration or application, of mind altering substances or other procedures calculated to disrupt profoundly the senses or the personality;—(C) the threat of imminent death; or—(D) the threat that another individual will imminently be subjected to death, severe physical pain or suffering, or the administration or application of mind altering substances or other procedures calculated to disrupt profoundly the senses or personality.'

American soil, even temporarily or, in case of a legal entity, that it has so-called 'minimum contacts' with the U.S. legal system (for instance, a secondary branch located in the United States).[5]

These particular features have allowed the development of human rights class actions, which a few scholars consider the 'new frontier' for group litigation (Johnson 2004, 643–670): a new frontier that will help this unique type of class action gain a truly international dimension that goes well beyond the use of the U.S. model of class action as the term of reference (both in the positive and in the negative sense) for designing a viable form of group proceeding acceptable worldwide.

3 Protecting the Victims of Human Rights Violations Through the ATCA and the TVPA: From Individual Actions to Class Actions

Before expanding on the specific topic of this essay, it is necessary to emphasize another particular aspect of the experience of human rights class actions. It is the aspect having to do with the older of the two statutes granting standing to sue before U.S. federal courts to the victims of human rights violations. As a matter of fact, the first human rights class actions were filed under the ATCA; they can be seen as the progeny of the first case in which the ATCA was invoked as the legal basis for a claim for damages asserted in a federal court by an alien plaintiff against an alien defendant for events that took place outside the United States. The case is *Filártiga v. Peña-Irala*, which was decided in the 1980s.[6] This case, which paved the road for many others, brought to U.S. federal courts both as individual lawsuits and class actions, shows how a very old statute can be revived, in this instance after almost two centuries of neglect.

A brief history of the *Filártiga v. Peña-Irala* case seems in order, keeping in mind that all the facts constituting the cause of action took place in Paraguay. Joelito Filártiga was the son of a member of the party opposing the dictatorship of Alfredo Stroessner. In 1976, Joelito was arrested by Américo Norberto Peña-Irala, who was a high-ranking police officer in Asunción, the capital city of Paraguay. Joelito (17 years old at that time) was tortured and eventually killed as retaliation against the anti-regime activities carried out by his father. All attempts by the Filártiga family to get justice in Paraguay not only failed, but were met with threats

[5]If my oversimplification here of the American concept of jurisdiction raises eyebrows, this author assures the kind reader that I chose this avenue only because of the constraints of limited space, within which it would not be practicable to elucidate the complexities of a subject matter that is among the most problematic ones concerning the way U.S. courts, both federal and state, can assert their power on the parties to a dispute. For a concise but clear commentary on the main principles governing the jurisdiction of U.S. courts, see Kane (2013, 7–27, 41–71).

[6]630 F.2d 876 (2d Cir. 1980).

and violence. A few years afterwards, Joelito's sister, Dolly, moved to the United States where she obtained political asylum. Dolly chanced to discover that her brother's killer also was living in the United States, as an illegal alien. The suit brought before a district court by Dolly Filártiga against Américo Norberto Peña-Irala (who, in the meantime, had been arrested and detained) for the wrongful death of Joelito was unsuccessful, since the court denied that abuses perpetrated by the officers of a country against the citizens of that very country could be deemed as a breach of the 'law of nations', as required by the ATCA. The judgment was reversed on appeal. The U.S. Court of Appeals for the Second Circuit stated, in a lengthy, cogent opinion, that the ATCA was applicable to the case at hand, making it clear that human rights abuses perpetrated by government officers against citizens are at odds with the principles of international law, since 'official torture is prohibited by the law of nations'.[7] Therefore, under the ATCA, official torture had to be considered as a tort for which a civil suit could be commenced before a U.S. federal court. Leaving aside the sophisticated legal arguments advanced by the court, the final part of the opinion held the promise of a 'new life' for the ATCA and its possible pivotal role in the development of civil human rights litigation. The last paragraph of the opinion reads:

> In the twentieth century the international community has come to recognize the common danger posed by the flagrant disregard of basic human rights and particularly the right to be free of torture. [...] In the modern age, humanitarian and practical considerations have combined to lead the nations of the world to recognize that respect for fundamental human rights is in their individual and collective interest. Among the rights universally proclaimed by all nations, as we have noted, is the right to be free of physical torture. Indeed, for purposes of civil liability, the torturer has become – like the pirate and slave trader before him – *hostis humani generis*, an enemy of all mankind. Our holding today, giving effect to a jurisdictional provision enacted by our First Congress, is a small but important step in the fulfillment of the ageless dream to free all people from brutal violence.[8]

The human rights class actions filed so far under the ATCA and the TVPA have been grouped into two categories, that is, cases against individuals under the doctrine of command responsibility, and cases against corporate entities allegedly involved in human rights violations. A third group of cases could be taken into account, namely, cases having to do with events that occurred in connection with the Holocaust and World War II, but these cases will not be analyzed here, since they raise issues (not only legal, but ethical and political issues as well) unsuited to this essay and its purposes.[9]

It is in the first category that the first reported human rights class action falls, that is, the class action brought against the dictator of the Philippines, Ferdinand

[7]630 F.2d at 884.

[8]The complete text of the opinion can be found at http://hrp.law.harvard.edu/wp-content/uploads/2011/04/filartiga-v-pena-irala.pdf. Accessed 7 June 2018.

[9]For this classification, see Van Schaack (2003, 282, 283).

Marcos.[10] This is an important case also because of the number of people involved (the class included no fewer than 10,000 victims of human rights violations) and, most of all, because, apparently, it is the only case in which the damages awarded by the jury were actually distributed to the members of the class. The case began in 1986, immediately after Marcos had fled the Philippines and retreated to the U.S. state of Hawaii, and over time had a convoluted development. When eventually the jury found for the class, awarding $2 billion in damages, the Marcos' estate had already been safely hidden in Swiss banks. Only in 2011 were the members of the class (or, more likely, their heirs) able to receive a portion of the damages, after long negotiations with the Swiss banks, the Marcos family and the government of the Philippines. The damages were essentially nominal and not compensatory, in consideration of the number of years that had passed since the human rights violations had occurred (Swift 2012, 38–41; Davidson 2017, 257–275).

The second category of human rights class actions encompasses several actions against multinational corporations engaged in, for instance, the extraction of oil and natural gas in third world countries. Worthy of mention here is the case of *Doe v. Unocal*, the class action commenced by the residents of a Burmese region against the Unocal Corporation, which was engaged in the construction of gas pipelines. According to the class representatives, Unocal had imposed forced labour and perpetrated systematic violations of human rights against the inhabitants of the region with the aid of local policemen. The case, begun in 1996, had a complex development before U.S. state and federal courts. More than one judgment issued in the case hinted at the principle according to which, under specific circumstances, a corporation is liable for damages when its agents have violated human rights either directly or with the aid of third parties. The case ended in 2005 with a settlement for an undisclosed (but presumably large) amount of money. Even though the conclusion of this long and convoluted litigation was welcome by many commentators, others emphasized the fact that the settlement prevented the establishment of important judicial precedents concerning the liability of corporations for human rights abuses perpetrated abroad in which they aided and abetted or from which they profited.[11]

For time and space considerations, it is not practicable to mention here additional human rights class actions. May it suffice though to point out that between the 1980s and the 2010s U.S. courts have been the stage for many judicial battles for the enforcement of fundamental human rights infringed abroad, showing that a domestic remedy (namely, an action for damages arising out of tortious conduct) can be adapted so as to redress even violations of international law.

---

[10]See *Hilao v. Estate of Ferdinand Marcos*, 103 F.3rd 767, 771 (9th Cir. 1996): actually, this is the final judgment issued by a federal appellate court at the closing of a proceeding that had begun, as mentioned in the text, ten years earlier.

[11]Out of an extensive bibliography, see, e.g., Collingsworth (2006, 115–132), with reference to many other cases similar to *Doe v. Unocal*; Rosencranz and Louk (2005, 130–147); Kielsgard (2005, 185–215).

4 *Kiobel v. Royal Dutch Petroleum Co.*: A Nonreversible Setback?

At present, the development of human rights class actions faces a predicament due to a judgment issued by the U.S. Supreme Court in 2013. In *Kiobel v. Royal Dutch Petroleum Co.*,[12] the Court stated that the ATCA does not have an extraterritorial reach. According to the Court, 'There is no indication that the ATS (ATCA) was passed to make the United States a uniquely hospitable forum for the enforcement of international norms.'[13] The case concerned a group of Nigerians who obtained asylum in the United States: they had fled their village in order to escape the human rights violations perpetrated by the Dutch company which was engaged in oil drilling in the area. The group sued the company before a U.S. district court, and the case reached the U.S. Supreme Court after a long and complicated procedural history.

With *Kiobel*, therefore, the U.S. Supreme Court set strict limits to the possibility of relying on human rights class actions brought under the ATCA to obtain satisfaction for the infringement of human rights when the alleged violations occurred outside the United States, were perpetrated against aliens and by citizens of other nations. If an extraterritorial application of the statute were upheld by the U.S. judiciary, the Supreme Court says, 'Other nations, also applying the law of nations, could haul our citizens into their courts for alleged violations of the law of nations occurring in the United States, or anywhere else in the world'.[14] That is why, the Court continues, 'The presumption against extraterritoriality guards against our courts triggering such serious foreign policy consequences, and instead defers such decisions, quite appropriately, to the political branches.'[15]

It will be interesting to see whether the 'new deal' inaugurated by the U.S. Supreme Court will have the effect of hobbling the development of human rights class actions. Certainly, the contemporary political environment is not promising, and that is really a pity. Let us not forget that in the past, class actions have been instrumental in so-called public law litigation,[16] meaning the litigation by which paramount results in the field of social justice have been achieved. It would be positive if a new pattern of public law litigation, a transnational one, could gain ground, in the United States or elsewhere, for the redress of the most egregious violations of the fundamental principles of international human rights law. It seems appropriate here to offer a definition of transnational public law litigation:

---

[12]*Kiobel v. Royal Dutch Petroleum Co.* (decided 17 April 2013). https://www.law.cornell.edu/supct/pdf/10-1491.pdf. Accessed 7 June 2018.

[13]Ibid., 12.

[14]Ibid., 13.

[15]Ibid.

[16]Two readings are a must on this subject (at least in this author's opinion): Chayes (1976), 1281–1316 and Kagan (2003).

> What makes transnational public law litigation unique, however, is its melding of two conventional modes of litigation that have traditionally been considered distinct. In traditional domestic litigation, private individuals bring private claims against one another based on national law before competent domestic judicial fora, seeking both enunciation of norms and damages relief in the form of a retrospective judgment. In traditional international litigation, nation-states bring public claims against one another based on treaty or customary international law before international tribunals of limited competence. ... Transnational public law litigation merges these two classical modes of litigation. Private individuals, government officials, and nations sue one another directly, and are sued directly, in a variety of judicial fora, most prominently, domestic courts. In these fora, these actors invoke claims of right based not solely on domestic or international law, but rather, on a body of "transnational" law that blends the two. (Koh 1990/1991, 2348, 2349)

What the future holds for the development of transnational public law litigation is difficult to predict. Similarly, it is difficult to forecast whether the principles laid down by the *Kiobel* case will shut the door to further advancement of human rights class actions, upholding the idea that they are a dangerous form of forum shopping, which may adversely affect the United States by raising serious barriers to its ability to entertain international relations and remain engaged in global trade.

5 Who Is Afraid of Universal Jurisdiction?

The idea of transnational public law litigation is predicated on the theory according to which the infringement of human rights is such disgraceful behaviour that every civilized nation should allow the victims to sue the wrongdoers for damages in its own civil courts, no matter if the event took place elsewhere or if the parties to the case are aliens. In other words, this theory postulates the need to acknowledge a universal civil jurisdiction. The concept of universal jurisdiction comes into play in the field of criminal jurisdiction and, in particular, international criminal jurisdiction. It is customary to say that a single definition of universal jurisdiction, generally accepted by the legal community, is lacking. More than a definition, what seems useful is an explanation of the goals that can be attained by relying on the concept of universal jurisdiction.

> Under the principle of universal jurisdiction a state is entitled or even required to bring proceedings in respect of certain serious crimes, irrespective of the location of the crime, and irrespective of the nationality of the perpetrator or the victim. The only connection between the crime and the prosecuting state that may be required is the physical presence of the alleged offender within the jurisdiction of that state.[17]

Less known but more controversial is the notion of civil universal jurisdiction, which has been described as follows:

[17]International Law Association, London Conference (2000), Committee On International Human Rights Law And Practice, Final report on the exercise of universal jurisdiction in respect of gross human rights offences. https://www.scribd.com/document/131960356/ILA-Report-on-Universal-jurisdiction-2000, p. 3. Accessed 7 June 2018.

> The principle under which civil proceedings may be brought in a domestic court irrespective of the location of the unlawful conduct and irrespective of the nationality of the perpetrator or the victim, on the grounds that the unlawful conduct is a matter of international concern. (Kamminga 2005, 123)

Scholars cite the U.S. ATCA and TVPA as the most significant examples of statutes granting this type of jurisdiction (e.g. Kenney 2015, 1053–1115; Curran 2012/2013, 799–809), insofar as they bestow on federal courts civil jurisdiction over extraterritorial matters. But it is obvious that such an extraterritorial reach of domestic courts is a matter of dispute: in particular, to admit that the courts of any country can set themselves up as the universal judge in charge of deciding over the liability for damages caused by the violations of human rights committed abroad can bring about the danger of a sort of 'jurisdictional imperialism', particularly despicable since universal jurisdiction is likely to be exercised in powerful states against crimes committed in weaker states.[18]

The idea of offering victims of heinous crimes a form of reparation to be granted by domestic civil courts of any country is intriguing, since it satisfies a concept of justice that goes beyond the criminal prosecution and the punishment of offenders. The problem is that universal civil jurisdiction does not seem to have a solid base, grounded, for instance, in an international treaty, so that at times it has been labeled as 'irrational', since it is devoid of any justification and, as opposed to universal criminal jurisdiction, cannot be upheld as an answer to impunity for those who perpetrate human rights abuses (Wallach 2014/2015, 803–835, 834). Even the supporters of universal civil jurisdiction find it hard to recognize its autonomy, and are inclined to support the theory according to which 'the well-accepted modern rationale for exercising universal jurisdiction to impose criminal penalties also justifies exercising it to provide civil remedies', since 'the goals of criminal and tort law overlap' so that 'punishment and compensation represent two distinct, but complementary, ways of condemning the past, and deterring future, wrongdoing' (Donovan and Roberts 2006, 154). But others object that the limited acceptance of universal civil jurisdiction depends primarily on an emotional factor, meaning that when crimes against humanity are involved 'the notion that these crimes could be monetized and viewed essentially as a tort is repugnant to many' (Roper 2016, 1).

While the debate on universal civil jurisdiction goes on and the future of U.S. human rights class actions is uncertain, what remains unchanged is the need for a model of aggregate litigation for human rights violations, a model that is acceptable and workable at the international level at-large, even though the obstacles to overcome are many, and the reluctance to allow collective actions in the field of international human rights law has undeniable and apparently unsolvable political overtones.

---

[18]International Law Association, London Conference (2000), n. 17 above, at p. 20.

References

Apostolova E (2010) The relationship between the Alien Tort Statute and the Torture Victim Protection Act. Berkeley J Int'l Law 28:640–652

Bassett DL (2011) The future of international class actions. Sw J Int'l Law 18:21–29

Chayes A (1976) The role of the judge in public law litigation. Harvard Law Rev 89:1281–1316

Collingsworth T (2006) Using the Alien Tort Claims Act to hold multinationals accountable for human rights violations in U.S. federal courts. http://apps.americanbar.org/labor/lel-aba-annual/papers/2006/05.pdf. Accessed 7 June 2018

Curran VG (2012/2013) Mass torts and universal jurisdiction. U Pennsyl J Int'l Law 34:799–809

Davidson NR (2017) Alien Tort Statute litigation and transitional justice: bringing the Marcos case back to the Philippines. Int'l J Transitional Justice 11:257–275

Donovan DF, Roberts A (2006) The emerging recognition of universal civil jurisdiction. Am J Int'l Law 100:142–163

Drinan RF, Kuo TT (1993) Putting the world's oppressors on trial: the Torture Victim Protection Act. Human Rts Q 15:605–624

Fitzpatrick BT (2015) The end of class actions? Arizona Law Rev 57:161–199

Harsági V, Van Rhee CH (eds) (2014) Multi-party redress mechanisms in Europe: squeaking mice?. Intersentia, Cambridge-Antwerp-Portland

Johnson KR (2004) International human rights class actions: new frontiers for group litigation. Michigan State Law Rev 3:643–670

Kagan RA (2003) American adversarialism. Harvard U Press, Cambridge, Mass, The American way of law

Kamminga MT (2005) Universal civil jurisdiction: Is it legal? Is it desirable? Am Soc'y Int'l Law Proc 99:123–125

Kane MK (2013) Civil procedure in a nutshell, 7th edn. West Publishing Co, St Paul, Minn

Kenney CC (2015/2016) Measuring transnational human rights. Fordham Law Rev 84:1053–1115

Kielsgard MD (2005) Unocal and the demise of corporate neutrality. Cal W Int'l Law J 36:185–215

Koh HH (1990/1991) Transnational public law litigation. Yale Law J 100:2347–2402

Lewis Humphrey JM (1980/1981) A legal Lohengrin: federal jurisdiction under the Alien Tort Claims Act of 1789. Immigr and Nat'lity Law Rev 4:327–354

Marcus RL (2016) Bending in the breeze: American class actions in the twenty-first century. DePaul Law Rev 65:497–533

Mullenix LS (2014/2015) Ending class actions as we know them: rethinking the American class action. Emory Law Rev 64:399–449

Roper S (2016) Applying universal jurisdiction to civil cases: variations in state approaches to monetizing human rights violations. J Civil Legal Sci 5:1–6

Rosencranz A, Louk D (2005) Doe v. Unocal: holding corporations liable for human rights abuses on their watch. Chapman Law Rev 8:130–147

Schwartz RE (1994) And tomorrow? The Torture Victim Protection Act. Ariz J Int'l Comp Law 11:271–338

Stephens B (2002) Translating *Filártiga*: a comparative and international law analysis of domestic remedies for international human rights violations. Yale J Int'l Law 27:1–57

Swift RA (2012) A human rights class action distribution in the Philippines. Philadelphia Lawyer, Winter 2012:38–41. http://www.philadelphiabar.org/WebObjects/PBAReadOnly.woa/Contents/WebServerResources/CMSResources/TPL.winter12_philipines.pdf. Accessed 7 June 2018
Van Schaack B (2003) Unfilled promise: the human rights class action. U Chi Legal F:279–352
Wallach D (2014/2015) The irrationality of universal civil jurisdiction. Geo J Int'l Law 46:803–835

Elisabetta Silvestri Associate Professor of Civil Procedure and Comparative Civil Procedure in the Department of Law at the University of Pavia, Italy. Scientific Director of the post-graduate programme for the training of ADR professionals at the University of Pavia. LLM from Cornell Law School. Visiting scholar at Yale Law School and the London School of Economics. Co-director of the Public and Private Justice seminar at the Inter-University Centre Dubrovnik, Croatia.

A New Model of Civil Litigation in Slovenia: Is the Slovenian Judiciary Prepared for the Challenges Presented by the New Law on Collective Actions?

Jorg Sladič

Abstract Slovenia has adopted a new law on collective redress under EU, US, Dutch and Belgian influence. This contribution gives an overview of the new law. However, a static presentation of the law would not give a sufficient overview of the challenges faced by collective redress vehicles in Slovenia. Slovenian law is a mixture of a civil law system with a socialist heritage, which can be seen in the extreme formalism in the judiciary. Collective redress is a vehicle for the regulatory function in civil litigation. Yet, such a regulatory function is very much disliked in civil law jurisdictions. The main ingredient from the socialist tradition is a fear of collective redress, for collective redress is seen as *regulation through litigation*. Claimants and other litigants autonomously determine their future behaviour. Under the socialist heritage, higher court judges consider law as an instrument of class rule, perhaps even exploitation and alienation. Collective redress as defined by the *regulation through litigation* doctrine is indeed the very opposite of the socialist conception of law. Small individuals go against corporate Leviathans and force them by virtue of law to change their behaviour. In this contribution the author argues that collective redress will be perceived by the judiciary as a legal irritant, and it will not have a bright future.

1 Introduction

Slovenia adopted new legislation on collective redress at the end of 2017. The new law will be applied from April 2018[1] when the ordinary courts will be open to hearing collective redress actions. Collective redress is said to have regulatory functions, any compensatory function is considered rather accessory. Thus, before

[1] Law of Collective Actions (Zakon o kolektivnih tožbah—ZkolT), Official Journal of the Republic of Slovenia No. 51/2017.

J. Sladič (✉)
Faculty of Law, University of Maribor, Maribor, Slovenia
e-mail: jorg.sladic@gmail.com

A. Uzelac and C. H. van Rhee (eds.), *Transformation of Civil Justice*,
Ius Gentium: Comparative Perspectives on Law and Justice 70,
https://doi.org/10.1007/978-3-319-97358-6_12

long in Slovenia collective redress, a clearly regulatory instrument, will be performed through proceedings held in the civil courts applying the laws on civil procedure.

This contribution explores the questions Are regulatory functions supposed to be performed in civil procedure? and How will the Slovenian judiciary react to the changed environment and apply the regulatory aim of collective redress?

Today, the regulatory aim of civil procedure is a hot topic in Europe (Seewald 2017, 566–568). There is also a dire prediction that the regulatory function of civil procedure will not be performed to satisfaction in a post-socialist environment.

2 Slovenian Collective Redress

In 2016, the Ministry of Justice unofficially started circulating within the legal community a draft law on collective redress.[2] The proposed legislative draft was based on the US Federal Rules of Civil Procedure, Rule 23 (Class Actions), the Dutch WCAM (Wet Collectieve Afwikkeling Massaschade) and the Belgian CdE/WER (Book XVII Code de droit économique/Wetboek van economisch recht).[3]

In Slovenia, a mixed opt-in and opt-out system similar to what exists in Belgium was chosen. Under the draft bill, collective redress should be applied in consumer, competition, securities and labour law. In the field of anti-discrimination law, the draft went very far by stating that no individual lawsuits would be admissible; in other words, only collective actions would be permitted. However, in the end, with the adoption of the Law of Collective Actions (Zakon o kolektivnih tožbah—ZKolT) the legislator also allowed individual lawsuits in anti-discrimination law (Article 57 ZKolT).

Standing in collective redress is given to representative, non-profit legal persons of private law and the State Attorney (Article 4 ZkolT).

The Law of Collective Actions incorporated follow-on actions. Such actions are admissible as of the day the administrative decision adopted by a public authority becomes final. The initiation of administrative proceedings (public enforcement) by a competent administrative authority suspends the collective action (Article 9 ZkolT).

However, a very interesting provision is to be found in Article 8, where the period of limitation for claims that are the subject matter of a collective action is suspended during the duration of collective proceedings (Article 8 ZkolT).

Under Dutch influence, a great amount of emphasis is given to negotiated settlements and the proceedings for declaration of the *erga omnes* compulsory nature of the settlement reached (Arts. 12–25 ZkolT). As in the Netherlands, only the

[2]EVA 2016-2030-0007.

[3]A conference on the draft law was organised for attorneys and judges in the second half of 2016 by the Ministry of Justice.

parties to the proposed collective settlement jointly apply for the declaration of the *erga omnes* compulsory nature of the settlement reached (Article 12 ZkolT). The court dealing with the compulsory joint request can refuse the settlement, e.g. if the party representing the harmed persons is not representative enough, if the amount of damages is too low, if the costs to be paid to the other party are too high, if the deadlines set for bringing individual claims is unreasonable, if there is no mechanism for verification of the merits of individual claims and if the interests of represented persons are not adequately ensured (Article 17 ZkolT).

Under Belgian influence, provisions on the collective lawsuit on damages and written submissions regulate matters in detail (14 compulsory elements to be mentioned in the application) (Article 26 ZkolT). In the final part of the law there are provisions relating to collective actions on injunctions (Arts. 47–57).

It should be noted that the European rule on cost-shifting applies. The party having lost the lawsuit will have to pay the costs and expenses of the other party (Article 60 ZkolT).

The question is, Will the Slovenian judiciary be able to apply this law in a satisfactory manner?

3 A "New Model of Civil Litigation"

Latin American law professors have described the difficulties in the application of traditional civil procedural law in a modern mass economy characterised by collective redress (Marinoni and Arenhart 2014, 44, 45). In the second half of the 20th century, US legal writers slowly started developing a devastating critique of individual traditional lawsuits in private law. Traditional lawsuits (in private law) are supposed to be bipolar (the party either wins or loses), retrospective (Van Boom et al. 2010, 2), self-contained (*res iudicata* is confined to the parties), party-initiated and party-controlled (absence of active managerial judges) and entirely linked to existing substantive law (Chayes 1976, 1282, 1283). In Europe, the main criticism heard among lawyers is that the US legal culture is litigation prone and extremely plaintiff-friendly (Amman and Meier 2017, 96), which could explain the collateral attacks on traditional civil procedural law by US legal writers. Rulings of US courts are, according to one German scholar, motivated by considerations of economic policy and politics (Schack 2014, 307, 308). Additionally, European common law jurisdictions do not offer a favourable view of US law. Lord Denning's degrading characterisation of the US judiciary in his famous opinion in the *Smith, Kline & French Laboratories* case is legendary. Indeed, the English judge wrote that "As a moth is drawn to the light, so is a litigant drawn to the United States. If he can only get his case into their courts, he stands to win a fortune." US legal scholars have colourfully described the difference between the United States and the European Union with the following words: "Instead of building a European-style regulatory state, the United States constructed the litigation state" (Glover 2012, 1148).

A solution to the negative status of individual private lawsuits was proposed by legal scholars from Harvard and Yale universities, i.e. a "new model of civil litigation" (Resnik 1982, 377). The new model of civil litigation could be described from the European point of view as the use of public law techniques in private law lawsuits. In other words, techniques European lawyers are familiar with in administrative or constitutional courts should be applied in ordinary civil and labour courts too. Could this "new model" also be applied in European states? Is it just a curious characteristic of US law where the judiciary is not specialised? Is it known in Europe? It certainly is known in European collective redress (Directive 2009/22/EC of the European Parliament and of the Council of 23 April 2009 on injunctions for the protection of consumers' interests).[4]

On a comparative level, the retrospective function of lawsuits in private law seems to be a very common legal tradition based on Roman law not applying actions for injunction (*actio condemnatoria*, *Leistungsklage*) in tort law (*omnis condemnatio pecuniaria est*) that was avoided in continental Europe by actions for injunction for enforcing rights under substantive law (Van Boom 2010, 14). Such a development is probably influenced by the extension of public law[5] to private lawsuits and supposedly requires the transformation of civil procedure into having something more than a purely compensatory function. As far as the USA is concerned, it is said that "civil litigation works as a policymaking mechanism" (Meurkens 2014, 25). All of the just-mentioned criticisms of the USA are acknowledged in Europe. However, all of the criticisms Europe has acknowledged are not in private law lawsuits, but rather in proceedings before administrative and constitutional courts, where litigation brought by individuals indeed works as a policymaking mechanism. Some contend that there is the phenomenon of the gradual convergence of the functions of lawsuits before ordinary (civil and commercial) courts and administrative/constitutional courts in Europe. Modern law is attacking the traditional private/public law divide rather than manifesting the inability of traditional lawsuits in private law. As far as the retrospective function of a lawsuit is concerned, in Europe actions before administrative and constitutional courts also contain a so-called *Normwiederholungsverbot*, i.e. the prohibition against enacting the same legal norm a second time (after it has been repealed once already by the competent court) (Detterbeck 1995, 443; Lange 2010, 203–205). The French term *contentieux objectif* is also known. Both terms contain a purely and completely regulatory function. Annulments of administrative acts and laws have an *erga omnes* effect, public law lawsuits are strongly controlled by the judges (*le principe inquisitoire*, *Inquisitionsmaxime*) and completely linked to substantive law (e.g. by special requirements of *locus standi* or interest in bringing proceedings understood as a direct interest due to a norm of law having a direct effect).

---

[4]OJ EU L 110, 1.5.2009, p. 30.

[5]As seen in Europe in, e.g., compulsory provisions in competition law intended to protect competition, such as in Arts. 101 and 102, Treaty on the Functioning of the European Union (TFEU).

4 The Dawn of the Regulatory Functions in the Law of Civil Procedure in Slovenia

Civil litigation in Slovenia and generally in Europe does not have a regulatory aim. It has, rather, a compensatory aim. This is also seen in the law of obligations with the postulate of *restitutio in integrum*. The aim of extra-contractual liability is to compensate the harmed victim and not to regulate the tortfeasor's behaviour. However, it is clearly understood that tort law in Europe has solely a compensatory aim and is not supposed to replace the role of policy decisions (Camilleri 2013, 534). A corresponding division of the judiciary into ordinary (civil and criminal) courts and specialised (labour—in collective actions concerning collective agreements, administrative and constitutional) courts can be observed in many countries in Europe, and also in Slovenia. The specialised judiciary (administrative and constitutional) does have primarily a regulatory function. However, in the USA tort litigation is used "to address a variety of social problems" and "to influence regulatory policy" (Lytton 2008, 1837). Tort law is constantly applied "to new societal questions, thus turning them into legal ones to be decided by the courts" (Loth 2015, 788). "The rationale of the American civil justice system is that tort litigants, among others, not only try to get compensation for their losses, but they also serve the public interest by revealing and deterring dangers in society" (Meurkens 2014, 29). Traditionally in Europe, where "remedies in tort cannot have other functions than exclusively the compensatory one", there can be no deterrence (Camilleri 2013, 534). In Slovenia, a patent dislike of using the law of obligations (extra-contractual liability) for policy issues can also be observed. On a comparative level, a very narrow scope of the law of extra-contractual liability in certain EU Member States can be observed. The narrowest field of application of such law is probably to be found in Germany. The German law of extra-contractual liability is indeed extremely narrow when compared to other EU Member States (§§ 823 I and 823 II Bürgerliches Gesetzbuch (BGB) and § 826 BGB); even cases such as slipping on the floor in a supermarket (*Linoleumrollenfall*) have to be resolved by using the *culpa in contrahendo* doctrine in the German law of contracts and not the law of extra-contractual liability.

> But the German reluctance to use civil procedure for the regulation of mass torts and to install [lege: introduce] more group actions does not mean that private actions do not strongly influence the development of law and social life. Often it is a public or private insurance [company], which is the powerful opponent of the wrongdoer in a civil action after legal assignment of the individual citizen's claim. In Germany, the consequences of the financial crisis are mostly regulated by court decisions or in-court-settlements. Until now, the traditional form of individual procedures prevails, and it happens often that the results of a first final decision are the basis of settlements between other reasonable parties and lawyers. [Stürner 2016, 77]

What seems to happen in Slovenian civil procedure is the extension of public law techniques to private law lawsuits. Public law is policy-driven; private law, on the other hand, was traditionally supposed to be neutral. Therefore, regulatory tasks are to be performed by public agencies as a part of the executive branch (Babić 2014, 220, 221).[6] However, the tactic of using the courts to induce regulatory decisions is most definitely a reality in the EU; environmental law is the clearest example. One might, for example, refer to lawsuits based in environmental law such as Court of Justice of the European Union (CJEU) cases concerning the now repealed Directive 85/337/EEC.[7] Newer European doctrine on consumer protection law is slowly acknowledging the fact that plaintiffs, e.g. in European collective redress actions before ordinary courts, might want to influence the behaviour of corporate defendants, i.e. perform a regulatory policy and change the future behaviour of defendants (Klauser 2016, 584, 585). But do the courts really exist to create regulatory policy? Are the courts in the conception developed by Montesquieu not solely the guardians just to say what such a policy cannot be?

A preference for regulatory private litigation in the form of injunctive relief may be witnessed in Europe as well, especially in the Netherlands.

> Private law systems and the rules designed for those systems mainly look backwards, not forwards, supplying possible solutions, that is, remedies, when something has gone wrong, for example when a duty was breached or a contract was not lived up to. Second, when reacting to such a wrong these systems mainly try to restore the former situation by way of compensation or restoration in kind for the harm done, and nothing more. Thirdly, private law rules typically react to a specific situation, problem or dispute without taking the broader picture into account. These flaws lead to, for instance, problems as regards compliance with, and possibilities of, enforcement of private law rules. [Van Boom et al. 2010, 3]

Under US influence, the possibilities offered by collective redress are considered by the CJEU. Where the compensatory function of civil lawsuits begins to be neglected and at the same time injunctive relief is stressed, then "the collective action as a means of enforcing collective rights not only provides access to this legal remedy but also has characteristics that make it an effective deterrent".[8] Furthermore, "The successful enforcement of rights by way of a collective action creates a just balancing of the interests of consumers and undertakings, ensures fair competition and shows that collective actions are just as necessary as individual actions in order to protect the consumer."[9]

In Slovenia, a very post-socialist and post-modern mistrust in the institutions of public law, i.e. agencies run by politicians or politically appointed civil servants, can be observed (typical discussion: A civil servant? Ah, an incompetent without capacity to think and without any knowledge, and having been appointed by political influence). Even though standard manuals on public and administrative law

---

[6]Such a tradition led to a peculiar situation in Serbia where consumer-oriented collective redress litigation as of 2014 will be conducted in administrative proceedings before administrative authorities.

[7]See e.g. *Bund für Umwelt und Naturschutz Deutschland, Landesverband Nordrhein-Westfalen*, C-115/09, ECLI:EU:C:2011:289.

[8]Opinion of Advocate General Trstenjak C-472/10, *Invitel*, ECLI:EU:C:2011:806, para. 41.

[9]Ibid.

place an important emphasis on the neutrality of public services and the executive branch, the public opinion seems to go the other way (Zobec and Cernic 2015, 131). Sociologists have found that due to the expansion of the modern market economy the growth of a new and very confident middle class of individuals who are the ideal plaintiffs in lawsuits has disempowered the classic voter (Maltsev and Skaskiw 2013, 53). As a consequence, the administrative actions undertaken by governmental authorities under the influence of the legislative branch are suffering. In other words, the growth of consumer awareness due to the deregulation of public services leads to regulation by the courts. The term coined in sociology is the "citizen-consumer" (Krastev 2014, 68, 69). That citizen-consumer is confronted with the fact that "capturing the government is simply no longer a guarantee that things will change" (Krastev 2014, 68).

Faced with the loss of influence of regulatory and executive agencies, individuals naturally turn to the courts in order to uphold their perceived rights or defend against the infringement of their legally protected interests. From the European point of view, in the USA class actions seem to be a powerful and efficient vehicle to defend against such infringements. This is a consequence of the typical US notion of the courts as balancing the authority of the government (Zoller 2011, 560, 561). However, as everywhere, there can be abuses. US legal scholars already offer devastating critiques of the regulatory enforcement of law by private individuals before the courts in private law lawsuits (Glover 2012, 1140).

Yet, there is also an inevitable counter-revolution by conservative wig and pen folk. Slovenia is obviously a part of Europe. Traditionally, the published opinion by the legal community as one part of the elites in Europe voices a strong preference for ex ante regulation and ex post public enforcement of the law. It is claimed that "both deterrence and compensatory objectives can be pursued by either the public or the private enforcement system, it is commonly accepted that deterrence is better pursued by … authorities, while compensation is better achieved by private damage actions" (Bučan 2013, 22). The European paternalistic,[10] autocratic and even totalitarian tradition sees the State acting through its agencies as caring for the individual and protecting the rights and interests of the individual.[11] The State's task is to regulate aspects of everyday life (like public safety, public well-being, public health). One might go back to the considerations in Articles 3[12] and

[10]See e.g. the Prussian Iron Chancellor Otto von Bismarck as the founder of the European welfare state after German unification.

[11]The totalitarian influence in the regulatory state in Europe will not be forgotten. When comparing Tito's Yugoslavia and Franco's Spain one could be surprised by the similarity and even identity of arguments used for the justification of the ever-expanding regulatory state at the individual's expense.

[12]*Le principe de toute Souveraineté réside essentiellement dans la Nation. Nul corps, nul individu ne peut exercer d'autorité qui n'en émane expressément* (The principle of any sovereignty resides essentially in the Nation. No body, no individual can exert authority which does not emanate expressly from it).

12[13] of the 1789 *Déclaration des Droits de l'Homme et du Citoyen*. It is even said that "the United States is a reactive rather than an activist state. The reactive state traditionally fulfils a relatively reserved role in society and attaches great value to the individual's own responsibility, whereas the activist state tends to improve economic and social life and implements policies accordingly" (Meurkens 2014, 23, 24).

In Slovenia, there is an inherent difference between the enforcement of private law and public law (usually even the procedure in law enforcement is different). According to the old perception, public agencies do not have an interest in the enforcement of private law. Solely substantive public law or some parts of compulsory private law (e.g. collective labour law, parts of consumer protection law) are supposed to be enforced by public agencies of their own motion or even upon request of interested parties (e.g. delivery of a building permit). The regulatory intervention in European thinking by public law is necessarily performed ex ante, regulation by private law, however, always ex post (Röger 2004, 825, 826; Corapi 2012, 3). According to the European understanding applied also in Slovenia, private enforcement can only be a complement to public enforcement (Roth 2016, 1137). According to Advocate General Jan Mazák:

> Regulation No 1/2003 and the case-law of the Court have not established any de iure hierarchy or order of priority between public enforcement of EU competition law and private actions for damages. While no de iure hierarchy has been established, at present the role of the Commission and national competition authorities is, in my view, of far greater importance than private actions for damages in ensuring compliance with Articles 101 and 102 TFEU. Indeed so reduced is the current role of private actions for damages in that regard that I would hesitate in overly using the term 'private enforcement'.[14]

US lawyers consider that the interplay between the compensatory element and the regulatory element in civil procedure is fundamentally different when comparing US law and the laws of EU Member States (Marcus 2014, 36). However, lawsuits necessarily belong to the ex post regulation engaged by private applicants (Corapi 2012, 3). As such, they do not necessarily correspond to the protection of the public interest and cannot be used in every case to obtain regulatory effects. In other words, the judge necessarily regards the past. This ex post phenomenon has been best theorised by Advocate General Giuseppe Tesauro in his opinion in the *Factortame* case when assessing the necessity of interim relief[15]: "The problem arises from the fact that in a structured and intricate context which a modern system of judicial protection demands there is a lack of contemporaneity between the two points in time which mark the course of the law, namely the point when the right

[13]*La garantie des droits de l'Homme et du Citoyen nécessite une force publique: cette force est donc instituée pour l'avantage de tous, et non pour l'utilité particulière de ceux auxquels elle est confiée* (The guarantee of the rights of man and of the citizen necessitates a public force: this force is thus instituted for the advantage of all and not for the particular utility of those to whom it is entrusted).

[14]Opinion of Advocate General Mazák, C—360/09, *Pfleiderer*, ECLI:EU:C:2010:782, para. 40.

[15]Opinion of Advocate General Tesauro, *Factortame*, C—213/89, ECLI:EU:C:1990:216, para. 16.

comes into existence and the point (later on) when the existence of the right is (definitively) established." One needs a procedure for enforcing an existing right. In that manner, the judicial recognition of a right that might be understood as a regulation through litigation has only a declaratory effect. In order to get a regulatory civil judgment, a right, or to be exact an infringement of an existing right, necessarily precedes any lawsuit.[16]

5 Can Future Slovenian Collective Redress Be a Success Story?

Slovenia is trying to follow a modern path in civil justice. A bill on collective actions (collective redress) has been prepared by the Ministry of Justice. However, is the Slovenian judiciary prepared for such actions? Slovenia is a former communist state with a typically East European civil justice system characterised by excessive formalism and inefficiency. "If a civil justice system does not dispose of organisational and procedural mechanisms and case-management techniques for handling complex multi-party and multi-claim matters, any collective litigation device will be inappropriate and will be perceived as a "legal irritant"" (Uzelac 2014a, 61). Where even in the western part of Europe voices can be heard saying US class actions as the modern form of regulatory lawsuits in private law stand for a loss of party autonomy and a transformation of class members, other than the lead plaintiff, into *kolkhozniks* (Stürner 2014, 631–633), it could be argued that such thinking will make collective redress a priori suspect to the judiciary in new EU Member States like Slovenia. If understood in a typically Central and East European formalistic manner, an active and managerial judge necessary in any successful form of regulatory lawsuit might even be the cause of procedural inefficiencies (Uzelac 2014b, 203, 211; Kühn 2011, 204). The typically Central and East European formalistic mindset of lawyers is still impregnated with decades of a

[16]COM (2013) 401 Final, 11 June 2013, Communication from the Commission to the European Parliament, the Council, the European Economic and Social Committee and the Committee of the Regions "Towards a European Horizontal Framework for Collective Redress", p. 10: "There is a consensus among stakeholders that private and public enforcement are two different means that should normally pursue different objectives. Whereas it is the core task of public enforcement to apply EU law in the public interest and impose sanctions on infringers to punish them and to deter them from committing future infringements, private collective redress is seen primarily as an instrument to provide those affected by infringements with access to justice and—as far as compensatory collective redress is concerned—the possibility to claim compensation for harm suffered. In this sense, public enforcement and private collective redress are seen as complementing each other. Collective damages actions should aim to secure compensation of damage that is found to be caused by an infringement. The punishment and deterrence functions should be exercised by public enforcement. There is no need for EU initiatives on collective redress to go beyond the goal of compensation: Punitive damages should not be part of a European collective redress system."

communist instrumental approach to law, where formalism was the only means used by the judiciary for avoiding committing injustices too often. Such reasoning is clearly not capable of dealing successfully with, for example, collective redress (Kühn 2011, 152, 153). It might be argued that the transition from a policy-implementing type of judiciary to a conflict-resolution type of judiciary will not succeed in Eastern Europe until the final removal (probably by force of biology) of lawyers who began their careers in communist times and were educated in communist legal academia.

Formalism and textual positivism in the interpretation of laws also allow closing the case on procedural grounds that can be avoided if managerial judges as in the US class action were known (Kühn 2011, 204). Logical legalism typical of a hierarchical judiciary is inherent in civil law legal systems. However, formalism is the Central and East European specific development of logical legalism. Formalism is used by courts in Central and Eastern Europe as a veil to hide either an inability or a fear of decision-making or even a hostility to a result in a lawsuit (Uzelac 2010, 383; Kühn 2011, 204; Sladič 2014, 211, 222). In other words, there is an inherent hostility against conflict resolution via judicial decisions on the merits by shifting the emphasis of the judicial process to the even more obscure question of procedure (hyperformalism). This is indeed a worrying development in regulatory lawsuits. Or to put it differently, the aim of the judicial process is not conflict resolution, rather it is the respect even for minor formal issues. A typical example can be found in the Slovenian judiciary. If a party wants to be represented by an attorney, a strictly formalised written power of attorney has to be given to the attorney for proceedings before the courts of first instance and appellate courts. Such a written document must be filed with the court. Representation without a written power of attorney is not valid and procedural acts submitted by an attorney without a proper written power of attorney are inadmissible. However, in order to plead before the country's highest ordinary court—the Supreme Court—a special power of attorney has to be given after the date on which the challenged decision was rendered, such power of attorney containing an express citation of the contested judicial decision. Now, why should courts have to deal with the regularity of mandates given by clients to their attorneys? No attorney sound in mind would plead without having a mandate, for an attorney without a mandate given by the client has no right to legal fees. If already the formalism in powers of attorney is a cause of inefficiencies in individual lawsuits, then collective redress where there is representation of a group by a qualified entity or a lead plaintiff without a mandate will not result in efficient conflict resolution.

Due to a civil service hierarchical career path typical of European judiciaries, Central and East European appellate and supreme courts are still staffed with judges educated in communist times who continue to be equipped with the methodological weaknesses of communist legal thinking that preclude any possibility of modern managerial techniques in judicial proceedings (Zobec and Cernic 2015, 145–147). It might be true that the transition period provided for many "opaque and illogical" rules (Emmert 2003, 297), yet this is the case with much modern legislation due to ever-expanding legislation and regulation. However, where settled legal methods of interpretation of written laws are applied, such lacunae are not a problem. This is not the case in Central and Eastern Europe. Judicial decisions are rendered by "mechanical and simplistic conclusions without trying to understand the purpose of the law and the impact of the advocated decision" (Galič 2015, 111).

The basis of the methodological weakness of appellate judges in Central and Eastern Europe as remarked and seen by West European lawyers is still the Marxist-Leninist political theory inherent in legal studies prior to the fall of communism (Reich 2004, 50, 51; Emmert 2003, 291–298). "Before 1989, a Marxist moral-political orientation was considered an essential qualification for a judge" (Sirc 2008, 137).[17] "The transition did not entail any revolutionary change in the structure of staffing of courts or the bar" (Mańko 2013, 10). This means that even in countries where politically contaminated judges were removed from office there are still weaknesses at the appellate and supreme court levels (Korenzov 2015, 241, 242 and 260, 261). Legal theory underlying legal education before the fall of communism in Central and Eastern Europe was inherently linked with three names as different as Stučka, Pašukanis and Vyšinsky. Even though the older generation of lawyers is ashamed of citing them in modern legal writing, they are the explanation of the formalist and conservative wig and pen folk in the Central and East European judiciary.[18] Communist legal thinking caused judges to perceive "judicial activity very much as an exercise of legal formalism and textualism" (Korenzov 2015, 261).

First the thinking of Stučka and then later that of Vyšinsky clearly explain that regulatory litigation intended to protect the individual's (human) rights cannot succeed when put to judges educated in communist legal academia. Law will perish under communist legal thinking (de Lara 2013, 881). According to Vyšinsky in his *The Law of the Soviet State*, "Marxism-[L]eninism … teaches that legal relationships (and, consequently, the law itself) … are merely the will of the dominant class, elevated into a statute." Another doxa promulgated by Vyšinsky is, "The rights of human being[s] cannot be considered outside the prerogatives of governments, and the very understanding of human rights is a governmental concept." It is indeed impossible to see any possibility of regulatory litigation when law is considered in this manner. Such a concept is then referred to as an instrumental approach to law. Law is only an instrument. Vyšinsky as the theoretician of the instrumentalist approach to law (i.e. law as an instrument used by the Communist Party for tyranny over every part of the population) considered that a judgment should correspond to the politically required outcome (Djilas 1956, 121–131). As a consequence, if Damaška's distinction of two types of judiciary (the behaviour-modification type and the conflict-resolution type) is taken as granted,

[17]However Sirc also explains that as in Slovenia no judges were dismissed after the fall of communism, those with the qualification of a Marxist moral-political orientation remain in situ.

[18]How does one cite a Latvian Soviet people's commissar of justice known for food theft and terror (Stučka) or Stalin's attorney general and inventor of political show trials (Vyšinsky) and then claim adherence to human rights and an independent judiciary?

then the conflict-resolution type of judiciary is still in *statu nascendi* in Central and Eastern Europe. Collective redress is indeed something that goes against politically motivated outcomes, as seen in, for example, environmental collective redress in the EU.

Under Marxist-Leninist legal thinking, Law and State are defined as instruments of class rule, exploitation and alienation, and are therefore unwanted. Law and State are typical figures in capitalist societies and will disappear in socialism (Uzelac 1997, 109, 110). Pašukanis created in his *General Theory of Law and Marxism* a legal approach that actually precludes any regulatory lawsuit. Social interference and social relations take precedence over law (Pavčnik 2013, 525, 526). "In material reality a relationship has primacy over a norm" and "categories of law have absolutely no significance other than an ideological one" (Pašukanis 2003, 73, 87).[19] Such thinking goes against regulation through litigation doctrine inherent in private enforcement and collective redress.

If the old expression by Rudolph von Jhering is to be used, collective redress and any regulatory lawsuit in general is a modern form of a struggle for law (*der Kampf um's Recht*) that requires a conflict-resolution type of judiciary. Collective redress is a response to failures of the enforcement of law. The research done in modern sociology (spurred by global protests in recent years and events such as the Tea Party, not to mention the 2016 presidential election in the USA or Brexit) has confirmed considerations according to which US class actions or any other form of collective redress with regulatory aims are based on the perceived failure by public agencies to comply with the expectations of individuals allegedly harmed by wrongful actions and omissions by enterprises and even other public agencies. In the context of Central and Eastern Europe, citizens do not see the government administration or the judiciary as delivering for the money paid (Euromaidan is one example, Viktor Orban is another). Where administrative and other public agencies do not offer a response to inefficiencies that is perceived as satisfactory by the public or by harmed groups, there will be a form of spontaneous collective redress created without the importation of legal transplants irritating to the judiciary. The reaction of the harmed strata in society is the autonomous creation of collective redress vehicles.[20] This is also known, for example, in Austria and Germany where legal practice saw the setting up of special purpose vehicles for the assignment of claims against tortfeasors, judicial collection and re-assignment to the original owners. Alas, the standard response to such phenomena consists in negating the

[19]English text also available free of charge at https://www.marxists.org/archive/pashukanis/1924/law/ch03.htm. Accessed 7 June 2018.

[20]The author of this study advised, in a preliminary reference to the CJEU, an association of Slovenian small shareholders, which acted for more than 500 harmed individuals after a bank bail-in operated by the Slovenian government (*Kotnik*, C-526/14). The special purpose vehicle was created by entrepreneurial, harmed individuals without any legislative or jurisprudential intervention, as a solution in the light of governmental, administrative and judicial failure to protect harmed rights.

need for large-scale regulatory proceedings by virtue of excessive formalism and even stating that such vehicles infringe the foundations of the law of civil procedure.

In the end, one could also say that the formalism of Central and East European laws is not to be overextended. West European legal orders might also have some formalistic, authoritarian leftovers (e.g. the Bismarckian tradition of the paternalistic state in Germany in social security legislation since 1870 precluded any need for collective redress). Even in Central and Eastern Europe the common style of legislation seems baroque because of the hyperprecision of the texts (see from the West European point of view Küpper 2015, 305–374, "legislation in Eastern Europe is hypertrophic, unstable, and of poor technical quality").

6 Conclusion

The transplantation of regulatory lawsuits (and the implementation of modern legislation on collective redress) seems to be an East European showpiece for proving that post-communist states run by an ex-communist civil service and judiciary have become modern and democratic commonwealths. However, the "East European judiciary" is not ready for such instruments. One might argue that the new EU Member States have grown up by acceding to the European Union. However, practical experience with the judiciary offers a different impression. Therefore, a negative prognosis will have to be given on collective redress in Slovenia. This prognosis is of course only a *praesumptio iuris tantum*.

References

Amman O, Meier N (2017) Verhältnis von nationalem und internationalem Recht in den USA. Aktuelle juristische Praxis/Pratique actuelle juridique 26(1):90–98

Babić B (2014) Zaštita kolektivnih interesa potrošača. Anali pravnog fakulteta u Beogradu 62 (2):215–228

Bučan N (2013) The enforcement of EU competition rules by civil law. Dissertation Radboud Universiteit Nijmegen. http://hdl.handle.net/2066/121821. Accessed 7 June 2018

Camilleri E (2013) A decade of EU antitrust private enforcement: chronicle of a failure foretold? Eur Competition L Rev 34:531–537

Chayes A (1976) The role of the judge in public law litigation. Harvard L Rev 89(7):1281–1316

Corapi D (2012) Class actions and collective actions. In: Fairgrieve D, Lein E (eds) Extraterritoriality and collective redress. Oxford U Press, Oxford, pp 3–14

de Lara P (2013) Prendre le droit soviétique au sérieux. Revue internationale de droit comparé 65 (4):879–903

Detterbeck S (1995) Streitgegenstand und Entscheidungswirkungen im Öffentlichen Recht: Grundlagen des Verfahrens vor den allgemeinen Verwaltungsgerichten und vor dem Bundesverfassungsgericht. Mohr, Tübingen

Djilas M (1956) Die neue Klasse, eine Analyse des kommunistischen Systems. Kindler, Munich

Emmert F (2003) Administrative and court reform in central and eastern Europe. Eur Law J 9 (3):288–315
Galič A (2015) The aversion to judicial discretion in civil procedure in post-communist countries: can the influence of EU law change it? In: Bobek M (ed) Central European judges under the European influence. Hart Publishing, Oxford and Portland, pp 99–124
Glover JM (2012) The structural role of private enforcement mechanisms in public law. William Mary L Rev 53:1137–1217
Klauser A (2016) Verbandsklagen von Verbraucherorganisationen auf Unterlassung von Menschenrechtsverletzungen und Unternehmensstrafrecht. Österreichisches Anwaltsblatt 2016:584–586
Korenzov A (2015) When david teaches EU law to Goliath: a generational upheaval in the making. In: Bobek M (ed) Central European judges under the European influence. Hart Publishing, Oxford and Portland, pp 241–265
Krastev I (2014) Democracy disrupted. U of Pennsyl Press, Philadelphia, The Politics of Global Protest
Kühn Z (2011) The judiciary in central and Eastern Europe: mechanical jurisprudence in transformation. M Nijhoff Publishers, Leiden, Boston
Küpper H (2015) Normsetzung in Osteuropa. Jahrbuch für Ostrecht 56(2):305–375
Lange FV (2010) Grundrechtsbindung des Gesetzgebers. Eine rechtsvergleichende Studie zu Deutschland, Frankreich und den USA. Mohr, Tübingen
Maltsev Y, Skaskiw R (2013) The tea party explained: from crisis to crusade. Open Court, Chicago
Mańko R (2013) Survival of the socialist legal tradition? a polish perspective. Comparative Law Rev 4.2. https://www.ssrn.com. Accessed 7 June 2018
Marcus R (2014) The big bad wolf: American class actions. In: Harsági V, Van Rhee CH (eds) Multi-party redress mechanisms in Europe: squeaking mice?. Intersentia, Antwerp, pp 35–49
Marinoni L, Arenhart SC (2014) Collective litigation and due process of law: The Brazilian experience. Intn'l J of Procedural Law/Revue internationale de droit processuel/Internationale Zeitschrift für Prozessrecht/Revista internacional de derecho Procesal/Rivista internationale di diritto processuale 4(1):42–61
Loth MA (2015) Corrective and distributive justice in tort law. Maastricht Journal of European and Comparative Law 22(6):788–811
Lytton TD (2008) Using tort litigation to enhance regulatory policy making: evaluating climate-change litigation in light of lessons from gun-industry and clergy-sexual-abuse lawsuits. Texas Law Review 86:1837–1876
Meurkens RC (2014) Punitive damages, the civil remedy in American law, lessons and caveats for continental Europe. Dissertation, University of Maastricht. http://www.dart-europe.eu/full.php?id=1253331. Accessed 7 June 2018
Pašukanis EB (2003) The general theory of law and Marxism. Transaction Publishers, New Brunswick, London, Second printing
Pavčnik M (2013) Teorija prava, 4E. GVZaložba, Ljubljana
Reich N (2004) Transformation of contract law and civil justice in new EU member countries: the example of the Baltic States, Hungary and Poland. Riga Graduate School of Law Working Papers No. 21. http://www.rgsl.edu.lv/en/research/rgsl-working-papers. Accessed 7 June 2018
Resnik J (1982) Managerial Judges. Harvard L Rev 96:374–448
Röger R (2004) Nachbarrecht im Spannungsfeld zwischen liberalisiertem öffentlichen Baurecht und verschärftem Zivilrecht. Österreichische Juristenzeitung 59(22):821–826
Roth H (2016) Private Rechtsdurchsetzung im Zivilprozess. Juristenzeitung 71(23):1134–1140
Schack H (2014) Internationales Zivilprozessrecht. CH Beck, Munich
Seewald K (2017) Tagungsbericht: Instrumentalisierung von Zivilprozessen. Juristenzeitung 72 (11):566–568

Sirc L (2008) Totalitarian features of the judiciary in the republic of Slovenia (1945–1990): disregard for the rule of law. In: Jambek P (ed) Crimes committed by Totalitarian regimes: reports and proceedings of the 8 april european public hearing on crimes committed by Totalitarian regimes. Slovenian Presidency of the Council of the European Union, Brussels, pp 135–144
Sladič J (2014) Appeals in civil procedure in Slovenia: why the recent reforms of civil procedure did not manage to avoid the endless cycle of remittals. In: Van Rhee CH, Uzelac A (eds) Nobody's perfect: comparative essays on appeals and other means of recourse against judicial decisions in civil matters. Intersentia, Portland, Antwerp, pp 211–227
Stürner R (2014) Liberalismus und Zivilprozess. Österreichische Juristenzeitung 69(14–15): 629–639
Stürner R (2016) The role of civil procedure in modern societies. Ritsumeikan Law Rev, Int Ed 33:73–81
Uzelac A (1997) Istina u sudskom postupku. Pravni fakultet, Zagreb
Uzelac A (2010) Survival of the third legal tradition? Supreme Court Law Rev 49:377–396
Uzelac A (2014a) Why no class actions in Europe? A view from the side of dysfunctional justice systems. In: Harsági V, Van Rhee CH (eds) Multi-party redress mechanisms in Europe: squeaking mice?. Intersentia, Antwerp, pp 53–74
Uzelac A (2014b) Croatia: omnipotent judges as the cause of procedural inefficiency and impotence. In: Van Rhee CH, Fu Y (eds) Civil litigation in china and Europe—essays on the role of the judge and the parties. Springer, Berlin, pp 197–221
Van Boom WH (2010) Comparative notes on injunction and wrongful risk-taking. Maastricht J Eur Comp Law 17(1):10–31
Van Boom WH, Giesen I, Ogus A (2010) Editorial: the power of injunctive relief in tort: an introduction. Maastricht J Eur Comp Law 17(1):2–9
Zobec J, Černič JL (2015) The Remains of the authoritarian mentality within the slovene judiciary. In: Bobek M (ed) Central European judges under the European influence. Hart Publishing, Oxford and Portland, pp 125–148
Zoller E (2011) La justice comme contre-pouvoir: regards croisés sur les pratiques américaine et française. Revue internationale de droit comparé 53(3):559–574

Jorg Sladič Attorney-at-law practising in Ljubljana, Sladiö—Zemljak, LLP, Slovenia. Assistant Professor of International and European Law at the University of Maribor, Slovenia. Ph.D. from the University of Saarland, Germany, LLM from the University of Trier, Germany, Diplôme d'études supérieures spécialisées at the University François Rabelais in Tours, France. Former Legal Secretary (*référendaire*) at the Court of Justice of the European Union.

The Brazilian Collective Redress System

Sérgio Cruz Arenhart

Abstract This contribution describes some of the Brazilian instruments used for collective redress, pointing out their main features and uses. It explains the origins of the Brazilian "class action" (currently named *ação civil pública*) and the relation between this action and the so-called "popular action" (still in use, but with a more restricted field of application and less effectiveness). The contribution focuses on the practical use of these instruments, outlining some jurisprudential restrictions and data, which may be useful to emphasize the importance of mass and collective litigation in Brazil. It also presents a critical analysis of the Brazilian judicial system, particularly focusing on the new Code of Civil Procedure, and the so-called "system of precedents" created by the new Code. Finally, it deals with a number of the features of this Code, presenting some of the new tools developed to face mass and complex litigation in the Brazilian system, particularly underlining the function of precedents and of the Brazilian "ancillary proceeding for solving repetitive questions", a tool similar to the English Group Litigation Order which allows for the collective management of claims on related issues of law.

1 Initial Remarks

Brazilian law has a highly consolidated tradition in collective redress. In part, this is because Brazil received from Portugal the Roman idea of a "popular action" (*action popularis*), which has always been present in the Brazilian legal system. Another factor that helped this development is the recent opening of Brazilian law (not so recent, in the field of constitutional law) to the Anglo-American experience. Brazil can be considered a mixed judicial system that sits between the European and the Anglo-American traditions, which makes it susceptible to influences from both systems.

S. C. Arenhart (✉)
Faculty of Law, Federal University of Paraná, Curitiba, Brazil
e-mail: arenhart@mpf.mp.br

A. Uzelac and C. H. van Rhee (eds.), *Transformation of Civil Justice*,
Ius Gentium: Comparative Perspectives on Law and Justice 70,
https://doi.org/10.1007/978-3-319-97358-6_13

For this reason Brazil has a complete system of collective redress, used as an example for many other countries in the world. Nevertheless, the practice of collective redress in Brazil still faces problems. In many situations, courts tend to restrain, inexplicably, the use of some "class actions", preferring to address mass claims individually. In other cases, outdated solutions offered by the law provide inadequate protection for collective interests, making these remedies fruitless in many situations.

This contrast between law and practice, and the need for the modernization of some ideas, shows that, although Brazil is an interesting country in terms of collective actions, it still has much to do in this field.

2 The Popular Action in Brazil

As mentioned, Brazil received from Portugal a remedy, dedicated to protecting public property, called "Ação Popular" (*action popularis*).[1] This tool has its roots in ancient Roman law, whose *actiones popularis* were also dedicated to protecting public interests. *Ação Popular* passed down through *Ordenações* (Ordinations) of the Kingdom of Portugal, which were applied in Brazil, a Portuguese colony until 1822.

For this reason, Brazil's first Constitution, enacted in 1824, established, in Article 157, that any case of embezzlement or corruption by judges or officers of the court could be the subject of a popular action, initiated by "any of the people". Although the Constitution of 1891 did not repeat the same idea, popular action itself remained, established by practice and by infra-constitutional law. The Constitution of 1934 reestablished the constitutional status of this remedy and stated that the popular action could be used to annul any sort of act that could harm federal, state or municipal public property.

Since then, all Brazilian constitutions established almost the same use for the popular action. The Constitution of 1988 extended the use of the popular action, defining that it can be used by any citizen, to annul acts harmful to public property, to public morality, to the environment and to historical and cultural heritage. It also states that this action is exempt from court fees and attorney's fees,[2] except where the plaintiff is deemed to be in bad faith.

The Brazilian Constitution—enlarging the scope within which a popular action can be initiated—gave a constitutional *status* to some rules already present in the statute that regulates this remedy. Law L. 4.717 of 29 June 1965, was the first

[1]About this instrument, see also Marinoni et al. (2017), Mancuso (2015), Silva (2007), Rocha (1968).

[2]Normally, in Brazil, the party that loses the case must pay the costs of the opposing party's attorney. This is called "succumbency" (*sucumbência*, in Portuguese), which can be freely translated as burden of defeat or loss of suit expenses. In popular actions, the rule of succumbency does not operate.

Brazilian statute to regulate this civil action, and it is still the law applicable to this subject. The statute enlarged the scope of application of the popular action, mentioning that it could also be used to protect assets and rights of economic, artistic, aesthetic, historical and touristic importance. This improvement was the result of the courts' interpretation of the term "public property" and enabled an important development of the popular action of the past.

So, currently, the popular action has a very wide usage, although always linked to some *public interest*. The plaintiff can be *any Brazilian citizen*, who is legally presumed to act in the interest of all Brazilian society, it being unnecessary to demonstrate any kind of "adequacy of representation". In other words, being a citizen suffices to have standing to sue for a possible harm to any of the interests listed above. The action is exempt from any fees, except in cases of so-called bad-faith litigation. The statute also grants some discovery powers to the plaintiff, compelling the government (and governmental agencies) to comply with any requests for documents important to a popular action within 15 days.[3] The fact that this kind of action always concerns public interests allows the government to take part in either side of the proceedings. In other words, upon service of process, the Brazilian government can decide either to defend itself regarding the act which is contested or to join the plaintiff, also seeking the annulment of the act and compensation for any harm incurred.

Even though the Public Prosecutor's Office is not allowed to initiate a popular action, its participation is mandatory. It is its duty to work towards an expeditious development of the discovery phase and, if necessary, to seek civil and criminal liability of anyone who may have acted against the public interest. It may also take the place of the plaintiff in case of unjustifiable discontinuance of the action. Furthermore, the Public Prosecutor's Office has the duty to enforce the judgment whenever the plaintiff fails to do so.

The statute also grants compensation for any damage to the public interest—independently of the claim—apart from the annulment of the act. The judgment has an *erga omnes* effect, binding everyone, except when it is dismissed due to a lack of grounds for the claim.[4] Whenever the lower court decides to dismiss the case, the dismissal is subject to an automatic review, by a court of appeals, even if the plaintiff or the Public Prosecutor's Office does not present an appeal against it.

Notwithstanding the protection the statute gives to the plaintiff, the use of the popular action has never fulfilled its purposes. One of the reasons for this is that, normally, people are not willing to go to court to protect interests that are not their own. The altruistic stance—assumed by the Brazilian popular action—is too much to expect from anyone, especially when there is no gain for a person who will be a party to civil litigation for many years. Therefore, many popular actions conceal a

[3]The only case in which such a request can be denied is in the case of public interest, properly justified.

[4]In this case, any citizen can initiate another popular action, provided that he presents new evidence.

private interest disguised as a public interest. Most of these actions are brought for selfish reasons, but present a "public cause of action".

The situation is aggravated when we consider that—even with no court fees for this action—there are, certainly, costs to initiate litigation. Why would anyone go to a Court of Justice, spending a considerable amount of money, just to protect the public interest? It simply does not make any sense.

On the other hand, even when a selfless plaintiff initiates a popular action—imbued with a republican spirit—it is obvious that his chances against the might of government power or of a corporation are very low. It is obviously a battle between David and Goliath. And, even though David wins the battle in the biblical tradition, on the judicial field the story normally ends in a different manner.

These reasons ended up decreasing the number (and the importance) of popular actions in Brazil. The action still maintains its role as a democratic tool to allow citizens to participate in public management, but it lost, long ago, practical significance in collective litigation.

3 The Birth of the Collective Action (or Public Civil Action)

The drawbacks of the Brazilian popular action resulted in a broad discussion about better approaches in the field of diffuse rights. From a bill presented to regulate environmental protection, following a suggestion from several São Paulo public prosecutors (who were also professors of law), a general Act was enacted, which allowed collective redress to be instituted to protect the same interests as those protected by popular actions,[5] but in a different setting. Instead of allowing any person to initiate this action, L. 7.347, of 24 July 1985, gave standing to sue to some public organizations and institutions, and to private associations, which are supposedly prepared to face large corporations or to defend social interests.

The Act gave *locus standi* for this "public civil action" (or *ação civil pública*, in Portuguese)[6] to many public and private institutions normally involved in the protection of collective and social interests. We shall return to this subject later, but the idea was to offer *locus standi* to entities that would be more capable of bringing a collective action. It also imposed the presence of the Public Prosecutor's Office in every collective action, either as a party or as *custos iuris*. Moreover, the Public Prosecutor's Office is obliged to take on a collective action in case of unjustified discontinuance by the original plaintiff.

[5]This Act has been amended many times since its introduction, permitting, nowadays, the protection of any diffuse or collective right.

[6]About the public civil action, see also Marinoni et al. (2017), Arenhart et al. (2017), Venturi (2007), Mancuso (2016a), Gidi (2008), Mazzilli (2000), Milaré (2015), Mendes (2014), Souza (2017), Almeida (2011), Lenza (2003), Vigliar (2001), Dinamarco (2001), Carvalho Filho (2007), Zaneti (2006), Leonel (2016), Rodrigues (2009).

Another important innovation brought by the Act was the "public civil inquest" (*inquérito civil público*). This investigative tool, employed by the Public Prosecutor's Office, is important for gathering information and evidence, to allow a better and higher quality protection of collective and social interests. In possession of all the information gathered, the Public Prosecutor's Office may seek extrajudicial relief for the case—such as an agreement for the offender to adjust his conduct[7]—or, if that is not possible, it may initiate a collective action. Such agreement, called "conduct adjustment agreement" (similar to a cease-and-desist) is an important instrument for resolving collective issues in Brazil. Its flexibility—as opposed to the rigidity of judicial adjudication—authorizes a more suitable solution in complex litigation cases, allowing to offer some time to comply with obligations or to stagger the implementation of the adjustment required.

The Public Prosecutor's Office, or any other *public entity* with standing to initiate a public civil action,[8] may also issue a *recommendation* to the lawbreaker. This instrument could be defined as a warning to the transgressor, explaining to him the reasons why his behavior is illegal and giving him time to rectify actions according to the proper rules. It is not an agreement, as the other tool is, and for this reason it does not have a binding force. Nonetheless, it may be used as an unequivocal sign that the public entity believes the conduct practiced is wrongful, and that other (more aggressive) measures may be taken afterwards (such as civil or criminal actions or even administrative sanctions).

In order to understand the importance of these instruments, it is useful to examine some numbers. Although Brazil does not normally provide reliable data and statistics, there is some information that may demonstrate the use and the success of such extrajudicial tools.

In 2015, the São Paulo Public Prosecutor's Office entered into 970 agreements, and issued 720 recommendations in collective disputes.[9] In the same year, the Federal Public Prosecutor's Office entered into 191 agreements and issued 5132 recommendations. The difference in the use of the two techniques at the state and federal level may be explained by the diversity of themes dealt with by each branch of the Public Prosecutor's Office. Since the Federal Public Prosecutor's Office deals mainly with the federal government, consensual solutions are less frequent due to

---

[7]Although the civil inquest was designed as a tool only for the Public Prosecutor's Office, the agreement mentioned in the text was not. The "conduct adjustment agreement" (*termo de ajustamento de conduta*) can be used by all the *public* organizations allowed to initiate a collective action in Brazil. Nevertheless, the most common user of this tool is the Public Prosecutor's Office.

[8]See, Sect. 4.2.

[9]São Paulo is the richest and most developed state in Brazil, and this is the reason for choosing it when discussing these mechanisms.

the restrictions commonly presented in this area. Nevertheless, these data demonstrate the relevance of the measures and the purpose of their use.[10]

The Act also offered an answer with regard to the compensation commonly sought in collective actions. Since the relevant rights do not belong to a particular subject, it is difficult to determine where to send the damages paid in such collective actions. For this reason, the Act created public funds to receive these sums of money and to manage their use, in the prevention of any new infringement of the laws or in the redress of damages to collective and social interests.

To facilitate the use of these proceedings, the Act also established an exemption from all court and attorney's fees (likewise the popular action) for the plaintiff in the action. So, except in case of bad faith, the plaintiff will not be charged with these costs.

Finally, in accordance with the nature of the rights protected by this sort of action, a special regime for *res judicata* was created. In the public civil action, *res judicata* operates *erga omnes* and *secundum eventum litis*. In other words, *res judicata* applies to everybody, preventing any other litigation over the same matter. On the other hand, if the judgment concludes that the relief sought cannot be granted due to lack of evidence, then there is no *res judicata* regarding the collective interest. In such a case, any other collective action may be initiated, provided new evidence is found.[11]

4 The Adolescence of the Brazilian Collective Action

Five years after the creation of the "public civil action", the Brazilian Consumer Protection Code (hereinafter, CDC) was enacted (L. 8.078, of September 11, 1990).[12] Even though the Statute's purpose was to regulate consumer law, it

[10]The CEBEPEJ—a private organization, also dedicated to gathering information and planning actions in the field of the judicial branch—has some interesting data. According to research conducted between 2002 and 2006, in São Paulo, the Public Prosecutor's Office was able to execute 8553 agreements (4899 of them were accomplished voluntarily, without need of enforcement). Just to compare these numbers, it is interesting to note that in the same period the São Paulo Public Prosecutor's Office initiated 12,216 public civil actions (while other entities—that have *locus standi* in collective protection—initiated 1899 actions). As may be noted, the number of consensual solutions was very high, almost equaling the number of collective actions initiated.

[11]More recently, this Act was modified to establish that collective *res judicata* only operates within the limits of the court's jurisdiction (e.g., in the city, the state or the region that it has authority over; we will return to this subject further on).

[12]Examining this Act, see Grinover et al. (2017), Ragazzi et al. (2017), Marques et al. (2016), Nunes (2015).

included a chapter to deal with collective protection, not only applied to the consumer field, but also to any sort of diffuse or mass litigation, creating, so to speak, a "microsystem of collective protection".[13]

In accordance with that idea, Brazilian courts tend to interpret all legislation on collective redress as though it belongs to a single statute. Any possible conflict of law should be resolved by the application of the "best collective protection principle". In other words, those conflicts should be resolved in favour of the solution that gives collective redress more effectiveness. However, courts do not always obey this principle. Although they frequently use the "microsystem" idea, in some cases it is invoked to impair collective protection, using sometimes older rules that tend to be less effective or specific rules designed to be applied just to some cases.

4.1 The Interests Protected

The first and main innovation is a legal definition of the rights that can be protected by a collective action. Article 81 CDC authorizes the use of collective actions for the protection of diffuse, collective and mass[14] rights.[15] *Diffuse rights* (in Portuguese, *direitos difusos*) are qualified as being indivisible, non-subjective rights that belong to an indeterminate community, such as the environment or cultural heritage. On the other hand, collective rights (*direitos coletivos*, in Portuguese) are those indivisible, non-subjective rights that belong to a defined class, group or category, for example, traditionally, indigenous people's rights or some consumer's rights. These two kinds of rights compose a proper "meta-individual" class of rights, because they are not related to subjective interests but, instead, to social or public interests.[16]

The other group of interests mentioned by the CDC is mass rights (called "homogeneous individual rights" or, in Portuguese, *direitos individuais homogêneos*). These are not collective rights; on the contrary, they are individual

---

[13]The expression is widely used in Brazilian doctrine and courts to represent the systemic view of all the Acts that deal with collective protection. In fact, the two statutes indicated in the text are just the main sources of Brazilian collective redress. Many other Acts discuss diffuse rights, such as the Children Protection Act, the Elderly Protection Act, the Writ of Mandamus Act and the Investor Act. All these statutes shall be interpreted as though they belong to a single unity. This is the idea behind the "microsystem" mentioned in the text.

[14]Mass rights are referred to by the Act as "homogeneous individual rights" (*direitos individuais homogêneos*). Nevertheless, they are better defined as the typical mass rights that authorize, in the USA, the use of class actions.

[15]For a deeper analysis of these rights, see also Arenhart (2014), Osna (2014), Vitorelli (2016), Gidi (2007), Andrade et al. (2017), Castilho (2004).

[16]The difference between these two categories is, from my point of view, irrelevant and should be abolished. Despite this, it is used by the Writ of Mandamus Act to narrow the use of collective writs, which, according to the Act, may not be used to protect diffuse rights. The rule's constitutionality is doubtful, and it is one of the few cases where the distinction may be of some use.

rights *managed by a collective instrument* (Zavascki 2006, *passim*; 1995, *passim*).[17] To facilitate their protection, the law authorizes bringing these interests together, to be protected in a single action, avoiding repetitive claims, waste of resources and preventing contradictory decisions.

As one can see, the Brazilian system deals with collective redress in two different manners. First, it offers protection to "non-personal" (non-individual) interests, allowing some special entities to defend them on behalf of the entire society or a specific class, group or category. Second, it offers a remedy for mass litigation, also allowing those entities to "concentrate" the discussion, eliminating the effects of multitudinous litigation.

4.2 *Locus Standi* in "Public Civil Actions"

As seen before, one of the main problems of Brazilian popular actions was the difficulty a single citizen faced to sue for a public benefit. Taking that into account, the Act addressing the "public civil action" chose to follow a different path. It opted to give *locus standi* for these collective remedies to a certain number of public and private entities which are better equipped to get involved in a complex lawsuit dealing with relevant interests and, usually, facing a powerful defendant.

Almost any public entity (or its bodies) may have standing in a collective action. The Acts, thus, mention: I—the Public Prosecutor's Office; II—the Public Defender's Office; III—Federal, State or Municipal Governments; and IV—Agencies, their bodies, "public companies" and public foundations. These entities may not only initiate a "public civil action", but, as seen before, may also seek an extrajudicial solution for collective issues.

As for private plaintiffs, Brazilian law allows any association, in existence for more than a year,[18] and whose institutional purposes include the protection of a collective interest/right, to initiate a "public civil action". Albeit *locus standi* for associations to initiate a collective action has been intensively and long debated by the courts—and there is a clear tendency to narrow their power to act on behalf of the collective—the authorization for organized private entities to protect social and collective interests is seen to be an important touchstone for the system. In the future, it is expected that these associations will assume the largest part of collective litigation, bringing organized society to participate in the public agenda.

[17]Brazilian doctrine usually makes a distinction between the protection of collective rights (diffuse and collective rights) and the collective protection of individual rights (homogeneous individual rights), although the public civil action may protect both kinds of interests.

[18]The requirement of this prior existence, for more than a year, may be disregarded by the judge, in consideration of the relevance of the case or the interest protected.

4.3 The Relief Sought

The first Act to regulate the public civil action (L. 7.347/1985) only permitted certain kinds of relief, particularly compensation or injunctions. The rule was highly criticized because some situations demanded other forms of remedy not expressly authorized by law.

For this reason, and to make clear that there are no limits to the relief that can be sought in a public civil action, the CDC expressly mentions the possibility to obtain any kind of protection, by any proceedings (Article 83). Furthermore, the Act created some interesting tools to provide appropriate protection for collective interests. It was actually the first statute to allow "specific performance" in Brazil, authorizing judges to use coercive measures to enforce specific conduct. This possibility was further increased by the new Code of Civil Procedure, which broadens the use of specific performance for any kind of obligation or act, including monetary compensation.

The Act also created a special procedure to collect individual compensation (in case of homogeneous individual rights). It established "two-stage" proceedings, first with a collective stage—conducted by one of those entities that has standing to sue for a public civil action—seeking a positive judgment, followed by an individual enforcement of the decision by the persons affected.[19]

Finally, it is interesting to mention that, despite of the lack of specific regulation for the subject, nowadays it is frequent to see the use of collective actions to obtain structural injunctions. Notably in the field of public policy conflicts—such as the public health system, the prison system and the education system—Brazil has seen many public civil actions seeking respect of fundamental rights. And the Brazilian judicial system, generally, grants relief in such cases, mainly due to the insufficient protection the government offers to such rights.

The interesting point of these structural actions is the judicial creation of new structures and a new approach to the relevant disputes, adapting the proceedings according to the needs of the situation and establishing an important dialogue with the public administration and the legislative branch to make the constitutional guarantees effective.

4.4 The Relationship Between Collective Actions and Individual Claims

One relevant matter with which the legislation had to deal was the relationship between collective and individual actions. Normally, this is a problem only related

[19]Using the same criteria employed by the Public Civil Action Act, if no individual presents himself to claim enforcement of the judgment in his own benefit, the amount of the award shall revert to the public funds, designed for the protection of diffuse and collective rights.

to homogeneous individual rights, since diffuse and collective rights are supposed to be non-individual interests. However, in the field of homogeneous individual rights, this is a major topic, mainly because it deals with the individual will (to sue) and the public interest in the efficiency of the judicial system.

Brazilian legislation conceived a relative autonomy between individual and collective actions. From this point of view, the existence of a collective action does not preclude an individual one or vice versa. Although a collective action dealing with homogeneous individual rights is supposed to gather all individual claims, there is no *lis pendens* between them. For this reason, anyone can initiate or continue with an individual action, despite the existence of a public civil action.[20]

Yet, to benefit from a collective action, the individual must request the suspension of his own claim (within 30 days, starting from when he is notified of the collective action). Otherwise, the collective action will not affect the legal position of the individual, who will be able to obtain an individual decision of his case.

If the individual asks for the suspension of his claim and waits for the collective proceedings, then he may benefit from a favourable judgment allowing the enforcement of his rights. Still, if the collective action is dismissed, the individual may ask to continue with his individual claim (which was suspended).

Regarding diffuse and collective rights, the CDC states that a favourable judgment in a collective action may be used by individuals, in a so-called "*in utilibus*" transfer of *res judicata*. In other words, individuals may benefit from this judgment, since the liability for the wrongdoing has already been established. So, they can avail themselves of this adjudication, in an "issue preclusion" manner, without the need for a new demonstration of liability. Consequently, all that individuals need to demonstrate is their own loss in order to receive compensation.[21,22]

4.5 Res Judicata in Collective Actions

The CDC created a very sophisticated *res judicata* system, one thought to offer better protection to collective interests. In this sense, it conceived a *res judicata* regime both *secundum eventum litis* and *secundum eventum probationem*.

Article 103 CDC states that *res judicata*, in diffuse rights cases, operates *erga omnes*, except in case of insufficient evidence. This means that *res judicata*, in such

[20]It is true, however, that the Superior Court of Justice—the higher court in interpreting federal law—stated, in a binding judgment, that the initiation of a collective action implies the automatic suspension of all individual actions on the same subject. This is not the rule present in the CDC, but an attempt to give more power to collective actions, clearly exceeding the legislative will.

[21]The same effect is given to criminal judgments, which can also benefit possible victims.

[22]There is a huge debate about the constitutionality of this "*in utilibus*" transfer, especially because the subject-matter of the collective action is the diffuse or collective right (and not individual rights). Nevertheless, if the idea of issue preclusion (presently adopted by Article 503 of the Code of Civil Procedure) is correctly understood, there is no more room for this question.

cases, affects everybody, and prevents any other action on the same subject. This consequence, however, does not apply if the decision to dismiss is caused by lack of evidence. In this case, any other entity may have standing to sue for another collective action, with the same objective, provided that it can offer new evidence.

In cases of collective rights, *res judicata* operates *ultra partes*, except in the event of insufficient evidence. The difference between *ultra partes* and *erga omnes res judicata* is supposed to depend on whether the group affected is defined or undefined. Since collective rights are related to a specific class, category or group, only that collective is affected by the *res judicata* (which leads to so-called *ultra partes res judicata*). Diffuse rights, on the other hand, are related to the whole society or, at least, to an unidentified group, and hence lead to *erga omnes res judicata*.

When dealing with homogeneous individual rights, the CDC offers a quite novel solution. *Res judicata* operates *erga omnes* only in the case of a favourable judgment.[23] If the case is dismissed, any individual may initiate his own individual action—or, if it was suspended as seen before, the plaintiff may request reinstatement of the proceedings. Within this framework, where the collective action can only benefit individuals, Brazilian legislation attempts to deal with the problems of proper control of representation, specific notification and some other issues commonly discussed in the realm of North American class actions.

As one can easily see, the system is very favourable to class protection. Of course, big companies, banks and the government (the most common targets of collective actions) take that into account and either include in their costs these types of litigation or lobby for specific amendments to the law, as a way to prevent major losses.[24]

[23]A modification was introduced in Article 16, L. 7.347/1985, establishing that *res judicata*, in public civil actions, shall be limited to the territorial jurisdiction of the court that decides the case. Doctrine fiercely criticizes the rule, pointing out either its unconstitutionality, or its lack of technique, or its irrationality. Obviously, such a rule can only be related to homogeneous individual rights, since diffuse and collective rights are indivisible and cannot be divided per jurisdiction. As for mass rights, the purpose of offering collective protection is precisely to preserve equality and to avoid repetitive litigation. This being so, there is absolutely no reason for the restriction just mentioned (except the intention to reduce the effectiveness of collective actions). The issue is still open for debate in Brazilian courts. The Superior Court of Justice tends to state (and has decided in this sense sometimes) that, although the rule is constitutional, it only relates to homogeneous individual rights and, whenever the collective action is initiated in a State capital, those limits do not apply and the judgment can affect individual interests all over the country.

[24]That is the reason for some important amendments, such as the one mentioned above—the limitations to *res judicata*—or Article 2-A, L. 9.494 (introduced in 2001), which imposes severe restrictions to collective actions managed by associations, particularly against federal, state or municipal governments.

4.6 *Enforcing the Public Civil Action*

The enforcement of collective redress in Brazilian law, nowadays, follows the same basic principles used in individual claims.[25] In this sense, and in accordance with the new Code of Civil Procedure (from 2015), one may use any coercive or subrogatory measure to ensure the effectiveness of a judicial order.

Thus, judges can enforce their judgment by injunctions, for instance, ordering compliance on pain of severe sanctions (such as fines, the restriction of rights or, in some very specific cases, even civil imprisonment). They can also allow third parties to perform the debtor's obligation (at their own expense) or even use law enforcement to obtain the specific performance imposed. This open system established by the Code of Civil Procedure (already prevailing in the past for some obligations) is limited only by the needs of the actual case and by constitutional guarantees. Consequently, it is possible to say that the Brazilian enforcement system stimulates "judicial creativity" to obtain the most feasible result.

One noteworthy point is a regime created by the CDC to enforce decisions on homogeneous individual rights. As noted before, to balance the purposes of a class action and individual rights, the statute created a two-stage procedure. The first part consists of collective proceedings, leading to the judgment of the dispute. Upon having determined the defendant's liability, the second stage begins, authorizing the victims (individuals) to initiate—to their own benefit—the enforcement of the decision. Therefore, the system operates within a collective-individual rationale, allowing the victim to choose to benefit or not from the judgment. In any case, if no individual shows up for enforcement, any potential collective plaintiff may request the enforcement of the decision. In this case, the money collected goes to the public funds mentioned before.

5 The New Code of Civil Procedure and New Instruments of Collective Redress

Despite all the system's possibilities, multiple lawsuits on the same issue continue to increase in Brazil. The numbers do not lie and show that the collective redress offered by the "microsystem" is not able to stop repeat players. Despite its efficiency in dealing with collective interests, mass litigation is still a major problem in the Brazilian system.

[25]For further references on the enforcement of Brazilian collective actions, see Shimura (2006), Venturi (2000).

In fact, in 1990, Brazil had 3.6 million claims. This number increased to 20 million in 2000, and to 25.5 million in 2009.[26] Currently, the Brazilian judicial system has more than 73 million cases.[27] On this basis, one can easily verify that many of these cases concern mass litigation. A report made by Fundação Getúlio Vargas, in 2010, demonstrated that in some of the most important courts in Brazil, most of the cases involve mass litigation. In the São Paulo State Court of Appeals, for instance, consumer litigation represented 51% of all cases, while public litigation represented 43%. In Rio Grande do Sul, 72% of the cases were related to consumer problems, while public disputes represented 20% of the total number. As experience demonstrates, these types of cases are normally repeat litigations, presenting the same factual or legal question, shared by many consumers or citizens.

A report from the Brazilian National Counsel of Justice, from 2011, demonstrates that more than 12% of all the cases in Brazil have the federal government as a party to the action, and more than 10% have banks. Municipal and state governments are parties in more than 10% of all cases. As a result, these repeat players are responsible for almost one-third of cases in Brazil. This indicates the impact of mass litigation on the Brazilian judicial system.

Aware of this situation, the new Code of Civil Procedure tries to offer new tools to tackle mass litigation. In fact, many new features were developed in this statute to address mass litigation in a better manner, but two of them are the most significant and will be addressed here.

The first of these instruments is a technique of examining repeated second appeals.[28] This tool is not new in Brazilian law, nor was it designed for the first time in the new Code of Civil Procedure. Brazilian legislation adopted this idea under the Code of 1973, with a change introduced by L. 11.672 of May 2008. According to this modification—and the rules presented by the new Code of Civil Procedure, which basically repeat the former regulation—whenever the same question of law is presented in many different second appeals, the superior court (including the Supreme Court) may order that all the cases (in which such question is also present) are to be stayed, until a model case is examined by the Court. In other words, the Court may select one single appeal or several appeals that are representative for the relevant legal question, meaning that all other cases should be stayed until that question is answered. The superior court's decision is binding for all present and future cases, avoiding the need to reexamine the same question multiple times afterwards.

---

[26]Despite this number, the report mentions that 63% of the people who had a dispute in 2009 did not seek judicial relief. This shows the level to which the reputation of the judicial system has been brought into disrepute, a state of affairs caused mainly by its costs, its delay and its bureaucracy.

[27]The data are taken from the national report on litigation, available at http://www.cnj.jus.br/programas-e-acoes/pj-justica-em-numeros. Accessed 7 June 2018.

[28]"Second appeal" is an expression used in this text to refer to an appeal directed to a Brazilian superior court, either in case of violation of federal law or in case of violation of the Constitution. Mainly, it represents an extraordinary appeal, which concerns the standardization of the interpretation of law, rather than reexamining all the questions of the case.

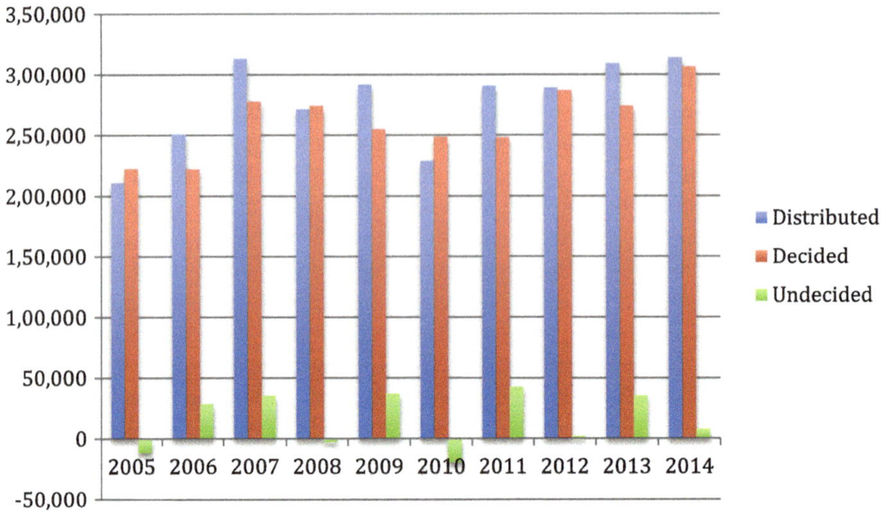

Fig. 1 Number of appeals in the Superior Court of Justice 2005–2014

This technique proved to be very useful in dealing with the excess of litigation on the same subject in superior courts. The numbers in Fig. 1 show a significant reduction of appeals in the superior court of Justice, after the use of this technique[29]:

The success of this tool ensured its continued use in the new Code of Civil Procedure. The new legislation provides a better and more detailed regime for the technique,[30] but its essence was maintained.

The main advantage of this way of examining second appeals is to optimize the Court's resources, avoiding the need to bring the same question over and over again, which frequently leads to different decisions and to uncertainty about the correct interpretation of the matter.

On the other hand, the technique is unable to prevent repetitive litigation and is also useless for solving the problem of excess litigation in courts of appeals and lower courts. In fact, the instrument only operates for superior courts, which means that litigation in all other cases will continue until the order to stay proceedings. Furthermore, there is no sanction imposed on parties who intend to litigate

[29]The data are taken from the Brazilian National Counsel of Justice (http://cnj.jus.br/noticias/cnj/79833-mecanismos-auxiliam-na-reducao-de-recursos-ao-stj. Accessed 7 June 2018). The data compare the number of second appeals received by the Superior Court of Justice from 2005 until 2014. The repetitive second appeals mechanism was first used in Brazil in 2008, and it is possible to see the impact of its use in managing the cases under this court's jurisdiction.

[30]The new Code of Civil Procedure—trying to overcome a number of flaws of the earlier regulation—provides several criteria for selecting the cases which may be brought on appeal and helps to distinguish cases; it also offers some guidelines by which to determine the participation of the interested persons in the judgment.

subject-matter already decided in other cases. Consequently, the tool has a very specific and narrow purpose (to help superior courts to deal with repetitive claims), not being of much use for other courts and for the judicial system as a whole.

In an attempt to take a step further, and considering the limits of the technique we just examined, the new Code of Civil Procedure created another instrument, called "Incidente de resolução de demandas repetitivas" (or IRDR, meaning an "ancillary proceeding for solving repetitive questions", in a literal translation).[31] According to this instrument, whenever there is a repetitive question of law, threatening equality and legal certainty, any party, the Public Prosecutor's Office, the Public Defender's Office or any judge may initiate this ancillary proceeding. It will be handled by the court of appeals (with jurisdiction over the case), and the decision will be binding for all cases subject to the Court's jurisdiction.

Once the motion is accepted, all cases that discuss the same question of law are to be stayed, until a decision of the court of appeals. Once a decision is rendered, it is binding for all courts hierarchically linked to that court of appeals. Thereafter, it is possible to take the same question further, to a superior court. In this case, since the decision will be delivered by a court with jurisdiction over the entire Brazilian territory, it will be binding for all courts in the country.

This instrument has the advantage of using courts of appeals to resolve repetitive questions, as a way of "decentralizing" the same task previously given to superior courts. Nonetheless, this virtue is also its major problem. Since repetitive questions do not normally pertain only to one state or region, for they tend to be widespread all over the country, a uniform solution of such question just for one state or region will obviously not resolve the issue. The dissent will still exist in other states or regions, which will result in multiple ancillary proceedings (initiated in different states or regions). Thus, this situation will lead back to the first instrument examined (the repetitive second appeal). Considering that there might be an important divergence between the interpretation of a question of law among the courts of appeals, the superior courts will normally be called upon to resolve this matter, giving a definite interpretation of questions of law.

In addition, this instrument may also lead to an important flaw. Ordinarily, the repeat player is the party more prepared to detect the presence of a repetitive question of law. As that party participates in all cases, it is correct to assume that it is in a better position to set up a question that might be subject to the ancillary proceeding. Taking this into account, it is also correct to conclude that the repeat player may choose where, when and with whom to litigate on this legal question. And, since ancillary proceedings only require the presence of the original parties to the case (since they are of no concern as to the party's ability to represent the group interested in the solution of that question), one may imagine the possibility that the repeat player chooses the weaker party, a weaker court or the best environment to litigate on the repetitive question, without allowing the group or the class to

[31]About this "incidente de resolução de demandas repetitivas", see also Marinoni (2017a), Mendes (2017), Mancuso (2016b), Cavalcanti (2016), Temer (2017).

participate in this discussion. Additionally, what is even worse, despite this lack of participation, the decision is still binding for all courts subordinate to that court.

Finally, it is important to highlight that all these instruments are only designed to deal with questions of law. All factual matters are automatically excluded, meaning that—except for the Brazilian class action—the national system still has not found a way to properly handle these issues.

Nonetheless, the experience so far with these instruments shows a substantial use of them. This points to some conclusions. First, that there is a great number of repetitive cases in Brazilian courts. Second, that many of these cases may be settled in a collective way.

However, the effort to use these instruments has some important consequences. Proceedings are stayed in a significant number of cases, waiting for the final decision of the common question of law. Although this stay of the proceedings is mandatory whenever these instruments are used, it nevertheless causes enormous frustration to the parties, who must wait—sometimes for years—for the resolution of their case.

6 Brazilian "Precedents" as a False Answer

The new Brazilian Code of Civil Procedure also puts its faith in the introduction of a theory of precedents, as a means to deal with repetitive cases and, as a consequence, to provide collective redress in similar situations.[32]

Regardless of the name used in Brazilian legislation, it is easy to perceive that what was created by national law is far from the Anglo-American type of precedents, well-known worldwide. Brazilian law naively believed that all the strength of precedents in the common law could be achieved just by giving a binding effect to some decisions, rendered by special courts or by special court divisions. In this sense, when the new Brazilian Code of Civil Procedure mentions the idea of "precedents", it is referring to special decisions (particularly the ones listed in Rule 927), which receive a binding effect by law. Among these special decisions, one may highlight the judgments in repetitive second appeals, analysed above.

The main concern, in Brazilian law, as one can see, is to impose the decisions rendered by superior courts or by courts of appeals in representative cases (involving questions of law), discouraging people to relitigate these issues. It is easy to conclude that the purpose of this instrument is far more modest than the issues involved in the Anglo-American theory of precedents. As one can construe on the basis of the reasons presented in the explanatory memorandum on the new Code of

[32]About the Brazilian "Theory of Precedents", see Marinoni (2016, 2017b), Mitidiero (2017a, b), Zaneti (2017), Mancuso (2016c), Cramer (2016).

Civil Procedure,[33] the explicit intention of the Brazilian "theory of precedents" is to deal with mass litigation, to prevent the same rule from being subject to different interpretations, which creates uncertainty and lack of isonomy.

The binding effect of these judgments, undoubtedly, can prevent *some* kinds of mass litigation (particularly about the same question of law). Nonetheless, this effect still has unpredictable consequences concerning the individual's right to a "day in court". As Brazilian law is not concerned with the suitability of the representation of the parties in the model case, it may happen that the case adjudicated does not present the entire scenario and all the possible arguments that could be relevant for resolving the issue. Despite this situation, there is no rule that allows further litigation on the issue. Consequently, one may be bound by that decision even if one's arguments were not examined or considered by the court.

It is still too soon to establish the success or failure of the "Brazilian precedent". What is certain, however, is the intention to use it as an instrument to deal with repetitive claims and, in so doing, as a collective way to resolve similar questions.

7 Final Remarks

It is easily recognizable that Brazilian law has plenty of techniques conceived to deal with collective litigation. Initially created to deal only with "non-personal" interests, these mechanisms were redesigned as a device to face repetitive litigation. Particularly in this field, Brazil is lavish in developing new tools, and it is correct to conclude that national legislation has a plethora of ways to manage mass litigation.

Nevertheless, all these techniques have shown to be unable to deal with repetitive litigation. Brazil still has a very important problem with this kind of litigation, which clogs the judicial system and prevents focusing on other issues.

Maybe this situation is a sign that the abundance of tools to deal with mass claims is not enough to ensure an adequate approach to this matter. It is imperative that Brazil change the culture of litigation and that it employ measures that are truly capable of inhibiting the excess of abusive litigation, and that stimulate the use of aggregating instruments. The mandatory use of collective redress in some cases and the use of techniques that prevent abusive litigation—such as punitive damages, so frequent in North American legal culture—may ensure better results in this field, rather than just making a massive number of proceedings available, putting them at people's disposal and waiting on the litigants' good will in making reasonable use of the judiciary.

Many other countries do not have such a variety of tools to deal with mass claims and collective matters. This may indeed be a symptom that these instruments

[33]These reasons, in Brazil, are normally provided for important statutes and can be used for the interpretation of these laws. The reasons underlying the Code of Civil Procedure are available at https://www2.senado.leg.br/bdsf/bitstream/handle/id/512422/001041135.pdf?sequence=1. Accessed 7 June 2018.

are not necessary, either because some other way has been found to deal with these claims or simply because they are not a real problem.

As a conclusion, it is possible to assert that the protection of collective and mass interests does not depend, solely, on the existence of the relevant procedural tools. It is far more important to have a culture of collective protection, and to understand the needs of interested litigants, so that it may be possible to develop (or to adapt) instruments that may protect the relevant interests. The lack of specific procedural techniques dedicated to collective and mass protection may indicate the presence of other ways to deal with these problems. On the other hand, the existence of such instruments when they are not properly used is probably the worst scenario, as it offers a promise of protection that is not made real in practice.

Brazil still has a very long way to go. Although it does not lack the formal instruments to deal with collective and mass litigation, it lacks the culture and the will to face these matters in a serious way. The superficial appearance of a very complete system evaporates in practice, which evidences the need for an extensive refresher course for judges and lawyers, allowing them to use these instruments in a proper manner.

The public civil action is a very powerful tool, but it depends on people to be really committed to and concerned about collective and mass claims. After all, the simple existence of adequate proceedings is not a guarantee of the correct protection of an interest, if not brought by people capable of using such proceedings.

References

Almeida JB (2011) Aspectos controvertidos da ação civil pública, 3rd edn. Revista dos Tribunais, São Paulo

Andrade A, Masson C, Andrade L (2017) Interesses difusos e coletivos. GEN, Rio de Janeiro

Arenhart SC (2014) A tutela coletiva de interesses individuais, 2nd edn. Revista dos Tribunais/ Thomson Reuters, São Paulo

Arenhart SC, Moreira EB, Bagatin AC et al (2017) Comentários à lei da ação civil pública. Revista dos Tribunais, São Paulo

Carvalho Filho JS (2007) Ação civil pública, 6th edn. Lumen Juris, Rio de Janeiro

Castilho RS (2004) Direitos e interesses difusos, coletivos e individuais homogêneos. LZN, São Paulo

Cavalcanti MA (2016) Incidente de resolução de demandas repetitivas. Revista dos Tribunais, São Paulo

Cramer R (2016) Precedentes judiciais. Forense, Rio de Janeiro

Dinamarco PS (2001) Ação civil pública. Saraiva, São Paulo

Gidi A (2007) A class action como instrumento de tutela coletiva dos direitos. Revista dos Tribunais, São Paulo

Gidi A (2008) Rumo ao código de processo civil coletivo. GEN, Rio de Janeiro

Grinover AP et al (2017) Código brasileiro de defesa do consumidor, 11th edn. Forense, Rio de Janeiro

Lenza P (2003) Teoria geral da ação civil pública. Revista dos Tribunais, São Paulo

Leonel RB (2016) Manual do processo coletivo. Malheiros, São Paulo

Mancuso RC (2015) Ação popular. Revista dos Tribunais, São Paulo

Mancuso RC (2016a) Ação civil pública, 14th edn. Revista dos Tribunais, São Paulo
Mancuso RC (2016b) Incidente de resolução de demandas repetitivas. Revista dos Tribunais, São Paulo
Mancuso RC (2016c) Sistema brasileiro de precedentes, 2nd edn. Revista dos Tribunais, São Paulo
Marinoni LG (2016) Ética dos precedentes, 2nd edn. Revista dos Tribunais, São Paulo
Marinoni LG (2017a) Incidente de resolução de demandas repetitivas. Revista dos Tribunais, São Paulo
Marinoni LG (2017b) Precedentes obrigatórios, 5th edn. Revista dos Tribunais, São Paulo
Marinoni LG, Arenhart SC, Mitidiero D (2017) Curso de processo civil, vol 3, 3rd edn. Revista dos Tribunais, São Paulo
Marques CL, Benjamin AH, Miragem B (2016) Comentários ao código de defesa do consumidor, 5th edn. Revista dos Tribunais, São Paulo
Mazzilli HN (2000) A defesa dos interesses difusos em juízo, 11th edn. Saraiva, São Paulo
Mendes AGC (2014) Ações coletivas, 4th edn. Revista dos Tribunais, São Paulo
Mendes AGC (2017) Incidente de resolução de demandas repetitivas. GEN, Rio de Janeiro
Milaré E (ed) (2015) Ação civil pública – após 30 anos. Revista dos Tribunais, São Paulo
Mitidiero D (2017a) Cortes superiores e cortes supremas, 3rd edn. Revista dos Tribunais, São Paulo
Mitidiero D (2017b) Precedentes, 2nd edn. Revista dos Tribunais, São Paulo
Nunes LAR (2015) Comentários ao código de defesa do consumidor, 8th edn. Saraiva, São Paulo
Osna G (2014) Direitos individuais homogêneos. Revista dos Tribunais, São Paulo
Ragazzi JL, Honesko VHN, Honesko RS (2017) Código de defesa do consumidor comentado, 2nd edn. Verbatim, São Paulo
Rocha JM (1968) Da ação popular. Recife, Recife
Rodrigues MA (2009) O novo processo civil coletivo. Lumen Iuris, Rio de Janeiro
Shimura S (2006) Tutela coletiva e sua efetividade. Método, São Paulo
Silva JA (2007) Ação popular constitucional, 2nd edn. Malheiros, São Paulo
Souza MC (2017) Ação civil pública e inquérito civil público, 6th edn. Saraiva, São Paulo
Temer S (2017) Incidente de resolução de demandas repetitivas, 2nd edn. Juspodivm, Salvador
Venturi E (2000) Execução da tutela coletiva. Malheiros, São Paulo
Venturi E (2007) Processo civil coletivo. Malheiros, São Paulo
Vigliar JMM (2001) Ação civil pública, 5th edn. Atlas, São Paulo
Vitorelli E (2016) O devido processo legal coletivo. Revista dos Tribunais, São Paulo
Zaneti H Jr (2006) Processo coletivo. Juspodivm, Salvador
Zaneti H Jr (2017) O valor vinculante dos precedentes, 3rd edn. Juspodivm, Salvador
Zavascki T (1995) Defesa de direitos coletivos e defesa coletiva de direitos. Rev Inf Legislat 127:83–96
Zavascki T (2006) Processo coletivo. Revista dos Tribunais, São Paulo

Sergio Cruz Arenhart Associate Professor of Civil Procedure at the Federal University of Paraná, Brazil. Ph.D. and LLM from the Federal University of Paraná. Post-doctoral Fellow of the Università degli Studi di Firenze, Italy. Former Federal Judge in Brazil. Federal Public Prosecutor at the Court of Appeals for the 4th Circuit, Brazil.

'Shadow of the Law' or 'Shadow of the Settlement': Experiences with the Dutch Act on Collective Settlement of Mass Damage (WCAM)

Annie de Roo and Rob Jagtenberg

Abstract Public and private justice may not be such mutually exclusive concepts as commonly viewed. Public court judgments may co-determine private settlements, but also conversely, private settlements may co-determine court judgments. The latter phenomenon can be found particularly in mass disputes leading to collective settlements that receive broad media coverage. This contribution analyses the practice in the Netherlands, where such collective settlements can even be endorsed by the courts under the Act on Collective Settlement of Mass Damage, or the WCAM Act. Individual parties that decline such a settlement and prefer to pursue their case in court may nevertheless be confronted with such a private settlement to which they themselves are not a party. The contribution rounds off with a non-exhaustive stocktaking of salient pros and cons of negotiated settlement and law enforcement, respectively.

1 Introduction: Public Justice Versus Private Justice?

The very theme itself of the public and private justice series prompts a closer look at the distinction between 'public' and 'private' justice. This is all the more so in the area of collective redress as analysed in this contribution, where in this area the line between 'public' and 'private' becomes particularly vague.

Along the curve of human dispute strategies, ranging all the way from 'flight' to 'fight', there is a linear relationship between the methods of negotiation, mediation, arbitration and litigation. These methods imply a steadily decreasing amount of *control* on the part of the disputants, and a shift from the private to the public sphere (Jagtenberg 2014, 282).

A. de Roo · R. Jagtenberg (✉)
Erasmus School of Law, Rotterdam, The Netherlands
e-mail: jagtenberg@law.eur.nl

A. de Roo
e-mail: deroo@law.eur.nl

A. Uzelac and C. H. van Rhee (eds.), *Transformation of Civil Justice*,
Ius Gentium: Comparative Perspectives on Law and Justice 70,
https://doi.org/10.1007/978-3-319-97358-6_14

Negotiation, or bargaining, usually signifies that we must give up something in order to get something else in return from our opponent. When we do not succeed in that, we can just walk away, and thus there is full autonomy. Typically, bargaining takes place in private conference rooms. Modern mediation refers to a structured process of negotiation under the guidance of a professional neutral third party. According to European legislation, nearly everything discussed during mediation is to be kept confidential, in order to incentivize frankness and creativity. Only the solution itself, once contained in a settlement contract, escapes secrecy in order to allow its enforcement.

Both bargaining and mediation are thus methods based on a mutually agreed solution. This is what is meant, in our view, by private justice: the contents of the solution are solely determined by the immediate parties themselves.

Arbitration and litigation, by contrast, are methods based upon an imposed decision, that is, imposed by a privately appointed neutral third party or by the publicly funded judiciary where party control is reduced to almost zero. The judiciary declares or enforces the law: the public norms to rule the dispute.

Thus, at first sight bargaining and in-court adjudication—to take the extremes—seem to be mutually exclusive concepts. Upon closer inspection, however, a court judgment (from the past or anticipated) may well leave its mark on the bargaining process. As Robert Mnookin observed in his seminal article 'Bargaining in the Shadow of the Law', court judgments rendered in prior, relevant lawsuits may serve as an objective parameter for negotiations that are about to get started (Mnookin and Kornhauser 1978/1979, 950–997), no matter whether these negotiations unfold directly between the parties or as mediations.

In another landmark contribution, 'Against settlement' by Owen Fiss, the author posited, rather, that where the law has any relevance to a dispute, the parties should precisely *not* bargain a private settlement but, instead, resort to the courts. Fiss emphasizes that law enforcement transcends the interests of the immediate parties in having their dispute resolved:

> The social function of the lawsuit is to explicate the values embodied in authoritative legal texts; in case of settlements, society gets less than what appears, and for a price it does not know it is paying. (Fiss 1983/1984, 1073–1090)

One may wonder to what extent this view is rooted in the real world of disputes. In many court cases, already the *facts* to which the law is to be applied are often contested; and the *law* itself may be unclear, if only because there is almost always a legal norm that could counterbalance a first norm invoked by one's opponent.[1]

For decades now, the proponents of mediation like to illustrate the advantages of private solutions in precisely such cases with an unpredictable legal outcome through the classic example of the two cooks who are about to litigate over the ownership of a shipload of oranges that has just arrived from, say, Morocco.

[1]The phenomenon of *contributory negligence* constitutes a good example.

One cook's name appears on the bill of lading, the other's name on the insurance certificate. With the additional necessity of collecting evidence from abroad, pursuing the case in court may take years. Unlike a judge who will be focused on the past, a mediator will help to identify both cooks' present and future interests. It appears that the first cook needs the *pulp* of the oranges for making juice, while the second cook needs the *peel* for making marmalade.

On that basis, an optimal solution serving both parties' interests can be worked out, and both parties may trade off the costs and uncertainty of a legal outcome against a commercially viable solution, with both cooks processing the oranges together from then on.

Still, Owen Fiss might argue: What price does *society* pay here?

Suppose the dispute over the documents arose because a shady agent in Morocco had found he could sell the same oranges *twice* every time by *forging* the documents (bill of lading and/or insurance certificate)?

A public lawsuit would likely expose the villain, and would thus be instrumental in preventing other cooks in society from falling victim to similar duplicity in the future (though these others could be said to enjoy a free ride then on this first and no doubt expensive public lawsuit).

Taking this macro perspective, law enforcement would yield larger returns for society as a whole.

Viewing the legal process primarily as a method of dispute resolution for the *immediate* parties seems to have become dominant in Europe, or perhaps one should say, dominant *again*. On the European continent there is a long existing practice of the 'multi-hat court judge', whereby the judge is statutorily authorized to make an attempt at reconciling the litigants that have appeared before him/her. This tradition has now been complemented (in both Continental and common law jurisdictions) with the relatively new practice of the 'multi-door courthouse' (a concept coined by Frank Sander), whereby the judge no longer attempts to reconcile the parties himself/herself, but refers them to an external, professionally trained mediator (Jagtenberg and de Roo 2011, 7–23).

These practices may make one wonder: How 'public'—in the sense of focused on public goals such as law enforcement—are courts today?

Government policy documents across Europe emphasize that it may be justified to refer those intending to bring their cases to court to external mediation *mandatorily* (de Palo and Canessa 2014, 36–41; Silvestri and Jagtenberg 2013, 7–19).

This objective is often justified by pointing out that many lawsuits do not 'belong' in a courtroom and that the parties themselves would be better off trying mediation. What transpires, however, through these arguments which are not necessarily evidence-based is the perceived need for budgetary restraints.

Meanwhile, the mere power of judges to bring up mediation as an alternative increasingly incentivizes lawyers to discuss direct negotiation or mediation with their clients *at an early stage*, in order to be better prepared in the courtroom. We have termed this phenomenon 'the shadow of the referral', and it amounts to a hidden (or pre-emptive) outsourcing of potential lawsuits to private conference rooms (Jagtenberg and de Roo 2011, 17).

In sum, in the world today court adjudication and bargaining appear to be intertwined in multiple ways.

2 Round Sourcing Between Public and Private Justice: Collective Redress

A striking example of how bargaining and adjudication may become intertwined is constituted by 'round sourcing' of legal dispute resolution. Here is what 'round sourcing' looks like. The court system refers lawsuits brought by large numbers of disputants affected by a single, particular event to a private bargaining scheme accommodating these multiple claimants. There, a mass private settlement may be reached between an agent representing those multiple claimants and the torfeasor(s)—usually a company. Yet, individual claimants may decide not to adhere to that settlement but pursue their claim against the tortfeasor(s) individually in court. If the mass private settlement, despite having been renounced by these claimants, nevertheless comes to guide the courts in adjudicating such claims, this constitutes 'round sourcing'. Having outsourced its public responsibilities to a private agency, the work performed privately eventually flows back to the courts, and is used there as if it were the court's own intellectual achievement.

This phenomenon can be observed notably in the area of collective redress.

Collective redress allows many claims relating to the same case to be bundled into a single court action. In these days of standardized mass production such redress is especially, though not exclusively, relevant for consumer claims following the sale and purchase of defective products or services. Out-of-court, private settlement is particularly promoted in this area.

It should come as no surprise that 'round sourcing' is encountered here, since settlements involving large numbers of disputants can hardly be kept confidential: for 'round sourcing' to operate, it is unavoidable that the terms of settlement become publicly known.

A European Commission Recommendation was issued in 2013 laying down common principles for injunctive and compensatory collective redress mechanisms.[2] The Commission found it necessary to encourage Member States to introduce and align such mechanisms, for two reasons:

1. to improve access to justice. In most consumer disputes the amount in controversy is likely too small to justify lawyer fees paid by an individual—a phenomenon that would result in under-enforcement of the law; and

---

[2]European Commission Recommendation No. 2013/396 of 11 June 2013 on common principles for injunctive and compensatory collective redress mechanisms in the Member States concerning violations of rights granted under EU Law. *OJ* 2013, L 201/60.

2. to avoid abusive 'American-style' class actions. The Commission therefore recommends that entities representing groups of claimants should operate on a non-profit basis. Moreover, contingency fees and punitive damages should be prohibited.

The Recommendation highlights collective *court* action, but emphasizes that *out-of-court* settlement (ADR) can be a particularly efficient way of obtaining redress in mass harm situations, and should thus always be available alongside judicial collective redress.

3 WCAM[3]: The Dutch Experience

The Netherlands has gained considerable experience in the area of collective redress over the course of about a decade. We will elaborate on the Dutch experience, which is increasingly held up as an example in European discussions, to illustrate the 'round sourcing' phenomenon.

A collective court action to obtain declaratory relief has been available in the Netherlands since 1994. One would expect then that a collective action for compensatory relief would also have been available since that same year. However, this is not the case. Compensation for damage sustained is only available through (subsequent) individual court action. This odd situation has been explained as a result of effective lobbying by Dutch industry. A bill introducing the possibility of collective recovery of damages is currently on the agenda of parliament, but a 2014 internet consultation of industry, consumers and the judiciary suggests there is still a long way to go here (Jagtenberg and Voet 2015, 6–32).

Although it is not possible (yet) to bring damage claims collectively, it *is* possible to negotiate settlements collectively over damage sustained.

Since 2005, Dutch law has been enriched by the Act on Collective (Out-of-court) Settlement of Mass Damage (WCAM).[4] This statute was inspired by the desire to facilitate negotiations towards a settlement in the early years of the new century in the high profile 'DES-daughters' drama, which had been lingering for nearly two decades by then.[5]

The system of WCAM can be summarized as follows. The Act is concerned with settlement agreements regarding compensation for damage caused by the same event; agreements, that is, that are concluded between entities representing claimants and (one or more) defendants.

[3]*Wet Collectieve Afwikkeling Massaschade*, wet van 23 juni 2005, Stb. 2005, p. 340.

[4]Technically, WCAM merely adds some new provisions to the existing Dutch Civil Code (BW) and the Dutch Code of Civil Procedure (Rv).

[5]Daughters of mothers who had taken diëthylstilbestrol (DES) during pregnancy had developed forms of cancer and as a consequence, they had filed massive lawsuits against the pharmaceutical industry.

These parties (i.e. the representative entities of claimants/victims and the defendants) may jointly request the Amsterdam Court of Appeal to declare their settlement agreement binding. Binding on whom? Basically, on everyone involved, that is—on the 'victim' side—all those persons to whom damage has been caused. Thereby, the negotiators of the settlement will have placed these persons into classes of sustained damage, a process referred to as 'damage scheduling'.[6]

WCAM then lists several criteria for court approval. The most important is that the judge must be satisfied that the settlement provides for levels of compensation that are reasonable, considering the likely *cause and extent* of the loss suffered, and the *simplicity and speed* at which compensation can be obtained.[7]

Judicial approval of the collective settlement then effectively bars the individual claimants represented by the entity that signed the settlement from pursuing their case further in court.[8]

How does that square with the fundamental right of access to court? The following solution has been found: individual claimants who are *dis*-satisfied after all with the terms of the settlement may yet opt out of the settlement within three months following court endorsement. Such claimants will have to submit a written statement to that end.

4 The *Dexia* Case

The workings of WCAM can best be illustrated through one of the largest disputes settled this way, i.e. the *Dexia* case. Dexia bank had concluded nearly 400,000 'securities lease' contracts with individual consumers during the economic boom of the 1990s.

Through such contracts, a consumer would borrow money from Dexia that Dexia would then immediately invest in shares traded at the Amsterdam stock exchange.

The expectation was that after some years, with share indexes continuously rising, a consumer would easily manage to pay off his/her loan using the expected stock exchange profits, while still having some money gained left.

However, between 2000 and 2003, the Amsterdam share index fell from 700 to 270 points, and all that was left was a huge pile of debts.

Initially, the bank abruptly started debt collection procedures against those unable to redeem their loans. Many felt though that Dexia itself was to blame for not having alerted its customers to the risk associated with such a securities lease product.

---

[6]Article 7:907 lid 2 BW.

[7]Article 7:907 lid 3 BW.

[8]Article 7:908 lid 1 BW; technically, the settlement constitutes a special category of contract (*vaststellingsovereenkomst*) that cannot be voided e.g. based on alleged defects in respect of consent. As such, this form of settlement is not enforceable per se.

Once the issue started to receive nationwide media coverage, individual consumers in great numbers began to report to the national consumer association (*Consumentenbond*) and/or to entities set up as special purpose vehicles for bringing a collective declaratory claim against Dexia, such as the Lease Loss Foundation (*Stichting Leaseverlies*).

Dexia felt somewhat cornered by this media attention and decided to offer its own settlement proposal that essentially allowed customers more time to pay off their loans.

A number of customers accepted Dexia's proposal, but the vast majority of aggrieved consumers registered with the entities to pursue their collective declaratory claims before the district court of Amsterdam (where Dexia's Dutch branch had its seat).

These claims generated mixed outcomes: notably, the district court asked for further and better particulars, which made it necessary for the entities to sort out the allegedly misguiding brochures that had been used to sell the securities lease product.

While these first claims were pending in court, the government decided to intervene, fearing harm to the reputation of the Netherlands as a financial hub. Former Finance Minister and European Central Bank (ECB) President Wim Duisenberg was put forward as a mediator.

His mediation effort took two months and resulted in an agreement between Dexia and the four largest entities representing the consumers.[9]

Slightly simplified, the gist of the agreement was that consumers would have to pay 40% of their outstanding debts, whereas Dexia would pay the remaining 60%.

This mediated settlement was submitted to the Amsterdam Court of Appeal under the aegis of WCAM. The Court of Appeal considered the 40/60 allocation reasonable, and it endorsed the Duisenberg settlement early in 2007.[10]

Over 165,000 claimants decided to adhere to this collective settlement, which brought the total number of cases settled to 230,000: 65,000 customers had accepted Dexia's one-sided offer earlier on. However, in the end about 30,000–40,000 claimants decided to continue the legal fight.[11] A considerable percentage of

[9]For completeness' sake, mention should be made of a further dispute, i.e. between Dexia bank and the AEGON insurance company, that had been lingering for a while but had been resolved just about the time when Mr. Duisenberg's mediation took off. Dexia itself had purchased the lease portfolio from AEGON and had intimated they would sue AEGON in turn. In the end, AEGON decided to contribute a considerable sum of money to the settlement fund that Dexia had started to build up.

[10]Hof Amsterdam 25 January 2007, ECLI:NL:GHAMS:2007:AZ7033; later on, some refinements were made as to the 40/60 ratio by the Amsterdam appellate court in its judgment of 1 December 2009, ECLI:NL:GHAMS:2009:BK4978.

[11]A quick calculation tells us that hence approximately 130,000–140,000 customers neither joined a collective settlement nor pursued their case in court (in all, nearly 400,000 securities lease contracts had been concluded). This remaining group may have undertaken no action at all—this is a likely outcome in view of the options that were identified in a large-scale Dutch survey of conflict strategies in 2003 (the 'Dispute Resolution Delta'): about 45% of the respondents in that

these 'stayers' had lodged formal objections with the Amsterdam Court of Appeal at the occasion of the settlement approval procedure.

They had argued, first, that too much of the financial burden was placed on the shoulders of the consumer. The Court of Appeal, however, considered that the 40/60 Duisenberg settlement had sufficiently differentiated between categories of damage, using the damage schedules. Moreover, according to the court:

> [I]t is inherent in a negotiated settlement that the amount of compensation reflects the end of uncertainty over the outcome of a prolonged court procedure.[12]

It is noteworthy that the court emphasizes the avoidance of uncertainty of litigation outcomes as the main argument why one should accept the settlement. Positive inducements are absent.

Finally, the court considered that while Dexia was to blame for not duly warning its customers, the consumers were not without blame themselves in this case, since a reasonable person should have properly read the terms of such a contract at issue before signing it.

A second objection submitted by the 'stayers' takes us to the 'round sourcing' phenomenon. The 'stayers' had argued that despite the opt-out facility, the WCAM regime constituted a violation of Articles 6 and 1 of the First Protocol of the European Convention on Human Rights (ECHR). This was because a 'reflex effect' emanating from the collective Duisenberg settlement had to be feared in any future court claim that an individual 'opt-outer' might bring for the recovery of damages ensuing from his/her particular securities lease contract with Dexia.

The Court of Appeal rejected the argument that Article 1 of the First Protocol had been violated. The court considered that even if the consumer, by adhering to the collective settlement, would have to satisfy himself/herself with an amount of compensation that might be smaller than what one *might* secure by pursuing and winning a court case, then still such a 'deprivation of a possession' (if a deprivation at all) is justified in the *public interest*, now that through such a collective settlement the major *social costs* involved in large numbers of civil litigations were avoided.[13]

In our view, this reasoning has several flaws. Why would large numbers of civil litigations harm the public interest? Other areas see large numbers of litigations too. Is the real problem that the courts are understaffed, and/or that individual consumers will face a financial access problem? However, if those are the real problems, might one, perhaps, better solve these first instead of simply manoeuvring claims away from the courts?

---

survey said they would just drop their case. Alternatively, at least some customers in this remaining group may have negotiated an individual settlement with Dexia. Such settlements would likely be governed by a confidentiality clause; hence, nothing can be said about the size, or even the very existence, of this category.

[12]Hof Amsterdam, n. 17 above, para. 6.6.

[13]Hof Amsterdam, n. 17 above, para. 5.11.

There are many litigations where the Court of Appeal also dismissed the objection based on Article 6, if only because of the existence of an opt-out option. Moreover, the court deliberated over the anticipated 'reflex effect':

> [S]pecific individual circumstances were not taken into account in the collective settlement endorsement, in the way these *would have to be* dealt with in individual court claims for recovery of damages. A court dealing with such individual compensatory claims in the future will be free to accord just that amount of authority to the collective settlement that it thinks is appropriate.[14]

This reasoning remains somewhat enigmatic. One would have to refer back to the indicators used in the damage scheduling process in order to ascertain how broadly formulated these were, and hence which 'specific individual circumstances' were left out there. One could possibly trigger a court's creativity by submitting such circumstances. Would the 'social status' and 'level of knowledge' of a consumer, once decisive factors in a landmark judgment on Dutch contract law, 'do the job'?[15]

5 Collective Settlement and Reflex Effect

In view of these considerations of the Court of Appeal, it is fascinating to see what actually happened in subsequent individual litigation.

First, a remark on how the remaining litigation was managed by the Amsterdam district court. That court was designated ten judges assisted by 20 clerks to form a special 'Dexia panel'.

Moreover, where individual cases were co-ordinated through entities that had objected to the Duisenberg settlement, some telling cases were sorted out by these entities themselves to be dealt with first, as test (or pilot) cases that could guide cases with similar individual characteristics.

One example of such a test case is singled out here, *De Treek v Dexia*, which was eventually decided by the Dutch Supreme Court (Hoge Raad) in 2009.[16]

Before the lower courts, De Treek had submitted that his case indeed involved a 'specific individual circumstance' that had not been taken into account in the collective settlement. He was a person with low income and very inexperienced in share trading. Consequently, De Treek had pleaded defect of consent, namely error (misrepresentation by Dexia). If this plea were honoured, the defect would have made the securities lease agreement concluded with De Treek void ab initio, meaning that De Treek would have to be reimbursed 100% by Dexia.

But the Supreme Court endorsed the lower court's decision that Dexia had fulfilled its duty to inform De Treek. A new variety of this duty was introduced though: the special relationship between a bank and an inexperienced customer

---

[14]Hof Amsterdam, n. 17 above, para. 5.14; emphasis added by the authors.

[15]HR 13 March 1981 (*Haviltex*), NJ 1981, 635.

[16]HR 5 June 2009, ECL:NL:HR:2009:BH2815.

such as De Treek implied a duty (for Dexia) to warn. However, Dexia's neglect of this duty had to be weighed against any contributory negligence on the part of De Treek (viz. De Treek's neglect of his duty to investigate). The Supreme Court continued that, therefore, and also being aware of the test case character, as a general guiding principle, a 40/60 allocation of remaining debts would be quite acceptable.[17]

This reasoning leaves the impression that the Supreme Court tried hard *not* to make the courts a more attractive avenue for consumers who had declined the collective settlement.

Does one observe here the shadow of the collective Duisenberg settlement then, hovering above this individual judgment?

It is difficult to give a straightforward answer. The Supreme Court operates rather cautiously. In the *De Treek* case, Dexia itself had also lodged an appeal in cassation, arguing that the court was legally bound by the collective settlement in individual cases. Since such a large percentage of Dexia customers had agreed to the settlement, the 40/60 ratio could be said to embody 'current juridical views' in the Netherlands, according to *Dexia*. Such current views in turn should be determinant of what reasonableness and fairness require, also in the *De Treek* case.[18]

Dexia's argument echoes the general position taken by industry, that collective settlements should be final and conclusive; no opting-out facility should be allowed, as this would leave too many loose ends for industry and undo a major advantage of investing in a settlement in the first place.

The Supreme Court however, explicitly rejected the argument submitted by Dexia.[19] It would be incompatible with the opt-out facility if the court were bound by the terms of the collective settlement in individual lawsuits. It would even be incompatible if the court had to explain why in such individual lawsuits it would deviate from the terms of the collective settlement.

A seemingly clear answer. Yet, many scholars feel that in this and other judgments the courts have started with the 40/60 ratio in mind and then reasoned backwards to a judgment, to avoid the impression that much more could be gained by pursuing an individual claim instead of joining a collective settlement (Van Boom and Lindenbergh 2010, 188).

Perhaps even more telling than the *De Treek* case is a case dealt with by the Amsterdam Court of Appeal on 8 November 2007. This case was about an appeal lodged by Dexia against a judgment by the Alkmaar district court in favour of an individual customer X. The Court of Appeal reasoned that this dispute raised a number of questions that the court had already addressed six months earlier, in its judgment endorsing the collective Duisenberg settlement.

---

[17]HR 2009, n. 23 above, at para. 4.4.5.

[18]The general principle of reasonableness and fairness, which plays an important role in Dutch private law, is not defined exhaustively in the Civil Code, although Article 3:12 BW mentions that current juridical views may be one of the factors to be taken into account in determining what is 'reasonable and fair'.

[19]HR 2009, n. 23 above, at para. 4.9.2.

> The Court assumes that counsel are privy to this settlement; deliberations of this Court at that time, that lend themselves for general application, will be guiding this Court in deciding future [individual] disputes.[20]

One cannot help but wonder what exactly makes a deliberation lend itself for general application. Arguably, the answer can only be found on a case-by-case basis.

An example of a 'specific individual circumstance' of the kind the Amsterdam Court of Appeal may have envisaged in its 2007 consecration of the Duisenberg settlement is provided by a 2016 Supreme Court judgment. In this case, a customer had not contracted directly with Dexia, but through the intermediary of a stockbroker. The stockbroker, *Spaar Select*, had acted beyond the scope of its business licence, however, by acting as an investment consultant to the plaintiff, persuading him to enter into a Dexia securities lease contract. Here, the Supreme Court held that Dexia had to compensate the plaintiff for the full 100%, since Dexia—as the professional party—should have checked whether the intermediary was licenced and thus authorized to bring in clients for the securities lease project.[21]

How would those customers feel who had accepted the 40/60 collective settlement and also had entered their securities lease agreement in the same way (through an unlicensed intermediary)?

6 Private Justice Reassessed: Hybrid Governance and Rule of Law

Does a 'shadow of the (collective) settlement' indeed exist?

The answer, based on the foregoing snapshot of Dutch case law, should be formally no, but informally, most likely.

A preliminary point to consider is whether a collective WCAM settlement can be regarded as 'private justice' at all. One could argue that the larger the number of private parties involved in a settlement, the less 'private' the settlement is bound to be, despite the fact that the content of the settlement still rests on an agreement between private parties and is not imposed by a court of law. The settlement, however, is bound to become more 'public' as a consequence of 'media-tization': if many people sustain damage due to a particular event, the media are more likely to show an interest, as clearly was the case in the Dexia affair (Huls and Van Doorn 2007, 58). Media attention entails a dynamic of its own; public outrage and the fear of one's reputation being damaged can push a 'hardliner' into making concessions. Once an affair has caught the attention of the media, it will be impossible to keep the terms of the settlement confidential, although the process of negotiating towards a settlement may still take place behind closed doors.

---

[20]Hof Amsterdam 8 November 2007, ECLI:NL:GHAMS:2007:BB8135, at para. 4.4 and 4.6.

[21]HR 2 September 2016, ECLI:NL:HR:2016:2012, at para. 5.2 until incl. 5.7.

Endorsement of the settlement by a court of law takes the settlement yet a step farther into the public domain. Such endorsement is by itself a multi-faceted phenomenon. In the WCAM system, the endorsement is perceived as a facility that both sides in the dispute (industry and multiple consumers) could find attractive: the industry may feel such endorsement will enhance the prospect of finality; the consumers may feel endorsement will reduce the risk of the industry not honouring its part of the deal. In addition, both sides may feel reassured that a court will have scrutinized the terms of the settlement as to fairness, and as to consistency with the law.

The latter point takes us back to an observation made at the outset of this contribution, following Fiss's quote: in many cases 'the law' may not be a single, unequivocal norm in need of enforcement. The Dexia example provides a good illustration that the balancing of countervailing norms in a complex dispute remains a matter of careful human observation, intuition and weighing skills. And this is not so different from what are considered typical mediator assets (with the fundamental difference that a court must speak out, whereas the mediator should let the parties speak out).

In the *Dexia* case, moreover, mediator Duisenberg could build on a case analysis, including a legal analysis, prepared by the Dutch National Ombudsman Marten Oosting. Mr. Oosting wrote this analysis at the instigation of the government (Jagtenberg and Voet 2015).

Earlier in this contribution, reference was made to Mnookin's thesis that a court judgment may well leave its mark on the bargaining process. What the individual cases decided in the wake of the Dexia collective settlement demonstrate is that, conversely, the (outcome of) a bargaining process may well leave its mark on court judgments. Moreover, more than that: it seems the courts could not function adequately anymore *without* private settlement. No doubt, processing the full 270,000 claims against Dexia would have burdened the Amsterdam district court (and possibly the higher courts as well).[22] In legal literature, the growing 'rights consciousness' or emancipation of consumers (and individual citizens generally) has long been associated with the litigation explosion, and it was thus assessed negatively (1977 1977, 71).

One could argue that the WCAM settlement facility 'solves' the litigation explosion, but this might be a solution that does not address the real underlying problem: the staffing of courts has not kept pace with the juridification of society. If rights are granted, then the addressees should be able to invoke and enforce those rights; that is a prerequisite of the rule of law. In addition, Owen Fiss might say: the members of a society should be willing to finance as taxpayers a system for enforcing the rules they have ultimately chosen themselves for the benefit of all.

Moreover, one may wonder whether the judicial role is not compromised if the judge (as an interested party in an understaffed court) is to persuade unwilling parties to question the soundness of a settlement no longer.

[22]Deducting the 130,000 cases that were presumably dropped from the overall number of 400,000 securities lease contracts gives 270,000 claims that remain.

7 Round Sourcing: Blessing or Betrayal?

Having established that 'round sourcing' *does* exist, we round off this analysis with the important question: Should such 'round sourcing' be regarded as a blessing or a betrayal?

This question brings into focus an issue that we have raised before: (the lack of) an evidence-based framework for assessing different modes of conflict resolution. One parameter could be costs and returns, with some important qualifications: Who decides which costs are to be acknowledged as costs? Costs (or returns) for whom? and, Costs (or returns) in the short run or in the long run?

To put it differently, Who, in the end, benefits most? In nominal, monetary amounts, the answer is the industry. This could be easily demonstrated through an example with neat figures: 1000 consumers suffer a €100 loss each from a deal with industry Z. Z risks losing €100,000 if each consumer brought a lawsuit and won. But on top of that, Z would have to engage lawyers in 1000 different lawsuits (for, say, €2000 per claim), which would bring the cost of defending against these multiple lawsuits to €2,100,000 (cost of damage to reputation and reduced turnover as a consequence thereof not included). If a 50/50 settlement were achieved, industry would pay €50,000 to its customers (€50 × 1000) and, say, €30,000 in legal fees to three lawyers for preparing and executing this deal. In all, €80,000 is spent to avert the risk of having to pay €2,100,000. A statistical probability analysis would be essential in order to accurately weigh the risk of losing the court case. The potential costs of a damaged reputation and decreased turnover would be (even) more complicated to calculate.

Each consumer, individually, will lose €50 in a 50/50 settlement, but would thereby avoid the cost of losing another €50 in the event of not winning the case in court. On top of that, the consumer would avoid spending €2000 on lawyer fees in his/her case (assuming the consumer has not taken out a legal expenses insurance policy, but assuming also that a consumer association will negotiate the settlement free of charge). In sum, industry can save itself the largest *nominal* amount. *Relatively* speaking, however, there is much more to gain (though in small nominal amounts) for individual consumers.[23]

Here, the problem of under-enforcement of consumer law (where mostly small amounts are in controversy) presents itself. This issue could be translated into the conflict management grid: where the most likely conflict strategy for consumers, in view of the huge cost of hiring a lawyer, would be 'avoiding' or 'yielding', the availability of a tool such as WCAM for collectivizing negotiations with industry brings the more positive strategy of 'solving' within reach. How is this to be valued, in monetary terms?

---

[23]The maximum loss for Z amounts to approximately 26 times the amount actually paid (€2.1 million versus €80,000); for the individual consumer, the maximum loss amounts to 40 times the amount actually received (€2000 vs. €50).

Lawyer fees were a major cost item in the foregoing example, and this corresponds to the real world situation. In the *Dexia* case, and WCAM practice generally, one could say the lawyers are the real losers—for a change. Only a few of them will be needed to assist in the negotiation process. However, in reverse, 'cutting out the lawyers' constitutes a major gain for the disputing parties.

It is a small step from lawyers to judges. Worthy of mention is that the Amsterdam Court of Appeal, when endorsing the *Dexia* settlement, referred explicitly to the social costs that could be avoided thanks to a collective settlement. To a considerable extent, these costs may be the opportunity costs involved were judicial staff capacity allocated to handle multiple individual lawsuits.

A complication might be that, occasionally, an individual case could entail such unique characteristics that it would deserve to be heard extensively in court. Here, the reflex effect or shadow of the settlement has a dark side, pre-empting a pristine analysis of such an individual case if pursued.

In any proper assessment, it is important to realize that consumers, industry, lawyers and judges are not the only parties involved. It has been suggested, for instance, that government regulators and supervisory bodies (notably in the *Dexia* case, the Supervisory Authority for the Financial Markets, AFM) should have taken part of the blame (and financial burden), since they were slow to react to such a defective product as 'securities lease' being brought into circulation (Huls and Van Doorn 2007, 30). But if such regulators, being publicly funded bodies, had had to contribute to the reimbursement of Dexia customers, the innocent taxpayer would have been burdened, and once again for the dubious activities of a bank.

It is clear that devising an accurate framework for assessing negotiated settlements versus court judgments (i.e. the law) is bound to be a very complicated and demanding exercise.

References

de Palo G, Canessa R (2014) The EU parliament study 'Rebooting the Mediation Directive': an overview of its key findings and a response to its critics. Neth Flemish Mediat Confl Manage Q 18:3641

Fiss OM (1983/1984) Against settlement. Yale Law J 93:1073–1090

Huls NJH, Van Doorn CJM (2007) De constructie van een massaclaim – een rechtssociologische analyse van de eerste fase van de Dexia-affaire. Rechtsgeleerd Magazijn Themis 2:58

Jagtenberg R (2014) Mediation: a desirable case management tool for the courts? In: Van Rhee CH, Fu Y (eds) Civil litigation in China and Europe. Springer, Dordrecht, p 282

Jagtenberg R, de Roo A (2011) Frame for a Dutch portrait on mediation court connected mediation in the Netherlands. The Judiciary Q. Council for the Judiciary, The Hague, pp 7–23

Jagtenberg R, Voet S (2015) When it takes thousands to tango. Neth Flemish Mediat Confl Manage Q 19:6–32

Manning B (1977) Hyperlexis, our national disease. Northwestern Law Rev 71:n6

Mnookin RRH, Kornhauser L (1978/1979) Bargaining in the shadow of the law. Yale Law J 88:950–997

Silvestri E, Jagtenberg R (2013) Juggling a red hot potato—Italy, the EU and mandatory mediation. Neth Flemish Mediat Confl Manage Q 17:7–19

Van Boom WH, Lindenbergh SD (2010) Effectenlease: dwaling, zorgplicht en schadevergoeding. Ars Aequi, 188 ff

Annie de Roo Associate Professor of ADR and Comparative Law at Erasmus University Rotterdam, the Netherlands. Director of the Netherlands Organization for Scientific Research (N. W.O.) sponsored project on Hybrid Governance in the Social Domain. Vice-chair of the Exams Committee of the Mediators Federation of the Netherlands (MFN). Editor-in-Chief of *TMD*, the Dutch-Flemish Mediation & Conflict Management Quarterly.

Rob Jagtenberg Senior Research Fellow of Erasmus University Rotterdam, the Netherlands. Former member of the Supervisory Committee for the national Dutch project on court-connected mediation, and Principal Researcher in projects commissioned by the World Bank and The Council for the Judiciary, The Netherlands.

Part V
Access to Justice and Fair Trial Rights

Transformation of the Croatian Legal Aid System: From Normative to Functional Insufficiency

Juraj Brozović

Abstract The establishment of the Croatian legal aid system in civil matters was a consequence of Croatia's accession to the European Union. Lack of comprehensive assessment of citizens' needs and lack of systematic research on the costs of legal aid resulted in an insufficient normative background. Uncertainty and the lack of flexibility of some of the provisions of the Legal Aid Act effectively precluded many citizens from obtaining legal aid. Matters were such that the Croatian Constitutional Court intervened by abolishing some of the Act's key provisions. The new Legal Aid Act was supposed to cope with all the identified problems. Simplification and increased flexibility of threshold rules, in combination with policy changes with regard to financing of legal aid providers, promised a greater possibility to access justice in civil matters. This contribution assesses the extent to which the normative transformation of the Croatian legal aid system was indeed successful in achieving the goals of recent reform attempts.

1 Introduction

Before 2008, effective access to legal aid in Croatia could be achieved only in criminal cases.[1] In order to facilitate access to justice in civil cases as well, Croatia enacted its first Legal Aid Act (LAA 2008).[2] The Act laid down the threshold for obtaining legal aid, making aid dependent on the overall income of

This contribution is the result of research supported by the Croatian Science Foundation (project no. 6988).

[1]Some of the defendants were statutorily obliged to appoint defense counsel, while others could apply to the court for legal aid if they could not afford one. See Articles 65, 66 Criminal Procedure Act 97.
[2]Legal Aid Act (2008).

J. Brozović (✉)
Faculty of Law, University of Zagreb, Zagreb, Croatia
e-mail: jbrozovic@pravo.hr

A. Uzelac and C. H. van Rhee (eds.), *Transformation of Civil Justice*,
Ius Gentium: Comparative Perspectives on Law and Justice 70,
https://doi.org/10.1007/978-3-319-97358-6_15

the applicant and his or her household members, their pecuniary and non-pecuniary assets, as well as their real estate (Article 8 LAA 2008). The Act narrowed the scope of legal aid to cover only the costs of legal aid in the proceedings before courts or administrative authorities if they adjudicated one of the client's intrinsic issues which the legislator named "existential" (Article 5 LAA 2008). The Act also envisioned a rather complex procedure in which clients were supposed to obtain so-called orders (vouchers) by submitting a formal application along with corresponding attachments and documents to the competent administrative body (Article 22 LAA 2008). The procedure was the same, regardless of whether clients were interested in obtaining simple advice (so-called primary legal aid) or representation in court proceedings (so-called secondary legal aid) (Johnsen et al. 2011, 50). This "voucher" was intended to be the basis for the funding of legal aid providers. While this type of funding was acceptable to lawyers, it was not adapted to primary legal aid providers, whose role conditioned the need for different funding schemes. In 2011, the normative non-effectiveness of LAA 2008 was recognized by the Croatian Constitutional Court. The Court abolished statutory provisions on threshold rules and the scope of legal aid due to their uncertainty and the lack of flexibility which effectively precluded many citizens from obtaining legal aid.[3] Several studies were made and experts called upon to address these issues and to make recommendations (Uzelac and Preložnjak 2012, 267). Although some of the problems were meant to be solved by the amendments to LAA 2008 in 2011, it was not until the new Legal Aid Act was passed in 2013 (LAA 2013)[4] that the Ministry of Justice finally decided to seriously cope with the problems recognized in the studies. The result is the simplified threshold rules which are supposed to increase the number of successful applications. The funding of primary legal aid providers, as well as the procedure for obtaining legal advice, was changed to adapt to their special position and role in the system.

Normatively speaking, LAA 2013 is a major improvement of the Croatian legal aid system. The criteria for obtaining legal aid in Croatia seem to be flexible enough to enable every citizen in need to access justice in his or her civil case. It is easier than ever now to obtain legal advice. However, it is not the law itself that settles the issue. In the end, it is its application that ensures the intended goals are reached. This contribution will assess whether the normative transformation of the Croatian legal aid system truly resulted in a satisfactory legal environment in which justice is accessible to everyone.

[3]Decision of the Constitutional Court of the Republic of Croatia (2011).

[4]Legal Aid Act (2013).

2 What the Transformation Was Supposed to Achieve

As a reaction to prior normative insufficiency, there were two major goals of the latest reform of the Croatian legal aid system: to increase the number of successful applicants and to simplify the procedure for obtaining legal aid.[5]

The first goal was supposed to be achieved primarily through simplified threshold rules which apply solely to secondary legal aid. Instead of complex rules based on the type of property or income, LAA 2013 made legal aid dependent on the overall income, and the overall movable and immovable assets owned by the applicant.[6] A new tax basis for the threshold calculation was introduced, so that more citizens fall within it.[7] Although the proceedings in which secondary legal aid can be granted are explicitly prescribed, there is a general rule that legal aid can be provided in any court or administrative proceedings when it is justified by the "concrete life circumstances of the applicant and his or her household members, in accordance with the purpose of the law" (Article 13 LAA 2013). LAA 2013 also laid down several important exceptions to the threshold rules. In some types of proceedings (e.g. child support) legal aid is granted automatically, regardless of the threshold (Article 13 LAA 2013). Additionally, some types of income and assets are excluded during the assessment of overall income either due to reasons of social justice (e.g. social benefit, real estate where the applicant and his or her household members live, etc.) or to the fact that there are objective reasons that prevent the applicant from disposing of that property (e.g. income is spent on medical treatments) (Arts. 14 and 15 LAA 2013). On the other hand, the criteria for obtaining primary legal aid are laid down only in general terms, allowing the providers to interpret and elaborate on them in their own internal procedures (Article 10 LAA 2013).

To reach the second goal, LAA 2013 completely simplified the procedure for obtaining primary legal aid. In order to obtain legal advice, the client is supposed to contact the provider himself or herself, without the need to obtain a "voucher" or any other formal type of administrative decision first (Article 11 LAA 2013). Since primary legal aid providers are no longer financed by cashing in "vouchers", project funding was introduced, thus making the amount the state invests in them dependent on various factors, such as costs and the social value of legal aid provided, territory covered by that provider, as well as the number of clients and their cases that the provider resolved (Article 36 LAA 2013). Although secondary legal aid is still funded in a fashion very similar to "vouchers", the proceedings have been significantly simplified. Also, applicants do not have to attach any documents to

[5]Legal Aid Act Final Proposal (2013) Vlada Republike Hrvatske, Zagreb. https://vlada.gov.hr/UserDocsImages//Sjednice/Arhiva//123.%20-%206.pdf. Accessed 7 June 2018. See specifically pp 24, 25.

[6]Cf. Article 8 LAA 2008 and Article 14 LAA 2013.

[7]Legal Aid Act Final Proposal (2013), 27, 28.

their applications, because administrative authorities are expected to obtain them *ex officio*. The application form was shortened as well.

Two mechanisms were reintroduced for the purposes of system monitoring. The Ministry of Justice is the first institution in charge of monitoring the progress of the law's application. It has a special Department for Legal Aid which has appellate jurisdiction with regard to denied applications for legal aid and exclusive jurisdiction with regard to the registration of providers, along with some other administrative roles. The Ministry gathers reports submitted by legal aid providers and submits its own report to the government. That report is then subject to parliamentary review (Arts. 43–46 LAA 2013). Furthermore, the Commission for Legal Aid was confirmed as the advisory body of the Ministry. Its principal tasks remain the monitoring and analyzing of the legal aid system, giving opinions on Ministry reports, giving opinions on tender applications for funding of primary legal aid providers, as well as opinions on their reports, and making recommendations for further development of the legal aid system (Article 48 LAA 2013).

3 Reality Check: Evaluation of the Current System

3.1 Growing Number of Approved Applications as an Indicator of Successful Reform?

As can be seen from the official reports of the Ministry of Justice, there is a noticeable trend of constant increase in the number of approved applications for legal aid. Indeed, as shown in the chart below in Fig. 1, the total number of approved applications has increased over the years from a modest 3182 in 2009 to a peak of 7945 in 2014:

The subtle decrease in recent years is presumably the result of the general decrease in the number of incoming civil cases in the courts.[8] Still, the bigger picture confirms the overall growing trend, which could be interpreted as a success of recent reforms. As mentioned earlier, one of the main goals of the 2013 reform was to include more citizens in the system by changing the method of the threshold calculation. However, it is not only the calculation method, but also the scope and notion of legal aid that has changed over the years. Court fees and advance on costs waivers are now granted by administrative authorities exclusively, without the intervention of the court which is in charge of the civil proceedings in question. This necessarily means that those waivers are no longer considered in the context of the court budget, but in the context of the implemented legal aid budget. Additionally, they are considered successful applications for legal aid which are

[8]Report of the Ministry of Justice on the Functioning of the Judiciary (2016) Vlada Republike Hrvatske, Zagreb. https://pravosudje.gov.hr/vijesti/izvjesce-o-radu-sudova-za-2016-godinu/14727. Accessed 7 June 2018.

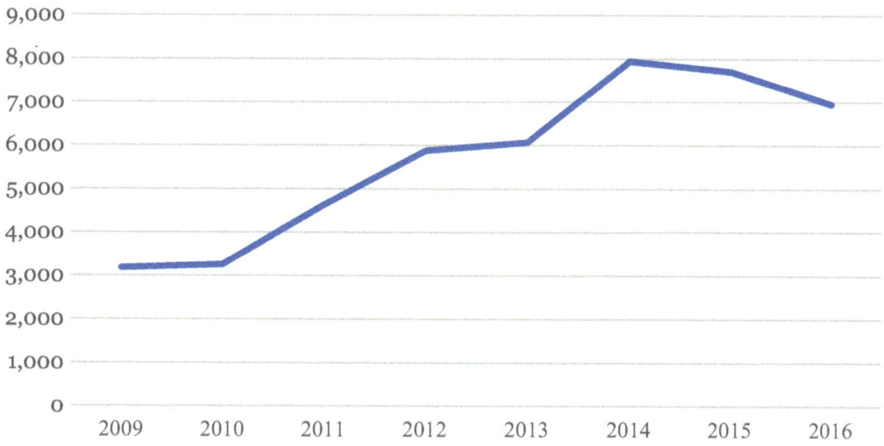

Fig. 1 Approved applications for legal aid since 2009. *Source* Reports of the Ministry of Justice on Legal Aid and Expenditure of State Funds 2009–2016

added to the total number of approved applications. This means that the *real* picture can be seen only if one considers the type of legal aid granted in the same period (Table 1).

Although the number of cases in which legal aid was granted in the form of representation[9] has slightly increased, it is evident that the real reason for the overall growth is the effective inclusion of court fees waivers in the legal aid system.[10] For instance, in 2015 there were 6151 court fees waivers, while the total number of approved applications equaled 7704. The rise in the overall number is thus merely a consequence of a different methodology and factual structural changes in the state budget, while the number of cases of representation stayed more or less the same.

Unfortunately, although the difference in the numbers seems to be significant enough to conclude that nowadays more people in need obtain legal aid, data on the types of the proceedings in which legal aid was granted refute such a conclusion (see Fig. 2).

In more than half of the cases legal aid was granted to the parties in family court proceedings, i.e. the only proceedings in which the court has full inquisitive powers and can render many decisions on its own initiative (Triva and Dika 2004, 757–761). These are also proceedings in which the Croatian Bar Association offers their

[9]The number includes cases in which lawyers represented clients before the courts, administrative bodies, in ADR and special types of proceedings.

[10]It could, however, be argued as to whether such inclusion was indeed effective. In a recent study, the number of waivers was shown to be more than five times smaller than the number of enforcement proceedings, which had been initiated due to the non-payment of court fees and which turned out to be unsuccessful for more than a year. Presumably, those court fees should have been waived, which shows that the waiver system does not function properly. See Brozović (2017).

Table 1 Type of legal aid granted from 2009

	Representation	Court fees waiver	Advance on costs waiver	Other
2009	3019	n/a	n/a	389
2010	2883	n/a	n/a	388
2011	3394	n/a	n/a	340
2012	4622	n/a	n/a	314
2013	4710	1004	263	–
2014	4372	1167	231	–
2015	4503	6151	2337	175
2016	3621	4906	2079	205

Source Reports of the Ministry of Justice on Legal Aid and Expenditure of State Funds (2009, 2010, 2011, 2012, 2013, 2014, 2015, 2016)

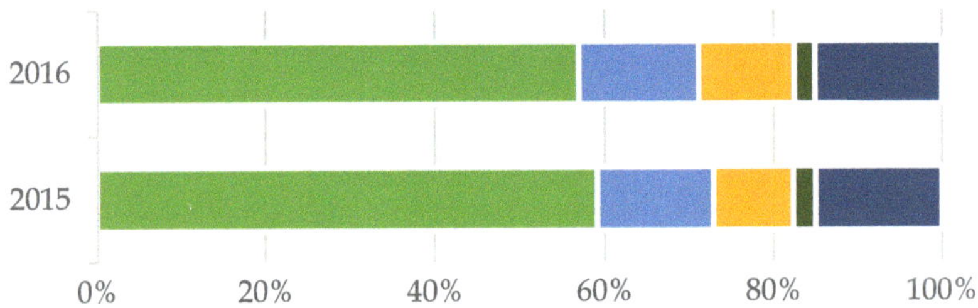

	2015	2016
Family	59.16%	56.82%
Enforcement	13.69%	14.13%
Property	9.49%	11.32%
Employment	2.63%	2.47%
Other	15.03%	15%

Fig. 2 Type of proceedings in which legal aid was granted in 2015 and 2016 compared. *Source* Reports of the Ministry of Justice on Legal Aid and Expenditure of State Funds 2015–2016

own parallel pro bono representation services, at least when the rights of a child are affected. In other words, Croatia spends the most money for legal aid in proceedings where legal aid is least needed.

3.2 (Mal)Functioning of the Commission for Legal Aid

Due to its statutory position, the Commission for Legal Aid had a chance to play a major role in the reforms of the legal aid system. During the reform of 2011, it warned that the amendments should be considered only temporary and that a new Legal Aid Act should be enacted as soon as possible (Jelinić and Knol Radoja 2014, 195). During 2013, when some of its members participated in the official working group, the Commission continued to insist on its earlier standpoint and strongly encouraged reform activities.[11] From the period of 2013 to 2015 it was rather proactive: it held 15 meetings during which it thoroughly discussed the situation of the legal aid system, opened a direct dialogue with primary legal aid providers,[12] and, most importantly, made proposals with regard to their financing.

Although it is the Minister who makes a final decision on the distribution of funds granted to primary legal aid providers, prior to 2015 it was customary for him to follow the recommendation of the Commission. In 2015, the Minister unilaterally decided to amend the Commission's proposal, without providing the reasoning for this decision. What followed was a chain of unfortunate events leading to the complete diminishment of the role and legislative purpose of the Commission. It no longer held meetings and eventually the mandate of its members lapsed. The complex political situation and lack of stable government in early 2016 prevented the appointment of new members, resulting in the Commission not being re-established for months. When the Ministry of Justice finally made new appointments, the choice of the members was, at the very least, dubious. To illustrate this by way of an example: as a representative of the legal clinics, the Ministry appointed a professor from the only faculty of law in Croatia (out of four) that does not have an actual legal clinic providing legal aid. Similar appointments and lack of meetings continued even during the next composition of the Commission. It was only recently that a meeting was held and the Commission partially participated in reviewing tendered applications of primary legal aid providers. However, Commission members were provided with a preset list with no real possibility to influence the final decision. This was one of the reasons why there was a problem establishing a sufficient quorum for making formal decisions. Thus, the Commission was prevented from fulfilling its statutory duty.

Disturbances in the work of the Commission did not have merely general, indirect implications for the whole system; on the contrary, they directly affected primary legal aid providers in their regular activities. Tenders for funding of their projects in 2016 and 2017 were published with more than two months of delay compared to the statutory deadline. Due to the abovementioned problems, the Commission did not review applications. Instead, an ad hoc committee, consisting solely of employees of the Ministry, which had not been previously disclosed to the public, made their own proposals to the Minister. He accepted their proposals without critical assessment, resulting in an arbitrary decision which essentially deprived some of the providers of the necessary funding. When several of them filed a complaint, the Minister simply rejected their grievance with a brief

[11]Statement of the Commission on Legal Aid (2013), 17 September 2013. Unpublished.

[12]A meeting was held in November 2014 to address the novelties in the system and to discuss various issues regarding the project proposals and their implementation.

explanation that failed to clarify the real reasons behind his decision. There were no legal remedies available to challenge either of those decisions before the courts. The Ministry of Justice thus single-handedly disregarded statutory provisions and enabled arbitrariness to enter into the interpretation and implementation of the law.

3.3 Budgetary Trends

Funding has represented the biggest challenge ever since the Croatian legal aid system was established. This does not come as a surprise, since at no point has the Ministry conducted systematic research regarding the costs of legal aid (Johnsen et al. 2011, 11). Naturally, without assessing the citizens' needs, it is impossible to estimate the amount of funds to be allocated to legal aid. The implemented legal aid budget in Croatia turned out to be one of the lowest budgets in Europe. For instance, in 2012 Croatia allocated as little as €0.04 per citizen to legal aid in civil cases, thus putting the country way below the European average (€8.63) and median (€2.30) too.[13] It seems that the situation improved in 2014, since Croatia allocated €2.59 per citizen, which is still below the European average (€9), but more than the European median (€2).[14] However, if we consider the country-specific data for Croatia, it appears that only €0.08 was allocated to legal aid in civil cases, while the rest went to legal aid in criminal cases, which was not taken into account in previous CEPEJ reports.[15] Again, it is methodology that helps to present statistics in such a way as to be better than they in fact really are. However, one should not forget that those numbers show the *implemented* and not the approved budget. The slight increase over 2012 is not the result of the Ministry's generosity, but the mere fact that civil proceedings in which clients were represented by lawyers finally ended. This enabled lawyers to cash in their "vouchers", as was envisioned under Article 55 LAA 2008. More of those can be expected in the future, which means that the *implemented* budget will continue to artificially rise without new, additional citizens having entered into the system.

Could this lack of proper funding be attributed to the general lack of resources? This is clearly the number one excuse offered to anyone arguing the financial insufficiency of the system. The approved budget for the courts has indeed decreased tremendously over the years,[16] but the allocation of the court budget has stayed more or less the same. Croatia spends most of its court budget on the gross

[13]CEPEJ (2014, 46).

[14]CEPEJ (2016, 72).

[15]CEPEJ STAT (2017). See specifically Quantitative data (for 2013, 2012 or 2014) for exact numbers and country-specific data (for 2013, 2012 or 2014) for methodology explanations.

[16]CEPEJ (2016, 49).

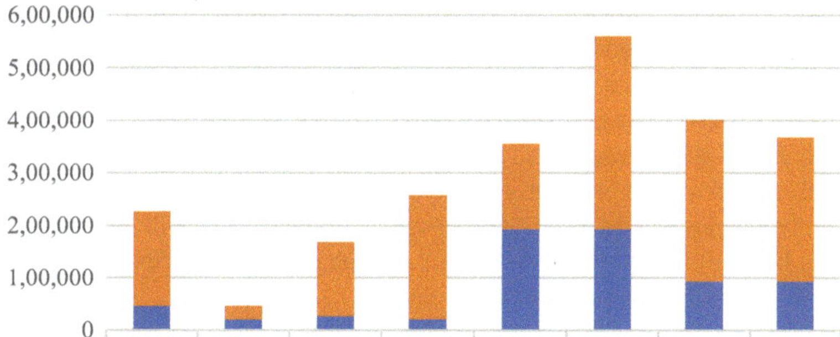

	2010	2011	2012	2013	2014	2015	2016	2017
Secondary legal aid	1,80,00	25,500	1,40,90	2,35,35	1,61,31	3,66,32	3,06,38	2,73,33
Primary legal aid	46,000	20,150	26,700	21,350	1,93,15	1,93,15	93,250	93,250

Fig. 3 Implemented legal aid budget (app. in euros). *Source* Reports of the Ministry of Justice on Legal Aid and Expenditure of State Funds 2010–2016

salaries of employees,[17] which is the result of a court system hiring as many as 41 professional judges for every 100,000 inhabitants. That makes it double the European average (20.7) and median (18.1).[18] The same goes for non-court staff.[19] It is thus rather cynical to state that there are no further funding options for legal aid in a situation where the judicial system is so irrationally organized.

It is not only the total amount allocated to legal aid that is worrisome, but also the distribution of those funds among primary and secondary legal aid providers, as shown in Fig. 3.

Except for 2014 and 2015, primary legal aid was immensely underfunded, directly affecting the work of primary legal aid providers. Even those providers who were lucky enough to be granted state funds faced numerous problems in their expenditure. Since in 2016 the tender for applications was published late, the decision was postponed until September, resulting in funds being paid in November. Some providers, who were subject to onerous bureaucratic auditing, got their funds only in late December. Those are the same funds that the Ministry expected the providers to spend beginning the 1st of January of that same year. Providers who did not have access to alternative funding options simply could not finance their activities. Even if the payment had been timely, the maximum amount

[17]Precisely, it spent 95.26% of its court budget on gross salaries in 2012 (CEPEJ 2014, 34) and 80.90% in 2014 (CEPEJ 2016, 37). The salaries of Croatian judges are below the European average and median (see CEPEJ 2016, 110).

[18]CEPEJ (2016, 90). The number is slightly higher since Croatia has special misdemeanor courts, as well as a High Misdemeanor Court. If they are excluded, the number would still be high: 32.29.

[19]Their number has increased over the years. In 2014, Croatia had 166.5 non-court officials for every 100,000 inhabitants, i.e. 2.5 times the European average (CEPEJ 2016, 149). If specialized misdemeanor courts are excluded, the number is 137.95, which still makes it double the European average.

which could be allocated to each provider (€10,000) could not cover the gross salary of a legal professional. The most worrying part is the fact that the same problem existed even before LAA 2013.[20] This shows continuity in the Ministry's lack of understanding of primary legal aid and its importance. Although the State Budget for 2018 shows a slight increase in the legal aid budget,[21] many primary legal aid providers will be forced to close their doors because those funds are simply insufficient to fund all of their activities. This will prevent more citizens from becoming acquainted with legal aid options and contribute to the stagnation of the number of successful applications.

3.4 *Overcomplexity of the System*

Even though LAA 2013 can be considered quite an improvement where the complexity of criteria for granting legal aid is concerned, the procedure for obtaining legal aid is still too complicated. The application starts with filling out a special form consisting of four pages which contains personal information about the applicant and his or her household members, details about their income, immovable and movable assets, as well as the legal aid applied for. The form is accompanied by a consent form granting access to income data accessible at tax authorities. The information needed is very detailed and precise. Even though competent administrative authorities are the ones who should obtain relevant documents on their own initiative, the applicant and his or her household members cannot fill out the forms without first contacting the competent tax, land and vehicle registry authorities. Since laypersons very often hardly understand the information required to apply for legal aid, the aid will remain out of the reach of the citizens who failed beforehand to obtain legal advice, including an explanation of the form and subsequent procedures. The simple fact that one needs legal aid in order to apply for it speaks for itself.

Besides being overcomplex, there is no place on the forms where one can explain objective reasons that prevent the applicant and his or her household members from disposing of their income or property (Article 14 paras. 2–3 LAA 2013). The rights guaranteed thus seem to be hidden from the eyes of their holders. The procedure is still very formalistic, to the insurmountable detriment of the applicant. For instance, should the applicant want his or her court fees to be waived, he or she should first be aware that the court proceedings should not be initiated prior to being granted legal aid. Waiver is valid only from the moment the decision is made (Arts. 19 and 20 LAA 2013), which means that court fees which became due before that date cannot later be waived.

[20]Statement of the Commission on Legal Aid (2013), 17 September 2013. Unpublished.

[21]See State Budget of the Republic of Croatia for 2018 Proposal (2017) Croatian Parliament, Zagreb. http://www.sabor.hr/prijedlog-drzavnog-proracuna-rh-2018. Accessed 7 June 2018.

The greatest proof of the system's overcomplexity is the need to constantly educate the officers who apply the Legal Aid Act in making decisions on legal aid applications. In the last couple of years, the Ministry has on several occasions held meetings with the representatives of the competent administrative bodies for the purpose of resolving their everyday issues in the application of the Act.[22] If the people applying the law are confused as to its correct implementation, how can one expect the citizens to fully understand it? They still need a considerable amount of help in the realization of their rights, as they need to be informed about the possibility of obtaining legal aid and about all the complicated procedural aspects. The constant decrease in the funds available to primary legal aid providers, described above, and delays with regard to funding tenders certainly exacerbate that problem.

3.5 *Ministry's Reports*

Even during the times of the previous Legal Aid Act, the Ministry of Justice had a statutory obligation to file reports (at the latest by the beginning of March each year) about the functioning of the legal aid system to the government, which, after accepting it, forwarded it to the Parliament (Arts. 68, 69 LAA 2008).[23] This was supposed to enable parliamentary review of the system, which should have resulted in necessary measures aiming at its improvement.[24] In order to achieve that goal, the reports should contain all the necessary information about legal aid providers, about their funding and about the legal aid provided to the citizens. Quite the contrary, being basically hidden from the public,[25] the reports regularly contained very rough information, which misinformed both the Parliament and the public about the real situation in the system.

In the last couple of years, the lack of seriousness in reporting reached its maximum level. Reports completely lack information about the number of primary legal aid providers, as well as the number of their cases. Furthermore, by careful presentation of statistics, the Ministry constantly tries to artificially present the situation as better than it really is. In the last three reports, while providing its own evaluation of the system, the Ministry literally copy-pastes the same sentence:

---

[22] Cf. Report of the Ministry of Justice on Legal Aid and Expenditure of State Funds (2014, p 13); Report of the Ministry of Justice on Legal Aid and Expenditure of State Funds, p 14; and Report of the Ministry of Justice on Legal Aid and Expenditure of State Funds (2016, p 14). All reports are published on the web page of the Ministry of Justice. https://pravosudje.gov.hr/vijesti/izvjesce-o-radu-sudova-za-2016-godinu/14727. Accessed 7 June 2018.

[23] Cf. Arts. 45 and 46 LAA 2013.

[24] Legal Aid Act Final Proposal (2008) Vlada Republike Hrvatske, Zagreb. http://www.sabor.hr/fgs.axd?id=11688. Accessed 7 June 2018. See specifically p 45.

[25] Reports are hidden within numerous other reports thematically unconnected to legal aid. There is no hyperlink on the web page giving information on legal aid.

> Establishment of an efficient legal aid system represents a significant factor in the improvement of the Croatian legal system, in which the Ministry of Justice plays a central role. By using an active approach and by expanding dialogue with all the providers, the Ministry of Justice, as the central authority responsible for the proper functioning of the entire legal system, contributed to the development of the legal aid scheme and made it closer to citizens and their needs, as well as the needs of the whole society.[26]

The greatest irony is that nothing in the above quotation is true. The Ministry's activities can hardly be considered proactive and the lack of proper dialogue with providers is evident from the very report itself, as primary legal aid providers have been almost completely ignored. As shown earlier in this paper, thorough analysis of the cases in which legal aid was granted proves that the needs and expectations of the citizens have not been met. This lack of self-criticism clearly shows there is no relevant political willingness in Croatia to establish an efficient legal aid system. Cynicism such as this surely does not build trust that the system is in good hands. If the system is not taken seriously by those who should supervise it and take care of its proper functioning, the situation is unlikely to change in the right direction in the future.

4 Conclusion

The normative transformation of the Croatian legal aid system only partially managed to solve its problems. Threshold rules were simplified and made more understandable. There is a certain degree of flexibility with regard to falling within the threshold, but the exemptions are too narrowly construed. The procedure for obtaining legal aid is still too complex for the average layperson. Although applicants are no longer required to obtain documents which accompany their applications, the forms cannot be filled out if those documents are not consulted beforehand. Basically, legal aid in the form of advice is required in order to correctly fill out all the necessary forms in the application process. Unfortunately, citizens' access to legal advice is rather limited. Difficulties faced by primary legal aid providers hinder them in their efforts to inform the citizens about their rights. Project funding, as the chosen method of their financing, is limited to one year exclusively. As such, it cannot guarantee successful finalization of their legal aid activities.

Nonetheless, it is not normative insufficiency that currently represents the biggest problem. Even in such form, LAA 2013 could represent an acceptable legal environment in which legal aid would be accessible to a greater extent for the citizens in need. Unfortunately, the factual transformation did not follow the

---

[26]Translation by the author. Cf. Report of the Ministry of Justice on Legal Aid and Expenditure of State Funds (2015, p. 14) and Report of the Ministry of Justice on Legal Aid and Expenditure of State Funds (2016, p. 14).

normative transformation. In other words, normative insufficiency was replaced by functional insufficiency.

It seems that Croatia has never truly comprehended the importance of legal aid in ensuring citizens' access to justice. In the years preceding its accession to the European Union, Croatia did as little as needed to ensure the closing of all the chapters in the accession negotiations. As soon as it entered into the European Union, enthusiasm for establishing an efficient legal aid system faded. The normative background, which was established under the influence of foreign experts, simply could not succeed without support of the political body in charge of the whole system. The Ministry of Justice has not exactly fit well into that role. Its activities have been half-hearted and counterproductive, aiming solely at budgetary cuts. The opinions of legal aid providers have ceased to be a factor in the making of its decisions, as there has not been sincere communication between the Ministry and the providers. Extensive interpretation of statutory deadlines has brought primary legal aid providers to the edge of a cliff. This necessarily affects the quality and quantity of legal aid provided, as has already been shown in the available statistics.

Perhaps the only solution to the problems identified in this paper is to entrust the system to a different body that would be competent enough to face all these challenges, an independent body led by professionals who will take the system seriously. Otherwise, no transformation of the Croatian legal aid system will ever truly succeed.

References

Brozović J (2017) Oslobođenje od sudskih pristojbi kao preduvjet ostvarenja prava na pristup pravosuđu. Pravni vjesnik. J Law Soc Sci Fac Law, Josip Juraj Strossmayer Univ Osijek 33(3–4):41–70

CEPEJ (2014) Report on European judicial systems—edition 2014 (2012 data): efficiency and quality of justice. https://www.coe.int/t/dghl/cooperation/cepej/evaluation/2014/Rapport_2014_en.pdf. Accessed 7 June 2018

CEPEJ (2016) European judicial systems. Efficiency and quality of justice. CEPEJ STUDIES No. 23. https://www.coe.int/t/dghl/cooperation/cepej/evaluation/2016/publication/CEPEJ%20Study%2023%20report%20EN%20web.pdf. Accessed 7 June 2018

CEPEJ (2017) Statistical database. https://www.coe.int/t/dghl/cooperation/cepej/evaluation/2016/STAT/. Accessed 7 June 2018

Criminal Procedure Act (*Zakon o kaznenom postupku*), Official Journal, No. 110/97, 27/98, 58/99, 112/99, 58/02, 143/02, 115/06

Decision of the Constitutional Court of the Republic of Croatia (2011), 6 April 2011, No. U-I-722/2009

Jelinić Z, Knol Radoja K (2014) Analiza hrvatskoga sustava besplatne pravne pomoći u građanskim stvarima u svjetlu dosadašnje prakse Europskoga suda za ljudska prava. Pravni vjesnik. J Law Soc Sci Fac Law, Josip Juraj Strossmayer Univ Osijek 30(2):185–211

Johnsen J, Stawa G, Uzelac A (2011) Evaluation of the Croatian legal aid act and its implementation. Human Rights Centre—Centar za ljudska prava, Zagreb

Legal Aid Act (*Zakon o besplatnoj pravnoj pomoći*), Official Journal, No. 62/2008, 44/2011, 81/2011, 143/2013
Legal Aid Act (*Zakon o besplatnoj pravnoj pomoći*). Official Journal, No. 143/2013
Legal Aid Act Final Proposal (2008) Vlada Republike Hrvatske, Zagreb. http://www.sabor.hr/fgs.axd?id=11688. Accessed 7 June 2018
Legal Aid Act Final Proposal (2013) Vlada Republike Hrvatske, Zagreb. https://vlada.gov.hr/UserDocsImages//Sjednice/Arhiva//123.%20-%206.pdf. Accessed 7 June 2018
Report of the Ministry of Justice on the Functioning of the Judiciary (2016) Vlada Republike Hrvatske, Zagreb. https://pravosudje.gov.hr/vijesti/izvjesce-o-radu-sudova-za-2016-godinu/14727. Accessed 7 June 2018
Report of the Ministry of Justice on Legal Aid and Expenditure of State Funds (2009) Ministarstvo pravosuđa, Zagreb. https://pravosudje.gov.hr/pristup-informacijama-6341/strategije-planovi-i-izvjesca/izvjesce-o-ostvarivanju-prava-na-besplatnu-pravnu-pomoc-i-utrosku-sredstava/6723. Accessed 7 June 2018
Report of the Ministry of Justice on Legal Aid and Expenditure of State Funds (2010) Ministarstvo pravosuđa, Zagreb. https://pravosudje.gov.hr/pristup-informacijama-6341/strategije-planovi-i-izvjesca/izvjesce-o-ostvarivanju-prava-na-besplatnu-pravnu-pomoc-i-utrosku-sredstava/6723. Accessed 7 June 2018
Report of the Ministry of Justice on Legal Aid and Expenditure of State Funds (2011) Ministarstvo pravosuđa, Zagreb. https://pravosudje.gov.hr/pristup-informacijama-6341/strategije-planovi-i-izvjesca/izvjesce-o-ostvarivanju-prava-na-besplatnu-pravnu-pomoc-i-utrosku-sredstava/6723. Accessed 7 June 2018
Report of the Ministry of Justice on Legal Aid and Expenditure of State Funds (2012) Ministarstvo pravosuđa, Zagreb. https://pravosudje.gov.hr/pristup-informacijama-6341/strategije-planovi-i-izvjesca/izvjesce-o-ostvarivanju-prava-na-besplatnu-pravnu-pomoc-i-utrosku-sredstava/6723. Accessed 7 June 2018
Report of the Ministry of Justice on Legal Aid and Expenditure of State Funds (2013) Ministarstvo pravosuđa, Zagreb. https://pravosudje.gov.hr/pristup-informacijama-6341/strategije-planovi-i-izvjesca/izvjesce-o-ostvarivanju-prava-na-besplatnu-pravnu-pomoc-i-utrosku-sredstava/6723. Accessed 7 June 2018
Report of the Ministry of Justice on Legal Aid and Expenditure of State Funds (2014) Ministarstvo pravosuđa, Zagreb. https://pravosudje.gov.hr/pristup-informacijama-6341/strategije-planovi-i-izvjesca/izvjesce-o-ostvarivanju-prava-na-besplatnu-pravnu-pomoc-i-utrosku-sredstava/6723. Accessed 7 June 2018
Report of the Ministry of Justice on Legal Aid and Expenditure of State Funds (2015) Ministarstvo pravosuđa, Zagreb. https://pravosudje.gov.hr/pristup-informacijama-6341/strategije-planovi-i-izvjesca/izvjesce-o-ostvarivanju-prava-na-besplatnu-pravnu-pomoc-i-utrosku-sredstava/6723. Accessed 7 June 2018
Report of the Ministry of Justice on Legal Aid and Expenditure of State Funds (2016) Ministarstvo pravosuđa, Zagreb. https://pravosudje.gov.hr/pristup-informacijama-6341/strategije-planovi-i-izvjesca/izvjesce-o-ostvarivanju-prava-na-besplatnu-pravnu-pomoc-i-utrosku-sredstava/6723. Accessed 7 June 2018
Report of the Ministry of Justice on Legal Aid and Expenditure of State Funds (2017) Ministarstvo pravosuđa, Zagreb. https://vlada.gov.hr/UserDocsImages//Sjednice/2017/04%20travanj/29%20sjednica%20Vlade%20Republike%20Hrvatske//29%20-%2010.pdf. Accessed 7 June 2018

State Budget of the Republic of Croatia for 2018 Proposal (2017) Croatian Parliament, Zagreb. http://www.sabor.hr/prijedlog-drzavnog-proracuna-rh-2018. Accessed 7 June 2018
Statement of the Commission on Legal Aid (2013), 17 September 2013. Unpublished
Triva S, Dika M (2004) Građansko parnično procesno pravo. Narodne novine, Zagreb
Uzelac A, Preložnjak B (2012) The development of legal aid systems in the Western Balkans. A study of controversial reforms in Croatia and Serbia. Kritisk Iuss. Utgitt av Rettspolitisk Forening (Liber amicorum – Jon T. Johnsen) 38(3–4):261–287

Juraj Brozović Research Assistant in the Department of Civil Procedure at the University of Zagreb, Croatia. Assistant to the Director of the Law Clinic Zagreb and one of the academic mentors supervising students' legal aid work.

The Transformation of Consumer Law in Times of Crisis: The Ex Officio Control of Unfair Contract Terms

Stephanie Law

Abstract Over the past decade, that is to say, post-financial crisis, national courts have identified rules of national civil procedure that they understand operate to impede the application of EU consumer law rules, as transposed into domestic law. The potential incompatibility of these national rules with EU law has come to the fore in the adjudication of disputes concerning consumer regulatory needs in consumer contracting for sales, services and credit. In responding to these references, the ECJ has rendered a line of judgments in an effort to establish procedural safeguards for the enforcement and protection of EU consumer rights. This contribution critically analyses one procedural mechanism, namely the establishment of the power and subsequent obligation on national judges to examine compliance with EU consumer protection rules ex officio. The contribution begins by providing a brief outline of the framework of EU and national consumer law, and the character of consumer rights enforcement. It then examines the tool (namely the preliminary reference procedure) by which the courts have engaged in the development of the ex officio regulation of EU consumer law, and outlines the key ECJ case law resulting therefrom. The contribution then evaluates the key shifts in national judicial cultures to which this mechanism of procedural protection gives rise and assesses the reach, limits and problematic dimensions of ex officio control in ensuring the effective and equivalent protection of consumer rights.

This paper was first presented at PPJ 2017 in Dubrovnik. I would like to thank Professors Alan Uzelac and Remco van Rhee as well as Marko Bratković, and the other participants at the conference, for an interesting discussion. The paper has also benefited from discussion with Professor Burkhard Hess and from the comments of Vincent Richard.

S. Law (✉)
Max Planck Institute Luxembourg, Luxembourg, Luxembourg
e-mail: stephanie.law@mpi.lu

A. Uzelac and C. H. van Rhee (eds.), *Transformation of Civil Justice*,
Ius Gentium: Comparative Perspectives on Law and Justice 70,
https://doi.org/10.1007/978-3-319-97358-6_16

1 Introduction

Since the 1980s the European Union (EU) has legislated for substantive rights for individuals and groups of consumers; EU consumer legislation is thus predominantly substantive in its nature. However, over the course of the past ten years—particularly in the aftermath of the global financial crisis—the EU legislature and the European Court of Justice (ECJ)[1] have begun to highlight the importance of procedural mechanisms to ensure the effective and equivalent protection of consumers at the domestic level. The aim of this paper is to critically examine an innovative procedural mechanism that has been established and developed by the ECJ and which has empowered and in some instances even obliged national courts[2] to examine and draw the consequences arising from possible infringements of EU consumer law of their own motion, that is to say, ex officio. Moreover, the paper aims to illustrate that the area of consumer protection is one in which the distinction between substantive and procedural rights has become increasingly blurred, particularly as issues relating to the enforcement of substantive rights and national procedural norms have come before the courts.

Narrowing the analysis from EU consumer protection in its entirety, the paper focuses on the regulation of contract terms. This is an area of "regulatory" private law (Micklitz and Reich 2014) which, while finding its basis in EU legislation (the Unfair Contract Terms Directive: UCTD) as implemented in the national legal systems, has been developed predominantly by the national courts and the ECJ. The paper begins by setting out the framework of consumer law enforcement and proceeds to examine the context in which the ECJ has established, advanced and refined this procedural device of ex officio control; the environment is one which has been dominated by the financial crisis and its consequences. The paper then provides an outline of the operation of the preliminary reference procedure, by which the national courts have referred questions of interpretation and the compatibility of national civil procedure with EU law to the ECJ. Against this background, the paper outlines the key case law, and therein the principles by which the ECJ has established and developed the mechanism of ex officio control of unfair contract terms. The key transformations at the national level are then set out. Finally, some brief conclusions are identified; these concern the limits of ex officio control, and necessary considerations relating to its continued use and long-term significance.

[1]ECJ is used here to refer to the European Court of Justice before the Lisbon Treaty; the term CJEU is used to refer to the Court of Justice of the European Union (encompassing the General Court and the Court of Justice).

[2]As well, potentially other dispute resolution bodies, although this will not be discussed here. Throughout, this paper endeavours to clarify the context in which the regulation of unfair contract terms is made, both by national courts and by other dispute resolution bodies.

2 The Consumer Protection Framework: EU Rights and National Remedies

Competence in consumer protection is shared between the Union and the Member States per Art. 4(f) TFEU. EU consumer protection legislation is usually—but not exclusively[3]—established through directives of a minimum harmonisation nature and in line with the internal market competence of the Treaties, that is, on the basis of Art. 114 TFEU. While the EU has competence in the realm of consumer protection on the (generally alternative) basis of Art. 169 TFEU, this provision has rarely been engaged as a legal basis without reference also being made to Art. 114 TFEU.[4] EU consumer law, including the UCTD, typically establishes mandatory rules by which consumers are attributed substantive rights. However, the EU itself has little power to enforce these rights or to adjudicate breaches of these rights. Having said this, EU consumer law—including the UCTD, in Arts. 6(1) and 7(1), as will be seen below—may require that the Member States protect consumer interests before the national courts and other relevant dispute resolution bodies, by ensuring, for example, that remedies are available.[5]

As the EU has a limited competence to legislate for domestic civil procedure,[6] the enforcement of consumer protection rules, and the procedural context in which this enforcement is made, is typically a matter for the national courts in line with their procedural autonomy.[7] This principle, confirmed by the ECJ in 1976,[8] has allowed for the maintenance of diverse procedural rules across the Member States. In specific regulatory areas like consumer protection, where claims are generally low-value and parties are typically not represented, distinct procedures—e.g. small claims or simple procedures—have also been established. Moreover, the principle of procedural autonomy can be said to ensure that an importance continues to be attributed to the

[3]The Consumer Rights Directive 2011/83/EU is an example of a directive with a targeted maximum harmonisation reach. Moreover, at the end of 2015, the European Commission proposed two directives of a maximum harmonisation scope: Proposal for a Directive on certain aspects concerning contracts for the supply of digital content COM(2015) 634 and the Proposal for a Directive on certain aspects concerning contracts for the online sale of (tangible) goods COM(2015) 635. These proposals aim to remove obstacles to cross-border e-commerce, by establishing single sets of rules for contracts for the sale and renting of digital content and contracts for digital services.

[4]As anticipated perhaps by Art. 169(2) TFEU.

[5]This requirement is also established in the Treaty structure; Art. 19 TFEU provides that the "Member States shall provide remedies sufficient to ensure effective legal protection in the fields covered by Union law."

[6]With a few key exceptions including European civil procedural norms legislated for on the basis of the EU's competence for judicial cooperation in civil matters in Art. 81 TFEU. For an overview, see Hess (2010).

[7]For further discussion on the underpinning debate, see Storskrubb (2008, 19–25).

[8]In the cases *Rewe* (Case C-33/76 *Rewe* EU:C:1976:188) and *Comet* (Case C-45/76 *Comet* EU: C:1976:191), in which the Court held that in the absence of rules which harmonise procedure, rights derived from EU law should be enforced in line with national procedural rules.

diversity of national procedural cultures. This is done alongside the construction of the EU regulatory space(s) via Art. 67(1) TFEU, which provides that the Union "shall constitute an area of freedom, security and justice with respect for fundamental rights and the different legal systems and traditions of the Member States". The principle of procedural autonomy is not unlimited however; the principles of effectiveness and equivalence operate (often inconsistently) to ensure that national rules of civil procedure cannot make it practically impossible or excessively difficult to exercise rights conferred by EU law, nor can the rules applicable to actions to which EU rights pertain be less favourable than in similar domestic actions.[9]

Individuals and groups of consumers therefore have to look to their own national law and national procedures (Reich 2010, 122) to enforce the rights derived from Union law (Dougan 2011, 407–438; Reich 2007). It can thus be said that there is a division of labour in terms of the establishment of rights at the EU level and their enforcement—as well as the provision of remedies—at the national level. As most EU consumer law has been promulgated in the form of directives and especially with a minimum harmonisation reach, it is necessary that the national legislature transpose and implement the EU legislation in the domestic legal system. This generates scope for different levels of protection in the Member States and a lack of uniformity across the EU. It is against this background that national courts may make a reference to the ECJ for a preliminary ruling on the interpretation of an EU rule or on the compatibility of national and EU law. The development of the procedural mechanism of the ex officio control of unfair contract terms reflects one instance in which this substantive/procedural division has become increasingly blurred as the ECJ has aimed to ensure that the consumer protection is both effective and equivalent across the Member States.

As noted, this paper focuses on the regulation of unfair contract terms; it is worth providing a short outline of the relevant EU legislation. The assessment of potentially unfair terms finds its basis in the UCTD, which arguably constitutes the EU legislature's first foray into the "core" of private law (Micklitz 1993, 533). Like most EU consumer law, the UTCD finds its legal basis in the internal market provision of Art. 114 TFEU. As a directive, the UCTD must be transposed into the national legal systems; as a directive with a minimum harmonisation reach, it has been implemented in diverse ways across the Member States.[10] The UCTD provides a framework for the control of potentially unfair terms where those terms have been included in consumer contracts and have not been individually negotiated.[11] The unfairness test is established in Art. 3(1) UCTD and provides that a term is unfair if it causes a significant imbalance in the parties' rights and obligations arising under the contract, to the detriment of the consumer, and contrary to the requirement of good faith. The directive also provides for an indicative and

[9]Joined Cases C-430/93 to C-431/93 *Van Schijndel* EU:C:1995:441.

[10]See Ebers (2008, 197–261).

[11]The notion of consumer being limited to a core definition, which certain Member States go beyond, that is, to natural persons acting outside their trade, business or profession.

non-exhaustive list of terms which may be regarded as unfair.[12] The unfairness review anticipated under the directive excludes terms concerning the main subject matter of the contract and the adequacy of the price or remuneration in so far as these terms are in "plain, intelligible language".[13] Written terms must also always be drafted in "plain, intelligible language".[14]

This paper will not focus on the substantive dimensions of the assessment of unfair contract terms but rather on the procedural characteristics of the regulatory framework and illustrate how the ECJ, notwithstanding the EU's limited competence in relation to procedure, has been able to make considerable inroads into national civil procedure. It is worth noting that, in line with the principle of procedural autonomy, the directive provides for few rules on the procedural dimensions of the regulation of unfair contract terms. Rather it simply makes provision in respect of the consequences that should be drawn by the national court and the requirement for the establishment of remedies at the national level. That is to say, Art. 6(1) provides that "Member States shall lay down that unfair terms used in a contract concluded with a consumer by a seller or supplier shall, as provided for under their national law, not be binding on the consumer", while Art. 7(1) establishes that the Member States must provide adequate and effective means of redress.

Before proceeding further, it should be useful to highlight the typical character of the relationships in the context of which disputes arise under the UCTD.[15] As noted, the directive aims to regulate potentially unfair, non-negotiated terms in consumer contracts. It is likely that in consumer contracts these will be provisions in standard contracts or sets of terms and conditions proposed by the trader or supplier on a "take it or leave it" basis. Two concerns are identifiable; these reflect the power imbalance that exists between the contracting parties: there is an imbalance in transaction costs in favour of the party proposing the standard terms and there is an information advantage also in favour of that same party (European Parliament 2013). This paper will return to examine the role that this power imbalance plays in the determinations of the courts.

[12]Per Art. 3(3) and the annex of the UCTD.

[13]Art. 4(2) UCTD.

[14]Art. 5 UCTD.

[15]In light of space constraints, it is not possible to identify and characterise all instances in which the UCTD—as implemented in the national systems—has constituted a matter of adjudication across the Member States. A brief overview of two points is instead considered: The social, economic and legal factors that have brought these issues before the national courts and which have incentivised those courts to make references to the ECJ for preliminary rulings necessarily diverge across the Member States.

3 Consumer Protection and the Preliminary Reference Procedure: Post-crisis Trends

The ex officio control of consumer law has been developed over the past ten to 15 years by the national courts and the ECJ, via the exercise of its interpretative jurisdiction as established by requests for preliminary references from the national courts. In light of the relevant regulatory framework of EU consumer law, with the establishment of rights at the EU level that can only be enforced at the national level, this paper proceeds to reflect on the role played by the preliminary reference procedure of Art. 267 TFEU in bridging this divide. In recent years, numerous disputes have arisen concerning the regulation of unfair contract terms in various types of consumer contracts, concerning both the substantive and, increasingly, procedural dimensions of the UCTD. Focusing on the latter, this part of the paper examines the context in which these cases have come before the national courts and have ultimately been referred to the ECJ for a preliminary ruling.

The preliminary reference procedure in Art. 267 TFEU is the principal—albeit not the exclusive[16]—way in which the ECJ's interpretative jurisdiction can be established. Art. 267(1) TFEU provides that the ECJ has jurisdiction to render preliminary rulings on the interpretation of the Treaties and on the "validity and interpretation of acts of the institutions, bodies, offices or agencies of the Union"; this operates alongside its obligation in Art. 19 TEU to "ensure that in the interpretation and application of the Treaties the law is observed". In the exercise of its jurisdiction, the ECJ should provide interpretations of Union law that can be applied in a uniform manner across the Member States, and provide for the compatibility of Union and national law, including the rules of procedure of the latter.

The preliminary reference procedure was extended by the Lisbon Treaty for the purposes of establishing a framework for increased judicial cooperation between the national courts and the ECJ, to ensure adequate remedies are available, and to promote effective judicial protection and the protection of fundamental rights. Only national courts and tribunals against whose decisions there is no judicial remedy under national law are required to make a reference to the ECJ, and while other courts and tribunals are not so obliged, the Lisbon Treaty has empowered lower courts to refer, a determination that has considerable practical consequences, particularly in the regulation of unfair contract terms. Indeed, almost two-thirds of the cases referred concerning ex officio control and the UCTD have come from first instance courts.

It is important to bear in mind that the determination of whether to request a preliminary ruling from the ECJ (with the exception of where there is an obligation to refer) is for the national courts. Various theories, along with explanations of structural, behavioural (Broberg and Fenger 2014, 37–58) and indeed institutional factors, have been advanced to facilitate understanding of trends in preliminary

[16]The ECJ may also hear appeals on points of law from the General Court, and infringement proceedings initiated by the European Commission.

references from different Member States.[17] As is clear from the data presented below, in relation to the UCTD, preliminary references are being made predominantly by the courts of certain Member States and, in particularly, by courts in Hungary, Romania, Slovakia and especially Spain.[18] By utilising the preliminary reference system, the national courts of these Member States in particular have created a situation whereby the ECJ has been attributed (the possibility to adopt) a role in advancing and refining the contours of the regulation of unfair contract terms and the interpretation of the UCTD in respect of both its substance, that is, predominantly the understanding of unfairness,[19] and the requirements of procedural protection at the national level. To this extent, the preliminary reference system can be said to play a role in facilitating the construction of a bridge between the legislative and judicial development of EU consumer law, on the one hand, and the rights and remedies established at the national level, on the other.

In a number of proceedings that were either initiated before the national courts (or made their way to courts from quasi or extrajudicial entities such as ADR bodies), national judges across the Member States have identified procedural rules that may constitute an obstacle to the examination of potential breaches of consumer rights derived from EU law. To the extent that the national judge has considered that these procedural rules may undermine the courts' implementation of Arts. 6 and 7 UCTD, as transposed in the domestic systems, a number of requests for preliminary rulings have been made to the ECJ concerning their compatibility with EU law. Examples of procedural rules that have been identified as constituting such an obstacle and which have been referred to the ECJ include formalities for bringing a judicial claim (e.g. standing),[20] time limits for the satisfaction of procedural requirements,[21] procedural rules that exclude the possibility to adjudicate certain issues at particular stages of the proceedings,[22] and the rules that govern concurrent proceedings.[23] Thus, the national courts have recognised that in this light, the national procedural systems might undermine the possibility for the national court to examine potential substantive violations of the UCTD, amongst

[17]Amongst others, these determinations have been described as a reflection of legal culture, whether monist or dualist, whether judicial review is engaged (Mattli and Slaughter 1998), as a reflection of the national courts seeking empowerment (Alter 1998), as a reflection of the significance of EU trade for that Member States (Stone Sweet and Brunell 1998), as well as a determination to engage in a type of judicial dialogue (see the contributions in Cafaggi and Law 2017) or political dialogue (Burgorgue-Larsen 2015).

[18]In particular, in Spain, over 55% of referrals concerning the UCTD and relating to its ex officio control—9 of 16 in total—were made from first instance courts. Data collected by the author from the website of the CJEU.

[19]On the substantive test of unfairness, see Case C-237/02 *Freiburger Kommunalbauten* EU:C:2004:209, Case C-240/98-244/98 *Océano Grupo* EU:C:2000:346, Case C-472/10 *Invitel* EU:C:2012:242.

[20]Case C-470/12 *Pohotovost* EU:C:2014:101.

[21]Case C-473/00 *Cofidis* EU:C:2002:705 and Case C-49/14 *Finanmadrid* EU:C:2016:98.

[22]Case C-618/10 *Banco Español, Banesto* EU:C:2012:349.

[23]Case C-415/11 *Aziz* EU:C:2013:164.

other directives, in such a way as to undermine the effective and equivalent enforcement of Union law.[24] Relatedly, returning to the notion of the power imbalance identified above, the national courts have recognised that these procedural rules constitute obstacles that shape the relationship between the parties and affect the possibility for the effective enforcement of EU consumer protection at the domestic level. That is to say, given the imbalances in economic, political and social power—essentially in terms of a lack of knowledge, time and economic resources—consumers are deemed to be less likely to engage their consumer rights of their own motion before their national courts, or even to appear before a court to defend themselves, a consideration that must be engaged by the national judge when applying and interpreting national rules of procedure.

In light of the ECJ's activity, it is worthwhile to identify the trends in the use of the preliminary reference procedure, in the whole and over time, concerning which directives of Union law and which Member States. Empirical data have been gathered from the website of the ECJ concerning preliminary references decided between 2000 and 2016; it is clear from the graph in Fig. 1 that there has been an increase in the number of preliminary references made by the national courts in relation to consumer protection directives generally.

Data also collected from the website of the ECJ indicate that the majority of these references concern the interpretation of the UCTD, or the compatibility of national law with its rules. Indeed, of 92 cases in which judgments were rendered between 2000 and 2016, 52 concern the UCTD (see Fig. 2).

It is also evident that the number of preliminary references concerning the interpretation or compatibility of national law with the UCTD in particular has increased over time, there having been a notable jump post-2008, indeed post-crisis.

A thorough analysis of the jurisprudence indicates that most of these cases concern unfair contract terms in agreements for consumer credit, either for personal loans or mortgages on property.[25] It is indeed clear that preliminary references have been made from certain Member States more than others. The evident outlier is Spain (see Fig. 3).

To recap, there has been an evident increase in the number of references for preliminary rulings concerning consumer protection matters over the past 16 years. Of decisions, 52 of 92 concern the UCTD; moreover, the number of references made has also evidently varied over the past 16 years, falling from nine in 2000 to

[24]While the questions referred are typically framed in terms of whether national procedural rules are compatible with the UCTD, the key questions underpinning the development of the ex officio regulation of consumer law have been the following: What is the character of the civil procedural systems in the Member States? What is the role of the judge/adjudicator? Is it typically adversarial or inquisitorial? Is it based on party disposition or does the judge/adjudicator have more of an investigative role? These issues are discussed in Sect. 5 of this paper.

[25]It is worth noting that data on housing, repossessions and evictions are largely irregular and not collected on the basis of harmonised approaches across the Member States. However, a considerable rise in the number of evictions and repossessions has been identified in a number of EU countries, including Spain (European Commission 2012, 43).

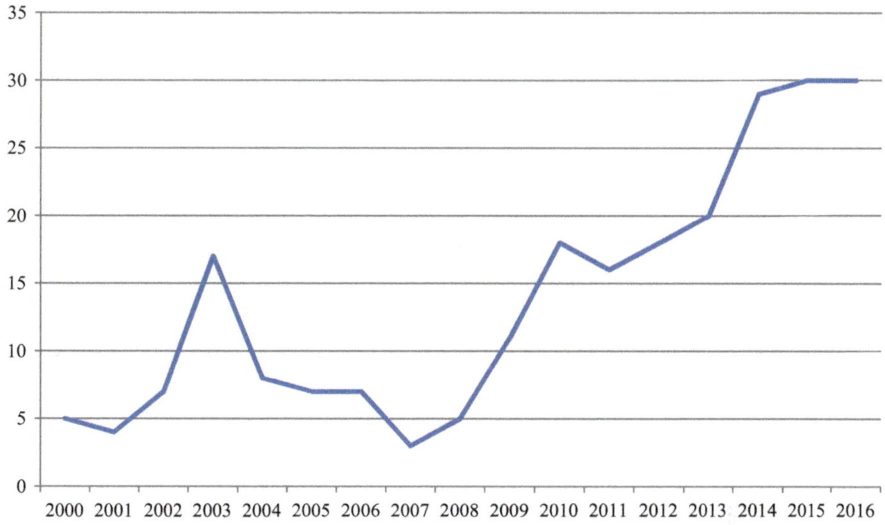

Fig. 1 Number of ECJ decisions from preliminary references concerning consumer protection: 2000–2016. *Source* Curia search for "consumer protection"; preliminary references; 2000–2016

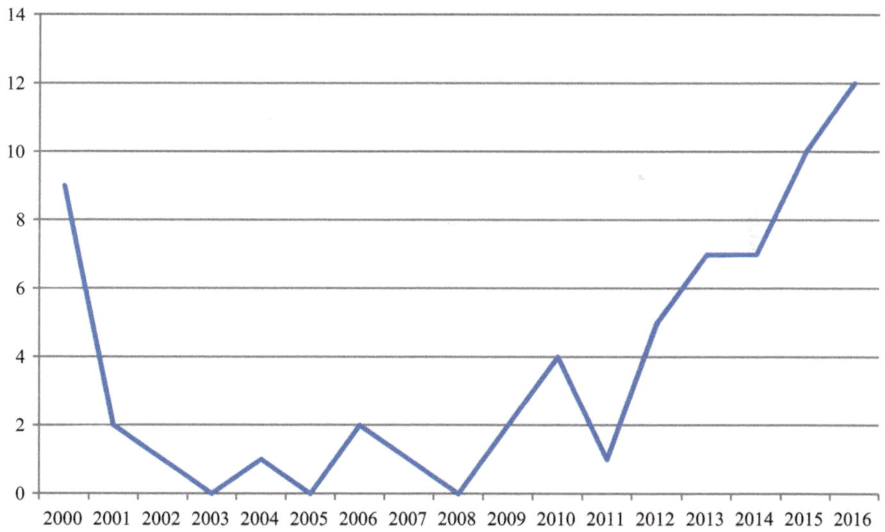

Fig. 2 Number of ECJ decisions from preliminary references concerning the UCTD: 2000–2016. *Source* Curia search by UCTD, per year; 2000–2016

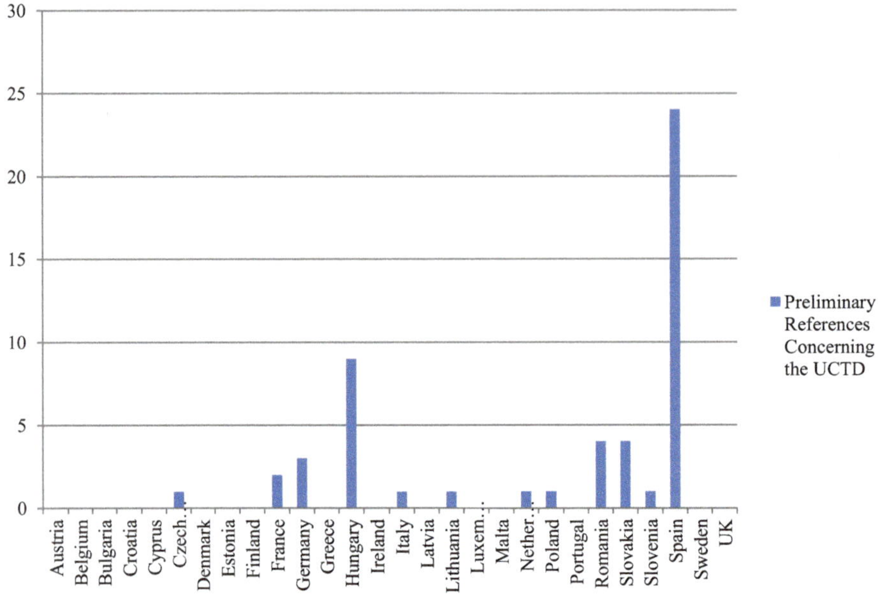

Fig. 3 Number of preliminary references by Member State concerning the UCTD: 2000–2016. *Source* Curia search for "UCTD"; preliminary references; 2000–2016 by Member State

zero in 2008 and rising to 12 in 2016. Finally, the vast majority of these references have been made by Spanish courts, followed closely by those in Hungary, Romania and Slovakia.

4 The ECJ's Proceduralisation of EU Consumer Rights: The Example of the Ex Officio Regulation of Unfair Contract Terms

This section will provide a short overview of the key case law in which the ex officio mechanism has been developed.[26] In the *Océano* case,[27] a reference from Spain (Fig. 3), the ECJ held that national procedural rules should not preclude the national courts from examining of their own motion contract terms that are

[26]It is worth noting that in relation to EU competition law the ECJ has held that the national court should apply EU Treaty law ex officio where the party that would benefit had never advanced their application; the ECJ has held that this obligation does not arise where such an examination would oblige the national court to abandon the rather passive role assigned to it under national civil procedural law (Joined Cases C-430/93 and 431/93 *Van Schijndel/Stichting Pensioenfonds voor Fysiotherapeuten* EU:C:1995:441 paras. 17, 19–22).

[27]Case C-240/98-244/98 *Océano Grupo* EU:C:2000:346.

potentially unfair by virtue of the UCTD. Indeed, it found that the national courts must be empowered to examine potentially unfair terms in consumer contracts. This power of ex officio control was confirmed in *Cofidis*,[28] a reference from the French *Tribunal d'instance de Vienne*, concerning the rules of prescription that limited the possibility for the assessment of unfair terms. The ECJ held that national law cannot prohibit the national court from examining and finding unfairness due to the expiry of a limitation period.

The ECJ subsequently identified a shift in *Mostaza Claro*,[29] a reference from the Spanish *Audiencia Provincial de Madrid*. The ECJ held that national procedural law should provide that the national courts are not only empowered but also obliged to engage in the ex officio control of unfair contract terms. This dictates that when the consumer does not raise the matter of potential unfairness initially in the proceedings (even in arbitration proceedings) but only subsequently in the substantive (judicial) action for the annulment of the arbitral award, the national court must nevertheless "return" to the issue and assess the pertinent term as to its putative unfairness. The mechanism of ex officio control, as established in this two-part test, operates to preclude a wholly passive role on the part of the national court. The key questions are: How is this obligation implemented in national systems? and What does the court understand as its role? This paper will come back to this consideration in the next section by examining the transformations at the national level to which the device of the ex officio control of unfair contract terms has given rise.

Before examining further the key case law of the ECJ, it is worth drawing a connection between the UCTD and the ECJ's reasoning. As noted, Art. 6(1) and Art. 7(1) UCTD are rare procedural provisions in substantive consumer legislation, requiring that the Member States ensure unfair terms are not binding on the consumer and that remedies are available. These articles provide a legislative basis for development of ex officio control, a characteristic of the UCTD that distinguishes it from the other consumer law directives. The ECJ has examined the power imbalance between the parties and considered that the consumer, relative to the trader or supplier, must be understood to be in a weaker position. Indeed, it determined that the existence of this power imbalance and its impact on the effectiveness of EU consumer protection requires that national judges should be empowered to play an active role in order to re-establish equilibrium and ensure that consumers can rely on their interests and rights, regardless of whether they actually invoke them. Taken together, the ECJ has held that if national judges do not examine unfair contract terms of their own motion and do not draw the consequences of a finding of unfairness, that is to say, discard the application of their own motion, the non-binding character of unfair contract terms might remain a purely theoretical concept. This would be the case where consumers do not know of or do not understand their rights, or are otherwise reluctant to act on or invoke them. The rationale is the protection of the weaker party and the establishment of equilibrium

[28]Case C-473/00 *Cofidis* EU:C:2002:705.

[29]Case C-168/05 *Mostaza Claro* EU:C:2006:675.

in respect of power imbalances, a "public interest underlying the protection which the Directive confers on consumers".[30]

Numerous cases have been referred to the ECJ post-*Mostaza Claro*, as the national courts have identified increasingly complex procedural obstacles arising in divergent national procedures and at different stages of the hearing of a dispute; moreover, cases have been referred concerning consumer law directives other than the UCTD.[31] This has led to the extension of the ex officio mechanism and (not entirely successful) attempts to clarify the scope of its operation, and to a deepening of the ECJ's reasoning so as to engage fundamental rights rationales. Via this case law, the ECJ has gradually "scratched away" at a rigid conceptualisation of national procedural autonomy, in light of the principles of equivalence and effectiveness,[32] particularly post-*Mostaza Claro*. While the core issues in each case may be the same—that is to say, at some stage of the hearing of a case the national court is precluded from examining the potentially unfair nature of a contract term—each case generates distinct, substantive and procedural considerations. For example, in the *Asturcom* case,[33] the ECJ held that the national court (or tribunal) hearing an action for the enforcement of an arbitration award which has become final and was made in the absence of the consumer is required to assess whether the arbitration clause in a contract concluded between a seller or supplier and a consumer is unfair, in so far as, under national rules of procedure, it can carry out such an assessment in similar actions of a domestic nature. The national court must ensure the consumer is not bound by the unfair term. Here the emphasis on equivalence is evident. In *Caja de Ahorros*, the Advocate General (AG) raised and for the first time engaged explicitly the economic rationale underpinning contract term regulation and thus demarcated the scope of contract term regulation with reference to the significance of party autonomy in respect of Art. 4(2).[34]

[30]Case C-168/05 *Mostaza Claro* EU:C:2006:675, Judgment, para. 38.

[31]The ECJ has held that the national courts must be empowered to examine possible violations of rights derived from other consumer protection directives. These include: Directive 87/102, amended by Directive 98/7 on consumer credit (Case C-429/05 *Rampion* EU:C:2007:575); Directive 85/577 on doorstep selling (Case C-227/08 *Martin Martin* EU:C:2009:792); Directive 1999/44 on consumer sales (Case C-32/12 *Duarte Hueros* EU:C:2013:637 and Case C-497/13 *Faber* EU:C:2015:357). Here, the focus is on the UCTD and so these cases will not be examined further. Only *Faber* is examined briefly.

[32]To the extent that national rules "cannot be less favourable than those relating to similar actions of a domestic nature nor render virtually impossible or excessively difficult the exercise of rights conferred by Community law": Case C-33/76 *Rewe-Zentral* [1976] ECR 1989, Judgment, para. 13, the limitation–essentially based on the principle of equivalence and effectiveness to be applied, "by reference to the role of that provision in the procedure, its progress and its special features, viewed as a whole, before the various national instances. In the light of that analysis the basic principles of the domestic judicial system, such as protection of the rights of the defence, the principle of legal certainty and the proper conduct of procedure, must, where appropriate, be taken into consideration"; Case C-312/93 *Peterbroeck* [1995] ECR I-4599, Judgment, para. 14.

[33]Case C-40/08 *Asturcom* EU:C:2009:615.

[34]Case C-484/08 *Caja de Ahorros* EU:C:2010:209.

The ECJ then delineated the obligation on the part of the national court in two subsequent cases. In *Pannon*, a case concerning the consumer's challenge to the fairness of a jurisdiction clause and the period within which this can be made, it provided that the national court is obliged to undertake an assessment "where it has available to it the legal and factual elements necessary for that task. Where it considers such a term to be unfair, it must not apply it, except if the consumer opposes that non-application."[35] In *Pénzügyi Lizing*,[36] again concerning a jurisdiction clause, the ECJ considered that the requirement of the national court to examine potential infringements of the UCTD is comprised of a two-part test: firstly, the national court must ascertain whether a contractual term, which is the subject of the dispute before it, falls within the scope of that directive. In a second step, if the term does fall within the scope of the Union legislation, that court must make an assessment "of its own motion, in the light of the requirements of consumer protection laid down by that Directive".[37]

Aziz concerned the limited opportunity for the unfairness of contract terms to be pled in mortgage enforcement proceedings as a defence to the enforcement and eviction that would follow; Spanish procedural law precluded grounds of objection based on the unfairness of a contract term to be advanced in enforcement proceedings. The ECJ held that a court hearing related declaratory proceedings (in which the consumer has brought an action for a declaration that the term is unfair) must be able to grant interim relief (including the staying of the enforcement proceedings) where this is necessary to guarantee the full effectiveness of its final decision on unfairness.[38] The decision not only gave rise to the scope for the ECJ to provide guidance to the national court in its assessment of contract terms to ensure effective protection[39] but also raised significant social considerations (especially in relation to eviction from the home), bringing to the fore the relevance of the constitutionalisation of private law via ECJ jurisprudence, a consequence that will be examined in further detail below.[40] The ECJ has also held that national courts must be able to determine ex officio whether a contract term is unfair in proceedings

[35]Case C-243/08 *Pannon* EU:C:2009:35, Judgment, para. 35.

[36]Case C-137/08 *Pénzügyi Lízing* EU:C:2010:659.

[37]Case C-137/08 *Pénzügyi Lízing* EU:C:2010:659, Judgment, para. 49.

[38]Effectiveness must be measured with reference to the procedural provision in the procedure as a whole.

[39]Case C-415/11 *Aziz* EU:C:2013:164. This criterion for the national court is clear from AG Kokott's Opinion, to the extent that she examined particularly the significance of rules on unilateral determination of the amount owed by the debtor in default, in light of national procedural rules, while the Court predominantly made reference to unfairness deriving from the limitation on the consumer's right to a remedy, per point 1(q) Annex, UCTD. See Micklitz and Reich (2014, 800).

[40]"Hidden constitutionalisation" per Micklitz and Reich (2014, 800), in light of the fact that while neither the AG nor the Court explicitly engaged the respect for housing, as found in Art. 7 CFR, their reasoning did engage constitutional considerations, in the relationship between domestic proceedings and contract law regulation, Opinion, para. 52, and the highlighting of the purpose for which the loan had been made, that is, the purchase of the home; Judgment, para. 61.

for the enforcement of a mortgage, which cannot be limited by a procedural time limit.[41] Similarly highlighting the need to ensure effective protection, the ECJ in *Banco Español*, following the Opinion of the AG, provided that national procedural norms must be deemed to be incompatible with Union legislation where their application renders the achievement of consumer protection established therein "impossible or excessively difficult", and thus violates the effectiveness principle. The Court further held that the national courts must ensure, where they identify an unfair term, that it has no further binding effect, and provide, where possible, for the continuation of the contract.[42] With regard to the contract's continuation, the ECJ has provided that national law which allows a national court, where it finds a contract term to be unfair and that the contract cannot continue without that term, to cure the invalidity of the term by substituting it with a provision of national law that is compatible with Art. 6(1) UCTD.[43]

In the *Kušionová* case,[44] referred from Slovakia, the ECJ held that national law which allows for the recovery of a debt by the extrajudicial enforcement of a charge on immovable property provided as security, which is based on potentially unfair terms, is not necessarily precluded by the UCTD. This will be the case provided that it is not excessively difficult or impossible in practice to protect the consumer debtor's rights; again, the ECJ highlights the effectiveness principle, and, more specifically, it is one of the few cases in which it engaged the right to an effective judicial remedy in Art. 47 Charter of Fundamental Rights of the European Union (CFR) in its reasoning. In *Asbeek Brusse,*[45] the Court clarified that the UCTD applies also to tenancy contracts concluded with professional landlords and held that appellate courts, acting ex officio to enforce public policy considerations, must similarly assess contract terms even if the issue of unfairness was not raised at first instance (equivalence). As to the consequences of unfairness, the ECJ followed *Banco Español* and held that the effective implementation of the directive requires a finding, ensured via national procedural rules, that the term is deemed never to have existed; any other determination must be understood to "weaken the dissuasive effect" of contract term regulation.[46]

The equivalency issue has arisen in a key case which concerns the extension of ex officio control beyond the UCTD.[47] As this paper focuses on the UCTD, this case is only considered briefly to highlight the special significance of the regulation

---

[41]Case C-613/15 *Ibercaja Banco* EU:C:2016:195; see also C-421/14 *Banco Primus* EU: C:2017:60.

[42]Case C-618/10 *Banco Español* EU:C:2012:349, Judgment, para. 65.

[43]Case C-26/13 *Kasler* EU:C:2014:282.

[44]Case C-34/13 *Kušionová* EU:C:2014:2189.

[45]In line with the notion that the national court must have the "legal or factual elements" available, explored in more detail below; Case C-488/11 *Asbeek Brusse* EU:C:2013:341, Judgment, paras. 41, 42. Similarly, in this case, like *Aziz*, noted above, the Court (there being no AG Opinion) raised the "social" issue of the "essential needs" of access to the home; Judgment, para. 32.

[46]Case C-488/11 *Asbeek Brusse* EU:C:2013:341, Judgment, para. 58.

[47]Case C-497/13 *Faber* EU:C:2015:357.

of unfair terms. Mrs. Faber had purchased a second-hand car on the basis of standard terms and conditions; the car later caught fire, was towed by a garage and kept in a yard before being scrapped, with no technical report having been made and without the knowledge of the purchaser. In bringing a claim alleging non-conformity, Mrs Faber did not assert her consumer status, and the court found the prescription period had expired and her claim should be dismissed; on appeal, she did not challenge the absence of consideration of the consumer nature of the contract. The ECJ held that as the consumer is deemed to be in a relatively weak position, the national court must determine of its own motion whether the purchaser may be characterised as a consumer "on the basis of the matters of fact and of law which they have at their disposal or may have at their disposal simply by making a request for clarification".[48] Furthermore, the ECJ held that Art. 5(3) Consumer Sales Directive (CSD), which provides for a presumption of the existence of non-conformity in the period of six months following delivery, must be understood as a provision of public policy, and thus engaged by the national court on an equivalent basis as national public policy, that is to say, ex officio. As the CSD contains no provision similar to Arts. 6 and 7 UCTD, which establish a legislative basis for ex officio control, alternative theoretical provisions have been advanced to explain the ECJ's finding that the national court must examine ex officio whether a purchaser is a consumer.[49] This is particularly significant, as the *Faber* finding—even if, as the author submits—is the correct decision for the purposes of ensuring the effective protection of consumers, provides the basis for the extension of the ex officio obligation across consumer law, and indeed for the spillover (Johnston 2013, 357–394) of this requirement into other areas of mandatory EU law, including, for example, environmental protection, in line with the protection of fundamental rights.

In *Banif Plus*, the ECJ confirmed that the consumer need not raise the issue to initiate an assessment as to unfairness and reiterated that the ex officio control must comply with Art. 47 CFR; rather, per Arts. 6 and 7 UCTD, the court must ensure that both parties are informed and can launch a defence, the assessment being undertaken in consideration of all contract terms.[50] The ECJ has also heard a Spanish reference in which it highlighted that the relevant Spanish jurisdiction rules must not completely preclude access to justice or render the enforcement of Union rights "impossible or excessively difficult" and furthermore that the UCTD should be demarcated in respect of the parties at whom it is aimed. That is to say, it was considered that the effective protection of rights to which it gives rise is aimed at

[48]Case C-497/13 *Faber* EU:C:2015:357, Judgment, para. 44.

[49]For example, Lenaerts et al. (2014, para. 4.40) refer to the principle of sincere cooperation (Art. 4 (3) TEU).

[50]Case C-472/11 *Banif Plus Bank* EU:C:2013:88, Judgment, paras. 28–30 and para. 41.

consumers and does not extend to consumer organisations (nor can the latter's budgetary difficulties be relevant with regard to the compatibility of national rules on the founding of jurisdiction).[51]

In addition to the extension of the ex officio obligation beyond the UCTD, another problem arises with respect to the extension of the obligation beyond courts to extrajudicial bodies, and the relationship between these institutions in ensuring consumer protection. The ECJ has held that the ex officio obligation applies to national courts engaged in the enforcement of payment orders, where the relevant decision is deemed to be a judicially enforceable instrument. For example, in *Finanmadrid*, it found that if the extrajudicial body (in this case, the Spanish *secretario judicial*) is not empowered to examine the unfairness of the penalty clause ex officio, then the court seised in the execution proceedings of the payment order should be obliged.[52] Similarly, the ECJ has held that the UCTD must be interpreted as precluding national procedural law, like that of Spain, which does not allow the court to review of its own motion *in limine litis*, in the subsequent enforcement procedure, the judicial enforceable instrument—an order made by the court bringing the order-for-payment proceedings to an end in the absence of any objections—in order to ascertain whether there are unfair terms.[53] *Sanchez Morcillo* was a case concerning a notarial act signed by a consumer and creditor for a loan secured by a mortgage on a property, which included a clause for accelerated payment. Spanish procedural law allowed an appeal to be brought against a decision which, upholding the objection raised by a debtor, terminates the enforcement proceedings; however it did not, by contrast, allow the debtor whose objection has been dismissed to bring an appeal against the judgment at first instance ordering the enforcement procedure to be carried out. The ECJ, also invoking Art. 47 CFR, held that Art. 7 UCTD must be interpreted as precluding such a national enforcement regime.[54] This decision, and the consequences to which it has given rise in the Spanish procedural system, is discussed in further detail in the next section.

This section has aimed to briefly outline and trace the ECJ's development of the ex officio monitoring of contract terms in the national courts, from its recognition of a power on the part of the national court to the imposition of an obligation. While it is clear that the ECJ has established the application of the ex officio mechanism in relation to unfairness in a number of cases, with regard to different procedures and

---

[51]Case C-413/12 *ACICL v. Anuntis* EU:C:2013:800, rejecting the scope for a consumer organisation to bring an action for an injunction in the courts of its place of business.

[52]Case C-49/14 *Finanmadrid* EU:C:2016:98; recent Spanish legislative reform aimed to ensure this ex officio control would be exercised at the earlier stage (i.e. obliges *the secretario judicial*) per the law on civil procedure of 2000, amended by Ley 1/2013 (LEC).

[53]Case C-122/14 *Aktiv Kapital* EU:C:2016:486.

[54]Especially one which provides that mortgage enforcement proceedings cannot be stayed by the court of first instance, which in its final decision can at most award compensation in respect of the consumer-debtor's damage, where that debtor cannot appeal against a decision dismissing his objection to enforcement, while the seller/supplier-creditor may bring an appeal against a decision terminating proceedings or ordering the disapplication of an unfair term.

at different stages of these procedures, numerous issues are still to be resolved, particularly relating to disputes arising beyond unfair contract terms and in respect of extrajudicial and alternative dispute resolution bodies. This is reflected in the fact that at the end of 2016, a further 20 requests for preliminary rulings were pending before the ECJ concerning ex officio control of consumer law.

5 The Transformation of Procedural Protection at the National Level

This section will set out key examples of the types of changes that have been made within the Member States in light of the ECJ's ex officio case law. The combination of the EU's limited competences to legislate for civil procedure and the principle of national procedural autonomy has ensured the maintenance of the diversity of the Member States. It is worth beginning with a brief overview of the framework of national civil proceedings.[55] Across the Member States, civil proceedings, including the roles of the litigants and the judge, are shaped, either explicitly or implicitly, by the principle of party disposition (Van Rhee 2005). This generally dictates that the initiation of proceedings, the subject matter of the proceedings and the relief sought, i.e. the *petitum* of the claim, are matters for the parties, by which the court is bound. Moreover, typically, the parties must advance the facts supporting the claim, the evidence supporting the facts, as well as the legal arguments that make up the action. Across the Member States, national courts may be more or less inquisitorial in respect of the determination of facts and the identification of the truth underpinning the dispute.[56] Increasingly, courts are also attributed a role in case management. These characteristics are enjoined by those of *iura novit curia* and *da mihi factum dabo tibi jus*, whereby the national court itself may be empowered to identify the parties' arguments, to identify the law of its own motion, to qualify the nature of the dispute and advance the arguments not advanced by the parties. Each of these considerations is dependent on the relevant national procedural culture. For example, in Spain, a very rigid conception of party disposition exists, which seems to underpin the number of cases referred to the ECJ.[57]

The national procedural systems are shaped by the principle of national procedural autonomy; the ex officio control of contract terms in principle operates in line with the procedural autonomy of the Member States but in practice limits it in line with the principles of equivalence and effectiveness (Hess 2010, para. 5 et seq.). That is to say, these principles have allowed the ECJ to build on Arts. 6 and 7 UCTD to provide for a balance to rigid and overly formalistic procedural rules. The fact that preliminary references are made from national courts on the basis of very

[55]For further detail, see Hess and Taelman (2017, para. 288 et seq.).

[56]See further, Hess and Taelman (2017, para. 298 et seq.).

[57]For an overview of the Spanish system in relation to consumers, see Gascón Inchausti (2005).

specific disputes, as well as the diversity of the Member States' procedural regimes, generates a considerable level of uncertainty both as to its operation and as to the impact in the national system. Unless the national courts actually engage the duty to engage ex officio unfairness, the effectiveness of the UCTD, which the mechanism aims to promote, will not be satisfied. Two sets of impacts are examined. The first relates to the way in which the ex officio obligation has been implemented in the national legal systems. The second concerns what is required of the national courts.

At the EU level, via two studies undertaken for the European Commission in relation to the Fitness Check of Consumer and Marketing Law, it has been proposed that there is a need for an increased awareness of ex officio control and for increased guidance and training to be provided to national judges. Moreover, in this report, it has been proposed that the ex officio control of EU consumer law, and at least the UCTD, might be codified at the EU level, in order to ensure the national courts are adequately and appropriately informed (Max Planck Institute 2017, para. 47 et seq.; Civic Consulting 2017, 91; European Commission 2017, 27, 28). In certain Member States, changes have been introduced via the code of civil procedure or specific legislation on procedural law. This includes Spain and Slovakia. In other Member States including the UK, Latvia, Lithuania and France, changes have been introduced in substantive law statutes. Still others, such as Ireland and Austria, have rather relied on judicial practice. It is possible to identify one Member State—Slovenia—in which no identifiable change has been made in order to ensure that ex officio control of the UCTD is understood to constitute an obligation that binds the national courts (Max Planck Institute 2017; Civic Consulting 2017, 90). A lack of clarity has, however, been identified in almost all Member States (Max Planck Institute 2017). A specific example can be given of the nature of changes in one particular national system, namely Spain. The examples of *Aziz* and the two *Sanchez Morcillo*[58] cases provide an indication of how the ECJ case law has had a direct impact on the Spanish system of civil procedure, via the higher and lower Spanish courts and the Spanish legislature. The *Aziz* case gave rise to a change to the Spanish Code of Civil Procedure. Following the ECJ's declaration that the existing procedural law was incompatible with EU law, the Spanish legislature enacted Ley 1/2013 amending the Code and related laws. Via this new law, the Spanish legislature introduced a new basis upon which mortgage debtors could object—within the execution proceedings, which was not previously possible—on the basis of the existence of an unfair term in the mortgage loan agreement. This had the aim of increasing the protection afforded to debtors. Per Art. 695(4) of the Code of Civil Procedure, if the mortgage debtor objected on the basis of an unfair term, separate (oral) proceedings were initiated within which the judge could—if he or she considered the objection to be relevant and well founded—suspend the enforcement of the mortgage and bring the execution to an end. Otherwise, the judge could dismiss the incidental proceedings and provide for the enforcement to

[58]Case C-169/14 *Sanchez Morcillo I* EU:C:2014:2099 and Case C-539/14 *Sanchez Morcillo II* EU:C:2015:508.

continue. Subsequently the issue that arose in the *Sanchez Morcillo* cases concerned the fact that while the creditor could appeal against the finding of unfairness, the debtor could not appeal to the finding that the objection was not well founded. The first instance court—the Tribunal of Aviles—hearing the dispute, advanced a number of questions before the Spanish Constitutional Court concerning whether this provision was compatible with the principle of equality; the Constitutional Court refused to entertain the question of constitutionality, considering that the lower court had not established why the response was necessary to resolve the dispute before it.[59] At the same time, the Audencia Provencial de Castellon heard an appeal against the decision of the first instance court of Castellon, in which the consumer's objection to the enforcement of a notarial act (allowing the creditor to demand the payment of the entire loan, ordinary and default interest and the sale of the property) was rejected. In this first instance decision, neither the court nor the debtor had raised the issue of unfairness. The appellate court referred the question of compatibility of Art. 659(4) with Art. 7 UCTD and Art. 47 CFR to the ECJ. The ECJ's judgment rested on the principle of effectiveness, finding the Spanish procedural system to be incompatible with Art. 47, to the extent that the system undermined the protection afforded to the consumer debtor and promoted the imbalance in power between the parties.

On the basis of the ECJ's judgment, the Spanish legislature amended Art. 695(4) with the Real Decreto Ley 11/2014; in so doing, it allowed an appeal to be made by the debtor following the rejection of his objection as to the existence of unfairness but limited the possibility for appeal to a complaint based on EU law, and not to all possible objections. The Audencia Provinial de Castellon did not consider this reform to be an adequate implementation of the ECJ's judgment. It then made a second reference, considering that Spanish procedural law violated the right to effective judicial protection, the equality of arms, the right to housing and the right to private and family life, and in particular Art. 1(q) of the Annex to the UCTD.[60] The ECJ considered that the amendments to Art. 695(4) of the Code of Civil Procedure did provide consumers with a satisfactory remedy per Art. 7(1) UCTD, as it allowed for evaluation and for the possibility of an appeal on the part of the consumer (thereby accepting a limitation of the right to appeal); moreover, the ECJ considered that the system was in compliance with the fundamental rights mentioned by the national court.[61] These three cases together highlight the roles of the

[59]AATC 70/2014 and 71/2014, of 10 March 2014 and AATC 111/2014, 112/2014, and 113/2014, of 8 April 2014.

[60]Which provides that terms which have the effect of "excluding or hindering the consumer's right to take legal action or exercise any other legal remedy, particularly by requiring the consumer to take disputes exclusively to arbitration not covered by legal provisions, unduly restricting the evidence available to him or imposing on him a burden of proof which, according to the applicable law, should lie with another party to the contract" may be regarded as unfair.

[61]It also found that the system did not violate the fundamental right to effective judicial protection, as it allowed for the opportunity for evaluation of the terms before the enforcement proceedings were finalised. With regard to the equality of arms, the ECJ held that for the purposes of the

national courts and the ECJ in engaging in a type of judicial dialogue, by which the national legislature will be required to amend and further clarify existing procedural law, in line not only with the UCTD but also with the protection of fundamental rights.

The ex officio case law of the ECJ has led to a shift—or at least, a push towards a shift—in legal cultures, particularly in certain Member States, largely depending on the more or less active role of the national judge within that system: while there are common law judges "who elaborate rules without legislative guidance based on the doctrine of precedent", and civil law judges "whose only source of authority flows from national legal codes", it is also the case that "both systems contain room for yet a third feature of national legal culture: relative judicial activism or restraint" (Mattli and Slaughter 1996). With regard to what ex officio control of the UCTD requires of the national courts, it can be said that the national court must examine EU consumer law (as transposed into national law), assess compliance and draw relevant consequences of its own motion, regardless of whether the consumer party has invoked applicable interests and rights. This obligation goes beyond *iura novit curia*. The national court has a duty to examine potential unfairness of its own motion and need not wait for the consumer's initiative,[62] where it has the necessary legal and factual elements necessary for such an assessment. However, as confirmed in the *Banif Plus* case, the ex officio obligation does not undermine entirely the principles that shape the national systems; in line with Art. 47 CFR, it must operate in a way that respects the principle of *audi alteram partem* (as such, via ex officio control of unfairness, the national judge should advise the parties of his or her assessment and then allow them both to react, i.e. both sides should be listened to).[63] The ECJ's case law—and particularly, its engagement of social considerations in its reasoning—has nevertheless led to a transformation from a negative assessment on the part of the national adjudicator (to ensure the exercise of rights is not impossible or excessively difficult) to the need for a positive one (to ensure that national remedies are satisfactory to ensure effective protection). This might require, for example, that the adjudicator introduce new remedies which are not currently in existence in national procedural law, a reflection of Art. 19(1) TEU which provides that the "Member States shall provide remedies sufficient to ensure effective legal protection in the fields covered by Union law."

Ex officio therefore has the effect of reframing the power of the national courts. Two avenues for the future development of the mechanism remain open, and one potential consequence arises where the national court does not satisfy the pertinent requirements underpinning this procedural protection. Firstly, the ECJ has indicated that as a procedural mechanism of protection, the ex officio control of consumer law should be supplemented with a proportionality assessment. This can be said to be a

---

UCTD, it is enough that the consumer can appeal to an objection based on unfairness; all others fall outside the scope of the directive and were not for the Court to evaluate.

[62]Case 618/10 *Banco Español* EU:C:2012:349.

[63]Case C-312/14 *Banif Plus* EU:C:2015:794, Judgment, paras. 29, 30.

further reflection of the constitutionalisation of European private law, integrating market and social dynamics. The constitutional underpinnings of ex officio control were, firstly, engaged by AG Trstenjak in *Asturcom* where she considered that the power of national courts to regulate ex officio unfair contract terms has its basis in the right to be heard, in Arts. 6 and 13 ECHR, and the right to effective judicial protection in Art. 47 CFR. Moreover, in *Aziz*, the Court explicitly engaged the relevant provisions of the ECHR and the CFR (Arts. 38, 47 CFR and Arts. 6 and 13 ECHR) and also highlighted the social consequences of the lack of effective consumer protection, namely the loss of a family home. Building on this reasoning, in the *Kušionová* case,[64] the ECJ highlighted the right to respect for private and family life in Art. 76 CFR, and held that the proportionality of the measures taken—the remedy of interim relief, rendered in favour of the consumer debtor to avoid his eviction from the family home—should be taken into account and analysed by the national court. For the ECJ, the possibility for national courts to adopt such measures was deemed to be adequate and effective.[65]

Secondly, a limit of the mechanism of ex officio control at its current stage of development concerns the lack of clarity as to whether its application extends beyond the UCTD and beyond the decisions of national courts to extrajudicial dispute resolution bodies, including notaries[66] and the *secretario judicial*. In relation to notaries, in the *ERSTE* case,[67] the Court held that ex officio control falls within the scope of the exercise of the judicial function and does not apply to the notarial function. The UCTD does not make explicit provision in respect of the role of the notary—or indeed other non-judicial bodies—with regard to contract term review. As such, the matter seems to be one for the procedural autonomy of the Member States: "[I]n the absence of harmonisation of national mechanisms for enforcement under EU law, and the role assigned to notaries within it, it is for the national legal order of each Member State to establish such rules, in accordance with the principles of procedural autonomy" and in line with the principles of equivalence and effectiveness.[68]

As noted above, further uncertainty arises in relation to the Spanish *secretario judicial*. Under Spanish procedural law, an order issued by the *secretario judicial* is deemed to be an enforceable instrument with *res judicata* force. As the ECJ had held in *Banco Español de Crédito* and *Sánchez Morcillo*, outlined above, effective protection is only deemed to exist if the national procedural rules permit the assessment ex officio of whether a term of the contract at issue is unfair, either before the order

[64]Case C-34/13 *Kušionová* EU:C:2014:2189.

[65]Moreover, in the cases of Case C-381/14 *Sales Sinués* EU:C:2016:909 and Case C-119/15 *Biuro* EU:C:2016:987, the ECJ held that the proportionality of national measures must be taken into account, particularly in the latter case where the issue concerned the balance between effective abstract control and the need to respect the right to be heard.

[66]On the understanding of notaries for the purposes of cross-border dispute resolution, see Mantovani (2017).

[67]Case C-32/14 *ERSTE* EU:C:2015:637.

[68]Case C-32/14 *ERSTE* EU:C:2015:637, Judgment, para. 49.

for payment proceedings is made or before its execution. This issue has arisen in two cases (thus far) and is at the heart of a number of other cases either currently pending before the ECJ. In *Finanmadrid*, the reference to the ECJ was made by a Spanish court. The ECJ found that where there is no possibility for the assessment of potential unfairness—on the one hand, because the court could only intervene where the amount claimed was incorrect or where the debtor challenged the claim, and, on the other hand, because the *secretario judicial* was only competent to check formalities and not substance—the procedural system cannot be understood to provide for the effective protection anticipated by the UCTD. *Panicello* was a case subsequently referred to the ECJ, not by a court but by the *secretario judicial*. The case concerned the *jura de cuentas*, a procedure for the recovery of unpaid legal fees, which could be heard exclusively by the *secretario judicial*. The question then arose as to whether the *secretario judicial* was a court or tribunal for Art. 267 TFEU purposes, which went to the heart of whether the request for a preliminary ruling should be deemed to be admissible. While the AG declared the reference to be admissible, the Court did not. For A. G. Kokott, as the decision of the *secretario judicial* cannot be appealed and is enforceable immediately, though is without *res judicata* force, its enforcement can be considered to be equivalent to the enforcement of a judicial decision. As such, as neither the *secretario judicial* nor the court enforcing the decision can examine potential unfairness ex officio, nor can the consumer advance a defence to halt the execution, the consumer's rights via the UCTD and in respect of Art. 47 CFR are undermined.[69] This issue for the moment remains open and will need to be examined further, particularly as the Court in *Panicello* refused to accept the admissibility of the reference.[70]

Turning to the third consequence arising from the ECJ case law brings the discussion to the issue of state liability. The scope for state liability[71] to arise where the national court fails to examine a potential violation of the UCTD of its own motion came to the fore in *Tomášová*. *Tomášová* was a case in which a credit agreement had been concluded in 2007 for €232 via a standard form contract which provided for an interest rate of 91.25% for late payments and a clause providing that all disputes should be referred to arbitration. The debtor was a relatively poor pensioner with limited school education. A dispute arose following non-payment and an arbitral tribunal—located 400 km from Mrs. Tomášová's home—found in favour of the creditor. The creditor then tried to execute the decision before the Slovakian court. In 2010, Tomášová brought an action for damages of €2000, alleging a breach of EU law (namely, that the arbitral decision had been made on the basis of an abusive arbitral clause, which the arbitral tribunal and the court had failed to assess). This was rejected by the court on the basis that she had not used all the paths at her disposition to challenge the finding and that as the execution procedure was not yet concluded, the damage could not yet have been calculated.

[69]Case C-503/15 *Panicello* EU:C:2016:696, Opinion of AG Kokott, paras. 104 and 138.

[70]Case C-503/15 *Panicello* EU:C:2017:126.

[71]Case C-168/15 *Tomášová* EU:C:2016:602.

She appealed, and the appellate court annulled the judgment and sent the case back to the district court, which made a reference to the ECJ on the issue of the existence of state liability. The ECJ reiterated that the rules for the assessment of damage as a consequence of a breach of EU law are matters of national law, to be applied in line with the principles of effectiveness and equivalence. Moreover, and importantly, the ECJ considered that state liability could not arise in the *Tomášová* circumstances on the basis of the date on which the case was initially heard; that is to say, the ECJ held that the obligation for the national courts to assess potential violations of the UCTD of their own motion was concretised only subsequently in the *Pannon* case. As such, the ECJ left open the possibility for *Köbler*-like[72] state liability to be established in cases heard post-*Pannon*.

6 Concluding Remarks

From the analysis above, it becomes clear that in light of the framework of EU consumer protection, the national courts have been actively engaged in identifying national procedural rules that may undermine the possibility for the court to assess potential infringements of EU consumer law. Via the preliminary reference procedure, these issues have come before the ECJ, which has established and developed the mechanism of ex officio control as a means of procedural protection for consumers. This mechanism has been fostered by the ECJ through the case law which has been set out and examined above, being initially established as a power and subsequently as an obligation on the part of the national court, initially in relation to the UCTD and subsequently extending to other areas of consumer law. The lack of explicit competence in Union law for making such inroads into national procedural autonomy[73] can be understood to have required that the ECJ use the above-mentioned general principles of EU law—that is, of effectiveness and equivalence—to empower the national judge where, per the judge's own national law, the judge does not have such procedural tools at his or her disposal; or, read another way, to use fundamental rights protections as a mechanism to make inroads into national civil procedure, where it is deemed insufficient and unsatisfactory. For this reason, it is important to note that this is one domain of EU law in which the ECJ has been accused of developing its own role in an area in which it may be deemed to be activist; this is so even if this might be conceived as the Europeanisation of national civil procedure in line with a dialogue-based

[72]Case C-224/01 *Köbler* EU:C:2003:513.

[73]Challenging the notion that procedural autonomy has ever concretely existed, see Bobek (2011, 305–324).

approach,[74] or indeed a trialogue with the national legislatures, initiated by the national courts and facilitated for the purposes of protecting the weakest and least empowered consumers.

References

Alter K (1998) Explaining national court acceptance of European court jurisprudence: a critical evaluation of theories of legal integration. In: Slaughter AM, Stone Sweet A, Weiler JHH (eds) The European court and national courts—doctrine and jurisprudence. Hart, Oxford, pp 227–252

Bobek M (2011) Why there is no principle of procedural autonomy of the member states. In: de Witte B, Micklitz HW (eds) The European court of justice and the autonomy of the member states. Intersentia, Antwerp, pp 305–324

Broberg M, Fenger N (2014) Preliminary references to the European court of justice, 2nd edn. Oxford University Press, Oxford

Burgorgue-Larsen L (2015) The constitutional dialogue in Europe: a "political" dialogue. Eur J Curr Legal Issues 21

Cafaggi F, Law S (eds) (2017) Judicial cooperation in European private law. Elgar, Cheltenham

Civic Consulting (ed) (2017) Study prepared for the European Commission: study for the fitness check of EU consumer and marketing law, final report. Civic Consulting, Brussels

Dougan M (2011) The vicissitudes of life at the coalface: remedies and procedures for enforcing EU law before the national courts. In: Craig PP, de Búrca G (eds) The evolution of EU law, 2nd edn. Oxford University Press, Oxford, pp 407–438

Ebers M (2008) Unfair contract terms directive. In: Schulte-Nölke H et al (eds) Consumer law compendium: the consumer acquis and its transposition in the member states. Sellier, München, pp 197–261

European Commission (2012) EU Employment and social situation quarterly review

European Commission (2017) Commission staff working document, report on the fitness check of EU consumer and marketing law. SWD (2017) 208 final

European Parliament (2013) Unfair contract terms in EU law: unfair terms directive and common European sales law. 130624REV1, 19 Sept 2013

Gascón Inchausti F (2005) La protección de los consumidores en el proceso civil español. Available at http://eprints.ucm.es/23856/. Accessed 7 June 2018

Hess B (2010) Europäisches Zivilprozessrecht. CF Müller, Heidelberg

Hess B, Taelman P (2017) Consumer actions before national courts. In: Max Plank Institute (ed) Study prepared for the European Commission: evaluation study of national procedural laws in terms of their impact on the free circulation of judgments and on the equivalence and effectiveness of the procedure protection of consumers. Max Planck Institute, Luxembourg

Johnston A (2013) 'Spillovers' from EU law into national law: (Un)intended consequences for private law relationships. In: Leczykiewicz D, Weatherill S (eds) The involvement of EU law in private law relationships. Hart, Oxford, pp 357–394

Lenaerts K et al (eds) (2014) EU procedural law. Oxford University Press, Oxford

Mantovani M (2017) Notaries as adjudicators? The circulation of notarial orders for payment under the Brussels Ibis Regulation (On file with the author)

[74]In Case C-137/08 *Pénzügyi Lizing* EU:C:2010:659, AG Trstenjak highlighted the significance of the dialogue between the courts and indicated the significance of the extent to which national civil procedure might be affected by the ECJ's case law.

Mattli W, Slaughter AM (1996) Constructing the European community legal system from the ground up: the role of individual litigants and national courts. Jean Monnet working paper

Mattli W, Slaughter AM (1998) The role of national courts in the process of European integration: accounting for judicial preferences and constraints. In: Slaughter AM, Stone sweet A, Weiler JHH (eds) The European court and national courts—doctrine and jurisprudence. Hart, Oxford, pp 253–276

Max Plank Institute (ed) (2017) Study prepared for the European Commission: evaluation study of national procedural laws in terms of their impact on the free circulation of judgments and on the equivalence and effectiveness of the procedure protection of consumers. Max Planck Institute, Luxembourg

Micklitz HW (1993) AGB-Gesetz und die Richtlinie über mißbräuchliche Vertragsklauseln in Verbraucherverträgen. ZEuP 522

Micklitz HW, Reich N (2014) The court and sleeping beauty: the revival of the UCTD. Common Market Law Rev 51:771–808

Reich N (2007) Horizontal liability in EC law: hybridization of remedies for compensation in case of breaches of EC rights. Common Market Law Rev 44:705–742

Reich N (2010) The interrelation between rights and duties in EU law. Reflections on the state of liability law in the multilevel governance system of the Union: is there a need for a more coherent approach in European private law? Yearb Eur Law 29:112–163

Stone Sweet A, Brunell T (1998) The European court and the national courts: a statistical analysis of preliminary references, 1961–1995. J Eur Public Policy 5:66–97

Storskrubb E (2008) Civil procedure and EU law: a policy area uncovered. Oxford University Press, Oxford

Van Rhee CH (ed) (2005) European traditions in civil procedure. Intersentia, Antwerp

Stephanie Law Senior Research Fellow of the Max Planck Institute Luxembourg. Former Post-doctoral Research Fellow, Faculty of Law, McGill University, Montréal (The Leverhulme Trust funding), Canada. Ph.D. from the European University Institute, Florence, Italy. During her doctoral research, she was a Visiting Scholar at Columbia Law School and a stagiaire in the Cabinet of Judge Christopher Vajda at the CJEU. Fellow of the HEC-NYU Public Interest Clinic and a member of the Academic Research Panel of Blackstone Chambers.

Safeguarding the Right to an Impartial Tribunal by Means of Challenging the Judge

Fokke Fernhout, Erwin Giesen and Oscar Vranken

Abstract The requirement of an impartial tribunal, as foreseen in Art. 6 ECHR, is the same for each Member State and the absence of a margin of appreciation makes it impossible to deviate from that requirement. However, the way to accomplish this objective is left to the contracting states. This implementation discretion has resulted in different challenge procedures within the EU Member States. It turns out that the differences cover all aspects of these procedures, including the ground on which a challenge may be based, the time limit within which the challenge has to be submitted and the judicial authority that has to decide on it. In this contribution, a method of assessing the predicted (a priori) effectiveness of such challenge procedures will be described. The method is based on a comparative research of characteristics of challenge procedures and a survey among lawyers and law students to establish the relative importance of each of these characteristics. The method is applied to the challenge procedures in the codes of civil procedure of 25 EU Member States.

F. Fernhout (✉) · E. Giesen · O. Vranken
Faculty of Law, Maastricht University, Maastricht, The Netherlands
e-mail: fokke.fernhout@maastrichtuniversity.nl

E. Giesen
e-mail: e.giesen@student.maastrichtuniversity.nl

O. Vranken
e-mail: o.vranken@student.maastrichtuniversity.nl

A. Uzelac and C. H. van Rhee (eds.), *Transformation of Civil Justice*,
Ius Gentium: Comparative Perspectives on Law and Justice 70,
https://doi.org/10.1007/978-3-319-97358-6_17

1 Introduction

All Member States of the European Union are parties to the European Convention on Human Rights (ECHR) and thus have the obligation to abide by the rules set forth therein.[1] Art. 6(1) ECHR requires, *inter alia*, that a tribunal falling within its scope should be independent and impartial. One procedural safeguard that is universally used by EU Member States is the ability of a party to challenge a judge whose impartiality is doubted by that party. Although this procedure is known under different names,[2] it seeks to accomplish the same objective in every Member State. If there is a legitimate reason for one of the parties to suspect a judge of being (subjectively or objectively) biased, then that party may seek the replacement of that judge.

The requirement of an impartial tribunal is the same for each Member State and the absence of a margin of appreciation makes it impossible to deviate from that requirement. However, the way to accomplish this objective is left to the contracting states. The European Court of Human Rights (ECtHR) determines whether or not the result of an impartial tribunal has been attained, but it does not prescribe the means by which the states have to obtain that result. The contracting states to the ECHR therefore have a significant degree of freedom to establish their own procedural rules with regard to the challenging of judges. The only condition is that the procedural rules fulfil their purpose effectively.[3]

Therefore, although the main objective of the challenge procedure is the same in the Member States, the way to accomplish the objective is not. When comparing the challenge regulations of EU Member States, one can distinguish certain procedural elements that recur in many or even all national challenge procedures, but the states tend to implement these elements in different ways. These differences in implementation could potentially influence the degree to which litigating parties can effectively challenge a biased judge in a particular state. By extension, the quality of a challenge procedure influences the degree to which states comply with the requirement of an impartial tribunal as imposed by Art. 6 ECHR.

In this contribution, a method of assessing the predicted (a priori) effectiveness of challenge procedures will be described and applied to the challenge procedures in the codes of civil procedure of 25 EU Member States.[4] The application of this

[1]This contribution is based on a research report written by the last two authors under the supervision of the first author. The title of the report is 'Safeguarding the Right to an Impartial Tribunal by means of Challenging the Judge: A comparative study of challenge procedures in the European Union', Report Maastricht University, The Netherlands, 2017. The report contains the full results of the research, including all challenge regulations that were studied. A copy of the report will be provided upon request.

[2]The terms 'challenge', 'recusal', 'removal' and 'disqualification' are used as equivalents.

[3]*Colozza v. Italy* (Application 9024/80), NJ (Reporter of Dutch case law) 1986, 685, European Court of Human Rights, 12 February 1985, Sec. 30.

[4]The research on which this contribution is based focused on the EU Member States following the civil law tradition. Whenever reference is made herein to 'the EU Member States' the United Kingdom, Ireland and Cyprus are not taken into consideration, unless explicitly stated otherwise.

method results in a 'scoreboard' which expresses the predicted effectiveness of a challenge procedure in a numerical score on a scale from 0 to 100. The higher the number, the more effective a procedure is considered to be. The basis of this ranking is predicted effectiveness, not objective effectiveness. It would thus be impossible to make definitive statements about conformity with Art. 6 ECHR based on this ranking alone. It would, however, be safe to say that, in general, low ranking states do have, at least as far as their challenge procedure is concerned, a lesser degree of Art. 6 ECHR conformity than high ranking states.

Section 2 will discuss the requirement of an impartial tribunal. In Sect. 3, an overview is given of the challenge procedures of EU Member States, breaking these procedures down into essential elements and describing them with respect to these elements. This will result in comparative tables for some of the most striking features of challenge procedures. In Sect. 4, a survey is described on the basis of which the relative weight of these essential elements can be assessed. This leads to the 'scoreboard' mentioned above. Application to the specific challenge procedures of EU Member States yields the table that is the subject of Sect. 5. Conclusions drawn from these results will be presented in the final section.

2 Art. 6(1) ECHR and the Requirement of an Impartial Tribunal

2.1 Applicability of Art. 6 ECHR in Civil Proceedings

Art. 6 ECHR imposes a positive obligation on contracting states to ensure the individual right of litigating parties to a fair trial. The individual rights listed in Art. 6(1) ECHR are applicable in cases where 'civil rights and obligations' are determined. To establish this, it must be ascertained

> whether there was a dispute ("contestation") over a "right" which can be said, at least on arguable grounds, to be recognised under domestic law. The dispute must be genuine and serious; it may relate not only to the existence of a right but also to its scope and the manner of its exercise; and the outcome of the proceedings must be directly decisive for the right in question. Finally, the right must be civil in character.[5]

If these general criteria are met, Art. 6 is, in principle, applicable.[6]

Art. 6 ECHR primarily concerns courts of first instance; it does not explicitly require the existence of courts of further instance. If, however, a contracting state has chosen to establish a court of appeal or a court of cassation, then these courts

[5] *M.S. v. Sweden* (Application 20837/92), European Court of Human Rights, 27 August 1997, Sec. 47.

[6] For a more elaborate overview on the applicability of Art. 6 ECHR in civil cases, see: Council of Europe (2013), Right to a fair trial (civil limb).

must also provide fundamental guarantees, including impartiality.[7] If there is, indeed, a court system with multiple instances, then the ECtHR, for the purpose of determining conformity with Art. 6(1) ECHR, takes the entirety of the proceedings into consideration.[8]

2.2 Objective and Subjective Impartiality

The ECtHR has repeatedly made the distinction between objective and subjective impartiality in its case law.[9] Whereas subjective impartiality relates to the personal conviction and behaviour of a particular judge, objective impartiality focusses on whether the tribunal itself and, among other aspects, its composition offered sufficient guarantees to exclude any legitimate doubt in respect of its impartiality.[10]

While the degree of objective impartiality tells us nothing about the actual presence of bias or prejudice inside the mind of the judge ruling on the case, the ECtHR still deems the appearance of bias due to objective facts and circumstances important enough to constitute a breach of Art. 6(1) ECHR.[11]

The ECtHR has created different methods to test whether the requirements for both objective and subjective impartiality are fulfilled. Specifically, for the subjective test, the Court holds the presumption that judges are impartial unless there is proof of the contrary.[12] The party who submits a challenge will therefore have to prove that a judge is indeed biased towards him or her. With regard to the type of proof required, the Court has, for example, sought to ascertain whether a judge has displayed hostility or has arranged to have a case assigned to himself or herself for personal reasons.[13]

The objective test is significantly easier to satisfy. In order to do so, it must be determined whether there are ascertainable facts which may nevertheless raise doubts regarding the impartiality of the court. In this respect, even the existence of

[7] *De Cubber v. Belgium* (Application 9186/80), NJ 1988, 744; NJCM-Bull 1985, 21, European Court of Human Rights, 26 October 1984, Sec. 32.

[8] *Bulut v. Austria* (Application 17358/90), European Court of Human Rights, 22 February 1996, Sec. 40.

[9] The first time in *Hauschildt v. Denmark* (Application 10486/83), European Court of Human Rights, 24 May 1989.

[10] *Micallef v. Malta* (Application 17056/06), European Court of Human Rights, 22 October 2008, Sec. 93.

[11] *Campbell and Fell v. The United Kingdom* (Applications 7819/77; 7878/77), European Court of Human Rights, 28 June 1984, Sec. 85.

[12] *Ekeberg v. Norway* (Application 11311/04), European Court of Human Rights, 31 July 2007, Sec. 32.

[13] *Olujic v. Croatia*, (Application 22330/05), European Court of Human Rights, 5 February 2009, Sec. 58.

circumstantial evidence can be a relevant factor.[14] There are a multitude of cases that elaborate on the requirements which need to be met in order to establish objective bias and which may vary depending on the circumstances of the case. The ECtHR notes that whether or not the accused's fear of a lack of impartiality can be considered to be objectively justified depends on the specific circumstances of each particular case.[15] For example, the fact that the same judge examines the questions of both civil and criminal liability arising from the same facts does not necessarily affect that judge's impartiality.[16]

2.3 Procedural Requirements Imposed on the Contracting States

The requirement of an impartial tribunal ensures the individual right of parties to a civil dispute to have their case decided by a judge who is free of bias. The impartiality of the judge therefore is a prerequisite for the effective protection of every other individual right. It should not be surprising then that the ECtHR has often held that the procedural rights stated under Art. 6 ECHR are of fundamental importance.[17]

Yet, the Court has also established in its case law that, while the result of an impartial tribunal is important, the means by which this result is accomplished are left to the discretion of the Member States. This is, for example, clearly stated in the *Colozza* case:

> The Contracting States enjoy a wide discretion as regards the choice of the means calculated to ensure that their legal systems are in compliance with the requirements of art. 6 para. 1 in this field. The Court's task is not to indicate those means to the states, but to determine whether the result called for by the Convention has been achieved … For this to be so, the resources available under domestic law must be shown to be effective.[18]

While every contracting state has to guarantee the effective protection of the rights mentioned in the Convention, this does not preclude states from exercising their own sovereign right to legislate and to establish their own body of procedural

---

[14] *Salov v. Ukraine* (Application 65518/01), European Court of Human Rights, 6 December 2005, Sec. 81.

[15] *Fatullayev v. Azerbaijan* (Application 40984/07), European Court of Human Rights, 22 April 2010, Secs. 138, 139. For another example concerning a minor, see *Adamkiewicz v. Poland* (Application 54279/00), European Court of Human Rights, 2 March 2010, Sec. 106.

[16] Ibid.

[17] See for instance *Delcourt v. Belgium* (Application 2689/65), European Court of Human Rights, 17 January 1970, Sec. 25.

[18] *Colozza v. Italy* (Application 9024/80), NJ 1986, 685, European Court of Human Rights, 12 February 1985, Sec. 30. For a further elaboration on the relation with procedural discretion and its relationship with the margin of appreciation and the principle of proportionality, see Aray-Takahashi (2001, 34).

rules (Greer 2000). To the extent that the principle of effective protection is respected, the contracting states have, with regard to their procedural law, a large degree of 'implementation discretion' (Schokkenbroek 1998).

Thus, it follows that very few procedural guidelines have been imposed by the ECtHR.[19] As regards the moment a challenge has to be submitted, the Court is not very strict.[20] In addition to this, the *Remli* decision can be mentioned, in which the ECtHR decided that all challenges have to be investigated by the court, unless the right to challenge has been abused.[21] This accounts for the wide diversity in challenge procedures that has been found, which will be the subject of the next section.

3 Comparing the Civil Challenge Procedures Found in EU Member States

3.1 Essential Elements of Challenge Procedures

Challenge procedures are diverse, but some of the elements of these procedures (such as the form in which a document has to be submitted) are not relevant when it comes to assessing their effectiveness. These elements were excluded from further analysis.

A procedural element is considered to be relevant if it could potentially have a more than insignificant degree of influence on the overall effectiveness of the national challenge procedure to which it belongs. Based on a study of the domestic law of the countries under consideration and on the expectations and experience of the researchers, a list was made of eleven procedural elements considered to be useful for determining the predicted (a priori) effectiveness of challenge procedures. These elements are displayed in Table 1.

Subsequently, the challenge procedures of the Member States were analysed and the presence or absence of the abovementioned procedural elements was determined for each state. The result of this process is an overview which establishes whether the relevant procedural elements are present in the code of civil procedure of a specific state and, if so, in what way these elements are implemented. In this contribution, a selection of the most interesting comparative findings will be discussed (Sect. 3.2).

---

[19]It is worth mentioning that there are some non-procedural requirements which should be taken into account. A state should, for example, protect the status of judges and should ensure that judges are not subject to any kind of pressure in the performance of their duties. See CCJE et al. (2016, 18).

[20]*Ekeberg v. Norway* (Application 11311/0), European Court of Human Rights, 31 July 2007, Sec. 44.

[21]*Remli v. France* (Application 16839/90), NJCM-Bull. 1998, 709, European Court of Human Rights, 30 June 1996.

Table 1 Essential elements of challenge procedures

Variable (procedural elements)	Definition/description
Imposition of a time limit for challenging	Whether a time limit has been imposed within which a challenge must be submitted
Legal representation needed	Whether a party may file a challenge in person, or whether he/she must do so represented by a lawyer
Oral and/or written challenge	Whether it is possible to submit a challenge in writing and/or orally
Possibility for additional motivation of a challenge	Whether additional grounds for challenge may be put forward at the hearing regarding the challenge
Suspension of the case after a challenge has been submitted	Whether a challenge suspends proceedings completely
Requirements imposed on person(s) who must decide on the challenge	Whether persons deciding on the challenge are selected from inside or outside the environment in which the challenged judge is working
Open and/or closed list of challenge grounds	Whether there are open and/or closed grounds on which a judge may be challenged
Possibility/duty to hear the challenged judge	Whether the challenged judge may/should be heard before the challenge is decided on
Possibility/duty to hear the party who submitted the challenge	Whether the party who submitted the challenge must be heard before the challenge is decided on
Anti-abuse rule	The presence/absence of anti-abuse rule(s) to prevent unmeritorious challenges
Self-assessment by challenged judge	Whether the judge is allowed to decide on the challenge submitted against himself/herself

Source of all tables: data collected by the authors

3.2 *Comparative Results*

3.2.1 The Imposition of a Time Limit

A limitation on the period of time within which litigating parties may challenge a judge is a procedural element that is present in all Member States. One can observe, however, that this procedural element can be implemented in different ways, offering parties differing degrees of opportunity to file an admissible challenge.

In most procedural codes, there are two separate periods of time during which an admissible challenge may be filed. First, there is a well-defined period which stretches from the moment at which the identity of the judge is known up until the moment the parties make their first appearance in the proceedings, either physically (by appearing at the hearing) or on paper (by submitting their pleadings).[22] In some countries, such as Estonia, Finland and Italy, parties potentially have an even

[22]This is the case in e.g. Austria, Poland, Latvia, Finland, Romania and Sweden.

shorter window of opportunity.[23] Litigating parties in these countries must submit a challenge as soon as the identity of the judge has become clear to them, which will usually happen before the first hearing starts. Some countries have a fixed deadline, which means that the challenge must be submitted five days prior to the hearing.[24] If this initial deadline passes without submission of a challenge, then the right of the parties to challenge the judge, in principle, is lost.[25]

If, however, a ground for challenging a judge becomes known during proceedings, the right of challenge might revive. The standard requirement for this is that the ground on which the challenge is based has only become known to the party during or after the hearing. The challenge then must be submitted 'immediately' after the grounds for challenge have become known to the litigating party. The terminology used tends to be slightly different in each Member State (e.g., 'as soon as', 'without delay'). While the exact amount of time that is meant by these terms might differ slightly for each state, we categorized this as taking roughly the same (short) amount of time. Some countries give more time, for example the Czech Republic and Slovakia,[26] and some less, as for instance Luxembourg, Estonia and Greece, where challenges must be submitted before the closure of the hearing.

Some countries do not distinguish between these two possibilities. Getting to know the identity of the judge is counted as the beginning of the period of time which is available to challenge that judge, when that identity alone is enough to raise doubts about his impartiality. Thus, in France, Slovenia and the Netherlands there is only one time limit for litigating parties to submit a challenge.

The rules regarding time restrictions on challenges seem to be most convenient for litigating parties in Malta. The Maltese rule is similar to one previously mentioned, that is to say, the parties can challenge a judge as soon as they become aware of a ground for challenge. However, the Maltese challenge procedure explicitly provides parties with an option to state, under oath, that they were not previously aware of the existence of the ground for the challenge in question, thereby settling any further discussion regarding the admissibility of the claim.

Finally, there is Denmark, which leaves a certain degree of ambiguity as to the exact time frame in which a challenge is admissible. A challenge must be submitted 'as much as possible before the first hearing'. The question remains whether judges are strict in maintaining this requirement, or lenient. In any event, the exact time limit could not be ascertained on the basis of the procedural code alone.

The fact that a challenge is not filed within a certain time limit can potentially hurt the effectiveness of the overall challenge procedure. A challenge could, for instance, stay without effect, not because it was ill-founded (indeed, the contrary

[23]Estonia: Art. 25 Code of Civil Procedure (CCP); Finland: Art. 8 CCP; Italy: Art. 52 CCP.

[24]Examples: Greece (5 days) and Italy (2 days).

[25]The question of whether this is in itself compatible with Art. 6(1) ECHR will not be discussed in this contribution.

[26]Both give 15 days (Czech Republic: Art. 15a sub 2 CCP; Slovakia: Art. 15a sub 2 CCP).

Table 2 Time limits for submitting a challenge

State	Moment until a challenge may be submitted				
	During the hearing, before substantive treatment	Before the hearing concludes, directly after the grounds have become clear	Before the hearing concludes	At any moment, directly after the grounds have become clear	At any moment, 15 days after the grounds have become clear
Austria				x	
Belgium				x	
Bulgaria				x	
Croatia				x	
Czech Republic					x
Denmark	NF	NF	NF	NF	NF
Estonia			x		
Finland				x	
France		x			
Germany				x	
Greece			x		
Hungary				x	
Italy	x				
Latvia				x	
Lithuania				x	
Luxembourg			x		
Malta				x	
The Netherlands				x	
Poland				x	
Portugal				x	
Romania			x		
Slovakia					x
Slovenia		x			
Spain				x	
Sweden				x	

might be the case), but just because it was not filed in time. This would subsequently form an unnecessary obstacle for the litigating parties to effectively challenge a biased judge. This explains the way in which the different possibilities have been ordered in Table 2.

3.2.2 Anti-abuse Penalties

Probably one of the most impactful procedural aspects that recurs in the procedural codes of Member States is the existence of anti-abuse rules. The purpose of these rules is to prevent litigating parties from abusing their right to challenge the judge. A party might, for instance, use this right not because he or she has reasonable doubts as to the judge's impartiality, but to purposefully slow down proceedings, or to express discontent. This would result in the loss of resources, since (usually) the hearing of the case needs to be suspended and the challenge must be processed by the competent authority. With regard to the anti-abuse rules, we observed four different ways of implementation in the procedural codes of the Member States.

Firstly, we observed that the majority of Member States have no anti-abuse rule. In the jurisdictions that fall within this first category, the court must, in principle, decide on every challenge submitted by a litigating party.

Secondly, there are five EU Member States in which the judge has an explicit legal ground for resolving repeated challenges in a simplified manner. This means that the judge does not have to substantively deal with a second challenge that is based on exactly the same grounds as the first one.[27] It might be plausible that a judge otherwise would also quickly dismiss a repeated challenge request without an explicit legal ground.

Thirdly, there are two Member States, namely Estonia and Finland, in which an unsubstantiated challenge can be disregarded by the challenged judge.[28] A judge in these states has the competence to dismiss a challenge against himself if he considers the challenge not serious or substantiated (enough). This rule will most likely result in savings of both costs and time for the court, but it also implies that some challenge requests will not be relayed to the person(s) who usually must decide on the challenge. It would thus be the challenged judge himself, and not a third party, who decides whether the challenge request is adequately substantiated. This would pose a problem in cases where the adequacy of substantiation of a challenge was debatable. In such situations it might, from the perspective of impartiality, be preferable to forward the challenge to another panel to decide.

Lastly, there are a few Member States where the party who submits a challenge can receive a fine or a costs order if the challenge is rejected. In this category, there is a wide range of possible fines that one might receive. For instance:

- in Italy, the fine may not exceed €250,
- the maximum fine in France is €3000,
- in Spain, the fine may range between €180 and €6000, and
- in Luxembourg, the fine must be at least €3, with no maximum given.[29]

---

[27]For example: Czech Republic: Art. 15 CCP; the Netherlands: Art. 37 CCP; Poland: Art. 53 CCP; Romania: Art. 53 CCP; Slovakia: Art. 15 CCP.

[28]Estonia: Art. 28 CCP; Finland: Art. 13 CCP.

[29]Art. 533 CCP of Luxembourg.

Table 3 Anti-abuse rules

State	Anti-abuse rules			
	No anti-abuse clause	Simplified resolution of repeated challenges	Simplified resolution when the challenge is unsubstantiated	(Penalty) fine when the ability to challenge is clearly abused
Austria	x			
Belgium			x	
Bulgaria	x			
Croatia				x
Czech Republic		x		
Denmark	x			
Estonia			x	
Finland			x	
France				x
Germany	x			
Greece	x			
Hungary				x
Italy				x
Latvia	x			
Lithuania	x			
Luxembourg				x
Malta	x			
The Netherlands		x		
Poland		x		
Portugal	x			
Romania		x		
Slovenia	x			
Slovakia		x		
Spain				x
Sweden	x			

While the risk of financial repercussions would certainly result in a party thinking twice before challenging a judge, the question could be asked whether such a measure would not exceed its initial aim and instead form a factor that deters parties from challenging the judge, not because their doubt as to the judge's impartiality is not serious enough, but because they are afraid of the potential imposition of a fine or costs order. The implementation of financial repercussions, especially if they are severe, might seriously hurt the overall effectiveness of a challenge procedure since parties would be too afraid to make use of it. The different modalities are to be found in Table 3.

3.2.3 Self-assessment on Impartiality by the Challenged Judge

Closely related to the previous procedural element is a rule which establishes whether the challenged judge is allowed to decide on the challenge submitted against himself. Such a rule exists, for instance, in the procedural codes of Malta and Latvia. If the judge who is challenged handles the case alone, that judge is allowed to decide himself on the challenge submitted against him.[30] The Portuguese procedural code even blocks the possibility to appeal against the judge's decision.[31]

This rule is expected to have a great impact on the effectiveness of the challenge procedure, since it effectively makes the distance between the challenged judge and the person deciding on the challenge disappear completely. A judge, in principle, has the obligation to recuse himself or herself from a case if that judge is convinced that he or she is or can justifiably be seen to be prejudiced or biased. The judge who hears the case thus has already made (or at least should have already made) a judgment regarding his impartiality. If a party subsequently forces the judge to reconsider that judgment by way of challenge, then there will be a fair chance that the judge has already made up his mind on the matter.

One might also consider an extreme scenario, where a judge was biased on purpose to help a favoured party or himself and wants to stay on the case in order to influence its outcome. The whole point of the challenge procedure—preventing biased judges from hearing the case—would subsequently become illusory. In this specific situation, the challenge procedure cannot protect a party's right to an impartial tribunal. With the exceptions of Malta, Latvia and Portugal, all the countries under consideration exclude the challenged judge from the decision on the challenge.

3.2.4 Requirements Imposed on the Panel Deciding on the Challenge

The procedural codes of the Member States all have in common that the person(s) deciding on a challenge must always be one or more fellow judge(s). The procedural rules differ, however, with regard to the professional distance that needs to exist between the challenged judge and the judge(s) who decide(s) on the challenge. This distance is usually created by requiring the deciding judge to be either of a higher hierarchical position within the same court, or to work in a different court altogether. In the absence of strict rules regarding this aspect, situations might occur where the challenge of a certain judge is decided on by (one of) his close colleague(s). This will inevitably affect the degree of impartiality with which the challenge is decided on.

In some countries, there exists the possibility to challenge the judge who decided on the initial challenge, but if the judge(s) deciding on this subsequent challenge

[30] Latvia: Art. 21 sub 3 CCP; Malta: Art. 738 CCP.

[31] Art. 738 CCP of Malta.

also comes from the same working environment, then one runs into the same problem again.[32] The exact requirements regarding the professional distance between the challenged judge and the deciding judge often differ depending on the capacity of the challenged judge. We observed that special requirements often apply for the challenge of court presidents and second instance judges.[33] For the sake of drawing comparisons between the requirements imposed by the Member States, the researchers chose to focus on the challenge of first instance judges, since they have to decide on the largest number of cases, and thus are likely to be challenged most often.

In most Member States, the choice is made to let another judge of the same first instance court decide on the challenge submitted against a colleague.[34] This gives rise to the aforementioned problem: there is a relatively good chance that the deciding judge has a personal relationship with the challenged judge, which would in itself be an obstacle for guaranteeing (at least objective) impartiality.

A noteworthy subsection of this group is composed of Member States where the deciding judge must be the president of the court to which the challenged judge belongs. While the higher hierarchical position of the president potentially puts a higher degree of professional distance between the challenged judge and the deciding judge, the impartiality of the deciding judge could still be questioned. The court's president may, for example, also have a decisive role in the initial assignment of cases to judges within his court, which could lead to a conflict of interest.

In contrast, a (rather small) group of Member States can be distinguished which allows a judge from the court of appeal to decide on the challenge.[35] The procedure of the Czech Republic goes even further than that, requiring the court of cassation to decide on the matter. This approach creates professional distance, both hierarchical and institutional, between the challenged judge and the deciding judge. While it is impossible to completely rule out the existence of any personal relationship which could (consciously or subconsciously) influence the decision on a challenge, this latter category of procedural elements is likely to decrease the chance of this happening. To simplify comparison, two categories are distinguished in Table 4.

---

[32]This possibility is not mentioned in the codes of civil procedure and thus was excluded from comparative analysis.

[33]See for instance Art. 73 of the Slovakian CCP.

[34]For example: Bulgaria: Art. 23 CCP; Denmark: Art. 62 CPP; Estonia: Art. 26 CPP; Finland: Art. 9 CPP; Germany: Art. 44 CPP; Greece: Art. 54 CPP; Hungary: Art. 18 CPP; the Netherlands: Art. 39 CPP; Poland: Art. 52 CPP; Romania: Art. 50 CPP; Spain: Art. 110 CPP; and Sweden: Art. 14 CPP.

[35]Belgium: Art. 838 CPP; France: Art. 349 CPP; and Slovakia: Art. 16 CPP.

Table 4 Panel deciding on the challenge

State	Panel deciding on the challenge	
	Judge(s) from the same working environment as the challenged judge	Judge(s) from outside the working environment of the challenged judge
Austria	x	
Belgium		x
Bulgaria	x	
Croatia	x	
Czech Republic	x	x
Denmark		
Estonia	x	
Finland	x	
France		x
Germany	x	
Greece	x	
Hungary	x	
Italy	x	
Latvia	x	
Lithuania	x	
Luxembourg	x	
Malta	x	
The Netherlands	x	
Poland	x	
Portugal	x	
Romania	x	
Slovenia	x	
Slovakia		x
Spain	x	
Sweden	x	

4 Effectiveness of Challenge Procedures

4.1 Survey

The effectiveness of challenge procedures could be measured by matching the procedures against the actual number of challenges and their outcomes. Unfortunately, although every EU Member State provides some statistical information about civil procedure, the facts and figures relating to the challenge of judges are either incomplete or not disclosed at all.[36]

Due to the lack of available challenge statistics it would be impossible to objectively test the effectiveness of challenge procedures. It is, however, still possible to measure this on a more abstract level, namely, by determining the relative effectiveness of the procedural elements that make up a challenge procedure, as predicted by persons with a legal background. The results would give a good indication of what legally trained persons perceive as important factors that would contribute to a more effective challenge procedure, and also to a higher degree of conformity with the requirement of an impartial tribunal.

Therefore, in order to be able to assess the a priori effectiveness of challenge procedures a survey was conducted among judges, academic staff, and law students who were at least in their second year of study.[37] A total of 42 people participated in the survey: 33 law students and 9 legal professionals. For a detailed description of the methodology used to design and conduct this survey, we refer to the report underlying this contribution. In short, the respondents were asked to order the most favourable option (for a challenging party) found for each of the procedural elements that was part of the comparative research in function of its contribution to safeguard the impartiality of the court. Since eleven elements were selected, the elements were ordered from 1 to 11.

The results per procedural element are presented in Table 5, which shows the relative importance (rank) of that element in relation to the other elements.

We can observe that, on average, persons with a legal background think that the elements that contribute (relatively) little to an effective challenge procedure are the ones that determine whether a challenge can be submitted orally during the hearing, whether additional grounds for challenge may be put forward during the hearing regarding the challenge, and whether a challenge can be submitted without mandatory legal representation.

Slightly more importance was assigned to the elements which determine whether a challenge completely suspends proceedings, whether a challenge can be based on a general/open ground, and whether the rejection of a challenge can result in the imposition of a costs order or fine on the challenging party, and also whether a time limit is imposed within which a challenge must be submitted.

It was deemed even more important whether the challenged judge and/or the party who submitted the challenge have the opportunity to be heard by the person(s) who must decide on the challenge. Interestingly, we see that the importance of the opportunity for the party to be heard was rated slightly higher than the opportunity for the challenged judge to be heard.

---

[36]At the time of writing, the EU Member State which provides the most statistical information on the use and success rate of challenges is the Netherlands. See, *inter alia*, Giesen et al. (2012); de Rechtspraak (2016, 48–52); van Rossum et al. (2012, 54).

[37]This survey was conducted in conformity with the basic principles and concepts for conducting empirical research in the field of law. See for reference: Lawless et al. (2010).

Table 5 Relative contribution of procedural elements to impartiality (N = 42)

Variable (procedural element)	Rank
A challenge can be submitted without mandatory legal representation	3.63
The challenge can be submitted orally during the hearing	4.08
Additional grounds for challenge may be put forward at the hearing regarding the challenge	4.33
No time limit has been imposed within which a challenge must be submitted	4.89
A challenge suspends proceedings completely	5.5
There is a general, open ground for challenging a judge	6.00
The rejection of a challenge cannot result in a costs order against the challenging party, or the imposition of a fine	6.16
The challenged judge must be heard before the challenge is decided on	6.26
The party who submitted the challenge must be heard before the challenge is decided on	6.93
Persons deciding on the challenge are selected from outside the environment in which the challenged judge is working	8.6
The challenged judge is not allowed to decide on the challenge submitted against him	9.63

Lastly, the elements that were found to be the most important for determining whether a challenge procedure is effective are the rules which determine the distance that should exist between the challenged judge and the person deciding on the challenge. It was deemed especially important that the challenged judge did not decide on the challenge himself.

4.2 *Designing the 'Scoreboard'*

The results of the survey were used to design a 'scoreboard' for challenge procedures, taking as a starting point the way each of the eleven elements has been implemented. The total score of a challenge procedure then is equal to the sum of all individual scores assigned to its relevant procedural elements.[38]

The individual score on a procedural element depends on three factors: a basic score related to the implementation of the element, the ranking of the element and a multiplying factor. The multiplying factor is only used to rank all procedures on a scale of 0–100.

The basic score is determined by the way in which a procedural element has been implemented. As discussed in Sect. 3, some implementations are less optimal than others. If the optimal value is fully present in a challenge procedure, then a basic score of '1' is assigned. If the optimal value is fully absent, then a basic score

[38]'Relevant' in this instance means: relevant for the purpose of measuring (on an abstract level) the predicted effectiveness of challenge procedures of EU Member States.

of '0' is assigned. If the optimal value is neither fully absent nor fully present, but lies somewhere in between, then a value between '0' and '1' is assigned based on the degree to which the optimal value is present. A further elaboration on this can be found in the report underlying this contribution.

The ranking of a procedural element is determined by the outcome of the survey discussed above. The ranking shows the relative contribution of an element to an effective challenge procedure. This ranking is multiplied by a factor to project the outcome on a scale of 0–100, thus guaranteeing that an optimal score on all elements results in a total score of 100.[39]

To assign a value to the implementation of a procedural element, three types of elements have to be distinguished:

1. procedural elements which can take one out of two mutually exclusive values (e.g., the existence of a right to orally submit a challenge or the existence of a right to challenge a judge without the need for a lawyer);
2. procedural elements which are observed to take one out of two non-mutually exclusive values (e.g., the degree to which a challenge request suspends the proceedings);
3. procedural elements which can take one out of three or more different values (e.g., the different time periods for challenging and the different anti-abuse rules).

If a procedural element falls within the first category, the maximum basic score of '1' was assigned if the element is present. If the element is absent, then a score of '0' was assigned.

If a procedural element falls within the second or third category, the researchers considered the degree to which an element is present or not and, consequently, the score that should be awarded. This inevitably introduces the subjective opinion of the researchers into the ranking process, which has an influence on the end results. However, if no scale were introduced, the resulting scores would fail to represent the actual contents of challenge procedures, which is crucial for a somewhat accurate indication of predicted effectiveness. For a detailed description of how different scales were introduced for the procedural elements which fall within the second and third categories, we refer the reader to the report underlying this contribution.

Due to the procedural discretion of the Member States, the layout and substance of the challenge procedure tends to be different in each of the procedural codes. This inevitably means that most of the aforementioned procedural elements are found to be present in some states and found to be absent in others. In the event that it could not be determined whether, or to what degree, an element is present or absent in the procedural code of a Member State, the researcher assigned the value 'NF' (meaning 'not found') to the respective variable. This means that, with regard to these specific elements, no definitive basic score could be determined.

---

[39]In fact, all rankings have been multiplied by approx. 1.513.

In order to give an accurate representation of the predicted effectiveness of the different challenge procedures, the 'scoreboard' must rank all these procedures on an equal scale. To create the scale, a basic score had to be assigned to the elements that were 'not found'. We considered that each procedural element that could not be found grants a procedural right to the litigating parties, which they otherwise would not have (as far as the civil procedural rules are concerned). For the purpose of ranking procedural codes on the 'scoreboard', the following assumption was made: when it cannot be (clearly) established whether, or to what degree, an element is present, that component is considered to be absent. Therefore, a provisional basic score of '0' was assigned to these components. The scores that are based on this assumption are tentative in nature and are therefore marked with a 'T' on the 'scoreboard'.

5 Results

Having elaborated on methodology and having made preliminary reservations in the previous section, we can proceed to the 'scoreboard', which is displayed below (see Table 6). On the 'scoreboard', the Member States are ranked in descending order, from the highest score to the lowest score. The table also displays the individual score for each procedural element.

When analysing this ranking, it becomes apparent that most of the procedural elements that contribute to an effective challenge procedure are found to be present in the codes of civil procedure of the Member States. Almost half of the states have a score of 75 or higher, and almost all states have a score above 50. The five highest ranking states are the Netherlands, Germany, Portugal, Belgium and Romania. It is noteworthy that the same procedural element, namely the right to provide additional grounds for challenge at the hearing regarding the challenge, is missing in the procedural codes of these five states. Across all other components these states have roughly the same (high) scores, which indicates that these states have very similar challenge procedures.

Another noteworthy observation is that twelve states give the challenged judge the possibility to be heard, while only six states give this right to the party who submitted the challenge. States provide for an opportunity either to hear the challenged judge or to hear both the challenged judge and the party who submitted the challenge. There are no states that only provide the party submitting the challenge with the opportunity to be heard. This is striking, given the fact that the survey made it clear in the way in which it is worded that the obligation to hear the judge and the obligation to hear the party are considered to be almost equally important. A possible explanation might be that states consider that the party who has submitted the challenge already had sufficient opportunity to substantiate and elaborate on the challenge. The judge should then be given a separate opportunity to elaborate on the matter as well.

Table 6 Ranking of countries according to effectiveness of the challenge procedure

State	Score per procedural element (relative importance determined by survey results)											Total score
	1	2	3	4	5	6	7	8	9	10	11	
The Netherlands	7.0	14.6	6.2	0.0	9.1	9.2	5.5	8.3	13.0	9.5	10.5	**92.97**
Germany	7.0	14.6	6.2	0.0	9.1	9.3	5.5	7.9	13.0	9.5	10.5	**92.65**
Portugal	7.0	14.6	6.2	0.0	9.1	9.3	5.5	8.3	13.0	7.1	7.9	**88.07**
Belgium	7.0	14.6	0.0	0.0	9.1	8.9	5.5	8.3	13.0	9.5	10.5	**86.42**
Romania	4.1	14.6	6.2	0.0	9.1	9.2	5.5	7.9	13.0	7.1	7.9	**84.6**
Lithuania	7.0	14.6	6.2	0.0	9.1	9.3	5.5	7.9	13.0	9.5	0.0	**82.15**
Spain	7.0	14.6	6.2	6.6	0.0	9.3	5.5	8.3	13.0	9.5	0.0	**80.03**
Slovakia	7.3	14.6	6.2	6.6	9.1	9.3	5.5	8.3	13.0	0.0	0.0	**79.94**
Sweden	7.0	14.6	6.2	6.6	9.1	9.3	5.5	7.9	13.0	0.0	0.0	**79.22**
Finland	7.0	14.6	6.2	6.6	9.1	8.9	5.5	8.3	13.0	0.0	0.0	**79.17**
Slovenia	3.7	14.6	6.2	0.0	9.1	9.2	5.5	8.3	13.0	9.5	0.0	**79.14**
Poland	7.0	14.6	6.2	6.6	9.1	9.2	5.5	7.9	13.0	0.0	0.0	**79.13**
Hungary	7.0	14.6	0.0	6.6	9.1	0.0	5.5	8.3	13.0	9.5	0.0	**73.61**
Austria	7.0	14.6	6.2	0.0	9.1	9.3	5.5	8.3	13.0	0.0	0.0	**73.08**
Greece	4.1	14.6	0.0	0.0	9.1	9.3	5.5	7.9	13.0	9.5	0.0	**73.01**
Croatia	7.0	14.6	6.2	6.6	9.1	0.0	5.5	7.9	13.0	0.0	0.0	**69.89**
Czech Republic	7.3	14.6	0(T)	0(T)	9.1	9.2	5.5	7.9	13.0	0.0	0.0	**66.69(T)**
Denmark	0(T)	14.6	0(T)	6.6	9.1	9.3	5.5	7.9	13.0	0.0	0.0	**66.01(T)**
Bulgaria	7.0	14.6	0(T)	6.6	9.1	9.3	5.5	0(T)	13.0	0.0	0.0	**65.13(T)**
Latvia	7.0	0.0	6.2	6.6	9.1	9.3	5.5	0(T)	0.0	9.5	10.5	**63.67(T)**
Estonia	4.1	14.6	0.0	0.0	9.1	8.9	5.5	7.9	13.0	0.0	0.0	**63.05**
Italy	1.5	14.6	0.0	0.0	9.1	0.0	5.5	8.3	13.0	9.5	0.0	**61.5**
Luxembourg	4.1	14.6	6.2	6.6	0.0	0.0	5.5	8.3	13.0	0.0	0.0	**58.26**
France	3.7	14.6	0.0	0.0	9.1	0.0	5.5	8.3	13.0	0.0	0.0	**54.24**
Malta	7.0	0.0	6.2	6.6	0.0	9.3	5.5	0(T)	0.0	0.0	0.0	**34.60(T)**

1 = The time limit imposed within which a challenge must be submitted. 2 = Participation of the challenged judge in the decision. 3 = The way a challenge has to be submitted (orally/in writing). 4 = The possibility to put forward additional grounds at the hearing. 5 = Closed or open grounds. 6 = Possibility of fines when a challenge is rejected. 7 = Need for legal representation. 8 = Suspending force of challenge. 9 = Selection of panel deciding on the challenge. 10 = Obligation to hear the challenged judge. 11 = Obligation to hear the challenging party

Among the lower ranking states we find Latvia, Estonia, Italy, Luxembourg and France. What these states have in common is that the time limit for submitting a challenge tends to be relatively short, that an oral submission is often not possible, that additional grounds may often not be put forward after the initial challenge, that a party might be deterred from challenging due to the potential imposition of a fine, and that the party who submitted the challenge may not be heard. Latvia even has a procedural rule stating that if a case is examined by a judge sitting alone, then that judge may rule on the challenge himself. Some of these procedural rules (by themselves, but especially considered together) form serious impediments for the party to effectively challenge a biased judge. With regard to the other procedural elements, these states obtained higher scores which resulted in their obtaining a total score above 50. While this overall score might be considered (barely) acceptable, the question should be asked whether the existence and enforcement of such impeding procedural rules does not in itself constitute a violation of Art. 6(1) ECHR.

The state that scored (by far) the lowest is Malta. Most of the procedural components that were regarded as being important by persons with a legal background could not be found in the Maltese Code of Civil Procedure. The judge may only be challenged based on a limited set of grounds, without any openly formulated residual ground. If a challenge is submitted, the challenged judge may still take action, where necessary, in the procedure by signing applications or warrants and—perhaps the most striking observation—if the court consists of only one judge and this judge is challenged, then the judge himself will decide on the submission with no possibility of appeal against this decision. Both the individual scores for each element, as well as the low overall score, raise serious doubts as to whether the Maltese challenge procedure (both as a whole and with regard to its individual components) can effectively safeguard the right to an impartial tribunal.

6 Conclusion

The European Court of Human Rights has made it clear that it does not impose procedural requirements on the Member States when it comes to protecting the individual rights guaranteed in Art. 6(1) ECHR. The contracting states, therefore, have procedural discretion to determine the means by which they choose to accomplish this goal. The ECtHR does, however, determine whether the result prescribed by the Convention has been achieved. Thus, the effectiveness of a challenge procedure determines Art. 6(1) ECHR conformity.

The goal of the research report underlying this contribution was from the outset to measure the effectiveness of the civil challenge procedures of EU Member States. Due to a lack of statistical information, this had to be done by comparing these challenge procedures on a more abstract level. To do so, a semi-empirical methodology was developed, which enabled us to operationalize the concept of Art. 6(1) ECHR conformity. This method resulted in a 'scoreboard' that gives a quick overview of the different regulations and facilitates a comparison on a more quantitative basis.

The results show us that, while most countries have procedural rules that are predicted to contribute to an effective challenge procedure, other countries have rules that are predicted to accomplish the exact opposite. An example can be found in the rules that deter parties from challenging a judge by imposing a fine or a costs order in the event a challenge is rejected. Most notably, there are Member States in which a judge, sitting alone, may decide on the challenge himself or herself. The question could (and should) be raised whether such procedural rules have a right to exist, given the obligation imposed on the Member States by Art. 6(1) ECHR to effectively protect the individual right to an impartial tribunal.

References

Aray-Takahashi Y (2001) The margin of appreciation doctrine and the principle of proportionality in the jurisprudence of the ECHR. Intersentia, Oxford, p 34

CCJE et al (2016) Challenges for judicial independence and impartiality in the member states of the Council of Europe (Report prepared jointly by the Bureau of the CCJE and the Bureau of the CCPE). Information Document SG/Inf(2016)3rev 2016, p 18

Council of Europe (2013) Guide on Article 6 of the European Convention on Human Rights, Strasbourg (report of the Council of Europe). Council of Europe Publishing, Strasbourg

de Rechtspraak (2016) de Rechtspraak, Jaarverslag 2016 (annual report published by the Dutch Council for the Judiciary). The Hague, pp 48–52

Giesen I, Kristen F, Enneking L (2012) De wrakingsprocedure, Een rechtsvergelijkend onderzoek naar de mogelijkheden tot herziening van de Nederlandse wrakingsprocedure. Sdu Uitgevers, The Hague

Greer S (2000) The margin of appreciation: interpretation and discretion under the European Convention on Human Rights. Bristol University Press, Bristol, para. 1.5

Lawless RM, Robbenholt JK, Ulen TS (2010) Empirical methods in law. Aspen Publishers, New York

Schokkenbroek J (1998) The basis, nature and application of the margin of appreciation doctrine in the case law of the European Court of Human Rights. Human Rts Law J 30(31):32–45

van Rossum W, Tigchelaar J, Ippel P (2012) Wraking bottom-up, Een empirisch onderzoek. Sdu Uitgevers, The Hague, p 54

Fokke Fernhout Associate Professor of Civil Procedure at Maastricht University, the Netherlands. Attorney-at-law and former Vice-President of the District Court of Maastricht. Coordinator of skills projects for lawyers and law students in the Netherlands and in Indonesia.

Erwin Giesen Master's student of Law at the Faculty of Law of Maastricht University, the Netherlands. Legal Counsel intern at the ARAG SE Insurance Group.

Oscar Vranken Master's student of Corporate and Commercial Law at the Faculty of Law of Maastricht University, the Netherlands. Assistant at the Maastricht Institute for Corporate Law, Governance and Innovation Policies (ICGI).

Part VI
Transforming the Apex of the Court Pyramid: The Changing Function of the Highest Courts

Roots of the Resistance to the Change in the Supreme Court's Role

Marko Bratković

That is, I wrote that same story four times. None of them were right ....
W. Faulkner on his novel *The Sound and the Fury*

Abstract In recent years, a paradigm shift in the supreme court's role from a private to a public purpose has been recognised in many jurisdictions. Due to growing backlogs at supreme courts in many countries, the private purpose of the just and correct resolution of every individual case has given place to a public purpose consisting in safeguarding and promoting the public interest of ensuring uniformity of case law, the development of the law, and offering guidance to lower courts. However, this paradigm shift has met with considerable criticism from a large part of the legal community. It has been argued that litigants will become exposed to judicial arbitrariness and that more restrictive access to the supreme court means less protection of equality before the law. In order to explore the possible roots of the resistance to the change in the supreme court's role, Faulkner's polyperspective technique of narration used in the novel *The Sound and the Fury* might be of some help. The retelling of more or less the same story from the perspective of the individual party, the attorney-at-law, the supreme court and the constitutional court reveals that in favouring the public interest of uniform application of the law some particular interests of all involved have to be suppressed, and the broader picture taken into account.

This contribution is the result of research supported by the Croatian Science Foundation (project no. 6988). I am indebted to Matthias Van der Haegen for his comments on the draft of this contribution. The usual disclaimer, however, fully applies.

M. Bratković (✉)
Faculty of Law, University of Zagreb, Zagreb, Croatia
e-mail: marko.bratkovic@pravo.hr

A. Uzelac and C. H. van Rhee (eds.), *Transformation of Civil Justice*,
Ius Gentium: Comparative Perspectives on Law and Justice 70,
https://doi.org/10.1007/978-3-319-97358-6_18

1 Introduction: The Supreme Court's Public Purpose

Following the latest civil procedure reforms in many jurisdictions in Europe and South America,[1] appeals to their supreme courts are now limited to cases that raise issues of general significance, i.e., issues that go beyond the immediate interests of the parties (Mattei et al. 2009, 509). At least, that was the legislator's intention in the jurisdictions that carried out the reforms under the pressure of the overcrowded dockets of their supreme courts. However, in some jurisdictions this change has been met with considerable resistance. For some scholars and practitioners, losing the opportunity of correcting the decisions of courts of appeal before the supreme court was not a welcome novelty (Mattei et al. 2009, 509).

Resistance was particularly strong with respect to the introduction of filtering mechanisms which enable the supreme court to decide whether the case at stake is worthy of a thorough review before the supreme jurisdiction (Galič 2014a, 14). The aim of the filtering mechanisms is not (only) to allow the best judicial minds to "cherry-pick the juiciest cases" for appellate reconsideration (Andrews 2011, 18), but to keep the caseload of the supreme court under control, hence enabling the supreme court to fulfil its public purpose. A supreme court that does not have some form of control over its docket is in danger of becoming so flooded with enormous numbers of small and unimportant cases that it can devote only insufficient time and energy to the truly novel and important issues of law coming before it (Jolowicz 1998, 60; Mattei et al. 2009, 509).

The supreme court's public purpose consists in laying down fresh precedents and statutory interpretations and updating old ones for the guidance of the lower courts in the court hierarchy. This means that its adjudication consists, in the first place, in clarifying the law, safeguarding and promoting the uniformity of case law and the development of the law in a given jurisdiction (Lindblom 2000, 105; Drewry et al. 2007, 145; Bobek 2009, 41; Galič 2014b, 163). It also consists in resolving legal problems of a particularly high order both as to difficulty and as to public importance (Drewry et al. 2007, 145, 146). This means that the supreme court gives preference to cases whose decision will make a contribution to the development and clarification of the law itself, and that it controls its own caseload (Jolowicz 1998, 57; 2000, 332).

If a supreme court focuses primarily on the public purpose, it means that its private function of correcting wrong decisions as far as they concern the parties to the dispute may not be fulfilled in every individual case (Jolowicz 1998, 41; Drewry et al. 2007, 145). The immediate interests of the parties and individual justice (in German *Einzelfallgerechtigkeit*) take a back seat to the supreme court's public purpose. Naturally, the extent to which the public purpose predominates in a given procedure depends on a number of factors (Jolowicz 1988, 2072). Among them, Jolowicz (1998, 56) recognises an interesting phenomenon—the heavier its caseload, the more

[1]See, e.g., for the Czech Republic, Bobek (2009); for German-speaking countries, Domej (2014); for Chile, Bravo-Hurtado (2014); for Slovenia (and Croatia), Galič (2014a, 2014b, 2014c) and Uzelac and Galič (2017); for Spain, de Benito (2017); for Belgium, Van der Haegen (2018) (in this volume).

willing the court is to concern itself with the private purpose; the more willing the court is to concern itself with the private purpose, the heavier its caseload.

The traditional civil law ideology is that the function of the supreme court is not only to ensure uniformity of case law throughout the country but also to fix mistakes of the courts of appeal in the interest of the individual parties (Mattei et al. 2009, 508; Domej 2014, 277). The discrepancy between tradition and new developments in assessing the role of the supreme jurisdictions raises resistance to the change in the supreme court's role.

The reader may wonder what William Faulkner's words quoted at the beginning of this contribution have in common with this change in the supreme court's role in many jurisdictions around the globe. Perhaps nothing at all; perhaps a great deal. In any event, in this contribution I will borrow Faulkner's polyperspective technique of narration which he used in his novel *The Sound and the Fury*. In that novel, more or less the same story is told from four different perspectives. And so I will try to do the same. But I will not imitate Faulkner's stream-of-consciousness style of narration; rather, I should adopt a more straightforward style, for my purpose is to explore from different angles the possible roots of the resistance to the change in the supreme court's role.

2 Four Stories: Four Perspectives

Story 1: It is my right to go to the Supreme Court The first story is told from the perspective of the individual litigant who has failed to win the case in the first and second instance proceedings. This party is thinking like this: If there is a possibility to take my case to the supreme court, I will go for it. Hopefully, the supreme court will realise that the lower courts decided wrongly and, at the end of the day, reverse their decisions to my advantage. After all, it is my right to go to the supreme court. Besides that, filing an appeal to the supreme court leaves open the door to the constitutional court and the Strasbourg court. So, I will definitely ask my attorney to lodge a second appeal with the supreme court.

Story 2: Filing appeals is my bread and butter The said attorney, who represented in court the party from the first story, is the main character of the second story. He is not quite sure whether lodging an appeal would make sense, but if his client wants to go to the supreme court, he will not try to talk him out of it. After all, why should he? Filing claims and appeals is his bread and butter. If he does not lodge an appeal, his client will hire another attorney who will.

On that account, the main character of our second story will file a second appeal for his client stating that, just to be on the safe side, all possible mistakes were made in the proceedings at the lower courts. That is to say, the substantive law was applied incorrectly, grave procedural errors were committed and the facts were established erroneously and incompletely.

He will most certainly not take a closer look at a case law database to find case law supporting his arguments. You see, the database is so heavily overloaded with all kinds of decisions that no one ever really reads them. After all, it is up to the supreme court to know the case law—*iura novit curia*.

Anyway, you never really know with the supreme court, for in many cases its case law is contradictory, so it is nearly impossible to advise his client whether his case has good prospects of success. Who knows. The supreme court might really set aside the lower courts' decisions and remand his client's case to the first instance court for a new trial. Or the decision might be something else, to the benefit of his client. In any event, the party will appreciate his assistance in dealing with all these never-ending court issues.

Story 3: We ensure a uniform application of the law The supreme court, from whose perspective the third story is told, receives tens of thousands of second appeals a year. The supreme court judges (even though there are many of them) do not have enough time to thoroughly examine each case, no matter how important it may be. They check whether substantive and procedural law were applied correctly, but due to the huge caseload, they decide on cases with, on average, a three-year delay. If truth be told, there are cases before the supreme court in which the original claim was filed as many as ten or more years ago. As for the reasoning of the decisions, the judges use standardised copy-paste formulas. Reasoning is therefore often superficial and unconvincing.

However, the task of the supreme court is not only to decide in line with the private interests of the individual parties to the case, but also to ensure the uniform application of the law and equality of all in its application. It is not quite clear how the supreme court, swamped with so many cases, can fulfil this task (but still that is what law students are taught in their civil procedure textbooks).

Story 4: Not only must justice be done, it must also be seen to be done The fourth and last story is told from the perspective of the constitutional court. As almost every legal dispute can be rephrased in terms of constitutionality and fundamental human rights, the constitutional court is afraid of being overwhelmed with too many constitutional complaints. In this regard, the constitutional court considers it is a good thing that the supreme court copes with as many cases as possible. If that were not the case, all litigants dissatisfied with the second instance decision would address the constitutional court directly, claiming that their constitutional rights had been violated in the court proceedings.

One more thing is to be pointed out. The constitutional court takes the view that all decisions delivered by the supreme court have to contain the reasoning for the decision. Even decisions of the supreme court denying permission to appeal need to contain written reasoning as to why the case is not considered important enough to be decided on by the supreme jurisdiction. Why is that so?

The answer can be summarised by the famous legal aphorism, Not only must justice be done, it must also be seen to be done.[2] By insisting on the supreme court's duty to give reasons for all its decisions, the constitutional court protects parties from arbitrary judicial decisions.

---

[2]Lord Chief Justice Hewart was the originator (paraphrased here) of the aphorism, "Justice should not only be done, but should manifestly and undoubtedly be seen to be done"; *R v. Sussex Justices, Ex parte McCarthy* ([1924] 1 KB 256, [1923] All ER Rep 233).

3 In Search of the Whole Elephant

Now that all four stories have been told, what is their common plot? Each of the actors involved (the litigant, the attorney, the supreme court and the constitutional court) speaks for his particular interests. The litigant wants to win his case. The attorney strives to please his client, earn a living and gain respect for his professionalism. The supreme court would like to have a manageable number of cases, and the constitutional court would like to achieve more or less the same. All of this sounds reasonable and legitimate. However, it does not look as though the desired goals have been achieved. Here, the chart presented in Fig. 1 may be helpful in shedding light on the situation.

Let us say that this chart graphically represents the common plot of our four stories. As we can see, the number of second appeals filed with this supreme court has (more or less) steadily grown year after year. In the period between 2006 and 2015 the number of second appeals filed annually increased threefold (from about 2,500 to 7,500 cases), while the backlog increased more than 17 times (from about 1,000 to more than 17,500 cases), in spite of the doubling of productivity. In 2016, the supreme court had a workload of over 24,000 cases. The average duration of unresolved second appeal cases is about three years. This means that in many cases it takes six, seven and sometimes even more than ten years from the filing of the claim to the obtaining of the supreme court's decision. If one asks for the cause, the attorneys will blame the judges, who in turn blame the attorneys.

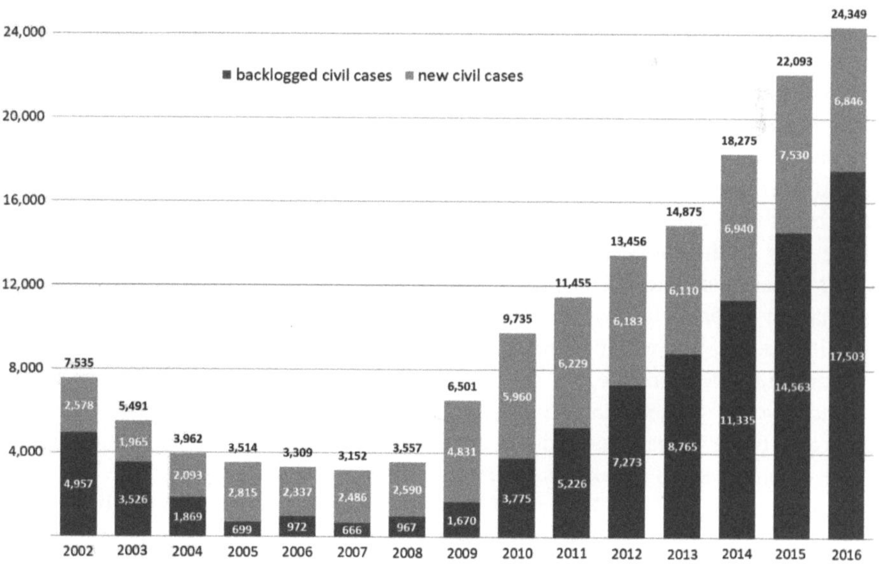

Fig. 1 Civil caseload of a supreme court (2002–2016)

Many authors argue that a supreme court should equally and fully serve both the private and the public purpose (Galič 2014b, 162). The humane desire of the judges to do justice to the parties and their natural reluctance to leave a perceived error uncorrected is understandable (Jolowicz 1998, 60). Be that as it may, case overload of a supreme court can have serious adverse effects on its ability to fulfil its tasks. If its caseload is too great, its judges will not be able to devote the time necessary for the proper consideration and discussion of cases which raise difficult and important questions of law (Jolowicz 2000, 332). A huge output makes it impossible for the supreme court itself to keep track of its own case law (Galič 2014b, 162).

In such circumstances, with court proceedings lasting a decade, the private interests of the litigants cannot be satisfied either. Dissatisfied litigants thus often turn to the constitutional court to seek relief. Consequently, the constitutional court becomes overwhelmed with too many constitutional complaints, and many of them are unfounded. Therefore, not only the supreme court, but also the constitutional court cannot function properly.

And what about the attorney from our second story? As the outcome of proceedings is difficult to predict in many cases due to contradictory case law, performing his duties as an attorney and advising his clients properly is not an easy task. However, since the tariff enables him to be paid by his client proportionally to the value of the dispute, the attorney is not motivated enough to insist on the quality of his submissions—for submissions of both excellent and poor quality are paid the same.

It is clear from the above that such a situation is unsustainable. Some changes are obviously needed. Why then has the proposal for the change from a private-oriented to a public-oriented supreme court been met with considerable resistance in many jurisdictions? I believe that the roots of this resistance lie in the very causes of this situation. I will try to substantiate this statement with the examples from the four stories I started this contribution with.

In those stories, largely the same content is told from four different perspectives. The classic illustration of the importance of perspective which comes to my mind is the old well-known story of four blind men who were asked to describe an elephant. Each blind man felt a different part of the elephant's body, but only one part, such as the side or the tusks. Each of them then described the elephant based on his partial experience, and each of their descriptions was in complete disagreement as to what an elephant really is. While each man's description was accurate, their inability to see the whole animal prevented them from understanding what an elephant really looked like.

And I would suggest that the unwillingness of all the actors involved (especially of the attorney and the constitutional court) to see the big picture—that is, to see the whole elephant, so to speak—is the main reason for the resistance to the change of the supreme court's role. If each of the actors involved is pushing only his own agenda, none of them will succeed. Why? Because each of their perspectives is partly false, based on a misperception. And this misperception becomes obvious only if seen from another angle.

4 Four Misperceptions: Roots of the Resistance to the Change

Misperception 1: It is my right to go to the Supreme Court First, I will address the perception that access to the supreme court is an individual's right. The appeal system, just like a lottery, rests on the litigants' irrational private hope that they will belong to the minority that will get the appealed judgment reversed by the supreme court (Lindblom 2000, 110). In many jurisdictions, notwithstanding the remarkably large caseload in their supreme courts and notwithstanding the fact that the vast majority of the cases presented to these courts do not at all concern a public interest, the right to take a case to the supreme court is jealously safeguarded (Jolowicz 1998, 57, 58).[3] It has been argued that access to justice would otherwise be unreasonably restricted, that litigants would become exposed to judicial arbitrariness (Galič 2014b, 164) and that a more restricted access to the supreme court means less protection of equality before the law (Bravo-Hurtado 2014, 320).

True. The right to turn to the supreme court is a constitutionally protected right in Italy, for example, and the amount of trouble it causes there is well known (Taruffo 1998, 121; Chiarloni 2008, 77; Silvestri 2017, 237–242). But it is telling that even in other countries which do not have such a constitutional provision access to the supreme court is conceived of as a right. In France, for instance, a distinguished president of the *Cour de cassation* once described the selection of cases for consideration by his court as contrary to the French understanding of democracy (Jolowicz 1998, 58).

An obsession with "running-through-instances" (in German *Instanzmentalität*) has been recognised as a feature of central and south-eastern European countries (Jolowicz 1998, 59). This means that, to a litigant, there almost always remains the tantalising possibility of going one step higher and then perhaps higher still (Drewry et al. 2007, 143) hoping that a more favourable judgment will be obtained in a higher court. It is hence not uncommon for a civil dispute to come before all five courts, that is to say, the first instance court, the appellate court, the supreme court, the constitutional court and, at last, the European Court of Human Rights. Even the possibility of going to the Court of Justice of the European Union in Luxembourg, in the event of a reference to that court on a point of EU law by one of the domestic courts, is not to be excluded.

Apart from the demands of economy and the value of bringing litigation to an end in the interests of stability, the "running-through-instances" practice reduces the courts of first instance to bodies which no one takes very seriously, because the real decisions are made at higher instances (Jolowicz 1977, 152; Bobek 2009, 65; Galič 2014b, 162). Moreover, so many possibilities of appeal may reduce rather than promote trust in the system of adjudication. If the first judge could have made a

[3] Conversely, in the common law countries, where the normal assumption is that the first word is also the last word, the right even of a first appeal has never been accepted as fundamental (Jolowicz 2000, 349).

mistake, why (Jolowicz 1988, 2062) should this not also be true for the second judge? "When a man keeps two clocks which tell the time differently, his fellows will receive with suspicion his weightiest pronouncements upon the hour of the day, even if one of them happens to be right" (Herbert 1966, 94). Where there are two courts of appeal, people cannot be blamed if they believe in neither.

In any case, at least as far as the European Convention on Human Rights is concerned, there is no right of access to the supreme court per se (Bobek 2009, 55). Contracting Parties to the Convention are not obliged to provide more than one instance of judicial protection in civil matters (Galič 2014b, 159, 160; 2014c, 308–313).[4] Limiting access to supreme jurisdiction by permission to appeal is thus not contrary to the Convention (Bobek 2009, 55).[5]

Misperception 2: By deciding thousands of cases the supreme court ensures a uniform application of the law More precedents simply does not mean more uniformity (Komárek 2007, 4). Deciding thousands of cases each year does not ensure the uniform application of the law. Exactly the opposite: in order to fully concentrate on legal research, debate and reasoning on the cases which are of general importance, the supreme court needs to deal with a relatively low number of cases (Galič 2014b, 164). Less quantity and more quality (Bobek 2009, 35). Overburdened supreme courts are unable, even when divided into numerous chambers, to adequately consider important legal questions in which their activity must be based not only on a considerable legal expertise, but also on the ability to see the wider societal consequences of decisions they make (Komárek 2007, 19).

Providing protection to the individual interests of the litigants should be the primary task of the lower courts, especially the courts of first instance, not the duty of the supreme jurisdiction (Bobek 2009, 62). Besides, one might wonder what kind of individual protection is being offered by a superficial review of thousands of cases (Bobek 2009, 56). The supreme jurisdiction protects the individual far more by providing clear guidance in the form of predictable case law than by reviewing each case for the third time.

In Italy, for instance, approximately 30,000 new civil appeals were brought to the *Corte di Cassazione* only in 2015; in the same year the court issued no fewer than 26,199 judgments just in civil matters (Silvestri 2017, 238).[6] The more case law the supreme jurisdiction produces, the more inconsistent and unpredictable the case law becomes, which in turn means that more and more cases arrive before the court (Bobek 2009, 63; Zobec and Letnar Černič 2015, 145). Some not so recent analyses done in Italy show that the Italian *Corte di Cassazione* contradicts itself several hundred times per year (Taruffo 1998, 110). It has been observed that its

[4]See, e.g., *Anghel v. Italy*, No. 5968/09, § 50, 25 June 2013.

[5]See, e.g., *Delcourt v. Belgium*, 17 January 1970, §§ 25, 26, Series A No. 11; *Tolstoy Miloslavsky v. the United Kingdom*, 13 July 1995, § 59, Series A No. 316-B; *Eliazer v. the Netherlands*, No. 38055/97, § 31, ECHR 2001-X.

[6]This is to be contrasted with the Supreme Court of the UK, which seems likely to hear c. 60 appeals a year, most of them in non-criminal matters (Andrews 2017, 41).

case law resembles a supermarket where the losing party can always find a favourable precedent (Chiarloni 2008, 79). As a matter of course, a contradictory and inconsistent case law flowing from the supreme court cannot produce consistency and uniformity in the interpretation performed by lower courts.

A certain "honesty" of the system is also to be mentioned here (Bobek 2009, 63). However conscientious the judges may be, it is pointless to pretend that they can produce work of the necessary quality in the thousands of cases dealt with (Jolowicz 1998, 57). Should the individual be allowed to believe that the supreme jurisdiction indeed has the means to deal with his or her case, only to receive, two or three years later, a standardized "copy and paste" decision, rejecting his or her application? It is perhaps better to acknowledge the fact that the supreme jurisdiction cannot handle thousands of cases, rather than insist on a façade (Bobek 2009, 63).

A reality check clearly demonstrates that the supreme court, swamped with thousands of cases, cannot fulfil its task of ensuring the uniform application of the law. Simplified views that the adoption of the new role of the supreme court amounts to a dramatic deterioration in the level of judicial protection have few or no merits (Galič 2014b, 163). The sooner this is acknowledged, the sooner a new and better system can be built. The predominantly public function of the supreme courts must be recognised and accepted openly (Lindblom 2000, 136). It must equally openly be admitted that the perception of a supreme court which takes as many appeals as possible and thus to the greatest possible extent ensures individual justice is merely a myth (Galič 2014a, 28).

Misperception 3: The meaning of the principle *iura novit curia* When taken too seriously, the principle *iura novit curia* becomes self-fulfilling, discouraging both the parties from contributing to the court's legal reasoning and the judges from drawing upon the attorneys' expertise (Kühn 2006, 25, 26). Especially in the legal culture of Central and Eastern Europe,[7] the principle *iura novit curia* is often (mis) used as an excuse for the attorneys not to undertake any legal analysis and legal research, particularly not to refer to case law (Galič 2017, 17). It is claimed that it is up to the supreme court to know its case law even without the litigants' assistance.[8] As a consequence, attorneys' pleadings to the court are quite brief, without a major enquiry into the legal issues (Kühn 2006, 21).[9]

---

[7]Rodin (2005, 7, 8) explains that the predominant discourse in Central and Eastern Europe was (and still is) authoritarian. The main characteristic of such discourse is the proclamation and imposition of one truth as universal and final. In this mode of legal thinking, judges are seen as agents mechanically applying legal texts to facts (*bouche de la loi* or *Subsumptionsautomat*) (Kühn 2011, 199–226; Mańko 2013a, 6).

[8]Conversely, the rule *iura novit curia* has never been and is not part of English law (Jolowicz 1980, 84). Anglo-American judges, for instance, draw heavily upon the parties' competing arguments as to what the correct statement of law is (Kühn 2006, 21). Cf. Damaška (1986, 139).

[9]Curiously, communist legal systems claimed that no party should gain an advantage from having a better lawyer (Kühn 2006, 22).

Nevertheless, providing legal arguments in the litigant's submissions, including references to case law, is the very reason why professional legal assistance is needed in second appeal cases.[10] The judges technically "know" the law, but they often need the parties' attorneys to help them find the relevant provision and to determine its best reading (Kühn 2006, 21). Besides, it is the parties' attorneys who should argue with previous decisions[11] and it is they who should engage in the technique of distinguishing when they are confronted with unfavourable settled case law, as invoked by the opposing party (Galič 2017, 17).

Attorneys and judges are both legal professionals, whose task is to do as much as possible, within the limits of their duties, to protect the rights of the parties seeking relief. That is the job attorneys are paid to do by the parties. Accordingly, in exploring the roots of the resistance to the change in the supreme court's role, professional remuneration as something that may influence attorneys has to be considered as well. It is normal for attorneys not to be indifferent to their financial rewards (Zuckerman 1995, 64). To some extent that could be the reason why in many countries attorneys are the leaders of the resistance to the change in the supreme court's role (Galič 2015, 114). The public role of the supreme court requires more effort on their part than just copying and pasting the appeal previously lodged to the court of second instance, as has been the practice of some of them.

The attorneys are also expected to explain to their clients the public role of the supreme court and the relatively low prospects of their case being selected by the supreme court for examination on the merits (Galič 2014b, 170). In that respect, attorneys should serve as a soft filter of important legal cases to be decided by the supreme jurisdiction of the country.

Misperception 4: Constitutional courts as courts of last instance One more misperception is very common in European countries that have a constitutional court as a separate, free-standing body, especially in Central and South-Eastern Europe. Since some constitutional courts are given the power to review individual judicial decisions, including the final decisions of the supreme court, by means of individual constitutional complaints, constitutional courts are often perceived—and they really often act in this way—as courts of last instance for all breaches of the law (Bobek 2009, 46, 54; de Visser 2014, 142, 382; Galič 2014a, 20–27).

As an individual may (after the exhaustion of all available remedies) appeal against a judgment which (allegedly) violates his fundamental rights (Galič 2014a, 21), the functions of constitutional courts and those of ordinary courts are bound to overlap, and this cannot but produce tensions and conflicts (Garlicki 2007, 65). However, since a duplication of functions is not an affordable luxury in public services (Drewry et al. 2007, 145), a constitutional court can be justified only if it

[10]In Germany, France and Belgium, for instance, in order to have access to the supreme court, the party needs to hire a specialised attorney.

[11]In that regard one has to be careful not to extend the factual and legal situations of another case if the cases do not really match (Galič 2017, 28).

can be shown that it performs a function that is different from that of the ordinary courts. It should not become a super-supreme court. Its scope should be much narrower, limited to questions of constitutional significance, leaving the interpretation of ordinary law to the general courts (Galič 2017, 3).[12]

If, on a constitutional complaint confronted with multiple possible interpretations, the constitutional court may be tempted to indicate which interpretation is constitutionally correct (Garlicki 2007, 49; Galič 2017, 10, 13) and if all interpretations are constitutionally acceptable, then it is not its task to decide which of them is correct. Questions concerning mistakes in interpretation and the application of norms which do not amount to violations of the constitution should be left out of the scope of the constitutional court's review (Galič 2014a, 22). However, experience has shown that constitutional courts are unable (or perhaps unwilling) to maintain a firm delimitation between the functions of the constitutional court and those of the supreme court (Garlicki 2007, 44; Galič 2014a, 22).

Something else is to be pointed out here as well. In some countries, such as the Czech Republic, Armenia, Poland, Hungary and Croatia (but not Slovenia[13]), the constitutional courts consider that even decisions of the supreme court denying permission to appeal need to contain written reasoning as to why the case is not considered important enough to be decided on by the supreme jurisdiction. Since judicial discretion is often viewed as behaviour that inevitably leads to arbitrariness (Uzelac 2008, 77), the response to the question Why were the "doors of the supreme court … shut on the party[?]" (Galič 2014b, 164) is, in the opinion of these constitutional courts, essential in order to ensure the legitimate and lawful exercise of the court's discretionary powers and an individual's confidence in a judicial act (Galič 2014b, 165).[14]

As a result, the supreme court judges and their clerks have to spend the vast majority of their time writing reasoned decisions in cases where they decide not to grant a second appeal (Bobek 2009, 49). It is believed that this is the way the constitutional court protects parties from arbitrary judicial decisions and prevents unreasoned supreme court decisions from being misused as a tool by less responsible judges in their efforts to get rid of cases (Bobek 2009, 57). In this situation, however, supreme court judges cannot fully devote their capacities to deciding cases of general importance (Galič 2014b, 161) and fulfilling the court's public role.

---

[12]The identification of constitutional matters, however, can be difficult especially in relation to the right to a fair trial, since almost any procedural violation by the ordinary courts could be seen as a violation of the right to a fair trial (Galič 2014a, 22).

[13]See Galič (2014b, 167, 168).

[14]While it is true that the European Court of Human Right has acknowledged that the supreme court is not required to give reasons for a decision not to grant permission to appeal, it nevertheless recently suggested on a couple of occasions (*Nersesyan v. Armenia*, No. 15371/07, § 25, 19 January 2010; *Wnuk v. Poland*, No. 38308/05, § 1c, 1 September 2009) that such a solution is not the preferred one (Galič 2014c, 307).

5 What to Do and How to Do It?

It has been acknowledged that the general perception of the extent of reasoning courts should provide in their decisions negatively correlates with the degree of trust these courts enjoy or deserve to enjoy (Uzelac 2011, 1566). Distrust of the judicial system holds true particularly for countries of the post-socialist legal tradition such as Poland, the Czech Republic, Hungary, Slovakia, Slovenia and Croatia. This holds true perhaps for the whole group of "Mediterranean systems" in the meaning this term was given by Uzelac (2008, 73, 74) and which could notionally cover not only post-socialist countries, but to some extent Italy, France and some South American countries, as well.

In a system that does not trust its own supreme court judges to do their work in a responsible manner, no procedural tool, however elaborate, would be a guarantee against misuse (Bobek 2009, 57, 58). In any event, the solution is to seek more trust, not more reasoning (Uzelac 2011, 1566). But if I am right in my belief that we agree that trust in the judiciary is important, then we must, after all, pay attention to the How? as well (cf. Jolowicz 1998, 63).

Lower courts have to take the decisions of the supreme court seriously, and the supreme court itself must take its new role seriously enough (Bravo-Hurtado 2014, 330). Only judges of the highest calibre and impeccable professional and personal integrity who use convincing legal arguments are worthy of public trust (Galič 2014b, 169; Zobec and Letnar Černič 2015, 148). In turn, public trust enables discretion in selecting important cases to be decided before the supreme jurisdiction. When this freedom concerns people's rights and duties, discretion in fact means power (Andrews 2003, 121). Since within the new role of the supreme court judges really exercise power, there should be a proportional relationship between the power and the responsibility of the judiciary towards the people (Bobek 2008, 111; Zobec and Letnar Černič 2015, 148).

The focus of the justice system in general should be on the interests of its users and not on any particular interests of other actors involved. The court of first instance should fulfil a predominantly private purpose of a just and correct resolution of every individual case. On the appellate level, the private purpose can be mixed with some public purpose features (rectification of errors and the overall interest in legality). The purpose of the supreme judicial level, however, should be a public one (Bobek 2009, 62, 63). In turn, the scope of the constitutional court should be limited to questions of constitutional significance. Within the limits of their duties, the attorneys are supposed to help their clients to protect their rights and explain to them the real prospects of their cases. Their professional remuneration should be in accordance with the complexity and quality of the work they perform.

Only through such a balanced interplay can the judicial system provide optimum protection of individual rights (Bobek 2009, 63), not only the rights of the (two) private parties in the litigation at hand, but of (all) prospective private parties in the future (Galič 2014a, 28).

6 Conclusion: The Place of the Stories?

Are all four stories and assessments of misperceptions based on reality? They are, as it is at least my impression, true for my country, Croatia. The statistical data on second appeals filed with the supreme court shown in the chart in Fig. 1 are official data of the Croatian Supreme Court.[15] However, are these stories only true for Croatia?

I assume that at least a few of my assessments are applicable to some other countries as well, and not only to the countries of the post-socialist legal tradition with a plethora of common normative and metanormative legal relics from the socialist legal culture (Uzelac 2010; Mańko 2013b, ch. 3). Some of the issues regarding an identity crisis of the supreme court have also preoccupied some Western European countries, for instance Germany and Spain (Gottwald 2008, 88; Galič 2014a, 7, 8), as has already been indicated in this contribution.

Not all the stories are applicable to all countries. For some countries, different stories can be added and for others some of the stories should be retold and other actors included. For instance, in a number of EU countries, where there is the trend of playing the EU law card in order to circumvent the authority of the national supreme jurisdiction (Komárek 2007, 8, 17), a special story concerns the Court of Justice of the EU.

Be that as it may, it is left for the reader to decide how much truth there is in the stories told here. Maybe, just like Faulkner's stories, none of them are right. Or maybe they are more right than we are willing to admit.

References

Andrews N (2003) Judicial discretion in common law jurisdictions: USA, England, Canada, Australia. In: Storme M, Hess B (eds) The discretionary power of the judge: limits and control. Kluwer, Mechelen, pp 119–242

Andrews N (2011) The United Kingdom's Supreme Court. Three sceptical reflections concerning the new court. Utah L Rev 9(1):9–24

Andrews N (2017) The Supreme Court of the United Kingdom: a selective tribunal with the final say on most matters. In: Van Rhee CH, Fu Y (eds) Supreme courts in transition in China and the West. Adjudication at the service of public goals. Springer, Cham, pp 37–51

Bobek M (2008) The fortress of judicial independence and the mental transitions of the Central European Judiciaries. Eur Public Law 14(1):99–123

Bobek M (2009) Quantity or quality? Reassessing the role of supreme jurisdictions in Central Europe. Am J Comp L 57:33–66

[15]Izvješće predsjednika Vrhovnog suda o stanju sudbene vlasti za 2016. godinu [Supreme Court President Report on the State of the Judiciary in 2016], Zagreb, April 2017, available at: https://vlada.gov.hr/UserDocsImages//Sjednice/2017/09%20rujan/57%20sjednica%20Vlade%20Republike%20Hrvatske//57%20-%2018.3.pdf. Accessed 7 June 2018.

Bravo-Hurtado P (2014) Two ways to uniformity. Recourse to the supreme court in the civil law and the common law world. In: Uzelac A, Van Rhee (eds) Nobody's perfect. Comparative essays on appeals and other means of recourse against judicial decisions in civil matters. Intersentia, Cambridge, Antwerp, Portland, pp 319–335

Chiarloni S (2008) Fundamental tasks of the *Corte di Cassazione*, heterogeneous objectives arosen from the constitutional right to appeal and recent reforms. In: Ortells Ramos M (ed) Los recursos ante los Tribunales Supremos en Europa (Appeals to supreme courts in Europe). Difusión juridical, Madrid, pp 77–86

Damaška MR (1986) The faces of justice and state authority. A comparative approach to the legal process. Yale, New Haven

de Benito M (2017) Civil cassation in Spain: past, present, and the future. In: Van Rhee CH, Fu Y (eds) Supreme courts in transition in China and the West. Adjudication at the service of public goals. Springer, Cham, pp 97–130

de Visser M (2014) Constitutional review in Europe. A comparative analysis. Hart Publishing, Oxford and Portland, Oregon

Domej T (2014) What is an important case? Admissibility of appeals to the supreme courts in the German-speaking jurisdictions. In: Uzelac A A, Van Rhee (eds) Nobody's perfect. Comparative essays on appeals and other means of recourse against judicial decisions in civil matters. Intersentia, Cambridge, Antwerp, Portland, pp 277–285

Drewry G, Blom-Cooper L, Blake Ch (2007) The court of appeal. Hart Publishing, Oxford and Portland, Oregon

Galič A (2014a) A civil law perspective on the supreme court and its functions. Paper presented at the conference the functions of the supreme court—issues of process and administration of justice. Warsaw, 11–14 June 2014

Galič A (2014b) Does a decision of the supreme court denying leave to appeal need to contain reasons? In: Adolphsen J et al (eds) Festschrift für Peter Gottwald zum 70. Geburtstag. CH Beck, München, pp 159–173

Galič A (2014c) Reshaping the role of supreme courts in the countries of the former Yugoslavia. In: Uzelac A, Van Rhee (eds) Nobody's perfect. Comparative essays on appeals and other means of recourse against judicial decisions in civil matters. Intersentia, Cambridge, Antwerp, Portland, pp 291–317

Galič A (2015) The aversion to judicial discretion in civil procedure in post-communist countries: Can the influence of EU law change it? In: Bobek M (ed) Central European judges under the European influence. The transformative power of the EU revisited. Hart Publishing, Oxford and Portland, Oregon, pp 99–124

Galič A (2017) The inconsistency of case law and the right to a fair trial. In: Uzelac A, Van Rhee CH (eds) Revisiting procedural human rights. Fundamentals of civil procedure and the changing face of civil justice. Intersentia, Cambridge, pp 17–51

Garlicki L (2007) Constitutional courts versus supreme courts. Int J Const Law 5(1):44–68

Gottwald P (2008) Review appeal to the German Federal Supreme Court after the reform of 2001. In: Ortells Ramos M (ed) Los recursos ante los Tribunales Supremos en Europa (Appeals to supreme courts in Europe). Difusión juridical, Madrid, pp 87–106

Herbert AP (1966) Wigs at work. Penguin, Harmondsworth

Jolowicz JA (1977) Appellate proceedings. In: Storme M, Casman H (eds) Towards a justice with a human face. The first international congress of the law of civil procedure (Faculty of Law, State University of Ghent, 27 August 1977–4 September 1977). Kluwer, Antwerpen, pp 128–165

Jolowicz JA (1980) Da mihi factum dabo tibi jus. A problem of demarcation in English and French law. In: Feuersten P, Parry C (eds) Multum non multa. Festschrift für Kurt Lipstein aus Anlass seines 70. Geburtstages. CF Müller Jurtistischer Verlag, Heidelberg, Karlsruhe, pp 79–99

Jolowicz JA (1988) Appeal, cassation, amparo and all that, what and why. Estudios en Homenaje al Doctor Héctor Fix-Zamudio III. Universidad Nacional Autónoma de México, Instituto de Investigaciones Juridicas, México, pp 2045–2074

Jolowicz JA (1998) The role of the supreme court at the national and international level. In: Yessiou-Faltsi P (ed) Reports for the Thessaloniki international colloquium (21–25 May 1997). Sakkoulas Publications, Thessaloniki, Athens, pp 37–63

Jolowicz JA (2000) On civil procedure. Cambridge University Press, New York

Komárek J (2007) In the court(s) we trust? On the need for hierarchy and differentiation in the preliminary ruling. Available at SSRN, https://ssrn.com/abstract=982529. Accessed 7 June 2018

Kühn Z (2006) The authoritarian legal culture at work. The passivity of parties and the interpretational statements of supreme courts. Croatian Yearb Eur Law Policy 2:19–26

Kühn Z (2011) The judiciary in Central and Eastern Europe. Mechanical jurisprudence in transformation? Martinus Nijhoff Publishers, Leiden, Boston

Lindblom PH (2000) Progressiv process – Spridda uppsatser om domstolsprocessen och samhällsutvecklingen. Iustus förlag, Uppsala

Mańko R (2013a) Survival of the socialist legal tradition? A Polish perspective. Comp Law Rev 4 (2). Available at SSRN, https://ssrn.com/abstract=2332219. Accessed 7 June 2018

Mańko R (2013b) Weeds in the garden of justice? The survival of hyperpositivism in Polish legal culture as a symptom/sinthome. Pólemos – J Law Lit Cult 7(2). Available at https://papers.ssrn.com/sol3/papers.cfm?abstract_id=2277857. Accessed 7 June 2018

Mattei UA, Ruskola T, Gidi A (2009) Schlesinger's comparative law. Thomson Reuters, Foundation Press, New York

Rodin S (2005) Discourse, authority in European and post-communist legal culture. Croatian Yearb Eur Law Policy 1(1):1–22

Silvestri E (2017) The Italian supreme court of cassation: of misnomers and unaccomplished missions. In: Van Rhee CH, Fu Y (eds) Supreme courts in transition in China and the West. Adjudication at the service of public goals. Springer, Cham, pp 229–245

Taruffo M (1998) The role of the supreme courts at the national and international level. Civil law countries. In: Yessiou-Faltsi P (ed) Reports for the Thessaloniki international colloquium (21–25 May 1997). Sakkoulas Publications, Thessaloniki, Athens, pp 101–126

Uzelac A (2008) Reforming Mediterranean civil procedure. Is there a need for shock therapy? In: Van Rhee CH, Uzelac A (eds) Civil justice between efficiency and quality. From *ius commune* to the CEPEJ. Intersentia, Antwerpen, Oxford, Portland, pp 71–99

Uzelac A (2010) Survival of the third legal tradition? Supreme Court Law Rev 49(2d):377–396

Uzelac A (2011) The need to provide reasons in court judgements, some developments in east and west. In: Gudowski J, Weitz K (eds) Aurea Praxis Aurea Theoria – Ksiega Pamiatkova ku czci Profesora Tadeusza Erecinskegiego. Tom I., LexisNexis, Warsaw, pp 1547–1566

Uzelac A, Galič A (2017) Changing faces of post-socialist supreme courts: Croatia and Slovenia compared. In: Van Rhee CH, Fu Y (eds) Supreme courts in transition in China and the West. Adjudication at the service of public goals. Springer, Cham, pp 207–228

Zobec J, Letnar Černič J (2015) The remains of the authoritarian mentality within the Slovene judiciary. In: Bobek M (ed) Central European judges under the European influence. The transformative power of the EU revisited. Hart Publishing, Oxford and Portland, Oregon, pp 125–148

Zuckerman AAS (1995) Reform in the shadow of lawyers' interests. In: Zuckerman AAS, Cranston R (eds) Reform of civil procedure. Essays on "access to justice". Clarendon, Oxford, pp 61–77

Marko Bratković Teaching Assistant in the Department of Civil Procedure at the University of Zagreb, Croatia. Visiting Scholar at the Max Planck Institute for Procedural Law in Luxembourg, and at the Max Planck Institute for Comparative and International Private Law in Hamburg and the Europa-Institut in Saarbrücken, Germany.

Transformation of the Cassation Model in France, The Netherlands and Belgium: Piercing the Legalistic Veil

Matthias Van Der Haegen

Abstract The supreme courts of France, the Netherlands and Belgium belong historically to the French cassation model. In recent years, these courts have witnessed profound changes that endanger this heritage. The reforms of their procedure and competence following years of case overload and backlogs pertain to some of the core features of the cassation model. The introduction of a preliminary procedure, the imposition of a stricter access regime, the use of a more elaborate reasoning style and the possibility to decide on the merits indicate that these courts of the cassation model are transforming their very nature from general guardians of the law into supreme appellate courts. This contribution discusses these reforms of the supreme courts of France, the Netherlands and Belgium and sheds light on their evolution away from the traditional cassation model.

1 Introduction

The supreme courts of France, the Netherlands and Belgium are built upon the French cassation model. This supreme court model is steeped in the legalistic ideals of the French Revolution. Reforms, both completed and currently proposed, threaten that heritage. In this contribution, I study the evolution of the cassation model through a comparative analysis of five recently reformed features of the cassation procedures of these three countries. The aim is to discern the direction in which the cassation model is moving, and the future that likely awaits the courts that adhere to this model. The goal is not to achieve completeness nor to give a

I am indebted to prof. dr. Dirk Heirbaut, prof. dr. Piet Taelman, dr. Sebastiaan Vandenbogaerde and Marko Bratkovic for their much appreciated comments on this text. Moreover, I would like to thank all participants of the PPJ 2017 conference, and in particular its organizers, for a week of fruitful discussions.

M. Van Der Haegen (✉)
Faculty of Law and Criminology, Ghent University, Ghent, Belgium
e-mail: matthiasr.vanderhaegen@ugent.be

A. Uzelac and C. H. van Rhee (eds.), *Transformation of Civil Justice*,
Ius Gentium: Comparative Perspectives on Law and Justice 70,
https://doi.org/10.1007/978-3-319-97358-6_19

detailed description of the cassation procedure, but rather to present an overview of the reforms that have taken place in order to sketch an ongoing evolution.

This contribution is structured as follows. I start with a brief history of the origin of the French cassation model in section two. This sets the stage for an overview in the third section of those changes in the cassation procedure that stand at odds with that origin. In the fourth section I discuss the future of the cassation model, before offering my conclusions in the fifth and final section.

2 History of the Cassation Model

The roots of the French cassation model date back to medieval France. Its origin lies in the principle of the *justice retenue*, the monarch's power to intervene at his own discretion in the judicial process through evocation of the case (Martinage-Baranger 1969, 285; Beauthier 1999, 13, 14). Formalized in several phases from 1303 onwards, two distinct mechanisms for revision of judgments rendered in last resort existed: the *proposition d'erreur* and the *requête civile*.[1] Both were brought before the king's (judicial) council. Even though in substance these mechanisms have little in common with the cassation appeal that exists today, the idea of revision of final judicial decisions links these precursors, across the French Revolution, to the present cassation mechanism.[2]

In the *Ancien Régime*, the cassation mechanism imposed a degree of administrative control on the judiciary (Boulet-Santel 1990, 23). During the French Revolution it served a similar purpose. The legalistic aspirations of the revolutionaries coalesced with the old means for revision, leading to the creation of the *Tribunal de cassation* in November 1790.[3] The Tribunal was tasked with ensuring the judges' compliance with the law and thus protecting the new legal order (Halpérin 1990, 27)[4] and guaranteeing the uniform application of that law throughout the nation, which was only shortly before characterized by the diversity of local customs and jurisprudence (Faye 1970, 1). Founded *auprès du corps*

[1]In short, the former aims at righting wrongs committed by the judge (both factual and legal errors), whereas the latter intends to remedy the (mis)conduct of the other party (Boulet-Santel 1990, 6; Beauthier 1999, 16–19). For a detailed study, see Dauchy (1988).

[2]The *Ordonnnance de Blois* of 1579 is widely considered the birth of the modern cassation mechanism (Boulet-Santel 1990, 6).

[3]More precisely by the Decree of 27 November 1790.

[4]This unequivocal mission is also emphasized in the alternative name that was proposed for the institution, namely the *Conseil national pour la conservation des lois*. See the Archives Parlementaires (1885, 337). See in this regard also Prugnon: '*[La cassation] est pour la loi ce que l'appel est pour le plaideur*' (Archives Parlementaires 1885, 330).

législatif,[5] the Tribunal acted as the parliament's watchdog, authorized to quash judgments delivered contrary to procedural rules or in violation of the text of the law,[6] but forbidden to interpret the law itself. In case of legislative ambiguity, the Tribunal had to ask the legislator for an interpretative law through the *référé législatif* procedure.

Despite its subordinate position vis-à-vis the law, the Tribunal, and later the *Cour de cassation*, expanded its authority and powers of its own accord, advancing from the mere explication to the interpretation of the law (Halpérin 1990, 51; Beauthier 1999, 62, 63).[7] This comes as no surprise, as already the drafters of the Napoleonic Civil Code recognized the fallibility of legislation and the consequent need for jurisprudence.[8] It was the court's task to guide the judiciary in that endeavour, and thus guarantee uniformity. The abolition of the *référé législatif* in 1837 only exacerbated this evolution,[9] so that by the middle of the 19th century the interpretation of the law was described as the court's first mission (Tarbé 1840, 82) and its case law as a beacon for the judiciary (Rivière 1862, v). From the guarantor of compliance the court became a pseudo-legislator itself. Its law-shaping activity is hidden behind a legalistic veil, however, as the court, true to its origin, remained deferential to the legislator and paid lip service to the law. Keeping up these appearances was necessary due to the reigning theory of legal sources, which denies binding force to anything other than acts bearing the legislator's seal.

3 Transformation of the Cassation Model

The supreme courts of France, Belgium and the Netherlands all inherited the above-described system to different extents (Martyn 2013, 218).[10] In all three countries, reforms have taken place in the last several decades, and reform proposals have been put forward recently that threaten this legacy and change the

---

[5]Article 1 of the Decree of 27 November 1790 reads as follows: '*Il y aura un Tribunal de cassation établi auprès du Corps législatif.*' The meaning of this last phrase has been much debated. Did the Tribunal belong to the judiciary, or was it rather part of the legislative branch of government? See for a discussion Halpérin (1990, 28–30) and Beauthier (1999, 38–41). Halpérin is of the opinion that this phrase merely settles the discussion on the location of the newly established institution in favour of Paris, which houses the seat of the *Assemblée nationale*.

[6]Article 3 Decree of 27 November 1790.

[7]This evolution was initially fuelled by the lack of (uniform) legislation (Bloquet 2017, 265).

[8]See e.g. Projet de Code civile 1801, xix.

[9]See Beauthier (1999, 66–70) for a discussion of the evolution of the *référé légisatif*. In Belgium, the *référé législatif* was abolished in 1865 (Beauthier 1999, 88–92).

[10]This is least true for the Dutch Cassation Court, which received at its inception in 1838 already some updates to the original cassation model. The Netherlands has, moreover, a more troublesome relationship with this heritage. In 1909, already the *Nederlandse Juristenvereniging*, the Dutch Society of Jurists, proposed to abolish the cassation mechanism completely (Haak 2008, 50; Veegens et al. 2015, 56, 57).

nature of the cassation model. The main impetus behind these reforms has been the massive case overload. Starting from the second half of the 20th century, the courts began accumulating a considerable backlog. Being corseted into a mindset of mass-production, this case engorgement endangered their normative mission (Tunc 1978a, 22, 23). The wish to tackle this backlog and strengthen the courts' normative mission led to reforms in several features of the cassation model. In this contribution, I will discuss five of these reformed characteristics. These are the competence of the cassation court, access to the court, the preliminary procedure before the court, remittal of the case after annulment, and the court's reasoning.

3.1 Competence

Express violation of the law defined the competence of the cassation courts, which was therefore often described as the guardian of the law. Law in this context must be narrowly understood as legislative acts of parliament. In recent years, reforms amended the competence of the courts by broadening the basis for annulment to include the violation of general principles of law.[11] This is a small but meaningful change, as the premise of the French legal system rests upon the reduction of the concept of law to legislation (Zenati 1992, 247).

3.1.1 France

The competence of the French *Cour de cassation* changed in 1979[12] when the court became authorized to quash judgments contrary to the *règles de droit* (legal rules), as opposed to the much narrower *loi* (legislation).[13] This sanctioned the court's earlier practice of annulling decisions that were contrary to general principles of law (Boré and Boré 2015, 249, 250).[14] In its decisions, the court must specify the legal provision for the violation of which it annuls a judgment.[15] In 2008, Article 1020 of the Code of Civil Procedure was amended to reflect the 1979 reform: the court now has to indicate the legal rule, rather than the statutory provision, that was violated.[16]

[11]The judiciary 'finds' these principles (Marchal 2014, 27, 28). This challenges the legalistic underpinnings of the Cassation Court and highlights its normative law-shaping, independent of the text of the law.

[12]Decree n° 79-941 of 7 November 1979.

[13]Article 604 French Code of Civil Procedure.

[14]These general principles of law are often used by the French Court of Cassation to limit or alter the field of application of a legal provision. See Gridel (2002). This practice is blatantly at odds with the origin of the cassation model.

[15]Article 1020 French Code of Civil Procedure. See also Article 17 of the Decree of 27 November 1790.

[16]Decree n° 2008-484 of 22 May 2008.

3.1.2 The Netherlands

In the Netherlands, a similar change occurred in 1963[17] when the competence of the *Hoge Raad* to annul judgments changed from violation of *wet* (legislative provisions) to violation of *recht* (legal rules),[18] comparable to the distinction between *loi* and *droit* in France. Again, this change was a legislative *ex post facto* approval of an earlier practice (Veegens et al. 2005, 171, 172), motivated by the need to bring uniformity in those areas of law aside from formal legislation (Memorie van Toelichting 1951, 4).

3.1.3 Belgium

In Belgium, a similar change has not yet materialized. The competence of the *Cour de cassation/Hof van Cassatie* is still limited to the violation of the law (*loi/wet*).[19] Just as its counterparts in neighbouring countries, however, the court accepted from the 1950s onwards the violation of a general principle of law as grounds for annulment (Hof van Cassatie 2003, 131).[20] This is the case even if that principle cannot be embedded within an existing legislative provision that encompasses its meaning. If, however, such a provision exists, artificial as the connection may be (Cornil 1952, 468), its omission in the appeal will result in its inadmissibility (Hof van Cassatie 2003, 131). The Belgian practice thus remains more legalistic compared to the practice in France and the Netherlands.

3.2 Access to the Court

The goal of the *Tribunal de cassation* at its inception was to guarantee the faithful application of the law by the judges who had a tendency to deviate from it, as the law stated.[21] This was achieved by annulling those judgments contrary to the law, as revealed by the systematic comparison of the appealed judgment with the

---

[17]Act of 20 June 1963.

[18]See Article 79 Dutch Act of Judicial Organization. For an overview, see Veegens (1965, 182–189).

[19]Article 608 Belgian Code of Civil Procedure.

[20]It is the court itself that decides what counts as such a general principle of law. See Verougstraete (2010, 451, 452).

[21]The legal provision reads: '*Le Tribunal de cassation n'est point en effet un degré d'appel ni de juridiction ordinaire, et il n'est institué que pour ramener perpétuellement à l'exécution de la loi toutes les parties de l'ordre judiciaire qui tendraient à s'en écarter: le but de cette institution suffit pour expliquer sa compétence.*' The Decree of 29 September 1791. See also the intervention of Robespierre and Chabroud in the parliamentary debate leading to the Decree of 27 November 1790 (Archives Parlementaires 1885, 336–338).

relevant statutory provision (Faye 1970, 1).[22] The general distrust of the judiciary required an open access to the court (Asser 2011, 72; Bloquet 2017, 258; Ferrand 2017, 186): given the admissibility of the appeal, every decision that is contrary to the law has to be annulled (Ferrand 2017, 188). From the outset, however, the court did have an institutional access filter in the *bureau des requêtes*,[23] which was tasked with either accepting or rejecting appeals depending on whether the court was competent to hear the case, and whether the grievances set out by the plaintiff in his appeal seemed to hold true (Tarbé 1840, 96).[24] This procedural step was primarily aimed at saving the defendant time and money.[25] The specialized bar at the courts also works as an informal access filter (Asser 2011, 72, 73).[26]

The open access to the court led to a torrent of appeals and rapidly growing backlogs, especially in the second half of the 20th century (Ferrand 2017, 188). Initially, institutional measures were taken to combat the growing docket, but with only temporary effect.[27] Salvation was to be found in limiting access to the court. Such measures can be divided into three categories: access can be denied before, at, or after the gate. The gate is used in this context as a metaphor for access to the court's procedure. The first system would negate the open access principle, one of the tenets of the cassation model (Barthölemy 2000, 189–191), and therefore selection mechanisms at or after the gate were adopted. Today, all three courts have procedures in place that allow for the passive selection of cases whilst adhering to the open access principle. Appeals can be lodged without substantial access restrictions, but unmeritorious cases that would unduly drain the court's resources are put on a procedural sidetrack that leads to their swift dismissal by a limited panel. The efficient management of scarce resources justifies the different treatment cases receive.[28]

---

[22]Le Chapelier during the parliamentary debate leading to the Decree of 27 November 1790: '*De quoi s'agit-il en effet? De comparer l'arrêt rendu avec la loi*' (Archives Parlementaires 1885, 485).

[23]Originally, the *Tribunal de cassation* was composed of two chambers: the *bureau des requêtes* and the *chambre de cassation*. The latter was split up into a civil chamber and criminal chamber by the Decree of 29 September 1793 (Tarbé 1840, 27).

[24]Article 5 of the Act of 10–15 April 1792 abolished this preliminary step in criminal cases.

[25]The proceedings only became contradictory after admittance of the case by the *bureau des requêtes* (Tarbé 1840, 94–96; Beauthier 1999, 43 footnote 102).

[26]In France and Belgium such a specialized bar has always existed. In the Netherlands, this is the case only since 2012 (Verkerk and Van Rhee 2017, 92, 93).

[27]Augmenting the number of justices, creating new chambers or hiring clerks are institutional measures that have been taken in the past in all courts. The disadvantage of these solutions is that with greater numbers comes an increased risk of contradictory decisions in the court's case law (Canivet 2005, 6, 7).

[28]See in this context also Zuckerman (2013, 2–5).

3.2.1 France

The basis of the two-track policy in France is the *formation restreinte*, a panel of three justices operating within each chamber. Founded in 1979, its main aim is to fight the growing caseload burden of the court (Marcilhacy 1978, 3, 4, 15, 16). As a filter mechanism competent to dismiss manifestly inadmissible or unfounded appeals, it is a continuation of the *chambre des requêtes* that was abolished in 1947.[29] Its competence changed in 1981, when it became authorized to hear all cases in which the solution seems obvious and was allowed to quash decisions instead of merely rejecting appeals.[30] Since 1997, all civil cases are brought before the *formation restreinte*. Only when the solution is not obvious will the case be sent for adjudication to the standard panel of five justices.[31]

This system allowed the court to allocate its resources more efficiently. More, however, was needed to combat the backlog. In 2001,[32] the procedure of *non-admission* was introduced, which gave the *formation restreinte* the possibility to declare inadmissible appeals or those lacking serious grounds of cassation 'not admissible'.[33] This term is partly confusing as, for the second type of cases it targets, it requires an examination of the merits of the case (Vigneau 2010, 107; Terrier 2013, 100; Ferrand 2017, 201). The decision in which an appeal is declared not admissible does not contain reasons but features merely a standard sentence.[34] The statutory provision did not, however, allow the court *expressis verbis* to reject cases without reasoning (Boré and Boré 2003, 62). And contrary to its plain meaning, the court sometimes declared certain grievances within an appeal 'not admissible', whilst giving a reasoned answer to others (Amrani-Mekki 2005, 23; Vigneau 2010, 105; Jobard-Bachelier et al. 2013, 15; Terrier 2013, 96). Given this ambiguity, Article 1014 of the French Code of Civil Procedure was amended in 2014.[35] The confusing term *non-admission* was dropped, and the provision presently states that the *formation restreinte* can decline to give an especially reasoned decision[36] when the appeal is inadmissible or can manifestly not lead to cassation. Now every panel of the court has the ability to declare an appeal (partially)

[29]The *bureau*, later *chambre des requêtes*, was suspended in 1947. This is perceived as one of the main reasons for the later case overload of the court (Corpart 1995, 4).

[30]Act No. 81-759 of 6 August 1981.

[31]See Article L431-1 French Code of Judicial Organization. The first president or president of the chamber may also decide to send the case immediately to the larger panel. Criminal cases are normally heard by a panel composed of five justices. They can, however, refer the case to the *formation restreinte* (Amrani-Mekki 2005, 21).

[32]Act No. 2001-539 of 25 June 2001.

[33]Article 1014 French Code of Civil Procedure.

[34]However, the court does send the report of the *juge-rapporteur* concerning the *non-admission* to the parties (Canivet 2005, 10; Fricero 2008, 28, 29).

[35]Decree n° 2014-1338 of 6 November 2014.

[36]The use of the term 'especially reasoned' (*spécialement motivée*) is quite ironic, given the fact that regular decisions of the court do not exactly excel in their reasoning either. See Sect. 3.5.1.

non-admis.[37] The court makes extensive use of this possibility. In 2016, 57% of criminal cases were dismissed following a decision of *non-admission* (Cour de cassation 2016, 325).[38] In civil cases, 26.7% of the appeals received a not especially motivated answer, which accounts for 42.5% of all dismissals (Cour de cassation 2016, 324). The court's caseload benefitted considerably from this new procedure (Boré and Boré 2015, 73).

The government submitted a profound reform proposal in parliament in 2016. Following this proposal, an appeal to the court would only be allowed in civil cases if it raises an important question, is of interest for legal development or important for the unification of case law.[39] Only certain predefined disciplinary grievances could still lead to annulment through a simplified procedure. For criminal cases, the violation of the law was added as a fourth admissibility criterion.[40] The goal of this reform was to allow the court to hear only those cases that pertain to its normative mission.[41] Before being put to a vote, however, the government withdrew the amendment.

3.2.2 The Netherlands

The possibility to hear cases with a panel of three justices was introduced in the *Hoge Raad* in 1986.[42] Two years later, the court was given the authority to dismiss grievances summarily.[43] The rationale behind this reform was the heavy workload and resultant growing backlog (Memorie van Toelichting 1987, 1). Whenever a grievance entails a workload for the court that is not proportional to its legal importance, summary dismissal was deemed appropriate (Memorie van Toelichting 1987, 3). Article 81 of the Act on Judicial Organization allows the court to not answer grievances if they cannot lead to annulment or if they do not require an answer to a legal question which is relevant to legal uniformity or legal development. If both conditions are met, the court's response to that grievance can suffice with stating as much. If all grievances meet these criteria, the entire appeal can be dismissed without reasoning. This system has proven to be invaluable in fighting the court's heavy workload (Hammerstein 2008, 18, 19; Veegens et al. 2015, 400). The dispensation from the need to provide reasoning in every case also led to more

[37]Previously, other panels had also declared appeals (partially) non-admissible, relying on the maxim '*Qui peut le plus, peut le moins*' (Amrani-Mekki 2005, 26; Terrier 2013, 96).

[38]Despite the fact that the term has been dropped from the provision, it remains in use for the purpose of describing the system.

[39]Amendement présenté par le Gouvernement, n° CL166, Assemblée nationale, 30 April 2016, 1. See Haftel (2016) and Ferrand (2016).

[40]Amendement présenté par le Gouvernement, n° CL166, Assemblée nationale, 30 April 2016, 2.

[41]Amendement présenté par le Gouvernement, n° CL166, Assemblée nationale, 30 April 2016, 2.

[42]Act of 21 June 1986. See Article 75 Act on Judicial Organization. The competence of the limited panel is understood as pertaining to uncomplicated cases (Verkerk and Van Rhee 2017, 90).

[43]Act of 16 June 1988.

extensive reasoning in cases that would benefit from it (Haak 2008, 66; Snijders 2010, 82).[44]

In 2008, the Commission for the Normative Mission of the *Hoge Raad*, better known under the name of its president, Alfred Hammerstein, as the Hammerstein Commission, concluded that although Article 81 had proven its worth, it was flawed in the sense that it only dismissed the cases that unduly arrogate the court's scarce resources at the final stage of the proceedings by relieving the court of its duty to provide reasons (Hammerstein 2008, 38, 39).[45] In order to deter such cases from being brought before the court in the first place, some sort of selection mechanism was deemed necessary (Hammerstein 2008, 39, 40). Parliament reacted in 2012 with the enactment of Article 80a of the Act on Judicial Organization.[46] The aim was to dismiss cases at an earlier stage of the proceedings than was hitherto possible, providing the court with the necessary latitude to focus on its core mission (Memorie van Toelichting 2010, 1).[47] In furtherance of that goal, Article 80a allows the *Hoge Raad* to declare appeals inadmissible if the grievances they contain do not justify the continuation of the proceedings because the party who lodged the appeal has apparently insufficient cause, or if the grievances can apparently not result in annulment. The Advocate-General identifies in which cases application of Article 80a appears warranted. A panel of three justices can subsequently decide to dismiss the case (Verkerk and Van Rhee 2017, 92).[48] If the case is dismissed, the court's reasoning can suffice with the acknowledgment that the conditions for application of Article 80a have been met.[49]

Before the introduction of Article 80a, the court made extensive use of Article 81. In 2011, 55 per cent of civil cases were entirely dismissed without reasoning on the basis of that provision (Hoge Raad 2013, 80). In criminal cases, it was 81.5% (Hoge Raad 2013, 82). Since Article 80a came into force, these numbers have changed. In 2016, 30% of civil cases were dismissed on the basis of Article 81, whereas 14% were dismissed through Article 80a (Hoge Raad 2016, 4). In criminal cases, Article 80a receives much more application: 12% of cases in which grievances were put forward by the claimant were dismissed through Article 81, compared to 62.6% through Article 80a (Hoge Raad 2016, 7).

---

[44]See also Sect. 3.5.2.

[45]Article 81 saved the justices much time, but less so for the Advocates-General whose opinions serve as the basis for the application of Article 81. See Schaffmeiste (1988, 103, 104) and Hammerstein (2008, 18).

[46]Act of 15 March 2012. The selection mechanism as enacted differs considerably from that put forward by the Hammerstein Commission. See Van Der Haegen (2015, 1266).

[47]This memorandum of explanation fails, however, to define what these core missions are, mentioning rather all missions of the court. Teuben (2012, 102) argues that these 'core missions' to which the memorandum refers are the court's tasks of providing legal uniformity and development, and to a lesser extent legal protection.

[48]Article 80a(3) Act on Judicial Organization.

[49]Article 80a(4) Act on Judicial Organization.

3.2.3 Belgium

The Belgian Court of Cassation has a panel of three justices since 1997.[50] Unlike its neighbouring countries, however, the court does not have a system in place that allows for the swift dismissal of cases without a reasoned judgment, except in criminal cases since 2014.

Originally, the limited panel was competent to hear all cases in which the solution seemed obvious, a criterion identical to the one used in France.[51] Its competence was broadened in 2014 by adding a new criterion: the limited panel can also hear those cases which do not require an answer to a legal question which is important for the uniformity of the case law or development of the law.[52] Only after the advice of the Advocate-General and the suggestion by the judge-rapporteur can a panel of three justices adjudicate the case. The lack of unanimity amongst the three justices suffices to send the case to a larger panel.[53] The court does not have the possibility to dismiss these cases without a reasoned judgement, however, even though the court has argued in favour of such a procedure and bills have been introduced in parliament to that purpose in the past (Van Der Haegen 2015, 1292, 1293). Currently, only the Dutch-speaking sections of the court make use of the ability to hear cases with three justices (Regout 2017, 196).

Further steps have been taken in criminal cases. Since 2014,[54] the president of the criminal chamber can declare appeals inadmissible without hearing the parties if the Advocate-General assents. This is possible when the case is manifestly inadmissible because it is clearly aimless or puts forward neither infringements nor irregularities that could lead to annulment.[55] The decision of inadmissibility must be reasoned, although only briefly, and cannot be appealed.[56] This procedure is used only for those appeals that are prima facie inadmissible, e.g. an appeal against a decision of the court itself.

3.3 Preliminary Procedure

In modern society, in which the law is as complex and fast-moving as the society of which it is a product, the need for legal certainty is increasingly pressing. The traditional way in which cassation case law is established, namely by a decision after the issue has matured in case law and doctrine, no longer fits a society in

[50] Act of 6 May 1997.
[51] Article 1105bis Belgian Code of Civil Procedure.
[52] Act of 10 April 2014.
[53] Article 1105bis(2) Belgian Code of Civil Procedure.
[54] Act of 14 February 2014.
[55] Article 433(1) Belgian Code of Criminal Procedure.
[56] Article 433(2) Belgian Code of Criminal Procedure.

which legislation has a relatively short lifespan. In order to strengthen its normative mission, the courts' method of legislative interpretation needed rejuvenation to accommodate this evolution. The preliminary procedure fits this purpose, as it allows the courts to shed their light on a novel legal issue more quickly. It was hoped that the consequently reinforced legal certainty would result in less litigation (Zenati 1992, 249; Boré and Boré 2015, 75). This technique has its drawbacks as well, however. It requires the court to rule on an issue before it has sufficiently ripened, heightening the risk of future reversals.

3.3.1 France

Since 1991 the *Cour de cassation* can render so-called *avis* in all areas of law.[57] The aim of this was to allow quicker unification of the interpretation given to (new) laws, and eliminate future litigation and diverging case law, as the highest court's view on the issue is immediately known (Coeuret 1991, 615; Rudloff 1991, 5; Buffet 2000, 1).[58] The legislator consciously labelled the procedure *saisine pour avis* ('referral for advice') in order to reflect its lack of binding authority (Boré and Boré 2003, 66).[59] An *avis* is considered to be merely an indication of the court's (future) position on the specific issue, serving as a starting point for the discussion between courts and doctrine (Libchaber 2003). The *avis*, however, do have substantial moral weight. To reflect their authority, the *avis* were initially rendered by an ad hoc panel consisting of the first president of the court, the presidents of the different chambers and two justices from the chamber that would normally be competent (Boré and Boré 2015, 78). In 2016,[60] this was changed: *avis* are now rendered by the chamber to whose competence the issue belongs.[61] The panel for appeals and *saisines pour avis* is now the same, which is thought to prevent possible disparities between *avis* and decisions[62] and make the procedure more popular (Piwnica 2017).

---

[57]Article L441-1 French Code of Judicial Organization. In criminal cases only since 2002 (Organic Act No. 2001-539 of 25 June 2001). The field of application is, however, limited in the criminal law area: the Court of Assizes cannot ask for an *avis*, nor can a court in cases dealing with pre-trial detention.

[58]The overarching aim was to combat the ever-growing backlog in the court (Darnanville 2001, 416).

[59]The initiating judge is not bound by the decision of the court, nor are any other jurisdictions or the court itself. It is, however, unlikely for the initiating judge not to follow the court's opinion (Zenati 1992; Boré and Boré 2015, 79). See Article L441-3 French Code of Judicial Organization.

[60]Act No. 2016-1547 of 18 November 2016.

[61]Article L441-2 French Code of Judicial Organization. If, however, the question belongs *ratione materiae* to the competence of more than one chamber, it is heard by a mixed panel. If a *demande pour avis* raises a question of principle, the plenary assembly will hear it. The plenary assembly comprises the first president and the president, the dean and a justice of each chamber of the court. See Article L421-5 French Code of Judicial Organization.

[62]Such disparities have occurred in the past (Ferrand 2016, 2417).

Several conditions must be met if a lower court wishes to request an *avis*: the legal question[63] must be of significant difficulty, novel and relate to a large number of other cases. The novelty requirement is interpreted by the court as pertaining to novel legislation (Boré and Boré 2015, 76).[64] Around 11 decisions are rendered annually in the *saisine pour avis* procedure (Cour de cassation 2016, 340). They share the same brevity as the court's judgments (Fulchiron 2015, 21).[65] In the recent past, the court has also published replies,[66] conceptually similar to *avis* but without any formal procedure, in response to questions from judges, detailing how new statutory provisions should be interpreted (Molfessis 2007; Fricero 2008, 26). This initiative presents yet a new step in the way the court fulfils its normative mission.

3.3.2 The Netherlands

In its report, the Hammerstein Commission indicated that important legal questions do not always reach the *Hoge Raad* (timely), which hinders its mission of legal development and endangers legal certainty and uniformity (Hammerstein 2008, 50; Stolp and de Groot 2012, 165). The Commission therefore advocated the introduction of a preliminary procedure in civil cases. Such a procedure, called *prejudiciële vraagstelling*, was enacted in early 2012.[67] Four years later, its scope was expanded to include tax law[68] following a generally positive experience with the procedure in the civil law area.[69]

---

[63]The question must be of a general and abstract nature and must not require any inquiry into the factual circumstances of the case. See Cour de cassation 23 May 2016, avis n° V 16-700.02, http://www.courdecassation.fr, conclusion of AG Vassallo, 17–20. Accessed 7 June 2018.

[64]It is unclear how the court defines novel. In one instance, the court dismissed a case relating to an old but unresolved controversy dating back to the original *Code civil* of 1804. Cour de cassation 14 June 1993, avis n° 0930006 P, http://www.courdecassation.fr. Accessed 7 June 2018. In a different decision, the court admitted a preliminary question even though it pertained to legislation over 20 years old. Cour de cassation 10 January 2000, avis n° 02020001 P, http://www.courdecassation.fr. Accessed 7 June 2018. See also Buffet (2000, 5, 6).

[65]See, however, Sect. 3.5.1.

[66]Albeit with the *Service de Documentation et d'Etudes* as intermediary.

[67]Act of 9 February 2012. Since 1963, the mechanism of *sprongcassatie* exists, comparable to the UK's leapfrog appeal, in which parties can agree after the first instance proceedings to bring their case directly to the *Hoge Raad*, bypassing the court of appeal. This differs from the *prejudiciële vraagstelling*, as it requires both a finished first instance procedure and the assent of the parties, and is solely aimed at cutting short the length of proceedings (Memorie van Toelichting 1951, 5; Veegens et al. 2015, 118–121; Den Dekker and Van Den Eshof 2015, 108). See Article 398 Dutch Code of Civil Procedure.

[68]Article 27ga–27ge Dutch State Taxes Act, as introduced by the Act of 23 December 2015.

[69]This was advocated by both the court and legal practice (Hoge Raad 2014, 43; Van Suilen 2012). Barkhuysen and Schuurmans (2013) defended the enactment of a preliminary procedure in administrative law as well.

The aim of the procedure is to provide guiding judgments for lower courts (Verkerk and Van Rhee 2017, 94). Article 392 of the Dutch Code of Civil Procedure outlines the criteria which a preliminary question must meet. First of all, the question must be a legal question. Secondly, the importance of the question must transcend the case at hand. The law details two such instances: the answer to the question must either be relevant to a substantial number of claims based on the same or similar facts or causes, or to numerous other cases sharing a similar fact pattern in which the same question is present.[70] Thirdly, the answer to the question must be necessary to decide the case. This criterion eliminates hypothetical questions (Stolp and de Groot 2012, 166). In its first preliminary ruling, the *Hoge Raad* argued that the constraints of the normal cassation procedure do not apply in the preliminary procedure: the facts as established by the lower court serve merely as guidance and do not bind the court.[71] Unlike in the French procedure, in the Dutch procedure the initiating judge is bound by the court's (*Hoge Raad*'s) decision.[72] An interesting feature is that the court can allow *amici curiae* to file written pleadings.[73] After a slow start, the number of preliminary rulings reached a peak in 2015 with 12 decisions (Hoge Raad 2015, 11).

3.3.3 Belgium

The Belgian Supreme Court does not have a preliminary procedure, except since 2006 in the area of competition law.[74] So far, only five such questions have been submitted to the court, and the reform plans of the current Minister of Justice include the abolition of this procedure (Van Der Haegen 2015, 1301). In 1995, a bill was introduced that aimed at introducing a general preliminary procedure at the Court of Cassation, but it failed to materialize (Van Der Haegen 2015, 1301, 1302). The implementation of a preliminary procedure has been defended in literature (De Corte 2008, 168, 169; Morbée 2013) and some justices appear to be favourable to the idea, but no parliamentary action seems to be underway.

---

[70]Article 392(1) Dutch Code of Civil Procedure.

[71]Hoge Raad 8 February 2013, ECLI:NL:HR:2013:BY4889, 3.1.

[72]Article 394(1) and Article 392(6) Dutch Code of Civil Procedure and Article 27ge Dutch State Taxes Act.

[73]Article 393(2) Dutch Code of Civil Procedure. The court has also allowed *amici curiae* to intervene in a cassation in the interest of procedural law as well (Hoge Raad, 6 June 2014, ECLI: NL:HR:2014:1342).

[74]Article IV 76 Belgian Code of Business Law. See for an extensive discussion: Bossuyt (2013).

3.4 Remittal

In the traditional cassation mechanism, the case is sent back to a lower court if an appeal is successful in obtaining annulment. The cassation court cannot hear factual issues, which makes it impossible for it to decide on the merits. The rules of remittal are a relic of the historical conception of the *tribunal de cassation* as an institution falling somewhere in between the legislative and judicial branches of government rather than a full-blown judicial court. In the traditional view, the cassation court is an independent review body, foreign to the normal court system, tasked with judging judgments and not cases (Leclercq 1953, 30, 31; Haak 2008, 57). As such, the Tribunal was explicitly forbidden to rule on the merits and was obliged to remit after annulment.[75]

The demands of modernization and economization left no sacred cows untouched, however. Annulment and subsequent referral drains the parties' time and resources and leaves more work to the lower courts, all of which could be avoided if the supreme court itself were able to rule on the merits (Tunc 1978b, 434, 435). To accommodate the requirement to do justice within a reasonable amount of time, reforms have been passed in the courts to allow adjudication on the merits (Boré and Boré 2015, 718). In order to square them with the original conception of the cassation court, these reforms rest on the premise that the procedure before annulment differs conceptually from the procedure afterwards. The drawback is that the ability to rule on the merits strengthens the conception of a cassation court as a third instance court, albeit with limited powers (Luxembourg 2006, 2358; Boré and Boré 2015, 718). Moreover, it partially cuts short the dialogue between the supreme court and the lower jurisdictions. Intrinsically linked with remittal is the question on the value of the highest court's decision in the procedure following remittal. This will be touched upon briefly.

3.4.1 France

The principle that the *Cour de cassation* cannot decide on the merits, so unequivocally stipulated in 1790, has lost some of its rigour: Article L411-2 of the Act on Judicial Organization explicitly allows exceptions. Following annulment, the case is in principle remitted to a court of the same nature as the court whose decision was annulled.[76] Since 1979, however, the court has the ability to annul decisions without remittal and put an end to the litigation itself.[77]

[75] Article 3 of the Decree of 27 November 1790: '*Sous aucun prétexte et en aucun cas, le Tribunal de cassation ne pourra connaître du fond des affaires. Après avoir cassé les procédures ou le jugement, il renverra le fond des affaires aux tribunaux qui devront en connaître, ainsi qu'il sera fixé ci-après.*'.

[76] Article L431-4 French Code of Judicial Organization.

[77] Act No. 79-9 of 3 January 1979. In 1967 already, the *Assemblée plénière* was able to judge on the merits under certain conditions. This reform remained a dead letter, however (Vexliard 2013, 103; Boré and Boré 2015, 718).

Currently the court can choose not to remit in three distinct instances, with the last change occurring in late 2016.[78] When the annulment does not imply that a new decision on the merits is necessary, the court can quash without remittal.[79] Secondly, when a decision on the merits is needed, the court may decide on the substance when the facts, as established and appreciated by the lower court, allow it to apply the applicable legal rule to those facts.[80] The court will then apply the same or a different rule to facts already established (Luxembourg 2006, 2360; Piwnica 2017). When new factual issues need resolving, the prerequisites are not met, and the court must always remit. Since the 2016 reforms, this second possibility is limited to criminal cases only. Thirdly, in civil cases the court may rule on the merits whenever the interest of the good administration of justice so requires.[81] This last condition was added in late 2016[82] and aims to prevent the unnecessary protraction of proceedings.[83] It was suggested that the court could make use of the possibility[84] this provision offers depending on the extent of the lower courts' backlog.[85] In order to guarantee the equal treatment of litigants irrespective of whether the court remits or not, it is vital that the court dispose of the same abilities when deciding on the merits as would a lower court upon remittal (Luxembourg 2006, 2361, 2362; Piwnica 2017; Texier 2017).[86] This entails *inter alia* the possibility to hear new claims, both factual and legal (Luxembourg 2006, 2361). The parties must be informed whenever the court wishes to annul without remittal or rule on the merits, and that the court may ask them to submit all information that could be useful for the decision on the merits.[87]

If the court does remit the case after annulment, the trial court is not bound by its opinion (Boré and Boré 2015, 699). If upon remittal that court contradicts the cassation decision, and a second appeal is brought, the appeal will be decided by the full bench,[88] whose decision will be binding upon the court to whom the case is remitted.[89] Although compliance is only rarely mandatory, the decisions of the

[78]Act No. 2016-1547 of 18 November 2016.

[79]Article L411-3(1) French Code of Judicial Organization. For example, when the court decides that French courts are not competent to hear the case. More examples can be found in Boré and Boré (2015, 717, 718) and Luxembourg (2006).

[80]Article L411-3(3) French Code of Judicial Organization.

[81]Article L411-3(2) French Code of Judicial Organization.

[82]Act No. 2016-1547 of 18 November 2016.

[83]Amendement présenté par le Gouvernement, n° CL165, Assemblée nationale, 30 April 2016, 1.

[84]Such discretion does not exist in Germany, where §563 of the *Zivilprozessordnung* requires the *Bundesgerichtshof* to rule on the merits whenever the conditions are met.

[85]Amendement présenté par le Gouvernement, n° CL165, Assemblée nationale, 30 April 2016, 1.

[86]See Boré and Boré (2015, 735–738) with regard to the competence of the court upon remittal.

[87]Article 1015 French Code of Civil Procedure as amended by Decree n° 2017-396 of 24 March 2017.

[88]Article L431-6 French Code of Judicial Organization.

[89]Article L431-4(2) French Code of Judicial Organization.

Court of Cassation have considerable authority. Compliance is in practice therefore the rule rather than the exception (Bell et al. 2008, 30; Boré and Boré 2015, 741).

3.4.2 The Netherlands

In the Netherlands, the situation is considerably different. The *Hoge Raad* has had the ability to rule on the merits since its inception in 1838 (Haak 2008, 57; Veegens et al. 2015, 406).[90] After annulment, the court will in principle decide on the substance of the case.[91] If for a decision on the merits, however, further factual inquiry is necessary, the court will remit unless it concerns only a subsidiary issue and the information found in the case dossier suffices for its resolution.[92] Although such a system is alien to the pure cassation mechanism, pragmatic considerations justified it (Memorie van Toelichting 1951, 6). If after an annulment only questions of law still need resolving, the court has the option whether to remit or not.[93] The court has interpreted its ability to decide on the merits broadly,[94] guided mainly by the interest of economization of the proceedings (Veegens et al. 2015, 410). At all times, the *Hoge Raad* is bound by the appreciation of the facts by the lower judge.[95] Nonetheless, the court sees itself as a court of third instance rather than a court of cassation when deciding on the merits of a case.[96]

In the event of annulment and remittal, the case is in principle sent back to the judge who rendered the annulled decision.[97] In practice, however, the court usually sends the case to another judge,[98] unless the court that rendered the appealed decision is unique (Dempsey 2012, 1; Veegens et al. 2015, 411, 412). The court to which the case is remitted is obliged to comply with the *Hoge Raad*'s decision.[99]

---

[90]The legislation on referral was thoroughly reformed with the Act of 20 June 1963.

[91]Article 420 Dutch Code of Civil Procedure. Although the Code stipulates this to be the standard *modus operandi*, it rarely happens in practice (Dempsey 2012, 1).

[92]Article 421 Dutch Code of Civil Procedure.

[93]Article 422 Dutch Code of Civil Procedure. According to Parliament, this decision should be taken with deference to the parties' wishes (Memorie van Toelichting 1951, 6). Veegens et al. (2015, 410, 411) argues, however, that parties generally do not comment on the desirability of remittal.

[94]For an overview of case law, see Veegens et al. (2015, 407–410).

[95]Article 419(3) Dutch Code of Civil Procedure.

[96]See Hoge Raad 30 June 1989, ECLI:NL:HR:AD0843, *Nederlandse Jurisprudentie* 1989, 769.

[97]Article 422a Dutch Code of Civil Procedure. This has been the case since 1838 (Veegens 1965, 177).

[98]See Article 423 Dutch Code of Civil Procedure.

[99]Article 424 Dutch Code of Civil Procedure.

3.4.3 Belgium

Belgium seems to have ignored the evolutions that took place in France and the Netherlands. The Belgian Constitution prohibits the Court of Cassation from ruling on the merits.[100] Together with other provisions this was construed as an obligation for the court to remit the case after annulment (Verougstraete 2010, 454, 455).[101] Nonetheless, often such remittal serves no purpose, as there is nothing left to decide.[102] In such cases, the court would sometimes annul without remittal. To accommodate this practice, a legislative change in 2014[103] permitted the court to decide on the costs of the litigation when it annulled without remittal.[104] A reform in the same year made it possible for the court to not remit in criminal cases when there is no cause to do so.[105] Further reform in 2017 explicitly allowed the court to annul without remittal in cases where there is nothing left to decide.[106] The court will only remit if there is cause to do so.[107] If the court does not remit, it must adjourn the case in the event that the Advocate-General did not point to that possibility in his or her written conclusion.[108] Another change is that the court has the choice to remit the case after annulment to a different court of the same nature, or to the court that rendered the quashed decision, but in a different composition.[109]

The 2017 reforms were fuelled by the installation address of the new Procurator-General in January of that same year (Thijs 2017). In his address, the Procurator-General proposed to allow the court to rule on the merits. Referencing extensively the procedures in France and the Netherlands, he emphasized that considerations of economization argue in favour of the adoption of a similar system in Belgium. The proposal copies the French system predating the 2016 reform:

---

[100]Article 147 of the Belgian Constitution.

[101]Cfr. the decision of the court in which it considers remittal to be legally prescribed (Hof van Cassatie 1 May 1888, *Pasicrisie* 1888, I, 231).

[102]For example, when the court annuls the decision of the court of appeal to admit an appeal that was inadmissible (Thijs 2017, 15). See De Vreese (1967, 569–571) and Verougstraete (2010, 459) for other examples.

[103]Act of 10 April 2014.

[104]Article 1111(5) Belgian Code of Civil Procedure.

[105]Article 435 Belgian Code of Criminal Procedure, as changed by the Act of 14 February 2014.

[106]Act of 6 July 2017. This rectified an anomaly created by the 2014 change that made it possible for the court to rule on the costs if it decided not to remit, although there was no provision allowing the court to refrain from remitting (Wetsontwerp houdende vereenvoudiging, harmonisering, informatisering en modernisering van bepalingen van burgerlijk recht en van burgerlijk procesrecht alsook van het notariaat, en houdende diverse bepalingen inzake justitie, Amendementen, *Kamer* 2016–2017, 2259/003, 37). However, there is also no provision that explicitly stipulates that the court must always remit after annulment. See Verougstraete (2010, 454, 455).

[107]Article 1109/1(2) Belgian Code of Civil Procedure.

[108]Article 1097(3) Belgian Code of Civil Procedure.

[109]Article 1110(1) Belgian Code of Civil Procedure as changed by the Act of 6 July 2017. In criminal cases, the court already commanded such leeway since the Act of 14 February 2014 (Article 435 Belgian Code of Criminal Procedure).

the court would be allowed to apply the applicable legal rule on the facts as established by the lower court.[110] From the moment the court needed to ascertain facts, remittal would be unavoidable.

The value of the decision of the Belgian Court of Cassation was drastically altered by the 2017 reform. Previously, its decision was only binding after a second annulment in the same case, on the same grounds.[111] Following the proposition of the Procurator-General,[112] the Act of 6 July 2017 made the decision of the court binding on the judge to whom the case is remitted.[113] The full extent of the Procurator-General's proposition was not honoured in the legislative reform later that year, but an evolution in the direction of our neighbouring countries becomes discernible.

3.5 Reasoning

The traditional reasoning style of the cassation model is etched into its core mission: upholding the primacy of the law.[114] In the traditional conception, the court's reasoning is built upon a syllogistic structure (Bouckaert 1997, 21–23; Steiner 2002, 135–147). The relevant legislative provision as construed by the court constitutes the major premise. The application or interpretation of that provision by the court whose decision is appealed forms the minor premise. The conclusion is then either the quashing of that decision or the rejection of the appeal, depending on whether the minor premise squares with the major premise (Touffait and Tunc 1974, 489; Lasser 2004, 34; Guillermet 2006, 86, 87). Besides having a syllogistic structure, the style is apodictic: the court does not explain or justify the choices it makes in constructing the major premise,[115] but presents its decision rather as the only logical interpretation of the legislative provision (Touffait and Tunc 1974, 490). Its judgments being solely based on pre-existing legislation, the court can suffice with the same brevity as the legislator's (Fricero 2008, 28). Anything that

---

[110]See also Verougstraete (2010, 456, 457) in this regard.

[111]The former Article 1120 Belgian Code of Civil Procedure. See De Vreese (1967, 578–583) for a discussion and Beauthier (1999) for a historical overview of this procedure.

[112]De Vreese (1967, 579), Bouckaert (1997, 17), De Corte (2008, 164, 165) and Verougstraete (2010, 457) had defended such a legislative change in the past.

[113]See Article 1110(4) Belgian Code of Civil Procedure and Article 435(2) Belgian Code of Criminal Procedure.

[114]The only provision in the Decree of 27 November 1790 dealing with the content of the judgements of the Tribunal is Article 17, which reads as follows: '*L'intitulé du jugement de cassation portera toujours, avec les noms des parties, l'objet de leur demande, et le dispositif contiendra le texte de la loi ou des lois sur lesquelles la décision sera appuyée.*'.

[115]The court does make such choices, see Verougstraete (2000, 1084, 1085) and Steiner (2002, 142).

would expose the relativity of the court's decision is banned (Van Gerven 1997, 220). The holding of the case therefore appears irrefutable, giving readers the impression that judgments are written out of thin air (Touffait and Tunc 1974, 497; Shapiro 1981, 143; Zweigert and Kötz 1998, 264). The rationale behind this syllogistic style and the brevity of its application is the concept of the court as the mere *bouche de la loi* (Tunc 1978b, 465). *Obiter dicta* or dissenting opinions are thus nowhere near to be found, and the same goes for autonomous arguments, such as references to case law, doctrine, equity or policy (Touffait and Tunc 1974, 499–501; Steiner 2002, 164). Only legal considerations (heteronomous arguments) are acceptable. The syllogism and scarcity of meaningful reasoning render the court's decisions formalistic, cryptic and anodyne.

This traditional notion holds true only if the decision is viewed in isolation, ignoring the judicial process that precedes it. The Advocate-General or reporting judge does weigh alternative solutions to the legal question at hand, and his or her opinion or report, respectively, abounds with autonomous considerations (Shapiro 1981, 143; Steiner 2002, 169, 170; Lasser 2004, 47–60; De Corte 2008, 152; Adams 2009, 1499–1501). The same arguments feature in the court's deliberation (De Vreese 1967, 589; Touffait and Tunc 1974, 490; Verougstraete 2000, 1072). But given the tenet of the French constitutional system that case law is only an authoritative and not a binding source of law, the court must appear to be merely applying the law rather than shaping its application. The real rationale of the court's decisions is therefore shrouded by the nature of its reasoning. In other words, its law-making activity is hidden behind a legalistic façade (Touffait and Tunc 1974, 489, 490; Steiner 2002, 169).[116]

In recent decades, however, cracks have appeared in the traditional reasoning style of the cassation courts. Numerous factors contributed to this evolution. Demands of accountability, transparency and legitimacy render the traditional reasoning style increasingly anachronistic (Welamson 1979, 512, 513; De Corte 2008, 142, 143; Louvel 2015, 10). The appearance of other supreme judicial bodies both within and above the national jurisdiction familiarizes legal society with other reasoning styles (De Corte 2008, 140, 141). The interpretation given by the European Court of Human Rights to Article 6 European Convention on Human Rights (ECHR) emphasizes the right of the litigant to reasoning rather than the duty of the judge to provide it (Terré 2007, 451, 454). The evolution in the nature of the cassation mechanism also necessitates a change in reasoning: a supreme appellate court requires a different reasoning style and method than a traditional cassation court. The apparent unaptness of legislation to comprehensively guide a fast-evolving society and, at the same time, a torrent of new, sometimes short-lived,

---

[116]The theory goes that the drawbacks of maintaining this façade are remedied by the more elaborate reasoning in the opinion of the Advocate-General, in an annotation of a law professor or in a note in the annual report of the court. This theory is, however, flawed, as the first two can at best only make an informed guess at the court's motives, and the latter can only hold true for a small minority of decisions. See Touffait and Tunc (1974, 493), Libchaber (2000), Verougstraete (2000, 1070, 1071) and Adams (2009, 1509).

legislation which sits sometimes uneasy with the existing laws necessitate an increasingly important role for case law as well (Dekkers 1955; Adams 2009, 1505, 1506; Boré and Boré 2015, 704), which influences the reasoning style. Upholding the legal façade has therefore become increasingly untenable.

3.5.1 France

The French reasoning style has not changed much since 1837, when the *référé legislative* was abolished (Service de Documentation 2015, 2). Since the current First President of the Court, Bertrand Louvel, was installed in 2014, however, long-held traditions have faced profound reform. A working group was established within the court to explore different possible reforms with regard to its reasoning style. The reform commission made several recommendations in its final report published in April 2017, including the use of the direct style and structuring of the decisions, and mentioning its own precedents when reversing previous case law or when consistently held case law is not adhered to (Commission de réflexion 2017, 154–157). In the meantime, the court has been experimenting with a more elaborate reasoning method (Commission de réflexion 2017, 149).[117] Moreover, the court has started to cite its decisions in *avis* judgments and when overturning its own case law (Commission de réflexion 2017, 154).[118]

Louvel also defended the inclusion of autonomous arguments in the *ratio decidendi* of the court (2015, 11), but so far no such propositions have been made. It is worth noting, however, that since late 2016 the *Cour de cassation* can invite *amici curiae* to comment on the case under review.[119] Necessarily, these would enlighten the court on societal and economic matters relevant to the case at hand, rather than on purely legal matters (Dreyer 2016, 2473; Ferrand 2016, 2416). As such, it is plausible that these arguments would also feature more explicitly in the decisions of the court (cfr. Service de Documentation 2015, 5). The recent change in competence of the Advocates-General is also relevant in this light: the law stipulates that they render an opinion in the interest of the law and the society,[120] the latter being an addition.[121] It is clear that a new dawn is breaking over the *Cour de cassation*'s reasoning style. This development is not limited to the French court

[117]See *inter alia* Cour de cassation 4 January 2016, avis n° 16001, http://www.courdecassation.fr. Accessed 7 June 2018; Cour de cassation 22 March 2016, n° 14-14218, http://www.legifrance.gouv.fr. Accessed 7 June 2018. The court also gives two other examples on its website: http://www.courdecassation.fr/cour_cassation_1/reforme_cour_7109/quelques_illustrations_8204/. Accessed 7 June 2018.

[118]Deumier (2016) and Laithier (2016) discuss some examples.

[119]Article 431-3-1 French Code of Judicial Organization. This reform sanctioned a previous practice of the court (Encinas de Munagorri 2005).

[120]Article 432-1 French Code of Judicial Organization. See also Ferrand (2016, 2416, 2417).

[121]Act No. 2016-1547 of 18 November 2016.

alone, for a leading example in this endeavour is also to be found in the Netherlands.[122]

3.5.2 The Netherlands

In 1978, Wiarda described the reasoning style of the *Hoge Raad* as the middle ground between the French and German supreme courts (1978, 289). Less concise and less apodictic, with room for extra-legal arguments, it had evolved considerably from the archaic style in use in the 19th century (Veegens et al. 2015, 412). This evolution has persisted, and the Dutch Supreme Court's current reasoning style is on many fronts more elaborate than its French counterpart, having abandoned a syllogistic nature for a more narrative style (Davids 2009, 224).

From the late 1970s onwards, a direct style and structuring of the decisions was adopted (Veegens et al. 2015, 413). The court mentions from time to time doctrine when it supports the court's solution, and *obiter dicta* can be found whenever deemed appropriate (Veegens et al. 2015, 416, 417, 421–423). The court references its own case law, either to indicate the existence of a consistent line of jurisprudence or to clarify its previous decisions (Veegens et al. 2015, 423, 424; Corstens 2009, 231). The practice of 'distinguishing' is in this regard not foreign to the court (Feteris 2016, 28). Since 1980, the *Hoge Raad* overturns its case law explicitly, and indicates the reason for doing so (Kottenhagen 1986, 12–35; Veegens et al. 2015, 424–426). The court regulates the consequences of its reversal when overruling prospectively (Schoordijk 1988, 60). The consequent downside of this elaborate reasoning in cases of legal and societal importance is that in less important cases, which constitute the large majority, the *Hoge Raad*'s reasoning can be quite succinct, or even absent (Veegens et al. 2015, 426).[123]

3.5.3 Belgium

The Belgian *Hof van Cassatie* updated its reasoning style at the start of the 21st century. In 2002, the court's decisions were given a clearer structure (De Corte 2008, 149).[124] Its characteristic indirect style was abandoned for a more direct style in 2006 (Marchal 2010, 408).[125] These reforms led to improved legibility (De Corte 2002, 6; Van Bossuyt 2011, 114), but not necessarily to improved intelligibility. The court does not cite doctrine nor does it refer to its own or other case law.

---

[122] The court translated a decision of the *Hoge Raad* into French to serve as an example of a richer reasoning style (Commission de réflexion 2017, 19).

[123] See also above under Sect. 3.2.2.

[124] See Soetaert (1979) for an overview of the old structure.

[125] Before 2006, the court's decisions formed one long sentence, each consideration starting with the infamous *attendu que* clause ('whereas').

Some exceptions exist, however.[126] When the court reverses its case law, it does so tacitly (Vanwelkenhuyzen 1978; Verstraelen 2015, 41; Verougstraete 2016, 455), as reversing explicitly would unveil its law-shaping activity. In recent years, however, an evolution towards more transparency is noticeable: the court has for example indicated that it is reversing its case law by referencing the overruled decision,[127] and recently also by saying so explicitly.[128] Whether or not this is a lasting change remains to be seen. Non-legal considerations are virtually absent in the court's judgments. Even though the manner of expression changed in recent years, the reasoning style of the Belgian Court of Cassation has remained very much the same, with some exceptions worth mentioning.

4 Future of the Cassation Mechanism

The discussed reforms constitute an ongoing process of reconciling the fictitious legalistic façade with reality. Changes in competence and reasoning, the enablement of a judgment on the merits, and the imposition of access restrictions and a preliminary procedure greatly affect features inherent to the cassation model. This begs the question, Which kind of supreme court will rise out of the debris of the traditional French cassation model? Some trends are already discernible.

The first noticeable evolution is the greater emphasis the courts place on their normative function by directing more resources towards it. The gain of the normative function is a loss for the disciplinary function, given the perennial scarcity of resources. Considering the legalistic history of the cassation model, this is an important evolution: rather than being enslaved to the law, the courts wish to shape it (Zenati 2016). The preliminary procedure serves the same goal of strengthening the courts' normative mission (Zenati 1992, 248). The more elaborate reasoning style which some courts have adopted is a by-product of this evolution. With this increased attention for the normative function comes the need to focus on important cases. By diminishing the resources devoted to the disciplinary function, the courts indicate that not all violations of the law are equally important and that only some

[126]See *inter alia* Hof van Cassatie 21 June 1928, *Pasicrisie*, 1928, 200; Hof van Cassatie 27 September 1928, *Pasicrisie* 1928, 235; Hof van Cassatie 3 February 1938, *Pasicrisie* 1938, 33.

[127]Hof van Cassatie 24 July 2007, P.07.0959.N, referring and overruling Cass. 6 June 2007, P.07.0689.F, and Hof van Cassatie 15 October 2009, C.09.0019.N, referring and overruling Hof van Cassatie 8 June 2009, S.08.0129.N. In the latter case, this was done by mentioning that the opinion of the Advocate-General, which was not followed by the court, was based on that previous, now overruled, decision. See Verstraelen (2015, 42).

[128]See Hof van Cassatie 12 June 2015, F.13.0163.N; Hof van Cassatie 3 April 2017, C.15.0508.N. Interestingly enough, the 2015 decision did not overturn the court's previous case law, as that had already been done in two earlier decisions of the French-speaking section (Hof van Cassatie 11 September 2014, F.13.0053.F and Hof van Cassatie 4 June 2015, F.14.0165.F). In fact, the Dutch-speaking section of the court merely made clear in its June 12 decision that which was only implicitly said in the earlier decisions (Verougstraete 2016, 455).

violations merit supreme court review. The French *Cour de cassation* is for example currently exploring the possibility for the courts of appeal to deal with disciplinary grievances themselves, such as vices in the procedure or reasoning defaults, rather than encumber the court with such cases that offer little added value for its normative mission (Commission de réflexion 2017, 236–240).

Secondly, the cassation courts of France, the Netherlands and Belgium are slowly changing the traditional cassation model into a supreme judicial court: originally conceived as a control mechanism on the judiciary, the courts are increasingly becoming third instance jurisdictions by venturing ever deeper into the factual realm,[129] deciding on the merits and allowing a greater procedural role for the litigants (Zenati 2016; Verougstraete 2010, 450). The French *Cour de cassation* has shown a tendency to replace the control of legality which it normally exerts with the control of proportionality and equity (Jestaz et al. 2014; Louvel 2015, 2–4; Commission de réflexion 2017, 158–170). A full-blown implementation of such revamped control would drastically change the nature of the court, becoming some sort of national outpost of the European Court of Human Rights in the process.[130]

Both evolutions necessarily lead to, and necessitate, a more restricted access to the court, as the courts' resources are by definition sparse. The access schemes currently in place do not amount to a filter mechanism, but merely enable the courts to manage their heavy workload more efficiently: the reforms of the last decades only allowed the court to diversify the adjudication process of cases in relation to their importance, and deal with those put on a side-track (more) swiftly (Guillermet 2006, 90; Ferrand 2017, 200; Commission de réflexion 2017, 264). A stricter access regime will be unavoidable if the court wishes to continue on the chosen path (Welamson, 1979, 516; Van Gerven 1997, 222; Pinna 2009, 175; Zenati 2016; Commission de réflexion 2017, 221). The French *Cour de cassation* is currently entertaining several options to do so. One option aims at extending the two-track policy currently in place by creating three categories of cases: simple, important and a residual category, with each having its own adjudication procedure (Commission de réflexion 2017, 63, 64). Another, more radical option, is the adoption of a real access filter. The court is currently considering two such mechanisms. In the first, external system, the courts of appeal would grant leave to appeal to the Cassation Court, with the possibility to appeal a refusal to grant leave, as is the case in Germany (Louvel 2015, 5; Commission de réflexion 2017, 271–274). The second system is an internal filter mechanism, based on the earlier withdrawn amendment,[131] in which the court itself decides on the admission of the appeal (Commission de réflexion 2017, 274–277). Throughout the reforms that have already taken place with regard to access, the moment of selection is constantly

[129]See already Tunc (1978a, 434).

[130]For an example, see Cass., 4 December 2013, N° 12-26066, in which the court discarded a provision of the *Code civil* because its application would infringe Article 6 ECHR given the factual circumstances of the case. See also Zenati (2016).

[131]See Sect. 3.3.1.

moving closer to the lodging of the case. The right of the litigant to an appeal before the court (Barthélemy 2000; Asser 2011, 72) is, as a consequence, increasingly under threat, and likely due to disappear.

The legalistic veil acted as both a scapegoat and a bulwark against critique from society and the legislator. The reforms of the last decades have pierced that veil. The denudation of the law-shaping quality of the case law and the sanctioning of such by legislative bodies fundamentally changes the game. With greater responsibility comes increasing public scrutiny. The courts will have to live up to their newly acknowledged role in society. This makes further reforms aimed at better enabling the courts to do so all the more likely.

The *summa divisio* between supreme courts of a supreme appellate tradition and those of a cassation nature is their possibility to select cases (Tunc 1978a, 17). The supreme courts of the German *Revision* tradition feature roughly as the middle ground on a continuous bipolar scale between the supreme court of the cassation model and those of the supreme appellate tradition. In 1997, Tartuffo (1998, 107) discerned the evolution of the French cassation model moving away from a guardian of legality towards a third instance court. The evolutions discussed in this contribution that took place following this statement prove his point. The reforms, both completed and proposed, indicate that the French cassation model is slowly but surely moving towards the other end of the divide. The recent French reform proposal indeed displays some similarities to features of the German supreme court model.

Tunc (1978b, 435) considered a hybrid court that combines elements from both traditions the ideal supreme court. The recent experience of some countries debunks that claim: the hybrid nature of the supreme courts of Croatia and Slovenia was found to be unstable and difficult to balance (Uzelac and Galic 2017, 225, 226). In moving away from the cassation model, the supreme courts of France, the Netherlands and Belgium will have to decide at some point whether they want to fully adopt the features typical of supreme courts of the other major tradition, or whether they want to muddle along without a clear objective. Hard choices will have to be made concerning the priorities of the future supreme court, bearing in mind that a half-hearted reform can only lead to half-hearted results. It is in this light important to note that changes to the nature of the supreme court, as the apex of the judiciary, affect the judicial system as a whole. A fundamental reform of the supreme court must therefore complement a complete overhaul of the judicial system, in order to make the dispute resolution system as a whole functional and efficient.

5 Conclusion

It is time for some conclusions. The similarity of the reforms is manifest. Faced with similar problems, the cassation courts of France, the Netherlands and Belgium adopted similar solutions, moreover, along a similar timeline. This attests to a considerable cross-border influence. Not every country has reformed its cassation procedure to the same extent, however. The *Hoge Raad* had from its inception some features that were only well over a century later embraced elsewhere. France initiated a major overhaul of its cassation procedure only recently. Despite having always been close to France in legal matters, Belgium seems to be missing the boat, lagging behind its southern neighbour (as well as its northern neighbour) on all fronts.

The method of reform is also similar. Often parliament merely rubber-stamps *post facto* an earlier practice of the court. The phased reforms also reveal their incremental nature. Most of the reforms are taken in response to perceived problems. No lasting, profound change can result, however, from such a stumbling and symptomatic approach. A systematic overhaul in which clear and conscious choices are made to further pre-defined goals is undoubtedly a better way forward. The broad reflection currently taking place in the French *Cour de cassation* is therefore to be applauded.

The cassation courts are moving in the direction of a leave to appeal system, clearing their dockets of cases that are not essential to their normative mission. From a general guardian of the law, the courts are developing into a supreme appellate court focused on producing precedents. This constitutes a major paradigm shift, finally freeing the cassation model from the shackles of an outdated legal sources theory (Tunc 1978b, 441). The legalistic façade is the first victim of that process. The French cassation model is on the road to *terra incognita*. And to those who warn *hic sunt leones*, the reply should be *tempora mutantur, nos et mutamur in illis*.

References

Adams M (2009) De argumentatieve en motiveringspraktijk van hoogste rechters: rechtsvergelijkende beschouwingen. Rechtskundig Weekblad 72:1499–1510

Amrani-Mekki S (2005) Les textes organisant la non-admission des pourvois en cassation en droit français. In: Amrani-Mekki S, Cadiet L (eds) La sélection des pourvois à la Cour de cassation. Economica, Paris, pp 19–31

Archives Parlementaires de 1787 à 1860 [X (1885)]: recueil complet des débats législatifs et politiques des Chambres françaises. Première série, 1787 à 1799, XX. Imprimerie Paul Dupont, Paris

Asser W (2011) Van selectie achter de poort naar selectie aan de poort. In: Hol A, Giessen I, Kirsten F (eds) De Hoge Raad in 2025. Boom Juridische Uitgevers, Den Haag, pp 71–92

Barkhuysen T, Schuurmans Y (2013) Een prejudiciële procedure in het bestuursrecht? Ars aequi 62:736–739

Bartholémy J (2000) Le droit au pourvoi. In: Guinchard S, Pluyette G (eds) Le juge entre deux millénaires: mélanges offerts à Pierre Drai. Dalloz, Paris, pp 185–202

Beauthier R (1999) La lente conquête d'une suprématie: l'exemple de l'organe de cassation de l'Ancien régime au XIXe siècle. Revue de droit de l'ULB 10:7–99

Bell J, Boyron S, Whittaker S (2008) Principles of French law. Oxford University Press, Oxford

Bloquet S (2017) La loi et son interprétation à travers le Code civil (1804-1880). LGDJ, Paris

Boré J, Boré L (2003) La cassation en matière civile. Dalloz, Paris

Boré J, Boré L (2015) La cassation en matière civile. Dalloz, Paris

Bossuyt A (2013) De in de gecoördineerde wet van 15 september 2006 tot bescherming van de economische mededinging voorziene prejudiciële vraag aan het Hof van Cassatie. In: Ghysels J, Vanlerberghe B (eds) Prejudiciële vragen: de techniek in kaart gebracht. Intersentia, Antwerpen, pp 145–164

Bouckaert B (1997) Hoe gemotiveerd is cassatie?. Kluwer, Antwerpen

Boulet-Santel M (1990) La cassation sous l'Ancien régime. Le Tribunal et la Cour de cassation 1790-1990. Litec, Paris, pp 1–24

Buffet J (2000) La saisine pour avis de la Cour de cassation. Exposé devant les premiers présidents de cour d'appel. http://www.courdecassation.fr/jurisprudence_2/avis_15/presentation_saisine_avis_8018/loin_expose_36050.html. Accessed 7 June 2018

Canivet G (2005) Propos introductifs. In: Amrani-Mekki S, Cadiet L (eds) La sélection des pourvois à la Cour de cassation. Economica, Paris, pp 5–11

Coeuret A (1991) Loi n° 91-491 du 15 mai 1991 modifiant le code de l'organisation judiciaire et instituant la saisine pour avis de la Cour de cassation. Revue trimestrielle de droit civil 89:615

Commission de réflexion de la Cour de cassation (2017) Rapport de la commission de réflexion sur la réforme de la Cour de cassation. https://www.courdecassation.fr/cour_cassation_1/reforme_cour_7109/reflexion_reforme_8182/. Accessed 7 June 2018

Cornil L (1952) La Cour de cassation: réformes mineures de la procédure. Journal des Tribunaux 71:465–474

Corpart I (1995) L'encombrement croissant de la Cour de cassation. Petites Affiches 383:4

Corstens G (2009) The legitimacy of the decisions of the Dutch supreme court in criminal cases. In: Huls N, Adams M, Bomhoff J (eds) The legitimacy of highest courts' rulings. TMC Asser Press, The Hague, pp 227–234

Cour de cassation (2016) Rapport Annuel 2016. https://www.courdecassation.fr/publications_26/rapport_annuel_36/. Accessed 7 June 2018

Darnanville H-M (2001) La saisine pour avis du Conseil d'Etat et de la Cour de cassation. Actualité juridique droit administratif 57:416–427

Dauchy S (1988) Les voies de recours extraordinaires: proposition d'erreur et requête civile. PUF, Paris

Davids W (2009) Judicial reasoning and legitimacy of the Dutch supreme court. In: Huls N, Adams M, Bomhoff J (eds) The legitimacy of highest courts' rulings. TMC Asser Press, The Hague, pp 223–226

De Corte R (2002) Cassatie wordt stilaan begrijpelijk. Juristenkrant 3(49):6, 7

De Corte R (2008) De eerste 175 jaar van het Hof van Cassatie. In: Hof van Cassatie van België, 175ste verjaardag. Larcier, Brussel, pp 139–172

De Vreese A (1967) De taak van het Hof van Cassatie. Tijdschrift voor Privaatrecht 4:567–597

Dekkers R (1955) Twee houdingen. Rechtskundig Weekblad 18:1497–1502

Dempsey N (2012) De procedure na cassatie en verwijzing. Tijdschrift voor Civiele Rechtspleging 20:1–8

Den Dekker G, Van Den Eshof L (2015) Sprongcassatie en de prejudiciële procedure. Tijdschrift voor de Procespraktijk 6:105–108

Deumier P (2016) Motivation des décisions de la Cour de cassation: mention de la jurisprudence constante. Recueil Dalloz 192:133

Dreyer E (2016) La main invisible de la Cour de cassation. Recueil Dalloz 192:2473

Encinas de Munagorri R (2005) L'ouverture de la Cour de cassation aux amici curiae. Revue trimestrielle de droit civil 103:88

Faye E (1970) La Cour de cassation: traité de ses attributions, de sa compétence et de la procédure observée en matière civile. Librairie Edouard Duchemin, Paris

Ferrand F (2016) La Cour de cassation dans la loi de modernisation de la justice du XXI siècle. À propos de la loi n° 2016-1547 du 18 novembre 2016. La Semaine Juridique édition générale 91:2415–2418

Ferrand F (2017) The French Court of cassation: on the threshold of a quiet revolution? In: Van Rhee CH, Fu Y (eds) Supreme courts in transition in China and the West: adjudication at the service of public goals. Springer, Cham, pp 175–206

Feteris M (2016) Les réformes à la Cour suprême des Pays-Bas: Lecture chez la Cour de cassation française. https://www.courdecassation.fr/cour_cassation_1/reforme_cour_7109/travaux_commission_8180/cassation_pays_34192.html. Accessed 7 June 2018
Fricero N (2008) Evolution des fonctions de la cassation française. In: Hof van Cassatie van België, 175ste verjaardag. Larcier, Brussel, pp 19–32
Fulchiron H (2015) Le juge et l'oracle, brèves observations sur la (non)-motivation des avis de la Cour de cassation. Receuil Dalloz 191:21
Gridel J-P (2002) La Cour de cassation française et les principes généraux du droit privé. Recueil Dalloz 178:228
Guillermet C-J (2006) La motivation des décisions de justice: la vertu pédagogique de la justice. L'Harmattan, Paris
Haak P (2008) De evolutie op lange termijn van de Nederlandse cassatieprocedure (in burgerlijke zaken) sedert 1838. In: Hof van Cassatie van België, 175ste verjaardag. Larcier, Brussel, pp 49–82
Haftel B (2016) La disparition ajournée de l'autorité des lois civiles en France. Recueil Dalloz 192:1011
Halpérin J-L (1990) Le Tribunal de cassation sous la Révolution (1790–1799). In: Le Tribunal et la Cour de cassation 1790–1990. Litec, Paris, pp 25–51
Hammerstein Commissie Normstellende Rol Hoge Raad (2008) Versterking van de cassatierechtspraak. https://www.rijksoverheid.nl/documenten/rapporten/2007/03/27/rapport-versterking-van-de-cassatierechtspraak. Accessed 7 June 2018
Hof van Cassatie (2003) Jaarverslag 2002–2003. Belgisch Staatsblad, Brussel
Hoge Raad der Nederlanden (2013) Verslag over 2013. https://www.rechtspraak.nl/Organisatie-en-contact/Organisatie/Hoge-Raad-der-Nederlanden/Over-de-Hoge-Raad/Publicaties/Paginas/default.aspx. Accessed 7 June 2018
Hoge Raad der Nederlanden (2014) Verslag over 2014. https://www.rechtspraak.nl/Organisatie-en-contact/Organisatie/Hoge-Raad-der-Nederlanden/Over-de-Hoge-Raad/Publicaties/Paginas/default.aspx. Accessed 7 June 2018
Hoge Raad der Nederlanden (2015) Verslag over 2015. https://www.rechtspraak.nl/Organisatie-en-contact/Organisatie/Hoge-Raad-der-Nederlanden/Over-de-Hoge-Raad/Publicaties/Paginas/default.aspx. Accessed 7 June 2018
Hoge Raad der Nederlanden (2016) Jaaroverzicht 2016. https://www.rechtspraak.nl/Organisatie-en-contact/Organisatie/Hoge-Raad-der-Nederlanden/Over-de-Hoge-Raad/Publicaties/Paginas/default.aspx. Accessed 7 June 2018
Jestaz Ph, Marguénaud J-P, Jamin Ch (2014) Révolution tranquille à la Cour de cassation. Recueil Dalloz 190:2061
Jobard-Bachelier M-N, Bachelier X, Buk Lament J (2013) La technique de cassation: pourvois et arrêts en matière civile. Dalloz, Paris
Kottenhagen R (1986) Van precedent tot precedent. Gouda Quint, Arnhem
Laithier Y-M (2016) Nullité relative pour vil prix: le revirement didactique de la chambre commerciale. Revue des contrats 13:435
Lasser M (2004) Judicial deliberations: a comparative analysis of judicial transparency and legitimacy. Oxford University Press, Oxford
Leclercq P (1953) De la Cour de cassation. In: Faurès J, De Meyer J (eds) La pensée juridique de procureur-général Paul Leclercq. Bruylant, Brussel, pp 29–91
Libchaber R (2000) Retour sur la motivation des arrêts de la Cour de cassation, et le rôle de la doctrine. Recueil Dalloz 176:679
Libchaber R (2003) La saisine pour avis, une procédure singulière dans le paysage jurisprudentiel. Revue trimestrielle de droit civil 101:157
Louvel B (2015) La Cour de cassation face aux défis du XXIe siècle. https://www.courdecassation.fr/publications_26/discours_tribunes_entretiens_2039/discours_2202/premier_president_7084/discours_2015_7547/face_defis_31435.html. Accessed 7 June 2018
Luxembourg F (2006) La Cour de cassation, juge du fond. Recueil Dalloz 182:2358–2362

Marchal P (2010) De stijl van de arresten van het Hof van Cassatie in civiele zaken (1832–2010). In: Dauwe B, De Gryse B, De Gryse E et al (eds) Liber Amicorum Ludovic De Gryse. Larcier, Brussel, 2010, pp 401–410
Marchal P (2014) Principes généraux du droit. Bruylant, Brussel
Marcilhacy P (1978) Rapport fait au nom de la commission des Lois constitutionnelles, de Législation, du Suffrage universel, du Règlement et d'Administration générale sur le projet de loi, adopté par l'Assemblée nationale, modifiant certaines dispositions relatives à la Cour de cassation. Sénat 1978–1979 n° 145
Martinage-Baranger R (1969) Les idées sur la cassation au XVIIIe siècle. Revue historique de droit français et étranger 47:244–290
Martyn G (2013) Belgium, the Netherlands and Luxembourg since 1800. In: Wijffels A, Van Rhee CH (eds) European supreme courts. A portrait through history. Third Millenium Publishing, London, pp 218–227
Memorie van Toelichting (1951) Wijziging van de regelen met betrekking tot het geding in cassatie. Kamerstukken II 1950–51, 2079, n° 3
Memorie van Toelichting (1987) Wijziging van de Wet op de rechterlijke organisatie (verkorte uitspraak van de Hoge Raad). Kamerstukken II 1986–87, 19953, n° 3
Memorie van Toelichting (2010) Wijziging van de Advocatenwet, de Wet op de rechterlijke organisatie en enige andere wetten ter versterking van de cassatierechtspraak (versterking cassatierechtspraak). Kamerstukken II 2010–2011, 32576, n° 3
Molfessis N (2007) Les avis spontanés de la Cour de cassation. Recueil Dalloz 183:37
Morbée K (2013) Het Hof van Cassatie als prejudicieel Hof in fiscale zaken? Tijdschrift voor Fiscaal Recht 14(191):192
Pinna A (2009) Filtering applications, number of judgments delivered and judicial discourse by supreme courts: some thoughts based on the French example. In: Huls N, Adams M, Bomhoff J (eds) The legitimacy of highest courts' rulings. TMC Asser Press, The Hague, pp 175–187
Piwnica E (2017) Commentaire des dispositions de la loi J21 relatives à la Cour de cassation. Gazette du Palais 137:76
Regout M (2017) Enkele recente ontwikkelingen in de cassatieprocedure in burgerlijke zaken. In: Hof van Cassatie, Jaarverslag 2016. https://justitie.belgium.be/nl/rechterlijke_orde/hoven_en_rechtbanken/hof_van_cassatie/documenten/jaarverslagen. Accessed 7 June 2018
Rivière H-F (1862) Revue doctrinale des variations et des progrès de la jurisprudence de la Cour de cassation en matière civile, et dans l'ordre du Code napoléon. Cosse et Marchal, Paris
Rudloff M (1991) Rapport fait au nom de la commission des Lois constitutionnelles, de législation, du suffrage universel, du Règlement et d'administration générale sur le projet de loi adopté par l'Assemblée nationale, modifiant le code de l'organisation judiciaire et instituant la saisine pour avis de la Cour de Cassation. Sénat 1990–1991 n° 297
Schaffmeiste D (1988) De rol van de Hoge Raad en de ontwikkeling van het cassatierecht in strafzaken. In: De plaats van de Hoge Raad in het huidige staatsbestel. Tjeenk Willink, Zwolle, pp 65–122
Schoordijk H (1988) Hoe vat(te) de burgerlijke kamer van de Hoge Raad zijn rechtsvormende taak op? In: De plaats van de Hoge Raad in het huidige staatsbestel. Tjeenk Willink, Zwolle, pp 3–63
Service de Documentation, des Etudes et du Rapport de la Cour de cassation (2015) Commission de réflexion sur la réforme de la Cour: groupe de travail motivation. https://www.courdecassation.fr/cour_cassation_1/reforme_cour_7109/travaux_commission_8180/motivation_arrets_7856/cour_cassation_32581.html. Accessed 7 June 2018
Shapiro M (1981) Courts: A comparative and political analysis. University of Chicago Press, Chicago
Snijders G (2010) Kronieken: cassatie. Tijdschrift voor Civiele Rechtspleging 18:80–85
Soetaert R (1979) Is een cassatiearrest leesbaar? Rechtskundig Weekblad 42:2609–2624
Steiner E (2002) French legal method. Oxford University Press, Oxford
Stolp M, de Groot J (2012) Een nieuwe procesvorm: het stellen van prejudiciële vragen aan de Hoge Raad (art. 392-394 nieuw Rv). Maandblad voor Vermogensrecht 23:165–170

Tarbé A-P (1840) Cour de cassation: lois et réglements à l'usage de la Cour de cassation. Librairie encyclopédique de Roret, Paris
Tartuffo M (1998) The role of the supreme courts at the national and international level: civil law countries. In: Yessiou-Faltsi P (ed) The role of the supreme courts at the national and international level. Reports for the Thessaloniki international colloquium 21–25 May 1997. Sakkoulas Publications, Thessaloniki, pp 101–126
Terré F (2007) L'hétérarchie juridique. La création du droit jurisprudentiel: mélanges en l'honneur de Jacques Boré. Dalloz, Paris, pp 447–457
Terrier F (2013) La pratique de la procédure de non-admission à la Cour de cassation. Justice & Cassation 9:95–100
Teuben K (2012) Kroniek: cassatie. Tijdschrift voor Civiele Rechtspleging 20:102–106
Texier S-L (2017) Réflexions sur le règlement du litige au fond par la Cour de cassation. Recueil Dalloz 193:63
Thijs D (2017) Installatierede Procureur-Generaal Dirk Thijs. https://justitie.belgium.be/nl/nieuws/andere_berichten_56. Accessed 7 June 2018
Touffait A, Tunc A (1974) Pour une motivation plus explicite des décisions de justice notamment de celles de la Cour de cassation. Revue trimestrielle de droit civil 72:487–508
Tunc A (1978a) Synthèse. In: Bellet P, Tunc A, Touffait A (eds) La cour judiciaire suprême: une enquête comparative. Economica, Paris, pp 5–83
Tunc A (1978b) Conclusions: la Cour suprême idéale. In: Bellet P, Tunc A, Touffait A (eds) La cour judiciaire suprême: une enquête comparative. Economica, Paris, pp 433–471
Uzelac A, Galič A (2017) Changing faces of post-socialist supreme courts: Croatia and Slovenia compared. In: Van Rhee CH, Fu Y (eds) Supreme courts in transition in China and the West: adjudication at the service of public goals. Springer, Cham, pp 207–228
Van Bossuyt H (2011) Toegang tot de rechtspraak en toegankelijke rechtspraak. In: Bossuyt A, Deconick B, Dirix E et al (eds) Liber spei et amicitiae: Ivan Verougstraete. Larcier, Brussel, pp 109–115
Van Der Haegen (2015) M Het Hof van Cassatie op het kruispunt van publieke en private belangen: pleidooi voor een versterking van de cassatierechtspraak. Tijdschrift voor Privaatrecht 52:1235–1309
Van Gerven W (1997) Creatieve rechtspraak. Rechtskundig Weekblad 61:209–223
Van Suilen A (2012) Pleidooi voor prejudiciële procedure in belastingzaken. Nederlands Tijdschrift voor Fiscaal Recht 13:2745
Vanwelkenhuyzen A (1978) La motivation des revirements de jurisprudence. In: Perelman C, Foriers P (eds) La motivation des décisions de justice. Bruylant, Brussel, pp 251–286
Veegens D (1965) Nieuw cassatierecht in Nederland. Tijdschrift voor Privaatrecht 2:177–197
Veegens D, Korthals Altes E, Groen H (2005) Cassatie in burgerlijke zaken. Kluwer, Deventer
Veegens D, Korthals Altes E, Groen H (2015) Cassatie in burgerlijke zaken. Kluwer, Deventer
Verkerk R, Van Rhee CH (2017) The Supreme Cassation Court of the Netherlands: efficient engineer for the unity and development of the law. In: Van Rhee CH, Fu Y (eds) Supreme courts in transition in China and the West: adjudication at the service of public goals. Springer, Cham, pp 77–96
Verougstraete I (2000) Het Hof van Cassatie en de motiveringsplicht. Mélanges offerts à Pierre Van Ommeslaghe. Bruylant, Brussel, pp 1061–1087
Verougstraete I (2010) Van cassatie naar revisie. In: Dauwe B, De Gryse B, De Gryse E et al (eds) Liber Amicorum Ludovic De Gryse. Larcier, Brussel, 2010, pp 445–462
Verougstraete I (2016) Les revirements de la Cour de cassation. Journal des Tribunaux 135: 453–456
Verstraelen S (2015) Rechterlijk overgangsrecht. Intersentia, Antwerpen
Vexliard C (2013) Le règlement du litige après cassation. Justice & Cassation 9:101–110
Vigneau V (2010) Le regime de la non-admission des pourvois devant la Cour de cassation. Recueil Dalloz 186:102–111
Welamson L (1979) La motivation des décisions des cours judiciaires suprêmes. Revue internationale de droit comparé 31:509–519

Wiarda G (1978) Le Hoge Raad des Pays-Bas. In: Bellet P, Tunc A, Touffait A (eds) La cour judiciaire suprême: une enquête comparative. Economica, Paris, pp 275–291
Zenati F (1992) La saisine pour avis de la Cour de cassation. Recueil Dalloz 168:247–254
Zenati F (2016) La juridictionnalisation de la Cour de cassation. Revue trimestrielle de droit civil 114:511
Zuckerman A (2013) Zuckerman on civil procedure: principles of practice. Sweet & Maxwell, London
Zweigert K, Kötz H (1998) Introduction to comparative law. Oxford University Press, Oxford

Matthias Van Der Haegen Ph.D. Fellow of the Research Foundation Flanders (FWO) at Ghent University, Belgium. Graduated from Ghent University, MJur from the University of Oxford. Visiting Scholar at Bergen University Faculty of Law, Norway, the Max Planck Institute for Procedural Law, Luxembourg and Washington University in St. Louis School of Law, United States of America.

Part VII
Historical Transformations

Does the New Always Prevail? Parallel Modes of Procedure in the History of Procedural Transformations

Henrik-Riko Held

Abstract This contribution provides a historical-comparative analysis of the phases of certain relevant civil procedural reforms in which for a certain period of time the old and the new mode of procedure existed in parallel, with the possibility of the parties' choice between the two. In the analysis, a threefold perspective is assumed, and the issue is approached from the perspective of Roman law, historical English common law and procedural law reforms in the lands of the Habsburg Monarchy in the 19th century. In the analysed periods, contrary to expectations, the parties disregarded the general evaluation of a new procedure's efficiency. Instead, they were inclined to prefer the procedure that suited their immediate interests the best, even if it was generally considered to be outdated. The presence of this phenomenon throughout millennia and in disparate jurisdictions indicates the necessity to calculate its effects in scholarly and practical assessments of any given procedural reform.

1 Introduction

In a number of certain key civil procedural reforms and transformations throughout history, the parties were afforded a choice between two different modes of procedure.[1] The older procedure, considered generally outdated, was concurrently opposed to a newer and presumably more efficient procedure. In the transitional

This contribution is the result of research supported by the Croatian Science Foundation (project no. 6988).

[1] The parties' choice here means either that the claimant had a right to choose the mode in which to pursue the claim against the defendant, or that both parties agreed as to the mode of procedure beforehand.

H.-R. Held (✉)
Faculty of Law, University of Zagreb, Zagreb, Croatia
e-mail: hheld@pravo.hr

A. Uzelac and C. H. van Rhee (eds.), *Transformation of Civil Justice*,
Ius Gentium: Comparative Perspectives on Law and Justice 70,
https://doi.org/10.1007/978-3-319-97358-6_20

period, the parties were, from a scholarly or a lawgiver's point of view, expected to recognise the perceived superiority of the newer procedure and prefer it over the older one. However, those expectations were in significant measure unfulfilled, and the main aim of this paper is to analyse the underlying reasons for and effects of that phenomenon.

The starting point of the analysis is Roman law. There is a standing controversy regarding certain developments in the transitional period from the *legis actiones* to the formulary procedure. In that event, a phase may have existed where the parties had a choice between the two procedures in the same matter. In essence, this controversy is related to the context of the *lex Aebutia*, the Act that is known to have played a very important part in the establishment of the formulary procedure, but in what way exactly is not known. The content of this *lex* is a matter of dispute, with the main contention being that it could not have introduced the formulary procedure as a parallel and equally viable procedure alongside the *legis actiones*. This conclusion operates under the main presumption that every generally simpler, quicker and less expensive procedure necessarily leads to the extinction of the other procedure if both are available to the parties. The flaw in this line of reasoning is that it overlooks certain immediate advantages for the parties in the procedure generally considered outdated and more complicated, advantages that may prompt the parties to avail themselves of that procedure, regardless of its general evaluation.

This observation has already been made in the literature, taking into account experiences in the history of the English common law, where it was noticed that the introduction of new writs and forms of action did not necessarily lead to the immediate extinction of the still accessible older ones, as parties found certain benefits in them. This is expounded upon in this paper, and similar considerations are added regarding the gradual disuse of the jury in civil trials in the 19th century in the same jurisdiction, whereupon parties had a choice between jury and non-jury trials. Finally, this paper analyses important procedural reforms that occurred in the lands of the Habsburg Monarchy in the 19th century. In them, a shift of paradigm may be observed in the transition from tenets of the Romano-canonical procedure to more modern procedural regulations. Therein also existed situations where parties could choose between an older, presumably outdated ordinary mode of procedure, and a more modern and generally more expedient extraordinary procedure (such as summary proceedings or small-claims proceedings). Theoretical analysis, together with an overview of the relevant judicature of the time, may shed light on the relevant development in that area.

A threefold perspective from disparate jurisdictions, both in a historical and a systematic sense, might help to provide an outlook on the issue not confined to specific social, political and economic circumstances. Rather, it might demonstrate universal tendencies in civil procedural reforms and transformations, regardless of the time and place in which they occur. In that way, experience from different legal surroundings of the common law systems and later developments in the Romano-canonical tradition may help to shed light on a controversy from Roman law. Conversely, a better understanding of the roots in Roman law, as always, may give context to later legal developments.

2 The Problem of *Lex Aebutia* in Roman Law

The *lex Aebutia*, as mentioned, is associated with the transition from the *legis actiones* to the procedure *per formulas* as the form of the ordinary civil procedure in Roman law. The *legis actio* procedure is considered to be the original and oldest Roman civil mode of procedure, stemming at least from the period of the Twelve Tables or the middle of the 5th century BC.[2] Five different *legis actiones* as modes of procedure existed (Gai. Inst. IV, 12). Each of them was designed for a specific purpose and set of circumstances; accordingly, each had certain peculiarities and in this capacity differed from each of the others.[3] However, overall the *legis actio* as a procedure had its own general distinctive features. It was essentially a verbal form of proceedings, where parties had to recite certain solemn words in a prescribed manner to initiate the process. It was notoriously excessively formalistic, inasmuch as the smallest mistake in the wording could lead to a failure of the case (Gai. Inst. IV, 11). In fact, this excessive formalism is usually referred to as the main reason for the abolishment of the *legis actiones* altogether and the establishment of the formulary procedure as the ordinary mode of procedure (Gai. Inst. IV, 30).

The formulary procedure, in other words the procedure *per formulas* or *per concepta verba*, had its origins probably sometime between the end of the 4th and the beginning of the 3rd century BC.[4] However, a long time passed before it became widely used, and it was established as the ordinary procedure only at the end of the 1st century BC with the famous *leges Iuliae iudiciariae*.[5] As its name

---

[2]For textbook references on the matter see Kaser and Hackl (1996, 34 *sqq.*), and in a less extensive manner Guarino (2001, 168 *sqq.*) and Jörs et al. (1987, 506 *sqq.*). For useful encyclopaedic references see Paulus (1999, 22 *sqq.*), Talamanca (1987, 4 *sqq.*), Mayer-Maly (1969, 546 *sq.*), Betti (1966, 1104 *sq.*), Weiss (1925, 1838 *sqq.*). For a monographic treatment of the subject see Albanese (1987), Cannata (1980), Pugliese (1961). Special treatment of the origins of the procedure can be found in Nicosia (1986).

[3]Alongside general literature on the *legis actiones* cited in the previous note, the following authors, in their respective works, deal specifically with five different forms of the procedure: Melillo (2007) and Fuenteseca (1964).

[4]For the formulary procedure in detail, with further references, see Kaser and Hackl (1996, 151 *sqq.*), less extensively Guarino (2001, 183 *sqq.*), Jörs et al. (1987, 524 *sqq.*). Encyclopaedic references can be found in Talamanca (1987, 24 *sqq.*), Betti (1966, 1106 *sqq.*). For a separate monography on the subject see Cannata (1982). Specific treatment of the origins of this procedure can be found in Magdelain (1991), Scherillo (1969), Luzzatto (1946).

[5]A significant role in the process during which the *legis actiones* were gradually superseded by the formulary procedure was played by the *lex Aebutia* from the 2nd century BC, which will be analysed in the text that follows. The *leges Iuliae iudiciariae* were subsequently passed in 17 BC. Alongside general references on the formulary procedure found in the previous note, which deal with the matter extensively, for a closer look at the sources relevant for the reconstruction of the

suggests, it was a procedure in which a written formula composed by a magistrate was used to carry out the proceedings before a judge.[6] In addition, since it was a procedure with *concepta verba*, it stood in contrast to the *certa verba* of the *legis actiones*. In other words, the wording of the formula used as a means to initiate and conduct proceedings before a judge was tailored to the circumstances of the case. This in itself contrasted with the rigid formalism of the *legis actiones* mentioned earlier. The formulary procedure, being much simpler and more appropriate for a more efficient and faster economy, was closely associated with the territorial and commercial expansion of Rome in the aftermath of the Punic Wars in the 3rd century BC (Cannata 1982, 50).

At any rate, the transition from the older regulations of the *legis actiones* to the more modern system of the formulary procedure may be considered a turning point in the development of Roman civil procedure, and definitely a major procedural transformation of the system. In this transformation, as suggested earlier, the *lex Aebutia* had a significant role. The limits of this paper, as well as its structure and purpose oriented towards a historical-comparative analysis of a specific issue across a wide divide of time and historical circumstances, do not allow a thorough study of the issue to be presented here. Nevertheless, a rough sketch of the issue is necessary as the framework of our present research.

Regarding the sources on the *lex Aebutia*, which is commonly situated sometime in the 2nd century BC,[7] only two direct references exist (Kaser 1953, 29 *sqq.*). One is found in Gai. Inst. IV, 30, where Gaius (2nd century AD), in continuation of his account about the petty-mindedness of the old jurists, states that because of it the *legis actiones* were 'put under' or suppressed (*sublatae sunt*) by way of the *lex Aebutia* and the *leges Iuliae*. The other reference is by Aulus Gellius (2nd century AD) who, in his *Noctes Atticae* in XVI, 10, 8, recounts how the majority of *legis actiones*, along with some other ancient legal peculiarities, were 'put to sleep' (*consopita sit*) by the *lex Aebutia*. Both accounts tell us precious little, only that *lex Aebutia* did play a major part in the abandonment of the *legis actiones*, and that this happened gradually over time. As with many other problems of earlier Roman law, this lack of clear and comprehensive sources posed certain difficulties and allowed for various interpretations of the matter.

For a certain period of time the dominant theory was the one propounded by the eminent Austrian Romanist of the 19th century Moriz Wlassak. According to his analysis, before the *lex Aebutia* was enacted *legis actiones* were exclusively used

contents of the said *leges Iuliae iudiciariae* see Rotondi (1962, 448 *sqq.*). For the most recent and thorough study of this transition and relevance of both the *lex Aebutia* and the *leges Iuliae iudiciariae* see Talamanca (1999, 63 *sqq.*).

[6]For a splendid collection of different formulas used in Roman law see Mantovani (1999).

[7]For a general account about this *lex* see Rotondi (1962, 304 *sq.*). Older discussions about the date of its enactment can be found in Girard (1893, 1908). For later discussions see especially Kaser (1953, 27 *sqq.*), Luzzatto (1946, 12 *sqq.*).

for claims based on *ius civile*,[8] and the formulary procedure was only used in the jurisdiction of the *praetor peregrinus*.[9] According to Wlassak, the main purpose of the *lex Aebutia* was to enable the formulary procedure to be used for all claims, whether based on the *ius civile* or not (Wlassak 1888, 104 *sqq.*; 1891, 18 *sqq.*; Kaser 1953, 27 *sq.*). However, he maintained that the *legis actiones* were potentially still available, which means that in the same civil matter the parties could, depending on their choice, use either a *legis actio* or the formulary procedure. This situation persisted until the passage of the abovementioned *leges Iuliae iudiciariae*, which abolished the *legis actiones* and established the formulary procedure as a regular and ordinary mode of procedure.

This theory was very elaborately and articulately criticised by the famous Romanist and Wlassak's compatriot Max Kaser, and his theory subsequently became widely accepted (Kaser 1953; Talamanca 1999, 72, note 45; Sacconi 1979, 63 *sqq.*; Birks 1969, 358, note 8). In his critique, Kaser offered a variety of arguments, with varying degrees of persuasiveness. For example, he argued that it is not likely that the Romans of the 2nd century BC would pass such a systematic reformative Act with far-reaching consequences for the whole procedure, because they lacked the proper methodology and terminology at the time (Kaser 1953, 38 *sq.*). Furthermore, he pointed out the fact that after the passage of the *lex Aebutia* there was not a single mention of one of the *legis actiones*, namely the *legis actio per condictionem*. This, alongside other arguments, led him to conclude that the *lex Aebutia* introduced formulary proceedings only for claims previously pertaining to the *legis actio per condictionem* (Kaser 1953, 28, 31 *sqq.*; 1949, 73 *sq.*, 93; Kaser and Hackl 1996, 159 *sqq.*).[10]

One of Kaser's arguments stands out in particular, especially in view of our present considerations. It is the contention that, if Wlassak's theory had any truth to it, the competition between the *legis actiones* and the formulary procedure would have been very short-lived. He argued that if there was a choice between the two procedures, the older one being dangerously formalistic and the newer one generally more advantageous and convenient, the older one would be extinguished almost instantaneously. However, this argument is not elaborated in detail, but rather mentioned in passing and taken as more or less self-evident (Kaser 1953, 50; Kaser and Hackl 1996, 160). This was shrewdly perceived by Peter Birks, the late

[8]Here, this term is used in the sense of a body of law based on *leges*, plebiscites, enactments of the emperor and the authority of the jurists, as it is defined in D. 1, 1, 7 pr. (Papinianus 2 def.), and is as such contrary to *ius praetorium* or *honorarium*, which is the law created by the *praetor* (Jörs et al. 1987, 13 *sq.*).

[9]He was a magistrate with jurisdictional powers in civil matters between foreigners, and between foreigners and Romans, who was accordingly allowed more freedom in the creation and application of the law, and was not strictly bound to the *ius civile* (Jörs et al. 1987, 12).

[10]Kaser himself admitted that this theory is not completely new, but stems from a work by Fridolin Eisele from 1889. However, he criticised this argumentation as partly based on untrue statements (Kaser 1953, 28 *sq.*). A similar line of reasoning as Kaser's is also proposed by the renowned Belgian Romanist Fernand de Visscher, in de Visscher (1923, 46 *sqq.*).

Regius Professor of Civil Law at the University of Oxford, to be the weakest link in the whole argumentation (Birks 1969, 359 *sqq*.). He maintained, rightly, that the parties might not necessarily prefer the more modern and more rational procedure, which is in any event a retrospective evaluation, since they might find certain immediate advantages in the older procedure.

This observation was used by Birks to support his theory, which is in our opinion entirely plausible, probably more likely than Kaser's, but at any rate one that need not be explicated in detail here.[11] Both accounts are actually in line with the sources mentioned earlier that are the sole direct references to the *lex Aebutia*. In this sense, the resolution of the issue depends on the question of the probable behaviour of the parties when they had a choice between two parallel modes of procedure, the *legis actio* and the formulary procedure.

In the situation at hand, we might speculate that after the *lex Aebutia* the parties had a choice between conducting the *legis actio* or formulary procedure in the same matter, as Wlassak and Birks suppose, or as Kaser supposes in building his argument for the contrary assertion. Undeniably, the formulary procedure had certain advantages, for example the possibility of representation, and was generally less prone to formalistic traps than the *legis actiones* (Birks 1969, 364). However, *legis actiones* still may have had certain advantages for claimants, as they could have hoped to prosper in the proceedings exactly because of its fixed and strict arrangements. Concretely, for example, they may not have wanted respondents to be able to file different *exceptiones* as defences, available in formulary proceedings, and thus sought out a *legis actio* for their claim (Birks 1969, 366). Therefore, it should be sound reasoning to conclude that it may not have been inevitable for the formulary procedure to quickly replace the *legis actiones* if the parties had a say in the matter, as is Kaser's supposition.

Despite the soundness of that assertion, there is a lack of sources from the time that would corroborate it directly. Under these circumstances, a historical-comparative analysis may be helpful. Birks in his analysis briefly points out certain developments in the history of the common law, drawing an analogy between the mentioned developments in Roman law and certain stages in the development of writs and forms of action in the history of civil procedure in the English common law (Birks 1969, 359 *sq*., 363.). The purpose of the following section is to expound

[11]In short, he opined that even before the *lex Aebutia* there was a choice between the two modes of procedure, but the *legis actiones* operated within the *ius civile*, and the formulary procedure within the *ius praetorium*. Consequently, conducting a suit in the formulary proceedings did not preclude a possible subsequent *legis actio* in the same matter. Claimants took advantage of this loophole by resorting to the *legis actio* after they failed in the same claim in formulary proceedings, thereby obviously abusing the system in their favour. The *lex Aebutia*, according to him, was designed to curb such behaviour, by providing that an adjudicated claim in the formulary proceedings consummates the matter *iure civili*, so that another suit cannot be brought in either mode of procedure. Birks's arguments are very clearly summarised in Birks (1969, 366 *sq*.). More recently, similar reasoning regarding the contents of the *lex Aebutia* can be found in Talamanca (1999, 75, 202 *sq*.), Crook (1992, 546), *cf*. Metzger (2015, 295 *sq*.).

on this analogy, adding further considerations from the history of civil procedure in the English common law.

3 Perspectives from the History of Civil Procedure in the English Common Law

The previous section mentioned how Birks drew an analogy between the transition from the *legis actiones* to the formulary procedure in Roman law and the development of writs and forms of action in the history of the English common law.[12] In that development, newer remedies were provided for matters in which older ones were still available. Another significant procedural reform in England may be added to the same line of argument. Namely, the one regarding the use of trial by jury in civil matters in English law, where the parties were able to choose between trials with and without a jury. In both situations parallel modes of procedure were available for choice by the parties, and the newer mode of procedure was considered generally better than the older one. Therefore, both are analysed in the following paragraphs.

Firstly, we are dealing with the development of writs and forms of action.[13] Specifically, we are analysing the action of *assumpsit* and its field of application. *Assumpsit* was a simple and non-formalistic action originating in the 14th century, used generally in the law of obligations, most importantly to enforce agreements (Plucknett 2010, 374 *sq.*, 637 *sqq.*; Baker 1979, 275 *sqq.*; Milsom 1969, 271 *sqq.*). In its simplicity, it was dissimilar to other actions that were used in comparable circumstances, namely the action of debt and the action of covenant. The action of debt was one of the early forms of action, with its origins before the year 1200, and was used against the debtor who owed certain things to the creditor (Plucknett 2010, 633 *sq.*; Baker 1979, 266 *sqq.*; Milsom 1969, 215 *sqq.*; Pollock and Maitland 1968, 203 *sqq.*; Hummel 1966). One of its characteristics was the 'wager of law', or the possibility to refer the resolution of the matter to compurgators or oath-helpers who would swear in favour of one of the parties and thus help that party to win the case (Baker 1979, 268 *sqq.*; Milsom 1969, 226, 237, 307). The action of covenant, stemming from the same time as the action of debt, had a similar field of application as the previously mentioned actions (Plucknett 2010, 365 *sq.*, 634 *sqq.*; Baker 1979,

[12]For a complete and extensive treatment of the history of English law see Holdsworth (1903–1966). An exceptionally clear and useful monography on the matter is Baker (1979). Further literature on the general history of the English common law includes Plucknett (2010), Van Caenegem (1988), Milsom (1969), Pollock and Maitland (1968). Specific treatment of the history of civil procedure in the English common law can be found in every cited source, to which may be added an encyclopaedic reference in Swain (2009), and a very comprehensive and detailed overview in Van Rhee (2005), especially valuable due to its analogies between certain developments in the English common law and those on the European continent.

[13]For their development generally see Van Rhee (2005, 133 *sqq.*), Baker (1979, 48 *sqq.*).

264 *sqq.*; Milsom 1969, 217 *sqq.*; Pollock and Maitland 1968, 216 *sqq.*). However, for it to succeed a sealed written document was needed. As suggested earlier, *assumpsit* lacked both characteristics, it did not involve wager of law as the action of debt did, nor did it require special formalities as the action of covenant did.

Owing to the fact that all three mentioned actions with different proceedings could have been used in similar circumstances stemming from the law of obligations, they may be said to have constituted parallel modes of procedure. The question at hand is what would be the expected course of development, given that *assumpsit*, the new mode of procedure, was quicker, cheaper, less cumbersome and generally more expedient than the other modes that could be used in parallel in the same circumstances. On the face of it, it probably should not be too unreasonable to suppose that the new mode of procedure will quickly replace the old one. However, exactly the opposite happened. The suppression of the action of debt and the action of covenant and the supremacy of *assumpsit* in the field happened slowly and gradually (Plucknett 2010, 637 *sqq.*; Milsom 1969, 271 *sqq.*). The ostensible reason is the fact that the parties obviously found certain advantages in the older procedures (Birks 1969, 360). The party that was not expecting to benefit from the bare facts of the case is actually likely to have insisted on the irrational wager of law, in which that party may at least have had some hope of achieving a decision in its favour. On the other hand, the party that was defaulting in the agreement is likely to have insisted on the requirement of a sealed document where none had existed, in order to avert an unfavourable judgment. In other words, it is most likely that the parties resorted to whatever available mode of procedure suited them best to achieve their immediate goals, and, accordingly, it may have been even somewhat naïve to have expected them to conform to retrospective evaluations about the expediency of procedure. This development confirms our considerations from the previous section about Roman law.

Another procedural transformation of interest to our present considerations concerns trial by jury in civil matters. Generally speaking, the jury in the common law procedure can be considered an immemorial institution, be it in civil or in criminal matters.[14] William Blackstone, the renowned 18th-century English jurist, labelled the jury as 'the glory of the English law' (Blackstone 2016, 249). However, during the course of the 19th century a gradual decline of the jury in civil matters is apparent, leading to its almost absolute abandonment in the first decades of the 20th century (Hanly 2005; Jackson 1937, 138 *sqq.*). In this development different phases existed in which the parties had an opportunity to choose between trial by jury and trial by judge alone. Since trial by judge alone in civil cases may be considered a more modern and expedient mode of procedure, these phases constituted parallel modes of procedure in the sense characterised in this paper, and therefore they deserve a closer look.

[14]For general information on the development of the jury in the English common law procedure, alongside further references, see Plucknett (2010, 106 *sqq.*), Baker (1979, 62 *sqq.*), Pollock and Maitland (1968, 616 *sqq.*). A useful monography dedicated solely to trial by jury is Devlin (1956).

The first major step in the attrition in the use of the jury in civil matters happened at the level of the lower courts, with the County Courts Act of 1846 (Hanly 2005, 266).[15] This Act provided that the cases brought before the County Courts, which were in essence small-claims courts, should be decided by the judge alone, but that the jury may be invoked by the parties if the amount of the claim exceeded £5.[16] In a sense, therefore, the parties had a choice between two different modes of procedure in certain cases. However, they did not avail themselves of the jury option in any significant measure.[17] The reasons for that are manifold, the most important one being the fact that the party making the request for a jury had to pay a sum of five shillings as payment for the jurors (Hanly 2005, 270 *sq.*).

What developed in the superior courts is of more importance, since it pertains to central courts of general jurisdiction (Plucknett 2010, 209; Baker 1979, 47 *sq.*). A momentous change occurred with the passing of the Common Law Procedure Act in 1854, which provided that civil proceedings are by default held before a jury, but may be decided by the judge alone if both parties consent to it in writing, and the judge approves (Hanly 2005, 277; Devlin 1956, 130; Jackson 1937, 139). In other words, again, the parties had a choice between two modes of procedure, of which the newer one was considered more expedient. During the decades that followed, reforms increasingly favoured the 'jury-less option' for civil matters. For example, in 1883 the court was allowed the discretion to order a trial by judge alone, save in certain exceptional circumstances (Jolowicz 2000, 377 *sq.*; Devlin 1956, 130; Jackson 1937, 139 *sq.*). The Administration of Justice Act in 1933 had similar provisions.[18] In 1965, the Court of Appeal held that civil cases should be tried by a jury only exceptionally, save when the statute provided otherwise, which was confirmed by the House of Lords in 1973 (Jolowicz 2000, 378). The Supreme Courts Act of 1981 upheld the main tendency of this development, enumerating certain cases that should be tried by a jury, but retaining the right of the court to order a trial by judge alone.[19] Most recently, jury trials in civil matters are very rare and confined mostly to defamation cases (Jolowicz 2000, 378).

---

[15]More about this Act and the County Courts, with further references, in Plucknett (2010, 208 *sq.*), Arthurs (1984, 137 *sqq.*).

[16]In smaller claims, the judge had the right to allow jury trial by discretion (Hanly 2005, 270).

[17]Out of the 267,445 cases that the County Courts dealt with in the first eight months of their existence, only 800 were tried before juries (Hanly 2005, 271).

[18]This Act provided that trial by jury was mandatory in the case of libel, slander, malicious prosecution, false imprisonment, seduction or breach of promise of marriage, unless the court was of the opinion that the trial required any prolonged examination of documents or accounts or any scientific or local investigation which could not be conveniently made with a jury (Jackson 1937, 141).

[19]This Act provided that the action should be tried by jury in the case of fraud, libel, slander, malicious prosecution or false imprisonment, unless the trial required any prolonged examination of documents or accounts or any scientific or local investigation which could not conveniently be made with a jury (s. 69 of the Senior Courts Act. Available at https://www.legislation.gov.uk/ukpga/1981/54. Accessed 7 June 2018). One can see how the provision from 1933 was changed only slightly, adding fraud and removing seduction or breach of promise of marriage as causes for jury trial.

Despite the obvious general indisposition of the lawgiver towards the jury in civil trials, the transition did not occur as nearly as quickly as it did in the County Courts. The parties were first afforded the right to choose a jury-less trial in civil matters in 1854, but in 1883, almost 30 years later, about 80% of the cases before the superior courts were still tried by juries (Hanly 2005, 277 *sq.*). This percentage shrank to 55% in 1913, to 36% in 1918 and to 16% in 1919 (Hanly 2005, 278). During the 1930s, the percentage fell further to 10%, and from the 1950s onwards it was around 2% (Hanly 2005; Jolowicz 2000, 378). In short, about a century was needed for the jury to all but disappear from civil cases.

This decline happened, without a doubt, steadily, but the end result was extremely slow in coming. The lawgiver was clearly intent on eliminating the jury from most civil cases, but the courts themselves, although having unfettered discretion, declined the request for trial in a negligible number of cases (Devlin 1956, 133). Therefore, the question may be asked as to the reasons for this development. Putting the matters in the perspective assumed in this paper may help in finding likely answers. Simply put, the parties may have held on to the older mode of procedure, disregarding the apparent expedience of the newer one, because they found certain immediate benefits in it. Concretely, parties, both claimants and defendants, may have wanted to have the opportunity to try to win the sympathy of the jury, and avoid a trial by judge alone if possible.

The fact that the same thing did not happen in the County Courts does not affect the main argument, the principal reason being that the jury there had to be paid for if requested. Actually, this may even strengthen the argument, seeing that the parties were protecting their immediate pecuniary interests, and thus most likely were not inclined to pay for the jury. This is supported by the fact that the County Courts dealt with simple and small claims, which were previously adjudicated without a jury (Hanly 2005, 271). Therefore, both the development regarding forms of action and the one concerning the decline of jury trials in civil cases support the main contention of this paper as set out in the context of Roman law in the previous section.

4 Reforms in the Lands of the Habsburg Monarchy in the 19th Century

In the lands of the Habsburg Monarchy, a major procedural transformation occurred over the course of the 18th and 19th centuries. In this transformation, a system with strong characteristics of the Romano-canonical procedure was gradually reformed to a more modern civil procedural system (Van Caenegem 1971, 95 *sqq.*). During the 19th century, periods existed in which parties had an opportunity to choose between an older and presumably outdated mode of procedure and more modern procedural arrangements. As that subject matter falls within the scope of this paper, the following text deals with it in more detail, considering relevant literature, legislation and judicature. Thus the main line of argumentation is brought into a more recent context, which is aligned with the Roman legal tradition in general, and within a setting directly relevant for a number of contemporary European states.[20]

Reforms introduced in the 19th century were directed against the procedural arrangements of the *Allgemeine Gerichtsordnung* (hereinafter: AGO).[21] That Act of 1781 had been passed after a prolonged period of preparation, and not without difficulties and opposition (Loschelder 1978, 26 *sqq.*; Engelmann 1927, 628 *sq.*). The Act did bring certain innovations, but largely remained within the field of Romano-canonical procedure and was more of a codification than a reform of the procedure (Oberhammer and Domej 2010, 255; 2005, 118; Oberhammer 2004, 220 *sq.*; Engelmann 1927, 629). In broad terms, it essentially provided for a written procedure, conducted non-publicly and indirectly, in which evidence had to be evaluated according to the formal proof theory, while the proceedings generally took a very long time to complete (Uzelac 2011, 184; Loschelder 1978, 86 *sqq.*).

There were a number of failed attempts at a comprehensive reform during the 19th century, but in the end change was brought about gradually, by introducing Acts providing for extraordinary proceedings intended to supersede the ordinary procedure little by little (Oberhammer and Domej 2010, 256; Oberhammer 2004, 221). Of these so-called *leges fugitivae* the most important ones were the *Summarpatent* from 1845,[22] introducing summary proceedings or *Summarverfahren*, and the *Gesetz über das Bagatellverfahren* from 1873 (hereinafter: GBV),[23] designed specifically for small claims (Oberhammer and Domej 2010, 256; 2005, 119; Oberhammer 2004, 221 *sq.*). The *Summarverfahren* was conducted orally and the judge had a stronger influence on the course of the proceedings in comparison to the ordinary procedure under the AGO (Oberhammer and Domej 2005, 119). GBV introduced a range of more modern procedural tenets such as the principle of orality, publicity and immediacy; formal rules of evaluating evidence were abandoned, while the judge was given significant authority to lead the course of the proceedings (Oberhammer 2004, 222; Engelmann 1927, 633). This type of procedure served as a model for the final result in the development of the civil procedural legislation of the 19th-century Habsburg Monarchy, the *Zivilprozessordnung*, which was passed in 1895 and came into force in 1898 (hereinafter: ZPO) (Oberhammer and Domej 2010, 256; Oberhammer 2004, 222;

[20]This includes in the first place countries that were previously in the lands of the Habsburg Monarchy, but also some other countries (Van Caenegem 1971, 97 *sq.*). Of course, those developments are of immense importance also for Croatia, since they were clearly reflected in its legislation, both before and after it ceased to be part of the state, albeit with certain significant delays (Uzelac 2011, 176 *sqq.*).

[21]*Justizgesetzsammlung* 1781/13. For a monography dealing with the AGO in detail see Loschelder (1978).

[22]*Justizgesetzsammlung* 1845/906. For more about this Act see Oberhammer (2004, 221), with references to further literature in note 23.

[23]*Reichsgesetzblatt* 1873/66. For a monography dedicated to the *Bagatellverfahren* see Schneider (2001), with further references to literature.

Engelmann 1927, 634). The ZPO was a modern procedural Act for the time, especially significant due to a substantial strengthening of the judge's powers in the proceedings, which led to a considerable decrease in undue delay (Oberhammer and Domej 2010, 256; Oberhammer 2004, 225). It is without question a landmark piece of legislation that influenced legal systems throughout Europe (Van Caenegem 1971, 96 *sq.*; *cf.* Van Rhee 2012).[24]

Summarverfahren and *Bagatellverfahren* were principally intended for cases with small and medium-sized claims.[25] What is remarkable for our current considerations is that both Acts also had clauses allowing their application by choice in other cases. The *Summarpatent* in its paragraph 6 stated that parties could choose summary proceedings through their agreement, regardless of the circumstances and the sum claimed. Correspondingly, GBV in paragraph 5 allowed for the application of the *Bagatellverfahren* if the parties agreed to it and the claim did not exceed 500 florins. In other words, in certain cases parties had a choice between an older and presumably outdated mode of procedure, conducted according to AGO, and the *Summarverfahren* and the *Bagatellverfahren* as the more modern procedures. Therefore, it could be said that parallel modes of procedure—in the sense characterised in this paper—existed, from which the parties could choose at will.

This situation persisted from the time of the passage of the *Summarpatent* in 1845 and the GBV in 1873 up until the ZPO came into force in 1898. In that period *Summarverfahren* and *Bagatellverfahren*, along with some other special procedures, ultimately superseded the older procedure from the AGO in the majority of cases (Oberhammer and Domej 2005, 119). Therefore, the period in which parties had a choice between different modes of procedure eventually ended with the triumph of a more modern and more expedient procedure. However, the transition itself may not have been without obstacles, and the surest indication of this might come from the judicature of the time.

One decision from 1885 by the supreme court of the State (*kaiserlich-königlich Oberster Gerichts- und Cassationshof*) stands out particularly in this regard.[26] Essentially, the issue was the validity of the parties' agreement with which they tried to exclude the application of the *Bagatellverfahren*, although it should have been applicable under paragraph 1 of the GBV mentioned earlier. In other words, the parties tried to opt out of the *Bagatellverfahren* in a situation that did not fall

[24]The ZPO and its conceptual derivatives also form part of the Croatian procedural tradition, and it has been said that the ZPO is actually a '*Grundstein des modernen Prozessrechts in Kroatien*' (Uzelac 2011, 175). A critical evaluation of the actual acceptance of its principles in Croatia can be found in Uzelac (2011, 183 *sqq.*).

[25]The *Summarpatent* in para. 1 provided that the *Summarverfahren* was to be conducted if monetary claims did not exceed 200 guldens. According to para. 1 of the GBV from 1873, the *Bagatellverfahren* was conducted for claims under 25 florins. However, that sum was changed to 50 florins in the *Gesetz vom 1. März 1876, Reichsgesetzblatt* 1876/23.

[26]Decision of the *kaiserlich-königlich Oberster Gerichts- und Cassationshof*, Nr. 32 *Plenissimarbeschluss vom 14. April 1885*, Z. 2553 (*Judicatenbuch* Nr. 117). It can be found in Entscheidungen (1885, 58–63).

under paragraph 5 of the GBV and for which choice actually was not available. The apparent basis was the fact that paragraph 88 of the GBV allowed for a subsidiary application of the general provisions of civil procedure, whereas the AGO in paragraph 15 and the *Summarpatent* in paragraph 24 generally allowed the parties to opt out of the special proceedings and resolve their dispute ordinarily (Entscheidungen 1885, 58 *sq*., 61). At any rate, several supreme courts of the constituent parts of the State had dealt with this matter previously. The same issue was addressed by the supreme courts in Graz in 1875, 1884 and 1885, in Zadar in 1878, in Innsbruck in 1881 and in Prague in 1883. Additionally, the supreme court of the State itself, though not in a plenary session, had already dealt with the problem in 1878 and 1881 (Entscheidungen 1885, 58). It was evidently a widespread and vital issue, which had to be resolved definitively and authoritatively by the highest judicial instance in the State.

The supreme court expressly held that the parties' express or tacit agreement with which they sought to evade the *Bagatellverfahren* in cases where it was explicitly prescribed is null and void (Entscheidungen 1885, 58). A range of arguments was put forward to justify the decision. Firstly, the court emphasised policy considerations, pointing out that the *Bagatellverfahren* was designed not only for the benefit of the parties, but also in the interests of the State. These included easing the courts' caseload and providing a trial test for the upcoming comprehensive civil procedural reform. Taking that into account, the court held that the provisions of the GBV should not be interpreted as allowing unfettered party choice, as that would be directly contrary to the interests of the State (Entscheidungen 1885, 60 *sq*.). Further on, the court pointed out that civil procedural law falls within the scope of public law, which is *ius cogens*, and thus its provisions cannot be abstained from save where explicitly allowed (Entscheidungen 1885, 61). Finally, the court resorted to the interpretation of the provisions of the relevant Acts, which very clearly stipulate obligatory *Bagatellverfahren* for certain claims, and allow a choice in others (Entscheidungen 1885, 62).

In a word, the court categorically denied the right of parties to circumvent a clear provision of the GBV that prescribed claims that fall within the purview of the *Bagatellverfahren*. This decision bears importance for our current considerations, since it directly relates to the parties' choice between an older and presumably outdated mode of procedure under the AGO and a more modern and expedient procedure under the GBV. It is true that this decision did not deal directly with the provisions allowing for a choice, but rather with those explicitly prescribing the *Bagatellverfahren*. However, there is no statistical data which shows how often parties chose a more expedient procedure over the older one when they were allowed to do so. In those circumstances, this decision is very illustrative. Namely, it shows that parties were more than reluctant to accept the *Bagatellverfahren*, even when they were explicitly obliged to do so. Instead, they resorted to a farfetched argumentation in trying to avoid it. The fact that this phenomenon was widespread over the whole area of application of the GBV only adds to the significance of the issue. It was obviously an internal systematic problem of the civil procedural reform in its initial stages.

Of course, there is no clear answer as to the reasons for this development. However, taking into account the considerations in this paper as well as the previously analysed historical examples may indicate possible causes. It is possible, or even likely, that the parties, both claimants and defendants, found certain benefits in the procedural system of the AGO, and thus sought to evade the *Bagatellverfahren* by any means possible. In this, they obviously disregarded the evaluation of the lawgiver and the judiciary of the time, as well as our own retrospective evaluation of the *Bagatellverfahren* as a superior mode of procedure. Instead, they were after their immediate interests. This conclusion is completely in line with our previous analysis regarding Roman law and the English common law.

There is another aspect from the judicature of the time that strikes one as important in the present context. In the already mentioned transitional period before the passage of the ZPO, there were a number of procedural Acts prescribing different proceedings and referring to one another regarding subsidiary application, recourse to higher courts, execution of judgments, etc. In those circumstances, it was probably very challenging for the courts to coordinate all those Acts and achieve a proper functioning of the whole system. Apparently, the supreme court of the State sought to standardise application of all the different proceedings by not allowing interpretations that would make the older procedure preferable over the more modern procedures of *Summarverfahren* and *Bagatellverfahren* due to certain procedural advantages.

For example, in a decision from 1890 the same supreme court as in the previously analysed decision dealt with a case in which the parties freely chose the *Summarverfahren*, but also agreed that the second appeal (*ausserordentliche Revision*) should be available, although it was otherwise not obtainable under the *Summarpatent*.[27] The court interpreted relevant law as allowing the combination of provisions of the ordinary procedure and those of the *Summarverfahren*. Effectively, therefore, the parties were allowed to conduct their proceedings by choice under *Summarverfahren*, while still having the option of the second appeal if so agreed. Similarly, in a decision from 1893 the same court contemplated grounds for the nullity of a decision reached in the *Bagatellverfahren* in comparison to ordinary proceedings.[28] Namely, the GBV allowed for nullification of a decision if brought under the *Bagatellverfahren* in violation of the subject matter competence of the courts (*sachliche Zuständigkeit*), apparently not mentioning the territorial competence (*örtliche Zuständigkeit*).[29] However, the court stated that according to the general rules applicable to civil procedure the request for nullity could be accepted if a court lacked territorial competence. It condemned a restrictive interpretation of the provision of the GBV, and invoked the lawgiver's explanation of

[27]Decision of the *kaiserlich-königlich Oberster Gerichts- und Cassationshof, vom 30. Jänner 1890, Z. 13552 ex 1889. I. Senat*. It can be found in Entscheidungen (1890, 59).

[28]Decision of the *kaiserlich-königlich Oberster Gerichts- und Cassationshof*, Nr. 915 *Plenissimarbeschluss vom 24. Mai 1893*, Z. 4365 (*Judicatenbuch* Nr. 125). It can be found in Entscheidungen (1893, 91, 92).

[29]See Sec. 2, para. 78 of the GBV indicating para. 1–7 of the same Act.

the motives for this Act, in which there was no differentiation between territorial and subject matter competence (Entscheidungen 1893, 92).

Both decisions could be interpreted as trying to suppress situations in which the older procedure could prove to be more advantageous than the more modern modes of procedure. In the first case, the supreme court allowed the second appeal in the *Summarverfahren* that the parties chose as a procedure to resolve their dispute, although the *Summarpatent* actually did not provide for that remedy. Had it decided otherwise, the parties might have been even more reluctant than usual to accede to the *Summarverfahren*, since it would lack an important legal remedy otherwise available. Likewise, in the second decision the supreme court held that a decision brought under the *Bagatellverfahren* could be declared null and void if the court in question lacked territorial competence, although the GBV lacked a clear provision in that regard. Again, had it decided otherwise, the parties might have been even less inclined to avail themselves of the *Bagatellverfahren*, since it would lack one ground for nullity otherwise available. In a word, the supreme court effectively tried not to give much reason for parties to evade the new modes of procedure.

Of course, this reasoning is mainly speculative, as the referenced policy arguments are not explicitly mentioned in the two decisions.[30] However, such a conclusion should be warranted by the previous analysis and historical examples presented in this paper. Moreover, the special proceedings did eventually almost completely supersede the old procedure under the AGO even before the passage of the ZPO, as stated earlier. Therefore, it could be said that this success retrospectively explains the supreme court's probable original objectives in the cited decisions. This conclusion could be both a confirmation of general historical tendencies in situations with parallel modes of procedure as outlined in this paper and an example of a successful judicial intervention that curbed their possible negative effects.

5 Conclusion

The main issue addressed in this paper deals with the transitional periods in certain procedural transformations during which parties had a choice between different modes of procedure, one of which was newer and more expedient than the other. The first part dealing with Roman law serves as a starting point and setting for further analysis, while analysis of certain reforms and transformations in the history of the English common law and in the lands of the Habsburg Monarchy in the 19th century provides a broader historical-comparative context.

[30]The decision of the supreme court from 1885 analysed in the previous text did have certain policy arguments favouring the *Bagatellverfahren* over the ordinary procedure, as was noted earlier.

The results of the analysis show a clear tendency in every procedural reform and transformation studied. When presented with a choice between two modes of procedure, the parties were most likely to choose the one that suited their immediate interests the best. This meant more often than not that they would choose the one generally deemed an outdated procedure, in which they nevertheless had certain advantages. In other words, historical analysis showed that the assessment of the lawgiver or of the legal scholar about the quality of a given procedure does not always conform to the immediate parties' interests. This discrepancy most likely stems from the unrealistic expectations of the lawgiver, and his inability to calculate this tendency in a reform in order to overcome its negative consequences.

In the context of Roman law, the procedural transformation analysed was the transition from the *legis actiones* to the formulary procedure. The main theory explaining that transition presupposed that the parties, when presented with a choice between the two modes of procedure, would nearly *en masse* and almost instantaneously favour the formulary procedure as the more expedient one. However, historical-comparative analysis showed that this supposition is faulty, as exactly the opposite happened in comparable circumstances in different jurisdictions and across a wide divide of time and historical circumstances. In the history of the English common law, *assumpsit* as a new form of action was introduced in the 14th century, and it was supposedly more rational and expedient than its older competitors, the actions of debt and covenant, which were available in parallel. Accordingly, it might have been expected that *assumpsit* would quickly and easily replace them, but that happened rather arduously and only after a long period of time. A similar situation existed when the English legislature in the 19th century and the beginning of the 20th century was largely indisposed towards the jury in civil trials in the superior courts. An option for the parties was created according to which they could choose between jury and jury-less trials, but it took about one hundred years before jury-less trials in civil matters prevailed. Finally, reforms of civil procedure in the lands of the Habsburg Monarchy in the 19th century showcase the same trend. In this gradual reform, during a certain period of time the parties could choose between a regular and presumably outdated procedure and the more modern special procedures of *Summarverfahren* and *Bagatellverfahren*. The judicature of the time shows that the parties were initially more than reluctant to accept new procedures, and the judiciary had to intervene to promote these procedures and carry the reform through. These conclusions run contrary to the supposition of the main theory regarding the content of the *lex Aebutia* analysed in the section of this paper dedicated to Roman law. Consequently, this indicates the necessity to support the theories that appreciate said tendencies of the parties, and which postulate the possibility of a choice between *legis actiones* and formulas as equally viable parallel modes of procedure in a given period.

The answer to the general question posed in the title of this paper is tentative, and contingent on different circumstances. In every mentioned procedural reform and transformation the new procedure eventually did prevail, but not before historical circumstances significantly changed, and not without decisive statutory intervention or judicial action oriented towards curbing the negative consequences of the parties' behaviour. The transition from *legis actiones* to *formulae* in Roman law lasted around three centuries and was completed only after the statutory abolition of *legis actiones* in most cases by the *leges Iuliae iudiciariae*. *Assumpsit* in the English common law prevailed over other forms of actions in due course of time, after their formalities and peculiarities became totally obsolete. The jury in civil trials in 19th- and 20th-century England was brought into disuse by careful and gradual legislative action. The parties' disregard for jury-less trials was only partly curbed in County Courts, where the privilege of a jury had to be paid for, which apparently lessened possible interest for a jury. Reforms in the 19th-century Habsburg Monarchy ended with a far-reaching general procedural Act, but not before many interventions by the judiciary in directing the course of the reform. In some of them, the courts actively sought to eliminate possible advantages of the older modes of procedure in order not to dissuade parties from partaking in the newer ones. In other words, the parties' behaviour was more often than not an obstacle to the reforms, and whatever hopes might have been placed in them to facilitate the reforms would have been in vain.

The reason for such a widespread phenomenon, stretching over millennia and different jurisdictions, may be an apparent proclivity of any given procedural system towards conservatism. Perhaps every procedural system—in other words the parties, their representatives and the judiciary as its principal actors—displays a general inertness and an inherent indisposition to change. This conclusion is apparently especially warranted in the case of the common law jurisdictions, which seem to exhibit particularly strong conservative tendencies.[31] Similarly, Roman law has been said to have displayed a general strong propensity to maintain and protect its traditions throughout its development.[32] Ostensibly, the reasons for such a tendency may be purely psychological on the part of the principal actors in civil procedural systems.[33]

Then again, before resorting to such explanations almost bordering on the irrational, perhaps a more rational justification could be proposed. As has been stated repeatedly in this paper, the parties may have behaved completely rationally in protecting their immediate proprietary interests while disregarding historical, theoretical or even ideological evaluations about the expediency of a given mode of procedure. This entirely reasonable behaviour by the parties has been obviously

[31]For example, the forms of action in England were gradually abolished during the 19th century (Van Rhee 2005, 142 *sqq*.). However, even after their abolition they still greatly influenced the pleading and the lawyers' mind-set generally, so much as to warrant Maitland to famously proclaim in 1909: 'The forms of action we have buried, but they still rule us from their graves' (1997, 1). This has been said to be true for the developments in the United States of America as well (Maxeiner 2010, 1275).

[32]On this characteristic of Roman law see especially Schulz (2003, 57 *sqq*.), with further references to sources and literature.

[33]For example, the psychological factor was emphasised regarding reforms of civil procedure in the United States of America in the 19th century and the beginning of the 20th century (see Fowler 1934; Proskauer 1928; and Sims 1911).

disregarded in a number of major procedural reforms and transformations throughout history. However, it is evidently an important factor to be reckoned with whenever and wherever parallel modes of procedure may be involved. One should be appreciative of this fact when considering procedural reforms and transformations in the past, such as those in Roman law. Conversely, its appreciation might also contribute to a general assessment of a reform in a contemporary context. It is true that parallel modes of procedure are likely to appear only during major civil procedural reforms. Still, the same logic may apply in any situation where an alternative to the ordinary procedure is offered, such as different ADR mechanisms. They may appear to be more expedient and modern, and seem to be a suitable tool to unburden the courts. However, if historical experience is any guide, they will be used in any significant measure only if the parties find them more suitable for their immediate interests than the ordinary procedure, totally regardless of their general evaluation by jurists. In any event, it may be concluded that we should consider this not only in hindsight, when analysing Roman law and different procedural transformations in history, but also in foresight, when considering contemporary and future civil procedural reforms.

References

Albanese B (1987) Il processo privato romano delle *legis actiones*. Palumbo, Palermo

Arthurs HW (1984) 'Without the law': courts of local and special jurisdiction in nineteenth-century England. J Legal Hist 5:130–149

Baker JH (1979) An introduction to English legal history. Butterworths, London

Betti E (1966) Processo civile (diritto romano). In: Azara A, Eula E (eds) Novissimo Digesto Italiano, vol 13. UTET, Torino, pp 1099–1120

Birks P (1969) From *legis actio* to *formula*. Irish Jurist 4:356–367

Blackstone W (2016) Commentaries on the laws of England, book 3. OUP, Oxford

Cannata CA (1980) Profilo istituzionale del processo privato romano, vol 1. Giappichelli, Torino

Cannata CA (1982) Profilo istituzionale del processo privato romano, vol 2. Giappichelli, Torino

Crook JA (1992) The development of Roman private law. In: Crook JA, Lintott A, Rawson E (eds) The Cambridge ancient history, vol 9. CUP, Cambridge, pp 532–563

de Visscher F (1923) La condictio et le système de la Procédure formulaire. A Buyens, Gand

Devlin P (1956) Trial by jury. Stevens & Sons Ltd, London

Engelmann A (1927) A history of continental civil procedure. Little, Brown, and Co, Boston

Entscheidungen des k.-k. (1885) Obersten Gerichts- und Cassationshofes in Civil- und Strafsachen, I. Jahrgang. Druck und Verlag der kaiserlich-königlichen Hof- und Staatsdruckerei, Wien

Entscheidungen des k.-k. (1890) Obersten Gerichts- und Cassationshofes in Civil- und Strafsachen, VI. Jahrgang. Druck und Verlag der kaiserlich-königlichen Hof- und Staatsdruckerei, Wien

Entscheidungen des k.-k. (1893) Obersten Gerichts- und Cassationshofes in Civil- und Strafsachen, IX. Jahrgang. Druck und Verlag der kaiserlich-königlichen Hof- und Staatsdruckerei, Wien

Fowler HH (1934) A psychological approach to procedural reform. Yale Law J 43:1254–1273

Fuenteseca P (1964) Las 'legis actiones' como etapas del processo romano. Anuario de historia del derecho español 34:209–233

Girard PF (1893) La date de la loi Aebutia. ZSS RA 14:11–54
Girard PF (1908) Nouvelles observations sur la date de la loi Aebutia. ZSS RA 29:113–169
Guarino A (2001) Diritto privato romano. Jovene, Napoli
Hanly C (2005) The decline of civil jury trial in nineteenth-century England. J Legal Hist 26:253–278
Holdsworth WS (1903–1966) A history of English law, vols 1–17. Methuen & Co Ltd, London
Hummel JD (1966) Die Vorläufer des 'writ of debt' und seines Verfahrens. Eberhard-Karls-Universität, Tübingen
Jackson RM (1937) The incidence of jury trial during the past century. Mod Law Rev 1:132–144
Jolowicz JA (2000) On civil procedure. CUP, Cambridge
Jörs P, Kunkel W, Wenger L (1987) Römisches Recht. Springer, Berlin
Kaser M (1949) Das altrömische *ius*. Vandenhoeck & Ruprecht, Göttingen
Kaser M (1953) Die *lex Aebutia*. In: Arangio-Ruiz V (ed) Studi in memoria di Emilio Albertario, vol 1. Giuffrè, Milano, pp 27–59
Kaser M, Hackl K (1996) Das römische Zivilprozessrecht. CH Beck, München
Loschelder M (1978) Die österreichische Allgemeine Gerichtsordnung von 1781. Duncker & Humblot, Berlin
Luzzatto GI (1946) Procedura civile romana, vol 3. Edizioni Universitarie, Bologna
Magdelain A (1991) Naissance de la procédure formulaire. TR 3-4:239–257
Maitland FW (1997) The forms of action at common law. CUP, Cambridge
Mantovani D (1999) Le formule del processo privato romano. CEDAM, Padova
Maxeiner JR (2010) Pleading and access to civil procedure: historical and comparative reflections on *Iqbal*, A day in court and a decision according to law. Penn State Law Rev 114:1257–1289
Mayer-Maly T (1969) Legis actio. In: Ziegler K, Sontheimer K (eds) Der kleine Pauly: Lexikon der Antike, vol 3. Alfred Müller, Stuttgart, pp 546, 547
Melillo G (2007) Le *legis actiones* e i quinque modi agendi. In: Cascione C, Masi Doria C (eds) Fides humanitas ius, vol 5. Editoriale Scientifica, Napoli, pp 3515–3535
Metzger E (2015) Litigation. In: Johnston D (ed) The Cambridge companion to Roman law. CUP, Cambridge, pp 272–298
Milsom SFC (1969) Historical foundations of the common law. Butterworths, London
Nicosia G (1986) Il processo privato romano, vol 1. Giappichelli, Torino
Oberhammer P (2004) Speeding up civil litigation in Austria: past and present instruments. In: Van Rhee CH (ed) The law's delay. Intersentia, Antwerp, pp 217–232
Oberhammer P, Domej T (2005) Germany, Switzerland, Austria (ca. 1800–2005). In: Van Rhee CH (ed) European traditions in civil procedure. Intersentia, Antwerp, pp 103–128
Oberhammer P, Domej T (2010) Delay in Austrian civil procedure and the legislator's response. In: Van Rhee CH (ed) Within a reasonable time. Duncker & Humblot, Berlin, pp 255–277
Paulus CG (1999) Legis actio. In: Cancik H, Schneider H (eds) Der neue Pauly: Enzyklopädie der Antike, vol 7. JB Metzger, Stuttgart, pp 22–24
Plucknett TFT (2010) A concise history of the common law. Liberty Fund, Indianapolis
Pollock F, Maitland FW (1968) The history of English law before the time of Edward I, vol 2. CUP, Cambridge
Proskauer JM (1928) A new professional psychology essential for law reform. ABA J 14:121–126
Pugliese G (1961) Il processo civile romano, vol 1. Ricerche, Roma
Rotondi G (1962) Leges publicae populi romani. Olms, Hildesheim
Sacconi G (1979) Appunti sulla *lex Aebutia*. Archivio giuridico 'Filippo Serafini' 197:63–93
Scherillo G (1969) La 'legis actio per iudicis arbitrive postulationem' e le origini del processo formulare. IVRA 20:5–48
Schneider G (2001) Das Bagatellverfahren im österreichischem Recht. MANZ, Wien
Schulz F (2003) Prinzipien des römischen Rechts. Duncker & Humblot, Berlin
Sims HU (1911) Problem of reforming procedure. Yale Law J 21:215–236
Swain WM (2009) Civil procedure in English common law. In: Katz SN (ed) The Oxford international encyclopaedia of legal history, vol 4. OUP, Oxford, pp 419–423

Talamanca M (1987) Processo civile (diritto romano). In: Moratti C, Pugliatti S (eds) Enciclopedia del diritto, vol 36. Giuffrè, Milano, pp 1–79
Talamanca M (1999) Il riordinamento augusteo del processo privato. In: Milazzo F (ed) Gli ordinamenti giudiziari di Roma imperiale. Edizioni Scientifiche Italiane, Napoli, pp 63–260
Uzelac A (2011) Kroatien: Rezeption des Ideenguts von Franz Klein als Aufgabe für die Zukunft? In: Rechberger WH (ed) Die Entwicklung des Zivilprozessrechts in Mittel- un Südosteuropa seit 1918. Jan Sramek, Wien, pp 175–201
Van Caenegem RC (1971) History of European civil procedure. In: Cappelletti M (ed) Civil procedure. JCB Mohr, Tübingen, pp 1–113
Van Caenegem RC (1988) The birth of the English common law. CUP, Cambridge
Van Rhee CH (2005) English civil procedure until the civil procedure rules (1998). In: Van Rhee CH (ed) European traditions in civil procedure. Intersentia, Antwerp, pp 129–159
Van Rhee CH (2012) The influence of the 1895 Austrian ZPO in the Netherlands. In: Chen L, Van Rhee CH (eds) Towards a Chinese civil code. Martinus Nijhoff, Leiden, pp 521–539
Weiss E (1925) Legis actio. In: Wissowa G, Kroll W (eds) Paulys Real-Encyklopädie der classischen Altertumswissenschaft, vol 12. JB Metzger, Stuttgart, pp 1838–1842
Wlassak M (1888) Römische Processgesetze, erste Abteilung. Duncker & Humblot, Leipzig
Wlassak M (1891) Römische Processgesetze, zweite Abteilung. Duncker & Humblot, Leipzig

Henrik-Riko Held Assistant Professor of Roman Law at the Faculty of Law, University of Zagreb. Post-doctoral studies at the Centro di studi e ricerche sui Diritti Antichi (CEDANT), Almo Collegio Borromeo, University of Pavia (2016), Italy. Member of the editorial board of the Zagreb Law Review.

Historical Uniformity and Diversity of Notaries in the Shadow of Their Modern Transformation

Ivan Milotić

Abstract The traditional understanding of notaries in Europe almost exclusively relies on the dictionary meaning of the term *notarius*. Etymology and the strict meaning of that Latin word reveal the essence of the roles and functions of notaries that have traditionally existed in European legal culture from late antiquity onwards. Despite the fact that the basic idea of the notarial profession relied on the same grounds, their positions and authority or credibility of the documents they produced varied considerably throughout Europe and during different historical periods. This contribution contains an overview of the traditional and continuous roles and functions of notaries in Europe. It puts emphasis on the question whether these roles and functions referred exclusively to documentary work or whether notaries of medieval and later Europe could reliably be ascribed some other (regulatory) powers.

1 Introduction

The process of dejudicialization in some parts of Europe, which has recently resulted in certain bypassing of the courts, has intensively highlighted the function and role of the public notary. Legislators in some countries recognized the potential of the public notary for the outsourcing of judicial tasks and functions. The legislators' reasoning for their decisions and policies in this matter was that these processes should generate savings and increase the efficiency of national civil justice. At the same time, the sudden and intensive transformation raised questions about the traditional functions and roles of the public notary. These questions gave rise to the search for the foundations especially of the Latin (European) public

This contribution is the result of research supported by the Croatian Science Foundation (project no. 6988).

I. Milotić (✉)
Faculty of Law, University of Zagreb, Zagreb, Croatia
e-mail: imilotic@pravo.hr

A. Uzelac and C. H. van Rhee (eds.), *Transformation of Civil Justice*, Ius Gentium: Comparative Perspectives on Law and Justice 70,
https://doi.org/10.1007/978-3-319-97358-6_21

notary, a search which often turned into the pursuit of historical analogies that could be exploited as sustainable arguments for the legitimization of the newly shaped (extended) roles and functions of the notaries.

The search for foundations often resorts to Roman law, because some activities which were later pertinent to the public notary were in origin closely bound up with Roman law and practice (Steinhoff 1976, 1, 29). A considerable amount of evidence from classical Roman law records various scribes (*scribae*, *tabularii*, *testamentarii*, *notarii*) whose scriptural activity and role in the production of documents was not constitutive or decisive and therefore cannot be qualified as the legal grounds of the formal credibility of documents. Their roles and functions should primarily be appreciated within the efforts of promoting the scribal culture and creating written proof of different legal transactions (Brown 1936, 8, 9; Stern 2000, 420, 421; Eck 1978, 277–295; Marino 1988, 634, 635; Amelotti and Costamagna 1975, 10 *et seq.*, 20, 21; Steinhoff 1976, 16, 18; Saradi 1999, 23). It was not until the late classical and postclassical period that the Romans developed the idea of persons who were professionally orientated on the production of private documents that enjoyed *fides publica* (Saradi 1999, 23). The most important compilers of private documents in the Roman period were *tabelliones*, whose activity was inseparably connected to *fides publica*. Their status of specialized professionals was profoundly regulated during Justinian's rule[1] with special normative references to the following fields: liability of *tabelliones*, *fides publica* which was linked to their activity, presumption of their documents' authenticity and judicial review of private documents they produced.

That the Romans themselves mentioned the term *notarius* does not necessarily mean that we can instantly (based exclusively on the meaning of that word) observe the existence of an idea or concept of public notary in Roman law. Though the technical term of notary historically derives from the Latin language (*notarius*), the formation of this profession dates to more recent times. Classical and particularly postclassical Roman law, including its transition to the early Middle Ages, represents a formative period of notarial practices which emerged from the perpetual tension between different judicial appreciations and evaluations of written and oral proof (Steinhoff 1976, 1, 2). In that period, the *notarius* was solely a craftsman, i.e. a routine scribe, copyist, penman or compiler (not a public office holder) who ensured that documents were properly set down. Because of that, the *notarius* enjoyed a certain degree of factual (informal) credibility and confidence (Milotić 2013, 693–724).

For these reasons, the search for the origins of the notary public should refer to the medieval period. Still, the analysis of the notarial phenomena in the Middle Ages requires caution since not all literal activities can be qualified as notarial. It is

[1]Ulpianus, D.48.19.9.4-8; Paulus, D.2.4.1; C.TH. 12.1.3; C.TH. 3.5.1; C.TH. 1.56.2; C.TH. 12.1.151; C.TH. 7.52.6; C.I. 4.42.2.pr.; C.I. 11.54.1.pr.; C.I. 1.2.14.6; IUST., *Novella* XLIV, c. 1.1; IUST. *Novella LXXIII*; Cuiacius, *Commentarius ad C.I.8.11.17*; Cuiacius, *Commentarius ad Novellam XLIV*; Brown (1936), 17; Pfaff (1905), 3–7; Saradi (1999), 3, 4, 7–13; Cannata (1986), 193, 194; Amelotti and Costamagna (1975), 24, 41; Steinhoff (1976), 20–23.

a great challenge for the researcher to set a clear and consistent distinction in that field because nomenclature linked to different medieval scribes and scribal activities is "often vague and fails to distinguish clearly between public notaries and others who were simple scribes or copyists" (Brundage 2008, 394).

With reference to these constraints, this paper will briefly analyse the basic lines of medieval development of scribal activities. Its intention is not to provide an exhaustive examination of medieval notaries, but rather to follow basic lines, concepts and tendencies which gradually shaped their development. The paper will provide an analysis of whether in the medieval notarial practices or persons of medieval notaries, or at least in some of their aspects, one could identify roles and functions which today represent a recognizable characteristic of the public notary. Finally, the paper will briefly examine whether the newly shaped (extended) notaries' roles and functions in Europe achieved through the modern process of dejudicialization have a traditional background in historical practices.

2 Scribes in the Vague Nomenclature of the Middle Ages Until the 13th Century

The increasing use of specialists who knew the techniques of writing and composing documents is an important tendency in the Middle Ages. In the minds of common, early medieval people, scribes who carried out this process retained close connections and associations with the Roman Empire due to their specific scriptural activity and their names (*tabellio*, *notarius*), which preserved a clear resemblance to the institutes and terminology of Roman law (Steinhoff 1976, 1, 2). In the West, especially in the former Roman imperial capitals of northern Italy, ancient scribal traditions cultivated by different types of scribes, compilers, editors, etc., were vivid and intense. Regardless of dramatic territorial and political changes in Western society, they formed continuity from Justinian's era and the early Middle Ages to the 13th century. Transition and permanent cultivation of notarial practices from antiquity to the Middle Ages is a key point in the long historical process of the development of notaries. M. W. Steinhoff qualified the *notarii* of that period as persons who enabled and carried out the transition between the ancient and early medieval civilizations and, consequently, between the ancient and medieval notarial traditions (Steinhoff 1976, 1, 2, 28, 116).

Reports in the medieval sources until the 13th century never designated scribal activities or scribes themselves with consistency and clear references (regarding concepts, names, terminology, etc.). Nomenclature linked to scribes was vague with no clear distinctions between their different types, which leads to the conclusion of a deficiency of any sort of system, uniformity, categorization and perception referring to specialized scribes who could be analogous to public notaries (Meyer 2000, 72–86; Brundage 2008, 394, 395). A single exception refers to *tabelliones* and imperial or curial *notarii* because the transition of their functions and roles to the Middle Ages was grounded in the direct continuity between Roman law and its legal tradition in the Middle Ages. For that reason, clearer perceptions existed on *tabelliones* and *notarii* because medieval people knew their names, functions and roles from before, i.e. from the period of Roman antiquity.

Because scribal activity before the 13th century was not uniform, standardized or adequately systemized, there are no arguments which could firmly support the existence of public notaries in that period. At the time, scribal activity was carried out by scribes whose work was highly routinized and merely relied on circulating diplomatic formularies and templates for certain types of legal transactions. No matter their names or Latin terms used for the purpose of their designation (*tabelliones*, *scribae*, *notarii*, etc.), the medieval scribes in the period before the 13th century should be perceived as craftsmen only, whose position and factual credibility depended solely upon the following factors: whether they performed their activity independently or not, whether they received formal training (usually legal) or not, whether they were employed in the *curia* or not, whether they performed basic scribal operations or more complex ones, whether they were rich and prominent citizens or not, etc. It should be emphasized that documents compiled by the scribes of that period had no formal credibility, which means they formally enjoyed no *fides publica*. The scribes' job was purely technical and consisted in simple copying, preparing or setting down a certain transaction in written form and ensuring that documents contained accurate descriptions of legal phenomena, adequate structure and all necessary components. The documents they produced were certainly regarded by people with a high degree of reliability and credibility, but these always remained of a factual nature only.

The production of documents markedly increased in the 11th, 12th and, particularly, the 13th century, which resulted in an increase in the number of scribes and gave rise to their importance. The increase was induced by demands set by the courts, judges and procedural treaties that the court materials should be delivered and procedures performed/recorded in written form. The continuous increase in document numbers was reaffirmed by the Roman-canon procedure that favoured written proof as the only means by which a relevant fact could be reliably and incontestably proved (*probatio plena*), and at the same time by diminishing the value of oral testimony (Gouron 1995, 84 *et seq.*). The importance of documents and the people who produced them was stressed by another factor which was adequately explained by M. W. Steinhoff: "With the spread of illiteracy the medieval notary was called upon to play a far more important role in the newly emerging civilization than that performed by his Roman ancestor in his more literate world" (Steinhoff 1976, 1).

3 Meaning, Function and Role of the *notarius* by the Late 13th Century

The Latin word *notarius* signifies *shorthand scribe*, *writer*, *recorder*, *stenographer* and *secretary*. In its genuine (dictionary) meaning, this word stands solely as the designation of a person, not of an office and service nor of an office or service holder. J. J. Murphy finds *notarius* to be a title which was originally attached to a function rather than to an official job or position (Murphy 1981, 263). Under the strong influence of the glossators (Stein 1999, 47 *et seq.*) at Bologna in the 12th century, the *notarius*' activities were qualified as *ars notaria*, which is a truly medieval invention. Such circumstances have even led scholars to the conclusion that the foundations of notaries in the West should be put in that period (Savigny 1834, 317 *et seq.*). Some 19th-century scholars thought that the invention of this *ars notaria* and its description should be ascribed to Irnerius (1055–1130), the first glossator, because he was at the time mistakenly attributed the authorship of the *Formularium tabellionum*, but later it was reliably determined that this work was written around 1205 in Bologna (Kantorowicz 1938, 36; Palmieri 1892). Still, Irnerius represents a point in time from which the growing interest in notarial matters at Bologna begins, primarily because the number of notaries grew rapidly along with the general population increase (Murphy 1981, 264; Brundage 2008, 397).

The earliest clear nomenclature references to a notary date from the mid 12th century (Meyer 2000, 72–86). The transition from the 11th to the 12th century brought clearer perceptions of scribes and scribal activities primarily because of the glossators' explanations. From that time, there are records of the glossators who wrote works specifically about the *ars notaria*: (1) Rainerius of Perugia, who demonstrates in the treatise *Ars notaria* (c. 1226–1233) the close connections between *ars notaria* and the legal system (Gaudenzi 1892, 25–67); (2) Rolandinus de Passageriis, who is the author of the *Summa artis notariae* ([c. 1256] 1492), in which, for the first time by anyone, he uses the term *doctor artis notariae* with an obvious tendency to qualify it as a preferred professional designation (Wahrmund 1917).

Around 1250, the *ars notaria* evidently reached a high level of importance because a specialized and institutionalized training was available in Bologna in the form of a school (faculty) for notaries (Murphy 1981, 264, 265; Wolf 1973, 509). In the second half of the 13th century, the notaries in Bologna organized themselves into an association (*societas notariorum civitatis Bononiae*), which confirms the strong tendencies of their professional affirmation (Rolandinus de Passageriis [c. 1256] 1492; Wahrmund 1917, 74). The spread of the notarial profession outside Italy in the 13th century took place parallel to the spread of the new glossators' (or Bolognese) learning across Europe (Stein 1999, 54 *et seq.*; Murphy 1981, 264, 265). All the same, notaries remained extremely rare outside Italy as of the late 13th century and even in subsequent centuries; the notarial profession in these regions (England, France, Germany, Scandinavia, central and southeast Europe, with the exceptions of southern France and to some extent the medieval cities in the Netherlands) would not reach a high level or importance nor would the notaries themselves represent the central figures of the bureaucracy, commerce or legal transactions (Wolf 1973, 506; Fournier 1984, 42 *et seq.*; Brundage 2008, 402). According to J. Brundage, the territorial core of the notaries should be placed in the areas south of the Alps and Pyrenees (Brundage 2008, 396).

If precisely studied, one can conclude that notaries of the 12th and 13th centuries were professionals in producing documents, shorthand writing (stenographers) and penmanship. A considerable number of notaries made their notarial practice their principal occupation. Their literary activity, though, should be understood merely as a technical job of producing documents by a legible hand for which knowledge of Latin was required, while a legal background might be useful, but not a decisive qualification.[2] Notarial activity in that period had close connections with the legal system, because in most cases the notaries' job consisted in producing the records of legal transactions. Furthermore, their job was to materialize the legal transactions in the proper form and structure for the purpose of written proof. "Notaries of the middling sort were skilled craftsmen, able to prepare original documents that accurately described fairly complex transactions. They often developed a distinct professional identity with their own professional organizations separate from those of professional advocates and proctors" (Brundage 2008, 395). No further roles and functions (regulative, adjudicative, etc.) of notaries existed at that time.

The production of documents by notaries in and of itself did not result in *fides publica*, i.e. in formal (public) trust in such documents. Public trust in a document was not something the notary was capable of awarding, because his authority was only factual and emerged exclusively from his professional skills. The context and circumstances of his activity a priori exclude any firm resemblance or analogy with the public notary as we perceive it today. Even the fact that from the Carolingian period the civil and ecclesiastical authorities occasionally employed notaries (which technically made them public servants) did not change the nature of their activity, because it was not the "notarial authority" or "notarial capacity" that awarded the documents public trust. Public trust, reliability and probative value depended solely on the authority of the person who employed the notary and authorized his activity.

4 Notaries in the Church After the Fourth Lateran Council (1215)

A separate line of development of the notaries' roles and functions existed in the Church bureaucracy. In the late 12th century, Pope Alexander III in his letter to Bishop Roger of Worcester described the phenomenon *instrumentum in formam publicam*. He declared that documents produced by the notary with public authority

[2]Durantis G, *Speculum iudiciale*, 2.2 *De instrumentorum editione* §8.1.

(*manum publicam*) had evidential value if they were prepared by him and authenticated by his personal sign (*sigillum authenticum*).[3] This view was reaffirmed in 1199 by Pope Innocentius III.[4] Alexander III's declaration that notarial documents enjoyed complete trust became a point of reference for the doctrine. Glossator Azo pointed out that a public document enjoyed public trust by itself (*soli autem publico instrumento habetur fides* per se), with no other support (*sine aliquo adminiculo*), and if it had no defect (*quod sine vituperatione appareat*), the content which the document contained was considered trustworthy unless it was proven to be false (*nisi is contra quem profertur probet falsum*).[5] This should be understood as follows: if a notarial document enjoys public trust, it should be qualified as a public act (Padoa-Schioppa 2017, 131, 132). From the procedural aspect of its probative/evidentiary value, this means that such a document is full proof (*probatio plena*) and that its authenticity could be contested only by using legal means and proofs which suggested that its content was false (Nörr 2012, 153).

Alexander III's considerations on notaries were expressed with reference to court proceedings and burden of proof. And so too at the Fourth Lateran Council held in 1215, when the Council promulgated the important procedural canon *Quoniam contra falsam* (canon No. 38), which evidently borrowed the language and norms from earlier decretals. The canon prescribed the legally binding requirement of making written records of court proceedings.[6] Pope Innocentius III made analogous declarations in the decretal of the following year (1216): a judge was obliged to keep written records of court proceeding in the Church courts by employing a

[3]*Scripta vero authentica, si testes inscripti decesserint, nisi per manum publicam facta fuerint [idest per notarium] publicam facta fuerint, ita quod apparenat publica aut authenticum sigillum habeant non vidnetur nobis alicuius firmitatis robur habere. Liber Extra* X 2.22.2; 1 *Comp.* 2.15.2.; *Corpus iuris canonici*, col. 344.

[4]Reg. Innoc. III, 2, 60–66, No. 37, 63. Fournier (1984), 44, 45; Meyer (2000), 99–103, 148.

[5]Azo, *Summa Codicis*, 4.21 *de fide instrumentorum*, n. 1.

[6][...] *statuimus ut tam in ordinario iudicio quam extraordinario, iudex semper adhibeat aut publicam (si potest habere) personam, aut dos viros idoneos, qui fideliter universa iudicii acta conscribant, videlicet citaciones et dilationes, recusationes et exceptiones, petitiones et responsiones, interrogationes et confessiones, testium depositiones et instrumentum productiones, interlocutiones, apellationes, renunciationes, conclusiones et cetera quae ocurrunt competenti ordine conscribenda, designando loca, tempora et personas. Et omnia sic conscripta partibus tribuantur ita, quod originalis penes scriptores remaneant* [..] Translation: [...] *We therefore decree, lest falsehood prejudice truth or wickedness prevail over justice, that in both ordinary and extraordinary trials the judge shall always employ either a public official, if he can find one, or two suitable men to write down faithfully all the judicial acts—that is to say the citations, adjournments, objections and exceptions, petitions and replies, interrogations, confessions, depositions of witnesses, productions of documents, interlocutions, appeals, renunciations, final decisions and the other things that ought to be written down in the correct order—stating the places, times and persons. Everything thus written down shall be given to the parties in question, but the originals shall remain with the scribes, so that if a dispute arises over how the judge conducted the case, the truth can be established from the originals*[...] 4 Comp. 2.6.3; X 2.19.11. See García and García (1981), 80, 81; Pennington (2016), 195, 196.

holder of a public office or two men.[7] These legal acts introduced a court writer (*scriptor*) in the Roman-canon process. Literature in the German language indicates the role of such writers as a specialized *Gerichtschreiber* and designates them as the clear forerunner of *Klerikernotariat* (Englemann 1895, 47, 49; Neschwara 2000, 1). He was a permanent court clerk exclusively engaged in writing *protocolla* and making judicial records. This notary was public, though he only functioned within court procedures, which made his role and function clearly different from other types of notaries otherwise employed by the Church bureaucracy in extrajudicial matters.

Besides *Gerichtschreiber*, several types of notaries can be traced in the Church bureaucracy: (1) lay-notaries employed by the Church who were then the Church's clerks; (2) clergymen who performed notarial duties within the Church's hierarchy —*notarii, protonotarii, vice-notarii*, etc.; (3) the *cancellarius*. Neither lay-notaries employed by the Church nor *notarii, protonotarii, vice-notarii* themselves could produce a public act of the Church. They were empowered to produce documents, make records of those documents in the registry (*bastardelli, imbreviatura*), but still their work was only of a preparatory nature. A document could not achieve the status of a public act unless a particular Church office corroborated (*roborratio, corroboratio*) the document and thereby awarded it with legal effect. *Corroboratio* was a further step after the document had been composed. It could be performed directly by the highest Church dignitary who had *munus gubernandi* or *regendi* (a bishop himself) or by a specialized office to which he delegated such powers. This office was the chancery (*cancellaria*), which awarded a notarial document with *corroboratio* through the *cancellarius* (who was the head of the chancery) or by means of other chancery officials delegated by the *cancellarius* (*vice-cancellarius*).

The role and function of notaries who acted within the Church should be understood with reference to the fact that *corroboratio* was introduced already in the 6th century and that thereafter it was constantly an infallible component (a part of *Contextus*) of the Church's public diplomatics.[8] This means that *corroboratio* which followed the production of a notarial document made it a public act rather than a notarial work alone. For these arguments, it is doubtful whether the foundations of the public notary as we perceive it today can be reliably traced within the Church's production of documents in the Middle Ages and in later periods.

The *sui generis* notarial phenomena in the Middle Ages can be found in the territories of Hungary and Croatia where cathedrals, monasteries and chapter houses acted as places of the production and authentication of documents. The legal grounds of such powers were decrees of Hungarian-Croatian kings, while the background to this activity, according to Hunyadi (2003, 25, 26 (esp. n. 4)), may be

---

[7] [...] *ut judex semper adhibeat aut publicam (si potest habere) personam aut duos viros idoneos, qui feliciter universa judicii acta conscribant* c. 71 X. de prob 2, 19 and c. 11 X. de prob 2, 19.

[8] Pope Gregory the Great introduced it. Santifaller (1976), 29. See Hunyadi (2003), 32.

linked to an act of Pope Alexander III issued in 1166.[9] The notaries (monks, canons, prebendaries, priests, etc.) served, among other roles, as compilers and witnesses to legal acts; they authenticated private documents with their seal and kept archives. Because cathedrals, monasteries and chapter houses enjoyed the status of *loca credibilia*, documents they produced were by themselves public acts, which means that they were awarded *fides publica* after they had been produced, with no further formal requirements. This applied in the 12th and 13th centuries to Croatian and Hungarian chapter houses and monasteries, and main cathedrals on the territory of the medieval Hungarian-Croatian kingdom.[10] Though convents and chapter houses were corporations, their notarial activity considerably resembles the main roles and functions of a public notary. It should be emphasized that the notarial phenomena that resembled the activities of the Croatian and Hungarian *loca credibilia* can be found throughout medieval Europe within the Church or imperial institutions involved in the production and authentication of documents (Hunyadi 2003, 35).

5 Divergent Notarial Practices, Functions and Roles in the Later Middle Ages

Before the modern period, Europe knew nothing of a universal and uniform concept of notaries. Notarial practices varied considerably, which was reflected in the nomenclature, types of notaries which differed enormously, diverse training requirements for notaries, legal grounds and the persons who appointed them, activities that they could perform and—above all—the probative/evidentiary value of the documents they produced. If the profession of notary in the Middle Ages and subsequent centuries is analysed from the perspective of a scale that stretches between two conceptual extremes—the *technician* at one end and the *public notary* at the other—one can conclude that there are many different levels on that scale which reflect considerable diversity. The diversity is modelled by the previously mentioned factors and can be clearly traced in the vast number of documents that were produced on a daily basis from the 12th century on in every corner of Europe and most of which are of a notarial provenance (Brundage 2008, 394; Meyer 2000, 72–86, 330, 331, 501).

The precise position of an individual notary on that scale largely would depend on the probative value of the documents he produced while "the probative value of a notarial document depended upon the authority who had appointed the notary

[9]Hunyadi (2003), 25 also states the following: "The *loca credibilia* were, however, rather more than *scriptoria*, 'copying shops', or institutions of witness. Besides their role in recording and verifying transactions and in drawing up deeds, the *loca credibilia* performed a vital function in discharging the tasks of royal government and in undertaking judicial and administrative duties on behalf of the ruler and of his principal agents".

[10]For Croatia see Gulin (2008). For Hungary see Hunyadi (2003), 25–35 (for a bibliography see n. 2).

who prepared it".[11] Notaries employed by the Church or imperial bureaucracy (Meyer 2000, 12–47) could not produce a public document themselves because in both cases the *corroboratio* of a chancery was required. It was the *corroboratio* itself, rather than the notarial activity, that gave the document legal effect and *fides publica*. These two analogous practices (here specifically linked to the notarial activity and evidently discernible in medieval diplomatics), each in its own domain (spiritual and civil), have a lot in common with the problem of investiture. Besides those notaries who were employed in the Church bureaucracy (whose number was small), the papal authority appointed notaries all over Europe who performed notarial functions exclusively in the civil domain. The pope surely had universal and factual authority in medieval Europe arising from his spiritual primacy. However, the legal powers or binding force of papal authority in civil matters were not universally recognized by the individual rulers, because of which the documents of notaries appointed by the pope failed to reach the effect that the documents produced by the public notaries would achieve.

The city-states of medieval Europe that were awarded municipal autonomy often developed a self-designed concept of notaries that bore the distinctive characteristics of each particular locality. Because no uniform notarial concept existed and because city-states could autonomously enact their regulations on notaries and award those specific notarial authorization, the roles and functions of notaries varied enormously from place to place. In most cases it was a matter of municipal statutory provisions and authorization whether a notary was solely a technician, or a part-time notary, or an authorized public notary, or he was awarded the (highest) imperial authority, or had powers for which he could be qualified as a public notary (Meyer 2000, 321–323; Brundage 2008, 401, 402). Such phenomena require locally orientated research. Apart from the authority that appointed or legal grounds that authorized him, the factual probative value of a notary's documents could be additionally enforced through his personal characteristics and extrajudicial factors: income, reputation, high office or a professor's position at university, skills, social networks, influential positions he held together with the notarial function, part-time legal practice, the status of elite notary, legal training or background, membership in professional associations, etc. The Dalmatian medieval municipalities (modern Croatia) by means of their statutory provisions instituted the function of *examinator* whose principal duty was to verify the authenticity and validity of these documents which were produced during their service. This clearly indicates that a person (notary) who produced the document did not enjoy full authority and credibility, and was subjected to supervision (Margetić 1971, 191–210).

The question may be raised whether a notary could assume some other functions, save for those previously mentioned in this paper. The answer is twofold. The notarial function was not necessarily a full-time position or principal occupation,

[11]Notaries needed to be created. Brundage (2008), 399; Meyer (2000), 12–47; Wolf (1973), 506, 507. Durantis, *Speculum iudiciale,* 1.3 *De procuratores* §3.1; 2.2 *De instrumentorum editione* §8.22–23.

which left enough room and time for a notary to perform different work concurrently, such as the administration of justice, state administration, advocacy, teaching law, holding public office and service or working in the private sphere, as a clerk, commercial trader, apothecary, etc. (Meyer 2000, 359–390; Brundage 2008, 397, 405). The second and considerably different aspect of this question is whether notaries could extend their notarial functions beyond producing and authenticating documents. For instance, the *loca credibilia*, which came closest to the public notary on the aforementioned scale, evidently assumed some other roles that they performed in a credible manner (administration of justice), but these were considerably different and evidently separate from producing and authenticating documents. It seems quite clear that these "other" roles were never considered or anyway treated as a part of their notarial work. In 1335 at Cologne and in 1340 on the island of Mallorca it was prohibited for notaries to practise advocacy in the same courts where they operated as notaries (Meyer 2000, 330, 331; Brundage 2008, 395). Durantis' *Speculum iudiciale* compiled in 1271 indicates that notaries received a university law degree sometimes only, which excluded them from a wide range of functions and practices linked to the judiciary and the administration of justice that required formal training in law.[12] Statutory provisions of the eastern Adriatic communities often record notaries attending the court, administrative procedures and legal transactions that took place outside their cabinets (in processes of enforcement, execution of warranties, imprisonment for debts, founding real securities, public auctions, preparing the records of court sessions, transactions which required witnesses, etc.). Their only role in such circumstances was nothing more than to provide written records or proofs and occasionally to produce a document of an event which would then be corroborated by the public authorities.[13] There are no records of notaries assuming the position of a judge, arbitrator or mediator, or performing any kind of regulatory or adjudicative operations within their notarial roles and functions. Finally, these views of notaries' solely "scribal" functions and roles can be reaffirmed if one analyses the official acts of authorization and lists of authorized notaries (*matricula*) in the medieval Italian city-states that represent a core of notarial activity in the Middle Ages (for example, Bologna, Padua, Lucca, etc.). The authorization exclusively refers to the production of documents. Even the requirements and preconditions that a person needed to fulfil to receive such notarial authorization (knowledge of Latin, penmanship, notarial skills, etc.) suggest that their functions and roles exclusively referred to literal activity, and to no other (Brundage 2008, 401, 402).

[12]Durantis G, *Speculum iudiciale*, 2.2 *De instrumentorum editione* §8.1.

[13]Durantis G, *Speculum iudiciale*, 1.4 *De teste* §7.2; Wolf (1973), 508, 509.

6 Conclusions

A basic understanding of notaries in Europe relies on the dictionary meaning of the term *notarius*. Though this term brings together a meaning referring to a certain person and the technical, literal operations he performs, it represents a framework and constraint of his professional activity which the notaries never exceeded. Regardless of on which grounds, by whom or to what extent their activity was authorized, the notarial job always and universally within Europe consisted exclusively of preparing, writing and producing documents, which is the elementary dictionary meaning of the Latin term *notarius*. From the time it reached its full formation in the 13th century, the notarial profession embodied functions and powers that were uniformly limited to these activities, which are precisely discernible in the vast number of documents they produced up until the 19th century. Additionally, the notarial profession did not assume any other functions (regulative, adjudicative or administrative). This should not be confused with the considerably different situation where certain persons who performed notarial activities at the same time had other jobs or held office and performed different services whose roles and functions were substantially different from notarial. They were not part of the notarial functions and roles either. It seems that no historical grounds or traditional legitimizations can be found of the newly developed (extended) roles and functions of notaries which exceed the threefold work (preparing, writing and producing documents).

Uniformity was, though, never achieved in the nomenclature and types of notaries in medieval Europe. Nor was it achieved in the probative value of notarial documents. Moreover, training and formal requirements for notaries differed greatly. Finally, the formation of the notarial profession and the number of notaries varied enormously, which suggests that the spread of notaries and the development of the notarial profession itself were not equal in different European territories. Naturally, such diversity resulted in considerable (substantial) differences and a wide range of notaries if they are analysed from the perspective of authority, evidential value and the legal effect that their documents were awarded. Diversity was even more supported by the enormous territorial fragmentation of Europe, the tensions which existed between the Church and the civil sphere, autonomous regulations on notaries in medieval city-states, the wide range of Church notaries, etc.

For these reasons, the notary is a complex historical phenomenon affiliated with the particular locality in which it developed. No general qualifications or description of a notary can be sustained without reference to particular notarial phenomena and the particular existing context. Whether a certain notary was solely a technician, recorder, writing-clerk, a notary employed by the bureaucracy or a purely public notary whose documents enjoyed *fides publica* is a matter that needs to be analysed and revealed in each particular case. Still, a general remark should be put forth that in the medieval and subsequent historical periods (until the 19th century) only a certain number of notaries can be traced that could be qualified as public notaries by modern standards.

References

Amelotti M, Costamagna G (1975) Alle origini del notariato italiano. Consiglio Nazionale del Notariato, Rome
Brundage J (2008) The medieval origins of the legal profession: canonists, civilians, and courts. Chicago U Press, Chicago
Cannata CA (1986) Aperçu *historique du notariat européen.* Revue Suisse du Notariat et du Registre foncier 67(4):193–206
Brown JC (1936) The origin and the early history of the office of notary. W Green and Son, Edinburgh
Eck W (1978) Zum neuen Fragment des sogenannten testamentum Dasumii. Z Papyrologie Epigraphik 30:277–295
Englemann A (1895) Der Civil prozess, Geschichte und System, Bd. 2, Hft. 3. Robner Verlag, Breslau
Fournier P (1984) Les officialités au moyen âge: étude sur l'organisation, la compétence et la procédure des tribunaux ecclésiastiques ordinaires en France, de 1180 à 1328. Scientia Verlag, Aalen
García and García (1981) A *Constitutiones Concilii quarti Lateranensis una cum Commentariis glossatorum.* Biblioteca Apostolica Vaticana, Vatican
Gaudenzi A (ed) (1892) Rainerii de Perusio Ars notaria. Biblioteca Iuridica Medii Aevi, vol 2, pp 25–67
Gouron A (1995) *Testis unus* testis nullus *dans la* doctrine juridique der XIIe siècle. Mediaevalia Lovanensia, ser. 1, stud. XXIV:83–93
Gulin A (2008) Hrvatski srednjovjekovni kaptoli—Loca credibilia Dalmacije, Hrvatskog primorja, kvarnerskih otoka i Istre (Croatian medieval chapter houses—*Loca credibilia* of Dalmatia, Croatian Coast, Islands of Kvarner, and Istria). Croatian Academy of Arts and Sciences, Zagreb
Hunyadi Z (2003) Administering the law: Hungary's *loca credibilia.* Custom and law in central Europe. In: Rady M (ed) Centre for European legal studies. Cambridge, pp 25–35
Kantorowicz H (1938) Studies in the glossators of the Roman law. Cambridge U Press, Cambridge, Newly discovered writings of the twelfth century
Margetić L (1971) Funkcija i porijeklo službe egzaminatora u srednjovjekovnim komunama Hrvatskog primorja i Dalmacije (function and origins of the examinator's office in the medieval communities of the Croatian coast and Dalmatia). Starine 55:191–210
Marino F (1988) Il falso testamentario nel diritto romano. Z Savigny-Stiftung Rechtsgeschichte, Romanistische Abt 105(1):634–663
Meyer A (2000) Felix et inclitus notarius. Studien zum italienischen Notariat vom 7. bis zum 13. Jahrhundert. Bibliothek des Deutschen Historischen Instituts in Rom 92. Max Niemeyer Verlag, Tübingen
Milotić I (2013) Pravno uređenje položaja sastavljača isprava te povjerenja u privatne isprave u rimskom pravu' (legal regulation of document compilers and trust in private documents in Roman law). Liber amicorum Mihajlo Dika, Faculty of Law, Zagreb, pp 693–724
Murphy JJ (1981) Rhetoric in the Middle Ages: a history of rhetorical theory from Saint Augustine to the Renaissance. U of California Press, Berkeley
Neschwara C (2000) Österreichs Notariatsrecht in Mittel- und Osteuropa Zur Geltung und Ausstrahlung des österreichischen Notariats. Manzsche Verlags, Vienna
Nörr KW (2012) Romanisch-kanonisches Prozessrecht: Erkenntnisverfahren erster Instanz in civilibus. Springer, Heidelberg
Padoa-Schioppa A (2017) A history of law in Europe: from the early Middle Ages to the twentieth century. Cambridge U Press, Cambridge
Palmieri GB (1892) [Pseudo-Irnerius] Il Formularium tabellionum di Irnerio. Appunti e documenti per la storia dei glossatori, vol 1, Bologna

Pennington K (2016) The fourth lateran council, its legislation, and the development of legal procedure. In: Witte J Jr et al (eds) Texts and contexts in legal history: essays in honor of Charles Donahue. U of California, Berkeley, pp 179–198

Pfaff I (1905) Tabellio und tabularius: ein Beitrag zur Lehre von den römischen Urkundspersonen. Manz, Vienna

Rolandinus de Passageriis (c. 1256) Summa Artis Notariae. Pub. (1492) by Simon Bevilacqua, Venice

Santifaller L (1976) Liber diurnus, Reihe Päpste und Papsttum, vol 10. A. Hiersemann, Stuttgart

Saradi GH (1999) Notai e documenti Greci dall'età di Giustiniano al XIX secolo, tom 1. Il sistema notarile bizantino, Giuffrè, Milano

Savigny KF (1834) Geschichte des Römischen Recht im Mittelalter, Kap. 8. Mohr, Heidelberg

Stein P (1999) Roman law in European history. Cambridge U Press, Cambridge

Steinhoff MW (1976) Origins and development of the notariate at Ravenna (sixth through thirteenth centuries). Dissertation, New York University

Stern Y (2000) The testamentary phenomenon in ancient Rome. Historia: Z Alte Geschichte 49 (4):413–428

Wahrmund L (ed) (1917) Die Ars Notariae des Rainerius Perusinus. Quellen zur Geschichte des römisch-kanonischen Processes im Mittelalter, vol 3, no. 2. Innsbruck

Wolf A (1973) Das öffentliche Notariat, Handbuch der Quellen und Literatur der neueren europäischen Privatrechtsgeschichte. Bd. 1: Mittelalter (1100–1500). Die gelehrten Rechte und die Gesetzgebung. Beck, München, pp 505–514

Ivan Milotić Professor of Roman Law at the Faculty of Law, University of Zagreb, Croatia. Member of the Legislation Committee of the Croatian Parliament. Editor of the journal *Law and Taxes*.

About the Authors

Sergio Cruz Arenhart

Associate Professor of Civil Procedure at the Federal University of Paraná, Brazil. Ph.D. and LLM from the Federal University of Paraná. Post-doctoral Fellow of the Università degli Studi di Firenze, Italy. Former Federal Judge in Brazil. Federal Public Prosecutor at the Court of Appeals for the 4th Circuit, Brazil.

Rashri Baboolal-Frank

Lecturer in the Department of Procedural Law. Lectures in Civil Procedure, Alternative Dispute Resolution and Legal Practice, and for the LLM Civil Litigation Programme. Certified arbitrator and mediator for the Arbitration Foundation of Southern Africa. Advocate of the High Court of South Africa having previously practised as an attorney in the lower and higher courts. Currently finalising her doctoral studies at the University of Pretoria, South Africa.

Marko Bratković

Teaching Assistant in the Department of Civil Procedure at the University of Zagreb, Croatia. Visiting Scholar at the Max Planck Institute for Procedural Law in Luxembourg, and at the Max Planck Institute for Comparative and International Private Law in Hamburg and the Europa-Institut in Saarbrücken, Germany.

A. Uzelac and C. H. van Rhee (eds.), *Transformation of Civil Justice*,
Ius Gentium: Comparative Perspectives on Law and Justice 70,
https://doi.org/10.1007/978-3-319-97358-6

Juraj Brozović

Research Assistant in the Department of Civil Procedure at the University of Zagreb, Croatia. Assistant to the Director of the Law Clinic Zagreb and one of the academic mentors supervising students' legal aid work.

Fokke Fernhout

Associate Professor of Civil Procedure at Maastricht University, the Netherlands. Attorney-at-law and former Vice-President of the District Court of Maastricht. Coordinator of skills projects for lawyers and law students in the Netherlands and in Indonesia.

Halvard Haukeland Fredriksen

Professor of European Law and Civil Procedure at the University of Bergen, Norway. Dr iur from the University of Göttingen, Germany. Ph.D. from the University of Bergen, Norway. Co-chair of the Research Group on Civil Procedure at the Faculty of Law in Bergen.

Aleš Galič

Professor at the Faculty of Law, University of Ljubljana, Slovenia, where he is engaged in teaching and research in the areas of Civil Procedure, International Private Law, Arbitration and ADR.

Fernando Gascón Inchausti

Professor of Civil and Criminal Procedural Law at the Complutense University of Madrid, Spain. Director of the Research Group on Current Problems of Justice and Procedure and the research project The Harmonization of Civil Procedure in the European Union.

Erwin Giesen

Master's student of Law at the Faculty of Law of Maastricht University, the Netherlands. Legal Counsel intern at the ARAG SE Insurance Group.

Henrik-Riko Held

Assistant Professor of Roman Law at the Faculty of Law, University of Zagreb. Post-doctoral studies at the Centro di studi e ricerche sui Diritti Antichi (CEDANT), Almo Collegio Borromeo, University of Pavia (2016), Italy. Member of the editorial board of the Zagreb Law Review.

Rob Jagtenberg

Senior Research Fellow of Erasmus University Rotterdam, the Netherlands. Former member of the Supervisory Committee for the national Dutch project on court-connected mediation, and Principal Researcher in projects commissioned by the World Bank and The Council for the Judiciary, the Netherlands.

Bartosz Karolczyk

Senior Attorney in the law firm of Domański Zakrzewski Palinka sp.k., Warsaw, Poland, with practice focused on civil commercial litigation and arbitration. Senior Lecturer in Civil Procedure at the Faculty of Law, Koźmiński University, Warsaw.

Stephanie Law

Senior Research Fellow of the Max Planck Institute Luxembourg. Former Post-doctoral Research Fellow, Faculty of Law, McGill University, Montréal (The Leverhulme Trust funding), Canada. Ph.D. from the European University Institute, Florence, Italy. During her doctoral research, she was a Visiting Scholar at Columbia Law School and a stagiaire in the Cabinet of Judge Christopher Vajda at the CJEU. Fellow of the HEC-NYU Public Interest Clinic and a member of the Academic Research Panel of Blackstone Chambers.

Richard Marcus

Horace O. Coil Chair in Litigation, UC Hastings College of Law, San Francisco. Co-author of leading American casebooks on complex litigation and civil procedure, and author of the discovery volumes of the leading US treatise on federal practice and procedure. Associate Reporter of the Advisory Committee on Civil Rules of the U.S. Judicial Conference. Principal author of rules for discovery and class actions adopted for U.S. federal courts since 1998.

Ivan Milotić

Professor of Roman Law at the Faculty of Law, University of Zagreb, Croatia. Member of the Legislation Committee of the Croatian Parliament. Editor of the journal *Law and Taxes*.

Annie de Roo

Associate Professor of ADR and Comparative Law at Erasmus University Rotterdam, the Netherlands. Director of the Netherlands Organization for Scientific Research (N.W.O.) sponsored project on Hybrid Governance in the Social Domain. Vice-chair of the Exams Committee of the Mediators Federation of the Netherlands (MFN). Editor-in-Chief of *TMD*, the Dutch-Flemish Mediation and Conflict Management Quarterly.

Elisabetta Silvestri

Associate Professor of Civil Procedure and Comparative Civil Procedure in the Department of Law at the University of Pavia, Italy. Scientific Director of the post-graduate programme for the training of ADR professionals at the University of Pavia. LLM from Cornell Law School. Visiting scholar at Yale Law School and the London School of Economics. Co-director of the Public and Private Justice seminar at the Inter-University Centre Dubrovnik, Croatia.

Jorg Sladič

Attorney-at-law practising in Ljubljana, Slovenia. Assistant Professor of International and European Law at the University of Maribor, Slovenia. Ph.D. from the University of Saarland, Germany, LLM from the University of Trier, Germany,

Diplôme d'études supérieures spécialisées at the University François Rabelais in Tours, France. Former Legal Secretary (*référendaire*) at the Court of Justice of the European Union.

Magne Strandberg

Professor of Law at the University of Bergen, Faculty of Law, Norway, where he teaches Procedure Law. Leader of the Research Group on Civil Procedure.

Alan Uzelac

Professor of Law at the University of Zagreb, Croatia, where he teaches Civil Procedure and Comparative Civil Procedure, Organization of the Judiciary and Alternative Dispute Resolution. Founding Member of the European Commission for the Efficiency of Justice (CEPEJ) in Strasbourg. Delegate in the UNCITRAL Working Group on Arbitration and Conciliation. Co-director of the Public and Private Justice seminar at the Inter-University Centre, Dubrovnik, Croatia. Director of the research project Transformation of Civil Justice Under the Influence of Global and Regional Integration Processes.

Matthias Van Der Haegen

Ph.D. Fellow of the Research Foundation Flanders (FWO) at Ghent University, Belgium. Graduated from Ghent University, MJur from the University of Oxford. Visiting Scholar at Bergen University Faculty of Law, Norway, the Max Planck Institute for Procedural Law, Luxembourg and Washington University in St. Louis School of Law, United States of America.

C. H. (Remco) van Rhee

Chair of European Legal History and Comparative Civil Procedure, Maastricht University, the Netherlands. Director of the research programme Foundations and Principles of Civil Procedure in Europe of the Ius Commune Research School. Co-director of the Public and Private Justice seminar at the Inter-University Centre Dubrovnik, Croatia.

Oscar Vranken

Master's student of Corporate and Commercial Law at the Faculty of Law of Maastricht University, the Netherlands. Assistant at the Maastricht Institute for Corporate Law, Governance and Innovation Policies (ICGI).

Matthias Weller

Professor of Law at the University of Bonn, Germany. Director of the Institute for German and International Civil Procedure and Dispute Resolution. Member of the International Association of Procedural Law, the German Association of Professors for Civil Procedure, the German Scientific Association for International Civil Procedure and the German Institution for Arbitration.

Margaret Woo

Professor of Law and Associate Dean of Research and Interdisciplinary Education at the Northeastern University School of Law, where she teaches Civil Procedure, Administrative Law and Comparative Law. Expert on the Anglo-American legal system and the Chinese socialist legal system. Former Fellow of the Bunting Institute (Radcliffe College). Associate of the East Asian Legal Studies Program at Harvard University.

Kolibri 360 GmbH
Ferdinand-Jühlke-Straße 7
99095 Erfurt, Deutschland
produktsicherheit@kolibri360.de